D0873839

INDUSTRIAL PSYCHOLOGY

McGraw-Hill Series in Psychology

Harry F. Harlow, *Consulting Editor*

Barker, Kounin, and Wright · Child Behavior and Development
Beach, Hebb, Morgan, and Nissen · The Neuropsychology of Lashley
von Békésy · Experiments in Hearing
Berlyne · Conflict, Arousal, and Curiosity
Blum · Psychoanalytic Theories of Personality
Brown · The Psychodynamics of Abnormal Behavior
Brown · The Motivation of Behavior
Brown and Ghiselli · Scientific Method in Psychology
Cattell · Personality
Crafts, Schneirla, Robinson, and Gilbert · Recent Experiments in Psychology
Deese · The Psychology of Learning
Dollard and Miller · Personality and Psychotherapy
Dorcus and Jones · Handbook of Employee Selection
Ferguson · Personality Measurement
Ferguson · Statistical Analysis in Psychology and Education
Ghiselli and Brown · Personnel and Industrial Psychology
Gilmer · Industrial Psychology
Gray · Psychology Applied to Human Affairs
Gray · Psychology in Industry
Guilford · Fundamental Statistics in Psychology and Education
Guilford · Psychometric Methods
Guilford · Personality
Haire · Psychology in Management
Hirsh · The Measurement of Hearing
Hurlock · Adolescent Development
Hurlock · Child Development
Hurlock · Developmental Psychology
Johnson · Essentials of Psychology
Karn and Gilmer · Readings in Industrial and Business Psychology
Krech and Crutchfield · Theory and Problems of Social Psychology
Lewin · A Dynamic Theory of Personality
Lewin · Principles of Topological Psychology
Lewis · Quantitative Methods in Psychology
Maier and Schneirla · Principles of Animal Psychology
Miller · Language and Communication
Misiak and Staudt · Catholics in Psychology: A Historical Survey
Moore · Psychology for Business and Industry
Morgan and Stellar · Physiological Psychology
Page · Abnormal Psychology
Reymert · Feelings and Emotions
Seashore · Psychology of Music
Shaffer and Lazarus · Fundamental Concepts in Clinical Psychology
Siegel · Nonparametric Statistics: For the Behavioral Sciences
Stagner · Psychology of Personality
Townsend · Introduction to Experimental Method
Vinacke · The Psychology of Thinking
Wallen · Clinical Psychology: The Study of Persons
Waters, Rethlingshafer, and Caldwell · Principles of Comparative Psychology
Zubek and Solberg · Human Development

John F. Dashiell was Consulting Editor of this series from its inception in 1931 until January 1, 1950. Clifford T. Morgan was Consulting Editor of this series from January 1, 1950 until January 1, 1959.

INDUSTRIAL PSYCHOLOGY

B. von HALLER GILMER
Carnegie Institute of Technology

With the collaboration of:

W. J. E. CRISSY
Michigan State University

R. M. CYERT
Carnegie Institute of Technology

LEONARD W. FERGUSON
*Life Insurance Agency Management
Association*

ROBERT GLASER
University of Pittsburgh

LEE W. GREGG
Carnegie Institute of Technology

THOMAS L. HILTON
Carnegie Institute of Technology

MYRON L. JOSEPH
Carnegie Institute of Technology

HARRY W. KARN
Carnegie Institute of Technology

EMANUEL KAY
The General Electric Company

ROBERT E. KRUG
Carnegie Institute of Technology

JAMES G. MARCH
Carnegie Institute of Technology

ROBERT B. MILLER
International Business Machines, Inc.

ROBERT M. MORGAN
Carnegie Institute of Technology

ROBERT S. RAMSAY
Carnegie Institute of Technology

KATHLEEN A. THOMPSON
Personnel Development Associates

McGRAW-HILL BOOK COMPANY, INC.

NEW YORK   TORONTO   LONDON   1961

INDUSTRIAL PSYCHOLOGY

23262

Dedicated

to

WALTER V. BINGHAM

PREFACE

Industrial psychology now embraces a number of specialties. Realizing that no one psychologist has the depth of knowledge of each area of specialization to write a well-balanced text, we have here combined the resources of many. We have assembled the contributions of experimental, social, and clinical psychology, together with certain phases of business organization procedures, into a unified description of how modern psychology fits into the industrial complex.

The principal author invited fifteen specialists to work with him in preparing a completely up-to-date text based on a review of some fifteen thousand publications in the several areas. The contributors have from the beginning been keenly aware that a text written by several people would lack uniformity of style and organization unless one person took the responsibility of putting the entire manuscript into a single style. To achieve this the senior author has worked closely with each contributor in the writing and rewriting of the chapters. The final product is a uniform presentation.

Each contributor to this textbook was chosen for his knowledge of and involvement in a particular field. Some of the authors work full time in industry; most are college professors experienced in industrial consulting. Each contributor's name appears on the chapter he prepared. Eight chapters were written by the principal author; eight were written by other Carnegie professors; and five by other professional colleagues.

A comment on each author is in order. The chapter dealing with the development of industrial psychology was written by L. W. Ferguson of the Life Insurance Agency Management Association. Most of the material in the chapter on the development of industrial psychology appears in print here for the first time. A more comprehensive history of industrial psychology will appear later in a book now being prepared by Dr. Ferguson. The chapter on business operating procedures was written by R. M. Cyert and J. G. March, specialists in the field of industrial organization. The chapter on personnel selection was written by R. E. Krug. The chapter on training was written by Robert Glaser, with the assistance of Murray Glanzer. Some of the material of this chapter is reproduced here for the first time through the courtesy of the Office of Naval Research and the American Institute for Research.

The chapter on executive behavior was written by T. L. Hilton, who brings together here a comprehensive picture of leadership studies from Europe and the United States. The chapter on labor-management relations was written by M. L. Joseph, a labor economist versed in the psychology of industrial conflict. The chapter on work was written by R. S. Ramsay, and the one on accidents and safety by H. W. Karn. The chapter on engineering psychology was written by L. W. Gregg, who is both an engineer and a psychologist. R. B. Miller of the IBM Corporation wrote the chapter on the newer roles of the psychologist in the development of systems.

The chapter dealing with advertising and selling includes some original materials normally not found in textbooks. This chapter was written by two practicing psychologists, W. J. E. Crissy and Kathleen A. Thompson, a specialist in women's buying habits.

In the final section of the book, which deals with the individual in industry, there are chapters by Emanuel Kay of the General Electric Company, and by R. M. Morgan.

Several new subject areas are introduced in this text. In addition to the chapter on the history of industrial psychology, a chapter on business operating procedures appears in an industrial psychology text for the first time. The latter was included because we believe that a more comprehensive understanding of the human problems of industry can be gained once the reader understands the rules and procedures of business organizations. And for the first time in an industrial text, there is a chapter on women in industry. Emphasis is also given to the newer roles of the industrial psychologist as he moves into development and systems planning. This chapter contains materials which are new in concept.

Some areas of psychology, notably the fields of leadership and human performance, have a wealth of research data which we have drawn upon. Other areas, like the subject of women in industry, come less endowed with research information. Some chapters, such as those dealing with human engineering and systems analysis, are, by their very nature, more difficult than others. We have made every effort to reduce to a minimum any unevenness which these factors may have caused. We hope we have succeeded.

Included in this rather comprehensive coverage of industrial psychology are chapters that may not serve the needs of some courses in industrial psychology. This text is, therefore, organized so that each instructor may have freedom in planning the material he will cover and in determining the way in which he wishes to use it. Some instructors, for example, may wish to omit Part II, which deals with the industrial environment. They will find that the book is organized so that these two chapters can be omitted without appreciable loss of continuity.

In making this book descriptive of the human aspects of the industrial setting, we have borne in mind the fact that many students taking courses in industrial psychology are not psychology majors. The text has been planned to give emphasis to description, with less detail devoted to methodology. Our aim in writing this text has been to help the student reach an understanding of life in industry rather than to give answers to problems per se.

To the many researchers and writers who could not be included in the bibliography because of space restrictions we wish to extend our appreciation for providing us with a base for planning this book. To the several professional people who critically reviewed either parts or the whole of our manuscript we wish to express our thanks. Some of their suggestions have been included in this final edition. We wish also to recognize the following organizations which in one way or another contributed to the preparation of this book:

Allis-Chalmers Manufacturing Company, American Federation of Labor and Congress of Industrial Organizations, American Institute for Research, American Psychological Association, Automobile Manufacturers Association, Bell Telephone Company of Pennsylvania, Chrysler Corporation, Coca-Cola Company, Congo Tire and Rubber Company, Corning Glass Works, Crown Zellerbach Corporation, Detroit Free Press, E. I. Du Pont de Nemours & Company, Inc., Eastman Kodak Company, Esso Standard Oil Company, Fisher Scientific Company, Ford Motor Company, Fortune Magazine, General Dynamics Corporation, General Electric Company, General Motors Corporation, Harper & Brothers, Harvard Business Review, Harvard University Press, Her Majesty's Stationery Office, Institute for Social Research at the University of Michigan, International Business Machines, Inc., John Wiley & Sons, Kaiser Industries Corporation, Kennecott Copper Corporation, Kraft Foods Company, Life Insurance Agency Management Association, Monsanto Chemical Company, New York Life Insurance Company, Office of Naval Research, Ohio State University, Pittsburgh Plate Glass Company, Princeton University Press, Procter & Gamble Company, Psychological Service of Pittsburgh, Raytheon Manufacturing Company, Robert Brunner, Inc., Ronald Press, Science Research Associates, Shenango China Company, Stromberg-Carlson Company, Triple G. Farms, United States Air Force, U.S. Department of Labor, United Automobile Workers, United States Steel Corporation, Universal Manufacturing Corporation, University of Chicago Press, Western Maryland Railway Company, Westinghouse Airbrake Company, Westinghouse Electric Corporation.

B. von Haller Gilmer

CONTENTS

PREFACE vii

PART I: PSYCHOLOGY IN INDUSTRY

1. THE AIM AND SCOPE OF INDUSTRIAL PSYCHOLOGY 3

Industry—A Place to Study Behavior. Why Study Industrial Psychology? What Psychologists Do in Industry. Cause and Effect in Behavior. Psychology as a Behavioral Science. The Methods of Psychology Applied to Industry. An Orientation. Your Personal Interests.

2. THE DEVELOPMENT OF INDUSTRIAL PSYCHOLOGY 18

First Psychologist to Industry. Early Research in Industrial Psychology. Psychology in World War I. First Organization for Personnel Consulting. Retail Training. First School of Life Insurance Salesmanship. Vocational Guidance. Industrial Psychology 1925, and Later. Psychology in World War II. The Present Era.

PART II: THE INDUSTRIAL ENVIRONMENT

3. THE STRUCTURES OF ORGANIZATIONS 41

The Meaning of Industry. The Anatomy of the Modern Company. The Organization Chart. The Structures of Labor Unions. The Psychological Climate in Industry. The Informal Organization. Status Hierarchies in Industry. Status at Different Ranks. Status Within the Union. Organizational Complexity and Human Relations. Toward a Global View of Human Problems.

4. BUSINESS OPERATING PROCEDURES 67

A Look at a Business Organization. Standard Operating Procedures. Types of Operating Procedures. Task Performance Rules. Records and Reports. Information Handling Rules. Plans and Planning Rules.

xi

PART III: PERSONNEL PSYCHOLOGY

5. Human Needs in Industry 91

A Basic Model of Behavior. Variations within Individuals. Reactions to Frustration. Toward Satisfying Needs. Success and Failure.

6. Personnel Selection 106

The Selection Problem. The Problem of Criteria. Some Available Criterion Measures. Combining Criterion Measures. The Prediction of Success. The Analysis of Predictor Criterion Relationships. The Current Status of the Selection Process. The Recruitment of Employees. Decision in Hiring. The Future of Personnel Selection.

7. Training in Industry 129

The Specification of Training Objectives. Input Control. Learning Principles and Training Procedures. Training Aids, Training Devices, and Simulators. Output Control through Proficiency Measurement. The Organization of Training. Training and Experimentation.

8. Human Relations in Supervision 152

A Historical Perspective. The Nature of Good Supervision. The Multiple Roles of the Supervisor. Empathy in Supervision. The Jobs of the Supervisor. The Supervisor and the Individual. Formal and Informal Counseling. Group Decision Procedures. Problem Solving in Human Relations.

9. Executive Leadership and Development 175

Functions of Executives. The Criteria of Success. Individual Leadership and the Environment. A Composite Picture. The Selection of Potential Executives. Executive Development Training. Conference Groups. Key to Successful Executive Development. Development: A Problem for the Individual.

10. Attitudes, Job Satisfactions, and Industrial Morale 197

Problems and Definitions. Information about Attitudes. The Extent and Nature of Job Dissatisfaction. Job Factor Comparisons. Effects of Attitudes on Productivity. The Psychological Climate for Work. Organizations and Morale. Employee Participation. Work Environment and Morale. Factors Related to Job Attitudes.

PART IV: LABOR PROBLEMS IN INDUSTRY

11. Labor-Management Relations 223

The Growth of Unions. Union Constraints on Management. Why Workers Join Unions. Problems within the Union. Institutional Goals. The Union Organization. Labor Union Membership. Officers of the Union. Management Meets the Union. Labor-Management Bargaining. The Settlement of Grievances. The Contract.

12. The Handicapped, Unemployed, and Aging Worker 242

The Handicapped Worker. The Psychological Aspects of Unemployment. Aging and Work. Retirement. A Perspective.

13. WOMEN IN INDUSTRY 266

One-third Are Women. A Historical Background. Differences between Women and Men at Work. Women's Jobs. Women in an Expanding Economy.

PART V: PROBLEMS RELATED TO WORK

14. THE NATURE OF WORK 285

Measuring Work Output. Measures of Effort. Fatigue. Boredom. Conditions Related to Work. Analysis and Evaluation of Work. Setting Performance Standards. Organizational Changes and the Worker.

15. ACCIDENTS AND SAFETY 305

The Concept of an Accident. Lost-time Accidents. The Causes of Accidents. The Accident Report. Investigations of Personal Factors Related to Accidents. Environmental Conditions Related to Accidents. Accident Proneness. The Problem of Accident-prevention Training. Techniques in Motivating Safety. The Engineering Phase of the Safety Problem.

16. ENGINEERING PSYCHOLOGY 324

The Job of the Engineer. The Problem of Complete Automation. The Field of Engineering Psychology. The Nature of Man-Machine Systems. The Behavior of the Human Operator. Inputs and the Human Sensory Processes. Control and Human Information Processing. Outputs and the Human Motor Responses. Human Motor-Ability Factors. The Analysis of Man-Machine Systems. Generalized Principles of Systems Design.

17. THE NEWER ROLES OF THE INDUSTRIAL PSYCHOLOGIST 353

Expansion of Psychological Problems. Research and Development. The Industrial Psychologist as Problem Solver. The General System. General System Factors. Overlap within a General System. Task Analysis. The Human Factors Subsystem. Design Variables of a Subsystem. Five Roles of the Industrial Psychologist.

PART VI: INFLUENCE AND SOCIAL INTERACTION

18. THE MARKETING MIX 383

The Ingredients of the Mix. Advertising. Selling. Analysis of the Selling Process. Perceptual Factors in Selling. Psychological Principles and Concepts Applied to Advertising and Selling. Changes in Research Directions.

19. THE INDUSTRIAL COMMUNITY 408

Importance of Knowing Community. The Yankee City Studies. Different Types of Communities. Power Structures in the Community. The Business Climate. Community Classes. Community Ties. Social Forces within the Community. The Struggle for Upward Mobility. Social Class and Personality. Industrialization and the Family. The Total Environment.

PART VII: THE INDIVIDUAL IN INDUSTRY

20. INDUSTRIAL MENTAL HEALTH 437

The Meaning of Mental Health. The Nature and Extent of Maladjustments in Industry. Adjustments of the Production Worker. Types of Work and Maladjustments. What Management Can Do. Adjustments of the First-line Supervisor. Adjustments of the Executive. Provisions for Good Mental Health. The Need for Understanding Personal Adjustment.

21. PERSONAL ADJUSTMENTS IN INDUSTRY 458

Toward Understanding Adjustment Problems. Frustration and Conflict. Motives and Emotion. Stress and Defensive Reactions. Neurotic Reactions. Psychotic Disorders. Dealing with People Who Have Psychological Problems.

BIBLIOGRAPHY 477

INDEX 499

PART I: PSYCHOLOGY
IN INDUSTRY

1

THE AIM AND SCOPE
OF INDUSTRIAL
PSYCHOLOGY

B. von Haller Gilmer

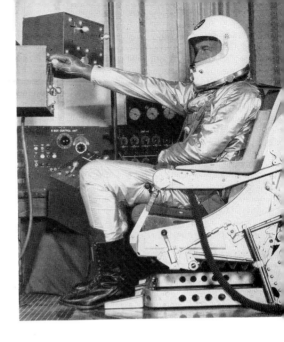

There is hardly a phase in the daily life of the man or woman associated with modern industry that is not in some way related to the study of psychology. This is not surprising, since psychology deals with the study of human behavior. And human behavior is of essential importance in every industrial activity, in the production and consumption of goods as well as in the rendering of services. Industrial psychology is interested not only in the man at work in the factory, but in the salesman on the road and the girl at work in the office. It is the study of people whose work is selling insurance, laying bricks, supervising the people producing goods, or directing the activities of the large corporation. The man who drives to work is guided by green and white road signs because psychologists have discovered that these colors are easily seen. As he listens to the advertising jingle on the radio, he is probably not aware that its quality, good or bad, has been influenced by a psychologist employed by the advertising agency.

INDUSTRY—A PLACE TO STUDY BEHAVIOR

Industry, at the present time, provides a good field in which to study the wants and needs of human beings. What does the psychologist in industry do? An answer to this question, of course, depends upon the size of the industrial organization, upon what the organization does, and upon the attitude of any given management toward psychology. There is hardly a nationally known corporation that does not employ the services of psychologists. Many smaller companies work with psychologists on a part-time consulting basis.

The psychologist working in industry does far more than give tests, a job popularly believed to be his activity [15]. True he has designed the tests and has validated them to see if they are accurately predicting what they are supposed to. But in the main the psychologist in industry has turned the testing program over to others. He is now advising the industrial relations department on the company's pending contract negotiations with the union, or he is designing a study to determine the buying habits of a suburban housewife as she walks through her local supermarket. In one hour, the industrial psychologist may be discussing the psychology of learning with the company's training director; in the next hour, he may be participating in a conference on a morale survey to be conducted in an out-of-town plant.

The Psychologist's Staff Position. The industrial psychologist usually holds a staff position, largely advisory, which enables him to apply his talents wherever they are needed. He helps to improve safety programs, and he works with engineers on the human aspects of equipment design. He assists the office of public relations in its interactions with consumers and with the community in which the company operates. He engages in the varied programs dealing with the mental health of the worker, and he assists management in finding ways to reduce absenteeism. The industrial psychologist may draw up a plan for the executive development of the newly hired college graduate on one day and discuss the problems of aging employees the next. From personnel selection to training, from supervision to job evaluation, from career planning to labor relations, the industrial psychologist moves in a wide and ever-varying scene.

WHY STUDY INDUSTRIAL PSYCHOLOGY?

"I do not plan to be a psychologist. Why then should I study industrial psychology?" This is a fair question, and quite possibly it has already occurred to the student reader. Here is our answer.

You and Industry. Most college graduates—whether they have specialized in the liberal arts, in science, in engineering, or in business administration—eventually find work in some branch of industry. One does not have to be involved in personnel administration, labor relations, or other phases of management to be confronted with human problems. From the hour the college graduate starts his new job in the small company or enters the training program of the large corporation, he moves in an environment swarming with human problems. Induction and training in this new job is in itself an involved human problem for the individual as well as for the company. It will help the student if he can find out in advance what he is getting into when he enters modern industry. Career planning today is much more involved than it was just a few years ago. Our first answer to the question, "Why should we study industrial psychology?" arises from surveys which reveal that students today more than ever before want to know what they are getting into. There is no better way to find out about the psychological climate of a work situation than to discuss the scientific and clinical studies about people who work in this climate.

A second reason for studying about human behavior in industry arises from the fact that more and more the leaders of modern industry are coming from the ranks of college graduates. Leadership in business is becoming more demanding, and the person without a liberal education is handicapped in getting the kind of position from which he can move upward in any business organization. The study of the human side of management, of supervision, is the province of psychology. It serves as a counterpart to the study of economic man.

The technical student, for example, the engineer, may ask, "Why take psychology?" Studies show that five years after graduation only about one-half of engineering college graduates are in engineering. A few years later, most are out of technical work altogether. What are they doing? Many advance to administration, a portion move into sales, some become entrepreneurs, but all seem to get more and more involved with the human side of industry. In one survey, for example, the graduates of a large engineering school who had reached supervisory or administrative positions in industry reported that more than three-fourths of their time was taken up by working with people. The importance of having skill in human relations can be illustrated by a study [2] of over four thousand white-collar workers from seventy-six different companies. Here it was found that 10.1 per cent were fired from their jobs because of a lack of technical competence. In contrast, 89.9 per cent were dismissed because they couldn't work with people.

Finally, whether we work directly in industry or not, as consumers and as citizens we find our lives influenced on every side by industrial changes. We are concerned with labor-management conflicts because the consequences often touch our pocketbooks; we are concerned with technological advances and their effect on the production of goods because this determines our material welfare; and we are concerned with the problems in industry, to at least some degree, because many of the people we know work there.

Man's behavior plays a part in all phases of industrial life. As educated people we should be aware of the significance of this force.

WHAT PSYCHOLOGISTS DO IN INDUSTRY

It is quite natural that people are confused about the function of psychology in industry. One writer [9] has suggested why this is so by saying that "psychology is probably misunderstood for the same reason it is so popular: it deals with a subject on which people have always considered themselves to be authorities." No place is this more true than in the general area of business and industry, where managers have prided themselves on being able to solve practical problems, to manage men. How can a science largely born and bred in ivory-tower lecture halls and attic laboratories attract the attention and money of the hard-boiled executive? A description of one typical research will provide the answer [7].

The publication describes a simple training experiment which saved money for the company. In a factory where new employees were customarily broken in on the job, the company wanted to know whether a part-time training program would pay. Under the psychologist's direction, one group of new employees was sent directly to work, and a comparable group was sent into a training program. The performances of both groups were recorded, and costs were evaluated by the accounting department. It was found that the untrained workers took twenty-nine minutes to change knives on a flying shears, even after six months' experience, whereas the group that had been trained properly was doing the job in only eighteen minutes. The eleven minutes saved in labor costs amounted to $20,880 a year. Furthermore, it was found that during the first thirty days of employment, accidents were 19 per cent fewer among the workers in the trained group than among those broken in on the floor. Waste and breakages were lower, labor turnover was not so great, and absenteeism was 51 per cent less among those given training under the direction of the psychologist.

Applications of Basic Principles. From laboratory work the psychologist has found out how people learn and how they can be trained more economically. In clinical situations he has found out how people feel, how they react to frustration. On the job the psychologist has discovered the basic principles underlying good supervision. The psychologist knows other things about human behavior that can be applied to product design, manufacture, and distribution; his knowledge not only is of economic value to the industrialist, but it can also make the conditions of work more pleasant for the employee.

Out of many psychological experiments have come answers to practical problems in the management of men and proof that many of the strong beliefs of the old-fashioned businessman are wrong. The idea that a "good judge of men" could look at the job applicant, talk to him, and tell right away what he could do and if he was a good worker has been disproved.

Gone is the notion that being a good foreman means being tough, and the belief that pay is the only thing the worker is after.

Today many psychologists, along with other behavioral scientists, are regularly employed in industry; others serve as consultants. They work with engineers on problems in the design of equipment. They help design the home telephone to reduce errors in dialing; they suggest changes in the cockpit of the airplane to make it less confusing for the pilot. The psychologist has helped change the aim of industrial design from what is easiest to make to what is best for the man.

Psychologists, along with other researchers, have discovered that human stress may be influenced more by one's emotional state than by hard work. A standard prescription for the harassed executive is to take a vacation. But the enforced idleness of an unwanted vacation may be the worst possible course for some people. Psychologists have studied the executive as well as the worker, and they know why he has been described as the most lonesome man in the organization.

The psychologist has uncovered many things about the needs of the worker in his struggle for status, for recognition, and for other elements that lead to job satisfaction. He knows that, contrary to some popular opinion, high morale does not always bring about high productivity. More importantly, he knows in part why.

Some Limitations in Psychology. Psychologists in industry have to spend some of their time restraining the enthusiastic administrator who believes that psychology has the answer to more problems than it really has. He has been impressed with the effectiveness of the company's program of selecting office workers and machinists and expects the psychologist to be able to do an equally good job predicting which of his younger men are the best bets for executive development. But for this problem the psychologist is not yet ready to supply all the answers. Nor is he able to select good salesmen. There are limitations as to what he can do in the areas of mental health [14]. The well-trained psychologist knows the present limitations of his science and its applications.

A particularly controversial area of industrial psychology is consumer research and advertising. Among the newest techniques attracting attention is what is called "motivation research." Some people in the advertising business believe they can get at the unconscious motives in people, and they gear advertisements to do so. For example, marketing people have called deep freezers "frozen islands of security."

Long-range Studies. The psychologist who works in industry is interested not only in day-to-day problems, but also in long-range programs dealing with the effective utilization of human resources. Although he does not have as complete control over the variables as does the psychologist working in the experimental laboratory or the clinician working in the confines of a therapeutic situation, the industrial psychologist is interested in basic problems as well as applications. Fortunately for the profession of psychology, the spirit of the laboratory and the clinic has been carried into industry.

Fundamental research is being carried on today in industrial and military settings. We have learned that psychology does not have to be locked in a laboratory in order to be scientific.

CAUSE AND EFFECT IN BEHAVIOR

No action, no emotion, no thought of a person ever occurs "spontaneously." Human behavior does not just happen; it is caused. Every act that a person performs is the result of sufficient antecedent causes. The antecedents of a thought are often hard to discover, but causal factors are always present even for the most evanescent of psychological phenomena.

The Individual and the Situation. How an individual responds to any particular situation depends upon what he brings into the situation in terms of his abilities, attitudes, skills, desires, understandings, and habits. Picture, if you will, the differences between what the union representative brings into the labor contract negotiations and what the representative of management brings in. Chances are that each has about the same abilities and many of the same skills for negotiation. But one thing is certain: they bring in different attitudes and desires from their respective backgrounds of experience. They have distinctly different economic goals. Labor is interested in high wages and certain related fringe benefits. Management is interested in profits. The importance of this difference is sometimes overlooked. One study, for example, showed that over two-thirds of a group of people surveyed had the opinion that in an average year few companies operate at a loss. However, the U.S. Treasury Department reports that in almost every peacetime year since 1913 at least 40 per cent of American corporations have shown no net income. It is therefore understandable that the goals of labor and management are in conflict. The solution of their problem hinges on a fair division of income from the goods produced. But what is fair raises the problem of "who determines." Understanding the basic differences of attitude each faction brings to the negotiations is important in determining cause and effect.

For labor to accept management's initial offer in negotiations is practically unheard of, because labor has its position of prestige and power to maintain. The labor leader must prove to the workers that he truly represents them in their demands, that he understands their feelings. Similarly, the representative of management has responsibility to his superiors, who in turn represent the stockholders. Although each recognizes the other's position, clearly each faction in the dispute tries to sell his particular side to the public. Misunderstandings are almost inevitable. It is of great help that the industrial psychologist who is working in this area knows what each side brings into the situation. He knows that the individuals representing labor and management come with somewhat prejudiced backgrounds as *individuals,* and he knows that the *situation* itself accentuates the differences in their points of view.

Finding the Cause. Sometimes the cause of a person's behavior is concealed. He may take an intense dislike to someone he has just met, without apparent cause, until he is made aware that this person acts just like someone with whom he has had unpleasant experiences. The worker who is reprimanded may feel that his foreman spoke without cause, whereas the concealed but quite real cause may be that the foreman is worried about a problem at home.

One may miss seeing the actual cause for behavior when something else seems more apparent. The apparent cause of a strike may be failure to get a raise in wages; this may even be the cause that is stated publicly. But often it is found that the real cause is something less easy to see, such as loss of status of the union leaders or dissatisfaction with supervision.

Sometimes we miss seeing the cause of behavior because of a prejudice we hold or because we wish to see some particular cause-effect relationship. We may see a situation as a cause of something, when the real cause does not lie within the situation but within the person involved. One may blame his lack of promotion on office politics rather than on his own lack of ability.

Cause-Effect Complexities. One pitfall in practical problem solving comes from transferring a cause-effect relationship which appears in one situation to another situation in which it is not valid. For instance, in considering a problem of absenteeism, it is possible to assume too quickly that the first cause suspected is the real one. Perhaps it has been found that improving the physical working conditions will reduce absenteeism among women; yet it may be a costly error to assume that such improvements will have the same effect upon men. The fact that most heavy drinkers are frequently absent from work should not lead one to generalize that this is *the* major cause of absenteeism; we may discover that most workers who have frequent absences are not heavy drinkers. High rates of absence on Monday in some plants may lead us to suspect that the workers have indulged in a big week end, but in actuality the cause may be poor supervision.

The psychologist working in industry has a particularly difficult job ascertaining cause and effect relationships. For one thing he is often dealing with multiple causation, and he does not have many conditions favoring well-controlled experimentation. Whereas industry is willing to spend time and money on product research, it is still not completely sold on human behavior research. Industrialists have been hoodwinked at times by non-professional people parading as scientists. This has made the job of the professional psychologist more difficult. But there is growing evidence that psychology itself is being accepted more and more in industry as managers are learning what the behavioral sciences have to offer.

PSYCHOLOGY AS A BEHAVIORAL SCIENCE

The behavioral sciences include a number of disciplines, such as anthropology, economics, history, political science, sociology, and psychology. Other specialties which are closely related to the behavioral sciences have a bearing on industrial psychology, namely, management engineering, industrial administration, industrial design, and labor relations. Differences among the behavioral sciences are not always clearly demarcated, but this does not cause confusion when a given discipline is problem oriented. Both anthropology and sociology are concerned with groups of people, and in both disciplines emphasis is given to the study of the cultures of various societies or groups. Social anthropology is particularly interested in primitive cultures and how societies have developed from them.

The events that make history are primarily events of human behavior. Economics touches on behavior as it deals with the making and distribution of goods, with market analyses, and predictions of what people may do next in buying stocks and bonds. Political science is closely related to industry through its studies of institutionalized governments.

By understanding how businesses are organized, how they are managed, and the complexities of the power struggles between management and labor, we get a wider view of how industrial psychology is related to many other specialties.

A Four-way Function. Industrial psychology is concerned with four relationships of man as he functions in industry. It is interested in relations between person and person, between person and group, between person and object, and in problems of the inner man himself.

The salesman who tries to get you to buy his company's product or service functions in a *person-to-person* relationship. The supervisor who gives orders to his workers is functioning in a *person-to-group* relationship, just as is the man who deals with groups in the school or in the community. The worker who operates a machine is engaged in a *person-to-object* relationship, the source of many psychological problems in industry. Perhaps most important of all are the problems of *intrapersonal* relations which arise when a man tries to understand his own desires, abilities, and frustrations.

Industrial psychology borrows from a number of fields within psychology itself as it utilizes the facts, theories, and methods of experimental, social, and clinical psychology.

THE METHODS OF PSYCHOLOGY APPLIED TO INDUSTRY

The experimental method of psychology teaches us to define the real problem, relate it to known principles, vary certain aspects in the conditions while holding others constant, make hypotheses, collect and analyze data, and verify our hypotheses. The experimental method requires that we conduct experiments in ways that allow for repetition and for control. It requires that we understand the variables involved.

Designing Experiments in Industry. In the laboratory it is relatively easy to design experiments so that they can be repeated. Let us say we are interested in the effects of exposure of white rats to gamma irradiation from cobalt, perhaps the effects it may have on learning ability. It is a simple matter to get animals that can be paired off into test groups and control groups, to describe and control precisely each aspect of the experimental situation, and to collect and analyze the data in standard ways. Such an experiment can be set up and repeated wherever appropriate animals and physical conditions exist. To date some sixty experiments of this kind have been reported in the literature, and each one is of a nature allowing for repetition. Indeed, a few of the studies have been repetitions, some by the same people, some by others.

Some experiments in industrial psychology can be repeated anywhere as easily as the one just described above. For example, one can determine with high certainty whether horizontal-type meters can be read with any greater degree of accuracy than vertical-type meters. However, many industrial problems are so involved and so complex that repetition under exactly similar conditions often is not possible. This does not mean that we should not try to apply the experimental method to the problems. It does mean that we have to be aware of the limitations of our study. It is not possible, for example, to learn with any great degree of accuracy just how effective human relations courses in supervision are in terms of their specifics. We can, however, get some fairly good approximations by applying problem-solving methods to our studies.

A second limitation in applying the experimental method to industrial human problems is that the experiment itself may interfere with the very thing we are trying to study. For example, we may wish to determine whether the severe noise generated by a jet plane has any effect on the performance of the mechanic testing the aircraft. If the people know they are subjects in an experiment the results may be affected by that awareness. But the situation may be such that if we are to get answers at all the subjects will have to know what we are doing. This is, of course, a limitation in our experiment. Nevertheless, important findings can be obtained even under such limitations (see page 213).

Another limitation of an experiment may be that it has some artificial arrangement in it. In an attempt to discover which variables are important to a problem, the psychologist must select the ones he wants to control. He may be lucky and select the variables which will give him results of importance. On the other hand, he may have poor luck and go through the motions of an experiment that leads nowhere. Sometimes he may get negative results, because the wrong questions were asked when he set the experiment up; yet he may find later that the results opened up a whole new set of important problems not considered before (see page 32).

But do not let these limitations of the scientific method discourage you. They are present in all the sciences: in physics and in chemistry and in the biological sciences. They just appear more frequently in the behavioral sciences. In the chemistry laboratory one can be given an unknown solution to analyze. If one cannot run his tests on Friday, one stores the solution in an appropriate place where temperature and pressure are controlled, and waits until Monday to make the analysis. On Monday the solution is just the same, and the analysis can be made just as accurately.

But if someone comes to you on Friday with a personal problem, you cannot defer listening until Monday. Neither he nor his problem can be put into cold storage.

Experimental Variables. Our picture of the experimental method is clearer when we consider the part played by *variables,* and by the *control* of variables. To do an experiment we must have at least two variables. For example, suppose we want to find out whether there is any relationship between taking salt pills and increasing productivity in making steel ingots under conditions of extreme temperature. Several things may be involved, but one important possibility is that the men may be influenced by suggestion. We therefore design our experiment to control this possibility. We select two groups of steelworkers, comparable in age, productivity, safety records, and a dozen other things, and give one group genuine salt pills and the other group a pill with only an outer coating of salt. The latter group is our control group; the group which gets the salt pills is the experimental group.

In this study we are dealing with two variables: the number of salt pills and the amount of productivity. In more technical language, we call the salt an "independent variable" because we can, if we wish, vary the amount independently of other factors in the experiment. Productivity, on the other hand, is our "dependent variable" because we are interested in whether or not variations in productivity of ingots depend upon the use of salt pills.

It is sometimes difficult in experiments to determine which is the independent and which is the dependent variable. Usually in setting up an experiment we have at least one independent variable and one or more dependent variables. Our problem becomes a little more confused when we include "intervening variables." In our example, it is possible that the amount of water in the worker's body at any given time is related to the effects that salt may have on fatigue and hence on productivity. Often it is these in-between variables that we have difficulty knowing about. Let us consider, for example, a question which on the surface seems simple to answer: "What is the relationship between the intensity of illumination and productivity?" How would you design an experiment to answer this problem? What variables would you have to deal with? (Think about this a few minutes before turning to page 33, where the results of one such experiment are detailed.)

Surveys and Clinical Information. Valuable data about human problems in industry come from surveys and from clinical observations. Much of what we know about the problems of labor-management relations, advertising and selling, human relations in supervision, and mental health has been learned by using these procedures.

One of the big contributions of industrial psychology has been to coordinate the methods of the experimenter, the survey psychologist, and the clinician into a resourceful attack on the problems of the people who work in industry, who live in the industrial community.

AN ORIENTATION

Part I of this book deals with several aspects of psychology in industry. Beginning with the following chapter, we describe the development of industrial psychology since its origin at the turn of the century. This history is an interesting story of the people and the events that led to the present-day practices and research techniques of the psychologist working in industry.

Some sixty years after the beginning of industrial psychology, we find the psychologist now entering into a new role, participating in systems planning and high-level decision making. We find the behavioral scientist bringing a knowledge of the human component to a system composed of machines, procedures, processes, information handling, and human beings. He is working with and constantly qualifying the productions of engineers, accountants, market analysts, and process specialists.

Organizations and Their Functions. Part II, "The Industrial Environment," is a description of how industries are organized and how they function. The physical and psychological structures of the modern industrial scene are described as they appear within the framework of both management and labor organizations. There is reason to believe that some people fail to adjust to the industrial world because they do not know what they are getting into. Likewise, some people who find jobs and rewards in industry to their liking attribute much of their success to an early understanding of and adjustment to the industrial environment. Through a description of the anatomy of modern companies, the structures and functions of labor unions, the psychological climates of organizations, we help set the stage for understanding the part played by the human element in engineering, producing, and marketing industrial goods.

Attention is given to how business is conducted in different kinds and sizes of organizations, how the controller determines decisions, how businesses function in meeting competition. We make an analysis of what different divisions and departments of a company do, how engineering works with sales, how industrial relations works with manufacturing. This material gives the background for understanding where the psychologist fits into the company, why he is restricted in his operation on the one hand, and why he is becoming more and more a key staff member on the other.

Human Resources in Industry. Part III is devoted to what has been called "personnel psychology." It begins with descriptions of the nature of human needs, the things that make men like or dislike their jobs, how people in industry react to frustration. Here we are concerned with the desires of people at all levels, ranging from factory workers to corporation executives. Chapter 5 is designed to give a background for understanding the many human behavior problems found in industry.

In the chapter on personnel selection we consider the several variables involved in fitting the man to the right job. Here the reader will be made aware of the important questions he will face when he begins plans for his own career. The chapter on training considers problems already of interest to the college student; it describes the efficient conditions for learning, human quality control, and the evaluation of training results.

Generalizations about human relations are discussed in the chapter dealing with supervision. The nature of effective problem solving in groups, and individually, is brought out as the reader is led through a maze of human relations situations found at the worker level. Since many college graduates who enter business soon find themselves in supervisory positions, we believe that the description of the multiple roles of the supervisor is valuable for practical as well as for academic use.

One of the areas of industrial psychology currently receiving much attention involves executive leadership and development. Modern business has expanded so rapidly that there is a shortage of people for middle management and top executive jobs. As the reader learns what is involved in executive development, he will discover ways to measure his own potential for high-level leadership. By considering the problems and the research findings presented, the student will be impressed with the necessity of separating fact from fancy in decision making, and he will learn the price one must pay in assuming responsibilities of leadership.

The bases for job satisfaction, methods of measuring attitudes, and ways to improve group morale are presented in a way that pulls together the constructs developed in the preceding chapters.

Labor in Industry. In Part IV, "Labor Problems in Industry," we describe the over-all framework of labor-management relations which cause industrial conflict. We discuss why workers join unions and the roles of unions in our society. Problems of the handicapped, the unemployed, and the aging worker are becoming more acute each year. Does the handicapped person make a reliable, productive worker? What are the effects of unemployment on the individual? Are our criteria for retirement sound? These, and similar specialized problems of labor, are considered. For instance, a chapter is devoted to women in industry. One-third of the entire labor force of the United States is composed of women. What do they do? How do their attitudes and capacities differ from those of men? What are the opportunities for women in industry? In answering such questions, we have given attention to the prejudices against women, as well as to the factors in their favor.

Work. The nature of work and such specialized problems as accidents and safety are described in Part V, "Problems Related to Work." Man's work is affected by the tools and machines which he has available to help him. Within the past decade engineering psychology, or "human engineering," as it is sometimes called, has expanded rapidly; it uses the knowledge of man's behavior that is gleaned from psychology to improve objects or devices in his environment. In the job of modifying the machines with which man works, it considers the man and the machine as a single over-all system, linked together and analyzed as a unit.

Consumers and Communities in Industry. The ways and means of distributing goods and services to meet consumer needs and wants are described in Part VI of the text, "Influence and Social Interaction." Attention is given to the psychological principles applied to advertising and selling and to the recent emphasis on the relations between industries and communities.

Mental Health. As never before, industrial leaders are concerned with mental hygiene, for the simple reason that an unhealthy mind is costly to industry. Attention is given in Part VII, "The Individual in Industry," to such problems as alcoholism, absenteeism, the fears of failure, the unpromotable executive, and status differentials—in effect, the mental-health climates of the several different aspects of industry. The chapter on personal adjustments in industry will be extremely useful to the student who will someday find himself in industry.

YOUR PERSONAL INTERESTS

Possibly most students of applied psychology, personnel psychology, human relations, or industrial psychology have elected the course. In a survey to determine some of the reasons students take such a course, it was found that a few did so simply because it fitted conveniently into their schedules or because they were interested in broadening their general education. Most students, however, reported that they chose the course because they planned to go into industry and they felt that a description of the human aspects of industry would help to prepare them for the job ahead.

This text has not been written to include just what the student wants. It has been prepared by professional men with firsthand experience in industry, either as part-time consultants or as full-time staff members, who have written on what they believe the student should know.

You will find that some of the problems described are familiar to you, particularly to those of you who have worked for pay. Few, if any, problems will be covered that are totally lacking in interest to you. You will possibly wish to project yourself into the situations and problems described. This is good. When we discuss the multiple roles of the supervisor, you are encouraged to picture yourself both in his position and also in the role of worker. When executive leadership problems are discussed, try to feel yourself in a position of having to make the right decision. Learn to look at advertisements within the framework of the psychology of influence, or consider what you would do about some strike situation you read about in the paper, once you know the real facts.

A Suggestion. The attitude one has as he reads a textbook strongly influences what he gets out of it. We suggest that you will get the most from this book if you ask yourself such questions as: How can learning about human behavior in industry apply to my personal experiences? How can I continue to learn about human behavior? How can I put to use what I will learn?

We suggest that when you sit down to read a chapter in the book you first read the headings in order to get a rough idea of the organization of the chapter. After this, you may find it of value to formulate a few questions to ask yourself before you settle down to careful reading. In the chapter on executive leadership and development, over one thousand articles and books were studied before the author started to write the chapter. You may speculate on the kinds of questions about leadership that have led to so many writings on the subject. No doubt your questions are much the same as those which others have asked and tried to get answers to. What are the requirements of a good leader? Do I have what it takes to be a leader? Seeking out the answers to such questions, of course, many of which may not be found in the text, is a good way to get an education. Asking good questions even without finding answers contributes to one's thinking. We hope that this book will stimulate your interest in the behavior of people who work in industry.

This text is focused on the understanding of psychological principles and their use in making the kinds of decisions businessmen must make in working with people. It is designed to help you acquire some specific understandings, skills, and desires which will prepare you to learn to work with others with increasing consideration, understanding, and effectiveness.

2

THE DEVELOPMENT

OF INDUSTRIAL

PSYCHOLOGY

Leonard W. Ferguson

Industrial psychology in America began for the simple reason that a few businessmen, faced with practical problems about people, wanted help. It began when academic psychologists trained in the rigors of the scientific method became convinced that industry offered a proper setting for the study of human behavior. From the very beginning the problems were challenging, but refined techniques and organizations for attacking them were lacking. Through the efforts and foresight of some two dozen psychologists and a number of businessmen in different companies, industrial psychology had its beginning. This chapter is the story of that beginning.

FIRST PSYCHOLOGIST TO INDUSTRY

In the fall semester of 1901 young Walter Dill Scott, associate professor of psychology at Northwestern University, received a visitor, Thomas K. Balmer, Western advertising manager of a chain of magazines. Balmer wanted someone to give a talk about how psychology might be used in advertising. He had been to see Münsterberg at Harvard, Thorndike at Columbia, and Coe at Northwestern, but they were not interested in his invitation.

Scott also refused to give the talk. Nowhere in his training at Leipzig under Wundt had he learned about advertising. Moreover, at that time no one could help his academic reputation by dabbling in the practical affairs of the business world. No, sir—he would stick to his laboratory.

"One can be just as scientific about advertising as about anything else," retorted Balmer. "Don't psychologists claim to know something about the normal adult mind? Don't they know about the various stimuli which confront this mind and how it reacts to them?"

After two hours of conversation, Scott agreed to give the talk. He thereby started the science of industrial and business psychology. Speaking before the Agate Club in Chicago on December 20, 1901, he said: "Psychology is, broadly speaking, the science of the mind. Art is the doing and science is the understanding how to do, or the explanation of what has been done. If we are able to find and to express the psychological laws upon which the art of advertising is based, we shall have made a distinct advance, for we shall have added the science to the art of advertising."

John Lee Mahin, head of a large advertising agency, was in the audience. He offered to establish a monthly magazine if Scott would write a series of articles for it. Encouraged by a fee of $250, Scott accepted. This is how it came about that Scott prepared the first series of articles showing how psychology could be used in advertising. And this is how it came about that Scott became America's first industrial or business psychologist.

Scott wrote articles. And he also wrote books, among them, *The Theory and Practice of Advertising, The Psychology of Advertising, The Psychology of Advertising in Theory and Practice, The Psychology of Public Speaking,* and *Influencing Men in Business.* He wrote reviews and accounts of the works of contemporary pioneers, such as Harlow Gale of the University of Minnesota, Daniel Starch of the University of Wisconsin, and Hugo Münsterberg of Harvard. Then, on June 1, 1916, he became the first professor of applied psychology. He was appointed to teach in the Division of Applied Psychology (the first of its kind) which had been established at the Carnegie Institute of Technology in 1915 under Walter V. Bingham.

EARLY RESEARCH IN INDUSTRIAL PSYCHOLOGY

Soon after Bingham arrived in Pittsburgh (in the fall of 1915), Arthur Arton Hamerschlag, president of the Carnegie Institute of Technology, introduced him to Edward A. Woods, a prominent Pittsburgh businessman.

"Can you not," asked Woods, "arrange to give in your newly formed Division of Applied Psychology a course in salesmanship?"

"What's the matter with the courses given in various commercial institutes?" asked Bingham.

"They are good as far as they go, but I want a course at the collegiate level that would really fit a man to be a salesman."

"Well, before we could give such a course," replied Bingham and

Hamerschlag, "we should have to do a lot of research. We should have to find out how good and poor salesmen differ from each other. This would take time, it would cost money."

"How much time, how much money?" Woods queried.

Industry Sponsors Research. Soon it was agreed that Woods, backed by two of his business acquaintances, would get each of thirty firms to contribute $500 a year for five years, a total of $75,000 for the program. As a result, on June 1, 1916, the Bureau of Salesmanship Research was established. And it was to head this bureau that Scott received his appointment.

In order to dramatize the work which the Bureau of Salesmanship Research was to undertake, Scott and Bingham journeyed to Detroit. There they met Guy Montrose Whipple, professor of education at the University of Illinois and noted pioneer in the field of mental tests. Together with Whipple they attended the World's First Salesmanship Congress. During this congress, in July, 1916, Scott, Bingham, and Whipple conducted the first widely acclaimed demonstration of the unreliability of the employment interview. Duplicating an experiment which Scott and his Northwestern University students had several times performed, Scott, Bingham, and Whipple showed beyond all possible doubt that twenty experienced sales managers differed widely and profoundly in their respective assessments concerning the suitability for employment of twenty-four bona fide sales applicants. To do this, Scott, Bingham, and Whipple allowed each sales manager five minutes to interview each of the applicants. They then found that the sales managers could agree on only six of the applicants. And the sales managers could agree only in terms of whether the applicant should be considered as belonging to the top half or bottom half of the group.

As indicated earlier, Edward A. Woods was motivated to back the plans which led to the Bureau of Salesmanship Research because he felt salesmen should be better trained. But Woods, who was the head of the largest and most successful life insurance agency in the United States, president of the National Association of Life Underwriters, and instigator and chairman-to-be of this organization's Committee of Scientific Salesmanship, might also have meant to encourage better selection. Better selection was almost imperative, because one of the toughest problems faced by the National Association of Life Underwriters was that of eliminating the rebater, i.e., the agent who offered to his prospect as an inducement for the purchase of a policy, part or all of his expected sales commission.

Research on Personnel Selection. From the very start of his membership in the National Association of Life Underwriters, Woods had been associated with a number of attempts to stamp out the rebate evil. In particular he identified himself with efforts to improve the selection of persons who were to enter the life insurance business. Therefore, Woods could not help but favor a plan introduced by Colonel Thomas L. Peters of the Washington Life Insurance Company of Atlanta, Georgia.

Peters said, at the 1894 Chicago Underwriters Meeting, that one way to stamp out the rebate evil would be for managers to require all applicants to answer a list of standardized questions, such as the following: Present residence? Residences during the previous ten years? Birth date and place? Marital status? Dependent or not dependent for support on own daily exertions? Amount of unencumbered real estate? Occupation during previous ten years? Previous experience in life insurance selling? For what companies? For what general agents? When and where? Claims, if any, for unsettled accounts? References? Such a list had been developed and used, said Peters, by his associates in the Georgia Association of Life Insurers. So it was not a group of psychologists, as many have believed, but a group of businessmen who created what is truly the granddaddy of standardized personal history and application blanks.

As we might suspect, there was nothing especially scientific about this early form. But Woods himself, early in 1915 and months before he had met Bingham, attempted a statistical analysis. Crude perhaps by modern standards, this analysis was based, nevertheless, upon a concept central in all modern selection research. This is the concept that the only items of predictive value are those which can be shown statistically to differentiate between carefully defined success and failure groups. For utilizing this concept Woods must be ranked with Münsterberg, who was the first psychologist to see the importance of comparing test scores with a criterion.

Aids in Selecting Salesmen. Taking over much of Woods's material and catching the spirit of his enthusiasm, Scott and his student associates readied for publication an impressive-looking volume, *Aids in the Selection of Salesmen.* By no means the first, (but clearly the most comprehensive) series of such aids that had by 1917 been made available, these aids, together with events we shall soon describe, set the pattern of selection research and practice which has been followed by industrial and business psychologists ever since.

First, there was an application blank or personal history record. This had resulted, said Scott and his students, from "the study of a large number of application blanks used by different firms." It had as its purpose, as did the form which resulted from Woods's earlier analysis, the organized compilation of "what appeared to be the most important parts of one's early training, environment, and experience . . . items . . . shown statistically . . . to have an important bearing on future success in certain lines of business."

Second, there was a Letter to Former Employers. Allegedly simpler than many letters then in common use, it was, said Scott and his students, a letter in which "all . . . essential parts . . . had been tested." It would be used to determine previous employers' opinions concerning the suitability of the applicant's industry, personal habits and conduct, and fitness for a selling position.

Third, there was an Interviewer's Scale, and fourth, an Interviewer's Rating Sheet. Together these comprised the basis of the Scott man-to-man rating system, a system designed to shorten the time of the interview by making the interviewer concentrate his attention on the few essential characteristics of a successful salesman.

To use the method, an interviewer had to proceed through several steps. First, he had to have before him the names of at least twenty salesmen. Second, he had to indicate which of these salesmen ranked highest, lowest, and intermediate on each of several traits: appearance, convincingness, industry, character, and value to the firm. Third, he had to indicate for each trait a salesman who ranked midway between highest and intermediate, and a second salesman who ranked midway between intermediate and lowest. These steps accomplished, the interviewer had in his possession what Scott and his students called the "master scale" (one for each trait).

Fourth, in order to provide an appraisal of a person to be rated, the interviewer compared the person with each of those listed on the master scale for the appropriate trait. Then by choosing a certain numerical value he indicated how closely the person being rated corresponded with which individual on the master scale.

Fifth, there were psychological tests. Among the most important of these, and the only one we shall mention here, was that known as Test I*a*, a forerunner of many modern-day spiral omnibus mental-alertness tests and, itself, modeled after an earlier test prepared by Scott.

PSYCHOLOGY IN WORLD WAR I

Just as Scott and his student collaborators were in the process of publishing their *Aids* and before many of the cooperating firms of the Bureau of Salesmanship Research had had a chance to put them into effect, the United States found itself at war with Germany.

An Emergency Meeting. On the day that war was declared, April 6, 1917, a meeting of experimental psychologists, was being held at Harvard University under Titchener's chairmanship. Promptly, Robert M. Yerkes, who was then president of the American Psychological Association, called an emergency meeting. Soon thereafter he also called APA's governing council into session in order to discover ways in which psychologists could be most useful to the war effort. In two sessions (on April 21 and 22,

1917) the council reached a number of decisions and appointed several committees to execute various courses of action.

One of the most important of these courses of action was that designed to establish a program whereby the Army would be able to eliminate those mentally unfit for Army duty, to classify according to their intelligence levels all or at least most of those who entered military service, and to select for promotion to officer status those of superior ability. A Committee on the Psychological Examination of Recruits, with Yerkes himself as chairman, was assigned specific responsibility for this program. With alacrity, the committee prepared two tests—*a* for literates, *b* for illiterates —and gave them to 3,501 recruits. The results were so satisfactory that the committee sought and received official governmental support.

Yerkes was commissioned a major and made head of a Section (later a Division) of Psychology under the aegis of the Surgeon General. This division restudied tests *a* and *b* and out of them created two new tests— Army Alpha and Army Beta. The tests were widely used, and they contributed materially to the effective selection, classification, and assignment of Army recruits during World War I.

FIRST ORGANIZATION FOR PERSONNEL CONSULTING

During the council meeting which led to the work just described, Scott found himself in disagreement with the majority decision. Particularly, he disagreed with Yerkes who had held that the testing of initial recruits was the one most important thing psychologists might do to help the war along. "Not so," said Scott. "The one most important way in which psychologists can contribute to the war effort is to aid in the selection of officers." And they could do this by seeing that the Army installed an adequate system of rating its officer candidates. Such a system was available, said he, in the Carnegie Tech man-to-man rating system.

Acting on his own responsibility, Scott secured the backing of Newton D. Baker, Secretary of War. As a result, a Committee on Classification of Personnel was formed in the Adjutant General's Office. Its organizational setup based on that of the Bureau of Salesmanship Research, this committee, under Scott, developed before the war was over a complete Army personnel program. This included (1) a set of qualification cards on which were recorded the qualifications for military duty of each enlisted man and officer; (2) an index of occupations which indicated what civilian occupations were valuable in various branches of military service; (3) a series of personnel specifications for military job assignment; (4) a series of trade tests; and, (5) a specialized Army Training Corps program.

The Scott Company. As the war neared its end, several members of the

Committee on Classification of Personnel, chief among them Robert C. Clothier (who later became president of Rutgers University) began to wonder if the Committee might not, with profit, organize a personnel consulting organization which could offer to civilian business and industry the same type of personnel service it had developed for the Army. Wonder begat interest. Interest begat action. So, in February, 1919, there came into existence the Scott Company, the first personnel consulting organization to be established.

The Scott Company adapted for civilian use the idea of the soldier's and officer's qualification cards. On the basis of results secured therewith, it suggested that its clients provide various training and educational programs for their employees. The company also proposed that organization and promotion charts and suggested avenues of employee development be made explicit and public and that, in the spirit of industrial democracy, organizations of employees be encouraged.

The Scott Company developed and installed for several clients (and even sold to a short-lived competing firm, Coburn & Hoadley of Boston) a mental-alertness test, Scott Test 1. Modeled directly after Army Alpha, this test looked very much like and, in fact, was a continuation or rather a revision once removed of Test 1 published by the Bureau of Salesmanship Research.

The company recommended to one of its clients, the United States Civil Service Commission, the establishment of a research section. Suggested specifically by Beardsley Ruml (known in a later day as the author of the pay-as-you-go method of income tax collection), this research section was to formalize work started earlier by John B. Watson, who in April, 1919, had been engaged "as an expert examiner to start experiments with a view to determining whether the principles observed by psychologists in testing . . . were applicable to civil service examinations." Under the direction of L. J. O'Rourke, this section (beginning its work on July 1, 1922) put into effect our modern system of standardized civil service examinations.

Tests and Training Aids. The Scott Company installed a large number of trade tests. These tests were developed under the direct supervision of Beardsley Ruml who, while serving with Louis B. Hopkins as the co-director of the Trade Test Division of the Committee on Classification of Personnel, formulated the basic rules by which such tests have been constructed ever since. Under the immediate supervision of Arthur Kornhauser a series of apprentice training manuals was developed. Based upon the elements involved in appropriate trade tests, these manuals provided a foundation for systematic and orderly individual instruction in a large variety of skills pertinent to shopwork and machine-tool work.

As an indication of its versatility the Scott Company originated, developed, and installed what today we would call "point systems" of job classification and salary evaluation. In this work it anticipated by a good five years the work of Merrill Lott, who has generally, but erroneously, been considered the originator of the point system of job evaluation.

The company invented and installed for several of its clients the graphic rating scale; this scale replaced the man-to-man rating system which businessmen found too cumbersome for routine practical use. The company helped its clients establish and staff their employment and other service bureaus. In some cases, in order to facilitate this work, the company released its own supervising staff member so that he could take on full-time employment with the client company.

A Philosophy about the Worker. The Scott Company installed, organized, and staffed complete personnel departments. In this connection it developed the philosophy, sparked by Ruml, of the worker-in-his-work unit. In other words, it developed the idea that the worker and his job were together an integral unit. This idea was opposed to Münsterberg's notion that there existed the worker, on the one hand, and the job, on the other; and that, since this was the case, the task of the personnel department was to look for square pegs, i.e., square workers, to fit square holes, i.e., square jobs. In contrast, said the Scott Company, the task of the personnel department was to develop harmonious, integrated worker-in-his-work-units, and in this task to recognize the fact that any given job could change a worker and that any given worker could change a job. Scott and his associates encouraged and assisted both management and employee organizations to develop a sound, adequate, and forward-looking labor relations philosophy and progressive arbitration procedures. It consulted, for example, with the Chicago Clothing Workers Federation and helped this organization and the Almagamated Clothing Workers of America to develop the sound framework upon which labor relations in the clothing workers industry has always rested. The Scott Company prepared technical articles and books. Ranking high among these is Scott and Mary Holmes Stevens Hayes's *Science and Common Sense in Working with Men,* and Scott and Clothier's *Personnel Management.*

A History-making Book. Shortly before the publication of the second of the aforementioned books, the Scott Company ceased to exist. In spite of an auspicious and profitable start, it suffered, as did many other business concerns, from the recession of 1921 and 1922. Old clients began to cut expenses and new clients became harder to get. Staff members, including Scott, who became president of Northwestern University, began to depart. The inevitable end came but, fortunately, not until Clothier had completed copy for his and Scott's history-making book, *Personnel Management.* Through this book, one that became and for years remained the bible of the personnel movement, the Scott Company extended its influence far beyond its own limited group of clients. From a scientific standpoint it set the pace for what today we know as modern personnel administration and practice.

RETAIL TRAINING

During World War I one of the original members of the Bureau of Salesmanship Research, the Kaufmann Department Stores, Inc., headed by the vigorous and forward-looking Pittsburgh merchant, Edgar J. Kaufmann, perceived from the way in which the work at the Bureau of Salesmanship Research was to be conducted that a long time would have to elapse before results specifically applicable to the field of merchandising and retail selling might materialize. Therefore, Kaufmann petitioned Hamerschlag and Bingham to establish a second bureau which could devote its attention exclusively to this field. If such a bureau were established, he along with six other Pittsburgh merchants, would be willing to subsidize it to the extent of $32,000 a year, for five years.

Specialized Training. Hamerschlag gave his approval to Kaufmann's plea, and on May 14, 1918, a Research Bureau for Retail Training came into being. Under the initial guidance of James Burt Miner, who was appointed acting director, this bureau set out "to give professional training to those planning to enter the field of retailing and to those who desired to become more efficient in that field, to train special teachers and supervisors in this field, and to conduct investigations for the improvement of methods of selecting, training, and supervising the employees in retail stores."

In 1919 Bingham secured W. W. Charters, professor of education at the University of Illinois, as permanent director for the Research Bureau for Retail Training. Charters, an expert in curriculum construction, saw that a great opportunity for the bureau lay in the possibility of its doing extensive research in his own major field of interest. In an environment where objectives had to be eminently practical, he and his associates could determine, or at least try to determine, the most effective ways of preparing curricula and of giving instruction. Unlike the typical academic course of long duration, a course in the Research Bureau for Retail Training was to be relatively short. If one method of curriculum construction or if one method of instruction didn't work, another could soon be tried.

Principles of Operation. Under Charters's leadership and in pursuance of the three aims established by its founders, the Research Bureau for Retail Training evolved and publicized a set of principles that have since guided work in this field. For example, bureau personnel, students as well as staff, were among the first to enunciate clearly the distinction between those persons who embark upon practical or applied research and those who choose to engage in what many scientists and academicians prefer to call "pure research." The former in contrast to the latter must, in the paraphrased words of Charters, study an organization to find its weaknesses, select one or more of these weaknesses as a problem for investigation, secure the best solution possible, install the solution, and maintain this solution in practice. Unlike the pure researcher who needs to study only those problems which interest him and who can stop whenever he wishes, the practical researcher must put his solution into practice. He must see that it works. And if it doesn't, he is obliged to start all over again.

A second principle of operation developed and publicized by the Research Bureau for Retail Training was that one should begin his investigation with a job analysis. This analysis should consist of two parts: duty analysis and difficulty analysis. In other words, when one has the task of building, let us say, a course for training department heads—as, in fact, the bureau did—the way to begin is by asking department heads what they do. A written description of these duties will constitute a duty analysis. Then one should ask department heads to describe their difficulties. A written description of these will constitute a difficulty analysis. Having the foregoing, one can then prepare course material in such a manner that a trainee will have the opportunity to learn ahead of time what duties and what difficulties he will experience when he enters upon the job of being a department head.

A third principle of operation developed and publicized by the Research Bureau for Retail Training, and one uniquely associated with Charters, is that contained under the rubric "the unrecorded specific." Said Charters, "There is more information on the problems of the department store which has never been written up than can be found in print. Go and collect these unrecorded specifics, write them down, and make them available for others to use." Thus, in publications such as the *Handling of Sales People, How to Sell at Retail,* and *Department Training,* the Research Bureau for Retail Training set the modern pattern for the preparation and construction of training guides and manuals.

That one must consider not only classroom instruction but on-the-job training came as a fourth principle. "This consisted," said Charters, "of five steps: analysis, demonstration, trial, correction, and follow-up." So here is the origin, or at least one of the very early versions, of the currently popular and much publicized PEDOS training formula: preparation, explanation, demonstration, observation, and supervision.

Finally, a principle developed and publicized by the Research Bureau for Retail Training was that the attitude of executives is most important. "For in these attitudes basically lies," said Charters, "not only the success or failure of any training or research program, but the very morale of the entire organization." Without good morale, said the bureau, little of a constructive nature in the way of better employee education or training could be accomplished. A point brought home to bureau students by Whiting Williams of the Hydraulic Pressed Steel Company, one of the first persons to assess, evaluate, and publicize (in his Carnegie Tech lectures as well as in his books, *What's on the Worker's Mind,* and *Mainsprings of Men*) the importance of employee attitudes.

The research and training experience which led Charters, his colleagues, and his students to the foregoing principles also brought about the establishment on a permanent basis in the Pittsburgh area of collegiate-level instruction in the field of retail selling, the establishment in retail stores of educational and research departments, the preparation and publication of many merchandise and training manuals, the publication of many trade and professional articles, and the publication of several books. Finally the bureau was put on a permanent and endowed basis at the University of Pittsburgh, where it is located today (following its transfer from Carnegie Tech in 1923). The Research Bureau for Retail Training now ranks as one of the major centers for research and training in the field of merchandising, retail selling, and department store management.

FIRST SCHOOL OF LIFE INSURANCE SALESMANSHIP

Working closely with Scott during the war years was an energetic and lively person by the name of Winslow Russell. A civilian associate of the Committee on Classification of Personnel and head of this committee's War Service Exchange, a placement bureau for those with special talent and skill, Russell was vice-president of the Phoenix Mutual Life Insurance Company of Hartford, Connecticut. He was also a very close friend of Edward A. Woods. For this and other reasons, he was present in Detroit in 1916 when, during the World's First Salesmanship Congress, Scott, Bingham, and Whipple demonstrated (so vividly and dramatically) the unreliability of the employment interview.

Association for Cooperative Research. Present also in Detroit in 1916 were a large number of life insurance agency or sales executives. These executives were in Detroit for a special reason. Edward A. Woods, a member of the executive committee which had arranged the congress, had invited them because Winslow Russell had asked him to do so. Russell wished to discuss with these executives the possibility of organizing an association of life insurance sales executives. Russell presented his case, and thereby laid the groundwork for what became soon thereafter (in October, 1916) the Association of Life Agency Officers. Its purpose was to promote discussion, the free interchange of ideas, and cooperative research on the selection and training of life insurance salesmen.

Under the prodding furnished by this organization, as well as that earlier and concurrently provided by Edward A. Woods, Hamerschlag and Bingham contacted Griffin M. Lovelace, superintendent of agencies of the Connecticut Mutual Life Insurance Company, and asked him to develop at Carnegie Tech a curriculum appropriate for the training of life insurance salesmen. (Remember, it was interest in training that had led Woods in 1915 to seek Bingham's help.) This Lovelace did. In a way now to be described, he completely revolutionized the technique of life insurance salesmanship.

Proceeding logically, Lovelace developed, first, a course on the *functions* of life insurance to show what purposes life insurance fulfills; second, a course on the *principles* of life insurance to show how a life insurance company operates; and third, a course on *practical selling* to show an agent what he had to do in the field. Next, reasoned Lovelace, there should be a course on the *theory of selling* to show the salesman why one approach or close was better than another. Not himself a psychologist, Lovelace asked Edward K. Strong, Jr., then a newcomer to the Carnegie Tech staff, for help. Strong replied that if Lovelace would outline a series of interviews giving typical examples of what actually took place when a salesman found himself face to face with a prospect, he would see what he could do. Lovelace wrote the requested outlines, and Strong assumed the task of developing one of the four courses to be offered in the curriculum of the School of Life Insurance Salesmanship. One of the results was his well-known text, *The Psychology of Selling Life Insurance.*

Recognizing Human Needs. Opening its doors on October 1, 1919, the School of Life Insurance Salesmanship (together with its followers, imitators, and successors) trained in a few short years several thousand life insurance salesmen. These were the vanguard of the modern life insurance salesman: the man who will analyze his prospect's needs, consider the events that may prevent the satisfaction of these needs, and show him how life insurance may guarantee their fulfillment. This contrasts sharply with the pre-Carnegie Tech approach, which consisted of an analysis of the contract, with no attempt to show how its provisions would meet a prospect's various needs. The revolution of which we spoke earlier lies in the fact that life insurance salesmen were made very much aware of human motivations, needs, and satisfactions. Prior to the Carnegie Tech School on Life Insurance Salesmanship, salesmen utilized these concepts hardly at all in their selling activity.

VOCATIONAL GUIDANCE

It is evident from the preceding discussion that applied psychology at Carnegie Tech took on an exceedingly broad interpretation following

World War I. Walter Dill Scott was succeeded by Guy Montrose Whipple; and Whipple, in his turn, was succeeded by Clarence Stone Yoakum. Under Yoakum the staff of the bureau was increased and the scope of research was extended. On June 1, 1919, three years to the day after its founding, the bureau's new name became the Bureau of Personnel Research.

Growth of the Measurement of Interests. From the research conducted by this bureau (1919 to 1924) came many significant findings. In this chapter, however, we select for comment only one—that which led to the now widely used Strong Vocational Interest Blanks. To begin this part of our story, let's turn our attention to four graduate students in psychology who earned their doctorates at Carnegie Tech between 1921 and 1923. We begin with Bruce V. Moore, widely known in later years as head of the department of psychology at the Pennsylvania State College and (later) executive officer of the Education and Training Board of the American Psychological Association. While at Carnegie Tech, Moore started a development which has had far-reaching consequences. During his stay on the campus, the Westinghouse Electric and Manufacturing Company, a supporting member of the bureau, had a problem. It could not distinguish as well, or as early as it would like, between those new employees who should be steered toward careers in sales engineering, on the one hand, and toward careers in design engineering, on the other. Would the bureau be able to help?

Yoakum, to whom the company brought its problem, immediately passed it on to Moore, and in discussing it with him suggested, among other things, that Moore experiment with an idea then being espoused by James Burt Miner. This idea was that vocational success or failure might be due in some measure to the presence or lack of appropriate interests. Earlier, in a study entitled "The College Laggard," Miner had thought he found evidence to indicate that many students bright enough to succeed had failed in their college work because of a lack of interest. Would the same thing be true in business and industry?

This question had frequently been discussed by Miner, Yoakum, Bingham, and others at bureau seminar gatherings. Here was an opportunity to try to find an answer. It was suggested to Moore that he see to what extent responses to items measuring interest could differentiate between those individuals who should become sales engineers and those who should become design engineers.

As matters turned out, of all the things which Moore tried, and he tried a good many, the only items of practical differential significance were those concerned with the applicants' interests. Sales engineers were found to have social interests. Design engineers were found to have mechanical interests. On the basis of these findings, Moore developed a system of scoring which enabled him to differentiate (in terms of their responses to twenty items) between the people who should become sales engineers and those who should become design engineers.

Picking up where Moore left off, Merrill J. Ream wondered if successful and unsuccessful salesmen could be differentiated one from the other in terms of their respective interests. Making use of an extended list of the type of item found useful by Moore, Ream concluded that they could not. But he may have reached this conclusion because he used such a small number of subjects (twelve in one group and twenty-seven in another) and because his subjects were students at the Carnegie Tech School of Life Insurance Salesmanship. Many of these had yet to demonstrate on a full-time basis their respective degrees of competence as life insurance salesmen.

Although Ream's findings were negative, he did contribute a positive idea in proposing that responses to interest items should be objectively weighted. In contrast with Moore's use of subjective evaluation (albeit with fourteen judges) to determine whether items reflected social or mechanical interests, Ream demonstrated that item responses might best be scored in terms of differences between the percentages of contrasting criterion groups which liked, were indifferent to, or disliked the objects, activities, or occupations in question.

Seeing value in this method, Max Freyd attempted to assess personality differences between those socially and mechanically inclined. This he tried by comparing the scores of students in the School of Industries, who, presumably, were mechanically inclined, with those secured by salesmen, who, presumably, were socially inclined. Finding a large variety of differences Freyd interpreted them in terms of a personality dimension of extroversion-introversion.

To Strong, who was one of Freyd's advisors, this interpretation missed the real significance of what Freyd had found. For, said Strong, Freyd's results—when considered along with those which Moore and Ream had reported—indicated that definable and scorable differences among a variety of occupational groups had been discovered. Why not use this information directly for vocational guidance? Why waste time trying to construct a scale for the measurement of a personality characteristic of rather dubious value? Couldn't Freyd reorient his thinking and possibly aim his inquiry at the problems involved in vocational guidance instead of at those involved in the rather vague field of personality measurement?

Apparently Freyd couldn't. During a period of time when Strong was absent from the campus Freyd turned in his thesis, and Bingham and Yoakum, neither of whom shared Strong's point of view, approved it. Freyd got his degree and went on his way to an instructorship at the University of Pennsylvania. As we might surmise, this *fait accompli* came as a shock to Strong, not so much because the thesis was approved in his absence (although this was a factor) but because of his feeling that the really important implication of Freyd's study had been rather cavalierly brushed aside.

Strong Vocational Interest Blanks. Strong carried this feeling of an opportunity missed with him to Stanford where he went in 1923. One day he chanced to discuss the problem with young Karl Cowdery, a Terman protégé on the lookout for a subject for a doctoral dissertation. Intrigued by what Strong told him, Cowdery extended the Miner, Yoakum, Moore, Ream, Freyd, Carnegie Interest Analysis Blank and asked small groups of professional lawyers, physicians, and engineers for their responses. Then using a differential system of weighting rather than the unit system used by Freyd and Ream, Cowdery discovered that he could distinguish very well indeed between each of his subject groups and the other two groups combined. Not only this, but he found also that students preparing for entry into each of the aforementioned professions could likewise be very clearly differentiated. Here was the result which Strong had long suspected. Consequently, he arranged to devote a major share of his own research time to the problem. As a result of his study, the Strong Vocational Interest Blank for Men was published in 1927, and the Strong Vocational Interest Blank for Women in 1933.

INDUSTRIAL PSYCHOLOGY, 1925 AND LATER

To this point we have discussed events which occurred in the first quarter of the twentieth century. It is evident that interest centered around what might be called "personnel" psychology. From 1925 to date, work has tended to center on what might be called (in fact, has been called) "industrial social psychology." So vast, however, have been the developments (as this entire book will make abundantly clear) that here we can cite only the bare beginnings.

The Classical Hawthorne Studies. In 1927 the Hawthorne (Chicago) plant of the Western Electric Company began a study designed to ascertain "the relations between conditions of work and the incidence of fatigue and monotony among employees." The work began with an attempt to determine the relationship between changes in plant illumination intensity and production. It was begun by, among others, Elton Mayo and a group from Harvard composed of Roethlisberger, Dickson, Whitehead, and Homans. In the beginning the study was conceived to be a one-year project, but it extended year after year as the maze of human problems affecting productivity became more and more involved. In 1939 Roethlisberger and Dickson published *Management and the Worker*—a classic in showing the nature of refinement in experimental methodology, and how a dozen new problems in human behavior evolve as solutions to one are being sought.

The series of experiments comprising the Hawthorne studies started by varying factors such as lighting, temperature, humidity, hours of sleep, and the like in order to see their effect on the workers' output. There were studies to determine the effect of rest periods, a shorter workweek, and wage incentives and production. The results were surprising; they opened up a new field of research on employee attitudes, a field which has grown so rapidly in recent years that a review of the writing on job attitudes published in 1957 records almost two thousand references (see page 197). The Hawthorne studies led to a change of methodology from the direct to the indirect method of interviewing, and they led to new approaches in the study of leadership. Studies began to show the importance of social organizations and their effect on production. The problems of communication became apparent. The beginning of industrial counseling came as a result of these studies. Although it soon became clear that no specific relationship existed between visual illumination and production, this original problem opened up an array of motivational problems still being worked on in industry.

A New Era in Psychology. In succeeding chapters, references will be made to parts of the Hawthorne studies. Let us record only the first study that was made, because here we find negative results that initiated a new era in industrial psychology.

The illumination experiment was conducted in three selected departments. In the first department small parts were inspected. In the second, relays were assembled, and in the third the work involved winding coils. For the control situation, production was measured under the existing lighting.

In the first department illumination was arranged so that the various levels of intensity averaged 3, 6, 14, and 23 foot-candles. In this department the production of the workers did vary, *but not in direct relation* to the amount of illumination.

The illumination intensities in the second department were 5, 12, 25, and 44 foot-candles. Production in this department increased during the study, but not entirely as a result of the changes in illumination.

Observations of the third department showed similar results, and the experimenters began to see the necessity of controlling or eliminating various additional factors which affected production output.

Here was a problem that was not so simple as it looked. The study was replanned, and a second experiment was conducted with more refined techniques. It was set up in only one department with two groups of workers participating, equated for numbers, experience, and average production. The control group worked under relatively constant illumination, and the test group worked under three different illumination intensities. Competition was eliminated between the groups by having them work in different buildings.

What happened? *Both* the test group and the control group increased production appreciably *and* to an almost identical degree. These results were perplexing and brought forth a third experiment in which further refinements in procedure were introduced.

In this experiment only artificial light was used to illuminate the working areas; all daylight was excluded. The control group worked under a constant intensity of 10 foot-candles. The test group began with an illumination of 10 foot-candles, and this was reduced 1 foot-candle per period until they were working under only 3 foot-candles of light. Despite the discomfort and handicap of insufficient illumination, this group of employees maintained their efficiency of work.

In a fourth experiment two volunteer girls worked in a light-controlled room until the intensity was reduced to that of ordinary moonlight. At this stage they were able to maintain production, they reported no eyestrain, and they showed even less fatigue than when working under bright lights.

A fifth experiment was conducted with girls whose job involved winding coils, but during this experiment there was no real change in production. At first the intensity of the lights was increased each day; the girls reported that they liked the brighter lights. An electrician then changed the light bulbs but kept the same intensity. The girls commented favorably on the "increased illumination." Finally, in the latter part of this experiment the illumination was decreased. For this condition the girls said the lesser amount of light was not so pleasant, *but* they reported feeling the same way when the lights remained constant, even though the electrician was supposedly reducing the illumination!

A Change in Thinking. As the publications from the several Hawthorne studies emerged, thinking about industrial psychology problems changed. No longer were problems in production conceived to be simply a function of illumination, physical fatigue, or working temperature. No longer was labor turnover thought of as being caused by the amount of dollar income. Questions about leadership, about supervision, about human relations, began to emerge. As a result of these and other studies, and of the demands placed on psychologists by the practical problems of World War II, applied psychology entered a new and bigger phase.

PSYCHOLOGY IN WORLD WAR II

With America's entry into World War II, psychologists were commissioned in both the Army and Navy to establish or expand programs for the selection and training of all sorts of military personnel. These programs not only aided the war effort, but also established the acceptability of psychology in practical situations. Much that was learned about the selection and classification of military personnel was also applicable to industrial problems; newer tests were developed; evaluation problems opened up new areas for investigation; and much was discovered about applying learning principles to realistic training problems. On the clinical and counseling side of the picture, World War II brought opportunities for studying reactions to combat stress, reorientations toward the problems of vocational guidance, and rehabilitation.

Expansion of Problem Areas. To a very large extent we can say that engineering psychology began with psychologists working on the design of equipment, particularly on the design of airplane cockpits to aid in better human perception. The several psychological research programs set up in the military services, such as the leadership studies sponsored by the Office of Naval Research and the criteria studies sponsored by the Air Forces, have led to many findings which are directly applicable to industry.

Over two thousand psychologists in one category or another served in a military or civilian capacity during World War II. Many of these men who had backgrounds steeped in a tradition of pure psychology became interested in applied problems. After the war some remained in military service, and some went directly into industrial work. A large portion of those who entered or returned to academic life have gone into part-time industrial consulting.

Growth in Status. World War II had three effects on the development of industrial psychology in the United States. First, it took the psychologist out of the stereotyped role in which he had been pictured as a "long hair" and showed him to be a sound behavioral scientist and practitioner. Second, many high-status psychologists became interested in applied problems, and this made working on these problems "more acceptable." Third, much of the interest found after the war in studying group behavior generated from wartime problems.

The establishment of a Division of Industrial and Business Psychology of the American Psychological Association in 1945 gave professional recognition to this field in a formal way.

THE PRESENT ERA

Developments in industrial psychology following World War II have been extensive. But, as with all such growth, the newer movements in the field, or related fields, have not yet received the test of historical perspective. Let us mention very briefly here a few of these new approaches to the human behavior problems of modern industry. Each will be discussed further in the chapters to follow.

People in Groups. In 1945 the Research Center for Group Dynamics was formed by Kurt Lewin at the Massachusetts Institute of Technology; three years later it moved to the University of Michigan. The researches of the center have awakened interest in problems of motivation and productivity as they are related to group structure. Going beyond a study of just the individual, group dynamics studies the way people work together in teams. In a company the different departments of engineering, manufacturing, sales, and the like often function in isolation. Sometimes conflict situations are created which generate hostile attitudes and even open disputes among the management groups concerned. The group dynamics approach attempts to solve such problems by creating an atmosphere in which various members come to understand the needs and problems of the other person or the other group. Just how best to create the team approach is still not too well known. It is important, however, that effort is being extended in getting people to *want* to work together. This is similar to the aim of another group of industrial psychologists working at Ann Arbor in the field of human relations, the Survey Research Center. Much interest, even controversy, has come from the theories and findings of this and other groups in their attempts to influence industry to operate within "an atmosphere good for its own sake." In other words, there seems to be a movement in human relations programs away from production merely for the sake of production. This approach does not deny the importance of production; it says in effect, "Let's have production and job satisfaction at the same time."

The Study of Organizations. Within the last decade scholars in industrial administration have given their attention to problems of organization and communication within companies. The psychologist has been concerned with determining where in the network of communication the individual fits into the group, the group into the department, the department into the plant, the plant into the company, and each into the community. The psychologist, along with the industrial engineer and the mathematician, has become concerned with finding out what kinds of communication networks and techniques will meet the demands for speed, accuracy, and efficiency in complex organizations. For example, can an organization achieve maximum efficiency of communication, production, and morale all at the same time?

Studies of the Executive. When one attempts a global view of what psychologists in industry have been concerned with in the past, the stress that has been put on the skills of the worker stands out immediately. It has been, however, only recently that work has begun on the higher levels of management. Executive development research is only now beginning in an organized way. Its future looks promising. This is a new frontier for psychological investigation.

Mental Health in Industry. Only within recent years has mental health in industry been of much concern. This is an area which is developing rapidly: considerable attention is being given to problems ranging from executive neuroses to ulcer successes. Similar to the way that personnel psychology has grown from merely giving tests to dealing with the important aspects of personnel planning, clinical psychology is being given increasing recognition. Programs of industrial mental hygiene provide vast opportunity both for professional practice and for research into such matters as absenteeism, turnover, and alcoholism—three of industry's most costly problems.

Industrial consultants in psychology, numbering only a few following World War II, now number in the hundreds. Consulting organizations in psychology are now found in most large cities; some of them employ full time as many as forty psychologists who hold the Ph.D. degree.

As for the growth of courses in industrial psychology in our colleges, one has only to look at the variety of texts related to industrial or applied psychology that have been published since the Viteles text defined the field in 1932. By 1959 over one hundred texts had been published.

Man-Machine Systems. Some of the latest thinking on the place of psychology in industry comes with the concept of systems analysis. A system consists of machines and men, plus the processes whereby they act and interact in an environment. No doubt there will always be psychologists in industry who specialize in personnel selection, others who concentrate their efforts on training, and others who function in this or that specialty. However, with the advances in automation, in operations research, and in centralized data processing, the industrial psychologist is entering into a new role of participation and responsibility where he is a key link in helping make man-machine systems function.

PART II: THE INDUSTRIAL ENVIRONMENT

3

THE STRUCTURES
OF ORGANIZATIONS

B. von Haller Gilmer

Some people experience feelings of uncertainty upon going into a new environment, and there is good reason to believe that the failure of many people to adjust to the industrial scene is due to the fact that they don't know what they are getting into. On the other hand, many people who find success in industry attribute it, in great part, to an early discovery of what the industrial environment consists of. In this chapter we will describe both the *physical* and the *psychological* structures of the modern industrial scene as viewed within the framework of both management and labor organizations. Although there is no such thing as a typical industry, it is possible to describe in a general way modern business firms and labor organizations so that the reader can see the essential nature of business enterprise in our economy, and come to understand the part played by the human element in the engineering, producing, and marketing of industrial goods.

THE MEANING OF INDUSTRY

Business enterprises are usually called "firms" or "companies," and they may differ in size as much as the family grocery store on main street differs from the United States Steel Corporation, with mills in many cities, iron and coal mines in several countries, and hundreds of ore ships sailing the lakes and high seas. The company, large or small, is owned and controlled as a unit, however scattered its parts may be. The company is thus a business unit under some form of coordinated management. The independently

41

owned grocery store is managed by the proprietor. He makes the fundamental policy decisions about his store, and this function the economists
call "entrepreneurship."

In large and more complex forms of business it is more difficult to determine the entrepreneur. For example, who runs the American Telephone
and Telegraph business? The million stockholders? The board of directors?
The president? The answer is that no single person or even group of people
acts as the entrepreneur; the functions of the entrepreneur are performed
by various individuals and groups through an intricate system of coordination. For example, the Dearborn plant of the Ford Motor Company is
operated somewhat differently from the Kansas City plant, although both
are largely controlled and coordinated by the general office. A plant, being
a group of buildings with more or less fixed physical equipment, has a
specific location, and this allows it to function with varying degrees of independence from some central authority.

This leads us into a consideration of the term "industry." Economists use
the term to denote the producing of any commodity. Farmer Gannaway is
a part of the beef industry if he raises cattle, or a part of the corn industry
if he produces corn. Some corporations engage in many industries. General Motors, for example, is in the auto industry, the appliance industry,
and many others. The process of making and distributing a commodity is
industry, whether the commodity is a concrete thing, like an automobile,
or something entirely different, like an insurance policy.

In the nineteenth century, manufacturing plants were relatively small,
and communication between the owner and the workman was comparatively easy. The workman was skilled in all the jobs required for the
manufacture of the product. The owner was frequently the president, the
manager, and the superintendent of the company all rolled into one, and
the worker reported directly to him. Many small industries of this type still
exist, but the rapid trend toward consolidation and merger has for the
most part made owner management a thing of the past.

Today companies, such as General Electric, General Motors, and some
of the aircraft and oil industries, operate in divisions scattered throughout
the nation and in some foreign countries. Each division may employ as
many as ten thousand men, and often each division is an industrial enterprise within itself. Yet each one operates in coordination with all other
divisions toward a common purpose, and each one conforms to established
over-all policies. This situation brings about complex problems of organization in which the human element is an important consideration. A modern
industry may be said to be structured in terms of a formal anatomy,
represented graphically by the flow-chart description of chains of command, of authority, and of responsibility. But it may also be structured in
terms of the less formal psychological climate in which the people work.

First, we will consider the business enterprise as it is organized according to a framework of management. Second, we will consider labor organizations. Following these anatomical outlines we will give a picture of the psychological climates of different managements and different union organizations, and we will describe the various status hierarchies within industry. Finally, we will consider the ways in which organizations are changing.

THE ANATOMY OF THE MODERN COMPANY

The administrative anatomy of a company is designed for the purpose of making decisions most effectively. Only in the smallest of firms are decisions made by a single individual. Ordinarily, even though the final responsibility for taking an action may rest on one particular person, there are usually formal and informal preparations made by a number of people which lead to the decision situation.

The decision-making process of converting policy into practice necessitates an administrative setup in which each division of a company is headed by someone who has both authority and responsibility for its supervision and control. Similarly each division may be broken down into a framework of departments with an operating head for each.

No two companies are identical. Company organizations vary not only in size, but also in the character of the people making up the company. However, there are five principal types of administrative organizations into which most firms can be placed.

Line Organization. This is a very simple structure. Responsibility and control stem directly from general manager to superintendent to foremen to workers.

Line and Staff Organization. As companies get larger they become more complex, and top executives can no longer be personally responsible for such different functions as research, engineering, testing, planning, distribution, public relations, and other activities requiring special training and experience.

In this type of organization executives and supervisors retain authority and control over activities in their particular departments. But this *line* function is aided by *staff* assistance from engineers, budget officers, and other specialists.

Functional Organization. This structure is an extension of the line and staff organization; here more attention is given to specialized skills, mainly at the supervisory or foreman level. One foreman may serve as the production boss to meet quotas, another as inspector, and a third may be responsible for maintenance. In this system the clear-cut lines of responsibility and authority of the line organization have been lost, but gains have been made in terms of getting more specialized work supervision.

Line and Functional Staff Organization. This type of organization gives the functional staff more responsibility and authority in consultation with the line organization in such specialized functions as inspection, purchasing, and shipping.

Line, Functional Staff, and Committee Organization. In order to facilitate communication involving decision making, some large companies construct a network of committees to work with the line and staff organization. In certain companies these committees are permanent and meet regularly. In others they are organized to serve a temporary function only.

THE ORGANIZATION CHART

The organization flow chart of a large corporation is presented in Figure 3.1. Here we see in the top-management section that the stockholders are represented by a board of directors under a chairman. Responsible to the board is the president, who is charged with the formation and supervision of the policies of the corporation. In some companies the rank of the board chairman and the president is the same; in some the chairman is superior in authority to the president. Most frequently, however, the president is the ranking working officer of the company. He in turn delegates to the treasurer responsibility for carrying out the financial policies of the company and to the secretary the responsibility for corporate records. As can be seen from Figure 3.1, the president may have staff officers, such as the legal counsel and the director of industrial relations, reporting directly to him.

Lines of Responsibility. In theory at least, organizational structure demands that the lines of responsibility do not require too many men to report directly to one man. In large organizations, industrial psychologists employed by the company often operate in the department of industrial relations. Their duties may range from those of human-factors specialist to those of consumer researcher. Consulting psychologists may work at any level within the organization. Consulting organizations function in an advisory capacity to the president and to other officers.

In the company of moderate size, employing some two thousand or fewer personnel, the organizational structure is less spread out. For example, a works manager rather than a vice-president may be in control of such staff functions as industrial relations, product development, and purchasing.

Size of Company. As one comes to understand business organizations of different magnitudes it soon is apparent that each size has characteristic strengths and weaknesses. Since no one man in the large company can have the personal knowledge of what is going on and personal contact with his

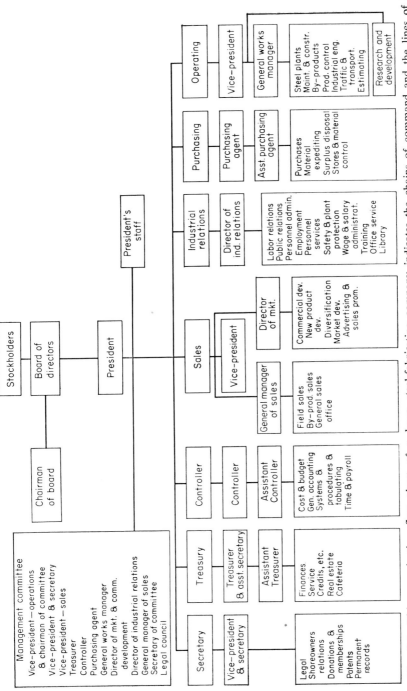

Fig. 3.1. This organization flow chart of a large steel-fabricating company indicates the chains of command and the lines of responsibility within the organization.

workers which an owner-manager has, the large company is forced more in the direction of coordination and group action. Personal ego interests, though always present in the "company man," may be placed more in the background in the larger organization.

The organizational structure of most companies of medium or large size has an inherent problem. There is not enough flexibility to meet emergencies when perfect coordination fails. Supervision at the foreman level finds itself in a myriad of what appear to be impossible demands coming down from the top. There is insufficient flexibility to overcome the gremlins of distribution, material shortage, and machine breakdowns. However, modern management is attacking such problems with systems analysis, mathematical programming, automation, communication control, or what has recently been called "information technology" [8]. Yet the biggest problem of the entire industrial scene involves the human element.

THE STRUCTURES OF LABOR UNIONS

Some people have the opinion that a labor union is something extraneous to the structure of industry. In actuality the labor union can be and, with all but the smaller industries, is as much a part of the total industrial structure as is engineering, accounting, or any of the other functions organized within a framework of management.

Importance of Labor Unions. Labor unions are important in our economy, in industry, in politics, and socially. Most of us become aware of the economic part played by organized labor when we see it exercising vast pressures on wages, hours, and working conditions. Within industry, the labor union is the power behind the worker in his daily grievances with the foreman. This important contact between labor and management rarely reaches public attention save in instances usually associated with publicized strikes. On the political front, organized labor is becoming more and more of a force in the selection of officeholders, both local and national. As lobbyists, its representatives are most effective. Socially, labor unions satisfy the need for "belongingness" of millions of industrial workers. Union organizations vary in size; very small unions may have only a dozen or so members, whereas, the AFL-CIO has about fifteen million. The number of local unions in the United States approximates sixty thousand.

Structure of the AFL-CIO Union. The organizational structure of a large union does not differ very much from the company flow chart. A close look at Figure 3.2 reveals that the AFL-CIO union is in some ways larger than the mammoth General Motors empire. The large national and international unions are primarily concerned with such broad policies as membership qualifications, area and trade jurisdiction, national politics,

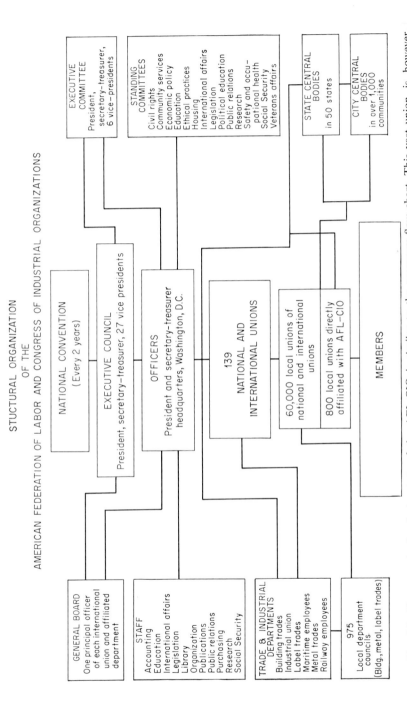

STUCTURAL ORGANIZATION
OF THE
AMERICAN FEDERATION OF LABOR AND CONGRESS OF INDUSTRIAL ORGANIZATIONS

EXECUTIVE COMMITTEE
President, secretary-treasurer, 6 vice-presidents

STANDING COMMITTEES
Civil rights
Community services
Economic policy
Education
Ethical practices
Housing
International affairs
Legislation
Political education
Public relations
Research
Safety and occu-
pational health
Social Security
Veterans affairs

STATE CENTRAL BODIES
in 50 states

CITY CENTRAL BODIES
in over 1,000 communities

NATIONAL CONVENTION
(Every 2 years)

EXECUTIVE COUNCIL
President, secretary-treasurer, 27 vice presidents

OFFICERS
President and secretary-treasurer headquarters, Washington, D.C.

139 NATIONAL AND INTERNATIONAL UNIONS

60,000 local unions of national and international unions

800 local unions directly affiliated with AFL-CIO

MEMBERS

GENERAL BOARD
One principal officer of each international union and affiliated department

STAFF
Accounting
Education
International affairs
Legislation
Library
Organization
Publications
Public relations
Purchasing
Research
Social Security

TRADE & INDUSTRIAL DEPARTMENTS
Building trades
Industrial union
Label trades
Maritime employees
Metal trades
Railway employees

975 Local department councils
(Bldg., metal, label trades)

Fig. 3.2. The organizational structure of the AFL-CIO is similar to the company flow chart. This vast union, is, however, much larger than any one corporation. It also operates differently in some respects from the company organization. (Courtesy AFL-CIO.)

47

and the sort of industry-wide bargaining which we shall describe in detail in a later chapter on labor-management relations.

Local Unions. It is the locals of the larger unions and the small company unions which function on the important day-to-day basis with management. The local in any one plant or department usually has a fairly simple structure. It has a chairman, an executive board, stewards, and general members.

The offices of the local are held by regular plant employees who are elected by the members. Depending on the particular practices of any given local, complaints or grievances may be taken to the steward, the executive committee, or its chairman. Since all the officers are working in the shops, they have direct contact with their fellow workers and often have a feel for the problems.

The Shop Steward. As a general rule the shop steward, or "committee-man," as the union's representative in each shop or department of the plant is called, acts as the contact point between the members and the higher union leadership as well as the intermediary on complaints with the foreman. When complaints or grievances cannot be ironed out at this level the steward may take them to the next level of management supervision directly. Usually if the problem has to be carried to a higher level the union executive board takes over.

Contact with Management. Administratively, the union serves as a link between management and the workers at three levels: (1) at the *communication* level, where the union is the recognized representative of the workers; (2) at the *collective-bargaining* level for hours, wages, and similar benefits; and (3) at the *worker-grievance* level. Psychologically, the union functions for its members in some additional ways. It gives the men recognition status and some feeling of belonging to a powerful group. Unionism has helped to break the notion of some people that workers are merely tools to be used in production. Workers often express the view that management's efforts to maximize profits ignores the men and their problems. The union is the workers' own organization, at least up to a point, and through it they get many of their needs satisfied.

The above account of the anatomy of industrial and labor organizations gives the reader some concept of the structure of business enterprises. However, the flow charts and anatomical descriptions tell only part of the story of what life in industry is like.

THE PSYCHOLOGICAL CLIMATE IN INDUSTRY

"Organizational charts do not fully describe our company," a recruiting interviewer remarked to a college senior. "It may interest you to know that our company differs from some others in personality. You will like working with us."

This statement brings up a most interesting question. Do companies have personality or character? Or, to rephrase the question in the language of the behavioral scientist: What are the organizational or psychological climates of the many and varied industrial environments?

The Character of the Organization. "Why does one company get excellent results from a particular job-evaluation plan while another company in the same industry, using the same plan, does not? Why does one company achieve lower turnover and less absenteeism from a particular supervisory training course that is of little if any benefit to another? In short, why do managerial programs that have been successful in some situations fail dismally in others?" These questions were posed by an educator in business administration [1]. He concluded that companies, or subunits of companies, have unique characters which vitally affect the results achieved by personnel management programs.

The more familiar one becomes with the anatomy of industrial organizations, the more he realizes that flow charts tell one kind of story and the behavior of people another story, often a contradictory one. It is the latter story which interests the college student who is planning to go into industry. If the student is an outgoing person, full of ideas, and likes to participate, then he may be better satisfied working in a democratic or permissive climate. On the other hand, if he prefers to be told what to do, does not relish taking part in decision-making conferences, then this student may be better off in an autocratic climate.

Some psychologists who have worked with different industries believe that companies fall into psychological patterns. One young engineer says, "In my company I am well paid, but I have the feeling that I never know where I stand." A second man is heard to remark, "Our company is demanding, but none of us feel any fear; we have both economic and psychological security."

Much has been written of the nature of business organizations in terms of channels of communication and hierarchies of authority; but missing from these descriptions are the portraits of the family-dominated business, of the corporation "permeated with fear," or of the place where employees "function in an atmosphere of permissiveness." Similarly, organization charts of labor unions fail to differentiate between the local which is run by and for the workers and that which is dominated by a power-mad union boss.

The idea that the character of an organization is a subject for study is a rather new concept in spite of the fact that the literature includes such terms as "quality of managers," "environmental factors," and "leadership climate" [4].

Studies on the Character of Companies. Some research on the character of companies seems to describe the "shadow of the organization" [1]; the inference is that the company is an extended shadow of the personality of its top executive. Studies have shown that authoritarianism in the higher levels of management can defeat any attempt to bring about a supervisory training program aimed at democratic leadership. A writer has shown that selection standards should include even such things as the employee's manner of dress in order to secure the persons most likely to succeed in a particular firm [9]. One observer reports that at a suburban party he was impressed with the fact that seventeen of twenty automobiles of junior executives of one large corporation were of the same make and model. And every one of the men wore a conservative gray suit. One might wonder how an aspiring young executive who is highly individualistic in his behavior could succeed in this climate!

Another writer [10] suggests that a business unit is best understood by viewing it as a social organization, and that measurements of social skills and adaptability may give a better prediction of employment success than do tests of the person's technical skills. The man who "fits into" the company which is authoritarian from top to bottom may be a misfit in the democratic organization. Why do we not pay more attention to this point of view? One industrial administration scholar [14] may have given the answer to this question when he said that administrative description suffers from superficiality, oversimplification, and lack of realism. An industrialist [6] exemplified this when he described the one-man-band executive as one who mistakenly considers himself a student of organization and a practitioner of delegation. Such an executive may display elaborate organizational charts in handsome bindings, but he fails to realize that delegation on paper only is mere theory. A man without much initiative may well go further in the organization where authority is not delegated than he will in the company which operates within a framework of permissiveness. Gellerman [5] has listed five steps for analyzing the character of a company: (1) identify the men in the organization whose attitudes count; (2) study these men and determine their goals, tactics, and blind spots; (3) analyze the economic challenges facing the company in terms of policy decisions; (4) review the company history, giving particular attention to the careers of its leaders; and (5) integrate the total picture with the aim of extracting common denominators instead of adding up all the parts to get a sum.

But lest we conclude too quickly that the top man of the company always casts the shadow for the organization, we need to be reminded that the personality of the local foreman may determine more company policies at a local level than some of the dictates of the head of the firm.

How Psychological Climates Can Change. The psychological climates of organizations change sometimes for good and sometimes for bad. A change may happen even where there is no turnover in company personnel. Let us illustrate how the character of one organization became quite different as the president modified his behavior over a period of some five years. The president initially worked cooperatively with his executives, often taking their advice and sharing in the give and take of conference behavior. The business expanded, profits increased markedly, and so did problems. Then gradually the climate of the organization began to change from the permissive toward the autocratic. Fewer and fewer conferences were held, and the president made more and more decisions without consultation. One observer described the process as "decision by desperation." Both staff and line officers, who had previously been quite free and open with constructive criticisms, now found that not only were criticisms not wanted, they were in effect forbidden.

What had happened? When the president began his term of office he never considered suggestions and criticism to be a reflection on his ability. A few years later, however, he took all such comments personally. He read into them an implication that he personally had failed for not having foreseen and forestalled the situation which was being criticized. Whether he also suffered from the ego inflation that goes with prolonged occupancy of a top administrative post is not so clear. It may be that he just grew tired of facing new disruptive problems.

The effect on the organization all the way down the line was one of clamming up. People began to censor what they would say and to whom they would talk. A few of the top people resigned, but on the whole the organization became adapted to the new climate.

Some recent studies aimed at determining the main variables which differentiate the activities of organization have shown that individual labor union locals show differences in character. Sometimes a clash in personalities between the company and the union may be a precipitating cause for strikes. Sometimes these clashes may change the climates of both organizations. There is evidence that certain industries are consistently strike-proof while others are consistently strike-happy. Keen observers of the labor-management scene report that some regions of the United States are known to be strike-happy while others are relatively strike-free. Often these strike-happy communities are the cities or towns where industry has not been very progressive in research on human relations.

Wives of Men in Industry. Another important aspect of the industrial environment to which industry has given some attention in recent years is the part played by the wives of men in industry. Consideration has been given to educating the families of workers in such company matters as health and safety. However, the most elaborate attempt to bring wives onto the industrial scene has occurred in the management structure. No picture of the psychological climate of modern industry would be complete without some description of the role played by executives' wives. This is a subject of particular import to the young man who is planning a career with one of the larger corporations (and to his wife also).

Surveys concerning management wives have been conducted across the United States [3, 11, 17]. The interviews were made on the basis of a rough sampling of management by age and by business (size and type); they were supplemented by interviews providing a cross section of particular corporation communities. Interviews were held with executive wives themselves, with executives as corporation officials, with executives as husbands; they were held with management consultants, sociologists, and psychologists. The husbands of the wives in question were in the age range of twenty-five to forty and in junior and middle management or with aspirations for getting there [16, 17].

Corporation officials sketched the ideal management wife as one who is highly adaptable, is gregarious, and who realizes that her husband belongs to the corporation. As the wife sees herself in this corporation culture, she is judged "good" by what she does *not* do: she is not to complain when her husband works late; she is not to fuss about a transfer; she is not to engage in any controversial activity. Above all, the wife feels that she is expected to be a good listener, to serve as the sounding board for her husband's frustrations. In a subtle sort of way the good management wife is expected to be a valuable publicity agent for the husband. She must be a good mixer, but not overly ambitious. The good wife must never be disagreeable to any company people; she must not get too chummy with the wives of associates her husband might soon pass on the way up. And never, never, should she get tight at a company party, because it might go down in a dossier!

Does the wife really belong to the corporation? In many ways, yes. She must conform or she will jeopardize her husband's status. Wives of prospective executives frequently are "selected" (in some social gathering) along with their husbands. The company may try to sell its point of view to her once she has passed the screening process, for she must be integrated into the corporation family. Whatever the differences between corporations in their organizational structures or their psychological climates, management wives are coming in for more and more consideration as a part of the industrial scene, and they are most certainly a part of the organization, although never portrayed in any flow chart.

THE INFORMAL ORGANIZATION

In the preceding sections we have discussed different formal organizations and the importance of psychological climates in industry. But what of the difference between the way a company is actually managed and the way it is commonly described? In Figure 3.3 Stryker [15] gives an "insider's organization chart" which shows some of the things which might happen to a formal organization chart if it were redrawn to reflect what *actually* goes on in a company. This company is hypothetical, but it is quite typical of the way many companies are run. Here the president is repeatedly asked to settle arguments among the manufacturing, purchasing, finance, and sales divisions, each of which wants its say on inventories. In this company, however, the most frequent conflicts occur between the people in line functions and those in the staff departments, such as engineering and marketing, who exercise authority over the line by virtue of their specialized knowledge.

Some Organizational Fictions. The managers of each department in this company are typically aggressive, and they pay scant attention to jurisdictional distinctions as defined on the formal organizational chart. For example, in this insider's organizational chart the authority of the industrial relations department completely overlaps that of the personnel department. There are two reasons for this situation. First, the president shows an enthusiasm for industrial relations. Second, a dominant member of the board of directors makes much of labor relations in his public utterances. Similarly, the company's finance chief has so much influence with the president that his department cuts right across all decisions handed down the line of command. The dotted circle (upper right in Figure 3.3) symbolizes the post held by the fun-loving brother of the president, who is totally incapable of managerial functioning. The president is surrounded by committees, one so dominant that it not only advises him, but can give orders down the line as well. His young assistant, in his confidential status, colors much of what the boss hears from the twelve executives who jealously insist on reporting directly to the chief.

Stryker makes the point that the statement that the president runs the company and is assisted by everyone under him is a fiction recognized by any manager who has experienced the politics and personalities of top management. The fiction is perpetuated in the formal organization chart whose neat little boxes and connecting lines strive to show who is running what and who reports to whom. The informal organization chart, which no one will dare to draw is quite different; yet it is the hidden operating structure which gets the work done.

It is convenient to try to wrap up organizational structures into orderly packages. But often these straight lines connecting symmetrical boxes are nothing more than what one industrialist referred to as "the organizational chart we depart from." The stereotyped cliches expounded by some management organizations rarely fit the real situation. Compare a few of these with the insider's organization chart above:

1. Always define responsibilities clearly.
2. Always give authority along with responsibilities.

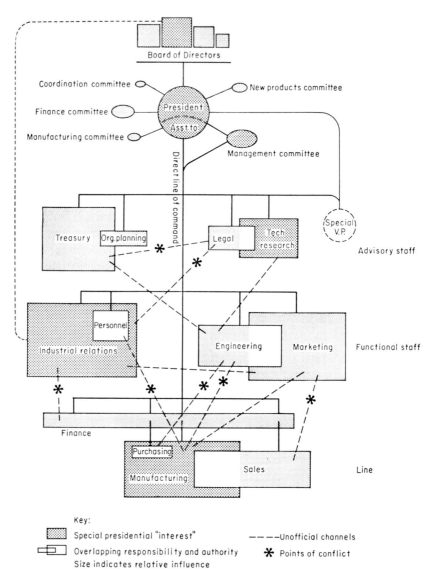

Board of Directors

Coordination committee

New products committee

Finance committee

President

Asst. to

Manufacturing committee

Management committee

Direct line of command

Treasury Org. planning

Legal

Tech. research

Special V.P.

Advisory staff

Personnel

Engineering

Marketing

Functional staff

Industrial relations

Finance

Purchasing

Manufacturing

Sales

Line

Key:

Special presidential "interest"

———— Unofficial channels

Overlapping responsibility and authority
Size indicates relative influence

✳ Points of conflict

Fig. 3.3. This array of lines, squares, circles, lozenges, and rectangles demonstrates what might happen to an orthodox organization chart if it were redrawn to show what actually goes on in a company that needs organization planning. In this hypothetical company the president is repeatedly asked to settle arguments among the divisions. He is surrounded by committees, one of which is so dominant that it can give orders down the line as well as advice to him. His young "assistant to," in his confidential status, filters and colors much of what the boss hears. The dotted circle symbolizes the post held by the fun-loving brother of the president, who is ill equipped to handle managerial functions. A dominant board member, on the other hand, directly interferes in industrial relations. Note also the points of conflict between "line" functions, such as manufacturing, and "staff" departments, such as engineering and marketing. (Reprinted from the July, 1953, issue of *Fortune Magazine* by special permission; copyright 1953 by Time, Inc.)

3. Never change a man's job responsibilities without informing all concerned.

4. Do not give the man more than one boss.

5. Do not give orders to another supervisor's subordinates.

6. Criticize subordinates only in private.

7. Settle promptly disputes over authority or responsibility.

8. Keep the man informed of his standing.

We do not wish to imply that formal organizations are valueless; far from it. We wish to stress the point that human behavior cannot be neatly put into a chart. Perhaps this is a good thing. At any rate, it is realistic.

The Organization's Social Structure. For better or worse the modern corporation has not only become the most efficient form for organizing large-scale production and distribution; it has virtually become a community within the community, manifesting a genuine social structure of its own.

The informal organization of the modern company has been called by various names: "the ropes," "the setup," "the system," or "our way of doing things." Basically it is a tissue of relationships which are never static and are revealed through symbols, subtle permissions, and taboos—the memo pad which reads "From the desk of . . . ," who sits with whom in the company dining room, whom you call by nickname, who has the key to the private washroom. One article introduces the problem of status hierarchies by this statement [11]: "It is ambiguity of status and not overemphasis that is most provoking—one has only to think of the subtle probing that goes on between two strangers in business to find out just where the other fits in."

STATUS HIERARCHIES IN INDUSTRY

An individual's status, who outranks whom, has long been a part of our culture. The GI is strongly conscious of status or rank because it is forcefully brought to his attention by the formalities of saluting, the clear-cut spelling out of what he can and can't do, including even certain restrictions placed on his family. It is certainly not customary for the wife of an enlisted man to associate with the wife of an officer in many situations.

The Nature of Status Differences. The tenet that all men are equal does not apply to the military organizations, nor does it apply to industrial organizations. As a matter of fact, it does not apply in the home, or in the school, or in the community. Even in the most democratic of societies, status differences are found at every economic and social level. The leading citizen in the political world may have much less status when he travels in financial circles. The lowly clerk may be "Mr. Big" on the public golf links. In many organizations, however, and particularly in industry, status position is more constant. The president of the company maintains his status position in the office and in the mill, at church and at the country club, whether or not he is a good golfer.

Within many business organizations, status not only is defined by the person's administrative rank, but also is often symbolized by rugs, pen sets, and other executive trappings. The visitor to the headquarters of a large modern corporation might well judge the relative importance of his vice-president acquaintance by whether he is taken to lunch in the executive dining room on the sixteenth floor or on the thirty-second floor.

Status Symbols and Need Satisfaction. Juggling for the perquisites of rank and the acquisition of status symbols is characteristic in many parts of modern industry. Certain needs of the executive are satisfied by attaining rank and status symbols. Often the little privileges that go with an office are more important to an executive than a raise in salary. Of course the men at the top get the best of everything in any case, so they do not have to play the game of "going one up on" the other fellow. The real struggle occurs among vice-presidents and those in middle management. One observer reports that a major crisis arose in a large company when it bought a new type of posture chair to test on a few of its executives. Those left out were so miserable that one man, to save face, bought a chair with his own money and smuggled it into the office. Another reporter tells of a group of foremen who walked out on their job until management agreed to provide them with a separate table in the workers' dining room adorned with a tablecloth and other appointments symbolizing their superior status.

One large corporation changed job titles and then made a study of the effects on the people involved. It was found, for example, that changing a title from "staff engineer" to "plant engineering associate" enhanced the status of the man involved. Other changes in a positive direction included changing the title "clerk" to "confidential clerk," "motor vehicle inspector" to "motor vehicle supervisor," "general plant employment supervisor" to "general plant personnel supervisor." When a title was changed from "draftsman" to "tracer" the study showed a loss rather than a gain in status. It was also found that even changing the name of the place where people worked was important. For example, employees preferred to say they worked "on the lower level" rather than "in the basement." Some workers prefer "incentive pay" to "piece rate." Even the word "company" often evokes a friendlier association than that of "corporation." However, some executives prefer to say that they work for a "corporation" because it sounds more prestigious.

The struggle for status and status symbols is not restricted to business. Consider the names of farms, the pictures of bulls and horses painted on doors of station wagons, large block letters on sweaters, fraternity pins on blouses, ornamental lodge pins, and colorful military ribbons. We all struggle for status, whether we are high or low in any given hierarchy. This universal form of behavior causes many of the problem situations which we must consider in our attempts to understand human relations in industry.

Status and Structure. One kind of status in business comes as a result of the administrative structure in which one man is boss and the other is subordinate to him. This status relationship establishes differences in rank and designates the right (and often the obligation) to give orders. In another kind of status relationship the executive is deferred to by the worker, but he has no right to command the worker. The worker may step back and hold the door open for the manager, but the latter, as a general rule, has no right to demand such service unless the worker's job involves opening doors. A third kind of status relationship is found among men of equal rank. Here conflict often arises as the men compete for subtle indications of status dominance. One may observe this by watching two foremen vie for the attention of the superintendent; the one who "gets told things first" may feel himself more in the know, and hence feel that he is in the position of more prestige.

Illogical Status Differences. Many of the status distinctions of our society do not make logical sense. The highly skilled master mechanic who works in the shop may be more important to the company than the clerk in the accounting office, and he may command much more pay. However, his status is generally considered inferior to that of the office worker. In effect, status hierarchy places the white-collar position above the blue-collar job, which in turn is higher than that of the day laborer.

The relationship between status and wages is sometimes paradoxical. The $10,000-a-year manager is expected to have a higher status than the $5,000-a-year man. On the other hand, the $15,000-a-year union official may not command the social status of either. Within the framework of most industries, however, status hierarchies are associated with wage gradations and job classifications, and the man who makes more money holds more status prestige.

Some aspects of status differences within a company make sense, and others do not. Most people would agree that the seniority of the older worker entitles him to a higher status than that held by a young worker, even though the younger person may be more apt in his job than the man with the longer service. However, it can hardly be considered logical that the office boy who works in the research department has a higher status than the office boy who works in the engineering testing department. But in many instances he is made to feel superior. An even more illogical status differential has grown up in some industries where women doing the same work as men are regarded as inferior to them. In one plant a strike was called when women were placed beside men on an assembly line, doing the same kind of work. The men maintained that this lowered the status of the job.

STATUS AT DIFFERENT RANKS

One way to portray status hierarchies in industry is to describe in detail the work situation of men in different ranks. For comparative purposes we shall describe the job of the foreman, the department head, the superintendent, the vice-president, and the president of a mythical manufacturing company. This will be followed by a description of the status differentials within the labor union structure, where the worker finds what little status he has.

The Foreman. The foreman is the first-line supervisor of the workers. In some companies he is definitely accepted as a part of management; in some he feels he is a part of labor. In other companies the foreman is in the awkward position of not being quite accepted by either management or labor. He spends a good part of the day on the floor, carrying out orders from above and seeing that work gets done. Though technically considered the first level of management, the foreman often feels that he really isn't in the know. At the same time, the foreman is not accepted as a worker. Rarely does he belong to the workers' union, and he must maintain a status position above those whom he supervises. His ability to maintain a distance from the workers and an identification with them at the same time is an indication of his degree of success as a foreman.

The foreman usually starts the day at his desk looking over the work orders. After he has done his turn around the shop, getting work started, he sometimes talks with neighboring foremen and with his department head about plans for the day and about yesterday's difficulties. Much of the foreman's time is taken up listening to problems and making decisions as he circulates among the workers. To the workers, the foreman is the boss. He judges their work, maintains discipline, enforces the rules, gives orders, listens to their troubles, and tries to maintain smooth relations with the shop steward (the workers' union spokesman).

The foreman often finds himself in a position so close to the work and the workers that he fails to get an over-all view and becomes impatient with those in the hierarchies above him. He feels that many of the orders which come down from above are unreasonable, while at the same time he feels that the workers do not understand the company's problems. The foreman is usually as impatient with paper work as is the enlisted man in the army.

Of course, foremen differ widely in their personalities and attitudes. Some of them try to cover up for their men and their mistakes and resist putting in changes that upset established routine. Other foremen play the "company-man" role and are critical of the workers.

Management often claims that the foreman needs more training, particularly in the area of human relations. (The foreman's superiors often fail to tell him that what they mean by human relations is that he is to follow orders, get the work done, and keep the problems at a minimum.)

As the workers see him, the foreman is to represent their views to management and to protect them from excessive pressures from above. He is viewed as the vital first link in labor-management relations and is expected to know all the answers.

And what does the foreman think about his status? There seems to be one universal attitude: he feels that he never has enough authority to carry out his responsibilities.

The Department Head. The department head, or "chief," as he is sometimes called, is unquestionably a part of management. His relationship to the workers is quite different from that of the foreman. Whereas the foreman deals directly with the workers in getting the job done, the department head uses the foreman as the buffer for his demands. In problems of discipline of the workers, of failure to meet production quotas, or in worker complaints, the department head centers his attention on the foreman. He thus avoids becoming involved in many energy-sapping frictions with the men, while at the same time he can play the role of the big boss.

The department head spends much of his time at his desk away from the work location. He reads reports, screens the type of information that should be passed up the line, and filters out the communications coming down which he feels should be passed along to the foreman. The head is in a position to know what is going on, since he spends a great deal of time in conferences with other department heads, with design and test engineers, with inspectors, and with other staff people. He has his ego boosted by showing VIPs through the department and by having his advice sought as a line officer.

The department head is actually too busy to find out firsthand what is going on in the shop. Hence he is quite dependent upon the foremen to keep him informed. This dependence is a club which the foremen may hold over the chief in order to get his cooperation when it is most needed. It is through the department head that foremen indirectly have a voice in the lower-level decision making.

The workers see just enough of the department head to know that he exists; hence they often let the foreman know that he, too, has a boss. The head can overrule the foreman or he can make a decision without having to cope with its consequences. If the chief is friendly, the workers feel he is a last resort to hear serious complaints. If he is unfriendly, then the workmen feel that no one will listen to them directly and they turn their complaints into formal channels through their union steward.

Psychologically, the department head is in an awkward position. He frequently does not possess as much formal education as the engineers with whom he works, but he is above the level of the foremen, the group from which he was most likely chosen for his present job. He is the last visible authority for the workers. He is consulted in some decisions and left out of others. Though primarily management-minded, and officially a part of management, the department head is nevertheless in the quandary of not quite knowing just where he does stand. The brass decide at any given time whether or not he is to be included in making policy or procedural changes.

The Superintendent. The superintendent, or works manager, is in the top-management bracket. Psychologically, at least, he is quite far away from the actual work of the plant. He keeps in touch with its activities through conferences, reports from department heads, memos, and data sheets. In the larger companies the superintendent often functions under the vice-president in charge of manufacturing, and as such he is the eyes and the ears for his boss who helps make policy recommendations above the level of everyday details. He is in a status position which allows him to disagree with the ideas of vice-presidents (up to a point!) as he upholds the importance of getting the work turned out. The manufacturing super-intendent is often a case-hardened old-timer who has risen through the ranks from foreman. He may or may not have much formal education, but he knows the plant and as a consequence has good cause for feeling secure in his job. At the same time the superintendent sometimes shows defensive behavior in resisting changes suggested by the top brass. In some respects the superintendent holds a status position, at least in the plant, above that of vice-presidents, even though they outrank him.

The Vice-president. Vice-presidents are frequently in an awkward status position. They have often come into the company from outside or have come up through staff positions in sales, engineering, accounting, or some other specialty, and hence do not have a detailed knowledge of the operations of the company as a whole. Vice-presidents sometimes hold the rank for public relations reasons (this is particularly true at the assistant vice-president level) and are the attenders of meetings and luncheons. They are often active in community affairs. Vice-presidents, save those who merely hold the title for prestige reasons, are in policy-making positions and hence have much power. By the time a man has reached the level of vice-president, he "is high enough to be shot at," as one observer put it. He has status, but he has to continue the competition game to hold his power—a situation clearly portrayed in the novel *Executive Suite*. It is at the vice-president level, as well as at certain lower executive levels, that we find the man's industrial status carrying over into the community. He is named to important civic committees and to boards of directors, and he usually expends much energy in playing the role of the important man around town.

The President. "The most lonesome man in the organization" is one way the top-management man has been described. He has status, and he possesses so many symbols of his status that he can afford not to flourish his rank for prestige purposes. Most presidents are professional managers and have attained their position because they have real ability and a strong constitution. The president is a lonesome man for several reasons. In the first place, he faces certain problems that only he can deal with. Not only does he have to steer his organization so that it will meet the ever-present problems of competition, but he must keep abreast of the social, economic, and political changes that affect business. Secondly, the president has virtually no one of his own status who can listen to his complaints or share his frustrations. He cannot become too confidential with other people in the organization for fear of revealing some of his own weaknesses. He must be very cautious of his statements because his every word may be interpreted as a commitment or policy indication. The new president soon finds that his old vice-presidential acquaintances gradually begin seeing less and less of him as he expands outward, as he attends more and more dinners and business meetings. These outside contacts which make it possible for him to get to know other top executives in other companies mean that he has less time for his old friends.

Although the president's attention is focused outward, he still must keep informed about how things are going within the company. Although he receives information prepared especially for him and is given advice by his staff, much of the problem solving is still his. With all that he has to do to keep up with his many jobs and the demands placed on him by his status, as well as by the company shareholders, the president soon finds his time and energy taxed to the limit.

As one president remarked: "When I was farther down in the hierarchy I wanted more status. Now that I have it, I do not have time to recognize it nor the energy to enjoy it."

STATUS WITHIN THE UNION

One mistake commonly made by the lay person is the belief that unions are organized along the same lines as management. To be sure, the usual structure of a union local presents a hierarchy made up of members, stewards, executive board, and a chairman of the board; the organizational chart of the large international union may look like that of any sizable corporation. But it functions quite differently.

Power-status Paradox. In the local union the hierarchy is not one of authority where the steward is over the members, and the chairman is boss. The chairman does not give orders or make decisions which can be forced on those below him. Although the chairman of the local may have status in one way, he does not have power status as does the foreman, the department head, or the superintendent in management. The workers do not have to take orders from the officials of their local unions, and locals do not have to follow the dictates of any higher headquarters. The president of a large union, such as the AFL-CIO, and his executive board may have the official right to negotiate contracts and to function in many ways in collective bargaining. They may agree to a new contract with a company, and they may use all the prestige of their office to get the locals to agree to it; but they cannot guarantee that the union membership will accept it. One of the frustrating situations facing management in negotiating with a union is that it must work out agreements which not only satisfy the union officials but are also acceptable to the union membership. Although unions are becoming better organized, they still are rather loosely coordinated. It is not just window dressing when we hear that the larger international unions at times refer problems down to the lowest levels for decision. They have to.

Worker Status. It is through his identification with the union that the worker has status. It is through the union that he feels strength and has a means to fight power with power. Whereas the man in management possesses symbols of status represented by titles, executive dining rooms, and company airplanes, the union man identifies himself with the heroic figures of union movements and the folklore of struggle. He can express himself through such traditional songs as "I'm a Union Man." The union leader, regardless of his power and prestige is never allowed to forget that he has risen to his position through his ability to get and maintain the support of his fellow union members. This is quite a contrast to the management executive who attains position through the approval of his superiors. We shall elaborate on this important point in a later chapter dealing with labor-management relations.

The Union Officers. When the union leader moves up from the local through regional and district offices into headquarters, he moves into a different world. While in the local, whether he was a steward or chairman of the executive board, he was still a worker, paid for his work. Union activities were extracurricular. As he moves up and his union activities demand full attention, the union officer goes entirely on the union payroll. In a psychological sense he has moved up above the rank and file and is no longer accepted as one of them. Consequently, even the most popular union leaders feel insecure when they lose touch with the boys in overalls. If a union official becomes too friendly with management, he jeopardizes his leadership role, unless at the same time he continues to make gains for the workers. Herein lies at least one basic cause of so much industrial conflict.

At most levels, union salaries are modest compared to executive jobs in industry, save at the very highest levels. (The salaries of the top officers of the AFL-CIO, for example, are above those of many top officers in business.) Men who work their way to the top of the union ladder and *hold their positions* are as much the executive type as any that may be found in high positions in industry. The rabble-rousing organizer type rarely, if ever, reaches a high union position. But however skillful the top union official becomes socially, economically, or politically, the system which put him into his status position constantly reminds him that his power comes from the group.

ORGANIZATIONAL COMPLEXITY AND HUMAN RELATIONS

The administrative organization of most companies is in effect a more complicated structure in terms of the responsibilities of its leaders than we are accustomed to thinking. Men in management now supervise expenditures of money on a scale that would have financed ancient wars or supported large kingdoms. They must, at least to some extent, understand the design and operation of specialized equipment, the complexities of modern accounting procedures; they must understand something of the importance of product research, the mechanisms of mass production, and the basic assumptions underlying the marketing of manufactured goods. The modern manager should know at least the fundamental principles underlying personnel selection, training, the division of labor, and the apportioning of rewards. Modern management must provide storage facilities, utilize transportation, set prices, scrutinize credits, direct publicity, and energize salesmanship. Management must raise funds, market securities, account for values, watch costs, meet liabilities, pay dividends, and stand answerable to public opinion. The evolution of business has compelled the formulation of principles and the invention of administrative mechanisms to aid proprietors in the task of management. The aim of an administrative organization is to establish such a series of relationships between the individuals involved in an enterprise that joint action without conflict is possible in the accomplishment of a common task.

The paragraph above was paraphrased from a textbook on industrial organization published in 1925 [7].

A Problem of Ego Identification. The problems of administrative organization are even more complex today than they were three decades ago. Worthy, writing on organizational structure and employee morale [18], says that the most important and fundamental cause of poor management-employee relationships is overcomplexity of organizational structure.

In viewing many business enterprises, one cannot but be impressed by the number of different departments and sub-departments into which they are divided, and the extent to which the activities of both individuals and groups have been highly specialized. In a very large number of cases, employees perform only elementary, routine functions because jobs have been broken down "scientifically" into their most elementary components. The resulting specialization undoubtedly has certain advantages, such as requiring less skilled people, shorter training time, etc. In many cases, however, the process has been carried to such extremes that jobs have little inherent interest or challenge; operations have been reduced to the simplest possible repetitive level and the worker makes nothing he can identify as a product of his own skill.

To a large extent employees in industry today have been deprived of the sense of doing interesting, significant work. They often feel little responsibility for the work tasks they are assigned. Increasing supervisory pressure to maintain production often creates resistance. At times the workers show only passive resistance by failing to respond to pressure or by finding some means to avoid it. In strongly unionized companies, however, resistance takes a more active form; the employees band together to exert pressure against supervision and management. In short, one of the basic human relations problems in industry is establishing some ego identification with the end product of the work the individual performs.

TOWARD A GLOBAL VIEW OF HUMAN PROBLEMS

The behavioral scientist must function within a complex organizational setting. Before turning to the following chapters which detail what the psychologist in industry does, let us take a more global look at the types of human problems which face organizational leaders in industry.

Lest the reader get the impression that it is a form of weakness to be concerned about human relations, let him ponder a significant statement by an executive vice-president [12] of a modern industrial corporation: "While I am very definitely *pro* human relations, I am also *pro* tough-mindedness, making practical decisions, self-discipline, profit consciousness, high standards of performance, individual initiative, creative imagination, hiring able men, firing misfits, and above all getting results. What is more, I do not see any conflict between one and the other."

To understand organizational behavior one must recognize that it is a product of human sentiments, sometimes nonlogical, affected by personal hopes and aspirations, and complicated by customs and traditions.

It is a matter of record that orientation of leaders toward the understanding of human behavior will make cooperative action easier, bring about better understanding between people, and reduce human frustration and conflict. Understanding human behavior has been shown in organization after organization to be the essential force in promoting group purposes without bringing about a loss of personal identity. In short, establishing effective human relations promotes not conformity, but individual integrity; not happiness, but the right to work out one's own salvation.

Elements of Effective Human Relations. What are the basic elements necessary for the establishment of effective human relations in industry? One writer [12] lists ten aspects of behavior which the effective industrial leader has learned to be concerned with in everyday practical situations:

1. An underlying element of his approach to other people is an attempt to understand them; that is, he tends to accept people as they are.

2. He has an awareness of and sensitivity to differences between his outlook and another man's, yet is able to maintain his own point of view in the face of such differences.

3. He has an ability to respond to and understand not only the logical content of what other people say but also the feelings and sentiments implied by their words and their behavior.

4. He has some awareness of his own nature and of the impact of his behavior on other people.

5. He understands clearly the nature of the social structure or social system of which he is a part.

6. He is realistic about the existence of a hierarchy of authority, responsibility, status, and position in his particular organization and is alert to how this hierarchy affects people's behavior, including his own.

7. In taking action in an organizational situation, he is able to predict (within limits) how the organization will respond.

8. In taking action, he makes use of those generalizations about social phenomena which he has constructed and tested by his own experience, and at the same time he continually watches for the unique elements in every concrete situation.

9. He realizes that human relations and its point of view are *not* concerned with making everyone happy or sugar-coating harsh reality.

10. He knows that human relations is *not,* and should not be equated in toto with, the job of management or executive leadership.

These ideas were written by a business executive in a business magazine. They cover, of course, only a small segment of what we regard as the subject area of industrial psychology. They are presented here to illustrate the point that the scientific and clinical approach to problems of human behavior is vitally important to modern industry. They are included also to show that the inherent problems of organizational complexities may be, at least to a degree, better understood when we can spell out more about human nature.

Organization Theory. Traditional organizational theory, which described the layout of jobs and how workers should perform their tasks, largely ignored man's psychological life, says Leavitt [8]. He points out that early "scientific managers" made the error of assuming that people on the job try to satisfy only one kind of need, physical need; he shows that they assumed that there is an automatic sharing of goals among members of the organization and that people try rationally to seek the best solution to a problem. They confused what people should do with what they actually do. The principles of traditional organizational theory do not resemble reality above easily programmed levels. To a large extent management creates its own unique set of human problems when it describes a given work flow and division of labor [13].

New ideas are coming into the picture, though they are not yet fully developed. These ideas come from mathematicians, engineers, psychologists, sociologists, economists, and other behavioral scientists. They deal with problems of social environments, of informal organizations, of work groups, communication, and decision making. To understand the part that man plays in industry we need first of all to know what goes on in industry. The following chapter on business operating procedures will lay a groundwork for our later discussions of the applications of psychology to industrial problems.

SUGGESTIONS FOR FURTHER READING

Argyris, C. *Understanding organizational behavior.* Homewood, Ill.: Dorsey, 1960. Although written primarily for a sophisticated audience, this book will give the student reader some insight into understanding what goes on in organizations.

Cornell, W. B. *Organization and management in industry and business.* New York: Ronald, 1958. This book gives a nonpsychological description of the structural analysis of a modern company.

Jennings, E. E. *An anatomy of leadership: Princes, heroes, and supermen.* New York: Harper, 1960. A book that helps in understanding the importance of organizational climates in terms of leaders driven to dominate, men dedicated to causes, and iron-willed individuals.

Lawrence, P. R. *The changing of organizational behavior patterns.* Boston: Harvard Univer. Bureau of Business Research, 1958. A case study of decentralization of importance for theoretical interpretations.

Leavitt, H. J. *Managerial psychology.* Chicago: Univer. of Chicago Press, 1958. Written by an industrial psychologist, this book explains some of the things about people in management.

McGregor, D. *The human side of enterprise.* New York: McGraw-Hill, 1960. An examination of the management of human resources in industry viewed in the light of current social science knowledge.

Rubenstein, A. H., & Haberstroh, C. J. *Some theories of organization.* Homewood, Ill.: Dorsey, 1960. An interdisciplinary collection of readings dealing with organizational theory, structures, and communication.

Whyte, W. H. *The organization man.* New York: Simon & Schuster, 1956. A description of the "psychological climates" found in some modern corporations.

4

BUSINESS

OPERATING

PROCEDURES

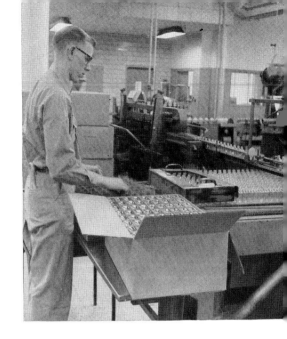

R. M. Cyert and James G. March

The structures of business organizations are somewhat complex, yet, as we know, their make-up can be understood with a little study. What happens in business likewise is understandable when one takes a systematic look at the operating procedures found in modern industry. The behavior of people in industry, how they face their problems, trials, and tribulations, can be understood better after one gets a picture of what a business organization looks like.

A LOOK AT A BUSINESS ORGANIZATION

Recently one of the authors asked a friend to describe a foreign car that had just appeared on the market in the United States. He proceeded to give a well-informed account of the automobile's rated and delivered horse-power, its compression ratio, its minimum turn radius, and other technical engineering characteristics. Such a performance is remarkable in at least two ways. First, assuming that the information provided is accurate, it is clear that some of our friends are considerably better informed about such matters than are we. Second, in this quite detailed description our friend assumed that we already knew a large number of the major characteristics of the vehicle. Indeed, some of the features that seem most important to an uninstructed layman were not even mentioned.

Does the car have wheels? How many? Is the motor an internal combustion plant? What does it use as fuel? The description was much like a baseball fan's attempt to explain the game to a Frenchman. The fan is likely to launch into a discussion of a hit-and-run play before he explains whether the bat is used to propel some object, to pole-vault around the bases, or to quell disturbances among the players. Similarly, analyses of business organizations will vary depending on whether they are set forth by an economist or by a psychologist. Although the two scholars may have much in common in their interest in studying industrial behavior, they take off from a somewhat different view of the industrial organization.

The Economist's View. In his interpretation of the industrial organization the economist is likely to describe it not as an organization at all, but as a single entrepreneur [5]. In economics the classical theory of the firm could be, and frequently is, written as though the decisions were made by a single entrepreneur acting on perfect knowledge rather than by a number of individuals provided by complicated organizational procedures with more or less accurate estimates of the environment. The focus of concern for the entrepreneur is a set of decisions—price, output, capital investment, and the like. He makes these decisions, according to the theory, on the basis of knowledge of the market demand, his own costs, and the plans of his competitors. And he makes the decisions in such a way as to satisfy some criterion. In the case of the economic theory of the firm, this criterion is profit maximization. Until quite recently, the theory of the firm ignored entirely the organizational characteristics of the firm.

The Sociologist's View. Sociological treatments of business organizations are likely to emphasize the complex problems associated with adjusting the demands of subunits within the organization [4]. Economic theory, on the other hand, assumes away conflict of interest within the organization. It does this by means of the employment contract. Sociological theory dramatizes the importance of such conflicts. The emphasis is primarily on what has been called the "unanticipated consequences" of organizational structure and survival needs—and particularly on those unanticipated consequences that are associated with goal setting in organizational subunits [10].

The Psychologist's View. When a psychologist looks at an organization, he is likely to perceive it as a large number of individuals pursuing their own goals, and certain goals of the group, within the context of a business corporation. He will argue that to understand what happens in a large organization you must be able to understand the factors that motivate the individual members of the organization. What is Joe Doakes trying to achieve in this situation? How can we harness Joe Doakes's wants to the requirements of the organization? This latter question leads naturally into the problems of selection, training, rewards, and evaluation which comprise a large part of this and other books on industrial psychology.

The Fable of the Elephant. A business organization is all these things. It sets prices, decides on the levels of output it will attempt to achieve, and invests in new plants and equipment. It encompasses a number of major subunits that tend to develop objectives at least somewhat at variance with one another. And it includes a large number of individuals each with his own values and reasons for being in the organization. The person who wishes to understand business organizations must recognize that each of the above descriptions is both accurate and incomplete. They are accurate in the sense in which a description of baseball in terms of hit-and-run plays, or of an automobile in terms of engineering characteristics, is accurate. But they are incomplete in the same way. All these approaches ignore an integrated view of the firm. This statement is not meant to be deprecatory. Any of these approaches is a useful and legitimate scientific technique which allows us to abstract from a mass of facts those details which are not directly relevant to a particular problem. However, after looking at the description of the various approaches, a logical question to ask is, "How does a business organization ever manage to function with so many diverse elements at work?" There are a number of answers to the question, but one important answer is that standard operating procedures are established. These procedures go a long way toward coordinating the varied objectives of the members of the organization. This chapter attempts to describe some of these procedures and to analyze their effects in an industrial firm.

STANDARD OPERATING PROCEDURES

To the outside observer, one of the most striking features of business operating procedures is their persistence. Presidents come and presidents go. Psychologists come and psychologists go. Lathe operators come and go. But most of the procedures followed by presidents, psychologists, and lathe operators in an organization survive with relatively little change. Some of the reasons for this will be examined later. For the moment all we assert is that procedures do persist despite change in personnel or in other features of the organizational environment. Of course, no one would suggest that operating rules and climates do not change. They do. But generally they change rather slowly and, except for rare instances, in small rather than large jumps. Assaults on standard operating procedures (SOP) are like earthquakes. They may cause considerable change within a local area and, if violent enough, tremors throughout a broad system. But most alterations, like most earthquakes, are directly perceptible throughout most of the system only by very sensitive recording devices. Frequently, of course, such direct perception is supplemented by secondary communication. Thus, knowledge of attempted major changes is usually much more widely shared than are any direct effects.

Why Standard Operating Procedures Persist. Basically, operating procedures persist for the same reason that human beings persist—because no
one has yet figured out a way to get along without them. Less succinctly,
they capitalize on two features of human behavior in organizations. First,
they capitalize on the limited capacity for the rational design of organizational systems possessed by human beings operating with the analytical
tools presently available to them. Second, they capitalize on the limited
ability to implement plans once adopted. Both of these limitations stem
from the extreme complexity of a modern industrial organization. We are
not suggesting that each person, or any person, in an organization has a
particularly complex task. The individual tasks themselves tend to be well
within the capacity of human beings. A description of the system as a
whole, however, frequently staggers the imagination. Even with recent developments in the use of high-speed electronic computers to increase our
problem-solving capacity, we are far, very far, from being able to solve
simultaneously all the design problems of an organization in the sense of
providing the optimum possible system. And if we concede the impossibility of finding the optimum solution to an organizational problem through
analytical techniques we can recognize why organizations will adopt a set
of procedures that will offer success enough to make the system work, that
is, to provide enough profit, a large enough share of the market, and the
like to keep the various participants in the organization satisfied [11].

Propositions about Organizational Changes. A simple difference in our
view of organizational goals has enormous significance for the way people
behave in organizations and particularly for the importance of standard
operating procedures to that behavior. The procedures specified in the
company manual, or comparable publication, and elaborated by custom
represent a plan of activities for the various parts of the organization. They
describe, frequently with considerable detail, how and under what conditions materials will be ordered, how these materials will be processed, what
reports will be prepared, and where these reports will be sent. To a great
extent this plan determines how things will be accomplished in an organization. Of course, if the organization were able to make a formal optimizing
analysis of its organizational problems, it would continuously reconsider
each of the elements in this plan and adjust them frequently. If, however,
such an analysis is not feasible, changes will be much less frequent. So
long as the plan represented by the SOP permits everyone involved the
opportunity to achieve whatever aspiration level he has set, there will be
little pressure for change. As a result, attempts to change procedures occur
rather infrequently. In general, the following propositions can be made
about changes:

1. Local changes in procedures will arise when there are local dissatisfactions with current achievement. Thus, changes in sales procedures will

arise when sales fall below (but not too far below) the goals of the sales department.

2. Major changes in over-all company procedures will arise when there is a sharp change in company achievement, for example, in profits.

3. Local or major changes may occur when similar firms or subunits have exhibited the apparent improvement in performance to be achieved.

4. Local or major changes may occur when reexamination of procedures is stimulated by technological innovation. Even where the innovation is not adopted, new procedures may be introduced.

The second factor which produces persistence in procedures is the difficulty of implementing new plans. Let us amplify this statement. By now we have all been disabused of the view of an organizational hierarchy of command as a simple push-button mechanism. The president of a business firm cannot, simply by initialing a memorandum, implement a major change in operating procedures. Some classic instances of this difficulty can be secured from the records of operations research teams. Time after time the report is that a new method was developed, tested, approved by the appropriate executive, and installed; but there was little or no significant change in the procedures used or the activities followed. Organizations are a bit like western Pennsylvania clay—it takes many a summer of adding miscellaneous elements to it before you have anything but clay by the time of the next plowing. We will not attempt to discuss here the reasons why organizations tend to be so impregnable. It is enough to note that this is generally true and to draw the patent implication this has for the rate of change of organizational procedures.

In addition, even if there were a one-to-one correspondence between top-level instructions and organizational action, the problems involved in changing a plan ought not to be minimized. Unless the proposed change affects an unusually autonomous operation, a relatively minor change involves a rather large number of side adjustments. This is, of course, one of the reasons why organizations resemble clay. The existence of unanticipated side adjustments may result in a failure of proposed changes through lack of implementation by relevant subunits. If a business executive realizes that there are a large number of such adjustments to be made, and that in all probability not all of them can be fully realized without considerable expense, he is likely to go slowly in proposing alterations in organizational practice. He will sometimes do this in situations other than those of the most routine type, unless he is deterred by the considerations indicated above.

Advantage of Standard Operating Procedures. In general, existing standard operating procedures have two great advantages over any potential set of new procedures. First, they work. There may be parts of the plan that seem inefficient or frustrating, but the existing mode of operation has demonstrated its feasibility. Second, they have no major costs of maintenance. Before an alternative set of procedures can be developed, there are search costs, design costs, testing costs, and costs of installation. In terms of money, time, energy, and risk, the costs are ordinarily much greater for change than for continuation.

Because of their persistence, standard procedures deserve close attention by the student of industrial organizations, as does the behavior of the people affected by them. But their importance does not stem solely from their longevity. It is also true that they represent one of the major parts of the environment for members of the organization. One of the perennial shocks of a professional psychologist entering a business organization for the first time is the discovery that much of what he does is prescribed rather precisely by existing procedures. He soon discovers that even what he does of a quasi-discretionary nature is done within the framework of budgets, interoffice memos, and record keeping specified by the organization.

TYPES OF OPERATING PROCEDURES

Our intention in the remainder of the chapter is to describe the major kinds of procedures found in modern industrial organizations, indicate their function in an organization, and explore the psychological consequences of using such methods for coordination, direction, and control. There are four major types of operating procedures with which we will concern ourselves. Although they are neither exhaustive nor wholly discrete, they encompass most of the important rules and will serve as a reasonable introduction to the subject. They give us details which are necessary for understanding the environment in which we find our human problems. Let us mention the four major types of procedures briefly, and then elaborate on them in detail.

Task-performance Rules. How is the part fabricated? What tests are given, and when? How are the books kept? In almost any recorded standard operating procedure, most of the words are devoted to specifying methods of accomplishing whatever task is assigned to the individual member of the organization.

Records and Reports. Every business organization maintains a set of more or less permanent records about certain aspects of its operation. Naturally, these records tend to be related to the elements of business operations that have seemed most important to the smooth functioning of the firm.

Information-handling Rules. In any large-scale business organization, transmitting information in the form of directions, estimates, results, etc., is a major concern of top management. In order to provide reasonable certainty that relevant information will be available at the proper place at the proper time, a communication system is specified in the regular operating code of the organization.

Plans and Planning Rules. Plans for organizational behavior represent one of the major outputs of high levels in the organization as well as a significant output at other levels. Such plans take the general form of an intended allocation of resources among the alternative activities available to the firm and/or its subunits. They include a range of items, from short-run budgets of operating expenses to long-run plans for capital expenditures.

TASK-PERFORMANCE RULES

Think for a moment about the fate of a new employee in an organization. He arrives on the scene and is given the simple instruction: "Maintain our inventory so that we neither run out of items nor have too much overstock." If such an employee lasted long enough in the organization, and the organization lasted long enough, some reasonably satisfactory ways for handling the inventory problem would eventually be developed. But such trial-and-error learning is exceptionally inefficient.

Need for Rules. If the conventional Skinner box found in some psychology laboratories were as large as an organization, many a pigeon would have long since starved to death. It is partly for this reason that organizations specify rules for task performance and communicate them to new employees. Rules permit the transfer of past learning.

There is another reason for such rules, however. Even if acceptable solutions to task-activity problems were rather easy to discover through trial and error, the organization requires not just solutions but ones which are consonant with a large number of other solutions to other tasks being performed in the organization. So long as there exist a number of different solutions to the inventory problem, each one may require a different set of mechanisms coordinated with other parts of the organization, and other adjustments in the behavior throughout the organization. Thus, the organization needs not only an acceptable solution, but also a solution that has some unique properties. The uniqueness is needed to permit other parts of the organization to coordinate their activities with those of the inventory unit. Where the task itself does not provide a unique solution, the task-performance rules and training are used to do so. In this way an internally consistent, feasible schedule of activities is developed for the organization.

Task Specification and Work Standards. Task-performance rules exist in considerable detail at many different levels in the organization. Highly trained engineers dealing with complex design problems may have their work as precisely described by performance rules as the individual member of a production line. Generally speaking, however, the specificity of performance rules decreases as we go up the organizational ladder. There are a number of reasons for this. First, in order for detailed performance specifications to make much sense the task involved must be one that is repetitive down to rather fine detail. Thus, the standard operating procedure for any army is likely to devote much more detailed attention to how the morning report is completed than to how wars are won. Such tasks are not the exclusive property of low levels in the organization, but they tend to cluster there. Second, the higher one goes in an organization, the more vague the objectives of the organization become. Vagueness here refers not to any obvious fuzziness of the language that is used to define those objectives but to the difficulty of determining precisely what activities are likely to lead to achieving the objectives or even the extent to which the objectives have been achieved after the activities are engaged in. The closer the tasks come to what might be called problem solving, the less likely are the performance rules to be particularly specific.

Early Scientific Management. Probably the best known of all attempts to specify in detail the rules for performing simple tasks are those connected with the scientific management movement typified by the early work of Taylor and the Gilbreths on time-and-motion study [12, 3]. Time study and motion study were major innovations in the attempt to standardize and improve the rules for performance of routine clerical or production-line tasks. Or let us use an illustration familiar to most of us. Time-and-motion study has been made on the efficiency of washing dishes. It has been found, for example, that it is of advantage to use very hot water and let the dishes drain dry by themselves. This eliminates the step of drying the dishes manually. Other rules that have been established by study suggest that one keep everything within easy reach, use a step-on garbage can, use both hands for putting away dishes, and, where possible, sit down to work. Today a large part of the procedures specified in most companies for performing tasks has been developed from studies made by industrial engineers using techniques developed by Taylor and more recently by psychologists and other professional people interested in human engineering.

It may seem rather surprising that time-and-motion study has been so widely accepted in industry and so persistently followed. Although under some circumstances it has had rather dramatic effects on production, it is subject to severe methodological limitations that have been widely noted. Moreover, despite the pollyanna hopes of Taylor and the Gilbreths, scientific management has not been accepted by labor with the wildest of enthusiasm. In fact, most labor unions have been, and are today, extremely suspicious of time-study methods. Particularly are they suspicious of the introduction of time standards or piece-rate wages based on such studies. The primary reason for the success of time-and-motion study seems to us to lie neither in its acceptability to workers nor in its demonstrated efficiency, but in the uniqueness and legitimacy it provides for work rules.

When we say that time studies are useful because they provide a standard, the emphasis frequently should be on *a* standard, not a *standard*.

Standards established by the organization for task performance are designed, at least in part, to specify minimum acceptable behavior. In general they do this. At the same time, however, they become goals for the individual workers and thus not only a minimum, but an effective maximum also. Such a tendency for standards to become goals is supported by external forces and by internal individual needs. Externally, resistance to the "rate buster"—the person who produces over the standard—appears to be well-nigh universal unless an accepted bonus plan is in operation. These effects on group production were first studied in detail by Roethlisberger and Dickson in the Hawthorne studies and have been confirmed by a number of observers subsequently [9]. At the same time, individuals seem to be more ready to accept standards as goals than such admonitions as "Produce as much as you can" or "Produce a fair day's work" or the classical "Maximize!" Some of the reasons why this is true are discussed in other parts of this text.

Training at the Skilled Level. Work procedures that stem from time-study methods are generally devised specifically for the performance of a particular job. In some cases this may involve aggregating from previously established standard times for basic activities, but ordinarily the major source of data is supplied by studies of the particular job. The procedures are, therefore, internally generated and introduced into the system through instructing and training workers in their meaning. This is only one form that task-performance rules take. A second major form at the basic productive level in the organization is introduced not by training, but as a concomitant of recruitment and selection. Many employees in an organization come to the firm with built-in task-performance rules.

Some obvious examples of such pretraining can be found in the standard craft areas. Electricians, plumbers, carpenters, machinists, and similar skilled workers have ordinarily been trained in standard procedures for dealing with standard situations. These craft rules become part of the organization's operating procedures not by formal promulgation and publication, but by the simple act of hiring a person with the indicated training.

Training at the Professional Level. Training is not a phenomenon limited to what are commonly called blue-collar activities; the white-collar man may be involved also. When a business firm hires an accountant or a dietician or a doctor or a sanitary engineer, it hires not only an individual, but also a large number of standard operating procedures that have been trained into the new member of the organization by outside agencies. Often groups which do not belong to an organization thus provide task-performance rules for the organization. Although some business college professors would probably find it difficult to believe, one of their major functions is to provide future members of business organizations with rules for performing tasks; these rules thereby become an important part of the organizational code, and college professors thereby become important parts of business firms in which they may have no financial, emotional, or ideological interest. We will note below some of the consequences of this separation of training and the organization in specific areas. Here it will be enough to note that it leads to standardization of task performance across firms as well as to some problems in organizational control.

This separation of training responsibility from organizational control has created problems for organizations that wish to emphasize the uniqueness of their particular activities. Thus, some steel companies have been urging that training in steel technology be the function of the organization rather than of the engineering school. Similarly, the United Mine Workers has expressed itself as not entirely happy with the professional training provided doctors by medical schools and the American Medical Association. In both cases the separation of organizational control and responsibility for the specification of operating procedures has produced problems. If professional training of executives for business firms continues to expand in importance and if the current movement toward a management profession grows, these problems may well become acute. Few business firms are currently aware either of the extent to which their operating procedures are determined by external groups or of how this will grow if the movement toward the professional training of management achieves significant success.

RECORDS AND REPORTS

The continuing records and reports kept by the organization are a second major component of the standard operating procedures. Just as we can describe an organization in terms of the task specifications it makes, we can also describe it by the kinds of records and reports it maintains over a period of time. In fact, an analysis of an organization's records should enable us to deduce some important characteristics of the firm's decision-making system. For example, the kinds of records kept tell a good deal about the firm's perceptions of its own internal structure and the kind of world in which it exists. Records tell us also some subtle things about the psychological climate of the organization.

One of the first steps in analyzing the significance of record and report keeping is to attempt to identify the purposes for which such activities are designed. In most organizations there are two main purposes: *control* and *prediction*. These are, of course, the general purposes of a number of organizational subsystems.

Records for Control. The concept of control has a number of different meanings in the context of a business organization. The accountant, for example, speaks of "internal controls." By this he means a system of checks developed in an organization to protect against a variety of factors ranging from fraud to clerical errors [6]. For example, the person who opens the mail in a department store frequently does not count the cash. The person who counts the cash frequently is not the person who makes the entries in the records. Thus, organizations capitalize on the problems of organization, in this case the problems of organizing fraud.

Generally, the organization itself does not issue reports or keep records on the functioning of the internal control system. The check on the internal control system is usually made by an outside person, the auditor for the organization. His report is made to top management and becomes, in part, an assessment of the quality of the internal organization.

Managerial Control. To the psychologist, a more interesting notion of control is that of managerial control. *Managerial control means control designed to stimulate behavior that the person in control would induce if he were physically present.* A foreman, for example, ordinarily would like the group he supervises to conform to some standard whether he is present or not. He attempts to build automatic control devices that will produce the desired behavior.

Automatic control devices are of course widely used to deal with modern machine systems. A simple example is the common thermostat used to control the output of a heating plant in a house. The desired outcome is a specified temperature. Whenever a deviation from that temperature occurs, or in more complicated controls when it is anticipated, the heating output is changed upward or downward. If the required temperature is maintained perfectly, the system is well controlled. Most household heating systems are not that well designed and produce perceptible oscillations around the desired temperature. The theory of such a dynamically controlled system, sometimes referred to as "servomechanism theory," underlies much of modern instrumentation and automation [1].

What is the relevance of such theory to the problems of managerial control? In a general sense, managerial control and servomechanisms have a common purpose, namely, to maintain controlled systems. In fact, it has been suggested that servomechanism theory is a useful framework for examining organizational systems. One analogy to the thermostat is the organizational record. It is assumed that the individual employee, knowing that a particular report will have to be made, behaves in such a way that there will be no adverse repercussions from the report. A common example of this is the usual profit-and-loss statement and balance sheet, the financial statement of a corporation. These are required by law at regular intervals for almost all business organizations of any size. Knowing that such statements will have to be made, the management of the firm presumably will behave in such a way that these statements will reflect a desired behavior. This is one of the primary uses of such statements, although sometimes they are justified in other terms.

Behavior and Organizational Demands. Another example of automatic control through reports is found in the use of standard costs and the standard costs report. Standard costs for doing particular jobs are calculated, usually by the accounting department or by industrial engineers. The actual cost of a job is compared in the form of a ratio with the standard cost. If the ratio is greater than 1.0, it means that the job costs more to execute than was estimated. Reports of such results are made periodically, sometimes as frequently as each day, sometimes weekly. These reports show the performance of particular employees or particular departments. As in the case of the profit-and-loss statement, it is assumed that members of the organization will behave differently when they know that cost records are being kept. Specifically, it is assumed that the behavior will, under such conditions, be more consistent with organizational demands.

Records, such as the financial statement or the standard cost report, have a control effect for a short while merely by the fact that they are kept. But in the long run, records will have little effect if they do not trigger organizational reaction when behavior is out of control. If a department substantially exceeds or substantially improves on standard costs, the records should induce action. Otherwise, the records become simply relatively ineffective parts of the corporate memory. Generally, the action involved is action by a supervisor or executive responsible for the department. It may also involve other workers, however. For example, the simple publication of quality-control statistics creates a reference group for the individual worker and generally results in modifications of behavior in the direction of homogeneity within the work group.

Resistance to Procedural Changes. At the same time, the records and reports specified in standard operating procedures affect the development of individual goals in the organization. They indicate, as they are intended to indicate, what is considered to be of importance in the organization. But where the organization is dealing with a relatively ambiguous goal (e.g., profit) and relatively precise records and reports (e.g., in accounting procedures or psychological testing), the justification of the reports in terms of the goal tends to be forgotten and the reports become important in themselves. This substitution of subgoals for the over-all objectives to which they are supposed to contribute is generally functional for the time being. But on occasion it can lead to considerable inflexibility in adjusting operating procedures when they are inappropriate. For example, it has been suggested that modern statistical decision theory appears to demand some revision in standard accounting procedures [13]. Yet accountants who have urged such changes have met with considerable resistance. This should not surprise us since it seems to be true of a large variety of proposed changes both in and out of organizations. But it exhibits the important goal-setting consequences of standard operating procedures. In connection with this kind of problem it is interesting to note that some men who succeed as top managers conceive their job to be more flexible than do many middle-management people. The latter often feel that their role in the organization is merely to "follow the rules."

Records for Prediction. In addition to control, a second major function of records is to help an organization predict its environment. Since the world in which business organizations live is extremely uncertain, industrialists place considerable emphasis on making estimates about future behavior. For example, they attempt to predict what their competitors will do, how fast demand for their products will increase or decrease, what labor demands will probably be, and what technological innovations are likely to be important over the next few years. In order to make such estimates, the firm needs first of all some ideas about relations between past events and future events, and second, it needs some records of the relevant past events.

Rarely does an organization have a unified plan for ensuring that only those records that are needed are kept. More frequently, new records are started when some special need for them arises, and old records persist long after they have served their purpose. At any point in time, however, the information maintained on records bears a reasonable relation to those variables that the organization considers important in predicting its environment.

Decision Making and Records. Two important consequences stem from the organization's dependence on a particular set of records for predictive purposes. First, the significance of records for the individual members of the organization increases substantially. Organizational decisions about the allocation of resources among the various subunits and individual employees depend on estimates of future events. Generally, advertising managers feel that they should, within reason, ensure records favorable to the proposition that increases in advertising more than pay off in increases in sales. Similarly, industrial psychologists learn the importance of having records which tend to show the efficiency gains resulting from selection and training procedures.

Secondly, the records that are kept determine in large part what aspects of the environment will be observed and what alternatives of action will be considered by the firm. Recent theories of business behavior place considerable emphasis on the process by which organizations find alternatives to consider [8]. Records of past behavior are one of the major sources for such a process. As a result, there is more stability of organizational decisions from one period to another than one would predict if the organization entered each situation without records of prior experience. Similarly, if the firm exists in an environment that changes suddenly in such a way as to make a new statistic important to decision making, the firm is likely to be relatively slow in adjusting to the new factor, and it is likely to attempt to use its existing model of the world and its existing records to deal with the changed conditions. Here, as in the case of task-performance rules, we observe the standard operating procedures serving an organizational learning function. They permit the organization to deal more effectively with previously experienced situations than it could if it were considering the situation without prior experience, but they normally retard adjustment to strikingly different situations. Thus we have here a reason why so many ambitious young men who enter business for the first time get frustrated when their "new" ideas take a kicking around.

INFORMATION-HANDLING RULES

Just as some people have described an organization as a massive servo-mechanism, others describe it as a "communication system." As a communication system, the firm can be defined in terms of four things. *The characteristics of the information taken into the firm* is our first consideration. Information comes to the organization from outside in a wide variety of ways and forms. Salesmen receive orders and confidences about competitors. Foremen hear about the toothache that Harry Stern's wife has. Executives read trade journals and formulate conclusions about general conditions in the industry. All these data comprise inputs for the firm. Second, we have *rules for distributing and condensing input information.* What does the salesman do with an order? What does the foreman do with the information about Mrs. Stern's toothache? What does the executive do with the trade-journal information? In the third place, we deal with *rules for distributing and condensing internally generated information.* Different parts of the organization make decisions, issue orders, request clarification. How are such pieces of information moved through the organization? Finally, we are interested in *the characteristics of the information leaving the firm.* The organization communicates with its environment through orders on suppliers, deliveries to consumers, advertising, petitions for patents, and a large number of other ways.

Information Sources. It is obvious that not everyone in an organization seeks or receives all the information needed by the firm to pursue its business. There is considerable specialization in securing information, just as there is in task performance and record keeping. In large part, this specialization is defined by operating rules linked closely to the rules for information flows, which we will discuss below. Generally, a firm will

allocate responsibility for securing particular information to subunits having either regular contact with the information source or special competence in securing the information. Thus, salesmen from their regular contacts with customers are expected to provide information on market demand. A labor relations department is expected to keep management informed of impending labor demands. A purchasing department would
ordinarily be responsible for providing information on the availability of
supplies. In each of these cases regular contact with the relevant outside
environment makes the department an obvious expert on the subject.

Often, however, the organization does not rely simply on contact as the
criterion for selecting information sources. Large firms now maintain staff
experts whose sole function is to secure and evaluate information. On the
payroll are market analysts, financial analysts, psychologists, and
economists, all providing services supplementary to the information
gathered by regular operating units.

Information and Confusion. Does it make any difference who gathers
the information? Certainly it does. It is important because the person who
gathers the information is also the first one to communicate it, condense it,
and evaluate it. It is also important in another way. The business world
is truly a big, buzzing confusion. The environment of the firm buries an
extremely large amount of information that might be relevant to decision
making within the firm. Some initial screening decisions are made at the
very periphery of the organization. Most of these are trivial. For example,
a salesman learns that one of his customers is driving a new automobile,
but he does not report the fact to his department because he does not
consider it relevant. But some screening decisions have important effects.
If the salesman decides to rely on a particular informant in an outside
organization, he links his own firm's policies to the accuracy of the informant's reports. Similarly, all parts of the organization, from clerks dealing with visitors to vice-presidents dealing with bankers, make decisions
about what questions they will direct to whom on the outside. These decisions depend on their past training and their perceptiveness in the situation.
Organizational decisions, in turn, depend on them. Understanding the
nature of confusions is important.

Information Flows. In a very simple organization it might be possible
to allow all information to be shared among all members of the organization and to permit this sharing in the informal manner characteristic of
small groups. In a large organization with specialization of functions, however, it is necessary to establish regular procedures for transmitting information—whether it be information from outside the organization or
decisions and instructions originating within the organization. We turn now
to a consideration of the rules regulating the movement of information
through a firm.

Routing Rules and Filtering Rules. There are two aspects of the standard operating procedures for information flows, namely, routing rules and filtering rules. Routing rules specify who will communicate to whom about what. The most obvious, best-known, and one of the most important of such rules is the through-channels rule. The organization requires that certain kinds of information be handled through channels. In such a system, the president talks only to the board of directors, his staff assistants, and vice-presidents. Vice-presidents talk only to their staff assistants, the president, and division managers or the equivalent. For many purposes the standard organizational chart is viewed as a rule for channeling communication. Obviously no organization can adhere strictly to such a rule without severe strains, as we saw in the preceding chapter. But most business organizations observe it for a wide variety of information handling.

The reason for the extensive use of through-channel rules is clear when one considers the reasons for organizational departmentalization. Departmentalization depends on the assumption that the activities necessary to accomplish the firm's goals can be grouped so that any given group can act more or less independently of other groups. The production division can ignore the finance division except for a few exceptional occasions. To the extent to which such atomization of the firm occurs, and is complemented by a similar atomization of relevant information, the departmental organization defines reasonably well the groups within which sharing of information is needed. Since information needs and task specialization are highly correlated, it is appropriate to process information through the hierarchy as it is defined in terms of task specialization.

By the same token we can predict when communication that is not through channels will become part of the operating procedures of the firm. Where there are needs for coordinating the activities of subunits in the organization, communication through channels is frequently quite inefficient. As a result, procedures for transmitting information across channels are developed. Here we find the filtering rules. These procedures are more likely to be the result of innovation than of conscious planning at the top, but in time they become as fully accepted as the routing rules.

What difference do routing rules make? Very little, by themselves. Provided the information is unchanged from receipt to final destination about all that can be affected by routing is the length of time required to transmit the message. What makes the routing rules important is their linkage with filtering at the various communication relay points. Information is condensed and summarized as it goes through the organization.

Useful and Unuseful Information. Condensation of information is clearly desirable for an organization. It is not important for top-management personnel to know how many times the secretary in the production department went out for coffee. Someone, perhaps, should have that information, but not the president. Two things complicate the filtering process, however. On the one hand, there is frequently considerable uncertainty in the organization about what information should and what should not be communicated. Sometimes, particularly in young organizations, top executives are inundated with information which they cannot use effectively. Under other circumstances, relevant information is not available when needed. Either situation is an unhappy one for the firm.

The other complication in filtering stems from having people rather than simple machines as relay points. The sales group can be expected to know more about sales and sales potential than other group in the organization. Consequently, it will have primary responsibility for filtering such information. But the sales group frequently will have a consistent bias with respect to sales estimates, particularly if its performance is linked to the relation between predicted sales and actual sales. Similarly, accounting departments will filter cost information differently from other departments. And although the computation center is obviously the best source of information on the efficiency of a computer installation, it is unlikely to be an unbiased filter.

Selective Filtering. Once we note that those places where information is received in an organization are different from those places where it is used to make decisions, and that much more information is received than can be communicated through organizational channels conveniently, we must acknowledge the importance of selective filtering and of inferences drawn at relatively low levels in the organization. The kind of information which is in the hands of the decision makers in the firm depends in part on the way in which information is processed in the firm. As we noted earlier, the data on costs processed through an accounting department will be treated differently from the same data processed through a different department.

As a result of these information phenomena, and the high dependence of the organization hierarchy on the information it receives, many of the more naïve views of organizational influence need to be reexamined. A boss who makes decisions on the basis of highly filtered information does so in only a very special sense. After he has received the relevant information, he is frequently given very little real discretion. An effective executive recognizes this fact and introduces control methods designed to improve the accuracy and completeness of the information he receives. But even with the best control techniques available, he still must operate several filters removed from the environment he is predicting. Consequently, in order to understand how decisions are reached we need to know in considerable detail how information is moved from one place to another in the organization.

And we need to recognize that the *actual* decision maker will often be rather far removed from the *formal* decision maker, as we shall see in the later chapter on executive leadership.

Communication Code. Information-handling rules affect perceptions in another, more subtle, way. When information is communicated from one part of the organization to another, a communication code develops. We use the word "code" in a very general sense. It consists of two things: a division of all stimuli into classes of stimuli and an assignment of a symbol to each such class. Communication then proceeds in terms of the symbols. The English language is an example of such a code. Consider the colors. The word "red" signifies a class of discriminable colors some of which are very hard to specify in the English language, though they may be somewhat more easily described in other languages. What difference does example make? For an organization it may make a considerable amount of difference. It develops a way of coding the environment that permits it to make the discriminations necessary in the current world. If the world changes, the organization code may be quite an awkward one with which to deal. The problem is comparable to what would happen if automobile traffic signals were changed from red and green to two different brightnesses of red. Neither our language nor our learned abilities to describe colors permit us to describe different intensities adequately. In general, the information-handling code in an organization functions the same way. It facilitates dealing with the usual environment. It makes dealing with the unusual somewhat more difficult [7].

PLANS AND PLANNING RULES

That planning is a major responsibility of the leadership of a firm has become increasingly clear in recent years. As a result, the procedures used in planning have become a subject for the specification of operating procedures. Manuals on the budgeting process are now used by a number of firms. In its planning activity the organization is face to face with the problem of resource allocation within the firm and the relation between that allocation and the behavior of other firms, consumers, investors. What new capital expenditures for plants or equipment will be authorized? How much will be spent for research and development? How much should be invested in the selection and training of employees? The way in which these allocations are made will, of course, determine such aspects of firm behavior as the kinds of products that will be produced and the ways in which the products will be sold.

Why the Firm Plans. If the environment were conveniently stable or easily predicted, planning would be relatively simple also. Where the best predictions are discouragingly crude and the planning commitments ominously large, rather elaborate procedures are used by the firm. More-over, under conditions of extreme uncertainty the organization will attempt to devise a system that is flexible enough to permit quick adjustments. Why under such conditions does a firm plan at all? We think there are three major reasons why organizations plan. First, organizations are composed of human beings. Recent research on human prediction of uncertain events suggests that human beings resist the adoption of strategies in the face of unpredictability and prefer to try to predict even in the face of considerable evidence that their predictive power is nonexistent [2]. Second, people in organizations expect to learn from experience and (possibly correctly) be-lieve that only through trying to predict the environment are they likely to develop techniques for doing so. Third, the organization's ability to achieve its plan depends on the willingness of members to implement it; and willingness is more easily secured where there appears to be some connection between the organizational plan and standard notions of rationality.

Basic Planning Phases. What is a typical procedure like? It can be de-scribed in terms of three basic phases. First, there is an estimation phase. A sales forecast is made by the sales department along with a tentative plan for marketing the product. The behavior of competitors is estimated. What will the reaction of Ford be to a 100 per cent increase in advertising expenditures by General Motors? What is Ford planning to do about price next year? The production division estimates costs of production and pro-duction needs over the budget period. How much material, labor, equip-ment, new plant will be needed? The finance division estimates the avail-ability of investment money for expansion for such things as equipment replacement.

The second phase is an evaluation of the tentative plans from the point of view of organizational objectives. Suppose that a firm wants to obtain a net profit of at least 10 per cent, a return on new investment of at least 20 per cent, maintain or increase its current share of the market, and maintain or increase current employment. It will examine the tentative budgets, summarized in terms of a cash budget and a capital expenditures budget, and determine whether the objectives can be achieved. If they can, a master budget will be adopted. Frequently, however, they cannot. The organization then passes to the third phase of the planning process.

In the third phase the original plans and estimates are reexamined to see whether savings in costs, gains in demand, and improvements in credit posi-tion can be secured. One thing about the planning process that frequently surprises outside observers is that in this third stage it is almost always possible to discover revisions in plans which will bring one closer to the objectives. This "organizational slack" permits business organizations to achieve plans in relatively hard times when on the surface it seems impossible to do so. If the reexamination of estimates does not produce a feasible plan, it then becomes necessary to lower the objectives.

The plans of the organization, as formalized in the budget and related documents, establish goals for the individual members and subunits of the firm. This dual role of the budget as both a prediction of the future and a goal to be achieved results in a tendency for organizational budgets to be self-confirming. The detailed consequences of this phenomenon are not particularly important here. What is important to remember is that any organizational plan will generate some force toward its own fulfillment, even where the plan is based on estimates of considerable inaccuracy. Where the estimates are high, fears of the consequences for future estimates will lead to a pacing of activity so that achievement is close to the estimate. Where the estimates are low, the organization subunits will search for new methods, designs, etc., which will allow them to meet the plan. For example, it is not uncommon in these days of inflationary construction costs for a business organization to construct a new facility within the budgeted amount by redesigning and reengineering the project.

Why Businesses Use Operating Procedures. The importance of standard procedures to the effective operation of a business firm is beyond question. They introduce uniqueness where variety would be disastrous, coordinate activities which if uncoordinated would create chaos, and in general permit a large and complex system to act more or less rationally. This is no small accomplishment. It also explains why a description of a business organization which ignores standard operating procedures is a most limited description.

At the same time, we have tried to discuss a number of important consequences of standard operating procedures for human behavior in business organizations. We can call these the "psychological" consequences of standard operating procedures in order to emphasize the way in which innocuous-looking rules can have substantial unintended effects on people, and of course, partially intended effects at times. The effects we have noted seem to fall into three major categories. First, standard operating procedures affect *individual goals* within the organization. The specification of a plan or other rule has a distinct effect on the desires and expectations of organizational members. Second, standard operating procedures affect *individual perceptions* of the state of the environment. Different parts of the organization see different environments, and the environments they see depend on the rules for recording and processing information. Finally, standard operating procedures affect the *range of alternatives* considered by organization members in arriving at operating decisions. The way in which the organization searches for alternatives is substantially a function of the operating rules it has. The standard operating procedures of any business are closely related to the needs of the people within the organization; at least there are those who think that they should be. The nature of human needs we will cover in the following chapter.

SUGGESTIONS FOR FURTHER READING

Grimshaw, A., & Hennessey, J. W. *Organizational behavior: Cases and readings.* New York: McGraw-Hill, 1960. Selections are concerned with decision-making problems in business at the various levels of the industrial organization. Useful in orienting the reader who is planning a career in management.

Haire, M. (Ed.) *Modern organizational theory.* New York: Wiley, 1959. This volume covers some of the latest theories on organizational objectives and decision making of interest to the sophisticated reader.

March, J. G., & Simon, H. A. *Organizations.* New York: Wiley, 1958. A detailed description of organizational behavior putting emphasis on the ways in which decisions are made in an organization.

Selznick, P. *Leadership in administration.* Evanston, Ill.: Row, Peterson, 1957. This book is an essay on the role of a modern organizational leader in the face of a changing environment.

PART III: PERSONNEL
PSYCHOLOGY

5

HUMAN NEEDS

IN INDUSTRY

B. von Haller Gilmer

Human beings want many things. All of us must have air, food, shelter. Other needs, which are just as real, include status, recognition for our efforts, and a feeling of belongingness; but these needs are often more difficult to satisfy. It is important to consider how they are related to the work environment of the person in industry.

Industry has made much progress in helping the worker as well as the executive satisfy some of their economic needs and obtain many of the physical comforts of life. But progress has been slower in other respects—in helping the man feel that he belongs, that he has the opportunity to measure up to his own ambitions. One reason for our lack of progress in helping motivate the man to acquire skill and use it in the development of his full potential lies in the fact that what a man needs changes with time and with circumstances. In youth, men look more for opportunity; in old age, for security.

A BASIC MODEL OF BEHAVIOR

In this chapter we will describe some of the more common needs and raise some practical questions of why people behave as they do. We hope that the presentation here, which will be amplified from time to time in later chapters, will help the reader to understand the sources of behavior.

The student of psychology is familiar with three interrelated assumptions about human behavior: Behavior is *caused*. Behavior is *motivated*. Behavior is *goal-directed*. We will present these three assumptions in terms of a basic model of behavior described by Leavitt [11]. This model is represented in Figure 5.1.

In this closed-circuit model, obtaining a goal eliminates the cause, which in turn eliminates the motive, which consequently eliminates the behavior. When one's stomach is empty, the emptiness stimulates a feeling of hunger, and this feeling stimulates action in the direction of food. When obtained, the food fills the stomach, causing cessation of the hunger impulses, and this in turn terminates the behavior in search of food. The description seems simple, but at this point Leavitt emphasizes that the closed-circuit conception has a limitation of which we should be aware. Whereas one can consume enough food to stop hunger and food seeking temporarily, it does not follow that one can consume a given quantity of prestige, for

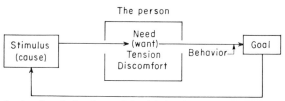

Fig. 5.1. A basic closed-circuit model of behavior, showing relationships between causality, motivation, and goal direction. Obtaining a goal eliminates the cause, which in turn eliminates the motive and, finally, the behavior. (From Leavitt, H. J. *Managerial psychology*. Courtesy of the University of Chicago Press; copyright 1958 by the University of Chicago.)

example, and feel satiated. This is important to remember if we are to understand the drives of people in industry.

Often human behavior does fit in with the system just described. Behavior may be an effort to eliminate tensions by seeking goals that neutralize the causes of tensions. For instance, a man thinks that he has a need for a new car. The more he considers the proposition, the more his tension increases. He explores the market and finds the car that will meet his needs. The more he thinks about a new car, the more he is influenced by advertising and the more a desire to obtain one builds up in him. Finally, when arrangements are made to buy the car, the tension is resolved.

Understanding something of the general nature of human wants sets the stage for dealing with many of the problems to be described later in chapters dealing with personnel management, work, and social and personal adjustments.

VARIATIONS WITHIN INDIVIDUALS

One of the main influences on a man's needs is his age. It is quite apparent that the needs of the child differ greatly from those of the adult. Similarly, the satisfactions that we expect from our job depend, in part, on the age and experience bracket we are in. Most industrial workers range in age from eighteen through sixty-five, and those in management range from the early twenties to retirement. There is evidence that the range of individual differences within the limits of man's working span is so great that one man may be as youthful biologically and psychologically as another who is fifteen or twenty years younger. But in spite of these individual differences, we can still say that psychological needs change with age, and these changes affect our attitudes toward work.

Needs in Youth. The youth is aware of and welcomes change. The individual is growing, his world is widening. The man just out of college, entering an industrial career in engineering, salesmanship, or the like, seizes every opportunity to get ahead, and he has the stamina to take the competition. He wants and expects challenge, for herein lies the path to recognition. In old age, change is unwelcomed and resisted. The dreams of better days ahead are over, and the world is narrowing. Competition is shunned because few have the stamina to keep up the pace.

The problems of early youth are numerous. The college student in his senior year must decide whether to take a job or to enter graduate school and study for a profession. When he begins working, he must try to adjust his psychological needs to meet new economic necessities. He must look for an opportunity where his anticipations can be realized and his enthusiasms rewarded. He may not succeed at first. But youth has one big advantage; disappointments are soon overcome by hopes for a better future. Dissatisfaction with one job may be remedied by taking another. The opportunities for youth in our expanding economy build up attitudes of both confidence and defiance—just the reverse of the kind found in the older person. A youth at the worker level, regardless of his limitations in education, is optimistic about the future. His physical strength and vitality to some degree make up for his lack of training and experience. Desires that are not readily fulfilled today are projected in terms of satisfaction in the future.

Needs in Middle Age. In middle age, status becomes of great importance; in this age, a man is determining whether or not he will be a success, as measured by his own goals. In occupations, such as engineering and science, in which long professional training is essential to productive activity and economic independence, men who have not yet been admitted to full standing may identify themselves as being young. A laborer, on the other hand, who may be the same chronological age as the newly licensed company lawyer may feel himself old at thirty-five. A steelworker or coal miner may feel he has reached his economic peak just at the age that the engineer and accountant are ready for promotion and their best work.

Along with decreases in physical stamina and sexual activity, such things as vanishing hairlines indicate the passing of youth, a stage soon to be followed in some people by what has been termed a "middle-age revolt" [3]. This usually comes earlier in the case of the worker, later with the manager or professional man; but it comes to many in terms of lost dreams and failure to meet cutthroat competition. This revolt comes when the man cannot plead the inexperience of youth or the frailties of age. The middle-ager sometimes expresses guilt feelings of failure and blames himself for not having gone into the right job. He frequently wonders whether he married the right woman. He may see his weight climbing and his hair thinning. When youngsters call him "Sir" and the lone courtesy candle appears on his birthday cake, the middle-aged man is quite ready to magnify his problems. His ego suffers another blow when he moves into the bifocal stage and he finds that his insurance rates are going up. It is in this stage that the middle-aged man sometimes begins to aggress against his family and against his job. During this period of emotional second adolescence, the middle-aged worker may be difficult to deal with and the manager may be hard to work for.

Variations between Individuals. Another factor influencing human needs involves class differences. A job considered good by the son of a day worker might be thought of as poor by the son of a vice-president. Job satisfaction has a relation to job expectancy. The young man who comes from the working-class family may regard the job of a toolmaker or bricklayer as very satisfactory. This class of job would probably be considered inferior by the young man from a higher social status. Thus job status and social status go hand in hand where there is some permanence involved. The president may brag that his college son is spending the summer with a drag crew in the steel mill. The worker may also brag about his son having a similar job. However, the needs being satisfied in the two cases are quite different.

When we think in terms of needs being satisfied, we must think in terms of goal expectancy. One young man from a lower-class family may be dissatisfied with the same job his neighbor likes because he or his family has set higher goals for him.

The level of aspiration of any given person in relation to his feelings of accomplishment determines in large measure his attitudes. The son of the worker who aspires to work his way up from the bottom, who pictures himself becoming a part of management, may play just such a role until he experiences failure and rebuff time after time. Being thus thwarted, he may turn his attention to union activities. If he is encouraged with success here he may well go on to become a leader and a strong union man. Some of the outstanding union leaders today, men with proven leadership and executive ability, have become union rather than management men because in the union they found the recognition they had been seeking.

Status Anxiety. The acceptance or rejection of a person, and his consequent attitude toward his work, is frequently a matter of status. The college graduate who may be competing with a high school man for recognition on the job may feel that he is in an advantageous position. He may well be taken aback to find that being known as a college man who works with noncollege people can have its disadvantages. The author has several instances in his files of engineering students who have had to buck the problem of being accepted on the job where their coworkers had never been to college. The thing that may make a person "belong" in one situation may well be a handicap in another. A Ph.D. in psychology is a union card in academic circles, and it can serve as an entree on many occasions. Any experienced consultant, however, can verify the statement that this advanced degree can be a handicap in being accepted in the shop. Status anxiety is found in every part of our culture, but it is particularly noticeable in industry. Here we can observe human tensions in a clear-cut way as one man compares himself with another in terms of the recognition he has received and the advancements he gets.

Differences in Ambition. Although we have seen how social status, age, and education determine, in part, an individual's ambitions and job satisfactions, it is important to remember that the drives of some people differ regardless of the influence of these factors. Many people seem quite adjusted to their job situation though it be of comparatively low status and low financial return. It is hard for the highly motivated person to realize that some people are not as ambitious as he. In one industrial situation, psychologists were employed to study the attitudes of people who had several times been passed over in promotions. Some were quite indignant because they had not received recognition, but a surprising number seemed quite contented to remain at their particular level. One man, who gave evidence of having more ability than he had used, was asked why he was content with his medium-status job. He pointed out that he valued other things in life more highly than job success. "I know what you are thinking," he said during the interview. "I don't have hypertension, I don't have an ulcer, I'm a failure!"

We know that there are variations of human needs from person to person and also that the needs of any individual change from time to time. We know that these variations are in some instances related to age, in others to status, experience, and education. But there are many changes of needs in the human being for which we cannot account. Industry has laid primary emphasis on improving the workers' environment, but only indirectly has it studied the worker himself to determine his needs.

Need Variation across Groups. Not only do needs vary from one person to another; sometimes they vary from group to group. A study [13] made during World War II offers us a good example. In an industrial plant, blue-green lighting had been installed after research had indicated that this would reduce eyestrain. Careful records of production were kept, and after the blue-green lighting had been installed the output of male workers increased. There were many comments about less eyestrain from the men. They were very happy with the new lighting. But with women employees the story was quite different. Output fell off, absenteeism hit its highest peak. Their production was greatly reduced. Why? Because the women felt that the new type of lighting made them look ghastly; and, in fact, it did. In this particular instance, an environmental situation which motivated one group of people in one way had just the opposite effect on another group with different specific needs.

REACTIONS TO FRUSTRATION

Attempts to obtain satisfaction of needs and desires frequently meet with obstacles, regardless of one's status or job. Many times these blockages are only temporary and are overcome easily. At other times, however, attempts to attain a goal are blocked time and time again with the result that there is an accumulation of tension within the individual. The work environment in our highly competitive American industrial system is in itself particularly frustration-inducing for workers and managers alike. The examples given below, all taken from industrial settings, illustrate several kinds of reactions to frustrations that normal people show.

Elementary Aggression. Elementary aggression as shown by the adult looks somewhat like the behavior of a naughty child. In an Eastern city, a union local called a strike which shut down all truck deliveries to and from the five largest department stores. As the strike, which involved hundreds of drivers, went into its second year, such childlike behavior was engaged in as heaving paint bombs into the homes of the store supervisors, and breaking plate-glass windows in the stores by throwing steel balls at them from moving automobiles.

Displaced Aggression. Displaced aggression reactions are shown in indirect and subtle ways; they are so named because the behavior is directed against some object or person other than the real source of the frustration. The frustrated worker, for example, who is sore at the boss, may rant and rave at his family. He cannot tell off the boss for fear of losing his job; so his wife and children become the innocent victims of his displaced aggression. The following example illustrates this kind of behavior.

A middle-aged woman employee was transferred from her regular operation of assembling parts in a metals fabrication plant to a new operation in the same department. The new job consisted of a repetitive type of task, machining springs for toy motors. After a day the woman became adept at the job and was able to produce about 250 pieces an hour, and after another day at the job, 350. The amount of production asked by the gang boss was 500 units per hour. The worker reported that she could not reach this requirement. The boss insisted that she could raise her production if she wanted to and that she was holding back purposely because she wanted her old job back. Her name was reported to the foreman as being one of several workers who balked at meeting production requirements. The foreman spoke to her in harsh tones, telling her, in effect, to produce or else.

The woman became upset and was able to do hardly any work for the remainder of the day. She did not say anything to the foreman. During the next three days her work improved slightly in quantity but decreased in quality. It was also discovered later that she had been the one responsible for stopping up the toilet in the ladies' rest room on three successive days following the instance. On each occasion she had placed a whole orange in the commode. Certainly this was displaced aggression!

Organized Aggression. Organized aggression may come about through well-laid planning, as is often found in prolonged labor-management conflict. But often closer to the real feelings of people is the aggression that becomes organized more informally. An example of this type of reaction to frustration is found in writings about the famous Western Electric researches [10]. In the study of a wage-incentive scheme, it became apparent that the majority of a group of workers, regardless of other differences, shared some common feelings. If an individual turned out too much work he became a rate buster; too little work labeled him a "chiseler." The person who would say anything to injure a fellow member of the group was a "squealer." It was also accepted practice that no member of the work group should act officiously.

The wage-incentive scheme was planned to encourage output by setting pay rates on the basis of group earnings. The experts who devised the scheme assumed that the group would bring pressure to bear upon the slower workers to make them work harder and so increase the earnings of the group. Actually what happened was practically the reverse. The workers put pressure not only on the slower workers but upon the faster ones as well. Pressure was applied in various ways. One informally organized aggression was "binging," as the men called it. If one of the workers did something which the group did not consider proper, a fellow worker had the right to bing him. This consisted of a quick, stiff blow on the upper arm. The worker who was struck got the idea and did not strike back. The punishment was, therefore, psychological, not physical. Why was such behavior engaged in? For one thing, the industrial worker has his own ways of doing his job, his own traditions of skill, and his own satisfactions from achieving goals set according to his own standards—this, of course, within certain practical limits. The worker hates to be "told" or to be "planned for" by experts. In a sense he rejects authority, particularly when customs of work are challenged by innovations put in without his approval. The resulting frustration brings out aggression. The aggression frequently becomes organized when the majority of the group feel the same way about the source of the frustration.

Work as Escape. Another kind of reaction to frustration, frequently found with the harassed executive, is attempts of escape through excessive work, more or less routine in nature. Such was the case with a former executive vice-president of a large corporation, whom we shall call Mr. Gregory.

Mr. Gregory was in his early fifties. He was a graduate of an engineering school and had worked his way up in the company over a period of some thirty years. Now he had held the position of executive vice-president for four years. To all outside appearances he was a highly successful executive; in the office before eight, he was the last to leave in the evening, carrying a loaded briefcase. It gradually became apparent to Gregory's superiors that he was working harder and harder and accomplishing less and less. There seemed to be no family or outside problems causing his difficulty. During a routine clinical examination held periodically for top executives, the following facts appeared. Gregory had been successful as an engineer, and he had made notable progress as the vice-president of manufacturing. In fact, his success in the latter position led to his appointment as executive vice-president. About two years after this promotion, the corporation expanded and the job became too big for Gregory, though he did not realize it at the time. He began to postpone more and more decisions and to become harder to see. He spent his time primarily on details of a clerical nature, working evenings and sometimes on week ends. When pressed for decisions, particularly from the lower echelons, he made it known that he was too busy, not verbally but by actually being busy.

Here is a type of reaction to a frustration caused by inability to cope with the important parts of a job; the reaction is to seek escape by concentrating on the unimportant things.

Excuses for Failure. One of the most common ways of reacting to frustration caused by failure to reach a goal is indulging in *rationalization*. The person tries for a way out by coming up with a plausible or good excuse for failure; he tries to justify his behavior. This is illustrated by the industrial clerk whom we shall call Harold.

Upon graduation from high school, Harold was employed by the ABC Company as a general clerical worker in the office. During the ensuing five years he made satisfactory progress, and at the end of that time he was transferred into the accounting department. Shortly after beginning work in the accounting department, he married. Within the next few years Harold's family responsibilities increased until his salary was not sufficient to sustain the standard of living to which he and his wife had become accustomed and which they desired to maintain. Harold requested an increase in salary from his superior in the firm, and he was told that he was receiving all that the job was worth. The head of the accounting department told Harold that the only way in which he could hope to receive an increase in salary was to qualify himself for a higher-rated job. He advised Harold to enroll in an accounting course in a local night school.

Harold had not participated in any formal educational training since graduating from high school where his work had been of only average quality. He enrolled for courses in accounting, but within a few months he began to experience difficulty with his schoolwork. His conduct in the office and at home became noticeably different. At the office he discoursed loudly and long to his fellow workers on the unnecessary attempts by accountants to make their work unduly hard for students and the unnecessary difficulty of standard accounting practices. At home, Harold's behavior showed a change. Whereas he had formerly taken considerable interest in his home and enjoyed playing with his children, he became surly toward his family.

As time wore on Harold's behavior went from rationalization to *withdrawal* through daydreaming. Instead of working on his lessons for night school he began spending more and more time hanging around the local beer parlor, drinking mildly, and making various plans to get a job in which he would make a great deal more money. No effort was ever made to carry through these plans.

Piling Up Frustration. Let us use one final example to show how frustration after frustration can accumulate to such an extent that a person will aggress in violent ways that may even lead to the loss of his job.

The XYZ Electrical Manufacturing Company decided to have a time-and-motion study made. Joe M. worked on the assembly line in one of the company plants. He was a hard worker and took pride in his speed on the job. Since he had skill and was fast he received one of the largest pay checks in the department. One morning Joe got up late and, while rushing around to leave for work, had a severe argument with his wife. When he arrived at work, he found a man standing a few feet away from his table. No words were exchanged between them, but as Joe worked he saw that this man was checking his movements with a stop watch. Joe found that he was slowing down, and as he attempted to work fast he began to drop some of the tiny parts making up the assembly. As time passed, Joe became more and more angry. Finally he lost control of himself and shoved the motion-study man to the floor.

One may at first interpret the aggression shown by Joe as resentment of this particular time-and-motion-study man. In the hearing that followed, however, it became clear that Joe had been frustrated all morning. It began with his getting up late and having words with his wife; the frustration was added to by Joe's having had a difficult time finding a parking space; and it was climaxed by the checking of the time-and-motion-study man. Any one instance in itself would probably not have induced the aggression, but the accumulation of pent-up tensions finally reached the explosion point.

TOWARD SATISFYING NEEDS

Later in the book we shall describe job attitudes and satisfactions in considerable detail. However, it is important to introduce the subject here in order to emphasize the point that industry does have some control over need satisfactions.

Attitudes and Needs. Installing a bonus system in a plant may not increase production at all. The failure may not lie in the inadequacy of the bonus system as such, but in the fact that no account is taken of the workers' attitude toward the system and their understanding of it. If the bonus system appears desirable to the workers and is meaningful to them, they are likely to increase production as a result. To know whether we can expect the horse to drink, we must know whether or not he is thirsty. To know whether or not a bonus system will increase production requires that we have information about the workers' reaction to such a system. The worker and the manager alike want to be included, to participate in what affects them. A number of experiments support this position. Let us briefly describe one from the meat industry [12].

During the meat conservation program in World War II, the government decided to try to convince housewives that they should use cheaper cuts of meat and thus stretch the supply. What was the best way to get them to change their old habits of buying choice cuts? Two kinds of test groups of housewives were organized: lecture groups and discussion groups.

The first test groups were exposed to lectures by competent speakers, who used excellent visual-aid charts and slides showing the various cuts of meat. The lecturers presented statistics to show that the family could get good nourishment from cheap cuts and save money at the same time. However, follow-up checks showed that, although the housewives listened attentively, they were not motivated to buy the cheaper cuts of meat.

For the second test groups, a different approach was used. There were no formal lectures. The group of housewives listened briefly to a leader who presented the facts and then let the women argue about prices, budgets, and health. Each member of the group had ample opportunity to express her opinion. The problem now belonged to the participants, not to some bureau in Washington. When the buying habits of this second group were checked and compared with those of the first group, it was found that the discussion group responded much more favorably.

We know that men want recognition; they want to feel that they belong. In one large industry with which the author is acquainted, the safety director told him that when the familiar "tell and repeat," "tell and repeat," was reinforced by giving more recognition to the workers—by having them submit suggestions on safety and serve on small safety committees—accidents declined more. He concluded by saying that although the safety problem was still of concern, he felt that the reduction in accidents was due partially to the fact that the safety program now belonged to the men. A need was being satisfied, at least in part.

Getting at Feelings. People working in industrial relations have found that one of the key problems in labor-management communication involves the understanding of feelings. No one knows better than the contract negotiator that employees want more than what they find in the pay envelope. Often negotiators have seen workers become angry and go on strike, and then look around for something to demand. Higher wages, fringe benefits, and shorter hours are ready demands, neat and easy to formulate. But in many cases they are only secondary demands substituted for wants or needs which the workers have difficulty describing. Both employers and employees frequently are not conscious of their real motives. Some of these needs may even be as simple as that stated by a union official speaking of a strike in a Midwest factory [18]. Asked what the real issue was, he replied: "The real issue wasn't the 15 cents an hour we asked for, or the 5 cents we got. The real cause of the strike was that we had to convince that guy he couldn't be a dictator any longer." One of the big issues in a recent nationwide strike of a large corporation was found to be essentially psychological. The company had made a substantial offer to the union for a long-term contract, but it was refused by both the leaders and the majority of the membership of the union. The strike went on for weeks, for months, and was finally settled for what was basically the original offer, plus a few face-saving agreements. What had happened was that the company itself had worked out all the details of what it would give the union. Little or nothing was left for the union negotiators to do. They had not participated in framing the offer. As the strike wore on, management was forced into letting the union officials have their way and argue *their* points. A psychological need had now been met; and with full public relations fanfare it was announced that a new contract had been signed, that *pay* demands had been met!

One of the best places to observe the nature of human needs is in any labor-management bargaining situation where there are quite diverse interests involved and where both management and labor bring into the situation both similar and different needs. During the conflict that results, we see that man is interested in seeking psychological satisfactions as well as economic ones.

Feelings of Accomplishment. To assume that all the problems of men working in industry can be solved entirely through wage systems is oversimplifying the nature of human needs. Just as we have evidence that high morale and high production do not necessarily go hand in hand, so we must say that wage incentives per se do not always result in enthusiasm for efficient work. Let us illustrate this point by describing an industrial study summarized in Figure 5.2. Here we see that when time rates, bonus rates, and piece rates were compared, some tasks (wrapping, for instance) increased in output as much as 46 per cent when bonus rate replaced time rate; there was a further increase of 30 per cent in production when a piece rate replaced the bonus system. Note, however, that one task (unwrapping) showed no appreciable difference in production, regardless of the pay system. The authors of this controlled study [19] on work output

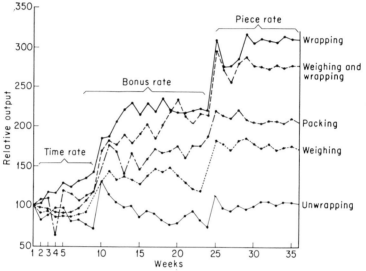

Fig. 5.2. Wage incentives in work per se do not always result in enthusiasm for work. We see in this illustration that, when time, bonus, and piece rates were compared, some tasks increased appreciably in output (wrapping), but others did not (unwrapping). (From Wyatt, S., Frost, L., & Stock, F. G. L. *Incentives in repetitive work*. London: Industrial Health Research Board, No. 69, 1934; courtesy Controller of Her Majesty's Stationery Office.)

also recorded the feelings of the workers toward their jobs. They pointed out that the most marked improvement in production came in tasks, such as wrapping, which involved behavior that aroused favorable feelings in the workers. There was no improvement when the task was disliked, where no feelings of accomplishment were evidenced, such as in unwrapping.

There is no doubt, according to experimental studies and practical observations, that there is some relationship between wage systems and the incentive to work. But wage systems alone are not sufficient to stimulate the will to work. If the work required seems aimless, futile, and unchallenging to a man, the economic incentive may have little or no effect upon him.

Need Satisfactions on the Job. Let us look for the moment at how a supervisor may apply effective human relations skills in a practical way. Let us assume that a plant worker comes to his foreman with a problem.

He is obviously upset. If the foreman is well trained in the principles of human relations he will try to get the man to see his own problem [14].

First, the supervisor will act as a sounding board for the man's frustrations. This means that he must get the man to talk about what is bothering him, to reveal his real feelings. It is wise for him to avoid making any suggestions to the man in this stage, because it is known that the frustrated person regards any suggestions as an attack on him and this leads him to some form of defensive behavior. The result is merely further frustration on his part. The effective supervisor will act only as a listener in this first stage of working with the man. He will encourage him to get his frustrations off his chest.

Second, the good supervisor will try to help the employee locate the cause of the trouble. He will try to discover whether the problem is restricted to the man or whether it is more general. If it is the man's alone, he will encourage him to talk about what he thinks is the cause of the difficulty; the supervisor will try to get *him* to locate the problem, to state it.

Third, the supervisor will try to get the worker himself involved in finding a solution to his problem. The employee is more likely to modify his behavior or his attitude if *he* decides to do something about the problem rather than if he is told what to do. He will be asked to tell what he thinks the facts are, what he thinks should be done. The effective supervisor will encourage the worker to give several possible solutions and then to choose the best one to try first. This makes the employee consider the consequences of his suggestions. Thus by listening and by asking questions the supervisor helps the man to be less emotional and more ready to work the problem out along rational lines.

We may now ask what needs in the man have been satisfied in this situation. First of all, he has received recognition; the supervisor has listened to his problem. Second, frustrations have been relieved. Tension has been reduced, and the worker feels more secure in the situation. Finally, the worker's ego has been boosted; he has gained the feeling of belonging. His thinking was asked for, and the supervisor considered it seriously.

SUCCESS AND FAILURE

In a man's attempts to achieve his goals, repeated frustration usually results in the lowering of aspirations. Repeated success in overcoming barriers tends to raise the level of aspiration. When levels of aspiration and levels of ability are not too far apart, occasional failure may become an asset to the individual in helping him learn to face ordinary frustrating situations. Having the confidence to take managerial types of risks, even when they may bring on reprimands or rejections, has been shown to aid one's striving. Men who have such confidence may be described as psychologically tough or resilient. They are, by and large, men who see themselves as active agents in their own progress, who are not willing to leave their future to the discretion of their superiors, and who hope to be rewarded for performance, loyalty, or patience [6].

Individual differences prevent us from establishing universal criteria for success. Socially accepted criteria may not meet the standards of success which an individual holds for himself; individual standards may not come up to those expected by society.

A person's own evaluation of his success may differ from the world's. The businessman may hold a position of responsibility, may possess authority and prestige, and may make money; yet in his own estimate he may still be a failure. Some people, as they come near the end of a career, may speak of themselves as did Abbe Sieyes. When asked, after the French Revolution, what he had done to distinguish himself during its most crucial period, he replied, "I survived."

In his writings on stress, Selye highlights the importance of considering the wear and tear of life when an individual sets up his short-range, long-range, and ultimate goals [16]. Selye emphasizes the fact that we must keep our smallest needs and greatest aspirations in harmony with our hereditary make-up. He points out that when an individual chooses his goals he should not attempt primarily to avoid stress, which is a natural part of life, but rather that each of us should watch our individual stress level. Excessive stress over a period of time may cause such a depletion of energy that success in terms of status, productivity, and money loses its meaning. But it would be erroneous to conclude that stress is limited to high level managers; evidence is to the contrary. For example, studies at Du Pont comparing the occurrence of stress diseases in the executive group with the occurrence of the same disease entities in the general company population show almost exactly the same rate of incidence [8].

One of the ways in which industry can help human beings to satisfy their needs, at least to a small degree, is to place the right person in the right job. The problems we face here will be presented in the following chapter.

SUGGESTIONS FOR FURTHER READING

Homans, G. C. *The human group*. New York: Harcourt, Brace, 1950. A readable description of the many human problems related to industrial production.

Lindzey, G. (Ed.) *Assessment of human motives*. New York: Grove, 1960. Cross section of contemporary thought and research in human motivation for the sophisticated reader.

Stacey, C. L., & DeMartino, M. F. *Understanding human motivation.* Cleveland: Howard, Allen, Inc., 1958. Readings covering such areas as levels of aspiration, frustration, and aggression and unconscious motivation, not directly related to industry.

Viteles, M. S. *Motivation and morale in industry.* New York: Norton, 1953. Human needs described within the complex environments of industry.

Whyte, W. F. *Money and motivation.* New York: Harper, 1955. Based upon sociological studies this book discusses the importance of incentives other than money in industry.

Zalenzik, A., Christensen, C. R., & Roethlisberger, F. J. *The motivation, productivity, and satisfaction of workers: a prediction study.* Boston: Harvard Univer. Bureau of Business Research, 1958. Illustrates some modern approaches in research on human needs in industry.

6

PERSONNEL

SELECTION

Robert E. Krug

The intentional selection of a person or a group in order to achieve a desired outcome has presumably occurred throughout most of man's history. Early man must have recognized differences in arm strength and running speed and used these facts in organizing hunting parties. Assuming that differential assignments based on these skills were in fact made, we can see that the selection would work to the satisfaction of both the community and the individual. We know that in some early tribes, the most successful hunter received special privileges in the hunt; thus the group's total kill was maximized, and the leader himself was rewarded by receiving choice portions of the meat. Through all recorded history, effort has been made by the chief, the knight, the prince, the skilled craftsman, or the leader of embryonic industry to choose from among the men available those whose visible or inferred characteristics were believed to be indicative of success in the venture planned.

THE SELECTION PROBLEM

History tells us that such selection occurred; and we are often told what characteristics in the applicant's behavior made him a desirable applicant; but we are given no unbiased account of how successful these early personnel specialists were. As a matter of fact, acceptable evidence on personnel selection is limited almost entirely to the twentieth century, and its development is almost the exclusive property of the psychologist, as we described in Chapter 2. It has been asserted that the development of psychological tests and the consequent quantitative investigation of relationships between human abilities and various "criterion behaviors" represents the outstanding achievement of the social sciences to date. Although this development is far from complete and our current practices contain considerable error, there seems little doubt that we are accomplishing the task more successfully than at any time in our past. There can also be no doubt, despite occasional published opinion to the contrary, that psychological tests are the most useful tools available in developing an adequate solution to the selection problem.

In general form, the selection problem may be expressed as follows: from a group of job applicants (n), we wish to identify a subgroup (k) which will be composed entirely of individuals who will be successful on a specified job. This rather formal statement implies the essential tasks which concern the psychologist working in personnel selection. First of all, we note that the statement implies the availability of an unambiguous measure of success. Second, we recognize that the number n is greater than the number k and that n must in fact contain at least k people who meet some critical level of performance which we call success. Unless this is so, effective selection cannot occur. A third factor in the formal statement is often taken as *the selection problem,* namely, the identification of those individuals who are to be offered jobs and the prediction of how well they will do on the jobs. Let us begin by discussing what indexes we will use as measures of success.

THE PROBLEM OF CRITERIA

A criterion is a standard. It is an index against which other indexes may be compared and evaluated. In our context, a criterion is a measure of job success. It therefore defines the desired end product of selection. Clearly, a program of personnel selection can be no better than the criteria which define it. It is well to indicate at the outset that the selection of criteria always involves an arbitrary judgment at some point. In one sense, the definition of success is always a policy decision made by the leaders of an organization. This decision may be stated formally as a series of objectives, informally as a general goal, or only as a vague generality about "staying in business."

Educational institutions are likely to state in formal terms the goals to be attained via the programs offered. Presumably, the successful student is thereby defined as one who attains the referent of each stated objective. Among such statements will be some like "it is the goal of this institution to develop the future leaders of an educated, democratic community," or "we wish to prepare students to continue to develop intellectually after their college years." Several comments may be made about such statements.

First of all, if the institution takes itself at all seriously, these statements demand attention as the ultimate objectives of any selection program. Second, most selection programs ignore such statements. Third, it is evident that the statements do not lead directly to indexes of their attainment. In contrast with this latter point, it would appear that an industry's objective, stated as "to sell soap," would lead directly to an index of success for a salesman. But we shall see that neither in educational institutions nor in industry is the development of a useful measure of success free of difficulty. A primary task of the personnel psychologist is to translate such statements of goals into adequate criterion measures.

An Example of Establishing a Criterion Measure. Let us consider for a moment the objective of selling soap, as a first formulation of a criterion of success as a salesman. Presumably, the gross value of sales per unit time is easy to obtain and directly relevant to the objective. This measure is quantitative, and it offers to rank all salesmen from best to worst. By deciding that a particular level is necessary to continued operation, we might designate a critical point as separating the successful from the unsuccessful. What kinds of error are associated with this so easily obtained measure? First, we might note that the unit of time selected is critical. Are we concerned with the amount sold per hour, per day, per week, month, or year, or over some still longer period? Or does any one of the time periods chosen give us information about all? This latter question is amenable to empirical inquiry. We may investigate the relationship which exists between measures gathered on a daily, weekly, monthly, or yearly basis. By considering such additional factors as the cost of hiring and training a new salesman, we may establish a minimal period of time to be taken as the unit in our criterion measurement.

Although the traditional methods of correlational analysis are available as aids to this subproblem, it is also true that arbitrary decisions may weigh considerably. For example, an organization may feel that for purposes of good customer relations, it is desirable to have a low turnover among salesmen. As a consequence, the organization may prefer a longer period of time for the definition of success than that demonstrated necessary for adequate reliability of the measure. As a result of such studies, we may select various units of time as criteria along a time dimension. Thus, a practically useful period, such as six months, may be employed as an approximation to a more distant criterion.

A second source of difficulty is the differences in experience which exist within the group of salesmen. If the organization is large enough, a sufficient number of salesmen with equal experience may be available for preliminary study, but this will certainly not always be the case. If adequate sales performance records are maintained, it may be possible to establish norms for various amounts of experience, but this will not always be possible either. Let us assume that we can by some method equate or allow for differences in experience, and that we have settled on a time period upon which to base the once-corrected (for experience) gross sales measure. We must consider what sources of error remain.

Sources of Error in Criteria. One source of error made up of several components may be termed "situational." This term refers to characteristics of the sales environment which will affect salesmen differentially. One neighborhood may contain more dirt than another. The amount of soap used per person for laundering purposes should be greater in a heavily industrialized city than in a mountain resort community. We might correct for this factor by obtaining data on the total amount of soap sold by retailers in each sales district and interpreting our gross sales figure as a percentage of the available market. This twice-corrected figure assumes that all competing companies apportion their sales effort, such as advertising dollars, similarly in regard to geographical area, so that the relative competition is equal for all salesmen. This is almost certainly not true; so in combating error of one form we introduce error of another variety. Since the concentration of population varies widely over sales districts, one salesman may contact more consumers per retailer visited. We would have to correct our measure for both absolute differences in population and for population density. We must also recognize that it is possible for a salesman to overstock a retail outlet. This can result in business failure and return of goods, loss of good will and resulting loss of future sales. We should correct our often-corrected gross sales measure by subtracting poor sales, for example, those that are later cancelled or do not lead to additional orders. We should also consider our company's position in a specific area when a given salesman entered it. A high sales figure may reflect the good work accomplished by the salesman's predecessor. Conversely, low figures may obscure the slow rebuilding of good will in an area where the organization's share of the market was reduced by the performance of a previous salesman. The point of all this is simply that considerable refinement may be necessary before the easily obtained gross sales figure is transformed into a useful measure of sales performance. The relationship between the original and final measure may be extremely low or even negative. If our measure is really to stand for "success on the job," all pertinent questions must be asked about the situation.

Success Is Multidimensional. In reality, the above discussion is greatly simplified, because we are talking about success as though it could be represented by a single measure. In the real world, no business just wants to sell soap. Success is always multidimensional. Furthermore, there is no reason to suppose that the components of success always go together and that we can safely ignore some aspects. The question of what the relationship is between various aspects of success is empirical.

It is evident that the construction of a good criterion measure is not a simple task. It should be equally evident that an enterprise based on an easily obtained, incomplete, error-contaminated, and possibly irrelevant criterion is doomed to failure. For example, if cumulative grade average (the usual criterion in educational selection research) is not related to all the objectives stated in the prospectus of the college, then a selection program based on this unitary measure cannot succeed. The better our job of selection according to the unitary criterion, the poorer may be our job of selection according to the total criterion field. Similarly, many programs of industrial selection employ predictors which are validated against the score earned in an entry training program. Again, unless this score is demonstrated to predict the more ultimate criteria of job performance, the reported validity coefficient is of little meaning. A primary deterrent to systematic progress in personnel selection is that the criteria employed are so unrepresentative of the total criterion field.

Eight Steps in Criterion Development. It may be well to spell out, at this point, the task of the psychologist in criterion development. *First, he must consider all stated goals of the organization.* In many instances, where no clear-cut statement of objectives exists, he may assist in the collection and formulation of such statements. *Second, he must select or construct a measure, however crude the first attempt, for each statement, or substatement.* At this point also, the task is a cooperative one between the psychologist and the policy maker. The first attempt at measurement may serve to clarify the original statement, the final resultant statement then demanding a new attempt at a measure. *Third, the measure must be refined by removing sources which introduce error.* As we have observed, this is primarily a rational process. *Fourth, the interrelationships between the various measures must be determined.* This idea is often difficult to sell to unsophisticated management people. *Fifth, we must organize the criterion field in terms of the now known relationships.* Practical as well as scientific goals call for parsimony. The final composite criterion should contain the minimum number of dimensions necessary for an adequate description of success. We can, as a consequence, eliminate any duplication of effort which characterizes our many measures. *Sixth, we must establish appropriate weighting systems to enable us to combine single measures.* Not all dimensions may be viewed as equally important attributes, nor will all measures be equally potent as representatives of the dimensions. The weighting, then, will employ both rational and statistical procedures. *Seventh, we must investigate time as a dimension underlying our criteria.* On this basis we select measures available early as representative of measures which can be obtained only at a much later date. *Eighth, we may revise measures according to considerations of economy, reliability, and face validity.* It is important to note that these final matters engage our attention at the end, rather than at the beginning of our program of criterion development.

SOME AVAILABLE CRITERION MEASURES

In practice, the criteria employed tend to be those most available when the selection program is installed. Subsequent development at times involves little more than improving the record-keeping process, so that the measures will be complete and will be collected under reasonably standardized circumstances. This development will at least increase the reliability of the measures, but will, of course, make no attack on the more crucial issues of relevance in terms of over-all goals. This should not be taken as an indictment of all industrial personnel research. It is simply an acknowledgment of the fact that much of our endeavor has stopped far short of what is so obviously required in the way of criteria. The pressures which lead to such behavior are easy to perceive.

A Practical Problem. Practical industrial problems are always accompanied by demands of immediacy; solutions are needed now, not in five years. In addition, the sponsors of the research are generally quite naïve about the problem. The uninitiated person tends to view the difference between successful and unsuccessful as roughly analogous to the difference between night and day; consequently he is surprised that the psychologist views the matter as a problem at all. The personnel man sees the need to educate his sponsor; but he will usually decide, probably correctly, that it is best to get started with what is at hand, and perform the educative function after some data are available.

Using the Company Records. A variety of measures are available in company records, all of which seem related to the objectives of most organizations, many of which are easily amenable to quantification, and most of which can be gathered routinely. Wherry [18] lists the following as suggestive of the measures which one might collect from the various records of most industrial organizations:

1. Items bearing on output per unit time
   a. Units produced
   b. Number of sales
   c. Items coded
   d. Earnings on a commission basis
   e. Words typed
2. Items bearing on quality of production
   a. Number of rejects
   b. Cost of spoiled work
   c. Coding or filing errors
   d. Returned goods (sales)

    e. Disgruntled customers (complaints filed)
3. Items bearing on lost time
    a. Days present
    b. Number of times tardy
    c. Days sick
    d. Visits to first-aid station
    e. Length or frequency of unauthorized rest pause
4. Items bearing on turnover
    a. Length of service
    b. Quits
    c. Discharges
    d. Transfers due to unsatisfactory performance
    e. Transfers at request of employee
5. Items bearing on training time and promotability
    a. Training time to reach standard production
    b. Cost of material spoiled during training
    c. Rate of advancement
    d. Training courses successfully completed since enrollment (number of jobs in plant for which employee is qualified)
    e. Merit ratings (times recommended for promotion)
6. Items bearing on employee satisfaction
    a. Number of grievances registered
    b. Morale survey standing
    c. Visits to plant psychiatrist
    d. Participation in plant athletic programs
    e. Contributions to "suggestion system"

It is evident that the above list contains measures of potential utility for a variety of jobs. It would provide a first approximation for most clerical, sales, and production jobs, sampling six potentially relevant facets of a complete criterion. In any program of criterion development, the simple records of performance which are available provide a reasonable starting point.

The Use of Ratings. Not all jobs leave a highly visible record of performance. We might hesitate to take a department's production records as indicating the same thing for a foreman that an individual production record indicates for a worker. In fact, for supervisory jobs, the majority of items on our list are pertinent only if we take a departmental aggregate as the supervisor's criterion score. Although ratings will often provide a measure possessing some relevance, it is generally true that as we move upward in an organizational hierarchy we become increasingly dependent for our criteria upon the evaluative judgments of men occupying the next higher position. In military organizations, for example, a score earned on a test may qualify an enlisted man for a higher rank, whereas for commissioned officers, a rating given by a superior officer carries considerable weight. Ratings of some kind have long been a frequently employed criterion device, despite the extreme subjectivity and typical lack of validity associated with them. Two recent developments in rating scale construction show promise of controlling the error, or bias, in earlier scales, and both will unquestionably see increasing use as criteria.

The Critical Incident Technique. Flanagan's Critical Incident Technique [6] is directed toward the elimination of an evaluative frame of reference and its replacement with a descriptive one. The construction phase consists of collecting descriptions of behaviors associated with conspicuous success or failure on a given job. The scale, in final form, consists of a list of those observable behaviors which for any one person might or might not have occurred within any given time period. The rater is *not* asked to decide whether the ratee *would* behave as a certain phrase suggests, but instead he simply checks those behaviors which *actually occurred* during the period being reviewed. Although intentional falsification by the rater is still possible, we doubt that this motive is responsible for much of the bias observed in ratings. Most of such error is, at least in part, due to the rater's inability to make accurate judgments in the absence of precise definitions of the things to be judged. A number of industries have reported that a check list containing critical incidents clearly makes the rater's task easier. In some ways it takes pressure off a supervisor when the worker puts him on the spot.

Forced-choice Technique. A different approach to the control of bias in ratings is the forced-choice technique developed by psychologists of the Adjutant General's Office, United States Army, during World War II and now used in some industries [13, 15]. The rationale of this method is to present the rater with alternative descriptions which are equally favorable, but which have differential significance in regard to job success. Again, the evaluative frame of reference is removed, and the rater is forced to *describe*. Construction involves the determination of favorableness (general preference, desirability, or goodness) for each item, as well as the relationship of the item to success on the job. The rater's task is to select the member of each pair which is most descriptive of the ratee.

COMBINING CRITERION MEASURES

Since we should always have several criteria of potential usefulness available, it is clear that we need some technique for dealing with this multiple measure. We might orient our effort toward predicting each measure singly, and then requiring that some minimal level of each be met or exceeded, but this would not avoid the problem. We would still be faced with the problem of evaluating persons who exceeded the minima by varying amounts. The most simple method would consist in adding the various criterion scores to form a composite, after first transforming each measure to some standard form.

The "Dollar Criterion." A plan for rational weighting of criteria is Brogden and Taylor's suggestion of the dollar criterion [1]. This approach is based on cost accounting principles, and assumes that if a suggested measure is related to the ultimate criterion of an organization, it should be translatable into monetary terms. For example, we are willing to accept absenteeism as a criterion because it is clearly associated with increased cost to the organization; output decreases while certain overhead costs remain unchanged. Brogden and Taylor suggest that this cost is computable; instead of expressing absentee rate in terms of so many days per hundred, we may express it as so many dollars, or fraction thereof, of cost to the company. Output per unit time, amount of material wasted, and the like are obviously computable on the same scale.

Certain criteria, such as friendliness, number of complaints, or consideration toward subordinates, may be more difficult to deal with in dollar and cents terms, but there is no reason to suppose that the problem of quantifying these attributes is made any more difficult by the restriction that they are to be expressed in monetary units. The method has the useful advantage of weighting measures in a fashion which is acceptable and understandable to management, the worker, and the personnel technician. The overlap between measures could still be investigated by any available method and removed if desired. Additional measures could be added by the same process of computing costs which was applied to the initially chosen ones, and the prior weights would not be changed.

THE PREDICTION OF SUCCESS

Let us assume that our criterion problem is solved and that we have an adequate quantitative definition of success. Logically, the next step is to obtain an estimate of ultimate performance for each applicant. Obtaining such an estimate will always involve three aspects. First, we must isolate a series of measures of attributes related to job success that are called "predictor variables." Next we must establish weights to assign each predictor which reflect the relative contribution of the attributes. As a final step we must specify the rules for combining the predictor measures. In other words, we want to determine an equation in which criterion performance is expressed as some function of weighted predictor scores.

Establishing an equation which is adequate for its purpose involves techniques which are beyond the scope of this text. Our discussion here is intended merely to acquaint the reader with the gross structure of the prediction process.

The Definition of a Predictor Field. As indicated above, our first step is to isolate the variables to be used as predictors. How is the initial pool of potential predictors defined? Throughout most of the history of personnel selection this definition has been made rather casually. Generally, the basis for initial selection of predictors is "general knowledge of the job," which represents an unspecified blend of observations, personal experience on the job, interviews with workers and supervisors, knowledge of what has worked in the past, and so forth. If considerable information is available from previous studies of the criterion, one can attempt to define the predictor field by matching each criterion component with a predictor.

The definition which emerges, from whatever operation, should be as inclusive as possible. Assuming that testing time is not a major problem for the early stages of research, errors of commission (including a measure which turns out to be of no value) are not harmful, but omitting a measure that would, if included, show validity, is serious. As a consequence, our definition of the field is likely to contain many rather than few characteristics to be measured. Some of the characteristics will suggest existing instruments as measures. A statement about "manipulation of verbal symbols," for example, suggests a test of verbal intelligence, and many such tests are available. Presumably, a test would be chosen on the basis of applicability to the group to be tested, time required, economy, and other such factors, assuming that several tests were adequate as measures of the required characteristics. However, one cannot assume that all tests labeled "verbal intelligence" are measures of the same thing. The value of a test as a measure of a construct like intelligence is inferred from the pool of public information available for the test. This information is primarily relational.

A test is known in terms of the relationships which have been demonstrated to exist between the test and other tests, and between the test and nontest variables. If one were interested in test X, which purported to measure verbal intelligence, he would be interested in three things: (1) the relationship between test X and other tests purporting to measure the same function, a positive relationship supporting the test's interpretation as representing the construct, (2) the relationship between test X and other tests intended to measure other factors, high relationships here permitting other explanations of test X's meaning, and (3) the relationships between test X and criterionlike measures assumed to reflect (or not to reflect) the operation of the construct.

Evaluation of Tests. The personnel psychologist does not start from scratch in his evaluation of tests. Such evaluation has been going on for a long time, and most of the results are public. Certain tests acquire status as "standards" by virtue of their demonstrated excellence; others are gradually used less and less, or they are used in a way different from that intended by the author. There are several standard sources in which one may seek information about the history of a test's use. One such source is the manual published for the test. In evaluating a test by its manual, one should be influenced not by the claims made, but by the data cited in support of such claims. The increasing adequacy of test manuals is a sign of progress in the field of testing.

Additional sources are: (1) the "Validity Information Exchange," published in *Personnel Psychology,* a quarterly journal devoted to personnel research, (2) the "Validity Studies" section of *Educational and Psychological Measurement,* another quarterly, (3) Buros's *Mental Measurements Yearbook,* published at somewhat irregular intervals by Rutgers University Press [2], which contains reviews of standardized tests as well as bibliographic information, and (4) standard texts on psychological testing [3, 7, 8, 15]. Further sources of information about tests are presented in the suggested readings at the end of this chapter.

Other Selection Measures. In addition to those aspects of the predictor field which suggest the use of existing tests, other aspects will suggest representation by nontest variables, and still others will appear to necessitate new construction. If the definition includes reference to specific experiences which are required background for the applicant, the measure suggested is the application blank, work-history record, or something similar. It should be noted that such information is treated in precisely the same fashion as a test score. For example, something from the work-history record itself becomes "a score" on a potential predictor which is yet to be validated. If some aspect of the definition concerns a personality variable for which no adequate test measure exists, and the personnel man doubts that he can construct an adequate one, he may decide to assess the characteristic in an interview. In this instance, the interview is to be considered as a measuring device which provides a score on certain characteristics; these scores will enter the same competition for eventual use as the tests, application blank, work record, educational history, and the like.

A number of critics have headlined the obvious, namely, that there are many aspects of human behavior which are not currently measurable by psychological tests. The intended corollary, that these characteristics can be assessed by other means, does not follow. Reasonableness demands that a required characteristic be represented by the best measure available, consistent with considerations of economy and practicality. All measurements, resulting from whatever operation, are evaluated according to the same rule; namely, that which predicts success is kept, the rest is dross.

Job Application Blank. It should be apparent from the above discussion that an instrument is included in the initial battery of predictors because its inclusion appears demanded by the tentative definition of the predictor field. The applicant does not complete an application blank simply because this is the traditional way to start the employment process, but rather because there are certain pieces of predictor information which can be collected most conveniently from such a blank. Clearly then, the construction of an application blank is guided by the definition. Since an organization hires people for many jobs, and since *one* application blank is preferable to many, the blank may collect information from an applicant which is not presumed relevant to the job for which he is being considered. Likewise, an interview schedule may be more or less standardized to fit a variety of jobs. The forms are thus constructed in accordance with a family of definitions rather than a single one.

Interviewing. There can be little question that many hiring procedures are maintained primarily because of the lag of culture. A face-to-face interview has been a part of the process for so long that it is often continued even though there is no clearly stated objective indicating what it is to accomplish. This is not a criticism of the interview; it simply calls attention to the fact that some of our procedures are at times permitted to remain outside the rules of the game. A face-to-face interview may well be justified in terms of the human relations value involved; as such it is a legitimate part of the induction program even though it may be extraneous to the selection process. In order to qualify the interview as a part of the selection process, we must specify the characteristics which are to be measured by it and then show that these measurements are related to subsequent criterion performance.

THE ANALYSIS OF PREDICTOR-CRITERION RELATIONSHIPS

We have said nothing about how to administer tests or how to ensure that criterion measures are not contaminated in the collection process, both of which are important issues. The reader may wish to consult the suggested readings for further study of this subject. Here we wish to discuss very simply the matter of relating predictors to criteria.

The Correlation Coefficient and Regression. Given scores on all predictors and all criteria for all members of our group, we are ready to construct a first approximation to a selection equation. The standard procedure for constructing this equation is via multiple regression. Although the formulas involved appear complex, the essential idea in multiple regression is no more difficult than that involved in the simple correlation coefficient. Though the latter concept may be familiar from previous courses, we will review the matter briefly.

You will recall that the correlation coefficient is an index of the relationship between two variables. It is also true that, given standard scores, the coefficient defines the slope of the straight line which best represents this relationship. For the two variable problems then, the *best estimate* of the criterion performance is equal to the correlation coefficient multiplied by the predictor score ($Z_{y'} = rz_x$). This use of the correlation coefficient is represented in the two examples of Figure 6.1. For any standard value of the predictor, the best estimate of criterion performance is easily determined in these examples.

A graph showing the relationship between predicted and achieved scores in a multiple regression problem (one where many variables are used to

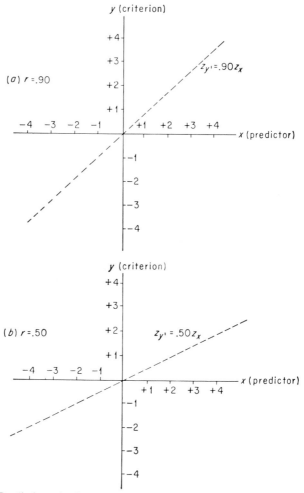

Fig. 6.1. Prediction via these regression-equation graphs shows the regression line (dashes) that relates a predictor and a criterion measure for two levels of correlation. In each case, the best estimate of criterion performance may be obtained by constructing the perpendiculars from the point on the x axis indicating the individual's predictor score. For example, a person with a predictor score of $+2$ is estimated to have a criterion score of $+1.8$ if $r = .90$, or $+1.0$ if $r = .50$.

predict the criterion) would look exactly like those in Figure 6.1. The difference would be simply that the predictor would be a composite of several independent variables. The method of obtaining an optimal composite cannot be considered here; it is sufficient for the moment to acknowledge the existence of such methods.

THE CURRENT STATUS OF THE SELECTION PROCESS

How successful is the personnel psychologist in his attempts to improve the selection process? What benefits may the employer reasonably expect

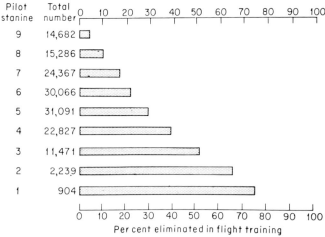

Fig. 6.2. This selection-of-airplane-pilots graph shows the relationship between the pilots' stanine (Aptitude Index) and the successful completion of flight training. (From Staff, AAF Training Command. Psychological activities in the training command. *Psychol. Bull.*, 1945, 42, 46.)

should he adopt the procedures we have described? These are eminently reasonable questions which demand a considered reply. Before attempting an answer, let us look at some examples.

Selection of Airplane Pilots. The first example is not offered as typical. It is a frequently cited result of the Aviation Psychology Program of the United States Army Air Force during World War II. Figure 6.2 shows the result of using a battery of tests to select pilots. The figure illustrates the percentage eliminated from Primary Flight Training for each of nine aptitude areas (pilot stanine). These results, based on over 153,000 cases, were obtained in a very large-scale program employing the talents of many of the nation's leading psychologists, in a situation where a failure in training was extremely expensive compared to the costs of quite extensive testing. From the figure, it is evident that by selecting only those candidates whose pilot stanine was 6 or above, 70 per cent of the potential failures would have been eliminated, but only 37 per cent of the potential graduates. The picture is actually a very conservative representation of the effectiveness of selection in this case. Observation of the number entering training at each aptitude level makes it clear that many of the lower-level candidates were eliminated prior to training, since for the total sample of candidates taking the test, the distribution of scores was normal; i.e., as many earned stanine 1 as earned stanine 9, as many earned 2 as 8, 3 as 7, etc. With this restriction on the range of those accepted for training, the validity coefficient between the stanine and the pass-fail criterion was approximately .60.

An Academic Example. The second example is taken from an academic selection situation, and it may be considered typical of results obtained from such programs. Since so many readers are familiar with College Boards, we choose this example. The predictor (Aptitude Index) is a composite of three College Board tests weighted to produce a maximal multiple correlation for an earlier sample of students. The criteria chosen to illustrate validity are: (1) the percentage at each level remaining in school after three semesters and earning a grade average of 1.25 (on a 4-point system) or above, and (2) the percentage still in school after three semesters and earning a 2.75 average or above. In other words, the first criterion measure represents performance that is above the minimum required for continuation, while the second represents performance which is significantly above average, as shown in Figure 6.3. In this instance, the validity coefficient is approximately .65. The figures clearly show that selection of only higher-aptitude students would significantly increase the percentage of entrants capable of superior performance. Although this would eliminate many successful students, it would eliminate very few outstanding ones. Restriction of range also enters this example, since the aptitude levels were established on a sample of accepted students; very low aptitude cases do not enter the picture at all.

An Industrial Example. Our final example concerns the selection of life insurance salesmen via the Aptitude Index devised by the Life Insurance Sales Research Bureau, a predecessor of the present Life Insurance Agency Management Association described in Chapter 2. Together, these organizations represent over thirty years of research on the subject. Figure 6.4 relates the Aptitude Index to a sales performance criterion. It is again evident that significant gains can be produced by hiring at the upper-aptitude levels only.

The three examples given above represent a considerable range of performance. The human characteristics required for success as an aircraft pilot differ considerably from those useful to the life insurance salesman, and both depart from the skills essential to success as a student in an engineering curriculum. Similar examples could be chosen for such jobs as truck driver, retail salesman, law school student, skilled machinist, street-car motorman, cablewinder, and so forth. We would search a long time however, before we found validity coefficients (cross-validated ones) appreciably above .60. This is one kind of summary statement. The success represented by a validity coefficient of .60 seems attainable for many jobs.

Interpretation of a Validity Coefficient. How good is a validity coefficient of .60? In one sense, it is not good at all. One way to interpret a

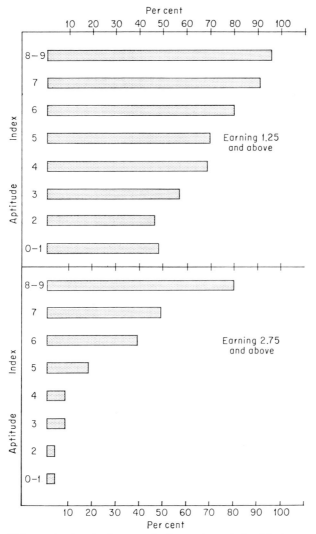

Fig. 6.3. This academic-selection graph shows the relationship between Aptitude Index and two different criteria of success in college. (Courtesy Bureau of Measurement & Guidance, Carnegie Institute of Technology.)

correlation coefficient is in terms of variance common to the two variables. This interpretation is via r^2, rather than r. If we square .60, we get .36; a validity coefficient of .60 tells us that 36 per cent of the criterion variance is predictable from or may be attributed to variation in our predictor variable. This does not appear at all satisfactory; yet the bar graphs in the three examples seemed to represent real success. A reason for this apparent discrepancy is that improvement in selection is dependent in part on factors other than the correlation between predictor and criterion.

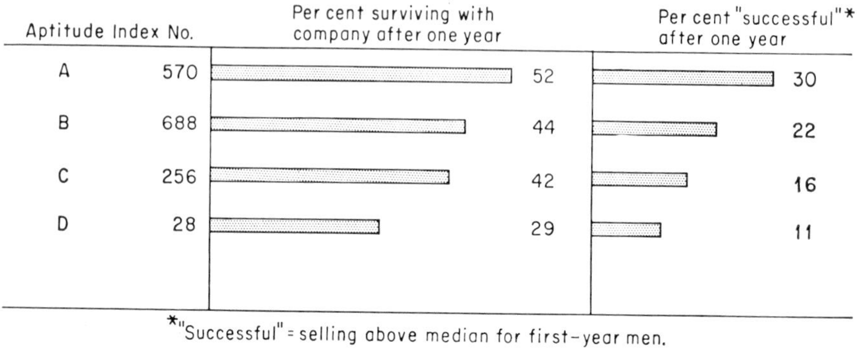

*"Successful" = selling above median for first-year men.

Fig. 6.4. Industrial-selection graph showing the relationship between Aptitude Index (of the Life Insurance Agency Management Association) and two different criteria of success in life insurance sales. (From LIAMA Report A14-48, 1951–52. Reproduced by permission.)

Imagine a situation in which the demand for employees is exactly equal to the number of applicants. If everyone must be hired, no improvement will result from a selection process regardless of the validity of the predictors employed. We noted, in examining the pilot selection results, that selecting only those candidates whose stanines were 6 and above would radically alter the average performance of the selected group. Similar statements apply to the student and life insurance salesmen examples. One factor, then, is the *selection ratio,* the percentage of applicants who must be accepted in order to fill the job quota. Improvement in performance is also a function of the *base rate,* defined as the percentage of people in an unselected population who would be successful on the given job.

Clearly, a job which can be handled adequately by 95 per cent of the total population will not justify the expenditure of funds for researching the selection problem. These three factors, the validity coefficient, the selection ratio, and the base rate, enable us to make a quantitative estimate of expected improvement due to selection. For practical purposes tables have been prepared by Taylor and Russell [14] which give the percentage of successful workers for given combinations of these three factors. Let us present an example to show the usefulness of such tables although they are of a theoretical nature (Table 1). This table is for a situation where 50 per cent of the population is considered satisfactory. If we enter the table with a validity coefficient of .60 and a selection ratio of .50, we see that our accepted group will be composed of 70 per cent successful workers

TABLE 1
TAYLOR-RUSSELL TABLES

The percentage who will be satisfactory among those selected for given values of the selection ratio and the correlation coefficient: Proportion of employees considered satisfactory = .50.

r	Selection ratio										
	.05	.10	.20	.30	.40	.50	.60	.70	.80	.90	.95
.00	50	50	50	50	50	50	50	50	50	50	50
.05	54	54	53	52	52	52	51	51	51	50	50
.10	58	57	56	55	54	53	53	52	51	51	50
.15	63	61	58	57	56	55	54	53	52	51	51
.20	67	64	61	59	58	56	55	54	53	52	51
.25	70	67	64	62	60	58	56	55	54	52	51
.30	74	71	67	64	62	60	58	56	54	52	51
.35	78	74	70	66	64	61	59	57	55	53	51
.40	82	78	73	69	66	63	61	58	56	53	52
.45	85	81	75	71	68	65	62	59	56	53	52
.50	88	84	78	74	70	67	63	60	57	54	52
.55	91	87	81	76	72	69	65	61	58	54	52
.60	94	90	84	79	75	70	66	62	59	54	52
.65	96	92	87	82	77	73	68	64	59	55	52
.70	98	95	90	85	80	75	70	65	60	55	53
.75	99	97	92	87	82	77	72	66	61	55	53
.80	100	99	95	90	85	80	73	67	61	55	53
.85	100	99	97	94	88	82	76	69	62	55	53
.90	100	100	99	97	92	86	78	70	62	56	53
.95	100	100	100	99	96	90	81	71	63	56	53
1.00	100	100	100	100	100	100	83	71	63	56	53

SOURCE: Taylor, H. C., & Russell, J. T. The relationship of validity coefficients to the practical effectiveness of tests in selection: discussion and tables. *J. Appl. Psychol.*, 1939, 23, 565–578.

(and consequently of 30 per cent unsuccessful ones). If we must take 80 per cent of the applicants, we will have only 59 per cent successful workers. The generalization is that improvement in performance of the selected group is most likely to occur in situations where both base rate and selection ratio are small.

Other Ways of Evaluation. There are other ways to evaluate the effectiveness of selection programs. In considering the Air Force example, we noted the expense involved in accepting candidates who were potential failures. Turnover is always associated with cost to the employer, and also to the unsuccessful employee, and the monetary savings made possible by a selection program is relevant to the question. Where a specific cost can be assigned to training, the number of candidates that must be accepted in order to meet a demanded output from the training program leads to a cost figure which is meaningful to the employer. Both of these methods possess a public relations value when selection is proposed to a potential sponsor. The validity coefficient is of interest primarily to the technician who wishes to improve the efficiency of his procedures; the Taylor-Russell tables or a set of bar graphs will be of greater value in illustrating the facts of the case to the industrialist.

The above considerations permit a reasonably precise answer to our original question if the question is asked in a specific job context. Although an equally adequate answer is impossible for the general case, some aspects of an answer have been indicated. For one thing, selection research has met with some success in a wide variety of jobs. To date, validities of .40 can usually be obtained, but validities above .70 are extremely rare.

THE RECRUITMENT OF EMPLOYEES

We noted at the beginning of this chapter that one of the requirements for effective selection is the presence in the applicant group of a sufficient number of potentially successful workers to satisfy the demand. Thus far, we have ignored the question of how this number is obtained.

You are already familiar with most of the devices used by employers. At one job level, the presence of an employment office is sufficient, except in time of manpower shortage. Occasionally, a newspaper announcement of openings is added. At higher levels, newspaper advertising is almost certain, listing with an employment agency likely, and advertising in professional journals or campus recruiting visits possible. During the post-World War II years, we have witnessed a vigorous campaign by industry to obtain the services of technical, scientific, and executive personnel. Recruiting teams are sent to the campus. Still greater effort is made in the search for higher-level executive personnel. Some agencies specialize in providing candidates for such openings, and if we can believe popularized accounts, companies engage in intense competition to secure such men.

The Need for Data. Considering the expense involved, it is surprising that there is no published evidence of the success of these efforts. We are unable to compare the relative effectiveness of newspaper and magazine advertising, personal visits, impersonal ads, agency referrals, and the nominations of current employees, all sources of applicants. A large company could compare the success of obtaining employees by each device and evaluate the cost per criterion gain. This has been done in a number of companies, but the data remain in their private possession. As a consequence, little authoritative advice can be offered. For the majority of jobs, recruitment does not appear to be a problem; the local office of the state employment service, classified ads, and the company's employment office suffice. If problems appear, one can emulate his competitor, or better, gather the necessary data from his own company's experience.

DECISION IN HIRING

Psychological testing in industry has become widespread. Many companies are using tests not only for initial selection of employees but also as aids in determining which employees should be promoted.

In the preceding sections, we have considered the central problem of industrial testing, that is, establishing the relationship between test results and job performance. We have shown that, within limits, testing can be a most useful aid in the personnel selection process. But it is not a panacea, by any means, and one of the worries of the industrial psychologist is that testing can be oversold. This has happened in recent years in the use of personality tests in industry. Since a number of tests of ability have worked out so well, industrialists, and some psychologists, have assumed that personality tests have the same degree of predictability. Experimentation has shown, however, that although we have a number of personality tests that are effective when included in testing batteries, others are quite useless. And some of the effective personality tests have been grossly misused, bringing about considerable criticism, particularly from psychologists themselves.

The Final Decision. Whereas testing research has largely been in the hands of the psychologist, the decision to hire or not to hire has been left to others. This decision involves a judgment. When we can use valid objective data as well as subjective interpretation in the decision-making process, the chances of our success may be increased. Now with electronic computers to aid us, we are able to give more attention to the scientific selection of personnel and thus aid management in making the final decision.

THE FUTURE OF PERSONNEL SELECTION

Several current trends suggest the direction of our future efforts. Predicting the future is always somewhat hazardous, but it is, after all, the stock in trade of personnel selection. If we are willing to predict the future performance of a group of applicants, we should be equally willing to predict the future of the science of personnel selection. We predict:

1. More attention will be given to criterion development. In commenting upon the history of personnel selection, Wherry [20] characterizes much of our effort up to now as belonging to a Dark Ages era. He believes that "this approach will disappear because those who rely upon it will disappear." It is clearly true that our technical capacity to construct adequate and representative criterion measures has outdistanced our actual development of such measures. We have only a few instances of adequate longitudinal studies which are essential to relating immediate and distant criteria. Too often we accept what is readily available and spend our time in polishing operations, such as improving the reliability of the measurement. Our future will consist, in part, of the expenditure of the necessary funds, time, and effort to develop worthwhile measures of success.

2. In predictor work, attention will be directed primarily toward the development of nonintellective measures. The early development, and subsequent wide acceptance, of psychological tests was concerned almost exclusively with general ability. Naturally enough, further development centered on structuring and refining in this area. Pioneering work by the factor analysts suggested that it would be useful to consider intelligence as composed of several independent abilities (such as verbal ability, ability with numbers, with space, etc.). A recent review of the cognitive area suggests that as many as *forty* such dimensions are reasonably well established [9]. Aside from the area of mental abilities, most of the progress evidenced has been in other ability or aptitude areas. Tests of mechanical aptitude, manual dexterity, clerical speed or accuracy, and the like have been a part of the psychometrist's kit for a considerable period of time and are included in most effective industrial selection batteries. Our accomplishment in the areas of interest, personality, and motivation has been less impressive. The Strong Vocational Interest Blank, the history of which was described in Chapter 2, might be offered as an exception to this generalization. The blank has been in extensive and careful use for over thirty years, and a number of relationships are well established. Even here, however, the blank is of demonstrated usefulness as a *selective device* in only a few occupations, the best known of which is life insurance salesman. While personality inventories have occasionally demonstrated apparent validity in job prediction, there is a dearth of cross-validated positive results. A tremendous amount of work is being conducted in this field, and we can confidently expect its continuation. Clearly the ultimate validities probable from tests of ability are not significantly greater than those already obtained. Improvement is possible only by extending our range of predictors. There can be little doubt that extensions of the current work on personality measurement will bring about such improvement.

3. The current emphasis on higher-aptitude personnel will be continued. In industry, most of our early progress in selection was with jobs in the semiskilled to skilled levels. For higher-level jobs, the task was left primarily to the training institutions. The presence of a college degree was sufficient to warrant favorable prognosis. Within the executive framework, selection occurred through promotion, a survival-of-the-fittest approach which appeared adequate. The factor responsible for change was the increased complexity of the jobs. As technology has grown, specialization has become commonplace. An engineering graduate may excel in one job, yet do mediocre or failing work in another. The position of an executive demands a range of knowledge and experience that cannot be gained casually, but needs to be planned; this requires that the potential executive be identified early in his career. Increasing effort may be expected in the area of executive and professional selection.

4. Labor-management agreements will result in increased attention to the general selection problem. It is clear that some form of guarantee of continued employment will be a commonly accepted obligation of the employer. This makes the act of hiring more crucial than ever before for both worker and employer. It is easy enough to see that the employer risks having to keep an inadequate employee; it should also be recognized that the employee who is hired for the wrong job risks failure and all the personal dissatisfactions that accrue as a result. Since it will become increasingly attractive for the employee to stay in one department of one organization, neither risk can be ignored. Effective selection will work to the advantage of both parties in the industrial enterprise.

5. Systematization of knowledge will occur. There are already a few signs that we are outgrowing the individual and piecemeal enterprise that personnel research has been. The work of military psychologists was a large step in this direction. Another has been the work of research agencies, such as those of the Federal government and of the life insurance industry. The industrial psychologist has generally obtained results which were specific to a given job in a certain plant of one industry. There will be increasing effort to broaden the applications of such results.

SUGGESTIONS FOR FURTHER READING

Cronbach, L. J., & Gleser, G. *Psychological tests and personnel decisions.* Urbana: Univer. of Illinois Press, 1957. A mathematical treatment of selection and classification problems utilizing concepts from decision theory. The approach represents a radical departure from the traditional orientation of personnel selection and may well lead to a new psychometrics. The reader must possess some sophistication (or at least be fearless) in regard to mathematics.

Dubois, P. *Multivariate correlational analysis.* New York: Harper, 1957. A concise and systematic presentation of the statistical basis for the procedures described or referred to in this chapter.

Fryer, D. H., & Henry, E. R. (Eds.). *Handbook of applied psychology.* New York: Rinehart, 1950. Volume I, Chapters 4 and 5, which contain twenty articles, deal with problems and fields of personnel psychology. Included are reviews of research in various occupational fields (sales, clerical, protective, etc.) and treatments of special problems (criteria, test selection, application blanks, etc.).

Gulliksen, H. *Theory of mental tests.* New York: Wiley, 1950. A systematic treatment of the traditional psychometric theory. This is a must for anyone interested in psychological testing. The treatment is primarily mathematical.

Kahn, R. L., & Cannell, C. F. *The dynamics of interviewing.* New York: Wiley, 1957. For the reader interested in the details of theory and techniques of interviewing. Contains case materials.

Thorndike, R. L. *Personnel selection.* New York: Wiley, 1949. An authoritative account derived largely from the work of psychologists in the Army Air Forces during World War II in regard to personnel selection. The book will remain a classic representation of what was known and what could be done at that time.

7

TRAINING

IN INDUSTRY

Robert Glaser

When we speak of the utilization of human resources in an industrial organization, or in a nation for that matter, we are almost inevitably led to think of training. We recognize that individuals need to be taught to perform in specific ways in order to accomplish certain aims. The aims must be specified and the behavior of individuals must be shaped and modified so that they can perform the tasks required as members of an organization. "Shaping" and "modifying" are key words. They define the meaning of training and, indeed, of all education. This is what training is, and this is what training agencies and educational systems do: *they begin with individuals who behave in certain ways and modify this behavior so that these individuals behave in ways which are defined as the end products of the training program.*

An organization is fortunate if the skills it requires exist in adequate quantities in the manpower resources available. An industry is even more fortunate if all it needs to do is pick out the appropriately trained individuals on its own roster. However, the widespread and firmly established existence of training departments in industrial and governmental organizations attests to the fact that things are not so simple. With both machines and operating procedures becoming more complex, training within industry is becoming more and more essential.

THE SPECIFICATION OF TRAINING OBJECTIVES

The first step in establishing a training program is to state the objectives of the program in operational terms. The behaviors to be learned as a result of training should be specified in terms of the particular actions and operations that men must perform. It is not enough to state that the objective of a training program is to produce a good executive or supervisor, a good salesman, a proficient repairman, or a loyal employee. The particular skills and attitudes that make up these job performances need to be analyzed specifically and set down as training objectives. These then constitute the behaviors which are the goals, or end products, of the shaping and modifying learning processes involved in training. In specifying training objectives it is important to get answers to questions such as:

1. What are the requirements for proficient job performance?

2. What are the special characteristics of a job with respect to the organizational structure in which it is performed?

3. How can the job be engineered, or organized, so that it fits into the general system most effectively? Can it be simplified? Can it be combined with other jobs?

4. To what extent is a man being trained not only for skill in an immediate job, but for possible conversion to other or future jobs?

5. What logistics problems are involved? That is, do we have the right number of people to be trained? Do we have equipment available for training?

Determination of the Requirements for Proficient Job Performance. Some ways of doing things are better than others, and certain ways in which people behave lead to more successful accomplishments than do other ways. In specifying the objectives of a training program, these behaviors must be identified. The ease with which they can be identified is, to a large extent, related to the ease with which they can be observed. This ease of observation is further related to the complexity of the behavior involved. Consider, for example, the differences between a training program for typists and a training program for first-line supervisors. The specific behaviors and skills of a proficient typist are relatively easy to define in terms of typing speed, accuracy, correct letter form, and neatness. Specification of a similar set of defining characteristics of supervisory proficiency in a particular organization is obviously more difficult, as we shall see in Chapter 8. Even more complex is the difficulty of defining the objectives of a course designed to develop good company executives.

Job Analyses. Although the specification of training objectives for certain jobs is difficult, techniques for carrying out systematic job analyses can provide a basic tool for accomplishing this task. With specific reference to training, the essential aim of job analysis is to specify the ultimate and immediate objectives of the training program. More directly, the aim is to specify the knowledges and skills which constitute the behavior to be displayed by an individual at the end of a course of training. It is unsatisfactory to say that an individual is being trained so that some time in the future he will be able to become an executive or an experienced technician. The subobjectives, or subgoals, of immediate training that are related to long-term and eventual job proficiency should be specified in detail as far as possible. Some of the best research in this area has been done by military psychologists. An example of the detail that is often required for specification of job characteristics appears in job analyses of Air Force tasks carried out as a basis for equipment and job redesign, and for establishing training programs with appropriate course content, manuals, and

TABLE 2

SAMPLE FORMAT FOR DESCRIBING A MAINTENANCE TASK

Operator: *Line Mechanic—Fire Control System*
Work Cycle: 1   *Adjust System Voltages.* Performed every 25 hours of aircraft operation.
    Task: 1.1   *Adjust Power Supply Regulated Voltages.* Requires 40 minutes. If any of the specified indications cannot be obtained, replace Power Supply unit.

Job element	Control	Action	Indication	Alternatives and/or precautions
1.1.1	POWER switch	Turn to WARM UP	Inverter hums, pilot light comes on	Make sure covers are on high voltage units before starting task.
1.1.2	AC VOLTAGE (screwdriver)	Turn as required	AC voltmeter aligns to 117 ± 4 volts	
1.1.3		Wait maximum of 5 minutes	READY light comes on	If READY light does not come on, use press to test button. If light is burned out, replace it.
1.1.4	METER SELECTOR switch	Turn to 300		
1.1.5	+300 VOLTS ADJ. (screwdriver)	Turn as required	Meter indicates within green area	
1.1.6	METER SELECTOR switch	Turn to −150		
1.1.7	−150 VOLTS ADJ. (screwdriver)	Turn as required	Meter indicates within green area	

training devices. Table 2 presents a segment of a task analysis for a maintenance job. Table 3 presents a similar description for a pilot task [22]. These tables are presented here merely to show the amount of detail required for the specification of the job characteristics for a single task. However, this detail is similar to that required for the more comprehensive time-and-motion studies in industrial engineering work. To the extent that the objectives of training (the end-product behaviors) are known, they should be stated so that we can have definite behaviors which we want our trainees to learn. To the extent that we do not or cannot specify these behaviors we must *guess* about the content of a training program.

How to Describe a Job. The crucial problem is how to describe a job in a detailed manner which is meaningful for training. Many of the job-

TABLE 3

SAMPLE FORMAT FOR DESCRIBING A PILOT TASK

Operator: *Pilot F–1000 Interceptor*
Work Cycle: 1   Climbing to altitude as directed by Ground Control.
    Task: 1.1   Accelerating to climb speed (in shortest possible time and in most favorable position to intercept and destroy unidentified aircraft).

Job element variables

Inputs

Needed input information
1. Position, speed, and direction of unidentified aircraft (provided by Ground Control)
2. Friendly or unfriendly aircraft
3. Amount of fuel
4. Position, speed, and heating of interceptor
   Disruptive or irrelevant inputs
1. Air turbulence
2. Background chatter from Ground Control
3. Radio static
4. Enemy jamming
   Critical time characteristics of inputs
1. If fuel is limited, intercept may have to be made before the most favorable position for attack can be reached

Decisions

1. Best course to follow in accelerating to climb speed
2. When climb speed has been reached

Required Control Actions

Controls	Actions
1. Control stick	Standard-power boost and artificial back pressure
2. Rudder pedals	Standard-power boost and artificial back pressure
3. Throttle	Standard

Feedback

Indications of adequacy of actions
1. Airspeed indicator reads attained speed
2. Direction indicator reads desired heading
3. Altitude indicator shows level flight
   Delay action to indication
1. Airspeed indicator lags about two seconds during rapid acceleration
2. Direction and attitude indicators have lag of less than .5 second

Characteristic Errors and Malfunctions

Climb may be started later than is efficient because of airspeed indicator lag

TABLE 3 *(Continued)*

Contingencies Which Will Affect Task

Contingencies	Effects on task
1. Ground Control loses target	Pilot must decide whether to attempt unaided intercept or return to base
2. Target changes course	Acceleration course may have to be revised
3. Ground Control detects target escorts	Attack attitude revised, changing point at which climb to altitude is started
4. Malfunction occurs	Must decide whether or not to abort

analysis schemes now in use in industry and elsewhere are not satisfactory for this purpose. One type of job-analysis procedure directly infers underlying abilities from observation of the job. According to this method, jobs are described in terms of abilities, such as numerical facility, verbal fluency, color vision, or ability to recall details. These terms, however, are ambiguous and are subject to different interpretations from job to job. For example, the presence of colored signals may not mean that color vision is involved. One should observe whether the operator must respond to the presence of a light regardless of its color or whether he must discriminate between differently colored signals. The specification of the kinds of discriminations an individual has to make among numerical, verbal, or other visual signals can help pinpoint the skills which must be learned. Another method of job description comes from time-and-motion study in which physical descriptions of movement are employed, such as "moves lever forward," "loads vehicle," "empties vehicle," and so forth. This kind of description is convenient to use and is unambiguous. However, it provides no indication of the behavior involved in initiating or terminating the movement. Moving a lever to shift gears in a truck requires different kinds of discriminations from those involved in moving a lever to start a production line rolling [8].

What the training specialist requires is a set of descriptive categories which tell him how to proceed. For certain kinds of tasks, one writer [8] suggests such categories as the following:

DISCRIMINATION. Examples of this are behaviors such as reading pointers, aligning dials and instruments, distinguishing typewriter keys as the typist does.

RECALL. Examples of this category are the identification of parts and the remembering of procedures. This may be very important to a warehouse foreman.

THE USE OF SYMBOLS. Examples are interpreting charts, diagrams, tables, and performing numerical operations.

DECISION MAKING. This is defined as making a judgment in which several possibilities must be considered, as is often the case in making management decisions.

MOTOR SKILL. Examples of this are various kinds of tool using and making control adjustments such as are necessary in running a lathe.

Six Job-analysis Methods. The advantages and limitations of various methods of obtaining task information for training purposes have been investigated. One study compared job practices with training course content using six job-analysis methods [3]. The different method were *direct observation,* an activity *check list* filled in by the job analyst and job supervisors, a job *questionnaire* filled out by the technician, investigation of maintenance *records* for each job, *reports* to the observer of jobs just completed, and *sorting* of descriptive task statements prepared by the observer.

These methods were compared in terms of the amount of observer time required, the amount of technician time required, the amount of time required for observer training, the amount of technical job knowledge required by the observer, the amount of total job coverage possible in one week, the type of data analysis required of the information obtained, and the difficulty of this analysis. The study showed that some combination of routine check list and questionnaire, supplemented with a large measure of concentrated on-the-spot observation is valuable for getting information for training purposes. Many industrial training problems could be dealt with more economically if just a little more time were given to the problem of determining what information will be most useful.

Procedures for the specification of the behaviors to be developed in a training program are extremely important because on the basis of these specifications the entire program is established.

Determination of the Structure and Organization of a Job. Certain considerations about the nature of a job and its relation to an organization are of value for training. It is most important in industry that the distinction be made between "training" and "education." Training is usually defined as the teaching of specific skills. Education usually refers to a broader type of teaching in which the objectives relate to proficiency in future situations by providing a basis for learning through experience or future training. It is often important for an organization to decide upon the goal of its training program. Within the limits of training time, is it more worthwhile to train individuals for a high proficiency level in a particular phase of a job, or is it more worthwhile to provide a higher degree of general training? Specific training gets people on the job faster and usually at a relatively high level of competence. Broad general training usually means that men will be more adaptable to fluctuations in job procedure and new equipment, but in any event, they require a period of specific on-the-job training. Each kind of training has its place. Instruction given the mechanic in running a new machine meets our definition of training. The instruction given in our graduate schools of business to young executive trainees we consider education.

Job Simplification. As jobs in industry and in the military become involved with increasingly complex equipment it often appears that lengthy training is required. One way of managing such a situation is by job simplification or "shred-out." Shred-out refers to the breaking up of jobs, or tasks, into more easily trainable units. Such units will then require shorter training periods and less background for the people entering training. These units can be developed by training specialists in cooperation with the persons responsible for the utilization of the trainees. Shred-out may require that a job be reorganized or redesigned so that it is performed in a new way. With appropriate job design a trainer may find that much less training time or fewer training demands are required. Industry has done little research in this area, but the military has done a great deal. An example of this research is reported for a control tracking situation where the task was redesigned to provide the operator with more immediate and direct knowledge of the effects of his own motions. Subjects who performed without task redesign were incapable of controlling in more than one dimension or coordinate. With task redesign, five out of six operators handled four coordinates with ease [1]. Studies of this kind highlight the principle that training should be considered in relation to equipment and job design. This will be exemplified in the chapter on engineering psychology.

INPUT CONTROL

A necessary aspect of the training process in industry is the selection of the "raw material" that is to be modified. Personnel for a training program are selected by a variety of procedures consisting of such devices as tests, interview judgments, personal history, previous training, and in some cases the whims of a supervisor or manager. Judgment based upon interview is an extensively used procedure, the effectiveness of which is not evaluated often enough. The more formal selection techniques, in comparison with other aspects of a training program, have quite a detailed body of methodology and relatively well laid out procedures, as was shown in the preceding chapter on personnel selection. However, some special considerations of these for training will be mentioned here.

Selection procedures and training methods are influenced by the adequacy of the manpower supply available. When there is a full manpower pool, less precise selection procedures can be employed in order to select the relatively small number of trainees with the desired qualifications. The precision of selection procedures becomes increasingly important as larger numbers need to be selected or as the amount of available manpower grows smaller [19].

Cost Considerations. Testing practice in industry is also related to the cost of training. If test scores are positively correlated with success in training and with subsequent job performance, then the selection of individuals with high test scores can decrease the average cost of training per satisfactory employee. However, setting too stringent a test score for acceptance into training may require the testing of a large number of applicants. Using such a procedure can increase testing costs so much that the combined cost for testing and training per satisfactory employee is higher than the average cost for training a group with a lower minimum test score. This is true because qualifying with a lower score would require fewer applicants from which selections could be made. In general, over-all costs increase when very high test scores are demanded. Refined selection techniques are especially necessary if classification for input into a number of different training programs is required [21]. Such a practice would take place, for example, if a large organization desired to select electrical engineers for placement in various company training programs leading to administrative, research, managerial, sales, or production careers.

Another aspect of input control is the determination of specific *training needs*. Training-needs tests can be of particular value for refresher courses and for on-the-job training courses to increase proficiency. On the basis of job-oriented knowledge and skill tests, individuals can be selected for refresher courses or advanced training. The main job of the training specialists in this connection is to develop a series of tests which can diagnose these training needs and assess levels of proficiency. Input for a training program often comes from the work force already employed in a company, and the problem becomes one of selection from this group. This kind of program entails the selection of foremen and higher-level supervisors who can benefit from training.

Selection and training procedures cannot be considered as relatively independent problems. The manpower available can determine the extent and nature of a training program. Similarly the time and cost of training is influenced by the kind of personnel selected. Attention to the interaction between testing and training permits evaluation of the relative utility of each function. If only applicants of high ability are accepted for training, then training can be less costly and perhaps be continued to a high terminal level. If lower-ability applicants are accepted, a longer training period and appropriate job reorganization may be required to reduce the need for high-level personnel.

LEARNING PRINCIPLES AND TRAINING PROCEDURES

We come now to the heart of the training process—the actual procedures and techniques used in shaping and modifying behavior, including the teaching of certain skills, knowledges, and attitudes. The instructor or the supervisor must determine the best procedures to use, recognizing the caliber of the input population and the nature and objectives of the organization.

Scientific Findings and New Applications. An individual learns as a result of certain events that take place in his environment. Determination of the characteristics of these events, and the relationships of these events to how behavior is acquired, is a primary study of the science of psychology. As psychology advances, it will probably be possible to state the kinds of training procedures required for particular kinds of behaviors, and for particular kinds of individuals. At this future time training and education will have become the applied psychology of learning. In furthering this end, psychologists spend much time working to discover the relevant considerations and variables that make up the "laws of learning." Applied practice often outruns catalogued knowledge, and so individuals are trained and educated on the basis of the informal knowledge gained by experience instead of on the basis of the more rigorous knowledge gained by formal experimentation. This is illustrated by the fact that bridges and steam engines were built before laws describing their underlying principles were formally specified. However, experience is neither an inexpensive nor an efficient guide, and it is likely that the individual who modifies traditional practice with available scientific knowledge can do a more effective job. It also may be that the individual who, on the basis of scientific findings, breaks with the practices built up from experience will discover new applications and techniques which far outdistance the old.

It seems clear that what is most needed for the advancement of training methods and the development of a psychology of training is fruitful and flexible interplay between the requirements of training programs in industry, government, and educational institutions, and an experimental approach to the modification of behavior. To have "pure" and "applied" endeavors operating in close coordination is an important undertaking. An experimental and research approach to training may be in the long run as valuable to an organization as a research laboratory for product development. Within the past decade industry has shown quite a willingness to work with professional educators and psychologists in attacking the practical problems of human learning.

Variables in Learning. A number of psychologists have attempted to draw together the results of the accumulated knowledge about learning and to state general principles that apply to training. These principles should be regarded primarily as *relevant variables* to be considered in developing training methods. The specific application of these variables in relation to the behavioral modifications required is a matter of determining their particular value in a specific training situation. This may be no more unreasonable than saying that here are some important considerations for building a new piece of equipment, but the exact application for developing this equipment, with certain desired characteristics, must be determined by field tests. If a consideration or variable is found to influence learning in a training situation, then it is important to ensure its appropriate use.

Repetition and Practice. Repetition can facilitate the learning of a task. A training situation should be designed so that the repeated practice of skills is possible. The amount of practice required depends upon the kind of task involved, training techniques, and individual trainee differences. The influence of these variables in a practical situation should be determined by observation and investigation. Too often, in industry as well as in college, time limits are set for training programs without knowledge of the amount and kind of repetition required for learning the tasks involved. Repetitions that are separated by a period of time are often more effective than repetitions that occur close together. Spaced repetitions, as compared with massed or concentrated repetitions, appear to result in more rapid learning and increased retention. The trainer must determine the optimal schedule of practice for the particular activities with which he is concerned, and he must also consider the size of practice units.

Task Guidance. Learning is facilitated when the behavior of the learner is controlled through guidance. The word "guidance" here refers to any procedure employed to ensure that the trainee performs a task or works through a problem in a way which the trainer considers correct. In many instances one of the most important functions of a trainer is to aid the learner in performing correct responses, such as selecting the best movement, using the correct form, or choosing the alternatives which give maximum information in making a decision. Training is most efficient, it seems, when the trainee is allowed to make only a minimum of incorrect or ineffective responses. As a task becomes learned, and the associated reponses become finely differentiated in the presence of task cues, guidance should be shifted to these new, more precise responses.

In relation to guidance, industrial psychologists often discuss the problem of training for accuracy versus training for speed. In general, it appears that the answer depends upon the extent to which fast task responses differ from slower responses. If the difference is great, it is probably best to approximate the speeded task to be learned at the outset of training. It is often pointed out that information to the trainee concerning the outcome of his efforts and the nature of his errors aids learning; this, too, can be considered a form of guidance. The trainer needs to determine the kind of information which, in particular training situations, can be best used by the learner, and he must decide upon the best method of presenting this information to him.

Reinforcement. The learning of a task is facilitated when the learner is stimulated by the successful consequences of his behavior. Psychologists refer to the reward that is contingent upon, or follows from, the performance of a task as "reinforcement." Reinforcement can take many forms in training and education; it can be information about successful results or achievement or about progress or improvement; it can be monetary reward, recognition, approval, or the feeling of accomplishment. In a particular training situation, it may be practical to make a survey of the events which are most reinforcing to the trainees. It is important that the trainee have realistic goals in the course of training. Unrealistic goals cause failure and are punishing rather than reinforcing. The appropriate establishment of realistic goals which are reinforcing is an important task of the trainer.

Positive and Negative Reinforcement. Another important task for the trainer is to determine the trainee's level of aspiration and to give the trainee practice in setting aspiration levels for himself which are reinforcing and contribute to learning (see page 425). Certain training programs use permissive discussion methods, which are designed to encourage the trainee to express his attitudes and viewpoints. Permissive discussion reinforces the trainee's behavior in expressing his views. The expression of these views is then reinforced by the acceptance, or nonacceptance, of the group, and by the reaction of the instructor. Certain general classes of reinforcers are distinguished by psychologists: positive reinforcers and negative reinforcers. *Positive reinforcing events* are effective because they are presented as a consequence of a response. Familiar examples are a good test score, the praise of the instructor, or information that a task has been performed accurately. *Negative reinforcers* are effective because they are withdrawn as a consequence of task performance. Examples include removing a trainee from a job he dislikes as a result of the successful completion of a training course, or transferring him to a new task which is less monotonous than his former job.

Reinforcement Schedules. Reinforcement is most effective if it occurs immediately after a task has been performed. Waiting until the end of a training session to inform a trainee of his success may not be as effective as immediate reinforcement. Determination of how various techniques and conditions of reinforcement influence learning and task performance has long been an important area of study for psychologists. Of particular interest in training is the frequency and pattern of application of reinforcement. How often and according to what kind of schedule should reinforcement follow the tasks being learned? Different schedules yield different characteristics in the behavior acquired [12, 17]. The effects of various schedules or programs of reinforcement in training curricula is an interesting matter for investigation and application. Optimal schedules of reinforcement can be of much practical importance. Skinner, who developed the idea of reinforcement schedules, points out that one kind of schedule of reinforcement depends upon the behavior of the individual himself— that is, when a reinforcement occurs only after a fixed number of responses. This is a common schedule in education where the student is reinforced for completing a project or a paper or some other specific amount of work. It is essentially the basis of selling on commission or of piecework pay. In industry such a schedule can result in very high rates of responding, which set unduly high standards of performance and result in excessive fatigue, and is dangerous to health. In view of these results, piecework pay is frequently strenuously opposed. Investigation of the effects of reinforcement schedules in industry, e.g., schedules of pay and the use of bonuses and incentive wages, could result in generating optimal productivity with the increased morale and happiness of the employee [17].

Reinforcement is not only an important consideration in the early stages of learning a task; it is equally important in shaping and maintaining the fine discriminations and fine behavioral modifications required for the increased effectiveness of task performance. At this stage of training, when a high level of skill is being obtained, the task of the instructor becomes critical in ensuring that appropriate behaviors are reinforced in the presence of appropriate cues.

Learning to Discriminate. It is important for the trainee to learn to discriminate between those aspects of a situation to which he must behave *differently* and those aspects to which he must respond in a *similar* fashion. In other words, whether he is learning to perform a fine motor skill or to make executive decisions, the trainee must learn to discriminate between certain classes of behavior and to respond similarly within these classes. This may be compared to what a child does when he learns to discriminate between a dog and a horse and learns to respond in a similar fashion by calling them both animals. Bringing out this within-class similarity of responses is called "generalization training." Here the individual learns to generalize his performance to cues other than those on which he was initially trained. Learning to discriminate between classes and to generalize within classes is considered a basic learning process involved in the formation of concepts [12]. Perhaps writers of training manuals have this kind of underlying learning process in mind when they point out that a training situation must contain an adequate variety of practice materials, that situations to be discriminated should be as little alike as possible, and that reponse interference is a function of the degree of proficiency attained in task performance. Other considerations of learning also indicate the desirability of a variety of practice material.

Experience shows that without guidance, and without appropriate arrangement of the training situation, reinforcement may not be effective in the right way. As a result, accidental connections may be established between certain task responses and the reinforcing event. In this way the operator of a machine may in a sequence of control manipulations give his controls some superfluous movements which are unrelated to the success of the desired operation. A comparable situation exists in certain games and sports like bowling and billiards in which the trainee develops a response referred to as "body English" which accompanies the true movements that contribute to a successful throw of the ball or shot with the cue [12]. In a similar fashion, accidental and wasteful behaviors may be learned in the course of learning to become a successful supervisor. Responses which are learned as a result of the accidental contingency of responses and reinforcement are often called "superstitious" responses. A trainer should be aware of this possibility in the course of training. Careful delineation and spacing of subtasks may avoid this situation.

Extinction. The modification of behavior through learning sometimes involves *removing* certain behaviors from a trainee's repertoire. In order to remove certain task responses from a learner's performance, reinforcement contingent upon the task can be withheld. When reinforcement is not forthcoming following a learned response, the response becomes less and less frequent and in effect becomes removed as a part of task performance. The process whereby a task response loses strength as a result of lack of reinforcement is called "response extinction." Often the process of response extinction is slower than that of acquiring a response through reinforcement.

Using the notion of extinction, trainers have often pointed out that bad habits, or incorrect responses, can be eliminated by practicing them in a situation where they are recognized as wrong and where reinforcement is withheld. It is also important to check on the growth and progress of trainees, because their falling behind may be the result of performing tasks for which they have not been appropriately reinforced. Lack of reinforcement may also lead to emotional behavior or frustration in the course of extinction. Inexperienced teachers can get booby-trapped in this situation. The trainer should be aware of this and make allowances for it. Extreme lack of reinforcement which can lead to extreme discouragement and lack of will to continue is, of course, to be avoided. In the development of attitudes it is often advised that procedures be designed to permit trainees to express hostile attitudes, to let off steam. It is desirable in these procedures to permit no reinforcement to occur, so that these attitudes can undergo extinction. Otherwise, it may be that the release of the hostile expression is reinforcement enough to guarantee its continuance. This may be particularly true in an industrial climate where one's boss is excessively autocratic.

A trainee's present task performance is dependent upon his prior conditions of practice and reinforcement. The extent to which a task response will be resistant to extinction, i.e., persist in the face of little or no reinforcement, will be the result of past training procedures. It follows from this that for certain job situations where the occurrence of failure is highly probable at times, tolerance for failure is best taught by providing a backlog of success or a history of reinforcement. Certain patterns or schedules of reinforcement, where success comes only intermittently in the course of practice, result in greater resistance of task performance to extinction.

Forgetting is not equivalent to extinction. Extinction occurs when a response occurs and reinforcement does not follow. Forgetting refers to a decrease in response proficiency as a result of the nonoccurrence or disuse of the response over the course of time. Some psychologists believe that forgetting is the result of learning competing responses which take place in the situation where the originally learned responses would have occurred. In general, as a result of forgetting, greater performance losses occur soon after the cessation of practice than occur later in the course of time.

Training Sequences. In the learning of a task, certain sequences of task performance are more effective for the learner than others. In fact, one of the major problems of effective training is not that of making training tasks similar to job tasks, but of *arranging successive tasks* in such a way that the behavior is efficiently learned. The systematic arrangement of practice on particular components of a complex motor skill may often lead to far greater improvement than direct practice on the task in its actual complexity. One investigator [14] found that requiring practice *first* on certain difficult visual-motor discriminations and later on the task itself was an efficient learning sequence. For some time, psychologists have debated the question of whether the "whole method" of learning an entire task was superior to the "part method" in the acquisition of a skill. It appears now that the answer depends upon the nature of the task and that a good trainer will organize a task into the most effective sequence for learning. The determination of effective learning sequences may be accomplished by careful job analysis and experimentation with suggested procedures.

In the course of learning complex behavior, the learner's performance progresses from unskilled, coarse responses to skilled, carefully differentiated behavior. The job of the trainer is to reinforce the correct responses in the correct sequence in a way that will lead to the desired behavior. He does this by reinforcing those task responses which approximate the behavior eventually desired and then continuing to reinforce behavior which gets closer to the performance of a skilled employee. The procedure of successively reinforcing a sequence of behavior approximating the finally desired task performance is called "successive approxima-tion." In this sense, a trainer should not expect perfection too soon from a beginner; early in learning, he should often concentrate upon actions rather than upon the quality of the end product. An analogy given by one writer [17] is that this procedure of shaping and modifying behavior is like shaping a lump of clay, where the sculptor begins with gross approximations to the final figure. If the trainer waits for a complete task performance be-fore reinforcing he may not be effectively teaching the early basic responses required in the educational sequence.

Learning and Effort. It is important to point out that as a task response is learned, and the learner becomes increasingly skillful, there is a *reduc-tion in the amount of effort* required to perform it. In many tasks this occurs to such a degree that a skillful operator seems to work effortlessly with little apparent concentration upon, or attention to, what he is doing. A trainer should be aware of this stage of performance if it occurs in the tasks with which he is concerned, so that he can permit the learner to drop out unnecessary responses and cues which were required in early training. At this time the trainer may also find it desirable to introduce further tasks which the learner can now perform but which would have interfered with early task performance. A related consideration in training is what is called "response tolerance" or "response precision." This refers to the range of precision that is permitted in responses during particular stages of training. Permitting practice on only the correct response restricts the range of tolerance so that the learner cannot make responses that are too fine or errors that are too gross. On the other hand, a wide range of response tolerances in the early stages of training allows the trainer to reinforce approximately correct responses and to refine his reinforcement through successive approximations. In deciding upon appropriate response toler-ances, the trainer must consider the interacting influence of many of the variables previously described, such as guidance of the correct response, reinforcement, and extinction.

Meaningfulness of Material. Learning is facilitated when the tasks to be learned are meaningfully related. If some general principles which the learner understands (has previously learned) underlie a sequence of tasks then these tasks will be learned more readily than tasks which are not meaningfully connected. Training sequences should, therefore, be organized around *connecting principles* whenever possible. The trainer should be aware of principles which do relate material meaningfully and those which do not. For example, the teaching of certain principles of basic electronics may assist a trainee in learning his job as a radio repairman. On the other hand, it may be that some principles which are traditionally a part of early training actually relate tasks only at more advanced job levels, e.g., at the level of radio design engineer.

In attitude and morale training it appears that free exchange of opinion should be encouraged if such discussion helps develop meaningful relationships which facilitate future learning. One of the important characteristics of learning sequences may be that effective sequences define meaningful relationships among the task responses to be learned.

Aversive Consequences. For efficient learning, stimulation by *unsuccessful* or aversive consequences of the learner's behavior appears to be less effective than positive reinforcement. A trainer can expect better results by stressing praise and offering a suitable incentive for correct or nearly correct performance than by stressing reproof or enforcing penalties for incorrect performance. Training under the control of rewarding consequences is preferable to training under the control of punishment. In training programs, aversive controls may take the form of docking pay, withdrawing privileges, discharge from the course, return to a lower-status job, or threats of these consequences. Research findings indicate that the immediate effect of aversive consequences is to eliminate the incorrect behavior. *However,* if the behavior is not removed by the process of extinction, the elimination may not be permanent. This may suggest that punishing consequences can be used to depress an incorrect behavior temporarily so that an incompatible correct response can be learned in its place. The term "incompatible" means that both responses cannot take place at the same time. An appropriate caution is that aversive consequences may often evoke emotional or defensive responses which are undesirable and which may be incorporated into the future job situation.

Plateaus. In many training situations involving complex behavior, the learner reaches a stage in which he exhibits no apparent learning progress or increase in task proficiency. Psychologists have called these stages "plateaus" because, in a curve showing learning progress, stages of no apparent learning result in flattened sections in the curve. An important function of the trainer is to analyze the characteristics of such stages of learning in his training program. The occurrence of a plateau may indicate both desirable and undesirable influences. With certain behaviors, a plateau or slowing down of learning may indicate that the learner is acquiring the responses and discriminations required for more proficient task performance. At the same time, early unskilled responses of the learner are undergoing extinction. These early responses may rely, for purposes of initial training, on certain training supports not required at advanced levels of proficiency. In such cases, learning and task proficiency following the plateau may increase at a greater rate than previously, since now a more efficient set of task responses is being learned and employed. In training circumstances of this kind, the trainer should be aware that learning is proceeding and that the apparent decrease in progress is temporary.

In some instances, stages of no learning may be quite real and may be influenced by a number of learning considerations, such as sequence, reinforcement, and motivation. A plateau may also indicate that the learner's limit of proficiency in the training situation has been reached. If there is a large discrepancy between this limit and the level of proficiency expected on the actual job, it is probable that the training situation has not adequately simulated the job conditions and the job equipment. If increased job simulation of the training task is not feasible, then it is necessary that the behaviors taught during training consist of responses that readily transfer to and provide a basis for increasing proficiency on the job.

Learning to Learn. Much can be gained in certain training programs if the learner is taught how to learn. Experimental studies indicate that when a trainee is presented with a series of different tasks he often develops greater facility in learning the later tasks than he displayed in learning the earlier tasks [11]. It has been pointed out that the training of a "set to learn" can be of important practical significance for job situations in which an individual must adjust rapidly to changing problems and changing equipment models [7].

Factors in a training program which influence learning to learn may be an important consideration for the trainer. A significant influence appears to be systematic variations in the learning situations presented to the trainee. The variables that are important in establishing learning sets need to be determined. These may consist of such aspects of behavior as habits of attending to critical discriminative cues, or habits of modifying behavior, when learning difficulties are encountered.

Active Learning. Learning that takes place by active responding permits more effective control by the trainer than does that which takes place through passive observation. Guthrie [10] writes that "in order to make listening profitable . . . it is essential that the student be led to do what is to be learned. . . . A student does not learn what was in a lecture or a book. He learns only what a lecture or book caused him to do." In this regard athletic coaches have a great advantage over trainers concerned with other kinds of behaviors. Many of the skills with which an athletic coach is concerned consist of overt behaviors which can be readily observed and shaped by appropriate reinforcement and sequencing. He can see the results of his training procedures and modify them accordingly to produce the behavior desired. The critical point here is that an important part of a trainer's job is to make the behaviors with which he is concerned as overt as possible. Only in this way can he see what he is doing. In teaching problem-solving tasks, such as the trouble shooting of equipment, it is important to use techniques and performance measures which make the learner's behavior overt.

Specially developed training exercises which require reasoning and integration of knowledge are useful ways of making the performance of such behaviors more available to the trainer [5, 9]. Training procedures which require a trainee to respond actively by summarizing a problem in his own words may be effective learning procedures of this kind. Despite the apparent advantage for trainer control that active responding permits, many training programs rely almost exclusively on a lecture method, which does not make available to the trainer the behaviors he is interested in shaping. In the chapter dealing with the training of executives we will discuss the reasons why lectures in industrial training are often useless.

Transfer of Training. The objective of a training program may not be to produce a highly skilled trainee capable of immediately performing the tasks required for a job. It may be, rather, to teach certain behaviors which will facilitate learning when the trainee is placed on the job. Often the aim of a training program is a dual one: to train for a specific task and also for transfer of training. Studies in the psychology of learning indicate that the validity of programs designed for transfer can never be taken for granted. It is necessary for the trainer to determine whether positive transfer effects occur as a result of training procedures. This is an important endeavor, because transfer effects can be positive or negative. They can either facilitate or hamper subsequent learning and performance. Furthermore, established behaviors which have an apparent similarity to subsequent task responses may show little if any positive transfer value.

It is difficult to determine those training tasks which facilitate subsequent learning and performance. Nevertheless, the trainer has the job of investigating and checking on the transfer value of his training program. If he does this, he can identify the training tasks and training procedures which maximize transfer for the tasks with which he is concerned. It seems that the considerations which are important for learning in general are equally relevant for learning behaviors which facilitate positive transfer.

The necessity of establishing dual objectives for a training program is often a complicating factor. The military service, for example, recognizes the need to train men to operate and maintain certain specific pieces of equipment, and at the same time to train them to adapt to frequent equipment changes. Training for a specific job requires certain kinds of input personnel and certain training procedures which demand a particular amount of time. Training for transfer and adaptability may require different considerations and usually requires a longer training time. Within the limits of a two- to four-year service period for many military personnel, a compromise program is necessary. In industries which have a large personnel turnover the problem is similar.

Motivation and Motivating Conditions. The influence of the considerations for learning so far discussed are enhanced or depressed by motivating conditions. A good example is the way in which the effect of repetition or reinforcement is influenced by such conditions. For the practical purpose of modifying behavior, a trainer may distinguish between the motivational possibilities that a trainee brings to the learning situation as a result of his past experience, and the motivational conditions that can be built into the training program. It is good practice for the trainer to assess the motivational states with which trainees enter a training program. For example, trainees can differ with respect to their desire to learn and their need for achievement. Also trainees can enter a training program with different degrees of anxiety or apprehension about aversive consequences that may occur in the training situation. The influence of anxiety upon learning has received considerable study. It appears that the learning of tasks at different levels of complexity is influenced differentially by varying degrees of anxiety [18, 20]. Although some degree of anxiety may be motivating, too intense a degree may result in emotional states which distract from learning. This may be true in industry where, let us say, the trainee has some feelings of insecurity anyway.

It is also important for the trainer to determine what motivating conditions he can introduce into his training program in order to enhance the effect of such variables as reinforcement. Trainers often suggest that this can be accomplished by setting up conditions of competition and cooperation in a training program. However, the long-range effects of motivating conditions during training which differ from the actual motivating conditions present in the future work situation needs more study, particularly in the industrial setting. Some experimental results do indicate, however, that learning under one type of motivating condition facilitates, or generalizes to, performance under another type of motivating condition [2, 13].

Individual Differences. Learning takes place on the foundation of existing behavior which a trainee brings to the learning situation, and trainees differ in this respect. An effective trainer will carefully evaluate the initial behavior of his trainees, since this comprises the raw material with which he must work. He should be aware of differences that exist between individual trainees or groups of trainees. As far as possible, training practices should allow for such considerations as differences in the initial ability of individuals to make certain required sensory discriminations, individual differences in the speed of learning, age differences which facilitate or retard learning, and the enhancing or hampering influences of the personality of a given instructor upon different individuals.

Emotional and Attitudinal Conditioning. The paradigm of Pavlov's dog should be described here to point out that during training emotional and attitudinal conditioning may take place which can persist in later job behavior. It will be remembered that in Pavlov's experiments, meat powder elicited salivation; then a tone was paired with the presentation of the meat powder over a number of repeated trials. After a time, the tone alone was sufficient to elicit salivation. Similarly, a pleasant instructor can elicit pleasant experiences. When the task to be learned is paired repeatedly with the instructor, then the training task alone can come to elicit pleasant experiences that will be elicited in the future job. In order, then, to contribute to good morale and to individual satisfaction, it is important for a trainer to be aware of this sort of conditioning.

TRAINING AIDS, TRAINING DEVICES, AND SIMULATORS

Training aids and devices are widely used in training programs, and psychologists have begun to study the characteristics of effective training aids [7, 15, 16]. The military services, for example, have official policies which require the development of training devices to accompany the construction of new equipment. In 1954 it was estimated that the Air Force spent more than 2 million dollars a year for the development of new training equipment, and that several million dollars worth of training devices would be in the field within a year. A major proportion of time in some training programs is spent using training devices. In industry, for example, commercial airlines have made sizable investments in flight simulators, because they reduce costs greatly by keeping operational equipment in use and because they provide opportunity for training and proficiency checking under supervision and low-hazard conditions.

The task of the psychologist in this work is to ask and answer such questions as: What are the characteristics of a training device that result in effective transfer of training to the job situation? How can a training device be built which will provide reliable measures of proficiency level? To what extent does a device have to simulate actual job conditions in order to provide effective training? In addition, these questions are important: To what extent do actual job conditions have to be deliberately altered to provide effective learning and reliable proficiency measurement? Does the use of a particular training device result in better transfer skills than less expensive classroom training aids? How can present aids and devices be used more effectively? The answers to these questions can be found by application and concurrent experimental investigation. From the psychologist's point of view, a major attraction of training aids and devices is that they offer a means of automatically controlling many of the variables which facilitate learning and transfer.

OUTPUT CONTROL THROUGH PROFICIENCY MEASUREMENT

At the end of a training program and during the course of training, it is important for the trainer to measure the performance of the trainee. In this way, he can determine whether or not the trainee has learned the behaviors specified as training objectives to the level of proficiency required. For training purposes, proficiency measures have three primary uses: (1) They provide information about the trainee's performance in the course of training which can be used to decide upon the subsequent course of learning; (2) They provide standards of proficiency which must be attained at the end of training; and (3) They can be used to diagnose inadequacies in training procedures so that training can be improved.

Tests of Proficiency. The main concern of the trainer in the development of proficiency tests is to measure those behaviors which have been specified as the objectives of training. This assumes that the specification of objectives adequately describes the behaviors necessary for job performance and for transfer of training on the job.

The validity of a measure is determined by how well the training objectives have been built into the proficiency test. The type of validity required for proficiency measures of this kind is called "content validity." In evaluating the content validity of a training achievement test, one asks, "To what extent does this test require performance by the trainee of the behaviors which constitute the objectives of the training program?" The more completely and reliably a test measures the attainment of these objectives, the greater is its content validity [4].

The determination of content validity is usually, like job analysis, a qualitative matter in which an essentially qualitative comparison is made of training objectives and the behavior elicited by the test. One use of training achievement tests should be to set standards of performance which most trainees can achieve by appropriate training. This could be accomplished by varying training procedures when necessary, such as by repeating certain aspects of the course or by employing different-size learning units for different individuals. Most trainees should then eventually perform satisfactorily on the established proficiency measures. In practice, however, training procedures and training time are relatively uniform, with the result that trainees perform with varying degrees of proficiency. A cutoff score is often decided upon below which achievement is unsatisfactory. This situation may require the estimation of predictive validity for appropriate use of the proficiency test. The predictive validity of a test refers to the extent to which it predicts future measures of behavior. This kind of validity is usually determined by correlating test scores with subsequent performance measures. With adequate validity of this kind, end-of-course proficiency measures can be used to estimate future job proficiency, and job assignment can be made accordingly.

Much of the work relating to the construction and interpretation of proficiency measures has developed out of general test theory which has emphasized individual differences. One emphasis in test interpretation in this context has been on relative measures, such as standard scores and percentiles which indicate the relative standing of an individual in a given group. In training, the emphasis is somewhat different. What is required is an indication of the level of attainment of training objectives. For example, a percentile or standard score on a test of a job skill would not indicate whether the trainee was highly competent or had little skill. The determination of proficiency attainment must be made in terms of training objectives. Levels of proficiency or achievement should be made by the training specialist and subject-matter experts on the basis of their judgments of observed performance and specified in terms of proficiency-test performance. Scores on such proficiency tests should indicate the degree to which training objectives have been attained by the trainee. These scores can then tell the trainer whether or not it is necessary to make changes in the training program in order to produce trainees with the desired proficiency levels.

THE ORGANIZATION OF TRAINING

This chapter has been concerned primarily with the principles which underlie training. In practice these principles need to be applied to many different types of training programs. Industrial training in general involves both on-the-job training and off-the-job training. In the former, a training program is organized to fit in with working operations and is carried out by experienced operators, foremen and supervisors, or special job trainers. Off-the-job training is carried on in a company school or by arrangement with outside technical schools and universities. Depending upon the job involved and the lines of employee development in an organization, training of many kinds can take place [6].

Training occurs at various levels in an organization and is concerned with shaping different areas of job behavior. For purposes of description, these areas can be classified in a meaningful way.

Orientation and Indoctrination Training. This training is concerned with new employees or employees who enter new job situations within a company. The objective is to provide information about the policies and goals of the organization and to develop attitudes such as pride, respect, and loyalty.

Vocational and Job Skill Training. Here the concern is to train novices or semiskilled individuals in the specific tasks required for skilled job performance. Many organizations have centralized training groups and well-defined procedures for accomplishing this.

Professional and Technical Training. In contrast to the vocational training just described, professional and technical training is primarily concerned with the acquisition of advanced job techniques and the learning of recent technological and scientific developments which are of direct or indirect benefit to the organization.

Managerial, Supervisory, and Executive Training. Although the special skills which contribute to success in jobs in this area are less well known than those in other areas, an increasing amount of training in industry is concerned with the development of executive skill. Training in human relations, supervisory procedures, and principles of scientific management takes place both on and off the job.

Specialized Training. An organization continuously requires a variety of specialized training programs such as job-rotation training, training in work simplification, salesmanship training, training in labor relations, safety training, training in employee evaluation, programs of general cultural and civic development, and so forth. As an individual and organization evolve, the need for specialized training appears to be ever present.

TRAINING AND EXPERIMENTATION

A training program in an organization has features throughout it which can be investigated by experimental study [23]. The industrial psychologist can bring to it hypotheses based on research findings, as indicated in the section on training procedures. Training personnel involved in day-to-day training operations can bring to it the results of their experience. From whatever source the problems or hypotheses come, they should be set up to give an adequate test of the practical alternatives and the general training variables being studied. This requires close cooperation between psychologists and training personnel. The psychologist may require experience in an organization's training programs. At the same time, training personnel may require indoctrination in a research point of view toward the training process. This interplay can contribute to improved programs of training for specific organizations and to the further development of training as an applied discipline based upon a science of learning.

SUGGESTIONS FOR FURTHER READING

Blum, M. L. Training. In *Readings in experimental industrial psychology.* Part I. Englewood Cliffs, N.J.: Prentice-Hall, 1952. A collection of four excellent articles on applied problems in training.

Fryer, D. H., Feinberg, M. R., & Zalkind, S. S. *Developing people in industry.* New York: Harper, 1956. Practical problems of training in industry.

Karn, H. W., & Gilmer, B. v. H. Training in industry. In *Readings in industrial and business psychology.* New York: McGraw-Hill, 1952. A collection of five papers dealing with the practical aspects of industrial training.

Maier, N. R. F., Solem, A. R., & Maier, A. A. *Supervisory and executive development.* New York: Wiley, 1957. A manual for role playing showing how to train people in solving realistic industrial problems.

Skinner, B. F. *Science and human behavior.* New York: Macmillan, 1953. This book describes some of the basic elements related to learning.

Wolfle, D. Training. In S. S. Steven, *Handbook of experimental psychology.* New York: Wiley, 1951. A basic chapter on training.

8

HUMAN RELATIONS

IN SUPERVISION

B. von Haller Gilmer

The first direct contact between management and the workers is made by the foreman, or first-line supervisor as he is also called. His position has been described in a number of ways: he is the key man in production; he is a man who always feels that he has more responsibility than authority; he is the pivotal factor in human relations; he is accepted neither by management nor by the worker. But his lot is improving somewhat. He has been elevated from "bull of the woods" to a person who holds the key to industrial morale. However, he is still in a position of "walking the tightrope of multiple loyalty." In this chapter, we shall analyze the principles of human relations in industry as revealed through the problems of the foreman.

A HISTORICAL PERSPECTIVE

Around the turn of the century, the foreman held a position in industry quite different from that which he holds today. Almost alone he had the responsibility and authority for running the shop. He hired and fired at will, acted as timekeeper, controlled production, and was, in effect, his own wage-and-hour administrator.

All this changed rapidly with the growth of unions, with the expansion of companies in size and complexity, and with increasing automation. Engineers and other trained specialists became essential people as technology advanced. Hiring was taken over by the personnel department, and union stewards became buffers between the foreman and his men. As the supervisor's authority and responsibility split in varying directions, management, for the most part, did little to help the situation. The foreman was bypassed in the chain of command and the worker found himself taking orders from a dozen bosses instead of one.

A Change of Status. Then, once again, as industry continued to grow in complexity, the supervisor's position became a key position. But this time it was different—the foreman was now an interpreter of policy, not a maker of policy. Training courses were established for him as he took on more and more responsibility for job instruction, accident prevention, and worker morale. This was the end of the bull of the woods who had become a supervisor only because he had been on the job a long time. One example in change of status of the supervisor was reported in 1959 by the National Foreman's Institute. This report states that only 17 per cent of the companies surveyed required supervisors to punch a time clock, compared with 39 per cent in 1953. In 1959 practically all of the respondents reported that their foremen participated in management meetings.

Now, whether the supervisor comes from the ranks (a yardmaster on the railroad, let us say, who slowly works his way up from trainman) or whether he is given his supervisory post shortly after joining the company (for instance, a young college graduate, expertly trained in technology or science, who rises swiftly in the chemical industry), a new dimension is added to his job—human relations.

Human Relations Emphasis. Emphasis on human relations in supervision has become most pronounced since World War II. But the seeds had been planted back in the 1920s by reports on surveys of company policies on the human aspects of supervision, by the writings of Bingham on human relations skills, and by the experimental work in human behavior begun at the Western Electric Company.

In this chapter we shall describe the nature of good supervision, the roles of the modern supervisor, and the tools he uses in applying good human relations. Although the psychological principles of good supervision apply at any level of management, in this chapter we shall deal primarily with the first line of supervision—the foreman. Supervision in middle and top management will be covered later in the chapter on executive leadership and development.

THE NATURE OF GOOD SUPERVISION

Information on the nature of good supervisory practices has come in recent years from a number of sources. Programmed experimental research from such organizations as the Survey Research Center of the University of Michigan has given us answers to questions involving the relationships between supervision and productivity. Reports of the Foreman's Institute include analyses of numerous case studies of industrial relations problems. Personnel associations and training societies have concentrated much of their efforts on supervisory selection and training. The National Industrial Conference Board, the various associations of business colleges, and government agencies have been focusing more attention than before on human relations in supervision. In this section we shall review experimental and observational studies of the human aspects of supervision.

Measuring Supervisory Results. Often two groups of workers, doing the same work under similar circumstances, produce results that differ significantly both in quantity and quality. If other factors are about equal, researchers have tried to answer the question: how does the way these groups are supervised affect their productivity?

One writer [11] has summarized the results of supervision on high-producing and low-producing groups in two diverse kinds of work: clerical work in an insurance office and section-gang work on the railroad. He found that the more secure the first-line supervisor felt with his superiors, the greater the group productivity; but the greater the amount of pressure exerted on the supervisor from above, the less the section productivity. There was more productivity from the groups of workers where the supervisor assumed a leadership role than there was from groups where the supervisor acted as just another employee. Of particular interest was the finding that where supervision was employee oriented, production was higher than where supervision was production oriented. One has to interpret these findings with caution, however. There must always be some emphasis on production, or little will get done. But exclusive emphasis on production without consideration of the employees can be self-defeating. Other investigators [14] report virtually the same results from studies made in a large utility company. Employees who felt free to discuss personal problems with supervisors were more highly motivated to turn out work than were employees who did not have such freedom. Being sensitive to employees' feelings, voluntarily letting the employees know where they stand in an informal way, and giving recognition were described as the behavioral evidences of employee orientation.

In a series of studies it was found that greater production resulted where the supervisor had influence with his superiors and used this power to help the employees achieve their goals. When power is used to block employees' achievement, the group's achievement suffers. These studies support the contention that close supervision of the section heads is not so effective for productivity as more general supervision, a factor related to the feelings of security of the supervisor [18].

An attempt to summarize the many findings of the Survey Research Center led to the observation that the effectiveness of the supervisor was not a problem to be solved only at the first-line supervisory level [7]. If a superior emphasizes production with the supervisors beneath him, those supervisors are, in turn, more likely to emphasize production with their workers. This emphasis frequently results in a production record lower than that of supervisors and superiors who emphasize personal relationships with employees. Good supervisory practices must be the concern at all levels of the organization. We must realize, however, that employee orientation is no magic solution to productivity; naïve interpretation of these findings can become a booby trap to supervision and productivity.

Other writers in summarizing studies on office employees, forest personnel, and skilled tradesmen concluded that supervisors in the more effective work groups were more democratic and more likely to share information with subordinates, who were thus kept in the know [29]. Such supervisors were effective in planning, in organizing, and in demanding adherence to regulations. They made decisions consistently and decisively.

One industrial relations professor [19], reporting on several studies, concluded that supervisors who achieved good teamwork in their groups were also quite loyal to the company. Those supervisors who perceived and prepared for future needs were found to be good counselors and good organizers. In general, the more effective supervisor felt that his authority was commensurate with his responsibility. In decision making, the better supervisors were reported to have good judgment and to be consistent, whereas poorer supervisors were often considered overly cautious.

Supervisory Complexities. When over one thousand insurance agents from five different companies were asked for suggestions on how their managers could improve their jobs, the most frequent recommendations centered around closer and more understanding agent-manager relationships [5]. Several studies have shown that the employee-oriented practices of the supervisor, combined with other skills, resulted in greater agent effectiveness. It was found that attitudes toward the company and how it is managed were favorable when attitudes toward the immediate supervisor were favorable [15].

Permissiveness, democracy, and flexibility in supervision do not automatically lead to good supervision. A study of the engineering department of a company illustrates how a work environment can become too flexible. Supervisory practices may be ineffective when policy practices of top management do not concur with those of immediate supervision [1].

This study reported bad morale in an engineering department of a company with the reputation of being an engineers' paradise. The structure of the department was such that each man had almost complete freedom; the major source of supervision was a committee which passed on research plans and checked on progress. In effect, there was no supervision save the vague pattern of control from top management, which gave the engineers no chance for advancement in responsibility. In fact, the environment was so flexible that the men felt insecure in their positions.

Much has been written on the techniques of good supervision, and it is of interest to note that many of the do's and don't's accumulated through practical experience serve as behavior samples of good human relations principles. Almost every book written on industrial supervision includes such good suggestions as: avoid getting into arguments with your men; learn to say "no" without harming the man's ego; praise people in advance so they will try to work toward your expectations; be honest in admitting your errors; tell the employees in advance of impending changes that will affect them.

Whether one regards human relations as an art, as a science, or as a combination of both, there is evidence to show that good human relations in supervision come only with hard work. Maintaining good human relations is a continuing problem.

How well one can go from effectiveness on the verbal level to effectiveness on the behavior level depends in part upon one's depth of understanding and one's ability to sense the local psychological climate. Good supervision is found at the *behavior level on the job*. Some men talk better supervision than they practice. As one observer put it in describing a certain supervisor: "He is big talk, little do." No doubt much money and effort are wasted on training programs that get no further than the verbal level. Later, in reviewing a study conducted at the International Harvester Company, we shall describe how one checks on the effectiveness of training at the behavior level (see page 189).

THE MULTIPLE ROLES OF THE SUPERVISOR

The supervisor has been described as a man who plays a dozen roles. He always belongs to two organizational groups, and sometimes to three. As management's representative to the employee, he must carry out company policy; as the employee's representative to management, he has a reverse role. Under some circumstances, the supervisor may find himself with a third loyalty—the foreman's union. In carrying through his major roles as a leader and key man of a communication network, the supervisor from time to time functions in selection, training, counseling, labor grievances, upgrading, record keeping, and public relations; in addition, he is something of a technologist.

Loyalty of the Supervisor. "Does your supervisor pull for the company or for the men?" This was one question asked of a group of employees by two investigators [14]. At the same time, ratings were given on the supervisors' performances by their superiors. These authors found that the supervisor who could understand the objectives of *both* the company and the workers was rated highest by management. More supervisors who pulled for the company were rated less effective by management. Many of the employees felt it was possible for the supervisor to pull for both the company and the men. Most significantly, this study showed that dual loyalty posed no serious problem where the goals of the company and the goals of the employees were compatible. However, when management fails to recognize this duality, the foreman may lose his ability to act for the employees and eventually lose his effectiveness in helping management gain its objectives. Failure on the part of the workers to recognize the duality may inhibit the supervisor's success as a representative of management. Apparently one of the factors that brings foremen, union leaders, and union stewards to positions of leadership is the ability to see both sides of the dual position.

Concern has been voiced because it is difficult to upgrade a man from the rank and file, and have him feel a balanced loyalty. A case in point came to the attention of this writer who had been giving similar but separate courses in human relations to supervisors and to middle-management administrators. Each group brought up an instance of a recently appointed foreman who would not cross a workers' picket line. The management group felt that his duties demanded that he cross the line. The supervisory group maintained that it would have been a violation of the spirit of unionism, since the supervisor himself belonged to a foreman's union. The man himself confided to the instructor that he was in conflict and did not know what to do. A search of the psychological literature to find what long-experienced consultants had to say about such problems showed that one psychologist [12] concluded that management needs to select and train supervisors more carefully, pay more attention to their dissatisfactions, make them feel more a part of management, and thereby forestall their joining a foreman's union. Another writer said that such problems are ones of communication between higher management and the supervisors [2]. A marked difference often exists between what management believes the responsibility of the supervisor is and what the foreman himself conceives it to be. Viteles [26] says it is a multidimensional problem involving status, pay, conceptions of authority and responsibility, and the opportunity to act and feel like management. Herzberg and his associates [7], in reviewing the literature on job attitudes, conclude that management must give proper attention to the supervisor if it expects him to identify with management. However, the relative value of such attention, its nature, and the conditions most appropriate for it are not yet known from concrete evidence.

EMPATHY IN SUPERVISION

Some psychologists believe that applications of the concept of empathy may lead to better selection and training of supervisors [8]. Here empathy has been defined as "the ability to put oneself in the other person's position, establish rapport, and anticipate his reactions, feelings, and behaviors." Some writers attribute a part of the conflict between labor and management to a lack of empathy on the part of both groups.

An experienced investigator, in one of his studies on industrial conflict, found that facts are not the same for people with different attitudes, and that leaders on both sides come to an industrial controversy ready to see only the good on one side and only the bad on the other [24]. Studies with the widely used File and Remmers test "How Supervise?" [4, 20] and the Kerr and Speroff Empathy Test [9] show that the abilities to perceive the feelings of others are related to supervisory success. But where does the balance in feelings come in? One psychologist [17] found, for example, in a study of empathy among people working in a textile factory that the supervisors tended to overestimate the worker's knowledge of the best methods of supervision and to underestimate management's knowledge of the facts.

One writer [15] who prefers to use the term "sensitivity" instead of empathy (since the word "empathy" carries a connotation of sympathy with the object empathized) found that, on the average, the better the supervisor is able to sense employee attitudes, the higher the productivity of the work group. He also found that supervisors were less sensitive to topics and attitudes in which they themselves might be ego-involved. For example, a foreman may be very sensitive about working conditions for his men, but insensitive to his own acts of favoritism.

The supervisor must play an interpretative role that extends beyond the job situation itself. The tensions which arise in the workers must be understood by the supervisor. He must understand the nature of the man's resistance to authority, his fears, and the feelings of insecurity. In this respect, it has been found that the more considerate the foreman's own supervisor, the more considerate he is himself. There are reports of a relationship between the pressures put on the foreman by his superiors and similar anxieties he creates in his men.

THE JOBS OF THE SUPERVISOR

Let us examine a little more extensively how thin the supervisor has to spread his talents and energies in carrying out the many roles of his position; how he has to be virtually a Jack-of-all-trades.

Inducting the New Worker. The supervisor's tact in getting the new man to talk about himself in a free and easy way is essential to good supervision. At this first session he must give the worker information about the company in general, its over-all policies, and the relationship between the employee's specific department and the whole company. Departmental rules and regulations have to be explained in relation to the worker's specific duties. The supervisor must judge how extensive he should make introductions and how he can best make the man feel he belongs to the work group. All of this has to be done with the knowledge that the new man can take in only so much and that his first impressions will be important.

Training Responsibilities. Some training responsibility falls to the supervisor. He must know how to prepare the best instruction sequence for the job at hand. The good supervisor must learn firsthand the principles of transfer in training, the nature of habit interference, and what to do about it. In short, he finds himself in education, but often unprepared.

Safety. Good safety practice is the responsibility of everyone, but to the supervisor goes the job of checking on the environmental and personal causes of accidents in his department. He must be alert for the man who operates without authority or bypasses safety devices, who uses unsafe equipment or operates a machine when emotionally upset. When he sees a worker committing an unsafe act, the foreman must "stop-study-instruct" and sometimes apply discipline right on the spot. The supervisor often must apply the principle of repetition in safety education. He is frequently the one who must tell the family when a man has been injured or killed.

The Handling of Grievances. In their initial stage, grievances fall to the supervisor. He must examine them for cause, whether attributed to work climate, to wrong job placement, to inadequate job training, or to personal causes. The good supervisor soon learns that gripes are often safety valves, not grievances. In some situations the supervisor finds a large part of his day taken up with the union steward, ironing out difficulties. He knows that the causes of grievances are legion: pay differentials, union contract specifications, unguarded work hazards, uneven distribution of overtime, favoritism, strict rules, credit stealing, disciplinary action, etc. The supervisor must be alert to them all.

Discipline Handling. The supervisor often finds himself in a difficult position as he tries to break bad habits of his men and to prevent wrong actions from going unnoticed. He acts as an analyst as he seeks the reasons for absenteeism or lateness to work, as a problem solver as he interprets facts that lead to correction of behavior, encouragement, warning, penalty by layoff or demotion, or finally dismissal. And in strongly unionized plants he deals with discipline under the watchful eyes of the union committee. His problem is even more complicated in those situations where the committeemen like to foment trouble for management.

Worker Rating. How to rate the worker is a problem that has not been effectively solved anywhere along the line. Rating scales or critical-incident techniques, regardless of their merit, depend upon supervisor observations and judgment. Whether he likes it or not, the supervisor must make judgments where objective standards of judgment probably do not exist. His ratings are often hampered by labor-management conflicts of interpretation. In the judgment of the supervisor, a relatively new man may be superior to the man with seniority, but the latter must be favored according to most union contract agreements. Rating, a rough problem even in the isolated confines of the ivory tower, is a most difficult task in the industrial complex, as we shall see in a later chapter (see page 298).

Managing the Budget. And, lest we forget, the supervisor has the role of budget manager. He must keep records—material cost, manpower cost; he must have a working understanding of profits and loss, and be able to tell the difference between "real" work and "soldiering." He must know how to plan for "waiting time"; he must know what to do with men who "make the job last." One executive summed up the situation thus: "The supervisor who does not pay attention to costs in dollars and cents can never really be a part of management."

Communication. The supervisor is a key in the communication network, whether communication be up, down, or horizontal. From giving orders to satisfying customer and public relations, the supervisor plays both a formal and an informal role.

A Check List of Supervisory Practices. One way to appreciate the many and varied demands placed on the supervisor in modern industry is to make a check list of his day-to-day activities. A review by the author of several such check lists taken from large industries and small industries, from office situations and plant situations, from closely confined work places and from the transportation industries shows that the human relations problems are the same, though activities from job to job may vary extensively. This check list states questions to the supervisor in a straightforward way.

Each question is phrased for a positive answer:

1. Do you know each of your men well enough to tell where he lives, where he came from, and what his interests are?
2. Do you know the general aims of the company?
3. Can you list in order your men who are ready for promotion?
4. Do your men work together well?
5. Do you know how to give an order?
6. Have you obtained better working conditions for your men?
7. Have you corrected the sources of grievances before they come up?
8. Do you listen to complaints?
9. Do you reprimand without building up ill feelings?
10. Do you avoid talking behind a man's head?
11. Do you reprimand in private rather than in public?
12. Do you have a check sheet for introducing a new man to his job?
13. Do you guide the new employee over rough spots?
14. Do you keep a progress chart on the new man?
15. Do you have good criteria for judging performance?
16. Are you a good listener?
17. Are your records useful?

18. Do you know how to get a man to talk in an interview?
19. Do you keep up to date on company policies?
20. Do you keep up to date on union activities?
21. Do you plan work schedules in advance?
22. Do you have adequate inspection procedures?
23. Are you familiar with the technical side of the men's jobs?
24. Does work go on efficiently in your absence?
25. Do you keep your superiors informed of your department's activities?
26. Do you avoid taking up bothersome details with your boss?
27. Do you answer correspondence on time?
28. Do you see where your job fits into the over-all organization?
29. Do you have a man who could take your job?
30. Do you know what the accident hazards are in your department?
31. Do you train for safety?
32. Do you give recognition to the man who does good work?
33. Do you ask workers for suggestions before attacking a new job?
34. Do you spread overtime work fairly?
35. Do you allow conversation at work on routine jobs?
36. Do you ever ask a worker to criticize his own work?
37. Do you admit your mistakes?
38. Do you believe that ability to handle workers is learned?
39. Do you know what goes on in departments other than your own?
40. Do you use conferences in getting ideas over to workers?
41. Do you keep cash and production records for your department?
42. Do you ever explain company policies to your men?
43. Do you keep your people informed on business conditions of the company?
44. Do you spend part of your time listening to worker complaints?
45. Do you believe the worker wants more from his job than just pay?
46. Do you believe most workers will cooperate in helping solve problems?
47. Do you believe that a worker who does not get promoted should be told why?
48. Do you believe in giving workers rest periods?
49. Do you believe people want to know where they stand on a job?
50. Do you believe in trying to sense how the worker feels?

Knowing what to do at the verbal level and actually carrying through at the behavior level is one of the big problems of supervision. Studies show that practically no supervisor does all the things which he knows should be done. For our purposes here the list is useful in emphasizing in another way the many demands put on this man of many roles.

Supervisor-Worker Relationships. Studies made by Hersey [6], involving over six thousand people, have led to some very practical understandings about supervisor-worker relationships. When employees were asked about the most irritating factor in their work situation, 75 per cent of them responded that the boss was. The response was strongest where the boss was closest to the worker in distributing work, supervising training, handling grievances, and enforcing discipline. But to these same people, the boss was also something of a father figure who meant much in their daily lives.

A great deal has been said about the worker's need to get a feeling of accomplishment from his work. The importance of this need has long been recognized, but how can the person in the low-level unskilled job, or the person who has reached his limits of job accomplishment, feel that he is making progress? Studies of workers in such categories show that feelings of accomplishment do not have to be directly associated with the job itself. If the job helps the man to feel that he can buy a car or build a cabin, then some degree of satisfaction may be present. A good foreman looks for these signs of progress as well as for the feelings of satisfaction that may come from the act of work itself, the so-called "intrinsic" aspect of work.

Hersey has brought out consideration of another aspect of the supervisor-worker relationship not often voiced. He found that over a period of time workers build up an emotional resistance against the driving foreman which hinders production. However, emotional pressures brought on by unavoidable events are quite different in their long-range emotional impact on the worker. Since these events are impersonal, they are unlikely to arouse antagonism and a desire to fight back.

Overgeneralizations in Supervision. One of the dangers involved in establishing do-don't rules of supervision comes from overgeneralization of selected facts. There is some evidence which supports the contention that a simple, repetitive operation involving no conscious thought produces in the worker a feeling of boredom or monotony and a consequent desire for change. This contention may well be true if the given worker is an intelligent, ambitious person who is made to stay on a simple, repetitive operation. On the other hand, a person of low intelligence may resist being taken off a job that is boring to others. Studies also show that workers performing the same simple repetitive operations are less likely to be affected by monotony if they see others doing the same thing and if they are allowed to talk and laugh with fellow workers. Permission to talk and laugh, however, must be limited to such tasks as making simple machine parts, where there are no adverse effects on production; card-punch operators in accounting departments (a task boring to some people) would lose considerably productionwise if allowed to talk and laugh with fellow workers on the job.

One other overgeneralization that has led to some misunderstanding is the belief that restriction of output by workers is found only in strongly organized union plants. Nonunion workers have been found to be just as prone to restrict output whenever the conditions of their employment lead them to fear layoff or a cut in rate. The good supervisor understands such subtleties of human behavior. He knows the importance of telling the worker why he is doing a particular job. In most higher positions people know the "whys" without being specifically told. Workers often do not have the opportunity to learn about a job except through the foreman.

But what of the morale of the supervisor himself as he attempts to carry out his many jobs? Why do employees frequently turn down the chance to become foremen? Much of the answer lies in the lack of clarification of the supervisor's role, as he is forced to deal with his workers individually and in groups.

THE SUPERVISOR AND THE INDIVIDUAL

The supervisor's relationship with any given man may well follow a pattern of helping to hire him, induct him into the job, train him, place him, rate him, upgrade him, counsel him, or fire him. As he gets to know his men, the supervisor becomes a student of the subject of individual differences.

The New Man. Although selection is today a function of the employment office or the personnel department, the supervisor, in many instances, still passes final judgment on who shall be hired. This gives him prestige in the eyes of the man. He is recognized as having authority and representing management. With the personnel department having recruited and screened applicants, the foreman first gets to see the man in the interview. Here he initially establishes his relationship with the man, a step that leads to inducting the worker.

Some people are insecure as they start a new job. In such instances, the supervisor functions in two ways. First, he tries to make the new employee feel some degree of belonging. Second, he often must skillfully break down ways of working carried over from the last job, ever mindful of man's resistance to change. Since first impressions tend to linger, the foreman can in this stage of induction "sell attitudes" as well as establish a cooperative relationship which will come in useful at a later date when the inevitable discipline problem arises.

Induction of the new worker is the beginning of his on-the-job training. The authors of a book on human relations in supervision maintain that the induction stage is crucial in helping to reduce costly employee turnover; about 80 per cent of all turnover takes place during the first three months of employment [16]. The attitudes which promote individual job satisfaction, as well as group morale, get established in the induction process.

How Supervisory Responsibilities Have Grown. One of the most difficult problems in industry is evaluating how well a person performs. No matter what formal criteria are set up, whether a worker is promoted, transferred, retained, demoted, or fired, the supervisor is a key man in the process. Many of the problems in this area are literally dropped in the foreman's lap without any plan as to how he is to solve them.

We find, for example, the supervisor in an unenviable role as he becomes trouble shooter and attempts to solve grievances at his level of employee relations. If he has too much trouble with the union steward, both labor and management can project their frustrations upon him. He must not only hear complaints, seek the facts, define the problem, and work out a solution, but he must promote good morale, too.

As a counselor, one of the key roles of the supervisor, the foreman must learn to discriminate between helping with personal problem solving and wasting time on unnecessary complaints. Here he sometimes finds himself in the role of a therapist without the preparation of a therapist.

FORMAL AND INFORMAL COUNSELING

Almost every individual relationship between the supervisor and the worker involves some form of counseling. By taking a look at the now classic Western Electric studies which were begun in 1927, we can get a picture of how counseling in industry took on at least a degree of formality.

Western Electric Studies. These studies set out to discover the effect of the working environment, such as illumination, working conditions, rest pauses, and the length of the working day, on production [21]. Through a series of circumstances one investigator of the studies found himself in the role of a supervisor in a department. Trying to obtain information from the workers, he noticed, as their comments were solicited, that they began to lessen their unfavorable attitudes toward management. As time went on it became apparent that factors other than working environment and working conditions were having an effect on the productivity of the employees. What was happening here?

At first, the investigators thought that asking workers about their job was the key thing. A series of systematized, structured interviews was set up, but with little success. Next came a more informal type of interviewing where the workers were allowed to discuss any topic of interest to them. The theory underlying this approach was that the worker would tend to talk about the thing that was bothering him most. But no ready-made system of effective counseling resulted from this approach; it did little more than give the workers a chance to get things off their chests. Finally, it was discovered that the key to the formalized employee counseling lay in giving the worker a chance to effect some *personal problem solving.* Thus in 1936 Western Electric instituted employee adjustment counseling by hiring full-time professional counselors.

In this program each counselor was assigned a given department or area within the plant. He had no supervisory or administrative responsibilities; his sole function was to acquaint himself with the employees with whom he was working and to counsel on personal problems in any informal situation: at the bench, at the desk, in hallways, washrooms, as well as in private counseling rooms. Experience showed that the interviews averaged a little over an hour; the employees were not docked in pay for the time they spent in the counseling sessions. Counseling could be initiated by the worker, his supervisor, or the counselor.

Evaluation of Formal Programs. How effective have these formal counseling programs been? Are they worth the money they cost? Answers to these questions, within and without Western Electric, are many. At one end of the continuum we find those in management highly endorsing such programs. At the other end, some managers have thrown the program out. Some other companies have established similar programs of counseling, some have tried them and later dropped the idea. Union reaction has, by and large, been negative to formalized counseling services. Spokesmen for unions regard them as a sop on the part of management to get more out of the worker.

Perhaps one can conclude that the lack of adequate objective evaluation procedures has led to the many pros and cons about formalized industrial counseling. There really is no clear answer to the question as to the effectiveness of the formal programs. The author, in conversation with a plant manager where a program had been well received for several years, heard the explanation of the sudden discontinuance of the program in these words: "We got a new vice-president, and he has interests other than the counseling program instituted by his predecessor."

When Do We Have Counseling? Regardless of the pros and cons for specific programs of counseling, much has been learned about the psychology of industrial counseling. Whether formal or informal, counseling is an important aspect of management-worker communication. Let us take a look at this communication of feelings, bearing in mind that in most companies the counseling that does take place is done informally by the worker's immediate supervisor. Often the foreman does not even think of it as counseling. The author had this brought to his attention when he spent a day with an industrial supervisor as part of a job-description study that was being made.

During the day, along with giving orders, making inspections, and planning for the next day's work, this particular supervisor helped six of his employees to work out solutions to individual practical problems. The six problems involved such diverse activities as listening to grievances about working conditions and handling a telephone call from the wife of a worker who wanted advice on a domestic problem (which wasn't given, by the way!). I mentioned to the supervisor that he was carrying out a good load of counseling during the day. His reply was to the effect that he didn't do counseling because this really wasn't part of his job. He did not regard the six individual problems he gave his time to as counseling. The writer would, however, for in each instance the foreman let the employee unburden himself by talking through his problem. In three of the cases, I received the impression that the employee *himself* worked out a solution to his problem as he talked and responded to the supervisor's questions. Since another interpreter might hesitate to call these informal instances counseling, let us describe a little more fully what goes on in the counseling situation, beginning our description with the use of professional counselors operating within a formal framework.

Nondirective Counseling. The formal counseling interview is, by its very structure, worker oriented. The counselor listens, does not argue, records what he hears, and uses the information he gets to try to help dispel anxieties. He does not discipline the worker, as the supervisor has to do at times. The counselor presents information to management which he believes is in the interest of the worker, not for use against the worker. Adherents of these formal programs have described them as "adjusting rather than paternalistic," "counselee-centered rather than authoritative," "clinical rather than disciplinary." The method is essentially the nondirective approach described by Rogers [22], where the subject himself does the most talking. Pauses of long duration sometimes occur, but the properly trained person will recognize these pauses to be good omens. Many times during these pauses the counselee is working out solutions to his problems. Often following long pauses the counselee says things which reveal that he is beginning to grope toward understanding.

In essence the nondirective approach in counseling is designed to provide opportunity for the counselee to work through his problems to his own satisfaction, without being given advice or guidance. Here the counselor establishes rapport, listens, and talks very little himself. He reflects his acceptance of the client's feelings and attitudes and lets the counselee himself break up the silent intervals, lets him bring out his own problems. Some counselors find the nondirective approach difficult because it does not allow for advice, argument, lecture, or cross-examination. It does not allow the counselor to ride his position of prestige or to take responsibility for final action.

Nondirective counseling demands that the counselor be secure and well adjusted himself, and that he be a good and interested listener who can use a language level appropriate to the occasion without losing the dignity of the counseling relationship. If the counselor can get the counselee to state his problem, to give its history, and to develop the problem—without having to ask leading questions—he has developed quite an art.

The counselor helps the counselee get insight into his problem by recognizing mixed emotions and by responding to how the man feels rather than to what he says. He gets the man to restate and discuss his problem without injecting his own personal opinion or experience. The counselor can usually feel that he has succeeded, whether or not a problem was finally solved, if the client feels some accomplishment upon coming out of the session.

Directive Counseling. There are times and places where directive counseling gets best results. Here the counselor takes an active part in bringing about an understanding or solution to a problem. He does not give the man the solution, but directs him toward a solution. And it must be remembered that there are times when people need to be told what to do.

Certainly there is little opportunity for most industrial supervisors to get much formal training in counseling. What little they can get, formal or informal, should enable them to do a better job in dealing with their workers.

GROUP-DECISION PROCEDURES

The development of human relations programs in industry has been approached from two directions. The impetus on improving the job satisfaction and morale of workers has come largely through attempts to improve first-line supervision by emphasizing the friendly personal touches. From the direction of the higher and intermediate levels of management has come an emphasis on the techniques of problem-solving conferences. Fortunately, the two approaches have a common base, since they deal with attempts to satisfy such psychological needs as status, recognition, and feelings of personal worth. Group-decision procedures, which have been proved so successful at the higher-participative management levels, are being used more and more at the first-line supervisory levels in dealing with a wide range of problems, from the coffee break, desk arrangements, and vacation schedules in the office to overtime work, safety practices, and job modifications in the plant.

Problem-solving Conferences. Some of the very best work in the application of the principles of behavior to group decisions has been conducted by Maier [13]. He has found that group problem-solving conferences are useful in several ways: (1) developing awareness of basic problems, (2) getting different points of view on problems, (3) providing for permissive participation of the people involved in any given problem, and (4) developing approaches to solving problems.

It is important, of course, that any given supervisor work out techniques best suited to his personal mannerisms and the psychological climates in which he finds himself. Conducting an effective problem-solving conference is a skill that has to be learned through experience.

Maier has described four stages of effective group decision-making procedures:

I. STUDYING THE PROBLEM. In this stage the leader checks his own responsibility to see if this is a problem he should deal with. He analyzes the situation to see if it is a problem to be brought before the group. It is important that the leader check his own attitude to see if he feels the group is capable of solving the problem, if he is willing to encourage the group to solve the problem. Following this comes a plan for presentation of the problem to the group, telling *why* there is a problem.

II. SHARING THE PROBLEM. First comes a statement of the question, presented in positive terms, never in terms of objecting to something. It is presented to the group as "our" problem rather than "my" problem, in a way that will stimulate interest rather than give rise to defense reactions. Facts are presented in this stage.

III. DISCUSSION OF THE PROBLEM. This is the stage that requires the leader's skill in human relations. Here he must establish an atmosphere of permissiveness, where everyone must feel free to talk without criticism. Here is where the supervisor pays as much attention to how people feel as to what they say. Every effort is made to get people to talk without putting anyone on the defensive. Even such behavior as eyebrow raising or a shrewd glance on the part of the leader of the session can destroy the atmosphere of permissiveness.

IV. SOLVING THE PROBLEM. Here the supervisor must recognize that group solutions come slowly because each person has to "catch up" with the other persons' thinking. He must get the feeling of group agreement on a solution without calling for a formal vote. Many solutions do not find everyone agreeing, and they should not be put on the spot by vote. An informal check or agreement can be obtained by such questions as: "We have had some good suggestions here. Do you feel they provide the answer to our problem?" Finally, it is important that each solution should specify some action. Discussion is often concerned with *what* should be done, but unless the *how* is included misunderstandings may occur.

Conference Leadership. Those who have used the group problem-solving procedures point out several do's and don'ts that group leaders should follow. Let us list twenty merely to show how important it is to understand how people feel in conference situations, and to get an appreciation of why resistance sometimes gets out of hand.

The supervisor who is leading a group-decision conference should:

1. Know the general types of things he intends to include in the discussion.

2. Have something prepared to start the meeting off.

3. Have brief warm-up sessions at the beginning.

4. Present the general problem area, and let the participants express their ideas on the way they see the problems involved.

5. Expect some resistance at the beginning of any session.

6. Let the men get aggressions off their chests.

7. Recognize all suggestions, but influence *direction of thinking* by asking further questions.

8. Protect individuals from criticism by other group members by interpreting all remarks in a favorable light.

9. Recognize his own position and prestige, and try never to be defensive.

10. Freely admit that he is wrong, if he is.

11. Keep the discussion *problem-centered.*

12. Respect minority opinions.

13. Have a recorder keep a list of suggestions.

14. Keep the discussion going by asking such questions as: "How do you see the problem?"

15. Not try to come to a solution too soon.

16. Not give personal suggestions as to a solution too soon.

17. Make his objective one of resolving differences.

18. Keep an optimistic attitude that the problem can eventually be solved.

19. Try to round out each meeting with the feeling that something has been accomplished.

20. *Listen*—let the others do most of the talking.

Example of Group Problem Solving. Aside from the more tightly structured group-decision conferences, participation in group problem solving can at times work well without the direct leadership of the supervisor. For purposes of illustration we shall describe a case taken from Maier's book, *Principles of Human Relations,* an excellent source of case studies [13]. The problem presented is a small one, but it shows that group decisions can be made applicable to small as well as to big problems.

This particular office problem involved a change of habits of the office worker. The office in question contained eighty girls, divided into four groups, each with a supervisor. The superintendent, Mr. Barr, was in charge of the entire office. The work of the girls was such that it was necessary for some to leave their positions, whereas others were quite stationary and spent a good deal of their time in telephone contacts. However, in taking relief periods, in leaving or returning to the office, all the girls, on certain occasions, had to move through the office to get to the only corridor exit, as shown in the plan of the office in Figure 8.1.

The problem concerned the manner in which the girls moved through the office. Instead of using the outer and center aisles, they cut through various units, and this activity disturbed the work of girls who frequently had phone contacts. Furthermore, the girls went out in pairs or larger groups, and this, too, caused confusion.

In other offices the same problem had been handled in this way: the supervisors indicated that only aisles were to be used in going from one part of the room to another. Since the regulation had not been favorably received

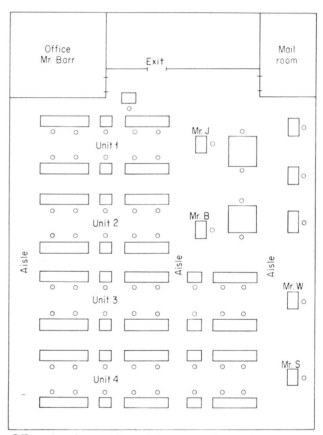

Fig. 8.1. Office plan for problem-solving case. The work positions of the girls, managers' desks, aisles, and exit are shown as related to the case described in the text. (From Maier, N. R. F. *Principles of human relations.* New York: Wiley, 1952.)

by the workers, violation became so general that management had no choice but to overlook the infraction.

Mr. Barr decided not to make an issue of the problem, but to try a more subtle approach. He noted that girls frequently deposited mail in the mailbox next to the door on their trips out of the office. He reasoned that if he placed the mailbox in the left front corner, it might draw the girls toward the outer aisles and reduce the amount of diagonal traffic through the middle of the room. However, all this planning was a failure. There were complaints about the unhandy position of the mailbox. With this personal experience and the failure to handle the problem in other offices as a background, Mr. Barr made no further attempts to correct the problem for a number of years.

Later while participating in a human relations training course, Mr. Barr decided to try the democratic method of solving his old problem. He decided to turn the problem over to the girls themselves. They soon made a plan for the correction of the problem and put it into effect almost immediately. Since there was general acceptance of the plan, good morale, and a high degree of execution of the decision reached, the problem solving was considered a success.

Since the solution to the problem had been worked out so easily and continued to work, Mr. Barr was curious to see if the democratic technique should be given the credit. He decided to make a test.

He decided arbitrarily to change the glass in the door at the front of the room from opaque to transparent glass. The change was made on Saturday. The next Monday he watched for reactions. They soon came. By noon he had three complaints.

On the basis of the complaints Mr. Barr put the problem to the group. He pointed out that he had replaced the glass without realizing that it made a difference. He was willing to make changes, but wondered what it was that bothered them. The criticism given was unclear until one girl mentioned glare. All the girls now mentioned this. He asked the group to help him find the best way to correct the matter. It was soon agreed that a shade be put on the window. The shade was purchased and installed. Since then no one has taken the pains or the interest to see that the shade is drawn!

Maier reports that two years later the traffic-problem solution was still holding up well and that practically no violations had occurred, despite the fact that several new girls had been hired during this period and management people had given them no instructions. Some way or other the new girls learned. The new manner of leaving the office had apparently become part of the culture of this office.

PROBLEM SOLVING IN HUMAN RELATIONS

The old adage that the best way to handle a problem is to prevent it has merit in supervision. We, of course, cannot prevent many problems from coming up, but we can often lessen them in degree and in frequency of occurrence. This can be accomplished by more self-understanding, by understanding why other people react to us as they do, and by familiarity with, and skill at, human problem solving.

Let us assume that we are aware of the *understandings* of human behavior. How can we handle the human relations problem when it does come up? There is nothing new or unique about the outline below on problem solving. It phrases questions to "you" as a matter of convenience. An examination of this outline offers one systematic method of working out solutions in human relations problems and often in personal problems as well:

I. Defining the problem
   A. First indication that problem exists
      1. What is bothering you?
      2. Is it a real problem?
      3. Is it a problem of your concern?
   OBJECTIVE: To recognize a problem
   B. Selecting the problem
      1. Does the problem need to be solved?
      2. Is the problem made of a number of problems?
      3. Is the problem within your capacity and knowledge?
   OBJECTIVE: To differentiate main problem from subproblems
   C. Stating the problem
      1. Can you write the problem out clearly and accurately?
   OBJECTIVE: To state the problem
   D. Setting up tentative solutions
      1. What ways can be thought of by which the problem can be solved?
      2. Why did you include these tentative solutions?
      3. What outcomes might be anticipated?
   OBJECTIVE: To see several ways of solving problem with possible consequences of each
II. Working on the problem
   A. Recalling what you know
      1. What do you already know that is vital to the problem?
   OBJECTIVE: To see what is at hand in the way of information
   B. Getting more information
      1. What additional information is needed?
      2. Where do you get it?
      3. How can you get it?
   OBJECTIVE: To get all the facts
   C. Organizing the information
      1. In what kind of order could you write down the information?
      2. Is any of the information irrelevant?
   OBJECTIVE: To have only pertinent information for use
   D. Interpreting the information
      1. How does the information relate to principles that may be involved?
      2. Does an examination of the information lead to other problems?

3. If so, what problem should be solved first?

OBJECTIVE: To see relationships

III. Coming to a conclusion
  A. Stating possible conclusions
    1. What are the possible conclusions?
    2. How do these conclusions stack up with your tentative solutions in I,*D*?

  OBJECTIVE: To clarify the alternatives

  B. Determining the best conclusions
    1. What conclusions can you eliminate?
    2. What conclusions do you want to draw?
    3. What conclusions seem most logical?
    4. What conclusions can you draw?
    5. What do you think will happen if you put the first-choice conclusion into effect?

  OBJECTIVE: To draw a logical and reasonable conclusion

IV. Carrying out the conclusion
  A. Doing something about the conclusion
    1. What *action,* if any, does the conclusion call for?
    2. If action is indicated, how and when can it be put into effect?
    3. If no action is indicated—what then?

  OBJECTIVE: To act on the conclusion

V. Learning from above activity
  A. Reviewing your behavior
    1. Did the problem solving work?
    2. If yes, what do you think made it work?
    3. If no, what made it not work?
    4. What would you do, or not do, the next time you have a problem similar to this one?

  OBJECTIVE: To learn from experience

The effectiveness of the supervisor in his many and varied roles comes down in the final analysis to how well he can solve problems. The person who has a good perception of the problem to be solved, who has an adequate command of the facts and observations that pertain to it, who understands why there is a problem, who can come up with possibilities of solutions freely and criticize them rigorously, is in a favorable position to do effective problem solving. One favorable aspect of problem solving in the area of human relations is that in most instances the supervisor has a ready check on whether or not his solution has been a good one. Feedback to the supervisor of his mistakes is not long in coming—from the individual worker, from the group, from the union organization, or from higher management.

SUGGESTIONS FOR FURTHER READING

Davis, K., & Scott, W. G. *Readings in human relations.* New York: McGraw-Hill, 1959. A balanced interpretation of recent developments in the general area of human relations.

Hersey, R. *Better foremanship.* Philadelphia: Chilton, 1955. A well-organized book on improving industrial supervision at the foreman level.

Maier, N. R. F. *Principles of human relations.* New York: Wiley, 1952. A sound book on the technique of human relations training. Includes excellent case materials.

Parker, W. E., & Kleemeier, R. W. *Human relations in supervision.* New York: McGraw-Hill, 1951. A very readable book on the practical aspects of supervisory training.

Whyte, W. F. *Man and organization.* Homewood, Ill.: Irwin, 1959. Human relations in industry analyzed in relation to research and practical applications.

9

EXECUTIVE

LEADERSHIP

AND DEVELOPMENT

Thomas L. Hilton

Defining the term "executive" is a difficult problem, as anyone will recognize who has ever tried to write a formal description for the job. One popular conception is given by the wife of a newly promoted man: "More money, more status, new clothes." Another, just about as useless, is that of the employee who identifies executives as "the ones who are allowed to use the private company parking lot." Likewise, though having a key to the private washroom may provide an indication of a man's status in the organization, it is hardly a workable description of the executive's job. What do people think executives do? What do they actually do?

FUNCTIONS OF EXECUTIVES

There are those who picture the executive as a person who sits at a great walnut desk surrounded by telephones, masterminding the fate of his company and its employees. This mythical executive spends his day making split-second decisions and issuing directives, like a master puppeteer who decides what each act shall be and who shall do the performing.

Then there is the conception of the executive, probably equally hypothetical, as the master expediter who is always on the go, never in the office. He has few, if any, scheduled routine responsibilities. If he were suddenly to leave for a six-months' tour of Europe, his absence would scarcely be noticed, save by those members of the organization who were perceptive enough to observe that things were not running quite so smoothly as usual and that morale was suffering a little. In general, we might say that in the absence of this executive, communication was more difficult, objectives not quite so clearly defined. In other words, the primary function of this second mythical person is to maintain a favorable environment for effective work by other people in the organization. This role requires that the executive be an expert in the motivation of human behavior to an almost impossible degree.

The Empirical View. The empirical version of the executive is quite different from those descriptions above. One group of psychologists [36] found through extensive interviews that executives spend their time on the following kinds of activities:

1. Inspection of the organization
2. Investigation and research
3. Planning
4. Preparation of procedures and methods
5. Coordination
6. Evaluation
7. Interpretation of plans and procedures
8. Supervision of technical operations
9. Personnel activities
10. Public relations
11. Professional consultation
12. Negotiations
13. Scheduling, routing, and dispatching
14. Technical and professional operations

These activities are somewhat like those found in organizational descriptions of executive functions, more realistic and less romantic than many popular views.

The origin of the written descriptions of executive functions stated in organization charters and manuals has been lost in antiquity. Many no doubt resulted from the laws, the military practices, the social customs, and even the tribal ways of early history. They have been modified and augmented over the years as the exigencies and opportunities of the changing industrial scene have demanded it. When a sales manager, for example, fails to function effectively within the company, his successor is likely to find a revised specification of his duties, responsibilities, and authority. But this does not mean that we can regard the accumulation of these operations procedures as the best guide for the executive.

Theoretical Versions. Written statements of executive job descriptions are necessary and helpful to officers, but it is equally clear that they are not necessarily valid prescriptions of efficient executive behavior. We cannot be sure that rules which have resulted from the needs which organizations have experienced in the past are applicable to twentieth-century organizations. A science of administrative behavior is required, one which will provide a framework of propositions by means of which we can test the validity of different conceptions of the role of the executive. Whether it is good to have a given executive spend 15 per cent of his time engaged in public relations activity can only be ascertained by considering the totality of functions which the executive should perform in the organizations. For some executives, in some situations, a 15 per cent bracket of time devoted to public relations may be highly effective, but for another executive, another company, or even another time, it may be a gross misapplication of effort. Important advances in a science of administration have been made, but we are still far from the goal of a science which enables us to answer many practical questions.

One writer on scientific management [4] defines an organization as "a system of consciously coordinated personal activities or forces of two or more persons." This definition brings out three vital elements of an organization—willingness to serve, common purpose, and communication. According to this theoretical conception, the executive must work to secure the willing performance of essential services from individuals and to define the purposes, objectives, and ends of the organization. Furthermore, it becomes the job of executives to develop and maintain the system of communication by selecting men carefully and offering them incentives to do the job. In other words, executives must provide techniques of control permitting effectiveness in promoting, demoting, and dismissing men, and they must understand the importance of the informal organizations within a company in which the essential property is compatibility of personnel.

These are functions of the executive organization, not the functions of any one man. In effect, it is the entire executive organization "that formulates, redefines, breaks into details, and decides on the innumerable simultaneous and progressive actions" of the company as we described in Chapter 4 on standard operating procedures.

The Standards of Successful Leadership. Having pictured the difficulty of describing the functions of an executive, let us now raise some other provoking questions. Can successful leadership be attributed to a man? To the situation? To a combination of the two? What kind of man is successful as a leader? Are leaders born? Can leaders be developed?

What evidence do we have that may help us answer these questions?

The success of an executive can only be evaluated *in terms of some criterion.* It is in the light of the functions an executive is called upon to perform that we examine industrial leadership. As we have seen, only a beginning has been made in conceptualizing executive functions; only now are researchers beginning to assemble data with which organizational propositions can be tested.

THE CRITERIA OF SUCCESS

Since we cannot unequivocally specify the proper functions of an executive and, in addition, would be hard put to obtain valid measures of the extent to which any one executive fulfills these functions, we make some inferences. One line of reasoning runs like this: (1) By objective standards organization X is highly successful; (2) Mr. Y is the executive of organization X; (3) Therefore, Mr. Y is a good executive. For example, let organization X be the production department of a paper mill. Mr. Y is the department head. It is observed that the net manufacturing cost per ton of paper produced in Mr. Y's department is less than that produced in any paper production department known. On these grounds, it is concluded that Mr. Y is a good executive.

Some Faulty Reasoning. In the foregoing example both the logic of the deduction and the validity of the premises are faulty. The argument implies that organizational success results only from executive functions, and that Mr. Y is the sole source of executive functions: obviously, we cannot accept these statements as logically valid.

Furthermore, net manufacturing cost per unit is not necessarily an adequate measure of the success of the manufacturing organization. We would want to be sure, for one thing, that the cost included all depletion of resources, including human resources, particularly the resources of the executive himself. In other words, low costs may have been achieved by making such demands on the personnel and rewarding them so little—monetarily and otherwise—that in the next time period, productivity would ebb markedly. Or the executive in question may have achieved a high level of performance at the cost of his own physical and psychic well-being.

The Problem of Delayed Effects. Again, we would want to ask whether organizational success results only from executive functions. In a broad way it does. For example, it can be argued that if production is costly because of defective raw materials or incompetent employees or obsolete facilities, then the executive has failed in so far as it is a responsibility of the executive to obtain these resources. But it is clear that the matter may well be beyond the control of any one executive. In the paper industry, for instance, a year of low rainfall can lower water levels to the point that cheap power is no longer available. Surely an executive cannot be held responsible for the external environment (rainfall, for instance) except in those cases where he can be expected to anticipate changes or to take steps ensuring his organization against unpredictable external factors.

In the long run, a chief executive probably can be held responsible for provision of adequate resources. But what is the length of this time period? This question introduces one of the most perplexing problems encountered in human performance evaluations, the problem of delayed effects.

Salary as a Criterion. Some other indirect measures of executive success are even less defensible. The salary received by an executive frequently has been used as a measure of his effectiveness. This measure can be regarded as a combination of several variables: (1) the worth of the executive as perceived by his superiors, (2) the supply of and demand for similar executive performance within the industry, (3) the ability of the organization to provide incentives, (4) the policy of the organization in regard to executive compensation, and (5) the value the executive places on nonmonetary rewards.

Who knows by what criteria an executive's superiors evaluate his worth? And even if we assume that the superiors do validly appraise his effectiveness, we also have to assume that the other factors mentioned do not influence the executive's salary. As a matter of policy in most organizations, length of service or age is an important determinant of salary. Consequently, in studies of effectiveness which use salary as a criterion, a minimum requirement is that some control or adjustment for age or length of service be made.

Studies of executive success usually employ *ratings* of the executive as criteria. The rating is done by the executive's superiors, by his associates, by subordinates, or by noncompany observers. The ratings vary from global judgments of over-all effectiveness to mere checking of whether the executive performs certain actions or not. The global judgments obviously are subject to the dangers already mentioned. At their best, they represent a valid appraisal of the extent to which the executive fulfills the rater's conception of what a good executive is, and thereby they usually tell us more about the rater's conception than about the executive himself. At their worst, they provide an unreliable indication of whether the rater wishes to present the executive in a favorable on unfavorable light for one or another irrelevant reason—personal friendship, animosity, hero worship, paternalism, sycophancy, to name a few.

Clinical Evidences. In spite of our problems with the criteria of successful executive leadership, there have been some studies of the correlates of success. These provide us with some appealing hypotheses in regard to the attributes of successful executives.

In a clinical study of 100 business executives extensive personal data were obtained [15]. Analysis of the data attemped to identify a personality pattern which was common to all the successful executives. These were the executives who had a history of continuous promotion, who were regarded by their superiors as still promotable, and who were at the time in positions of major responsibility and were earning salaries within the upper ranges of the then current business salaries. Executive effectiveness was, therefore, defined primarily in terms of the perceptions and preconceptions of the executives' superiors.

The attributes of the successful executives were perceived to be the following:

1. High drive and achievement desire.
2. Strong mobility drives, a need to advance and to accumulate "the rewards of increased accomplishment."
3. A perception of superiors as "controlling but helpful," not as "prohibiting and destructive."
4. High "ability to organize unstructured situations and to see the implications of their organizations." Their time orientation is to the future.
5. Decisiveness—the "ability to come to a decision among several alternative courses of action." It is proposed that the loss of this trait is "one of the most disastrous for the executive; his superiors become apprehensive about him."
6. Strong self-structure. They are able to resist pressure from other people and have high faith in themselves.
7. Active, aggressive striving. The aggression is not necessarily overt, nor is the constant activity physical for they are mentally active as well.
8. Apprehension and fear of failing.
9. A strong reality orientation. "They are directly interested in the practical, the immediate, and the direct." If sense of reality is too strong, the executive may be handicapped.
10. Identification with superiors and detachment from subordinates. But the successful executive may be sympathetic with many subordinates.
11. Emotional independence from parents but no resentment towards them.
12. Loyalty to overall goals of the company rather than complete concentration on the self.

The author concludes that the successful executive "represents a crystallization of many of the attitudes and values generally accepted by middle-class American society." But, he points out, "he pays for his virtues in uncertainty and fear."

Executives versus Supervisors. In another study fifty executives were compared with fifty lower-level supervisors of the same age and occupational history [29]. The authors concluded: "The executive considers mobility to upper levels essential for success, since his need for esteem and feelings of personal accomplishment can be satisfied *only* by securing a high position. The supervisor, on the other hand, has a much lower level of aspiration and less mobility drive and considers success achieved when he has attained personal and family security, respect, and happiness."

Although we are far from being able to spell out with any high degree of confidence the attributes of a successful executive, additional insights can be gained from the studies of leadership in general, by piecing together the accumulated wisdom of those who have worked closely with executives, and from executives themselves. Let us continue by taking a look not only at the individual as a leader, but also at the environment which helps make leadership possible.

INDIVIDUAL LEADERSHIP AND THE ENVIRONMENT

Interest in studying the behavior of people in groups began prior to World War II and gained momentum during the war as problems of leadership and communication became vitally important. The researches inspired by Lewin [21, 22] brought new emphasis to an old problem—essentially the point of view that the behavior of a person at any given moment is a function of his individual characteristics and his psychological environment.

Individual Differences. The individual characteristics which Lewin had in mind were not traits in the sense of observable uniformities in the overt behavior of individuals, but rather the momentary state of the needs of the person. He argued that the fact that the observable behavior of two people is similar is by no means proof that their individual characteristics are the same. Two people behaving aggressively may be doing so for entirely different reasons. One may have a pressing acquired need to do harm to the lives of other people, and the situation which we observe is perceived by this person as an opportunity to satisfy his aggressive need. The people or objects against which he aggresses are means to an end in the same way that food is a means to a hungry man.

The strongest momentary need of the second person may be a need for autonomy, a need to be left alone. He acts aggressively toward the people in the given situation because he sees them as insurmountable barriers to his achieving his independence. He may be mild-mannered and kind in other situations; here his frustration manifests itself in belligerent acts against the agents of his frustration. Note that the physical environment of the two men is identical but each perceives it quite differently.

Leadership Stereotypes. American efforts to predict human behavior have been dominated by an emphasis on traits and abilities, something of a carry-over from the beginning days of industrial psychology. For instance, several efforts to predict leadership skill have focused on the physical trait of height. To this day, there is a popular stereotype of the leader as a tall man. For example, a recent construction job in downtown Pittsburgh was observed to have three different observation windows cut in the tall wooden guard wall along the sidewalk. The lowest window was labeled "Junior Superintendent," a higher window "Assistant Superintendent," and the highest window "General Superintendent."

The evidence for this stereotype is contradictory. Although some studies have found height to be correlated with leadership, other studies have produced negative results. These findings are not surprising. For some groups in certain environments with certain tasks, tall men are perceived by the group as more able to serve its goals; for other groups in different situations they are not. The crucial determinant of successful leadership is not the trait make-up of the leader, but the needs of the members of the group and the nature of the situation in which the potential leader and his potential followers find themselves.

Situations and Leadership. In the furnace room of a steel foundry, a burly, aggressive, outspoken foreman may provide highly successful leadership, but his traits are not likely to further the cooperative goals of, say, a group of physicians. After an extensive survey of personal factors associated with leadership, one investigator [38] has come to this conclusion: "Leadership is a relation that exists between persons in a social situation, and . . . persons who are leaders in one situation may not necessarily be leaders in other situations."

Despite the convincing theory and evidence in support of a situational theory of leadership, many investigations have proved that certain personality variables do differentiate between leaders and nonleaders. Intelligence, for instance, is almost always found to be higher among leaders than among nonleaders. Likewise, such traits as self-confidence, sociability, will (initiative, persistence, ambition), and dominance are generally found to be significantly different [6, 12, 38].

Do these findings of the researchers who have studied personality variables serve to refute the situational theory of leadership? In one sense they do, for the personality variables mentioned seem to be common to many leaders. On the other hand, it can be argued that there are problems which are common to all situations, and that these common problems uniformly require the same characteristics of leadership for their solution. For instance, all group activity has a purpose. This is true by definition; a collection of individuals without a common purpose is just that—a collection of individuals, not a group. It seems likely that the group will appoint or otherwise accept a leader who is superior in those activities, including intellectual activity, which are required for the fulfillment of its purpose.

Social Interaction. A leader ordinarily must have some social interaction with the group, or at least some social proximity to it. The more sociable a man is relative to the sociability of the other members of the group, the more likely he is to become the leader. Similar arguments can be proposed for the other personality variables. It is conceivable, however, that exceptions to the usual situations will be found. For instance, it is not overly difficult to imagine a group and a situation in which successful leadership will require a low level of intelligence on the part of the leader. Nevertheless, for practical purposes, we can accept the personality variables mentioned as likely to be found in leaders, provided that we are always mindful that group needs and the nature of the situation are the primary variables.

Some Generalizations on Leadership. Psychologists interested in industrial leadership problems have drawn several useful conclusions for industrial consumption:

1. The major problem of leadership is not one of providing inspiration and achieving obedience, but one of creating a situation in which the followers willingly accept the leader as their agent in cooperative endeavor.

2. The major determinant of behavior is how a person perceives the need-fulfilling possibilities of the immediate situation. Achieving changes in the behavior of employees, for instance, is primarily a matter of achieving a change in their perception of the immediate situation.

3. Authority which is maintained by threats of punishment is clearly undesirable; it achieves only acquiescence, not voluntary acceptance.

4. Employees are more likely to accept group or organizational goals as their own when they have personally participated in setting up these goals.

5. The security, support, and, sometimes, anonymity which participating in a group provides, as well as the pressure which group members exert on each other, make groups unusually effective instruments for achieving change.

6. Communication among a number of people is greatest when they face each other as members of one group, provided that the group leader permits free interaction; groups themselves, then, provide the best way to disseminate information, opinion, and ideas.

It is important to recognize that typically the industrial executive is not in the same position as the leader of a small group. A basic distinction which must be considered is the difference between "leadership" and "headship." The executive in the business organization receives his authority from the organization itself. He is appointed from above. By his control of sanctions and incentives he has the power to achieve obedience. In addition, his goals as a leader are not necessarily compatible with the goals of his employees. The group leader, on the other hand, maintains his leadership by virtue of the "spontaneous recognition" of fellow group members when he contributes to group goals [12]. Here the goals are chosen by the group itself.

Leadership Methods. The behavior which a leader evokes depends somewhat on his leadership methods. Knickerbocker [19] has proposed that there are four methods a leader may use for directing the activities of people:

1. Force—the leader uses his control of means to force the choice of certain activities which he desires as means. The alternative to following him is reduction of need satisfaction.

2. Paternalism—the leader provides means, and hopes for acceptance of his leadership out of loyalty and gratitude.

3. Bargain—the leader may arrive at a bargain, a more or less voluntary

choice, made by each party to furnish certain means in return for certain means.

4. Mutual means—the leader creates the situation in which certain activities of his and of the group, if performed together, will serve as mutual means, means for all to satisfy their own (perhaps different) needs.

Knickerbocker says that the present-day leader is in a dilemma, since "he must succeed as a leader despite the fact that he cannot control the conditions in terms of which he leads." But he believes that "when management successfully creates the necessary conditions, the organization and its objective become a means not only to management but also to labor." In other words, here is expressed the belief that the industrial leader can become the kind of leader that theory and research in group psychology suggest would be highly effective. Our conclusion can only be that this remains to be seen; at present the industrial leader typically is in quite a different position from the small-group leader, and great caution must be exercised in applying the principles of small-group leadership to industrial leadership.

A COMPOSITE PICTURE

We have seen that the functioning executive is a complex person in a complex situation. To date there exists no means by which his behavior can be accurately predicted or his effectiveness evaluated. The integration of the myriad of personality, situational, organizational, social, and economic variables still is best performed by the experienced human observer. Professor Melvin Anshen [2], long experienced in the study of executive behavior, has this to say:

Even in a world of incomplete knowledge, we can develop reasonable projections of characteristics it will be useful to strengthen in the next management generation. The following list is offered simply as one man's suggestions, subject to any amendments each one of you may care to add.

1. Knowledge of the technical aspects of the business—as a basis for understanding their meaning in relation to the making and executing of policy.

2. Understanding of the relationships among the functional parts of the business—as a basis for thinking beyond departmental limits.

3. Understanding of the environment in which the business is carried on: economic, social, and political; special emphasis attaches to a grasp of the causes and significance of change.

4. An imaginative approach to management problems, particularly with respect to the ability to think beyond the routines of normal operation both in defining problems and in exploring alternative lines of solution.

5. Courage in making decisions—and equal courage in refusing to make decisions when the time is not ripe, or when decisions should be made by others as part of their own exercise of delegated responsibility.

6. Understanding of the tools of administration and control, and skill in using them to get results.

7. Ability to work with and through other people, individually and in groups: to stimulate their best efforts and to win and hold their confidence and loyalty.

8. Ability to encourage the development of subordinates: to delegate responsibility, to coach effectively, and to provide challenge for growing ability.

9. Power for continuing personal growth in performance and capacity.

Self-evaluation and Leadership. In the book *Executive Ability: Its Discovery and Development,* Cleeton and Mason [7] point out the importance of self-evaluation of one's behavior as he exercises responsibility for the efforts of others, makes decisions on questions of policy and practice, and sees that the decisions are carried out. Executive ability is not an all-or-none quality. It is important to recognize that varying degrees of executive ability are required in the large variety of positions involving administrative and supervisory responsibility.

An unusual kind of evaluative summary of the responsibilities of the leader has been given by an industrial psychologist in his farewell presidential message to the faculty, alumni, and friends of Antioch College:[1]

It will require time to think back over the many events that have been crowded into these few years and to draw a proper meaning from them. However, two related convictions have developed slowly but steadily out of this experience.

The first is a conviction which has been derived from my personal struggle with the role of college president. Before coming to Antioch I had observed and worked with top executives as an advisor in a number of organizations. I thought I knew how they felt about their responsibilities and what led them to behave as they did. I even thought that I could create a role for myself which would enable me to avoid some of the difficulties they encountered.

I was wrong! It took the direct experience of becoming a line executive and meeting personally the problems involved to teach me what no amount of observation of other people could have taught.

I believed, for example, that a leader could operate successfully as a kind of advisor to his organization. I thought I could avoid being a "boss." Unconsciously, I suspect, I hoped to duck the unpleasant necessity of making difficult decisions, of taking the responsibility for one course of action among many uncertain alternatives, of making mistakes and taking the consequences. I thought that maybe I could operate so that everyone would like me—that "good human relations" would eliminate all discord and disagreement.

I couldn't have been more wrong. It took a couple of years, but I finally began to realize that a leader cannot avoid the exercise of authority any more

[1] Reproduced with the permission of Dr. Douglas McGregor, formerly president of Antioch College, and now professor of industrial psychology at the Massachusetts Institute of Technology.

than he can avoid responsibility for what happens to his organization. In fact, it is a major function of the top executive to take on his own shoulders the responsibility for resolving the uncertainties that are always involved in important decisions. Moreover, since no important decision ever pleases everyone in the organization, he must also absorb the displeasure, and sometimes severe hostility, of those who would have taken a different course.

A colleague recently summed up what my experience has taught me in these words: "A good leader must be tough enough to win a fight, but not tough enough to kick a man when he is down." This notion is not in the least inconsistent with humane, democratic leadership. Good human relations develop out of strength, not of weakness.

I'm still trying to understand and practice what is implied in my colleague's statement.

THE SELECTION OF POTENTIAL EXECUTIVES

In view of our paucity of knowledge in regard to the functions and attributes of executives, there appears to be little that can be said with certainty as to which men should be selected as executives. At best, executive selection is, at present, educated guesswork. The research that has been conducted on executive selection suggests some possible profitable variables for which to look. The leadership research likewise provides some hints in regard to the personal attributes which may contribute to successful executive performance. Observations from experienced observers offer additional cues.

Some Major Assumptions. However we slice our problem, selection is still guesswork when the problem is one of selecting young men who are likely to develop into executives ten or more years from now. Knowing the attributes of today's successful executives is of particularly questionable value since it involves at least the assumption that today's executives have been properly selected, i.e., that today's executives are performing more effectively than other men who might have been selected for their positions. It is conceivable that our present beliefs and stereotypes are resulting in the wrong men being appointed to executive positions, particularly since, as described earlier, we do not fully understand executive functions. Contemporary successful executives may not be as successful as others who might have been selected. Two writers [20] have predicted that by 1980 the requirements of the executive may be radically different from the requirements of today. Computer machines may well take over some decision-making functions of the executive; they may even reduce the status of the man in middle management to that of a clerk.

Situational Testing. Aside from, or in addition to, the conventional procedures of personnel selection described in Chapter 6, one method of selecting potential executives is situational testing, first used extensively by the Office of Strategic Services during World War II [27]. The first objective of this technique is to envision the kind of problem situations which the executives of the future will be likely to encounter in fulfilling executive functions, e.g., marketing, planning, labor, public relations problems. Next, replicas of these problem situations are devised in the testing center. A large staff, which may even include professional actors, a communications system, and any other equipment needed to simulate operating conditions are required.

The candidates are given "real" problems, which often involve a task to be accomplished with only limited resources. For instance, they are sometimes given a group of "workers" to assist them, but the workers are instructed to obstruct progress as much as possible. The reactions of the candidate—how he handles the "incompetent" workers, how he reacts to frustration, and whether he is able to get the job done—are meticulously observed and recorded [27].

Situational testing of the type just described would still involve the assumption that those men who perform best in the test situation will perform best under actual control operating conditions, say, ten years later. The validity of this assumption can only be tested by longitudinal investigations. The present need for this kind of investigation is great.

If situational testing is desirable, why not expose candidates to actual operating conditions rather than to costly simulated test situations? Why not let each candidate work for the company for a trial period during which his performance would be carefully observed.

Despite the advantages of this trial-by-fire type of selection, it is questionable whether adequate test conditions can be created on the job. Good selection requires a broad range of test situations and ample opportunity to obtain valid observational data. These conditions are seldom attainable under operating conditions. In addition, an intensive situational testing program lasting, say, two or three days, allows companies to select the successful candidates without any obligation to provide employment for the unsuccessful candidate.

Whether or not we have valid ways of picking the people we wish to groom for executive positions, industry still has to pick somebody. One way or another a man has to be selected as a potential executive. The word "potential" is important because, except for the small minority of experienced administrators who enter companies as higher-level executives, most executives develop within the companies they serve. For example, 90 per cent of 900 top executives studied by *Fortune Magazine* had been with their companies ten or more years [10].

EXECUTIVE DEVELOPMENT TRAINING

Types of Practices. Current practices in executive development vary from complete *laissez faire* to highly organized systematic training. The former involves no formal efforts on the part of the company. Potential candidates merely mature in the company, picking up from their day-to-day experiences what skills they can. At the other extreme, the early years a potential candidate spends with the company consist of continuous training. His positions are carefully chosen to provide him with the experience he will require as an executive. He is transferred from time to time to provide him with a broad range of experience in all aspects of the company's operations. There are frequent conferences, during the working day and evenings, at which he has the opportunity to learn new skills (often human relations skills), to learn about new technical developments, and to make up for any deficiencies in his educational background. He is asked to attend week-long training sessions and may even be encouraged to attend formal programs given in various schools of business. Even his wife may be given the opportunity to acquire the social skills she will need. He will receive regular reports on his progress and hold extensive discussions with regard to his shortcomings. In some instances, even the services of a clinic will be available to him if personal psychotherapy is necessary.

Whether such an extensive program is justified is, of course, difficult if not impossible to ascertain. The first question is whether the product of such a system is in actuality a more qualified man than the product of a laissez-faire system.

A rigorous controlled study of the value of executive training has never been conducted. There is good reason for this; the situation is like that encountered in mental-health research. To validly test the efficiency of a new method or new mental-health program requires that a comparable control sample be excluded from participating in the new program. But if you are confident that the new program will be highly beneficial, what right have you to deprive a sample of its benefit, particularly if they earnestly seek the benefit? And what effect will the mere act of being deprived have on the control sample? In addition, how do you hold all other things equal, particularly in an industrial setting. As was learned in the Hawthorne experiment (see page 32), you cannot manipulate the experimental group without influencing the control group. Also there is the problem of criteria. Just how does one measure the value of a training program? Although we do not have an answer to this question, a lot of industries seem to think their training programs are worth the money they cost.

Educational Programs for Executives. Educational programs for executives have expanded rapidly until at the present time some quarter-million executives go back to school each year. There are three main ways in which the various programs have been run. First, university schools of business have instituted programs that run for periods of about ten weeks where the executives come and live on the campus. They are taught by the regular faculties and hear lectures by outside experts. Second, there are the company-run institutes, such as the one conducted by General Electric at its own educational center. Here top executives from every G.E. division live together for thirteen weeks; they attend classes together, have their meals together, and sleep in a dormitory. They hear lectures on subjects ranging from geopolitics to economics; they also work on individual projects. Some of the faculty are company executives and some are brought in from university faculties. Most companies with such programs design their curricula around courses closely related to their particular business.

The American Management Association, along with a number of other management-training associations, maintains programs for companies that are too small to run their own show. The training programs last anywhere from five days to several weeks.

In general, these programs cover studies in management principles, the nature of organizations, planning and controlling, and appraisal of operational performance. Some programs set up problem-solving situations where teams of executive students compete in such areas as making decisions on awarding advertising contracts, problems in promotion, and merit rating. Most of the programs include courses or workshops in human relations.

Effects of Training. It is doubtful that we will ever have a monetary measure of education, any time or any place. But the few studies which have been conducted on industrial training of personnel below the executive level give us an indication that we had better not expect too much from *individual* training when the *situational* setting for the person is not improved. We use the research example below for our illustration for two reasons. First, we do not have comparable studies in this area dealing with executive-type personnel. Second, this study emphasizes the point that we need to do some basic research on the effects of executive training.

International Harvester Study. Three investigators have reported on extensive efforts to evaluate a supervisory training program conducted under the supervision of the Personnel Research Board of Ohio State University with the cooperation of the International Harvester Company [9]. This was the first attempt to obtain measures of certain leadership variables both before and after a training session, and then to observe changes in the variables after the foremen returned to their jobs. The two-week training stressed principles of human relations, and made use of role playing, visual aids, group discussion, and lectures.

Prior to the training the foremen were given a Foreman's Leadership Opinion Questionnaire which was designed to measure crucial aspects of leadership. A factor analysis of the instrument indicated that there were two important aspects of leadership; the first, which was labeled "consideration," appeared to be related to friendship, mutual trust, and warmth between the leader and his group; the second, "initiating structure," appears to measure how much the foreman is concerned with "well-defined patterns of organization, channels of communication, and ways of getting the job done."

The day the foremen completed the course they were given the

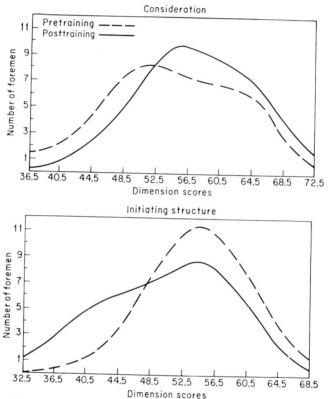

Fig. 9.1. Distribution of scores on the Foreman's Leadership Opinion Questionnaire before and after a course in human relations. The foremen showed an increase in "consideration" (friendship, mutual trust) and a decrease in "initiating structure" (getting job done, communication). (From Fleishman, E. A., Harris, E. F., & Burtt, H. E. *Leadership and supervision in industry: An evaluation of a supervisory training program.* Columbus: Ohio State Univer. Bureau of Education Research, No. 33, 1955.)

instrument again. The scores for consideration and initiating structure are given in Figure 9.1.

As expected, since the course concerned human relations, the foremen showed a general increase in consideration and a decrease in initiating structure. Most research in this area has stopped at this point, with all concerned happily assuming that an enduring change in the foremen's attitudes has been achieved. But Fleishman and his associates asked about the *permanent* effects of the leadership training. These were evaluated in a number of ways.

They compared a group of foremen who had not attended the training school with a group of foremen who had; the latter were divided into sub-samples according to the time elapsed since their training. Contrary to their expectations they found that the most recently trained group were *lower* in consideration behavior than the untrained group, and that some of the trained groups *increased* in initiating structures. These disquieting results were explained partially on the grounds that "the course makes the foreman more concerned with human relations, the whole project makes him more aware of his part as a member of management." Apparently the researchers believed that this resulted in the foreman showing less consideration and more initiation of structure.

The Company Climate. An extensive additional study indicated that the company environment or climate to which the foremen returned was an important variable. The climate was measured by giving each foreman and his boss modifications of the instruments already described. "The results showed that foremen who operated under leadership climates high in consideration scored significantly higher themselves in both consideration attitudes and behavior." The trend for initiating structure was the same.

Fleishman and his associates asked whether it is good for foremen to be high in consideration and less so in initiating structure. Many researchers have simply taken it for granted that the answer is "yes," but the analyses of Fleishman and his associates indicated that the foremen whose workers had the highest morale were the most considerate and were less inclined to initiate structure. The correlations for rated proficiency were variable. Further analysis indicated that much depended on the extent to which a department was under the pressure of a time schedule. In those departments where pressure was high, proficiency and initiating of structure were highly related in a positive way, whereas in the low-urgency departments (the nonproduction departments) proficiency and consideration were positively related.

It was found that the foremen with the higher consideration scores had less absenteeism whereas the opposite was true for initiation of structure. Finally, it was found that there was a tendency for more initiation of structure to go with more grievances.

Leadership and the Social Setting. One of the conclusions drawn from this study is a notable statement which should be impressed on the minds of all those who study leadership. Leadership behavior is not a thing apart but is imbedded in a social setting. In addition, the authors concluded that the ultimate answers as to what kind of leadership is most effective in various settings "may require an evaluation of long-range objectives as contrasted with those of short range."

For our purposes, this study raises some questions about the effects of human relations training. If nothing else, it shows that we must not blithely assume that the training will have the expected effects on the trainee. But this is not to say that all formal executive development is futile, far from it. This study concerned only a human relations training session conducted away from the plant and with lower-level supervisors. In answer to the larger question of whether executive training is justified, we adopt the point of view that executive development is going on all the time, that growth is inevitable. Therefore, the real question is whether we want to proceed willy-nilly or with planning, direction, and support. When the question is put this way it seems quite clear that continued efforts to facilitate desirable development are not only advisable but mandatory.

CONFERENCE GROUPS

Planned work assignments and informal on-the-job training are vital and irreplaceable types of training. Together they include informal instruction, work assignments carefully planned to provide varied and informative experiences, continual observation, extensive opportunity to discuss problems encountered and progress made, and suggestions for ways in which the potential executive can improve himself by the assignment of reading and recommended professional activities.

An important additional type of training involves the structure and operation of the organization—namely, the use of conference groups. The conference method has been widely used in industry. A scheme for the permanent incorporation of conference groups into the organization in such a way that there can be both formal and informal communications between various groups has been proposed by K. E. Moyer. This scheme shows how an organization can use its own structure to provide for continuous executive development [26]. Let us include it here as an example of still another way of giving attention to training.

A diagram of organization structure for "optimal communication and perpetual executive training" is shown in Figure 9.2.

A feature of Moyer's proposal is the way in which horizontal communication between the groups is achieved by means of a junior-management group, composed of selected junior members of the second-echelon groups. These men may be the most outstanding members of their groups or they may be selected by systematic rotation, staggered to minimize disruption of group operation. This group makes recommendations only. (The other groups are responsible for policy at their level and recommend policy to higher levels.) Not only does the junior-management group provide for coordination between the departments at their own level, but as a result of their several perspectives on company problems they are able to provide original, perceptive suggestions to top management.

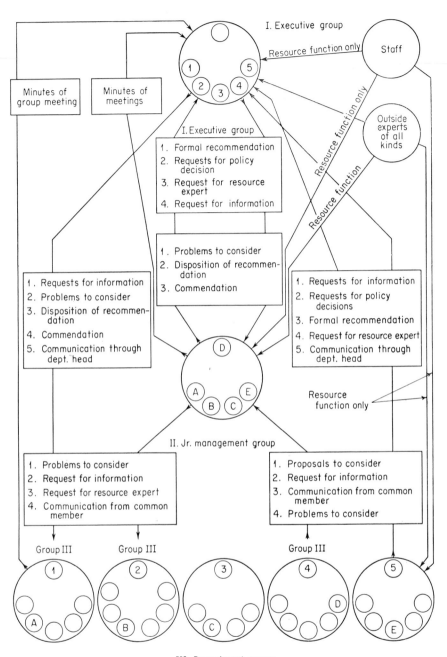

III. Department groups

Fig. 9.2. This schematic diagram for organization structure of optimal communication and perpetual executive training shows how conference groups can be organized, providing for both formal and informal communications between executive, junior management, and department groups. Such schemes enable executives to observe their subordinates actively engaged in problem solving. (From Moyer, K. E. *Conference communication and executive development*. Mimeographed edition, 1959. Pp. 1–41.)

Conference groups provide the potential executive with knowledge of the problems and accomplishments of other departments and give him a broader point of view. By freely participating in the group, he learns to contribute to cooperative problem solving, to respect the opinions of his associates, and, frequently, to see the shortcomings and narrowness of his own point of view. In addition the trainee also learns to express himself cogently and confidently. In the course of analyzing problems he acquires relevant incidental information, such as accounting techniques and labor relations, for example. Such a conference situation provides all the people concerned with an opportunity to get a global view of problems. Conference groups enable executives to observe their subordinates *actively engaged in management problem solving* and provide a source of valuable data on which to base recommendations for promotion.

We suggest that all conference groups be led in a permissive but controlled way; that is to say, let free discussion be encouraged, let no votes be taken, since the objective is to achieve unanimity—but let the leader maintain orderly discussion. The improvement of employee relations, safety, and selection are suggested as initial topics of discussion. After the ice is broken many other problems for discussion will flow to the groups.

KEY TO SUCCESSFUL EXECUTIVE DEVELOPMENT

Currently, executive-development programs consist of planned work assignments, informal on-the-job training, including ideas for self-improvement, and organization aids to development, including formal training classes and conferences. Techniques usually employed incorporate formal lectures with or without visual aids, discussion groups, role playing, and problem solving. Experienced observers report that regardless of its methods and techniques of training, an executive-development program is good and meaningful only in proportion to the degree to which the company is committed to development in general.

If a training program is viewed as a segregated peripheral effort which need not be tied in with the long-term planning and development of the resources of the company, then it may well do more harm than good. What use is there in providing a group of young men with advanced skills and heightened aspirations if their new skills are neither appreciated nor needed and their new aspirations are likely to be frustrated?

DEVELOPMENT: A PROBLEM FOR THE INDIVIDUAL

The primary opportunity for the development and training of a potential executive is in the work assigned to him; how far he gets is up to him. The key man in his development is his immediate superior.

A superior who is mindful of the future needs of his subordinate and also the future needs of the organization can thoughtfully and systematically assign varied and significant tasks providing invaluable experience for the potential executive. It is important to note that this is not variety simply for the sake of variety. Each new assignment must be selected in the light of the developing needs of the candidate; i.e., it should build on previous experiences and prepare him for the next assignment. In addition, each new assignment must enable the candidate to use his growing skills productively. It is said that some companies rationalize assigning men to menial berths by saying that the different experience is good for them. If this is the only motivation for such assignments, then the practice is, of course, indefensible. On the other hand, it is possible that a sympathetic, penetrating analysis of a candidate's record might indicate that, in the case of this particular man, assignment to a menial task would provide a beneficial experience.

It is important to keep good records on the man being groomed for a higher position. A long-range effort such as this requires that a full description of the candidate's development be kept, including statements of the reasons which motivated his assignments, summaries of experiences and skills acquired, and constructive evaluations of his performances.

It is likewise important that the motivation for development originate in the potential executive himself. The company can provide opportunities, aids, incentives, and, initially, direction. To be fully effective in the long run, however, the guidance of the development process should subtly shift, as time passes, from the organization to the individual.

Portrait of a Successful Executive. The successful executive is usually completely immersed in his work; he identifies himself totally with the organization. At the same time, however, there are many other demands on his time and energy. He is frequently called upon to participate in community work, and he probably has strong family ties. There is, therefore, almost inevitable conflict among his roles, resulting in cross pressures, frustrations, and feelings of guilt and self-incrimination.

The conflict is intensified by many factors. There are the ample monetary awards and status symbols with which the executive's services are purchased. There is, however, no specified contractual relationship between an executive's compensation and the number of hours he works. Surely most executives must feel an obligation to devote a supernormal amount of their time and energy to their work.

Long hours and hard work do not in themselves cause breakdowns. It is probably true, within limits, that hard work never killed anyone. It appears to be the conflict and consequent tension which results from these demands which exhaust an executive, as is the case with many people in lesser positions.

Another problem is that many executives, particularly lower-level executives, are deprived of the security and support which a stable and settled community life provides. A transferral every two or three years obviously precludes the establishment of deep roots in the community. The frequently moving executive becomes adroit at establishing himself and his family quickly, but his ties are at the same time kept fluid and superficial [42].

As a consequence of the factors mentioned above, as well as other stresses in any executive's life, it is no wonder that so-called "executive breakdowns" are not infrequent. An executive is no different from a worker so far as his needs are concerned. In fact, his needs are no doubt more elaborate and intense than those of company employees who have less responsibility.

Frequently, the executive is viewed as a tower of strength who can adapt to any situation, but he too can be discharged without warning, or transferred to a distant office on a moment's notice, or capriciously shuffled in the organization, or expected to reject all noncompany interests, or humiliated by his superior. It may be true that good executives can withstand all such strains; in fact, at present we tend to define the term "good executive" as one who can withstand the strains. The question is, "Are these strains necessary and desirable?" The answer seems clear. Surely even the hardiest individuals are not as effective under these conditions as they would be otherwise. We need not, however, lose the services of those executives who cannot function effectively in such an environment. Let us add to the several skills stressed in executive selection and development programs one other: the skill of being able to practice good personal adjustments.

SUGGESTIONS FOR FURTHER READING

Barnard, C. I. *The functions of the executive.* Cambridge, Mass.: Harvard Univer. Press, 1951. A classic effort to conceptualize the role of the executive systematically. Not an elementary book, quite provocative.

Dalton, M. *Men who manage.* New York: Wiley, 1959. A provocative book on the dynamics of the industrial environment.

Elliott, O. *Men at the top.* New York: Harper, 1959. A popular account of some of the problems of the executive.

Gibb, C. A. Leadership. In G. Lindzey (Ed.), *Handbook of social psychology.* Vol. II. Reading, Mass.: Addison-Wesley, 1954. A view of leadership within a framework of interaction theory.

Shartle, C. L. *Executive performance and leadership.* Englewood Cliffs, N.J.: Prentice-Hall, 1956. A comprehensive account of the many problems of studying the executive.

10

ATTITUDES, JOB SATISFACTIONS, AND INDUSTRIAL MORALE

B. von Haller Gilmer

What does the worker want from his job? How do benefits influence his feelings about his job? How do attitudes affect the amount and quality of production? These and similar questions were raised in various ways in the preceding chapters dealing with human needs, personnel selection and training, supervision, and leadership. Here we shall pull together the several aspects of what people think about their jobs in terms of the *feelings* they have. An extensive review of nearly two thousand writings on research and opinion about job attitudes was recently completed by the Psychological Service of Pittsburgh [13]. From this study came the conclusion that there is an urgent need in industry for a better understanding of the attitudes of people—both managers and workers—toward their jobs. Understanding feelings provides a base for interpreting a number of problems we shall discuss in later chapters dealing with labor relations, work, and individual and social adjustments.

PROBLEMS AND DEFINITIONS

Industrial leaders are becoming increasingly aware of the discrepancy between our technological success in creating the machinery for production of goods and services and our understanding and dealings with the people who operate and manage these modern tools of production. On the practical side, the review made by the Psychological Service states the over-all problem clearly:

Much can be gained by employees, their supervisors, and top management by stress on "effective" attitudes. Often this stress is carried out with the best of intentions in "human relations problems." However, "human relations" is not something that can be accepted or rejected perhaps according to budgetary considerations. Human relations exist in every organization whether they are planned or not. Planning a "program" for special consideration of human relations is greatly underestimating the extent of the effects of human relations problems *at all times*. Such programs are frequently "over-institutionalized" in that they are installed as a matter of course, a matter of fad, or a matter of display. Instead, human relations must be considered as a matter of policy affecting organizational decisions in the same way as other administrative policies. . . . The need for human relations considerations is a continuing one affecting the organization at all times.

The terms "employee attitude," "job satisfaction," and "industrial morale" are in many instances used interchangeably. Blum [3], however, has made the point that they are not synonymous. An attitude may contribute to job satisfaction since the latter is comprised of a number of attitudes. Similarly, job satisfaction is not the same as industrial morale, although it may contribute to morale.

Job attitude is the feeling the employee has about his job, his readiness to react in one way or another to specific factors related to a job. *Job satisfaction* or *dissatisfaction* is the result of various attitudes the person holds toward his job, toward related factors, and toward life in general. *Industrial morale* is generated by the group. For the individual it is a feeling of being accepted by and belonging to a group of employees through adherence to common goals. In a company, industrial morale is the composite expression of the attitudes of the various individuals in the company.

In this chapter, we shall discuss the ways that attitudes are determined, the extent of job satisfaction and dissatisfaction in representative industries, the factors related to attitudes, and the dimensions of good morale.

INFORMATION ABOUT ATTITUDES

We all have attitudes which govern our tendencies to react positively or negatively to people, to things, to situations. We like, or dislike, our work in different ways and in different degrees. Our morale may be good or bad depending on the adequacy with which a group functions in carrying out its purposes. Management has several ways of getting information about employee attitudes.

Formal Communication Channels. Higher management depends extensively upon the analyses of foremen and other supervisors to evaluate what the worker thinks. Such reports appear to be a normal method for trying to find out about employee attitudes. Unfortunately, in many places they are an unreliable source of information. The expressions of attitudes are screened on the way up, and false ideas are fostered. Bellows [2] reports that many foremen do not know how to handle men in the first place; hence, how can they effectively interpret workers' feelings? In one study, he found that one-fourth of the foremen felt that the best way to handle tough men was to be tougher than they were, and that about 40 per cent of the supervisors erroneously believed that workers were little interested in what others thought of their job so long as the pay was good. Few workers ever see top management. If they depend on their supervisors to interpret how they feel, one can readily see that there is little chance of an objective evaluation of job satisfaction through the normal communication channels.

Grapevine Channels. Rumored attitudes are a part of all organizations. However, the information that rumors carry becomes altered and often distorted as it makes its upward movement. More dangerous still are the attitudes communicated by the grapevine, for they may reflect only the extremes. Within this structure, attitudes of the majority of the workers never get impartially expressed.

Behavior Manifestations. Griping on the job, slowdowns, early quits, and excessive absenteeism are true revealers of attitudes, but they come too late. By the time such manifestations are evidenced, damage has been done. All too frequently, however, in some companies this is the only way information about employee attitudes is communicated.

Interviewing. Talking with people has long been used as a means of getting at attitudes. In the guided interview, there is the attempt to get answers to predetermined questions. This is in contrast to the unguided interview where the employee is encouraged to talk about anything he wishes. In the counseling interview and the exit interview, attitudes may also be uncovered.

The Questionnaire. The questionnaire technique is most economical and has certain advantages of objectivity of measurement providing for a quantitative treatment of responses. Answers may be gotten through check lists, multiple-choice questions, yes-no answers. Space for write-in comments is sometimes included on questionnaire forms. In order to provide for complete anonymity, some blanks have holes that can be punched, or some have a tear ballot where one can tear the appropriate arrowhead to indicate an answer. Various attitude scales have been used in practical ways to determine employee feelings.

THE EXTENT AND NATURE OF JOB DISSATISFACTION

The average figure of job dissatisfaction found in varying industries is around 13 per cent. Age as a factor here has been shown from twenty-three studies. In general, job satisfaction is high among young workers but tends to go down during the first few years of employment. The low point is reached when workers are in their middle and late twenties, or early thirties. Then it increases steadily until a temporary middle-age revolt sets in (see page 93). Initial enthusiasm for work is apparent among the younger group, but any failure to get ahead lowers job satisfaction for a period. Gradually, really dissatisfied workers are weeded out, and the rest struggle to survive and move ahead. In late middle age, positive attitudes toward the job are found in the man with seniority [13].

The Dissatisfied Worker. There is considerable evidence that job dissatisfaction is often associated with generalized maladjustment of some kind. People who are dissatisfied with their jobs are less outgoing and friendly, are more emotionally unbalanced, and show more boredom, daydreaming, and general discontent than do their satisfied coworkers.

The dissatisfied worker finds it difficult to adjust to arbitrary standards of work or to rigid requirements of the employer. For example, in one study of nearly 1,400 workers, in seven different occupations, it was found that people dissatisfied with their jobs had levels of aspiration far exceeding their levels of ability and opportunity [21].

Occupation Level. The literature review of almost two thousand articles reports the unequivocal fact that the higher the level of occupation, the higher the level of job satisfaction. One study, conducted on a large national sample, showed that 25 per cent of unskilled workers were dissatisfied with their jobs compared with 0 per cent of businessmen. Sustained job-interest studies have shown that professional people lead the list in degree of job satisfaction, that salaried workers are next, and that factory workers are least interested in their jobs.

Follow-up studies of college graduates show that dissatisfaction is directly related to income. Often it is more a matter of comparative incomes that affects feelings than the absolute rate of pay. It has been discovered that among executives in the middle-pay bracket, the best morale is found in small companies. This apparently is due to the fact that middle-management executives in the small company are not isolated either from the workers or from decision-making top management.

It is not at all uncommon to find low job satisfaction among workers in the lower social strata where family ties are weak, housing is substandard, and the opportunities for achieving stable work habits are limited. Such habits as shiftlessness, irresponsibility, and lack of ambition are normal responses which the worker has learned from his physical and social environment [8]. The well-educated girl from a professional family may scorn a job as a waitress whereas someone from a lower social class may be happy with it. There is considerable evidence that the attitude people have toward their jobs is more than just an individual matter; it is related to the value system of the class.

JOB-FACTOR COMPARISONS

Many studies concerned with job attitudes have dealt with what the worker wants from his job. Table 4 gives a list of ten job factors in order according to the number of times each was mentioned in about 150 studies. Under each heading are listed the specific aspects of the job factors. In Figure 10.1 the importance of factors in employee attitudes is shown graphically.

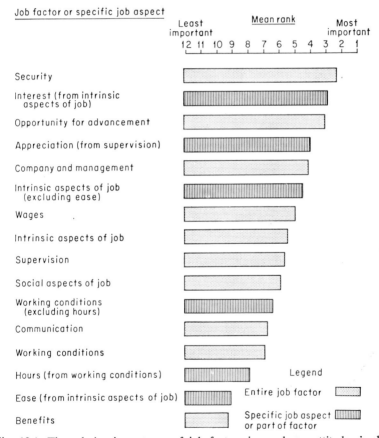

Fig. 10.1. The relative importance of job factors in employee attitudes is shown graphically. Here is an over-all comparative view of what the worker wants from his job. (From Herzberg, F., Mausner, B., Peterson, R. O., & Capwell, D. F. *Job attitudes: Review of research and opinion.* Pittsburgh: Psychological Service of Pittsburgh, 1957.)

TABLE 4

SPECIFIC JOB ASPECTS OF THE TEN MAJOR FACTORS

Intrinsic Aspects of Job

Appropriateness to training and preparation and abilities
Appropriateness to aspirations and plans
Opportunity for learning knowledge and skills
Pride in accomplishment and workmanship
Prestige, status, dignity, importance, respect, power
Recognition, public and private, appreciation, fame
Self-respect
Public service, altruism
Service to company
Personal contacts with outsiders
Contacts with management
Freedom and independence of research, action, and planning
Well-defined work project and duties
Creativity and self-expression
Opportunity to participate in decisions
Responsibility and authority
Initiative
Challenge
Thought and attention
Interest
Variety or repetition, specialization
Ease
Opportunity for travel
Opportunity for mobility
Personal convenience and preference
Appeal and desirability of work
Effects on health
Adventure
Tension and pressure
Work load and routine demands, distribution of work
Speed requirements
Distasteful job duties

Supervision

Foremanship
Consideration, fairness
Courtesy, tact
Proper evaluation
Information on status and progress
Appreciation
Credit, recognition, praise

Keeping promises, sincerity
Cooperation
Encouragement
Understanding, empathic ability
Ability to handle people
Opportunity for employee decision making
Sociability
Availability for assistance and consultation
Loyalty to workers
Permissiveness, closeness
Personal counsel
Delegation of authority
Manner of criticism and discipline
Consistency of orders, discipline, etc.
Technical competence and aptitude

Working Conditions

Attractive surroundings
Clean and orderly workplace
Adequacy and condition of equipment, supplies, and tools
Lighting
Temperature and ventilation
Absence of smoke, noise, excessive heat, odors
Safety conditions
Music
Recreational, food facilities
Medical facilities
Parking facilities
Geographical location and community
Hours

Wages

Pay, income, salary, earnings
Economic factors, motives, values
Economic advantages
Profit
Wage satisfaction
Financial adjustment
Profit sharing
Frequency of raises
Enough to live on
Fairness or equitableness of compensation

Opportunity for Advancement

Advancement on merit
Advancement on seniority

TABLE 4 (*Continued*)

Professional advancement
Economic advancement
Advancement in social position
Aspiration or ambition in relation to advancement
Merit system of advancement, etc.
Promotion from within the company
Promotion policies

Security

Steadiness of employment
Company stability
Continuous work prospects
Self-adequacy
Seniority
Feeling of being valued by firm
Having a trade
Opportunity to learn trade, job, skills, career
Influences of political processes on government positions

Company and Management

Company attitude toward and cooperation with labor unions
Company sponsorship of athletic teams, employee home development, candidates for city government, playgrounds
Contributions to charities
Interpreted fairness, intentions, and good sense of management
Administration cooperation and assistance
Company procedures and policy
Pride in company and product
Company interest in individual worker
Company training program
Meeting of company obligation

Structure of organization
Size of organization
Company reputation and public relations
Management's foresight and planning

Social Aspects of Job

Congenial coworkers, on or off the job
Social approval
Interpersonal relationships
Group dynamics
Team balance
Cooperation and group effort
Size and functions of work groups
Pride in belonging to team, belongingness
Pride in team accomplishments
Inter- and intradepartment relations
Department reputation
Competent coworkers
Prejudices

Communication

Information of employee as to status
Information on new developments
Information on what company is doing
Information on personnel policies, procedures
Information on company lines of authority
Suggestion systems
Instructions and orders
Annual report
Company magazine, newspaper

Benefits

Retirement provisions
Provision for emergencies: illness, accidents, etc.
Leave, vacations, holidays

SOURCE: Herzberg, F., Mausner, B., Peterson, R. O., Capwell, D. F. *Job attitudes: Review of research and opinion.* Pittsburgh: Psychological Service of Pittsburgh, 1957.

EFFECTS OF ATTITUDES ON PRODUCTIVITY

Within the past thirty years, the writings in the area of worker productivity have shown a shift from an emphasis on wage incentives and environmental working conditions to an emphasis on human relations. This shift is due, in part, to the fact that working conditions and wages have been improved in recent years. Mainly, however, industry leaders are finding that there is another important side to the economic man. A poll of the executives of several hundred companies emphasized that business leaders are beginning to realize how important worker attitudes are.

Work and Attitudes. Do attitudes affect the amount and quality of work production? This is an involved question. What are the facts? In 1957, twenty-six studies were cited in which some quantitative relationship between productivity and job attitudes in a variety of jobs had been measured [13]. Fourteen of these studies found that workers with positive job attitudes showed higher productivity than those with negative attitudes; for nine studies, there was no relationship; and in three studies, workers with positive job attitudes actually showed poorer production records than those with negative attitudes. The contradictions in these studies may be due in part to differences in the research methods involved, or in the workers surveyed, or in their work situations. One basic consideration is that high productivity accompanies high morale only when the attitudes of the work group favor maximum output. This is particularly true when the work group is very cohesive, when the atmosphere is friendly, and when belonging to that specific work group is highly desirable to its members. A group of this kind can either restrict or raise output independently of the degree to which its members are satisfied with their jobs.

The findings of studies relating attitudes to job turnover and absenteeism are in general in agreement. Twenty-one of twenty-four studies cited in the literature report that workers with positive job attitudes have less turnover and absenteeism than workers with negative attitudes [13].

Two studies report no effects, and one study showed workers with positive job attitudes as having more turnover. Wickert [30] has shed some light on the problem in his investigation of telephone company employees. He found that those who quit their jobs felt they are less personally involved in these jobs than those who stayed; they left, in part, because they had had no chance to help make decisions, and they felt they had not contributed to the success of the company. Another investigator found virtually the same thing with bricklayers and carpenters who were less likely to leave their jobs when they were given some say-so in the composition of their work groups [28].

It has been found that the critical employee is not always a poorer producer than the uncritical one, but the preponderance of evidence adds up to the position that workers with positive job attitudes outproduce workers with negative job attitudes when the psychological climates favor high production, where there is good supervision, and where the employee really wants to produce and get ahead.

Aspiration and Productivity. Morse [20] has made the point that employee satisfaction is a function not only of how much a person receives from the job situation, but also of where he stands with respect to his level of aspiration. When the environment provides little possibility for need satisfaction, those people with the strongest desires, or highest aspirations, will be the least happy. Or as she has put it another way, "The greater the amount the individual gets, the greater his satisfaction, and, at the same time, the more the individual still desires, the less his satisfaction." From her interview studies of white-collar clerical workers and supervisors, she makes the point that if an employee is in a situation where he is not making any decisions, *and does not want to make any,* he will tend to be highly or moderately satisfied with his work, but if he is not making any decision, *and would like to make some,* he will tend to derive little satisfaction from his job.

With satisfaction seen then as a function of both the strength of needs in a particular area and the amount of "environmental return," we can see how education increases the strength of needs for pay and for job status. This factor is of vital consideration to the college student in planning his career. As the person grows older, the need for pay and job status increases. This can lead to job dissatisfaction when the discrepancy between levels of aspiration and possibilities of attainment gets too great.

THE PSYCHOLOGICAL CLIMATE FOR WORK

The social aspects of the job-work groups, leadership, and organization of the company all add up to a psychological climate for the person to work in (see page 48). It is known, for example, that work groups which are cohesive, which have a sort of pride in the group, have higher morale than those which are not cohesive. However, it appears to be substantiated that high morale is not always associated with high productivity. Why? In part, we will get an answer to this question as we take a look at the complexities of how people work together or fail to work together.

Informal Group Structures. Logically, we may think that all people are ambitious, but they are not. We may think that people are motivated to keep accidents from happening; statistics show otherwise. We may think that work which is planned for convenience and efficiency will be accepted by the work groups, but experience sometimes proves otherwise.

Both the formal and the informal structures of an organization, as we indicated in Chapter 3, can be described by the roles that the people play, by the ways in which they communicate, and by the final decisions that are made. Formal structures are, of course, the official way a company is organized. Informal organizations, on the other hand, result from friendships, car pools, nearness of workplaces, community interests, union associations, and the like.

Kinds of Informal Organizations. Brown [4], writing on the social psychology of industry, describes three kinds of informal organizations. First, we find the formation of groups based on some issue. For example, a revolt in the ranks of the United Steel Workers lined up people for and against existing policy-making groups. Second, we have the clique, which, for example, may be based on a common workplace or on the sharing of some common task. The formation of a group consisting of intimate friends constitutes a third kind of informal organization. How these groups interact determines the morale of an organization to a large extent and often serves as the key element in productivity. Many informal groups have leaders who may actually set production norms. The real power of these informal groups was first adequately observed in the Hawthorne studies. These

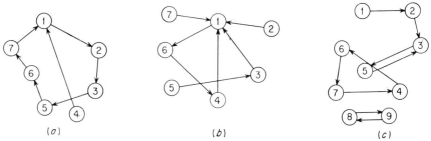

Fig. 10.2. These sociograms represent one way to portray communication between people graphically: (*a*) a cohesive group without a strong leader as contrasted to (*b*) one with a strong leader, and (*c*) an unstructured group with cliques, isolates, and mutual admiration societies. (From Blum, M. L. *Industrial psychology and its social foundation.* New York: Harper, 1956.)

studies pointed out that such devices as trading jobs, helping one another, talking, engaging in horseplay, and teasing were all prohibited by management rules; but the foremen did little more than wink at them. As a matter of fact, some studies have shown a high degree of labor turnover in jobs where there was little opportunity for conversation among workers.

On mass-production jobs in the automobile industry, one investigator has explained low job satisfaction among the workers on the basis of the lack of social contact due to the impersonal pressure of the assembly line. A number of findings have revealed that work situations in which the formation of informal work groups is inhibited are not conducive to optimal employee morale.

The Sociogram. The sociogram was developed by Moreno in the early thirties to describe relations among people. This unique instrument offers a graphic way to look at communication. One can see how these "who works with" structures can have a bearing on morale, either at the worker level or at the management level [19]. Let us illustrate some patterns these relationships can take.

Figure 10.2 shows kinds of sociograms found among workers (modified after Blum [3]). A diagram of a cohesive group without a strong leader is

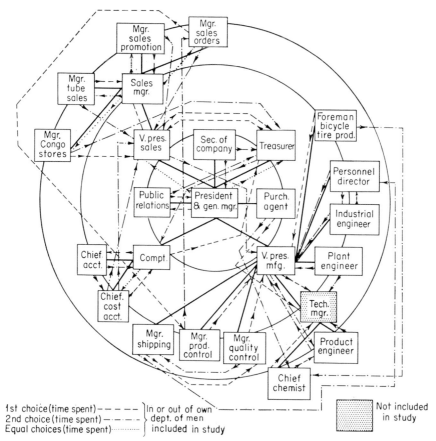

1st choice(time spent) – – – – ⎤ In or out of own
2nd choice(time spent) –·–·–·– ⎬ dept. of men
Equal choices(time spent)········· ⎦ included in study

Not included in study

Fig. 10.3. This sociometric pattern for the Congo Tire and Rubber Company is the result of a study of twenty-four executives who were asked to report with whom they spent the most time in the course of business. Note that the "choices" center around the vice-presidents for manufacturing and sales and the treasurer. (From Browne, C. G. Executive leadership in business. IV. Sociometric patterns. *J. Appl. Psychol.*, 1951, 35, 34–37.)

shown in (*a*). The sociogram of a group with a strong leader is represented in (*b*). An unstructured group with cliques, isolates, and mutual admiration societies is shown in (*c*).

Figure 10.3 shows a sociogram of a group as found at the management level in a rubber company by Browne [5].

ORGANIZATIONS AND MORALE

The manipulation of the variables affecting morale in a "live" business organization has certain limitations as to experimental control. Hence, why not build a miniature organization in the laboratory? True, such laboratory experimentation has limitations when it comes to relating results to real organizations. But the laboratory situation holds the advantage of manipulating one variable at a time, and it is possible to get at some of the relatively isolated factors operating in job satisfaction.

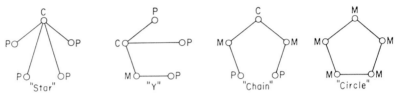

Fig. 10.4. Four communication nets show how the group is hung together. In the "star" the men on the periphery send information to the central person, who then transmits answers back. In the "chain" middlemen are interposed between the center and the periphery. The "Y" network combines the "star" and the "chain." Problem solving is more difficult in the noncentralized "circle" network. (After Leavitt, H. J. Some effects of certain communication patterns on group performance. *J. Abnorm. Soc. Psychol.*, 1951, 46, 38–50.)

Laboratory Studies. In a series of laboratory experiments [1, 11, 25, 27] answers were sought to such questions as:

¶ What difference does it make in an organization if communication is limited to certain channels?
¶ How will the morale and performance of an individual member be affected by the centrality of the position he occupies?
¶ What is it about a central position in an organization that is so satisfying?
¶ Does the position of "autonomy" affect job satisfaction in the individual?

Communication networks were established where subjects in any one group were seated around a circular table separated from each other by radial partitions which extended out so that the subjects could not see each other. They communicated by means of written notes passed through slots in the partitions. The communication network of any group was controlled by having some slots open and others closed. Problems were provided by the experimenter. The groups developed their own system of pooling information and working out answers.

The drawings in Figure 10.4 represent the "organizations" or different groups. In the "star" group all information is sent to a central person who then transmits the answer back to each individual member. In the "chain" network the information is sent by the end men, the men on the periphery (P), to the middle men (M), and then in turn to the man in the center (C). The "Y" network is a combination of the "star" and the "chain." The "circle" network lacks centralized organization; thus problem solving is made more difficult. In such a network, pieces of information could bounce around for some time before someone accumulated all of them and took the leadership in sending out answers.

Results of the experimentation showed, first, that for efficiency in problem solving the "star" and "Y" nets did better than the "chain" and "circle." Second, the members differed both within and across nets in the amount of satisfaction derived from their jobs in the group, and in the amount of status accorded them by other group members, as measured later by questionnaire. Even in these experimental situations, devoid of much reality, the persons occupying central positions expressed greater job satisfaction and were seen as having higher status than the occupants of middle positions. The latter, in turn, expressed more satisfaction than the occupants of the peripheral positions.

Satisfaction of Individual Needs. The descriptions above represent only a few of the experiments on this problem. As far as job satisfaction is concerned, they add up to the following conclusions:

1. A central position in a communication net usually has associated with it a larger amount of autonomy. Its occupant can decide for himself what to do next. The person on the periphery has to be *told* what to do. In our culture, at least, being able to decide for oneself what to do is more satisfying than having to be told.

2. Being autonomous has more effect on satisfaction than does merely being central.

3. In positions where the person is in a position of being both central and autonomous, satisfaction is highest.

4. Members of the groups whose personalities (measured before the experiment) showed strong psychological needs to be independent were more dissatisfied with positions of low autonomy than were members who had weaker independence needs.

Why do people get together in certain groupings, derive satisfaction from belonging to a particular group, and leave it only with reluctance? It is here that the *individual* finds a climate suitable to his individual needs where other members of the group help him satisfy his desires for recognition and status, his feelings of being wanted, and most of all, his feelings of security. When these needs *in the individual* members of the group are satisfied, group cohesiveness produces high morale, and, in turn, high productivity, especially where leadership and company loyalty are also a positive part of the psychological climate. When there is good reason for suspicion, the group can sometimes limit production *and* get by with doing so. A good example of this can be found in the Hawthorne series of studies [23].

Group Behavior. In the Bank Wiring Observation Room study, an observer was placed in the room to record as much as possible of the group's behavior as the people worked at wiring, soldering, and inspecting switchboard banks. In due course of time it became apparent that the men had become distrustful of the observer. The informal structure of the group began to operate. They set a low standard of output, which was rigorously enforced by group pressures. The men worked hard in the morning and early afternoon until they had reached their "informal quota." From then on, the day was filled in with trivial work, helping the slower fellow worker. Social pressure was exerted on the chiselers to maintain their quota by stepping up their work; it was exerted on the rate busters to slow it down.

A number of studies of rate busters have been reported in which it has been shown that the work group can close ranks against these deviates. Dalton [7], in a study of the individual rate buster, describes him as a person who is relatively maladjusted socially and unable to gain acceptance in the work group on a personal basis. Another writer has found that highly cohesive groups tend to enforce the group standard of productivity more rigorously than do less cohesive groups, but high productivity results only where the attitude toward the company is favorable [24].

Resistance to Change. There is some tendency, both within and without industry, for people to resist change, even though the change may be best for the individual or for the group. As simple a situation as introducing safety devices on machines to prevent accidents has even caused strikes among workers where the devices necessitated changes in work habits.

One investigator describes how a wage-incentive system was introduced into an automobile factory without any explanation of the reasons for it, or of the results it was supposed to produce [12]. The plan was a failure. Others tell of the failure to increase production in coal mines by changing from technical obsolescence to the use of modern machinery which had been shown to be effective in other mines. The workers not only resisted verbally, but they failed to produce with any appreciable change in output. The modern machinery caused the men to lose identification with their jobs. They had not been consulted about the change, and therefore, they were not conditioned to accept it [26].

In a somewhat similar situation in a textile plant, a proposed change in production operations was put to the workers *as a problem.* The workers themselves, thus being involved in a solution affecting them, accepted the change. The workers also increased their productivity during the course of the problem solving [22].

EMPLOYEE PARTICIPATION

There are numerous illustrations of how participation on the part of employees can help bring about their adjustment to changing conditions. People tend to support what they help to create. Let us describe one such situation in a small manufacturing company in southwest Virginia where psychologists had virtually a free hand in trying out the principle of participation.

The experiments are described by Marrow and French [17] and Coch and French [6], who participated in the projects. In this particular plant, a long-standing prejudice existed among supervisors against hiring older female workers. Exhortation from higher management and from the psychologists did not shake this prejudice. But when the supervisors met in small groups to discuss the problem and their own attitudes, they arrived at the conclusion that their attitudes had been wrong. More important, they changed their hiring practices.

Again in this plant situation, a problem of a different sort of resistance to change was met. The company had especially severe turnover problems among workers who were forced to transfer from one job task to another because of changing market conditions. Many of these workers quit shortly after the retraining started or before they had attained competence at their new jobs. The retraining became a slow and costly process.

Through cooperation with top management, the psychologists set up a controlled experiment. Work groups were established. They were briefed on the problem and asked to plan how the factory could adapt to shifts in the market and in technology. By group discussion, these workers soon arrived at the conclusion that their own retraining was necessary, and they launched into it. Turnover dropped practically to zero, training time was decreased, and the change was made more smoothly. With a control group the picture was different. They were merely told that a change in their job was necessary and that they would have to be retrained for a new job. This group showed high turnover and a longer, more costly training period. Subsequently, this no-participation group was reassembled for participation in the decision-making process. Figure 10.5 summarizes the results, contrasting the response of this group to retraining when they did participate and when they did not participate in the change.

These studies are dramatic, but they also raise a practical question: Is our problem just one of "get in there and participate?" A large-scale survey of General Motors employees indicates that workers do wish to be involved in day-to-day decisions [14]. In this study, it was found that workers' attitudes toward both the company and the union are strongly affected by the degree to which foremen and shop stewards welcome the participation of the worker. The workers will show a strong attachment to the company if the degree of participation they feel in the decision making with the foreman is more than the participation they have with the shop steward. Since, however, the shop steward is himself a worker, participation is often easier at the union level. Loyalty comes with feelings of participation. Other writers maintain that participation in decision making is a major factor in the morale of all levels of employees.

Lawrence [16] points up that participation is not something which can be conjured up or created artificially. You cannot buy it as you would buy a typewriter. You cannot hire industrial engineers to put it in. Participation will not work so long as it is treated as a device to get somebody else to do what you want him to do. Real participation is based on respect; it is acquired when the staff man faces the reality that he needs the contributions of the operating people.

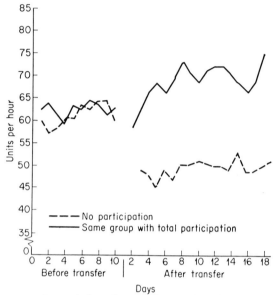

Fig. 10.5. A comparison of the effect of "no participation" with "total participation" on the same group in a decision-making process. Measurements were made in terms of work output in relation to transferral from one job task to another. (From Coch, L., and French, J. R. P., Jr. Overcoming resistance to change. *Hum. Relat.,* 1948, 1, 512–532.)

Four Dimensions of Morale. One of the big problems faced by the staff psychologist, or the consulting psychologist in industry, is to deal with the gimmick-minded manager who is looking for quick, easy answers. The building up of good morale is a complex process. The vast amount of experimental research in this area carried on at the Survey Research Center of the University of Michigan has led Katz [15] to offer four dimensions of morale:

1. Morale involves intrinsic job satisfaction.
2. Morale involves pride in the work group.
3. Morale involves satisfaction with wages and promotional opportunities.
4. Morale involves identification with the company.

There is much evidence to support the position that both attitudes and productivity of employees are geared to the quality of supervision. The morale of the first-line supervisor himself, however, is often neglected. As a foreman, he doesn't belong to the worker group, and often he is not fully accepted as a part of management. He wants to participate in management functions with his supervisor, who in turn wants the same thing from his superior, and so on up the ladder. At all levels in the industrial organization, we find that morale in its simplest terms involves the *feelings* of people.

WORK ENVIRONMENT AND MORALE

What of the feelings of people who are exposed to working conditions deleterious to man's well-being? This is a problem of increasing concern in this day of rapidly advancing technology. Can people be found who will be willing to work in high-noise-level areas around jet aircraft and guided missiles? What about absenteeism and turnover among workers whose jobs can possibly cause illness or even death? Are other factors in the work environment more displeasing to the man than physical discomfort? Are there positive factors in a job situation which counterbalance the negative factors?

Morale and Working Conditions—An Experiment. A recent series of studies has been made of the morale of workers exposed to high levels of occupational noise and other undesirable work conditions. These studies, reported by Felton and Spencer [9], indicate two important things. First, in this day of technological change more attention than ever needs to be given to the scientific selection of people for hazardous jobs; consideration must be given to both their technical skills and their ability to work with others. Second, in the evaluation of worker morale it is very important to know the psychological conditions of work before predicting that bad physical work conditions per se will cause low morale.

The investigation was made at Tinker Air Force Base in Oklahoma, a jet plane base, where the noise exposure was at times as high as 140 decibels (db). (For comparison, a pneumatic drill has a loudness level of 80 db, a boiler factory, around 100 db, and loud thunder, around 120 db. A level of 140 db can induce severe pain). In control rooms the noise levels were around 88 db; in the ready room the level reached 109 db; inside the test cell one jet engine at idle speed reached 119 db. The maintenance of jet aircraft just prior to flight reached 140 db. In this study, however, no subjects were exposed to these painful levels at 140 db. The subjects were aware, however, that even medium-range intensities could be a hazard to health.

The problem was simply to determine whether a high degree of morale can be maintained around intense noise, and if so, why? Some previous work of Miles [18], made aboard an aircraft carrier, showed that maintenance and other personnel engaged in servicing and operating jet planes are efficient in their work and willing to continue in their jobs, even without using earplugs.

The Air Force study was planned so that 100 jet-engine testers could be studied and compared with 100 welders and grinders. The two groups worked under different environmental conditions. The engine testers worked as a team under bad physical conditions. The welders and grinders worked in isolation under less severe physical conditions. The groups were matched for age, race, sex, pay status, and length of service. The experimental design of the study included personal interviews, environmental noise measurements, psychological tests, sociometric investigations, and reviews of absence due to illness, injury experience, and frequency of visits to the industrial medical dispensaries on the base.

The noise to which the experimental engine-tester group was exposed reached a maximum of 119 db. The control group (the welders and grinders) worked in a much less intense noise area of 76 db, about the average of factory noise. The skill requirements of the workers were classified as repetitive, average, and diversified, and the "social geography" of the jobs was identified. About three-fourths of the workers had received only a high school education, most of them were born in the state, and they were in the middle-age range.

In the personal interviews the workers were encouraged to talk about their social contacts and their attitudes toward each other, as well as about their jobs. Sociograms were developed which described a knowledge of the group structure, the leaders and dominant figures, the integration and cleavages, the clique formations, the amount of social interaction, and the hierarchical status of each member.

The experimental group (engine testers), because of the very nature of their jobs, was highly integrated; cohesiveness among them was intense. There was just no place for isolates on the test teams. The job requirements were diversified. On the other hand, the welders and grinders operated alone. They worked in booths, behind protective eyewear, and completed a work assignment on a single engine part. To them, their work seemed unrelated to the engine as a whole. Their jobs, although requiring some skill, were quite repetitive.

The results of the study showed *very high morale* among the engine testers, although these workers were exposed to levels of noise not far below the threshold of pain. The welders and grinders were found to have *low morale*, although their noise-environment level was no more than that of the average factory. Why the difference in morale?

Among the engine testers there was common motivation: the group goals were to turn out good engines which could be sold to the inspector. "Selling an engine" meant protecting a pilot's life, building a stronger air force, and making a better country. Leaving the men to work out the details of procedure, supervisors gave the assignments to the workers in groups, but stood by to offer help when needed. Since these workers felt an over-all satisfaction at accomplishing something worthwhile, they complained very little about the unpleasant features of the work situation. There was little or no complaint about the exposure to noise and outside temperatures or about the job being greasy and the area slippery. Little was said about the ever-present vibrations, the threat of engine explosions, and the potential danger of hearing loss. Complaints stemmed not from the work per se or from the physical environment. They came from such things as favoritism, inequities in giving raises, ratings, overtime, loan-outs, and demotions.

In short, these engine testers had to work together. Cooperation was basic to getting the job done. The purpose of their job was clear to them, the work itself was tangible, concrete, and easily grasped.

The welders and grinders were physically separated; the work was individual and repetitive and required no cooperative effort in any way. Many of the workers were found to be isolates or near isolates. Their morale was found to be low. Complaints from these men were numerous and centered around their isolation, their being dealt with arbitrarily, or their being discriminated against. They described their work as strenuous, unhealthful, nerve-racking, and fatiguing. They expressed deep feelings of job insecurity. For the most part the sociogram of these people demonstrated a sparseness of friendship choices, tenuous connections. The grinders in particular expressed no satisfaction in their jobs. There was no ego involvement or identification with the work. Although the physical hazards involved in the grinding work were of less potential danger than those involved in engine testing, the dangers here were mentioned more frequently. There were many complaints about dust, flying steel particles, impaired illumination, eyestrain, and standing; and believe it or not, these workers complained far more about noise than did the more cohesive group of engine testers.

Although most of the welders and grinders were highly dissatisfied with their jobs, a small minority were found to have a high morale. These were a group of nine welders who were found to belong to an informal clique. Although their jobs were separated, they got together at lunch and at other times. There was no common goal for these men such as that which existed among the well-integrated engine-testers group. Their clique had a clear status hierarchy dominated by a few individuals, but nevertheless this group complained far less than did their nonclique counterparts.

The Perception of Working Conditions. Several important conclusions can be drawn from these studies for our understanding of industrial morale. First of all, the results substantiated some earlier work that such factors as noise, exposure to bad weather, slippery operational areas, and other undesirable physical working conditions *do not* determine morale per se. Morale results from the worker's *perception* of his working conditions and his job. How the job is perceived is a function of his ego involvement with it. Associated with ego involvement is a feeling of belonging, a sense of responsibility, and an opportunity to contribute knowingly to a worthwhile effort.

Through worker selection and placement, adequate programs of training, and work situations favoring cohesiveness, workers' needs have a better chance to get fulfilled. When one feels that he is needed as a part of the organization, then his morale can be high in spite of the undesirable aspects of the physical environment.

But why, we may ask, do men work in the first place? One man may feel that something important needs to be done, that he is the man to do it. He needs no other motive to get the task completed. In the upper levels of the industrial hierarchy we may find economic forces pressuring an executive to work hard purely for financial reward. At another time he may work to avoid penalty for shirking. But generally he works, as do most people gainfully employed at any level, not for some special reward or for fear of penalty, but for a *combination of reasons*. We work for different reasons at different times, but in the main we are all after very much the same things in our work.

FACTORS RELATED TO JOB ATTITUDES

At the beginning of this chapter we listed in Table 4 the specific job aspects of the ten major factors related to job attitudes. Let us now consider each of these in a summary way as they contribute to our understanding of why people work. They are average ranks in the way they are presented, as determined by the analyses of Herzberg, Mausner, Peterson, and Capwell [13]. It is possible, of course, that no single individual would rank these factors in the order in which they are presented. We also know that at any given time, for any given person, a certain factor may rank high. With changing circumstances this high factor may shift to a relatively low comparative position. For example, for a newly married man wages may be of primary importance. At some other time, or under other conditions, it is quite possible for wages to be placed low in any comparisons. Opportunities for advancement or some other factor may well take first place.

1. *Security.* This factor deals with the steadiness of employment, where the manager or worker feels he has a reasonable chance of working under conditions of company stability. The man with security feels that he is valued by the firm and that he has the abilities and the opportunity to keep his job. Security is a strong reason for liking a job and is generally mentioned first by both men and women as contributing to job satisfaction. The lower one gets in the occupational scale, the greater the importance attached to the security factor. The greater skill and responsibility demanded in higher-level jobs gives the employee more "salability" and hence creates a demand for his services both within his own company and in others.

Security is a job-attitudes factor which increases slightly in importance with an increase in age. There is evidence that security is less important to employees with more education. It seems to be equally important to employees regardless of their dependents, with the possible exception of the single man who is entirely on his own.

2. *Opportunity for Advancement.* What are the chances of getting ahead? This factor ranks high in importance, particularly to the person striving for upward mobility. Opportunity for advancement is quite a different problem for persons at opposite ends of the socioeconomic scale. The professional man and the corporation executive have this factor primarily within their own individual control. To the man in middle management, however, the problem of opportunity is of greater concern, for his future is tied in largely with what happens to and within his company. To the worker, advancement is related to merit, to be sure, but seniority plays a big role where union contracts are in effect. The young, ambitious, good worker may find advancement held back because of seniority agreements.

The results of many attitude surveys show that the lack of opportunity for advancement is frequently a strong reason for disliking a job, but rarely is opportunity for advancement mentioned as a contributor to satisfaction. Men are much more expressive in giving importance to this factor than are women as will be spelled out in Chapter 13 (see page 270). There is some evidence that there is a decrease in the importance of the advancement factor with increasing age. Once a man has reached his "opportunity level," and becomes adjusted to his situation, other factors become more important to him, length of service in a stable company, for example. Intelligence and education are substantially related to the opportunities factor. As a matter of fact, one serious problem for the bright and ambitious college graduate is to realize that promotional opportunities are often slower in coming than he would like. Some studies show that college seniors select their jobs largely because they think they will have a good opportunity for advancement.

3. *Company and Management.* What constitutes a good company and management? To one employee it may mean how well the company gets along with the union. Another man may rate the company on its sponsorship of athletic teams. Whether we are dealing with the size of the organization, reputation, earnings, or public relations, the employee believes that a good company is one which helps him feel some stability in his job. Like security, this job factor is seldom a strong reason for dissatisfaction, but it contributes substantially to the employee's satisfaction.

In terms of occupational level there is some evidence that the higher the skill level, the greater the satisfaction with the company. Older workers show a slightly greater concern for the rating and reputation of the company than young workers do. Perhaps their years of service to the company have made them a little more ego-involved with it.

4. *Wages.* When this factor is ranked with nine other job factors, employees give it fourth place. It is interesting that employers generally rank this factor near the top when they are asked what the employee wants. Although there is some indication that wages and opportunity for advance-

ment are related through the element of money, employees consistently have rated wages as much less important than either opportunity for advancement or security.

Studies show that the factor of wages contributes more to the dissatisfaction than to the satisfaction of the worker. Rarely ever does a man express satisfaction with the amount of money he is making.

Wages are more important to men than to women workers, and are generally more important to factory workers than to office workers. Herzberg and his colleagues conclude that there is a tendency for the importance of wages to drop as the employee grows older, at least until the age of forty. After forty, the employee attaches more importance to the factor of wages, whereas the factors of job, company, security, and so on seem to have become fairly well established.

5. *Intrinsic Aspects of the Job.* There are many reasons why people like their job simply for the sake of the job. One man may like what he is doing because he has just the right ability and training for it. Another may like his job per se because it brings him recognition; a third person may like his job because it is easy, gives him an opportunity to travel, or is free of tension and pressure. Whatever the reason, what the man does at his particular job contributes to both satisfaction and dissatisfaction.

There is an important relationship between a person's skill and education and the requirements of a job. It has been found, for example, that a reduction in the skill requirements of a job increases the dissatisfaction of the more skilled worker, whereas it would not affect the less skilled worker. The higher the occupational and skill level of the person and the higher his education, the more important the challenge of his job becomes. Most people in executive or supervisory positions say they like their job because intrinsically it challenges and stimulates them. One difficult thing for successful leaders to realize is that employees in lower-status jobs often do not like jobs with challenge. For them there must be other things involved if the job is to lead to satisfaction.

6. *Supervision.* To the worker, his supervisor is both a father figure and an irritating boss who is an equally strong contributor to both satisfaction and dissatisfaction. Women seem more sensitive to supervision than do men, but for both bad supervision can be a primary reason for absenteeism and labor turnover.

Supervision seems less important at the high levels in spite of the fact that people in high positions have a greater tendency to verbalize the things that are wrong with their particular supervisory structure. College graduates voice criticism of their supervisors more than less-educated people. They are particularly critical at times of the supervisor's ability to handle people. There is some evidence that married workers with dependents are more conscious of the problem of good supervision than are single men. One could interpret this as meaning that the man with family responsibilities feels more necessity for supervisory approval. And, of course, we cannot overlook the fact that the supervisor, in playing his many roles with the worker, is a focal point for attitude formation.

7. *Social Aspects of the Job.* This is one of the most difficult of the job-attitudes factors to describe. It involves such needs as belonging and social approval. This factor contributes to both satisfaction and dissatisfaction of the employee. A man who feels himself a member of a productive, cohesive group is happier with his job than is someone who finds himself a misfit. The social factor appears only slightly more important to women than to men; it is relatively independent of age and occupational level.

8. *Communication.* An old military expression which says that "there is always someone who does not get the word" is expressive, but hardly a complete definition of the factor of communication. The lack of good communication may be a reason for disliking a job, but it is never a specific reason for liking a job. What, then, is really meant by communication? To be sure, it means the formalities of conveying information, giving orders, turning out annual reports. But to the employee it also means being listened to, receiving recognition, and "knowing why." Good communication, as far as feelings go, means the opposite of being ignored. The factor of communication seems to be more important at the higher educational levels.

First-line supervisors list the lack of good communication as one of their chief annoyances. Perhaps this is because they feel that they are "told" by higher management rather than "conferred with." In one company an attitude survey was made among 120 foremen. When asked to describe their biggest problem, most of these supervisors listed communication. In a few months these men were brought together to discuss company policies and problems. After a one-day session they returned to their jobs. One year later when they were asked to identify problems, communication was far down the list. A follow-up study showed that merely being brought together and asked for views on company problems had made the men feel that communication was now good. Recognition that he is a part of management may well be what the supervisor wants when he asks for improved communication.

9. *Working Conditions.* Temperature, lighting, ventilation, parking facilities, cafeteria, toilets, and the like are always a place affording criticism when the employee wishes to let off steam. Actually this factor has been found to make an equally low contribution to both satisfaction and dissatisfaction. Working conditions are substantially more important to women than to men as we shall point out later in the chapter entitled "Women in Industry." Hours are more important to men than any other specific aspect of working conditions; but among women, especially married women this aspect has even more significance. To the more educated and higher-level

employee, hours are almost negligible in importance. Few, if any, executives work the limited hours of the union man! To workers in hazardous jobs, safety conditions are most important; but when they are ranked with nine other job factors, working conditions come in next to last.

10. *Benefits.* Retirement provisions, hospitalization, leaves, vacations, and holidays are now somewhat a standard part of most jobs; there is greater uniformity throughout industry in this factor than in any of the other major factors. This factor has not been mentioned as a real contributor either to satisfaction or to dissatisfaction in the many studies of job attitudes. It is interesting to note, however, how much attention is paid by union representatives to fringe benefits at the time of contract negotiations. We shall see the reasons for this in the following chapter on labor relations.

The student giving serious consideration to his or her career may find the ten factors described above useful in helping him to establish an individual "need hierarchy." He will no doubt find that he wants all these factors in the job that he chooses, but he will want them in different degrees. As time goes on he will find his attitudes shifting, but it is important that he have a base of understanding from which to operate in making decisions about his life's work.

SUGGESTIONS FOR FURTHER READING

Brown, J. A. C. *The social psychology of industry.* Baltimore: Pelican Series, 1954. This publication describes the formation and functions of large groups, cliques, and small intimate groups within industry, and how they are related to morale problems.

Gardner, B. B., & Moore, D. G. *Human relations in industry.* Homewood, Ill.: Irwin, 1955. A book that pulls together the many and varied problems related to industrial production and job satisfactions.

Herzberg, F., Mausner, B., & Snyderman, B. *The motivation to work.* New York: Wiley, 1959. Utilizing the results of some 200 studies, the authors develop a practical theory of job motivation, job satisfaction, and job attitude.

Schutte, W. M., & Steinberg, E. R. *Communication in business and industry.* New York: Holt, 1960. Combining the latest findings from psychology, semantics, and linguistics, this book deals with the practical aspects of written and spoken communication and problems related to attitudes.

Walker, C. R., & Guest, R. H. *The man on the assembly line.* Cambridge, Mass.: Harvard Univer. Press, 1952. A detailed study of the satisfactions and dissatisfactions of workers and supervisors on the assembly line in an automobile plant.

PART IV: LABOR PROBLEMS
IN INDUSTRY

11

LABOR-
MANAGEMENT
RELATIONS

Myron L. Joseph

The American industrial scene is pervaded by the image of the rugged individualist and by a strong concept of private property rights. It is difficult for many employers to accept the fact that they are not completely free to run their own plants and that their employees are unwilling to rely on competition among themselves to uncover and reward the most productive. The current institutional pattern is the culmination of a long period of development and change. Taking a look at the ways of union organizations helps to give us a perspective for understanding the many problems of psychological conflict found within labor-management relations.

THE GROWTH OF UNIONS

Even before the spread of industrialization, workers in this country were banding together in organizations to protect themselves against the competitive pressures of expanding markets. This was not the action of oppressed workers against their exploiting employers; rather, it was the reaction of the skilled craftsmen against economic forces which threatened to dilute their skills and lower their wage scales. In the American environment, with its rapidly expanding economic opportunities, the new labor organizations had a difficult time taking root. The legal, political, and social forces were extremely antagonistic to organizations that interfered with the "natural" laws of competition and constituted a threat to private property.

Early Hardships of Labor Unions. In prosperous times when their bargaining power was high, the labor unions had some success, but prior to

223

1880 they virtually disappeared during periods of depression. Their susceptibility to economic reversals was due in part to the attractiveness of the political movements of the period, each of which had its own answer to the worker's depressed conditions. Programs for education, homesteads, easy credit, and producer cooperatives attracted the efforts and loyalty of workers, who could not see any hope in the more mundane direction of improving their working conditions. They could escape the risk of unemployment and low wages if they could become self-employed.

In spite of these difficulties unions managed to find a pattern for survival. In the latter half of the nineteenth century, paralleling the growth of industrial markets, national unions grew in number and in strength. The newly organized American Federation of Labor formalized a philosophy which enabled the movement to overcome some of its major obstacles in this country. The leaders recognized the necessity of following the narrowly defined interests of their members, and they vowed to avoid the alliances, political panaceas, and internal disputes which had weakened the earlier organizations. Union membership continued to grow slowly and fluctuated as in the past with economic conditions. However, unionism was not wiped out again in periods of depression, and each revival of industry brought new growth.

Fights against Unions. In these days the industrial and legal environment remained basically antagonistic to organized labor. The earlier conspiracy trials were succeeded by prosecutions under the antitrust laws and the free use of a powerful antiunion weapon, the injunction. With the threat of unionism spreading to the newly developing mass-production industries, management waged a furious battle to keep its plants nonunion. Employees suspected of union sympathies were discharged without hesitation. The weapons brought into play against labor organizers included the so-called "yellow-dog" contract, which was an agreement to stay out of unions as a condition of employment, the black list, private police, barbed wire, and tear gas. At the same time company welfare plans and new approaches to individual employees were instituted in the hope of eliminating the attraction of the unions. In the face of this vigorous campaign, and with a unique period of declining living costs in spite of prosperity and high employment levels, union membership fell from five million in 1920 to less than three million in 1933. The leaders of the labor movement were not successful in breaching the walls of the mass-production industries which employed large numbers of semiskilled and unskilled workers. Their efforts were hampered by the fact that each craft union wanted to make sure that it would not lose potential members in newly organized plants to any other organization. The drive for unionization seemed to have lost its steam.

Depression Stimulates Union Membership. The Depression of the thirties brought about a dramatic reversal of the declining trend of union membership. Unemployment and declining wage levels made workers less willing to depend upon employer generosity for satisfactory working conditions. The political atmosphere reflected a general disillusionment with the business leadership of the community and produced legislation which protected labor's right to organize. With the mass of workers ready for unionization and a favorable government administration, labor unions grew rapidly. Dissatisfaction within the labor movement with the old-fashioned organizing techniques, and an internal power conflict produced a split in the ranks of labor. Far from slowing down the process of organization, the rivalry between the newly formed CIO and the older AFL stimulated a race for new members.

The Mass-production Industries. One by one the mass-production industries succumbed to the organizing drive; new unions were formed; and the older organizations expanded vigorously. By 1937 more than seven million workers had joined labor unions, a figure which increased to more than fourteen million in 1949, and was close to eighteen million in 1957. The process of growth was uneven. The U.S. Steel Corporation and more than a hundred producing and fabricating firms in the industry signed contracts with the union in early 1937 after an organizing campaign that was largely educational. In contrast, the "little steel" companies refused to recognize the union and in a violent struggle completely defeated an organizing strike. The automobile industry was organized only after bitter fighting and a series of sit-down strikes, but the United Automobile Workers soon became powerful in the labor movement.

One-fourth of Labor Is Organized. Through a combination of bitter warfare, grudging retreat, and peaceful accommodation, more than 25 per cent of the American labor force has been organized by the union movement at the present time. Some sectors of industry continue to resist organization with all the weapons at their command, and the labor movement itself is in a continuing state of change. Nevertheless, collective bargaining appears to be an enduring institution. Although the political atmosphere has shifted considerably since the early 1930s, it is still public policy to protect the right of workers to form and join unions of their choice. In most modern industry the employer-employee relationship has been displaced by the complex of employer-union-employee relations. Labor unions have become a major institution with which modern management must develop a way of life.

UNION CONSTRAINTS ON MANAGEMENT

Almost by definition unions constitute an interference with managerial freedom of action, but that does not explain the violent rejection of unionism by employers when the problem first faced them, and the continued emotional antagonism displayed today by many management people who have dealt with unions for years. Management works to achieve its objectives in a generally restrictive environment. Competitors, banks, suppliers, customers, and the government place constraints on business decisions. Some of these groups enter directly into the decision process through representation on boards of directors, whereas others control parts of the environment within which the firms must operate. Although business organizations are usually reluctant to accept any of these restrictions, their strongest reactions have been traditionally against the intrusion of labor organizations.

A Challenge to Management. After a plant is organized, the paths through which management achieves its goals depend upon the reactions and cooperation of union leaders. To management, the goal of economic security is threatened by the impact of unions on the efficiency of operations and by shifts in the organizational structure that make the path to advancement less clear. The union-enforced constraints, and the fact that the labor leaders are not within their span of control, interfere with the desire of management to control its own affairs. This restriction is particularly disturbing because it is exercised by "outsiders." Union actions challenge many of the folkways that serve as guides for management decision.

In spite of the fear they have evoked, unions now constitute an important part of the industrial environment. Many managers may have to redefine some of their goals, but they will also find new ways to achieve satisfaction in the new organizational context. An important step in this direction is to develop an understanding of the internal bonds of labor unions. As we discussed in the chapter on the structure of organizations, union officers and members do not function within the familiar hierarchical pattern of the firm.

WHY WORKERS JOIN UNIONS

Why do workers join unions, and what satisfactions do they derive from their membership? The motives for joining a union vary with economic conditions and the circumstances of the individual plant. Positive reasons include the desire for greater security, the liking for such an organization, and a feeling that a union is the only way to get results. On the other hand, many workers join because of contract requirements, social expediency, or informal group pressures from their fellow workers. The evidence suggests that irrespective of the immediate reason for joining, most workers accept unions with some degree of conviction [19, 20, 21]. In one study of the situation it was found that 46 per cent of the members joined because of the union-shop requirements, but 93 per cent of the workers reported that they needed a union to buck the employer [15]. A wage problem or some other specific grievance may serve as the last straw, but the act of joining a union usually reflects some more basic need, such as seeking job security.

PROBLEMS WITHIN THE UNION

Although an organization does not exist apart from its members, its behavior must be examined independently. In order for a labor union to advance the goals of its members and officers it must be able to make decisions, take actions, and overcome its internal organizational problems. The labor union's organizational needs and problems constitute an important factor in determining its behavior. To survive, a union must be able to maintain its strength and resist the multiple dangers of an antagonistic environment.

Threats to Survival. Labor unions feel that employers remain a strong potential threat to their survival. The continuing resistance to organization in many industrial areas and the reluctant acceptance of collective bargaining in industries that have been organized for many years serve to reinforce the still vivid memories of the violent antiunion campaigns of the past. Today's union officers and staff workers are drawn for the most part from the ranks of the early organizers and activists. They retain much of the suspicion and antagonism which developed out of their experience, and help maintain a word-of-mouth tradition of the hostile employer based on the period of struggle. The absence of a strong working-class identification in our society has increased the difficulties of recruiting and maintaining union membership [13].

Value Conflicts among Workers. The middle-class values of many American workers are in conflict with union objectives and methods. In rural areas and among some white-collar groups this has made organization a slow and difficult process. In established unions, the younger workers cannot compare the preorganization working conditions with their present state, and they may not see any important reasons for paying union dues. Even if the worker recognizes the benefits of collective bargaining, union membership is not required for him to share the negotiated improvements. In organized plants, the collective agreement covers all employees without regard to membership, and in many nonunion firms employers follow a pattern of matching the wage increases obtained through collective bargaining in the organized sector of the industry.

INSTITUTIONAL GOALS

How does the labor organization function to further its objectives of survival and growth? To a limited extent the members will accept union policies which strengthen the organization in so far as they see union strength as a means to the fulfillment of their needs. The connection, however, is not always clear, and in some cases may not exist. The members may not understand the economic and political forces which would threaten the union if their contract demands are too extreme. The time period within which the danger exists is likely to be much longer than the span of the members' immediate interests. They may be reluctant to sacrifice an immediate gain for a long-run advantage. In addition, the members may not feel that their own objectives are related in any way to the growth of the organization. They may be more interested in results than in continuing any particular organization as their representative.

Union Leadership View. It is the union officials whose goals are much more closely linked to the organizational needs of the union. The leader's position depends on its survival, and his status is a function of the size, power, and reputation of the union. The difference between the leaders and members is illustrated by their perception of strikes. Union officers often tend to justify strikes and strike threats as a means of increasing the union's power in the long run; inactive members weigh the issues and the chances of success more pragmatically [21]. From the union leader's point of view, even an unsuccessful struggle proves willingness to fight, and will give greater weight to future strike threats. In addition, the conflict may solidify the membership behind their leader and provide evidence that the organization is fighting vigorously for the workers' interests. It may be particularly important to demonstrate this if the union is threatened from within by member apathy, or from without by a rival organization.

Union Organizational Needs. The fact that union demands and the actions of union officials are frequently related to institutional goals provides an important source of misunderstanding and conflict. As in the case of a hopeless strike, the union's behavior is considered irrational by management standards. It is difficult to see why a union will be willing to strike for a union security agreement when 90 per cent of the employees are already members, unless the union's perception of a threatening environment is taken into consideration. Similarly collective bargaining can become hopelessly bogged down over very small differences, because management does not understand that the importance of the union's figure is based upon its organizational needs.

The union may not be able to accept any contract which provides less than that won by a rival union without losing members, or even the local. It might be safer for the union to risk a strike than to sign a contract which could be compared unfavorably to its rival's. The demands for industry-wide bargaining are more likely to increase the security of union organizations than to enhance their bargaining strength. The increased scope of the bargaining relationship would protect them against internal comparisons and raids by other unions, and would make it more difficult for individual employers to eliminate the union from their plants [10].

THE UNION ORGANIZATION

A factor which must be considered in dealing with a union is the nature of the organizational constraints within which union officers function. Unlike the hierarchical management structure, a union is a political organization.

Power Delegation. The authority for the decisions of the officers comes from the members as delegated by the organization's constitution and by-laws. That authority may be withdrawn through the election process, and there is always the possibility of rival claimants for the leadership roles. Even while the officers are advancing the organizational goals of the union, then, they must protect their own positions in the official hierarchy. Compared with the survival problems of management personnel, the cost of repudiation for a union officer is high [16]. His only alternative, particularly at the local-union level, may be to go back to his job in the shop. The greater the status difference between his office and the available job, the heavier the penalty for losing the political struggle.

It is true that the national officers of the union are better insulated against the attitudes of the members, but internal revolts occur with sufficient frequency to affirm the necessity of protecting their political positions. Lack of opposition in elections does not demonstrate the absence of potential threats or a lack of responsiveness to membership pressures. As long as the path of democratic process remains open, as it does in most unions, even the top leadership must answer to the members. The attempted revolt within the ranks of the United Steel Workers in 1957 illustrates this point.

Power of Union Officers Is Limited. Union officers are constrained not only by the power of the ballot, but also by the fact that the members constitute the basis for their power. The ability of the union leader to gain concessions from management, the keystone on which his status depends, is a function of the support his members are willing to give. We are not suggesting that the union policies, which are for the most part formulated by the leadership, are identical with those which would have been established by a membership referendum. We are saying, however, that the officers must estimate the amount of pressure behind various membership demands and the possibility that they could be used as a steppingstone for a potential rival. They must also base their decisions on the willingness of the members to take strike action for a set of demands and to abide by the negotiated agreement. The power of union leaders to enforce their decisions on their members is very weak. Union officers can refuse to support grievances which are not based on current agreements and can withdraw official sanction and financial support from unauthorized protests. Rebellious officers at the local and intermediate levels can be disciplined by supporting rival candidates, or in extreme cases by removing the dissident from office. However, if these rebels have any substantial support from the rank and file, intervention of this type can be extremely dangerous because it may serve to stir up potent political opposition. As a result most cases of disciplinary action by national unions are for the purpose of protecting their locals against dishonest, dictatorial, or negligent local union officers [25].

Action against rank-and-file members who do not cooperate with union policy is difficult. The most extreme penalty that the union can impose is loss of membership. But this is a realistic alternative only against individuals or very small groups, unless the principle involved is worth the loss of a local.

Dependence on the membership forces labor leaders to keep one eye on their political fences. Unlike their management counterparts, there is no single measure, like profits, which can be used to evaluate their performance [16].

Behavior in Negotiations. Collective bargaining differs markedly from other commercial negotiations in that the union officials are communicating with their constituents through their preparations for bargaining, their behavior at the bargaining table, and their comments on the course of the negotiations. Table thumping and complaints that management representatives are not acting in good faith are often part of the process of gaining membership acceptance of the eventual agreement. Some unions formalize the process by requiring membership ratification of the terms of the collective agreements. It is ironic that the union officers who protest bitterly when management bargaining representatives do not have sufficient authority to make concessions must themselves be extremely wary that they do not accept an offer which the members would reject or which could serve as a weak spot in their political armor. On occasion, seemingly innocuous issues are very difficult to resolve because they are important to a group of workers who hold a strategic position in the local's politics, or because the officer is afraid that a concession can be twisted about by his opponents in such a way as to endanger his position. This unbusinesslike and illogical behavior of union officers, which is a cause of considerable friction, results from the fact that the pressures under which they function produce a different "logic" from that of management [1, 2]. Nevertheless, the labor leader's interaction with his members serves an important management function. The working conditions arrived at through negotiation will probably constrain management more than they would like, but the process of collective bargaining increases the probability that the employees will accept the conditions. Since there is no simple way to define what is right, or what is best, employees are more likely to accept conditions which were arrived at through a process in which their interests were adequately represented [3].

LABOR UNION MEMBERSHIP

"The interest of the members" is as difficult to define as "the public good." The membership ranks of labor unions are homogeneous only in the sense that they are employees. At the national level one union will represent a variety of occupations in several industries working throughout the country. Even within a local the members' interests and attitudes will vary in accordance with their racial and ethnic backgrounds, levels of skill, age, years of service with the company, and social groups, to mention just a few of the variables by which union members can be stratified. Each group has its own set of priorities for the demands to be made on management. Within the limits set by management's willingness to make concessions, more for one group means less for the others. On some issues the interests of different classifications of members are diametrically opposed. Better opportunities for promotion for one group will make it more difficult for some others to move ahead; more job protection for older workers often makes the younger workers less secure.

Union Democracy. Union constitutions and bylaws formalize the process of membership participation in union decisions, and they usually follow a very democratic pattern. The leaders will generally arrange for the major interest groups to be represented on the committees which determine the collective-bargaining demands and conduct the negotiations. If the pressure is strong enough, a group may be given the right to negotiate a separate contract, or to be represented in the union organization by a department of its own. In one instance a major industrial union was forced to give more autonomy to its skilled members after a series of wildcat strikes demonstrated their unwillingness to accept the terms of a contract that had been approved by the general membership.

In spite of the formal provisions, bargaining policy tends to be a leadership function [16]. The demands that are formulated by the rank and file cover too wide a range to serve as a realistic guide, although they provide a useful sounding board for the officers who cannot ignore an issue for which there is widespread support. Frequently the demands are initiated by members under the guidance of the officers or their representatives. They are then funneled through leadership committees which formulate bargaining policy in the light of the political and strategic needs of the organization. In many cases where the industry's products compete in national markets, union bargaining decisions must be controlled at a level far removed from the local unions and their members. In addition, the increasing complexity of negotiations places a premium on expert knowledge and bargaining skill.

An Organizational Paradox. The competing forces within the labor union organization create an organizational paradox. In order for the union to respond to the needs of its members, each member or group of members must be free to influence decisions and participate in the political process. However, the ability of the union to force concessions from management is a function of its bargaining strength, which in turn is closely related to the ability of the organization to maintain a solidly united front. Although it has many other functions, a union is basically a fighting organization, and anything which limits its ability to stand up to management in a crisis will weaken its ability to advance the interests of its members. Consequently, union constitutions and mores enforce the requirement of individual loyalty to the organization, and it is difficult to draw the line between dissent and disloyalty. The individual's right to defend his own interests must therefore be tempered in the light of the effect of protest on the ability of the organization to function in the interest of its members.

OFFICERS OF THE UNION

The forces leading to centralization and the loyalty requirements for organizational strength tend to protect the national union officers from membership political pressures. Other characteristics of labor unions increase their independence [8]. Probably the most significant is the relative indifference of most union members to the government of their organization. Very few feel any need to participate in the functioning of the union. There are typically large membership turnouts at meetings called to consider a new contract, or to conduct a strike vote, but extremely small attendance at all other times. This should not be taken as a sign of indifference to the organization, but rather as an indication that the union is perceived as performing a particular function for its members, and that as long as there is general satisfaction with the results the members have little reason to participate in its affairs.

Protection for Union Officers. The officers are protected from the rank and file by the power which their tenure in office gives them over strategic parts of the organization. The loyalty of the paid staff of the organization, who owe their jobs to the incumbent officers, provides the leaders with an effective political machine. The international representatives who service the local unions constitute the only direct contact which most union members and local officers have with the national organization. They can give support to local leaders friendly to the administration and make things difficult for their opponents. As long as the union staff remains loyal, it is difficult to break the rule of the incumbent officers.

National Union Officers. The preponderant position of the national officers in determining union policy facilitates their implementation of the organizational objectives, which are tied more closely to the personal goals of the leaders. As union leaders gain more experience and develop a more sophisticated understanding of their economic environment and the problems of the companies with whom they deal, their perception of the collective-bargaining situation will tend to deviate more and more from the view held by the rank and file [5, 21].

The officers' continuing relationships with management representatives take on value, both in terms of long-run bargaining strategy and the personal need to hold their respect. The further removed from the rank and file the leaders are, the more their behavior is conditioned by the values of other groups in the society with whom they have increasing contact. The net result of the relative independence of the national union officers are labor unions that are more stable and responsible and less responsive to membership attitudes. It should be noted that policies designed to force purer democratic behavior on labor organizations may entail a social cost in terms of less stability and responsibility.

Local Union Officers. At the local level, the political potency of membership pressures is less easily confined. A candidate can make himself known to the members with relative ease. Handbills, personal contacts, and informal communications within the plant minimize the electioneering advantage the incumbents may have. The campaign issues are likely to be very personal ones, relating to the personalities, behavior, and reputations of the candidates. Anything can be picked up by an opponent and blown up into a damaging accusation. Between elections, dissident groups can always pack a local union meeting as a means of putting pressure on the officers. When a local president finds a large turnout from a particular department at a meeting, he knows he is in for trouble. If one officer is unwilling to support a grievance, the member may be able to find another who is willing to build his own political strength by pushing it [17].

The fluidity of the political situation forces the local officers to devise techniques to protect themselves as best they can. The widespread "rule of two" serves to discourage accusations and rumors of selling out to management. This custom requires that no union officer will meet with a company representative unless at least one other officer is present. A local officer can be criticized if he does not win enough grievances, but it is politically difficult to refuse to accept grievances that have little chance of being granted. Partial protection is gained by establishing a committee which passes on the merits of grievances. Although this takes the blame away from any one individual, it does not prevent factions within the group from claiming that they would have pushed the grievance, but that others prevented it. The record of wins and losses can be improved by taking credit for concessions and passing the less hopeful cases on to the next step in the grievance process. The less insulated an officer is from membership pressure the more difficult it is for him to explain to a grievant that his claim is unwarranted. Consequently, many cases are appealed to the international representative and even to arbitration, although they are basically without merit. The effectiveness of this relief will depend on the relations between the local officers and the international representatives, and this is one of the tools that the latter can wield to exert influence at the local level. Even if the case is not passed on to the next level, the local officer may soften the blow by going through the motions of arguing a hopeless case, so that he will receive some credit for supporting his members.

The political advantage to be gained from winning concessions is hotly contested. A cooperative international representative will be careful to give credit to the local officers, even if he conducted all the negotiations. Opponents, on the other hand, may try to undermine an officer by claiming that he is too dependent on the international representative and has accomplished nothing on his own. To prevent this situation, some locals handle all of their own cases, taking their chances on losing cases, but claiming all the credit for the successes.

It is difficult for management to be neutral in this situation, because its behavior can be very influential in determining the political success or failure of the local officers. A policy of making important concessions only at the top local level can give the officers at that level more security in their positions and more influence on union policies. The timing of concessions can be very important to the outcome of local elections. Local union politics frequently reflect management's industrial relations policies.

MANAGEMENT MEETS THE UNION

When faced with the prospect of unionization, employers have a wide range of possible response. Federal legislation does not permit interference with the free choice of the employees, but management may express its attitudes toward unionization with reasonable freedom as long as no promises or threats are implied. Even if an employer would rather not deal with a union, a policy of opposition frequently carries considerable risk. In the heat of an organizing campaign, grievances are magnified and charges are pressed by union representatives in order to gain adherents. Attempts to correct any unsatisfactory conditions at such a time would simply provide the organizer with proof of the union's effectiveness, and answering exaggerated or fabricated charges might embroil the employer in an emotional interchange in which the objective situation played only a minor role. If the employees do not already have the information which would demonstrate the exaggerated nature of the organizer's claims, it would be very difficult to communicate it to them in an objective way without having the attempts turned around to the union's advantage. Many employees would say, "After all, if the employer is so anxious to keep the union out, perhaps it can really help us!" The greatest dangers of opposition are the implications of failure.

Behavior Patterns. The behavior patterns of the union leaders are developed in this formative period, as are the attitudes of the management organization. If the union succeeds, the employer must treat union officers as representatives of his employees. The type of leadership which succeeded in overcoming the employer's opposition is not likely to have the qualities he would like to meet over the bargaining table. If exaggerated promises and emotionally charged accusations were the path to victory, as they may well be, in a hotly fought contest the new officers will be expected to make good on their claims. If the employer escapes the danger of having to deal with overly aggressive or irresponsible leaders who were trained in combat, he must still face the problem of developing in his own ranks, trained in the same school, the attitudes necessary to maintain a stable bargaining relationship. Although for many employers the economic and noneconomic costs of unionization may be high, the costs of opposition should be fully realized.

A number of authors have categorized management policies along a continuum which is closely related to the conflict-cooperation classifications used to describe patterns of union-management relations [22]. At one extreme there is forceful and open resistance to unionization through the use of coercive techniques which shade into the various forms of aggressive persuasion of which employers may avail themselves within the constraints of the Labor-Management Relations Act. Further along the continuum are the employers who reluctantly accept the legal obligation to bargain with unions, but who do everything possible to restrict the influence of the unions with at least the hopeful expectation that some day they will be eliminated. In such situations there is a continuing struggle over the loyalty of the employees, and the unions will have to act to guard their institutional security. There is a better chance of a stable relationship when employers are willing to accept unions and collective bargaining as a permanent part of their decision process and guard against actions which would threaten the unions' survival. Here again there are degrees of acceptance ranging up to a level of cooperation which includes the recognition of many joint problems and the establishment of a decision process in which the responsibility for many decisions is shared.

LABOR-MANAGEMENT BARGAINING

As we know, *bargaining is basically a power relationship.* Each side must consider the costs and gains of alternative bargaining positions. The ability to inflict penalties and the capacity to survive penalties are implicit in the bargaining process. If a union could not strike or inflict damage on management through such techniques as the slowdown, it would have no strength as an organization to enforce costly demands on management. Similarly, management would be unable to resist union demands if withholding agreement did not inflict monetary or organizational costs on the union.

Commitments as Strategy. If one of the parties can succeed in convincing the other that it is unable to retreat from a solution within the acceptable range, the act of commitment will force the opponent to accept the offer [18]. Management and unions go to great lengths to convince each other that they are firmly committed to particular positions. Employers make public statements and establish a situation in which their status would clearly be in jeopardy if they retreated. Strike votes by union members and strike deadlines are among the techniques used by union negotiators to cut themselves off from retreat. Part of a good strategy would be to help the opponent to rationalize his retreat from a committed position so that he does not lose the ability to commit himself in the future. The difficulty of accurately comparing the multiple issues covered in negotiations makes it easier to compromise issues because the compromise need not be interpreted as a retreat.

The Limited Use of Facts. The nature of bargaining helps explain the limited function of facts [4]. They may be used to support demands or to help establish patterns, but they are infrequently used as a basis for agreement. If the parties could agree on the principles which should determine the outcome of bargaining, recourse to facts could settle the issue. The nature of the power conflict is such, however, that each side will support those principles which favor its own cause, and disagreement over facts usually disguises a more basic disagreement.

Working toward the Contract. The negotiation of labor agreements differs in a critical aspect from the process by which most other contractual arrangements are reached. Unless one of the parties fails to survive, agreement must be reached eventually. The alternative of simply breaking off relations if negotiations are not successful, and seeking a more satisfactory agreement with another organization, is not available. Most strikes are not aimed at the destruction of the union or the company, but are simply moves in the process of reaching an agreement. This mutual interdependence of labor and management serves as a major constraint on bargaining behavior. For one thing, the negotiators must provide a basis for the continuing relationship, recognizing and adjusting to the existing conflicts of interest. In attempting to agree on mutually acceptable working conditions for the period of the agreement, they must recognize the impossibility of covering the multitude of specific problems which will be the content of disputes that will arise. If we think of collective bargaining as an orderly process for adjusting conflicts of interest, it must include both the negotiation of a contract as general or as specific as the parties feel will meet their needs and a continuing method for handling disputes and issues which arise within the framework of the collective agreement.

Contract Violations. Damage suits are rarely a satisfactory remedy for breach of labor agreements—unlike most other contracts. The parties must consider the impact of their actions, including legal action against each other, on the quality of the ongoing bargaining relationship. An antagonistic bargaining committee may be a heavy penalty to pay for the satisfaction of proving damages against the union, and, in fact, most such suits seem to be withdrawn as part of the general settlement of disputed issues. More important is the fact that most of the problems which arise during a contract period will not involve a formal breach of the agreement by the union. The failure of individual members to abide by the contract does not automatically make the union liable for damages, and frequently the union officers are as anxious as management is to bring the dispute to an end. In any event, so long as the union officers disavow the actions which violate the contract and make some attempt to obtain compliance, management is left with disciplinary action against the individual employees as their only recourse.

Management may also be guilty of contract violations, and normal court procedures are equally inappropriate for employee satisfaction. The delays and costs of legal procedure and the lack of familiarity of the legal tribunals with the complexities of labor relations weaken the civil courts as a method of enforcing collective agreements. In recognition of this, most labor contracts are to a considerable extent self-enforcing. A formal grievance procedure enables an employee to appeal managerial decisions to higher levels of the management hierarchy through his union representative. Typically the union steward, the grievance committee, and the staff representative servicing the local will meet with their respective counterparts in the management organization. If the union is not satisfied with the results of the last stage of consultation, most contracts provide that the grievance may be appealed to arbitration.

THE SETTLEMENT OF GRIEVANCES

Some firms stress the judicial function of the grievance process and insist on a strict legalistic interpretation of the labor contract. This tends to curtail the number of grievances and places emphasis on the formal procedure. At the other end of the spectrum is the "clinical approach" which recognizes the dynamic nature of industrial relations and the need for adjusting the problems which arise out of the process of change. Although a legalistic approach may keep complaints which are not covered by the contract out of the grievance machinery, it will not eliminate the sources of conflict which may well find less desirable outlets for expression [9].

First Level of Grievance. In most cases the vast majority of grievances are settled at the first step, involving the shop steward, the foreman, and the grievant. At this level, the process is very informal and settlements which do not cause trouble for the higher levels of either organization are unlikely to be scrutinized with any care. In fact, such scrutiny would be impossible in many cases because of the inadequacy of the records. Even in companies which attempt to maintain a policy of strict contract interpretation at higher levels, the first informal stages of the process are characterized by rule and contract evasion by stewards and foremen [6]. They make informal concessions to each other which help meet their respective needs. The steward is able to meet his political commitments, reward his followers in the shop, and minimize the danger of costly appeals and less favorable contract interpretations from higher-level management. The foreman gains greater flexibility, fewer bad grievances, and guards himself against the actions his superiors might take if he were not able to handle his own problems. This informality helps to stabilize industrial relations, but the higher levels of both organizations may have a completely erroneous conception of relations in the shop.

Liabilities of the Grievance Process. The existence of a grievance procedure does not, of course, ensure a frictionless adjustment of difficulties. A problem of growing importance is the delay between the time of filing a grievance and its final disposition. If the employees are frustrated in their expectations of obtaining a fair handling of their cases in a reasonable time, the grievance process may create more problems than it solves. The delays are partly the fault of management, and partly the result of the political nature of the union. If answering grievances is not given sufficient priority by the employer, the union committee may be forced, in response to pressure from interested members, to accuse management of stalling tactics or at least of negligence. It is a particularly frustrating situation, because, short of direct action, there is no practical way for a union to force management to answer a grievance. The contract provisions which specify that a grievance must be answered in a particular period of time serve only as evidence of good faith and a standard for normal procedure. Union officers are often reluctant to put too much pressure on management to answer a grievance, because, as one officer said in explaining delay to his members, "It is always easy to get a 'no' answer." Membership discontent may build up to the point where the local officers are forced to prefer any answer to a continued delay, since the delay is interpreted as weakness on their part.

The effectiveness of the grievance process is hampered by the fact that it is unavoidably an integral part of the internal political process of the local union. Particularly in the industrial unions where national or pattern bargaining plays a major role in contract negotiation, grievance handling and contract administration become the primary function of the local officers. As a result, the stage at which the grievance is won or lost becomes political currency. If the answer is to be favorable, the steward, grievance chairman, or local president would like to get the credit. If the grievance is denied they would like to appeal it to another step so that the final negative answer will not be attributed to them. It takes a strong local officer to explain to a member that his grievance has no basis and that he will not process it. It is not unusual for the number of grievances, and the level of aggressiveness with which they are argued, to jump markedly in the period before a local election.

Arbitration. Arbitration should be considered an integral part of the grievance procedure. In addition to providing a method of disposing of unresolved issues of contract interpretation, arbitration helps to make the grievance steps more meaningful. Management and union officers are better able to eliminate unwarranted complaints, since the final result does not depend on relative force or the effectiveness of the pressure. Without arbitration, the balance of rights, as seen by the employees, is uneven. In the process of performing managerial functions, the employer could violate employee rights at will, and the only effective employee protests would be force. Arbitration provides a fair method of determining whether or not rights have been violated, and makes the contract something more than a temporary halt in the power struggle [11].

Arbitration is not universally accepted, and many contracts exclude certain areas, such as production standards, from their mandatory arbitration provisions. In such cases the union is free to strike if it is unwilling to accept management's answer at the highest level of consultation in the grievance process. From the employer's point of view there has been a great reluctance to allow an outsider to make a decision which is not in the strictest sense an interpretation of the provisions of the contract.

THE CONTRACT

The collective-bargaining agreement is a contract between management and the union as the representative of all the employees in the bargaining unit. It represents the only enforceable constraints, other than those which are a part of our legal structure, on the personnel and labor relations activities of management for the period of the agreement. Many contracts make this explicit by including a "management-rights" clause which states in various ways that the restrictions on management are limited to those contained in the contract.

Each contract is the product of its own environment. The extent to which different issues are important to the parties, the arrangements which are available to meet their needs, and their relative power to obtain their demands vary. Control of hiring has been extremely important to the unions in the construction industry, but of no significance in the industrial unions; their attitudes toward seniority provisions show the reverse pattern. Each collective-bargaining situation should be examined in the light of its own economic and organizational pressures.

Typical Contract Clauses. Some of the provisions of a labor contract can be identified as primarily union oriented. They do not relate directly to the employee's working conditions, but serve to strengthen and stabilize the organization.

One example is the checkoff clause which requires that management deduct union dues from the members' wages and remit them directly to the union. This cuts down the manpower necessary to administer a large union, but more importantly it makes it more difficult for a member to resign, since the positive act of revoking the checkoff authorization would be required. When collections were made by hand, each dues date presented the possibility of nonpayment, and the local officers had to do a continuous job to keep up the resources of the organization.

Many contract provisions restrict management's freedom to exercise control over the labor force. Clauses relating to discipline, layoff, promotion, and transfers come under this category. In part, the union seeks to protect its members against arbitrary or unfair decisions and to use the force of the union to balance the interests of the individual worker against the interests of the company. These restrictions give protection against antiunion discrimination and make it more difficult for the employer to put pressure on his employees to increase their level of output.

Wages. Wages are, of course, a major focus of labor agreements. In spite of the fact that current research has been unable to demonstrate that unions have succeeded in gaining any substantial comparative advantage for their members through collective bargaining, the bargained increases are perceived by officers and members alike as a measure of the success or failure of the union organization [12]. There is no union-management agreement on the appropriate criteria for wage determination, and the factors stressed by the parties change as changing conditions make them more or less consistent with the interests of either side. An additional source of difficulty is that some of the factors which influence a union's wage position are perceived by management to be irrelevant. Coercive comparisons with wages in other areas, other industries, and other unions are a function of the organizational pressures on union leaders and may be as important to them as the economics of the firm [16].

The Costs of Collective Bargaining. Labor contracts contain a great variety of employee benefits ranging from holidays and vacations to supplementary unemployment compensation. Although negotiations are primarily a union leadership function, the political nature of the organization suggests that in most cases the contracts correspond in a general way to important needs of the members. In some areas the resulting patterns may help achieve management goals as well. For example, a rational job-evaluation program may be as important to an employer as to the union, and the positive implications of improved morale for increased productivity should not be neglected. However, in many cases union gains are made at the cost of some efficiency. Even if management responds by improving in other directions, the restrictions enforced by collective bargaining limit the efficiency of production. We can go further and take note of the costs of the process of bargaining. Strikes curtail production and on occasion cause considerable discomfort to the general public. Society should be aware of the gains and costs of collective bargaining in evaluating it as a social process.

Labor-Management Cooperation. The problem of industrial harmony will not be solved until we develop techniques for sharing certain ego goals, concludes Stagner in his writings on industrial conflict [23]. One way to work in this direction involves understanding the nature of conflicts between unions and companies. In this chapter we have given descriptions that can lead to such understandings. Although the reader may get the impression from time to time that labor and management never cooperate, in actuality there is considerable cooperation between the two. Some of our social progress in health, education, and welfare is due to their extensive cooperation. One general problem area where management and labor are working toward common goals involves improving certain aspects of the life of the handicapped, unemployed, and aging worker. A description of the psychological problems in this area is given in the following chapter.

SUGGESTIONS FOR FURTHER READING

Barbash, J. *Unions and union leadership.* New York: Harper, 1960. A collection of readings helping with the understanding of the labor movement in the United States.

Kornhauser, A. W., Dubin, R., & Ross, A. M. *Industrial conflict.* New York: McGraw-Hill, 1954. This book brings together a number of significant writings on the nature of strikes and lockouts, of union attitudes and practices, and on the practical aspects of industrial relations.

Seidman, J., London, J., Karsh, B., & Tagliacozzo, D. L. *The worker views his union.* Chicago: Univer. of Chicago Press, 1958. Here is an up-to-date picture of what workers think about unions.

Stagner, R. *The psychology of industrial conflict.* New York: Wiley, 1956. A comprehensive examination of union-management relations as a psychological problem.

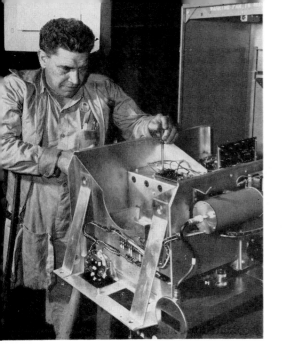

12

THE HANDICAPPED,

UNEMPLOYED,

AND AGING

WORKER

B. von Haller Gilmer

The leaders of industry in recent years have shown an increasing awareness of the psychological as well as the economic problems of the handicapped individual, the unemployed, the migrant worker, and the worker
approaching retirement. The social community and local and national
government agencies are likewise showing concern over such questions as:
Does the handicapped person make a reliable, productive worker? What
are the effects of unemployment on the individual? What of the insecurities
of the migrant worker? Are our age criteria for retirement from industry
sound? These questions are of interest to each of us as individuals. At
some time or other, we, too, may be faced with one or all of them.

THE HANDICAPPED WORKER

In one sense of the word we are all handicapped. There is no job that
really demands all our capacities. This is fortunate in that no one of us
is physically, mentally, and emotionally anywhere near perfect. Thus, we
are normal workers in relation to the jobs we can do successfully and
handicapped workers in relation to the jobs we are physically, mentally, or
emotionally unable to perform satisfactorily.

Productivity of the Handicapped. Through adequate job analysis,
physical and psychological measurement, training, and job orientation, it
has been shown that the vast majority of handicapped people can be placed
on jobs where they can produce as well as nonhandicapped workers.

Fortunately, attitudes toward the handicapped are beginning to shift away from emphasis on what the person cannot do to what he can do, away from the idea that the handicapped individual is a charity case to the belief that he is an economic asset.

The handicapped worker is very much like the nonhandicapped worker in many ways. The loss of an arm, leg, or eye does restrict the number of things a man can do. But a poor aptitude for mathematics or a lack of mechanical skill is also a restraint. If we possessed all these things, we would have a wider range of jobs to choose from. Physical defects in themselves do not destroy working capacity; they merely make the person incapable of performing certain jobs. In fact, the handicapped worker may be outstanding in some jobs.

Statistical surveys and clinical case studies by local and state governments, the Veterans Administration, U.S. Department of Labor, Civil Service Commission, the U.S. Chamber of Commerce, the National Association of Manufacturers, labor unions, and private companies have been published on the various behavioral aspects of the physically handicapped worker.

Typical of the findings is one report from over a hundred corporations involving thousands of workers which states that about two-thirds of the physically handicapped workers produce at approximately the same rate as their able-bodied fellow workers, and that 24 per cent produce at a higher rate. Only 10 per cent of the handicapped are reported lower in production than their nonhandicapped counterparts [26]. Accident rates, absenteeism, and turnover are frequently lower for the handicapped.

The Handicapped as an Economic Asset. Several factors favor the physically handicapped worker as a good economic bet. In the first place, handicapped employees usually have been screened, and their abilities have been matched with job requirements. Often more attention has been given to training and job orientation than among able-bodied workers. Moreover, individual motivational factors often operate in favor of the handicapped person. He is conscious of his handicap and often has feelings of job insecurity. He may well put forth more effort to hold his job, to report for work, or even to excel at his job. Other things being equal, the handicapped worker holds a very favorable attitude toward his job.

Although some information shows that handicapped workers occasionally are problems to an employer, the consensus of professional publications favors employing the handicapped person who has been properly rehabilitated. Success depends on finding out accurately the person's potentials and preparing him physically, vocationally, and psychologically for the job he will do. It also depends on helping the man find the right job—not just a job which he can do, but a job in a place where the work climate is such that he will be accepted.

Effects of Rehabilitation. Under the right kind of rehabilitation, the handicapped person is "adaptable, productive, careful, regular, reliable, and capable," concludes the National Rehabilitation Association from its study of thousands of cases. Evidence of adaptability is shown by the way the handicapped adjust quickly and satisfactorily to the conditions of the job. Where productivity can be objectively measured, handicapped workers are equal to and sometimes superior to other workers in job performance. They are careful workers, showing safety records equal to or superior to those of their fellow workers. Their handicaps seem to make them want to be safe. Unless there is something unusual about the nature of the handicap, regularity on the job is as good as, and sometimes better than, that of the other workers on the same job. Statistics indicate the reliability of the handicapped; they are not job hoppers. The handicapped are capable of doing superior work where they have skill to meet the job demands.

Who are the handicapped? They include young people, grownups, and elderly men and women. Some are clerks, others are executives, some are farmers, and others are machinists and housewives. The handicapped are veterans and nonveterans, college graduates and illiterates, blue-collar and white-collar workers; they may have a high IQ or be mentally retarded. In short, the handicapped are a fair cross section of the American people. An analysis of 66,000 persons rehabilitated during one typical year showed that 56 per cent were disabled by disease, 30 per cent by accidents, and 14 per cent by congenital conditions. Of this total the greatest single group had lost the use of arms, legs, or back. Next in order came amputees and blind or visually impaired workers [26].

Studies of adult industrial workers who have suffered sudden disablement show that they not only have to adjust to physical limitations, but also to psychological disturbances which may be more crippling than the physical disabilities. In many respects the rehabilitation of the mentally and emotionally handicapped person is more difficult than is that of the physically handicapped.

The industrial worker who becomes handicapped may be able to find placement within the same company and sometimes at the same job. The man who becomes a heart case may be able to carry on his regular duties within limits.

The Job Climate. The psychological climate of the job is important to the handicapped man. Some counselors feel that it is important to impress upon the men on the job that a handicapped worker should be treated in a normal matter-of-fact way. More than average curiosity, undue cheerfulness, or excessive helpfulness may indicate to the handicapped person that his colleagues are sensitive to his condition. Once fellow workers become accustomed to seeing the handicapped worker around, they will accept him, handicap and all. Fortunately, the recognition that the handicapped worker can be an economic asset to society and to himself is gaining ground.

Employing the Handicapped. Much has been written on the pros and cons of employing the physically handicapped. One opinion holds, for example, that the impaired person is more likely to be injured, since his actions and movements are hampered by his handicap. An opposite view is held by those who believe that the impaired person is less likely to be injured because he tends to be more safety conscious. What are the facts?

Neither of these statements is completely accurate in light of accident studies, yet there is some truth in each. The answers depend in great measure on how well handicapped persons are fitted to their jobs and their work environment. One study in the Western Electric Company of 685 handicapped workers well matched to their jobs found that 23.5 per cent became injured at work compared with 39.1 per cent of the control normal group. In this same study, it was found that there were 7.9 per cent more resignations among the normal workers than among the handicapped workers; 7 per cent more absences occurred among the normal workers; 5.6 per cent more discharges for just cause among normal workers; and 4.6 per cent more earnings were received by the handicapped workers [16].

The Pennsylvania State Bureau of Rehabilitation found that less than 1 per cent of 29,000 physically handicapped automobile drivers were involved in accidents one year as against $4\frac{1}{2}$ per cent of 2 million drivers of normal physical fitness. Superior selection, training, and attitude may have favored the handicapped group. It is also possible that the handicapped did less driving, but, even so, they appear to be good risks.

The many successes achieved in the rehabilitation of war veterans have opened up for the handicapped a number of areas generally thought to be the exclusive province of normal people. For example, 388 totally blinded veterans were put into new occupations never before open to the blind. They soon became highly successful in these jobs, which ranged from technical occupations and industrial management to sales and service-type work. At present, there are more than 6 million known handicapped workers; most of them are employed in factories, offices, and on farms—in situations similar to those held by nonhandicapped persons [26].

THE PSYCHOLOGICAL ASPECTS OF UNEMPLOYMENT

One way to appreciate, at least to some extent, the place of work in the lives of all of us is to get a view of the man who is out of work. Who is he? How does he feel? What can we learn from studying the behavior patterns of the unemployed?

Unemployment Is Always Present. Unemployment has a serious impact not only on the individual, but also on society, and nowhere is this impact felt more, economically or psychologically, than in the industrial community affected. Unemployment exists in good times as well as during recessions and depressions. In a study sponsored by the Twentieth Century

246   LABOR PROBLEMS IN INDUSTRY

Fund, it was found that the United States has not been free of unemployment since the turn of the century; it never disappears and rarely falls below 5 per cent of the labor force [28]. Unemployment includes both those workers who are out of jobs for short periods of time when changing jobs and those who are forced into longer periods of unemployment by seasonal variations and depressed market conditions. Only a few of the unemployed really do not want to work. There are around 250,000 domestic migrant workers in any normal year. Technological advances, although beneficial to employment in the long run, contribute to temporary loss of jobs. Since 1900 unemployment of one to three million people at any one time has been considered normal. At one time during the Great Depression of the thirties, unemployment in the United States reached a total of 10 million men and women either partially or totally out of work. One-third of all those normally employed were out of work in 1932.

The College-trained Unemployed. Typically, about 75 per cent of the unemployed are men and 25 per cent are women. During the Great Depression from 1930 to 1940, one-half of those persons out of work were in the 15- to 34-year age bracket, with the largest single group between 20 and 24 years of age. A survey made in 1935 showed that 1 million people were idle who had never been gainfully employed.

Statistics show that college graduates as a group are usually favorably placed in economic life. However, in 1937 a study of 1,000 college-trained persons of one large state university reported that four out of ten men and three out of ten women interviewed said they had been out of a job sometime or other since leaving the university.

A study of over 10,000 graduates of 1,000 colleges made in 1940 found that 2.1 per cent of the men and 3.3 per cent of the women questioned listed themselves as unemployed or on relief. These figures are low, to be sure, compared to those for production workers and physical laborers out of work at the same time [18].

Seasonal Unemployment. Cyclical and seasonal unemployment is a menace to stable career patterns. Although it hits hardest at semiskilled and unskilled workers, it touches others indirectly. Style changes and model innovations affect production schedules; holidays influence consumer buying patterns; the supply of young, school-age workers fluctuates. All these factors contribute to the up-and-down swing of employment here and there.

Seasonal unemployment patterns differ for men and women, for the young and the adult. During the first four months of the year, unemployment is higher among men over twenty-five years of age. It reaches a peak in February because of reduced activity in the construction industry and in agriculture. Unemployment for this group is below the annual average for the remainder of the year. Men and women under twenty-five years of age find jobs harder to get during the summer school vacation months because of the influx of young people into the labor market. For the most part, women over twenty-five years of age find employment relatively stable.

Psychologically, seasonal unemployment comes to be accepted, and hence the unemployed seasonal worker does not lose status; on the other hand, the worker who is accustomed to steady employment may fear a great loss of status when he is confronted with prolonged unemployment. Unemployment insurance has come to be a part of the normal pattern in our society and hence different from being on relief.

The percentage of workers affected by seasonal layoffs varies. In the beet sugar industry, canning, and ice manufacture, 50 per cent or more of the workers may be off during the slack time. About 25 per cent of automobile workers may be laid off temporarily during model change-overs.

Such industries as the manufacture of fertilizers, woolen goods, and furniture are quite sensitive to both seasonal effects and to economic depressions. On the other hand, employees of telephone companies, electric power industries, and the like enjoy more stable employment.

For the young person getting started, the lack of work is common even in prosperous times. For teen-agers ready to begin careers, unemployment often runs as high as 10 per cent. However, little or no psychological damage normally results from these conditions.

Prolonged Unemployment and Status. But what happens to the individual as a result of prolonged unemployment? A few studies were made of this problem during the Great Depression in both the United States and in England. From these studies, which are summarized below, we will get a descriptive picture of the changes which take place in the individual as well as an insight into the nature of human needs and the place that work holds in the routine of modern living.

Unemployment, of course, affects individuals differently, but there is a general pattern in the way the unemployed feel and act. Two major factors govern both individual and general behavior among the unemployed: the cultural background of the person and the length of time he has been out of work.

A man from middle-class circumstances may find his ego deflated sooner and more deeply than will the laborer who has always lived on the borderline of poverty. The unemployed man from the poorer environment probably has more associates who are also out of work than does the person who lives in a better community. In this environment, contrast may not be so noticeable. But middle-class people live in a psychological environment where the incentive to independence and self-support prevails. When economic opportunity is lacking, not only does the individual feel it directly, but he feels the social sanctions that his neighbors apply. Although the man from the lower-class group may be worse off economically, the social pressures on him are less. Ginsberg [8] summarized this status problem: "The unemployed were able to adjust to the loss of their jobs, the exhaustion of their savings accounts, even to the cashing in of their insurance policies, but they broke down on the day they asked for relief."

Stages of Behavior of the Unemployed. For most people the course of unemployment runs through three stages, according to Blum [5]. First, there comes the feeling of shock regardless of any forewarning that the loss of the job was imminent. In this stage, the individual reviews the sequence of events leading to his unemployment and rationalizes about the wisdom of having taken the job in the first place. He soon settles for the idea that he can use a much-needed vacation. This is followed by an appraisal of his abilities and the formation of plans to get another job.

The second stage includes the active search for a job. Most people begin looking for one better than the one they had, and then for a similar one, if unemployment continues. As time passes, they begin to look for work anywhere doing almost anything. "During this period," Blum says, "the individual is rather unresigned. His spirit is unbroken, and although he is unhappy about his predicament, he is still hopeful of success."

The final stage in unemployment involves the breaking down of the individual. Failing to find a job, he becomes anxious and pessimistic and begins to lose hope.

Some people pass through these stages rapidly, particularly the person who has experienced more failure than success. Each stage lasts longer for the individual who has had more success than failure in the past.

Effects of Prolonged Unemployment. There are several aspects of the psychological effects of prolonged unemployment:

1. There is a loss of the sense of security, both economical and psychological.

2. The worker comes to blame himself for his condition; then he takes an aggressive attitude toward the situation.

3. There is the problem of time. For the man who has a job the day's activities center around that job because it takes the greatest share of his time. For the unemployed man, time hangs heavy.

4. Daily routines of the household become interrupted. Regular hours of getting up or going to bed, of eating or performing chores are disrupted. This adds to the feeling of "being lost."

5. Early in unemployment, the individual attempts to conceal his status from others. He may even leave for his "job" at the regular time and return home at the usual time at night. He fills in this time by job seeking, watching movies, or just loafing around. Bakke [3] reports that in England during the Great Depression, the unemployed did not frequent the pubs during working hours, but rather at the closing time of the factories—when those employed went in for their beer.

6. Irrational spending has been noted among the unemployed; they often spend their money on luxury items instead of on necessities; some

even take up relatively expensive hobbies which rapidly deplete unemployment insurance funds or the relief check. This is one reason why relief is often given in goods rather than in money.

7. Some unemployed attempt to retreat from their situation through fantasy and dreaming. Others escape through psychosomatic illness. Some seek illegal outlets; others become radicals. But in the main, most unemployed men remain good citizens. Suicide and drinking are apparently not common escapes.

8. The unemployed man becomes excessively depressed if his family, relatives, and friends change their attitude of sympathy and understanding to one of criticism of the former breadwinner.

9. One of the most interesting psychological changes that occurs with prolonged unemployment is the intensification of daily habits. For example, the person who has read extensively when employed reads even more when unemployed. The person who reads only a little while holding a job will probably read even less when out of work. Those who were religious while employed become more religious during unemployment, whereas those people normally not very religious become even less so during unemployment.

10. The effects of prolonged unemployment of parents soon show up in the insecurities and anxieties of their children. This throwback to the parents reinforces all the other effects on the head of the family, lowering the morale as well as the authority of the father.

11. Personality changes related to unemployment show up eventually in irritability, new faults, a breakdown in morale, and loss of emotional stability. Prejudices may increase, and scapegoats are sometimes set up as a defense for the position the person finds himself in. Unemployment may well bring out into the open a person's previously concealed feelings of inferiority.

Aspiration and Unemployment. Although the unemployed do show behaviors in common, the *degree* to which unemployment affects the individual depends upon past experience and individual aspirations. The migrant worker without a home comes to expect less than the person who has seen better times. One study of over four thousand migrant families made in 1932 showed that 69 per cent were on the move because of economic distress. Some were following the seasonal employment route; some were looking for a permanent home; all hoped for little more than a place where body and soul could be held together. In another study of some twenty six thousand migrants, made in the prosperous year of 1954, the goal was essentially the same—economic survival. Ambitions for the children and hopes of becoming a part of some community were further goals, but little was expected. Aspirations of community status could not be verbalized too well by these people because most of them had never experienced it [2].

Somewhat in contrast to this group who "had little to lose psychologically" is a group of established families in New York City who "had more to lose" (9). A psychiatric study of the latter revealed that most of these people had been established in jobs, carried life insurance, and were on the way up when the Depression put the breadwinner out of a job. To these people, the emotional experience of losing a job may be compared to the loss of love which a child suffers from a rejecting parent, especially a child who has done nothing to deserve the loss. This feeling of rejection was especially strong among men who had worked long, arduous years for one employer, to whom, as well as to the job, they had understandably formed real attachments. "Deprived of 'love,' their first reaction was one of fear and bewilderment, combined with optimism, born of wishful thinking, obviously over-compensatory in nature."

It was found that the shame and embarrassment of being on relief was so great that a number of families persisted in hiding the fact for years. They refused to use commodities which would at once identify them as relief recipients. This study further reports that many of the children refused to eat the hot lunches provided for them at school, since this would identify them as "reliefers." In some cases there were attempts to "cheat" on relief investigators in petty ways affording the recipients some slight ego gratification of the kind a child gets from teasing teacher or pilfering his mother's purse for pennies.

Lasting Effects of Unemployment. The jobless man who eventually gets employment is not the same man he was before his unemployment experience. He has different attitudes, often colored by bitterness and disillusionment. His skills are lessened, his self-discipline relaxed, and often his habits of neatness, punctuality, and getting along with others have to be relearned. He has acquired fears that may remain with him a lifetime.

Studies show that women suffer less than men during unemployment. This may well be related to the fact that, generally speaking, women have never really been accepted in industry, that they often work on a temporary basis, or that they resign to have babies (see page 271). Although unemployment can hit the woman worker just as hard economically as it does the man, psychologically women seem to be exempt from many of the problems which face men who are out of a job.

Of the many writings on the psychological effects of unemployment on the individual, practically all focus upon one basic problem: satisfaction in life comes from the feelings of accomplishment that the person gets from work.

AGING AND WORK

"I was classified as a has-been. Instead of 'How's business?' the question was 'When are you heading for the warm climate?' What am I expected to do?" This businessman, describing his own attitude toward retirement, has in large measure raised the basic question of the aging worker. More attention is being given to this problem today than ever before, because we are rapidly becoming a nation of older people. The average human life span in the United States has increased from 48 years in 1900 to over 70 in 1960.

The Criteria of Aging. When is a man old? "Aging, true physiologic aging, is not determined by the time elapsed since birth, but by the total

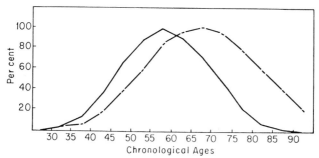

Fig. 12.1. Age and industrial leadership. The solid curve shows the ages of 2,795 outstanding commercial and industrial leaders. Higher executive posts are most likely to be filled by 57-year-olds; only 80 per cent of 66-year-olds are as well placed. The broken curve corrects for the fact that young people exceed older people in our population but that, proportionately speaking, older men are more favorably placed. (From Lehman, H. C. *Age and achievement.* Princeton: Princeton Univer. Press, 1953.)

amount of wear and tear to which the body has been exposed. There is, indeed, a great difference between physiologic and chronologic age." These words of Hans Selye [24], who has worked on the problems of aging and the stress of life for some three decades, gives us a key to the problem of how long any given individual should continue to work.

Among the unskilled and semiskilled workers, work accomplishment is primarily of a physical nature. Some get old in their thirties, others are capable of work into their sixties. Among skilled workers in our industrial society productivity continues as long as general health and opportunity permit. Little information is available from which it is possible to determine the role of age per se in industrial output. On the whole, there is little evidence that the output of older workers is less than that of younger ones.

In other areas, age is a factor in productivity. Lehman [14] has shown that the age for winning championships in sports comes early, often in the teens. The peaks for notable intellectual creativity come a little later, but fall off rapidly, during and after middle age. In contrast, professional recognition and leadership status in business, education, medicine, law, and politics tend to come in later life. In Figure 12.1, taken from the data of Lehman, we see the ages at which a sample of 2,795 commercial and

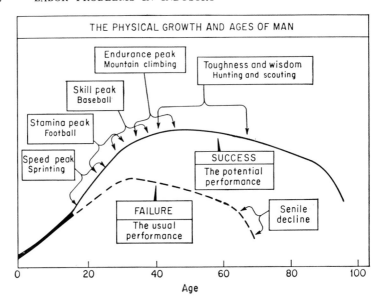

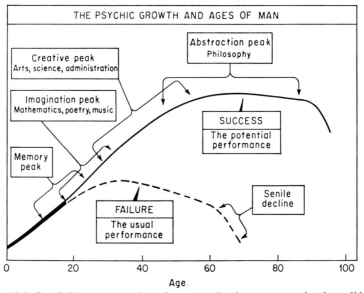

Fig. 12.2. Possibility and actual performance. In these two graphs the solid curve indicates the physical or psychological potential of normal people, with peak periods for various activities. How most people fail to measure up to these potentials is indicated by the broken curve. (From Still, J. W. Man's potential—and his performance. *The New York Times,* Nov. 24, 1957. Cited by Hurlock, E. B. *Developmental psychology.* New York: McGraw-Hill, 1959.)

industrial leaders became outstanding represented by the solid line. The broken line of the figure is the same as the solid line with the exception that it makes allowance for population differences at successive age levels.

Figure 12.2 gives an over-all view of the physical and psychological growth of man in relation to age brackets.

Effects of Age Sometimes a Myth. Before we conclude too hastily that the "scientist is through at forty," let us examine the kind of change that frequently takes place in a creative field. The physicist, for example, becomes personally involved in some technical problem and produces numerous research papers. As he gains in professional stature, his interests broaden, graduate students require more of his attention, and administrative problems become more demanding. Gradually our scientist moves from a "do-it-yourself" role into one of leadership in science.

Compensation takes place for every deviation in age; often, if certain capacities diminish, others are enhanced. Older people may make up for slowness in some job through steady work and good attendance. Since the greatest occupational mobility takes place under age thirty-five, older workers are an asset in terms of continuance on the job. This factor of stability, often enhanced by stronger loyalty, is of considerable importance in those industries where training periods are long and expensive.

Age is a convenient factor on which to attach status differentials. The young beginner on a job has little or no status; the older worker may be called "Pops" and treated with a certain deference. Some popular opinions about age are supported by research evidence; others are found wanting. For example, in general, research supports the opinion that people become more conservative as they grow older. On the other hand, a reason commonly offered for discrimination against the older worker is that he is more of an accident risk than the younger worker. This view is not justified in light of the facts. Tiffin [27], for example, in a study of 9,000 steel workers has shown that older people are even better accident risks than younger workers.

Another easily measurable aspect of industrial behavior is absenteeism. Let us cite one recent study [12] showing again that we should be careful in selling the oldsters short. This study was made in the Baker Chocolate Division of the General Foods Company. It will be noted from Table 5, which gives a summary picture of the number of absences and days lost, that workers over 45, the traditional dividing line between young and old, show up well in comparison with workers under 45 years of age. Actually, total absence per employee is a shade less among the older workers.

When we examine absence rates for the total firm in relation to age and length of absence (Table 6), we see that the age bracket 45 to 55 has a decidedly better absence record than either those older or those younger. In fact, it will be noted that the under-35 group has the worst record of all. It is important to note the distinction between kinds of absenteeism. Older workers are absent *for longer periods* (severity rate) but younger workers are absent *more often* (frequency rate).

TABLE 5

NUMBER OF ABSENCES AND DAYS LOST, BY AGE, SEX, AND LENGTH OF ABSENCE

	All employees			Male			Female		
	Total (619)	Under 45 (330)	45 and over (289)	Total (479)	Under 45 (250)	45 and over (229)	Total (140)	Under 45 (80)	45 and over (60)
I. Number of absences:									
Total absences	1,624	1,061	563	1,162	748	414	462	313	149
1 day	960	683	277	703	486	217	257	197	60
2-5 days	498	307	191	337	206	131	161	101	60
6 or more days	166	71	95	122	56	66	44	15	29
II. Days of absence:									
Total days	4,931	2,845	2,086	3,394	1,962	1,432	1,537	883	654
1 day	960	683	277	703	486	217	257	197	60
2-5 days	1,520	930	590	1,027	615	412	493	315	178
6 or more days	2,451	1,232	1,219	1,664	861	803	787	371	416

SOURCE: Kahne, H. R., Ryder, C. F., Snegireff, L. S., & Wyshak, G. Don't take the older workers for granted, *Harv. Bus. Rev.*, 1957, 35, 90-94.

TABLE 6

ABSENCE RATES FOR TOTAL FIRM, BY AGE AND LENGTH OF ABSENCE

	Disability rate*				Frequency rate†				Severity rate‡			
	All absences	1 day	2-5 days	6 days	All absences	1 day	2-5 days	6 days	All absences	1 day	2-5 days	6 days
All employees	3.4	0.6	1.1	1.7	1.1	0.6	0.3	0.1	3.2	1.0	3.2	15.2
Under 35	4.0	1.2	1.3	1.5	1.7	1.2	0.4	0.1	2.4	1.0	2.9	18.3
35-44	3.4	0.6	1.0	1.7	1.1	0.6	0.3	0.1	3.3	1.0	2.9	15.6
45-54	2.9	0.4	0.9	1.6	0.8	0.4	0.4	0.1	3.5	1.0	2.5	14.8
55 and over	3.6	0.3	0.9	2.2	0.7	0.3	0.2	0.1	4.8	1.0	3.8	18.3

* Average number of days absent per 100 scheduled workdays ($DR = FR \times SR$).
† Average number of absences per 100 scheduled workdays ($FR = DR/SR$).
‡ Average length of time lost per absence ($SR = FR/DR$).
SOURCE: Kahne, H. R., Ryder, C. F., Snegireff, L. S., & Wyshak, G. Don't take the older workers for granted, *Harv. Bus. Rev.*, 1957, 35, 90-94.

The results of this study are important in raising the practical question, "Are different kinds of absences important?" We need to know answers to this question when considering how suitable older people prove themselves to be on the job. Certainly, if frequent short absences, particularly of the unexpected and unnecessary kind, are annoying to management or impede production seriously, the older workers are preferable. If, on the other hand, staffing is not flexible enough to fill in for workers justifiably absent for several days at a time, then younger workers may be preferred by management.

A number of other aspects of absenteeism will be discussed in Chapter 20. We cite the results of this investigation here merely to illustrate that older workers are not necessarily absence prone, and that under certain circumstances they may even be preferred to younger workers.

To be sure, older people may be less adaptable to changes in job assignments; they may be more set in their ways. They may show less muscular strength and agility than younger people, but at the same time, experience and judgment may compensate for these things. Just as the handicapped worker may be an asset to business if he has been adequately analyzed as to what he can best do, trained to take advantage of his assets, and properly oriented and placed on the job, so can the older worker become an asset. Greater attention should be given to aptitude tests and to measurement of physical reserve in placing the older worker on the right job.

RETIREMENT

The worker, the manager, the professional man, if he lives long enough, must face the problem of quitting work. What are the problems of retirement?

The Magic Age of Sixty-five. For most workers there is no retirement, because they are either forced out of work or they die before retirement age is reached. In the United States, the age for industrial retirement is widely assumed to be sixty-five for men, and in some industries as low as sixty for women. The magic age of sixty-five for retirement seems to have come about when the Federal government originally selected a base for paying old age and survivors insurance, that is, "social security." Although it has been an age generally accepted by both business and union officials, sixty-five is still a controversial figure. Everyone seems to agree that some people are old at forty and that others are still young at seventy. Until there are good, measurable, and acceptable criteria of physiological and psychological age, then, it can be expected that the retirement age will be determined chronologically. There does seem to be some relaxation of retirement age during periods of labor shortage for skilled workers. Executives who are still productive may be carried on as consultants, or in some instances optional age levels for retirement may be put into effect, such as is now being done among college teachers who are in short supply.

It is believed that the number of retired workers will increase at an accelerating rate until at least 1980. A fair assumption may be made that there will be steps taken to lower retirement age if the supply of workers is adequate, or to adjust it upward when there are labor shortages.

Individual Differences in Aging. Individual differences among older people are enormous, both mentally and physically. That our bodies gradually wear out during life has always been known. The sensory processes decline, motor skills slow down, and attitudes change. With advancing years, people require increasingly more rest, but the process of aging does not progress at the same speed in each person, nor does each need the same amount and type of rest. Many a man who could still have given numerous years of useful work has been made physically ill and prematurely senile by enforced retirement at an age when his requirements for activity were still high and his ability to produce was still ample. This psychosomatic illness is so common that it is now called the "retirement disease." Every person has his own individual requirements for rest and activity. And certainly to lie in bed all day is no relaxation for an active man.

Studies of the reactions of older people can teach us much about energy conservation. Experiments on animals have clearly shown that excessive stressful activities use up reserves of adaptability which cannot be replaced. Selye [24] has stated the concept thus: "Vitality is like a special kind of bank account which you can use up by withdrawals but cannot increase by deposits. The only control is the rate that withdrawals are made."

When we consider the problems of personality changes that take place in older persons, let us bear in mind that chronological age per se should not be the criterion for judging when the person is past his prime.

The Loss of Status. In our culture the person who has reached retirement loses status. He may be treated as a has-been, consciously or unconsciously, through overattention or neglect. The man of status who has made decision after decision as a daily routine gets retirement shock when he is no longer called on for decision making, or even for advice. This has been such a serious problem for management personnel who have reached retirement age that some companies now have planned programs of preretirement counseling and of easing-up practices over a period of time. The person gradually gets used to doing less; it is a sort of "job-decompression" program.

Aside from the economic burdens of the retired person, he experiences some of the losses felt by the unemployed—feelings of not accomplishing anything through work. This comedown was described by a retired executive, formerly a vice-president and treasurer of a large corporation, who said he looked forward each month to a meeting of his local shuffleboard club. Much discussion of finances was always in order—what to do with a balance of $35 in the treasury!

No Typical Pattern in Old Age. Time hangs heavy on the retired individual's hands. Although some take up hobbies, these activities do not seem to relieve tensions as they formerly did. Working in a woodshop may be good to take the executive's mind off his office problems, but without these problems, the hobby may become only a time killer.

For those elderly people who become somewhat senile, the clinical picture is not good—mental rigidity, suspiciousness, hoarding, overtalkativeness, untidiness, and the like give a pessimistic picture of growing old. But this picture is not completely typical of old age. There are many oldsters who remain in good health and avoid the crisis of retirement. It may well be that we have not given enough attention to the proper placement of the reasonably healthy retired person. Why shouldn't he resent "made work" that just keeps him busy? A retired business executive could hardly get much satisfaction from building furniture all day in his hobby shop or from helping his wife around the house.

Just as we have seen how good planning and effective rehabilitation of the physically handicapped has made these people economic and social assets in our society, so too some of the programs now under way to reevaluate the assets of the aged show promise.

Through a projection of the problems of the handicapped, the unemployed, and the aging worker, we may be able to get a better concept of the meaning of work, a meaning which is individual to each of us.

A PERSPECTIVE

When we look at the various needs for adjustment in middle age and old age, the over-all problems related to work may become more meaningful to us. In one sociological study [7] word portraits were made of various people as they reached the time of retirement. As we take a look at these eighteen descriptions, it is possible to see at a glance the different kinds of problems arising from age. The descriptions show that *individual differences* exist and that they may even be greater in maturity than they are in childhood, adolescence, and middle age. Industry is coming to recognize this more and more as our expanding economy places additional demands upon the effective uses of human resources. Some men must retire; some can work part time; and some can keep going strong.

A is getting along in years but has good health. He has had to give up his more vigorous activities but still attends clubs and parties and looks after his business. Or, if he has retired, he carries on with hobbies and other interesting activities. His sight and hearing are not as good as formerly, but do not give him any great troubles. He has faced the fact that he is not as strong as he was and has adjusted his activities accordingly.

B is definitely showing his age. He walks slowly and lets his shoulders sag. There is nothing very much the matter except that he dosen't get around as fast as he once did. He can't do his work very well and he tires easily. He is content to sit quietly and let others carry on.

C has definite physical ailments characteristic of old age (such as high blood pressure or partial blindness or deafness). These interfere greatly with both work and recreation. He is inclined to complain.

D has not had to make any upsetting changes in his way of living. The family is still intact, and when members are absent, they keep in touch by correspondence. Finances are still adequate for the usual standard of living. No unusual or sudden illness has come either to D or his immediate family.

E has had to meet some sharp changes. He has lost a member of the family dear to him or has had a moderate decrease in income or has been retired before he was ready for it. He has shown normal sorrow and the ability to accept his losses fairly well.

F has had to make drastic changes in living. The death of a dear family member has left him desolate. Or he has had to give up his home and go to live with a relative or in a home for the aged. He says he sees no reason to go on living.

G talks occasionally about his adolescence. When he does, it is to relate some humorous incident or some exciting or interesting adventure. This was apparently a good period in his life.

H reminisces about adolescence along with other earlier periods of his life. His comments are neither doleful nor thrilling but simply matter of fact.

I dwells much more upon his adolescence and the difficulties he had then. He tells of the unjust severity of his parents, the unfair treatment he received from brothers and sisters, the troubles he had at school, among friends, and at work. He remembers adolescence as a very difficult period, when he was not well treated by others.

J has achieved a comfortable position for his old age. He is respected by his family and his friends. He has no financial worries. He has retained his old friends and enjoys their respect. He lives in as good a house as when he was younger.

K lives in his old neighborhood, or one of the same type, but he has to struggle to keep up appearances. His clothes are shabby and his house and furniture need repairs. He tries to keep up his contacts with old friends and succeeds by working hard at it.

L has had to accept an unsatisfactory standard of living. He has parted from his old friends and seldom sees those who knew him in better days. He is quite sensitive about his situation. His former friends feel that he has gone down since they knew him.

M has always been a cheerful, happy person. He has met his problems courageously and has worked out the best solutions possible for his situation.

N has always been inclined to be a worrier and to look on the gloomy side. Nevertheless, he has met his small problems fairly well and has been only mildly unhappy. He has had to have help from family and friends to face major problems.

O has never been able to face his problems. He has always gone to pieces easily, blamed others for his troubles, and complained a great deal. He is nervous and unstable. In a severe crisis he would probably have a complete breakdown.

P has led a successful life. He has done as high a type of work as he was capable of doing and has met his family responsibilities. He has been interested in the welfare of his community and his fellow workers. He feels satisfied.

Q has never been able to meet his own standards. He has tried to reach good standards but has never been quite able to make it. He therefore looks on his past life as a failure and is either bitter or full of excuses for his failure.

R has been a failure through and through. He has had low standards and has failed miserably to do what the community expects in the way of regular work and family responsibilities. But since his standards are low, he does not express any regret.[1]

Age and Speed. Turner [29] has emphasized the point that individual differences in performance increases with age. Almost always there are some older people whose performance equals or surpasses the average performance of the younger group. There is a tendency for older people to place more emphasis on accuracy and less on speed. However, surveys show that comparatively few older people are placed on jobs where there is unusual pressure for speed or where the pace of working is mechanically determined, as on a moving assembly line.

Attitudes toward the Aged. Another point concerns the importance of part-time work for older people. There are a number of people beyond the age of retirement who are willing and able to work part time. What should be employment policy in such cases? This question is not so simple to answer. Just as we have seen that individual differences exist among older people, so do individual differences exist among companies. Let us describe two particular firms. In company A, no one apparently had to retire or wanted to. In company B, retirement was compulsory at age sixty-five, and apparently no one wanted to stay on the job even that long [29].

Company A has 650 employees, of whom 307 are 55 years of age or older. There are 99 employees between 60 and 70 years old, 46 over 70. The company manufactures small metal products and machinery. The philosophy of the company is in effect that there is no age barrier to employment. "We have never believed that a man in good shape at 59 or 64 becomes suddenly useless the day he is 60 or 65," said the superintendent. It was the feeling among the younger men in the company that "older men are kept on too long." Among the older workers the attitude is that "a man should be allowed to work as long as he is able." This company is described as never having adopted modern personnel and safety practices,

[1] Cavan, R. S., Burgess, E. W., Havighurst, R. J., & Goldhamer, H. *Personal adjustments in old age.* Chicago: Science Research Associates, Inc., 1949. Reproduced by permission of Science Research Associates, Inc.

and many of its methods are old-fashioned. But it makes money, and older people like to work there.

Company B is an automobile assembly plant where the entire working environment puts a premium on youth. Retirement is compulsory at age sixty-five. The attitudes of the men were that there was a "compulsion to keep the line moving." Even the younger men believed that as they got older they would not be able to keep up with the pace of their jobs. A prevalent belief was: "They have no use for you when you get older."

These two cases illustrate the point that uniformity in retirement policy cannot effectively take care of individual differences either among individuals or among companies. More and more, both management and labor unions are recognizing the fact that responsibility toward the older employee does not begin and end with a retirement plan. There seems to be a movement in some places toward job analysis and job reassignment for the older worker. This philosophy is not unlike that of personnel selection and placement now in common use for the new employee. In some places, procedures have been carried an additional step and the reengineering of jobs for certain older workers is going on.

Redesigning the Job. Abrams [1] reports an interesting case of a factory in Syracuse where older women working as clay-press operators were turning out a diminishing amount of work. Rather than get rid of these older workers, the company reengineered the job by installing special hydraulic and pneumatic presses which decreased physical demands and awkward working conditions. With these modifications, the workers were quite capable of keeping up with the work.

In another case, older employees working on an operation in a shirt factory, which required them to match materials, were found to be losing their visual acuity. The firm rescheduled their work so that they did not receive any material which was hard to match by color or design. The same company, when confronted with workers who had developed arthritis or heart disease, redesigned machine controls or relocated workers' lines to better fit the job to the employees' physical capacities.

In his survey of over two hundred companies Abrams found a number of techniques employed in job engineering for older workers, such as:

1. Rescheduling the pace of production to eliminate fatiguing "quick sprints"
2. Reshuffling work so that the older worker receives large, easier-to-handle materials
3. Reducing production rating on incentive positions filled by oldsters
4. Providing better leverage for tools and controls
5. Relocating control levers and wheels
6. Providing power tools
7. Rearranging work area to bring motion into normal working area

8. Providing power feed of stock to machines
9. Substituting "pull" motion for "push" motion
10. Providing better grip on tools

Some of the effects of such changes were most encouraging. The job engineering had helped combat declining production in certain places. Labor turnover was reduced, and savings on costs enabled management to retain experienced workers.

Job Reassignment. Where job reengineering may not be practical, some companies have found it profitable to reassign a worker to a job within his capacity. It was reported by Abrams that large concerns usually have such a diversity of available positions that they can usually find some suitable post for an aging worker without much difficulty [1]. Job reassignments have included shifting older workers to jobs outside the line of production, to jobs requiring custom or quality work, or to jobs calling for part-time work on a more desirable shift. The following reassignments are typical of those made in different industries which have worked well for older employees:

The Blackstone Corporation employs workers on incentive or day rate, and transfers aging men who request it from incentive pay to daywork.

At the National Biscuit Company, operations must keep pace with the ovens; on most positions paced with the ovens there can be little slowing down. So the aging man who can't maintain the pace is shifted outside the sphere of jobs revolving about the oven.

At the Republic Steel Company operators of mobile equipment whose eyes are failing are shifted to other types of work not requiring visual acuity.

General Mills, Inc., reports switching aging workers from nightwork to daywork, and bringing outside salesmen into the office.

The General Motors Corporation, through its Chevrolet Central Office, says, "Size and diversification of the Chevrolet organization has in the past made it possible to move the aging and physically impaired employee to a job which he could do. A review of this matter shows the older workers gravitate to the less arduous tasks in the plant. As a result we have not found it necessary in many cases to engineer the job to the older worker." This is the refrain heard commonly from big industry: "Transfers are no problem; we transfer aging personnel quite regularly."

The Kroehler Manufacturing Company reports having "many workers over 65 and even beyond 70," but it has numerous jobs that can be handled by older men without undue fatigue.

Sylvania Electric Products, Inc., similarly reports that it is "fortunate in being able to reassign older employees to jobs fitting their capacities." The operations in the radio and television plant are such that subassembly and inspection departments are capable of handling aged people.

The H. J. Heinz Company and the General Electric Company both report that job transfer is a commonly used technique. The food concern says it has been "very successful" in solving its problems of making adjustments for older workers by transferring them to different jobs, "in most instances without down-grading." Therefore it reports not engaging in job engineering for declining capacities.

The International Business Machines Company also reports that a "great diversity" of jobs enables them to transfer workers easily.

The Procter & Gamble Company since 1923 has had a guarantee of regular employment which assures workers forty-eight weeks of work a year. The company reports that this has resulted in a low turnover, with a consequent aging of the labor force. The company says that it has developed an understanding among its workers that successful operation of the plan depends in part on willingness of the employees to accept occasional transfers which may be necessary because of schedule changes, installation of technological developments, or physical or mental impairments which may arise.

The American Sugar Refining Company, Link Aviation, Inc., and Winthrop Stearns, Inc., also report that transferring is common. The latter transfers employees, using a "limited service" category. "When we have a square peg and a round hole, we simply shift the peg to where it fits rather than re-design it," the firm reports.

The National Cash Register Company, with almost thirteen thousand employees, has one department especially arranged to take care of those with declining physical capacities, so that they can sit at a bench and perform work which does not require much physical effort. There are sixty workers in this department who sit at benches and disassemble registers, and the parts disassembled are sold as scrap. The company transfers aging employees to small assembly jobs, such as light filing of metal, and also arranges for a shorter workday if necessary.

A large perfume company hiring a high proportion of persons fifty to seventy years of age says that age doesn't severely handicap their workers. Most work is done by hand, and few operations are paced by machines. Nor are there many heavy lifting operations. "We find we have a sufficient variety of these operations for us to set up our incentive groups in such a manner that those who by reason of age have lost the necessary rhythm required for the machine operations can perform certain of the necessary hand operations on the final assembly line," the company reports. Having a variety of shipments, it uses younger personnnel on the heavier freight shipments and older workers on light mailings and shipments.

The U.S. Gypsum Company prefers to shift an older employee to a lower-level job than to hire a new employee, because his experience will allow him "to handle it more efficiently."

Moore Business Forms, Inc., reports that transfers are made to similar types of presses if operating complicated large presses becomes too much for older workers.

"Closely allied with the relocation of an employee who is unable to perform his primary job is the matter of wage rates to be paid on the new job," points out the Rochester Community Survey. It found that it is customary in Rochester plants to pay the employee the rate of his assigned occupation. In some instances this results in a lower rate, but occasionally the amount earned is increased.

Prejudice against Older People. In spite of what industries and some unions have been able to do for the aged person, there still exists much prejudice against older people. In a study of a nation-wide sample of elderly people, Barron [4] found that 53 per cent of them lacked any club or other organizational affiliation, and 40 per cent were rarely ever asked for advice by their family and friends. About a third claimed to have no really close friends. Social isolation was found to be most conspicuous among the unemployed aged. The aged tend to demonstrate such typical minority-group reactions as hypersensitivity, low morale, defensiveness, self-hatred, and isolation.

Of the aged unemployed, 70 per cent who had tried to secure reemployment reported that they were unsuccessful, largely because of "prejudice against older workers." Barron concludes that the social isolation of the older person is a basic factor in the tension which exists between the young and the chronologically aged in our society. Unless people have frequent and meaningful contact with each other, they build up stereotypes of each other and develop prejudiced attitudes.

Some Facts Worth Noting. Bowers [6] made a study of 3,162 men and women workers ranging in age from eighteen through seventy-six years who performed various duties in an organization that included a variety of operations. Data were gathered on each worker from personnel records. Supervisors made appraisals of the person's work, of any administrative actions taken affecting the employees, of any completion of training courses, of grievances, and of any similar information important to the study. Men and women in the age groups 18 to 29, 30 to 44, 45 to 50, and 60 and up were compared in ability, character, and faults. Included were such traits as accuracy, initiative, job knowledge, efficiency, cooperativeness, dependability, attendance, thoroughness, steadiness, tactfulness, slowness, and instability.

The results of this study indicate that age differences in traits were relatively small. Older workers of both sexes with over two years' service were reported to learn less readily and to be slower; on the other hand, they more frequently showed good attendance, steadiness, and conscientiousness. These trends were reported by Bowers to be quite consistent. In other traits covered in this study, age differences appear to be negligible or not consistent. For example, the difference in efficiency between the oldest and youngest groups of men was 9 net percentage points favoring the younger, but there was only a 1 per cent drop between the 30 to 44 group and the 60 and up group. Of interest is the finding that the oldest women were considered more efficient than the younger by 7 percentage points, although women under 30 years of age were fairly often mentioned as rapid workers. No consistent age differences were found in job knowledge, accuracy, dependability, or emotional stability. Physical differences were not mentioned often enough, even for the oldest group, to indicate that such handicaps were of importance. In this company, attitudes favorable to older people were evidenced by the fact that it employed new people over 45, and that several were hired as new employees who were over 60 years of age.

The author concludes with the following statement: "Quite evidently workers should be employed and retained on the basis of merit without reference to age. Biases and misconceptions limiting the use of older persons should be replaced by facts. Oldsters can maintain productivity, thus making an extended productive life worth while, strengthening man-power resources, and lessening possible economic burdens which often result from dependency of large numbers of non-productive older persons."

Job Demands and Age. McFarland [17], who has studied the psycho-physiological problems of aging in air transport pilots and the age problems of professional truck drivers, and who has reviewed the over-all psychological aspects of aging, concludes that aging is a highly individual matter; chronological age alone, he says, is rarely a reliable index of a person's physical or mental development and adjustment. He points out that the natural process of aging is of more significance for some occupational groups than others by virtue of differences in the demands made upon individual abilities. A defect in vision or hearing may be important for one occupation, but not for another. Slowing reaction time may lead to loss of confidence where a task requiring quick responses is involved. The problem is one of matching the abilities of workers to the requirements of their job *throughout the life cycle.*

A Favorable Trend. Attitudes toward older people and their role in society have tended to force them into corresponding behavior patterns. There is evidence that, as people age, individual differences tend to become more marked. Instead of retiring people arbitrarily when they reach a given chronological age, we might better think in terms of helping to place them in jobs more suited to their abilities. Until around 1940 only a few psychologists had worked on problems of old age [21]. Today there is a growing interest in the problems of old age on the part of medical people, social scientists, governments, forward-looking industrial leaders, and responsible union leaders. The trend of thinking of most of those people who are studying the relationship between age and work today is in the direction of helping the oldsters who are capable of working to continue working. A number of industries are keeping good workers on the payroll through programs of job engineering, job reassignment, and job counseling. These programs, limited as they may be, denote a favorable trend toward dealing with some of the problems of the aging worker. For the retired executive some plans are in operation promoting part-time consulting. For example, in Pittsburgh there is an organization called Associated Senior Executives. The members are retired professionals in administration and research and development. A small company, for example, which cannot afford a full-time man in their product development may call on a senior associate for assistance. Between jobs he returns to his "retirement activities."

SUGGESTIONS FOR FURTHER READING

Crook, G. H., & Heintein, M. *The older worker in industry.* Berkeley, Calif.: Univer. of California Institute of Industrial Relations, 1958. A study of the attitudes of industrial workers toward aging and retirement.

Ginsberg, E. *The unemployed.* New York: Harper, 1943. A description of what unemployment means psychologically to the man of middle-class status.

Pressey, S. L., & Kuhlen, R. G. *Psychological development through the life span.* New York: Harper, 1957. A comprehensive treatment of the problems of development in our society.

Switzer, M. E., & Rusk, H. A. *Doing something for the disabled.* Public Affairs Pamphlet, No. 197. New York: Public Affairs Committee, Inc., 1953. This pamphlet describes the ways in which disabled persons can often become productive.

Wright, B. A. (Ed.) *Psychology and rehabilitation.* Washington: American Psychological Association, Inc., 1959. A summary picture of current thinking on the basic and applied problems of rehabilitation.

13

WOMEN

IN INDUSTRY

B. von Haller Gilmer

"It would not be much of an exaggeration to say that if all women who are employed in industry stayed home on Monday, our economy would suffer a headache," said one industrialist. And he added, "If they stayed out for the remainder of the week, we would suffer an economic disaster." Whatever one may learn from such expressions of opinion, it is certainly true that women are playing increasingly significant roles in industry. What do they do?

ONE-THIRD ARE WOMEN

Almost one-third of the total labor force in our country is made up of women. By "labor force" we mean all people who work for pay, whether as production workers in a plant, as office managers, or in professional jobs, as doctors or engineers. Figure 13.1 shows the relative numbers of women working in various types of jobs in the United States.

The subject of women in industry is more interesting to college students today than it has ever been before. An increasing number of young women, both married and unmarried, are entering industry after graduation from college. Older women, including many who do not need to work for a living, are coming into or returning to industry after their family responsibilities become less demanding. In this chapter we hope to tell what kind of work these women do and how they are accepted, and to point out some trends in the changing place of women in industry.

266

At the present time there are about 50 per cent more women at work than there were just before World War II. It has been predicted that by 1975 our total labor force will be about ninety million persons [11]. Where will these people be found? In any good business year, women comprise about 90 per cent of the total labor reserve, and here we find the answer to this question. Of necessity about half the growth will be made up of women, largely from the married group in the 35- to 54-year age bracket.

Much has been written about women in industry, but there are few scientific studies of the subject [8]. We shall approach the psychological problems peculiar to the woman worker and manager by looking back a few years into our industrial history.

A HISTORICAL BACKGROUND

The rapid progress of women in industry has been contemporaneous with the growth of our mass-production economy. The accompanying changes in customs and modes of living have been important to women workers. The social revolution at the turn of the century which brought the young single woman into the office gave her some economic independence. It also brought new life to a host of industries, such as garment factories, beauty shops, and women's magazines.

The expansion in manufacturing, construction, and transportation was followed by growth of commerce, trade, and service industries. But the dramatic appearance during World War II of Rosie the Riveter, of the woman welder, truck driver, and lathe operator, directed attention to the abilities of women in occupations which had never before been considered suitable for them. Mechanical power has made difference in strength between the sexes less important in many jobs. For example, the use of fork trucks allows women to accomplish much of the heavy lifting which was once performed solely by men. In the three years following Pearl Harbor, over 6 million women entered the labor force for the first time.

Women in World War II. Before World War II, it was generally accepted in steel mills that "skirts were bad luck"; this kind of work was the province of men. But at the height of the war, women were performing every job formerly done by men in ore mines, steel mills, and shipyards, except jobs requiring heavy physical exertion or calling for many years of training and experience. During the year 1944, for example, about 40,000 of the total of 315,000 employees of one large steel corporation were women. Approximately 15,000 of these were in office occupations and 25,000 were working directly in war production. These women came from all walks of life; formerly they had been housewives, saleswomen, stenographers, teachers, musicians. One subsidiary of this corporation listed 275 different jobs filled by women.

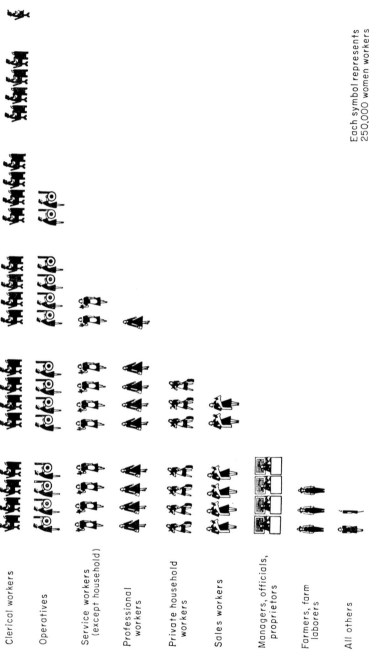

Clerical workers

Operatives

Service workers
(except household)

Professional
workers

Private household
workers

Sales workers

Managers, officials,
proprietors

Farmers, farm
laborers

All others

Each symbol represents
250,000 women workers

Fig. 13.1. Relative number of women in various types of jobs. Of the women working in the United States, the largest single group is in clerical work. Relatively few are found in managerial positions. (Courtesy U.S. Department of Labor.)

268

By "conveyorizing" operations, one plant of the United States Steel Corporation was able to increase its number of women employees to 48 per cent of the total. Overhead cranes and electrically driven dinkeys carried materials from department to department, thus obviating the need of lifting heavy material. Of the 153 crane operators in this plant, 79 were women. In the chemical laboratory, 80 per cent of the personnel were women who had not gone beyond elementary chemistry, taken either in high school or college; they were given on-the-job training [5].

Women in steel mills broke tradition and gave to their sex a power status never before experienced in heavy industry. Their presence introduced many changes, such as the installation of modern sanitary facilities and the employment of women counselors to guide new employees into the strange world of the steel mill.

Changes in Cultural Attitudes. In the half-century since 1910, there have been significant changes in terms of the socioeconomic groups to which women workers belong. Whereas only about a quarter of all working women were nonmanual workers in 1910, the proportion has now risen to about one-half. The number of women in nonagricultural work has increased nearly 100 per cent in the past half-century. This increase has been due to changes in cultural attitudes as well as to economic influences. The breakup of the old middle-class pattern of respectability, in which the wife did not work if her husband could afford to keep her at home, has affected all levels of society. Apparently women need the feeling of accomplishment which comes from earning money. In one survey 74 per cent of the women said they would continue to work even if they inherited enough money to live comfortably [2].

For many years, domestic service remained the largest single occupation for women. The rise in new mass-production industries and the vast technological changes taking place in more recent years have brought clerical workers and machine operators into the pattern.

At the professional level, teaching and nursing are still the most obvious choices of careers for women, although business, engineering, and the sciences are gaining in proportion as women's status changes.

Various factors have affected a change in women's occupations. The change-over from an agricultural to an industrial economy created the need for a new labor supply; this supply of new workers became available as women became less tied down with household duties.

The rise of our highly industrialized economy has been accompanied by social changes. During pioneer days most women directed their efforts to production and service for the family. Later, as a result of new inventions, spinning, weaving, sewing, laundering, and many personal services were taken over by commercial companies. As the luxuries of living came more and more to be necessities, there was an increasing need for women to help with the family budget. Thus the status of both the part-time and the full-time woman worker was raised considerably. Gradually women were offered more extensive opportunities to obtain education and specialized training. Some companies claim that although they originally put women into certain jobs because of a manpower shortage, they have found that special characteristics of women make them better suited to some tasks than men. These changes have been coming about slowly and are still in process.

Technology Opens up Jobs. The increase in the number of public service and welfare agencies has opened up new opportunities for women in such areas as social work and government offices. Since there was little or no traditional competition from men in these occupations, they, like teaching and nursing, have become known as "women's work." Technology, with such inventions as the typewriter and the telephone, created new kinds of jobs which went mostly to women. As automation increased, more new places appeared for women. In the craftsmen's occupations the traditions of long apprenticeships and prejudices against women began to give way as machines eliminated the necessity for physical strength on the job. Both the public and employers have gradually been changing their common belief that certain types of work are not appropriate for women.

DIFFERENCES BETWEEN WOMEN AND MEN AT WORK

Do women like their jobs? Do they have the same job dissatisfactions as those expressed by men? Do they have much interest in unions? Do they make good managers? Questions like these are important not only to personnel people, but also to college students who are trying to decide what kind of job to prepare for or what particular job offer should be accepted.

Differing Attitudes. Of several questionnaire-type studies reported in the literature comparing men and women in job satisfaction, some indicate that women are more satisfied than men; others show the reverse; and still others show no differences. Qualitatively, women seem to express themselves more freely, either by written comments or in interviews, about such things as cleanliness of working conditions, pleasantness of social relationships on the job, and treatment by supervisors. Women verbalize loyalty more than men, but show less interest in pay, benefit programs, and opportunities for advancement. The author had the opportunity recently to make a good comparison between the attitudes of men and women working together on the same types of jobs in a company employing about equal numbers of each sex. In response to a question of what they liked least about their jobs, two-thirds of the men mentioned low pay, but very few women mentioned money, in spite of the fact that their rate of pay was below that of the men. On an item concerned with cafeteria conditions, 600 women made a specific complaint which only 2 men mentioned. Noticeable differences between men and women in their questionnnaire responses were found in areas involving supervision and cleanliness in working conditions; the women were more sensitive than men. On questions involving a proposed installation of automatic laborsaving machines, the men expressed fear of losing their jobs, but the women were apparently not interested in the problem [8].

Problems of Adjustment. The employed woman who has to divide her energies between the working world and her traditional role as a woman faces adjustment problems peculiar to her sex. The married woman has both home and job responsibilities somewhat different from those of her male counterpart. The social and psychological pressures on the single woman complicate her attitudes toward marriage, toward her job, and toward her associates. A major consideration of the young single woman in selecting a job may well be the opportunities which it offers her to meet eligible men of marriageable age.

Married Women Workers. Women differ from men in their original attitudes toward work. Most young women today take a job until marriage or a few years after. The married women are more likely to leave the labor force during the years when their small children require care. Many return to jobs when their children are partly grown and no longer need constant attention. Because of this cycle, the largest proportion are in the labor force between the ages of 20 to 24. The proportion declines in the age range from 25 to 34, and increases again around 35.

Statistical surveys show that an increasing number of married women are going into industry. Part-time work is more likely to be sought by women than by men, since women frequently need to combine a paid job with household cares. Data show that 60 per cent of all part-time workers are women, most of them married and over 35 years of age. They usually do the same type of work as full-time employees. Apparently part-time work has resulted from the normal needs of management and is not merely a by-product of full employment. Women work part time because of a need to increase or supplement the family income, or to have outside interests. Management uses them during busy periods, for relief schedules, or for temporary peak loads.

Barriers to Employment. Women must face age barriers to employment earlier than men. Opinions of employment service personnel indicate that women around 35 years of age meet difficulties in getting jobs equivalent to those met by men of 45 to 50 years of age. Figure 13.2 shows the kind of shifting in jobs for women that takes place by age group.

In 1955 a study was reported by the Women's Bureau of the U.S. Department of Labor on twenty-three training programs for middle-aged and older women looking for work [18]. The programs included such items as industrial sewing, institutional housekeeping, domestic work, selling, and production work in the electronics industry. Without exception, the instructors and administrators of the training programs stressed the fact that

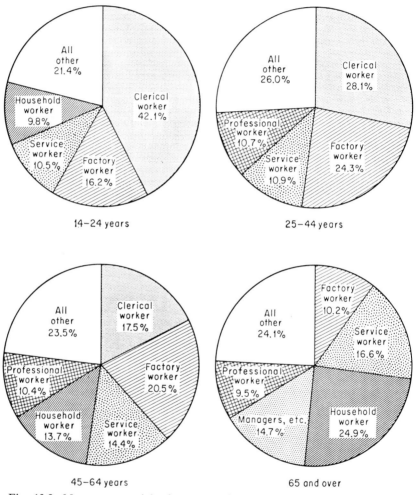

Fig. 13.2. Most common jobs for women by age group. These graphs illustrate the relationship between age and types of jobs held by women workers. (Courtesy U.S. Department of Labor.)

learning proficiency in these highly practical jobs depended on individual ability regardless of age. There was some evidence that older women did not do as well as younger students in classwork and theory but were better in demonstration and practice work. The instructors felt that since the mature women had been away from school for several years, they were no longer accustomed to studying. One important finding of the study was that mature women had a great need for individualized counseling and guidance. Their self-confidence had to be developed. The over-all results achieved in these twenty-three training programs showed clearly that women who have never worked, or have not worked for several years, can, with proper counseling, training, and placement, become both productive and satisfactory employees.

Some Traditional Beliefs Are Wrong. It has been a generally accepted idea that certain kinds of work are unsuitable for women. Many groups and agencies concerned with problems of social welfare have condemned nightwork as being bad for women. Before World War I, it was commonly believed that working at night was dangerous to the health of women. As scientific evidence failed to support this view, more attention was given to the idea that nightwork for women created a social hazard, disrupted family living, and deprived the workers of recreation and participation in community life. The pressure of public opinion led a number of states to pass laws regulating or prohibiting certain kinds of night employment for women. Some industries tried to prevent "the possibility of annoyance or criminal assault" by ending the swing shift an hour earlier for women than for men, so they could leave the plant at a separate time.

But what of the facts? Do women object to nightwork more than men do? One study may help to give a new perspective to this problem. A total of 270 men and women who worked nights in hotel and restaurant occupations were asked about their views on nightwork for women [14]. A preponderance of the women found nightwork acceptable. Some had chosen it deliberately because they liked the night shift, or because it was the most convenient time to work. Others had taken a night job because this was the only thing they could find. In contrast, the men who were interviewed expressed more objections to nightwork.

Equipment Redesign. Society's concern for protecting the woman worker has had a long history; it has been expressed through the enacting of state laws and varying social customs. In recent years, however, an even more significant change in industry has occurred because of the influence of the woman worker herself. Some of the initial work of human engineering in industry—fitting the machine or job to the worker—began with women. Since they are shorter than men, women had to use platforms when standing at machines. With the large influx of women into industry during World War II, many plant changes were brought about which were good for men as well as for women. More and more frequently levers and pulleys were substituted for muscles. Rest rooms were modified and lunchrooms were improved. More safety practices were introduced. It even became fashionable for a woman worker to dress to suit her job.

Facts versus Opinions. A great deal has been written about the physical limitations of women for various jobs. For example, a Soviet Russian commission reported an investigation which revealed that almost three-fourths of the women required to do heavy lifting in such industries as coal and steel had menstrual troubles, twice as many as had similar troubles when engaged in lighter work [12]. It has generally been assumed that women are more susceptible to fatigue than men. One finds statements that overtime work causes more accidents among women than men. It has also been reported that absenteeism is as much as 100 per cent higher among women than among men. Such statements are often made without citing valid statistical data, and one should use caution in generalizing from them. Some authorities attempt to prove that women are more accident prone than men; others claim the reverse. When adequately documented studies are considered, the evidence indicates that in the areas of safety, absenteeism, and general adjustment to the job situation, factors other than sex differences are often more likely to be the reasons for variations in human behavior. Some writers maintain that it is women's psychic dependence on man and her feeling of inferiority engendered by male domination which cause her to be less successful in the industrial world. But we would do well to consider their statements to be opinions only, not evidence.

It is difficult to separate facts from opinions in what has been written about women workers. To say, as several writers have, that women are not as good long-term investments as men is indulging in hasty generalization. In some kinds of clerical positions they have been shown to be better investments. It may be true that a smaller proportion of women than men qualify for upgrading or advancement to supervisory jobs in manufacturing industries. But what criteria are used here for upgrading or advancement? Maybe our stereotyped conception of the woman has placed her in such a role that she cannot meet the standards for promotion.

WOMEN'S JOBS

About two-thirds of all women in industry (21 million) are employed in manufacturing, retail trade, or personal services. The largest numbers are in clerical and operative jobs; but only a few are in executive positions. Somewhere around one-fourth of all women workers are in factories, primarily those manufacturing apparel, textiles, or foods. About one-fourth of the workers in the executive branch of the Federal government are women.

Traditions and Discriminations. There are still many prejudices and traditional discriminations against women in factory-type jobs, but enough traditions have been broken to show that changes can be made. Even such small things as changing physical working conditions and introducing schedules which allow the women time to get their housework done can reduce women's absenteeism below that of men. In the more professional types of jobs (accounting, science, engineering, mathematics), once thought to be the exclusive province of men, women are being accepted in many quarters. Some writers feel that our shortage of scientists and technologists can be partially overcome by selecting and training more women.

Although women are going into many "men's" professions, the proportions are still small. Most female college graduates who work go into traditional "women's jobs." Women constitute about 90 per cent of all librarians, 60 per cent of all welfare workers, and 80 per cent of all public school teachers.

At another level, women have a hard time fitting into some of the skilled trades. Lack of training facilities is a part of their problem, but their greatest difficulty is that they have to fight tradition and union politics, even at times of peak employment. For example, studies have shown that among tool and die makers two out of three men entered the trade through apprenticeship; among molders 57 per cent entered this way [16]. During the peak employment of the middle 1950s there were only 9 apprentices for every 100 journeymen tool and die makers employed in the metal-working industries, and none were women. In many trades women apprentices are unheard of. In another way women have not quite fitted into the union picture. Whereas women may be aggressive and courageous in emotional situations like strikes, they take little interest in the day-to-day business routine of the union. They are apathetic about paying dues and fighting for fringe benefits. Some union leaders have expressed concern about the possible dangers to unionism in this feminine attitude, and well they might.

Higher-level Positions. Apparently it takes a long time to establish a tradition favorable to women within the higher-level positions in industry. In the home offices of insurance companies, women hold only about 20 per cent of the supervisory positions; and in banks, the figure is even lower. Both of these industries employ large proportions of women. Two-thirds of all insurance company employees are women. They constitute about one-half of the number of employees in banks. Only in department stores does one find an even distribution among women and men in the so-called "higher-level" positions. Here women make up about two-thirds of all employees [2, 6].

Women officers in industry are no more than 4 per cent of the total. Only a handful hold board directorships. In production operations in manufacturing, few women are found above the level of forewoman. Aside from prejudice, lack of education and training has been cited as one of the principal reasons women do not advance. One writer summed the problem up well by pointing out that the young woman does not take specialized training because she fears it will be wasted in a hostile market, and she has little chance for advancement because she lacks the training. This circular dilemma must surely be avoided if our economy is to continue along its predicted course [19]. The women in middle-management brackets with no more than a high school education are usually older than those in the general labor market, and more of them are single. Women in personnel work, training, publishing, job testing, social service, science, and engineering are usually college graduates.

The opportunities for women at the administrative level are increasing in such positions as research analysts in banks and insurance companies, in merchandising, public relations, advertising, and personnel work. However, very few women in any field occupy the top executive jobs. One business magazine estimated that not over five thousand women could be found among the quarter million "real" executives [2]. A market analysis of women holding positions of responsibility in industry and commerce indicated that the way women *behave* on the job rather than the way they *perform* the technical operations of their position is a chief determinant of their acceptance as administrators. Apparently there is a widespread belief that women are "too emotional" or "too personal" to hold down supervisory jobs or executive positions. Most evidence, however, that seems to point in this direction is more subjective than objective.

Opportunities in Administrative Jobs. One of the most illuminating studies on opportunities for women in administrative jobs was conducted by the Harvard Business School [6]. In effect, the study was a market analysis to find out what women do if they hold responsible positions in business and how they are accepted. Of particular interest to the college girl thinking about a business career were the findings on the kinds of jobs opening up for women, what things are in their favor, and what barriers to advancement must be met.

The research team interviewed 175 persons in 95 organizations. Forty-seven of the administrative people interviewed were women, and the fields represented included accounting, advertising, banking, credit, food, government, heavy industries, hospitals, insurance, law, management consulting, manufacturing, publishing, retailing, textiles, utilities, and wholesaling.

There was a general acknowledgement of the increasing importance of women in business, but very few women were found to be holding top executive jobs. "Second in command" was the way several executives described the highest level that a woman could hope to attain. One management consulting firm expressed a prevailing sentiment that the highest position women are going to reach in the foreseeable future in any large numbers is that of assistant to a top executive, primarily an expansion of the secretarial function. Exceptions to this apparent limitation on women's advancement were found in the more creative fields, such as merchandising, promotion, public relations, and magazine publishing. In the more specialized positions, such as home economist for large food companies and women's magazines, the field is wide open, as are such comparable areas as the fashion industry. Working as buyers for department stores was strongly emphasized as a lucrative occupation for women.

New Opportunities. The study showed further that there is a growing place for women in certain types of research jobs—investment analysts in banks and insurance companies, technical research positions in laboratories of food and chemical companies, and statistical jobs in nearly all large organizations, regardless of their business.

The job area of "consumer contact" seems to be opening up for women. One bank executive expressed the general idea in this way: "A woman would rather talk to a woman about financial matters, particularly if she is afraid she'll ask a foolish question." Similarly, in fields such as retailing, merchandising, and promotion, it was pointed out that women have long been used in jobs requiring a knowledge of the woman consumer as well as of the product.

Many executives who were interviewed regarded personnel work as a natural field for women. An important consideration should be included here, however. The study pointed out that the level of organization to which women can rise in this field seems to depend on the kind of business they choose. Where women constitute a major part of the working force, there is apparently more chance of a woman's becoming head of the personnel department than in companies where men predominate. Strongly unionized industries and those requiring a large number of skilled employees, such as engineers, offer less chance for women to become head of personnel. Heavy industry, steel for example, is a most unlikely place for a woman to become an executive.

Limitations to Advancement. With women entering the sciences, law, and other professions in greater numbers than ever before, but without full recognition, we find a warning sign for those college women planning careers in industry. There are barriers to the success of women in business —barriers which are mostly psychological in nature. What are these barriers?

The Harvard study of ninety-five organizations showed that the limits on women's advancement to the administrative level as imposed by the general attitudes of the business community vary from industry to industry. In certain fields, where the primary function is to serve other businesses, a woman is at a disadvantage. One businessman summed the attitude up by saying: "While a woman performs very effectively *within* the walls of many banking organizations, the prospect of her representing the organization to business units outside is still unacceptable to most businessmen."

In nearly every line of business represented by the interviews, the comparative shortness of a woman's stay in an organization was pointed out. Among the common opinions expressed by men on the limitations of women in business were: she is barred from executive dining rooms; she doesn't play golf with customers; women regard their jobs as of secondary importance in life; women do not really want careers; and women do not like to assume responsibility. From the women interviewed came such statements as: women are too ready to attach themselves to a pleasant working situation and to refuse advancement opportunities because their current situation is so nice and easy; or women do not choose a career but "fall into one."

The analysis of other attitudes frequently expressed in the interviews pointed out that men resent working for a woman and women do not like to work for other women. Apparently, both men and women feel there is less status in working for a woman than in working for a man. Most negative sentiments concerning women in supervisory positions seemed to be based on the belief that women "are more emotional than men" and "take everything too personally." Several men in top positions acknowledged that there was very little difference between men and women so far as emotional attitude toward their jobs was concerned, but that women were less likely to hide their feelings and keep them from influencing business decisions.

Attitudes and Interests. Attitudes toward married women working in business fall into two schools of thought. The older, more traditional businesses, such as banking, have only recently begun to hire or retain married women. Adherents of one school hold the belief that a married woman shifts her allegiance from her job to her home. In contrast, there is the idea that marriage is a stabilizing factor which makes the woman more confident and dependable.

One interesting aspect of the executives' discussions was the frequent reference to the fact that administrative training and business experience should make a girl a much better wife for a businessman.

There is enough evidence to conclude that attitudes of women, and about women, can and do change. It may well be that the wise personnel man should take a hard look to see just where he may profit by employing women even though men may be available for the job. The woman worker, the woman executive, and the professional woman may hold the key to our expanding economy.

WOMEN IN AN EXPANDING ECONOMY

Technological innovations are expected to continue. They will bring the development of new skills, some of which may be generally accepted as women's work. Witness, for example, how women have moved into the relatively new field of electronic computer operations. Curricula and subject matter in our schools are beginning to be attuned less to older patterns of women's employment and more to meeting the needs of modern technology.

Let us examine several of the reasons given by employers in the past for hiring or refusing to hire women.

In certain manufacturing fields, in professional service, and in sales work, some jobs are often closed to women because it is taken for granted that they should be held by men. This belief has been so generalized that some employers say women would induce negative reactions not only among male supervisors, fellow employees, and customers, but also among the public at large. The mere fact that a particular job has traditionally been held by a man or by a woman often determines who will get the job when a replacement is needed.

Certain cultural patterns help to decide who will get what job. The idea that women should have easier, cleaner, and lighter tasks has been a part of the pattern of male chivalry. Some employers frankly admit that the economic factor operates in job assignments. Women can be hired for less money than men; hence certain jobs get labeled as women's, and men tend to avoid them.

With employers setting higher educational requirements for their new employees, many men are failing to qualify for jobs that women are prepared for. The realities of meeting labor competition at the more technical levels, plus the fact that women now have a better opportunity to get into the newer technical jobs, make job opportunities for women better now than at any other time in our industrial history.

A Changing Pattern. Another factor which favors the entry of more women into industry is "age acceptance." Although there are still prejudices against hiring the older female worker, the percentage of older women in the labor force has been increasing [11].

In the year 1890, 70 per cent of all women workers were single, and over half were under 25 years of age. Less than 3 per cent of the white wives in the country worked. In that year, half of the women in the country had never worked for pay. Most of the other half stopped working for pay when they married, and they did not return to work unless their husbands died or were incapacitated. The women who followed a different pattern were mostly immigrants, the daughters of immigrants, or Negroes. These were mainly concentrated in a few localities.

Conditions are quite different today. Over one-half of the working women are married and over forty years of age. We now find the working wife in all communities and among all social, racial, and ethnic groups. An increasing number of women now remain in the labor force for most of their adult lives, save for short periods taken out to bear and raise children. In some circles this work pattern is even becoming fashionable for wives of economically secure husbands.

Several circumstances have been responsible for this change. The employment of women in wartime had the effect of breaking, at least in part, certain attitudinal barriers against women in industry. But more important, our expanding economy has put new demands on the labor supply, and technological changes have created a need for more highly skilled people. Whereas automation will probably have little effect on the major fields of women's employment (teaching, nursing, service, sales, the apparel industry), it is opening up many new jobs for women in the electronics industry.

The National Manpower Council predicts that the reason for the employment of women will bear less and less relationship to their low income and social status. The number of middle-income families continues to grow and women in the middle- and upper-income groups have been going to work in steadily increasing numbers. In the future, fewer women may be working because of economic necessity, and more and more because they choose to. Women, although still restricted, are finding greater freedom to choose for themselves the particular pattern of employment which best satisfies their own needs.

In the past, girls have been penalized in their initial employment opportunities because of a lack of education. About 45 per cent of all girls, compared to about 30 per cent of all boys, terminate their formal education with high school graduation. This has served to restrict the types of jobs they can find. Only about 10 per cent of all women complete college [11].

Womanpower in the Future. There is certain to be more effective utilization of womanpower in the future, and we dare say it will be accompanied by a number of adjustments:

1. Attitudes about women working and attitudes of women working in industry will undergo more change.

2. Many women appear to get satisfaction from combining work for pay with homemaking functions. Adjustments will be made to allow for this.

3. Discontinuity in employment poses a problem of skill maintenance when women temporarily leave the labor force to raise families. Provision will be made for retraining the older woman when she returns to work.

4. Shortages of highly trained personnel will bring about excellent opportunities for women who are prepared for a specific job or profession.

5. Sex labels of jobs will tend to disappear as women are allowed to show what they are capable of doing. Advancing technology will help give them the chance.

6. Nonindustrial jobs in government and the armed forces will help to break the barriers of tradition unfavorable to women.

7. The increased emphasis by union organizations on raising pay for women will tend to level women with men in certain jobs.

8. The increasing fear of insecurity may motivate women to develop some kind of employment skill, even though they plan to marry.

9. The growing independence of women will expand opportunities for them in industry.

10. The current strong pull toward early marriage will lead more women to work to help support the family budget.

Of the several factors related to the prediction that women will play more and more important roles in industry, we believe three are primary. First, except in periods of economic adjustment, women will be needed in industry more than ever before. Second, technological advances will create many jobs highly suitable to women. Finally, women are gradually acquiring more status in industry, and this in itself will induce more women to work.

SUGGESTIONS FOR FURTHER READING

Fisher, D. A. *Steel in the war.* New York: United States Steel Corp., 1946. Includes some description of women at work in the steel mills during World War II.

National Manpower Council. *Womanpower.* New York: Columbia Univer. Press, 1957. The present and future position of women in our industrial society.

Wolfle, D. L. *Commission on human resources and advanced training.* New York: Harper, 1954. Some discussion of the place of women in our total human resources outlook for the future.

PART V: PROBLEMS
RELATED TO WORK

14

THE NATURE

OF WORK

Robert S. Ramsay

Through the application of time-and-motion methods half a century ago it was found that a bricklayer could increase his output from 120 bricks per hour to 350 per hour for short periods of time. With continued improvement in tools and know-how, as reflected, for example, in scaffolding, it should now be possible for the skilled modern bricklayer to lay 2,000 bricks per day without undue effort. It is well to note, however, that at the present time union bricklayers may lay as few as 250 or 300 bricks per day and come up to quota.

We use this illustration to emphasize that factors enter into the understanding of work which might easily be overlooked should we restrict our discussions of work to laboratory situations. In addition to describing the criteria and characteristics of work, and the effects of working conditions and methods on efficiency, we need to consider the influences of labor organizations in setting work standards and their reasons for setting them. We need to take into account the personal feelings and emotions of the worker and the psychological climates for work.

The production chart hanging in the office of the superintendent tells us some of what we want to know about work, as does the graph pictured in the report to the stockholders and the statistics compiled in the controller's office. The total number of units produced in a given period of time at such and such a cost is valuable information, but it is an incomplete representation of work since it omits the picture of the grimy-faced miner or the secretary's hurt feelings.

In general one may think of work as the use of the individual's physiological and mental processes in the accomplishment of some goal. The goal may be the production of a steel ingot, the sale of an insurance policy, or the decision to pay a stock dividend. But in every case, activity on the part of the individual is required, and the utilization of the worker's skills and knowledge means a cost in terms of effort expended in reaching the goal. In previous chapters we have described the supervisory and management activities related to production goals. In the three chapters that follow we shall tell in detail how changes in work systems through engineering psychology and organizational structure may lead to greater accomplishment of industrial goals. In this chapter we shall deal primarily with the activities of the individual production worker.

MEASURING WORK OUTPUT

How can we measure the effectiveness of the individual worker in accomplishing his production goals? In the case of the steel ingots or similar products represented by real objects, we can of course simply count the number produced in an hour, a day, or a week, or in any appropriate time period. Where the consequences of the individual's efforts lead to a clearcut event, as in the sale of an insurance policy, a similar count per unit time or production rate can be established. However, not all sales are of the same amount, and hence a dollar value might serve us better. Even less clear is the measure that would be appropriate for decision-making tasks where the quality of the decision may be much more important than the quantity of decisions. In fact, the mark of a good executive may be that he makes as few decisions as possible and these only of major policy. He delegates to his staff the authority to make lower-level decisions for which they are held responsible.

The problem of criteria in measurement was introduced in Chapter 6, dealing with personnel selection (see page 107). Here again we face the criterion problem. The solution is clear in principle, but often difficult in practice. We must:

1. Make sure that the measure is relevant to the production goal, i.e., is *valid* for the job.

2. Determine that the measure reflects the performance of the individual worker, i.e., is *unbiased,* not contaminated by systematic factors other than the worker's own skills and knowledge.

3. Be sure that the measure is sufficiently *reliable* for whatever purpose it is intended.

To measure rate of output without proper consideration of the number of parts rejected at inspection would not be a valid measure where quality or tolerance limitations are of primary concern. Bias may enter into a situation where work complement is not controlled and one worker receives assistance from a helper while another does not. Reliability of a measure refers, of course, to freedom from random fluctuations or errors for which no cause can be determined. An unreliable measure is one which is not consistent when we attempt to repeat it under supposedly identical circumstances.

One general relationship stands out in attempting to measure work output. For many tasks, an attempt on the part of the individual to speed up his rate of production means that accuracy will suffer. Quantity of work and quality of work are conflicting aspects of work performance. As a result of this relationship, measures compounded from these two aspects of performance are often very useful. Thus, typing proficiency is usually given in words per minute, but from the total number of words typed the number of errors is subtracted.

Some Characteristics of Work. A number of changes take place in our behavior when we work. Common to almost every activity are the pauses that accompany work. Attention wanders, perhaps, for only a matter of seconds. Often we are unaware of the pauses or blocks, as they have been called. The effect may be a momentary inability to remember a name or recall material read only a moment earlier. Another characteristic with which we are familiar is the ability to recover from near-exhaustion to meet an emergency.

These phenomena are not generally seen when we attempt to portray the changes in performance measures over time—the pauses are too fleeting and the emergencies too rare. However, a wide variety of behavior changes are easily seen when we plot proficiency against various time periods. This we have done in Figure 14.1 *a* through *f*.

In *a* we see what has been termed the "warm-up effect"; after a person works on a familiar job for a short period of time he does better than when he first started. In *b* we have a curve of "acquisition." This represents a person's output when he is learning. Motor skills in particular are learned slowly; they show improvement over months and even years of practice.

A very common phenomenon in work occurs when the individual levels off in his performance, as shown in *c*. In this period of nonimprovement we see plateau. It is usually temporary. In *d* we have a picture of variation in work output related to the time of day.

A phenomenon of work often observed is the end spurt, where output may go up during the last part of the day's work. This is represented in *e*. Under certain conditions, as the individual continues to work, both the speed and quality of his performance gradually decrease. This work decrement is seen in *f*.

The learning curves illustrate not only that increased production is the result of a learning process, but also that adequate training is important. Plateaus in learning and in production, end spurts, or other compensatory spurts are related to a number of factors, such as lack of motivation, misdirected effort, fatigue, and boredom, as we shall see in some of our later descriptions of work. Problems of work decrement and variability in output are of particular importance in industry.

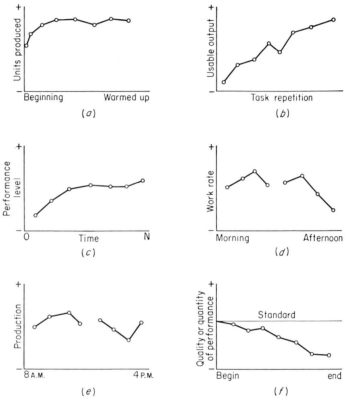

Fig. 14.1. These hypothetical curves show six common characteristics of work: (*a*) *warm-up* effect; (*b*) curve of *acquisition,* representing a person's output as he learns through repetition; (*c*) *plateau* of nonimprovement in performance, a common phenomenon in work; (*d*) *variation* in work output related to the time of day; (*e*) end spurt of increased production near the workday's end; (*f*) *work decrement,* which, under certain conditions, occurs as a person continues to work.

MEASURES OF EFFORT

Activity of any kind requires effort on the part of the individual. Apart from the performance criteria by which we evaluate work output, we are also interested in determining the amount of effort expended in work.

Physiological Measures. Measures of heart rate, blood pressure, oxygen consumption, breathing ratios, electrical resistance of the skin, and muscular responses have been used as indexes of physiological changes in the organism. In general, it is known that physiological changes are greater during work which is predominately physical rather than mental. As an example, we know that bodily temperature does not change greatly during mental work, but changes extensively under conditions of physical work. We know that electrical resistance of the skin is related not only to emotional conditions, but also to work effort. We also know that pulse rate and blood pressure are affected by effort.

Of the several physiological indexes that have been used as indicators of effort, muscular changes have long been considered important. One reason for this is that muscular changes can be measured in several ways. Where a physical task requires some movement, it is easy to measure the force, direction, and amplitude of the movements. Improved methods of recording electrical potentials from the muscles are giving rise to new concepts about effort expenditure. Although studies of this kind may seem remote from practical industrial problems, it is from such basic researches that progress is being made in describing the nature of work. Let us summarize one of these experiments.

Gregg and Jarrard [8], in seeking to learn more about the impairment of muscular responses under conditions of physical work, measured electrical potentials generated by muscle action. The apparatus for measuring the potentials provided separate indications from five different body locations. The muscular movements involved lifting bar-bell weights under varying experimental conditions. It was found that the electrical energy coming from the muscles increased with increases in the magnitude of the weights lifted. But, more importantly, with prolonged work there was an increase in the values. With repeated liftings of the same weight, the electrical activity within the muscle groups became greater. We know, however, that individual muscle fibers will fatigue; their contractility becomes impaired with prolonged work. In this situation, there must be a change in the method of lifting. Different, and larger, muscle groups must be brought into play in order to maintain the desired output.

The practicality of such findings as these lies in the possibility of deriving an index of working efficiency in quantitative units. We may soon be able to get indexes of mental effort, as well. It is known, in a general way, that greater muscular effort is expended in solving difficult problems than in solving simple ones.

Psychological Indexes. Most people are familiar with such descriptive terms as "fatigue," "tiredness," "boredom," and "monotony." We use these words from time to time in describing how we feel. We do not have, however, clear-cut measures of boredom or of subjective fatigue. Psychological means for evaluating the effort expended in work are less precise than are the physiological measures, but the reports of our feelings may actually be more relevant than the physiological measures, especially for work of a nonphysical nature. Let us indicate some things we do know about psychological fatigue and boredom.

FATIGUE

Feelings of fatigue, feelings of tiredness, are subjective or psychological states that may accompany prolonged work. We might suppose that all work decrements, the actual decreases in proficiency over time, lead directly to such subjective feelings. This is not true.

Feeling Tired. Feelings of tiredness are, of course, related to physiological changes. But there are different kinds of tiredness related to different kinds of work, and herein lies one of the complexities involved in measurement. An emotional upset may involve a kind of tiredness different from that resulting from a hard day of physical labor free from frustration. Although we have no good measures of tiredness, the descriptions we can give of it are useful in certain practical situations. One personnel manager reports the case of a worker who frequently complained of feeling tired on the job. Following up on the suspicion that the man was not being accepted in his particular work group, he had the man transferred to a similar job with a different group of workers. Here he soon came to feel that he belonged, and he made fewer complaints.

A university counselor tells of the case of a male client, a newly married student of twenty-four, who was having difficulty with his courses. He complained of being tired each night when he sat down to study. Though he fought the impulse, he would invariably fall asleep over his books; finally giving up, he would retire with his lessons unprepared. His decreasing scholastic performance brought him before the counselor. He and his wife moved out of his mother-in-law's home, and in two weeks the symptoms of fatigue were completely gone. He was working quite effectively. One day he stopped the counselor on the street and recounted the following: "I took my wife over to visit with her mother last night, and had a most remarkable experience. Ten minutes after we entered the house an overwhelming need for sleep came over me, the first time that has happened since we moved."

Reduction in Work Output. One might suspect that the reduction in the *capacity* for work would be a good measure of fatigue. Ryan points out otherwise [15]. He suggests that much confusion has arisen in industrial studies of fatigue because change in capacity for performance has been confused with change in actual rate of work, i.e., performance decrement. In some instances it has been concluded that no fatigue was present because there was no decline in output near the end of the day. Conversely, some people have taken declining output as a measure of fatigue. Neither conclusion is justified, says Ryan. Output may fail to decline because the individual sets a pace for himself even though there has been some loss of capacity. Output may go down without any change in capacity if the individual is ahead of his schedule for the day.

We know, in general, that beyond a certain point a man's production rate gets lower the longer he works at a job. He may get less work done for each operation, it may take him longer to complete some piece of work, or the quality of his work may be affected. We do know from laboratory studies that errors in work and lack of precision and coordination occur as a result of fatigue on psychomotor tasks. Where it can be determined that reduction in work is not due to quotas of some kind, it may be practical to consider errors, lack of coordination, and accidents under certain conditions as indexes of fatigue. Quality-control systems in the mass-production industries often provide statistical data which are useful in analyzing the results of fatigue.

Rest from Work. Most of our reliable information dealing with the problem of recovery from fatigue due to muscular work has come from laboratory studies. We know, for example, that a subject can become so tired from lifting a weight that he can no longer move his arms until he has had a given period of rest. Recovery, though quite rapid at first, is followed by a long slow period of comeback. The more fatigued we are, the longer it takes to recover.

From laboratory studies under ideal controlled conditions and from less controlled industrial situations has come a practical principle of work which says, in effect, that fatigue should be prevented by taking rest periods before the fatigue sets in.

It is generally recognized that rest pauses improve worker performance. If formal rest pauses are not allowed, employees take unauthorized ones. It has been found in some instances that these are just as effective in combating fatigue as are those scheduled by management. Just when to schedule rest periods varies from situation to situation. One way to get at the problem is by plotting production records throughout the working period and observing drops in production. It is important to schedule rest periods before the drops occur. It is also important to keep an eye on production records routinely, because not all drops in production are caused by fatigue or corrected by rest pauses.

Rest on the job can be obtained in a number of ways. One way is to slow down activity. Here, in effect, the worker actually rests while he works. Some people resort to pacing their activities, as most all workers on a piece rate learn to do. Daydreaming may be thought of as a form of rest which allows the person to leave his job mentally. Late starts and early quits, with interruptions in between, are other forms of work stoppage.

And of course, physical departure from the work scene is a possible form of rest.

Rest at one time may involve doing nothing; at another time, it may mean engaging in some other activity. To lie in bed all day may be a form of rest for some people, but not for others. An important part of rest is change or deviation from the usual or routine course of work. Fishing may be restful for the executive, but it is hard work for the man who makes his living by it. Deviation involves turning something away from its course, and it is most important in combating mental stress. It can, for example, be helpful in alleviating certain distressful mental habits which we have fallen into. We know that worry can sometimes be lessened by putting something in the place of the worrisome thoughts.

There have been several studies in industry which show that rest pauses during work are beneficial to production. In one study [10] it was found that the introduction of a twelve-minute rest pause in the middle of the morning and a similar pause in the middle of the afternoon increased the output of comptometer operators 29 per cent. It also decreased the length of voluntary rest pauses 60 per cent. This study showed that rest pauses should be introduced just before production begins to fall from its maximum.

No doubt some unauthorized work stoppage is in response to an honestly felt need for rest, but other stoppages are ways of rejecting something in the work situation. The introduction of rest pauses which result in an increased work output have been found to have a beneficial effect both physiologically and psychologically; they improve the attitudes of the employees toward the working situation. Loafing on the job, slowdowns, and unauthorized work stoppages often are indications not that the worker needs rest, but that something is wrong with the work climate.

The shortened workday or workweek may set the stage for increase in production while the person is working, but there is little chance of an over-all increase unless the entire work context is favorable.

The attitude a person has toward his work determines to a large extent his need for rest. The average executive works longer hours, and in many ways harder, than do many of the men down the line, yet he may not tire unduly from his efforts. He sets his own pace to some extent, and this is important.

Work has different meanings to different people. The manager's position requires him to think of work in terms of profit maximization. He may be held responsible if production rates are not maintained. The worker may see the job as a daily social hurdle, an opportunity to show up poorly or well. In the case of the manager or the worker, the job situation is a stage upon which he will expend effort, become tired, and seek some form of rest.

BOREDOM

Boredom is characterized by a lack of interest, usually associated with repetitive work activity. It is differentiated from fatigue in that it involves the desire for change in activity rather than for rest or relief from the work itself.

Boredom Factors. The two factors determining boredom are the amount of repetition in the work and the degree of attention demanded by the work.

Whereas boredom is frequently experienced by individuals engaged in repetitive work, some workers prefer repetitious jobs. This is where attention, or concentration, enters the picture. Jobs which require continuous attention tend to be interesting, and those which require little or no attention leave the individual free to talk with his neighbors or to think of other things. Although such jobs may be highly repetitious, they can be automatized to the extent that they may be pleasant for some people. The more boring jobs, according to this theory, would be those which have enough variability to require part of the worker's attention, but not enough to keep him fully occupied [15]. This theory, which still needs to be substantiated, seems to jibe with case studies on job satisfaction.

Change in Activity. A practical way to relieve boredom is to change one's activity. If such a change is not possible in the job situation itself, then a change of pace may be accomplished by taking up a hobby. The important thing involved here is the *change* of activity. Bowling might be an excellent way for the production worker to relax, but not for the professional bowler. Neither would fishing be quite so pleasant for the retired person if this was all he had to do.

Generalizations about boredom in industry have been given by Wyatt and his British coworkers [20]. They point out that when activities provide little or no interest, the prospects are discouraging, and the effect seems to bear some relation to the magnitude of the task to be accomplished. As an example, the person who does not like walking will not look forward to a twenty-mile tramp over uninteresting country. Although he may start with a certain amount of enthusiasm, it soon disappears. At this stage the magnitude of the task may seem appalling, but as the time for lunch and rest draws near, interest is awakened. The remaining distance now appears to have lessened considerably and he continues with increased enthusiasm. Although this enthusiasm may diminish after a few miles, it will reappear with increased intensity as the person nears his goal. The worker at some uninteresting repetitive task will usually find his enthusiasm very low toward the middle of the morning. It is revived by the expected and actual recuperative effects of the midday break and the diminishing magnitude of the task as the end of the afternoon is approached.

The bored worker is inclined to overestimate the duration of time. Although a repetitive task may not be attention-demanding, and may leave time for revery, the worker may have varied and discordant thoughts during which he keeps coming back to the amount of time still to be worked. This type of mental activity may well happen on the continuous assembly line where the work is automatic, where there is little or no chance for conversation, and where there is little or no personal interest in the final product or its destination. Wyatt also suggests that the additional incentive and satisfaction which accompanies a piece-rate system of payment tends to retard the onset of boredom. On the assembly line, experience of boredom is also dependent to a certain extent upon the method by which material is supplied to the operatives. Quantities which take about an hour to complete give more satisfaction than an endless flow along a conveyer, because of the interest associated with awareness of achievement.

There seems to be general agreement that susceptibility to boredom is individualistic. A person who is temperamentally lively and has a high degree of intelligence may tend to be more bored by repetitive work than the person of lower intelligence who is submissive.

CONDITIONS RELATED TO WORK

There is an extensive literature in the areas of the human senses and the response mechanisms, and much has been written in the fields of illumination, sound, and ventilating engineering. In the three chapters which follow, details will be given about conditions of work as they apply to problems in safety, engineering psychology, and systems development. Here we shall present a preview of some of the physical and psychological conditions that have some influence on work. However, it should be stressed that we still do not have the answers to many practical questions about working conditions—such problems, for example, as whether color schemes for walls and machinery have anything to do with efficiency of work, or whether noise actually reduces work performance. Let us here summarize, in a general way, what is known about conditions related to work.

Illumination. It is not too difficult to find the kind of lighting for a given work area which will permit the job to be done effectively once certain conditions are specified, such as the nature of the job and the visual acuity of the workers. There is no single set of recommendations to cover all situations, but rough guides are available. It has been shown that glare causes discomfort in workers and affects performance. The spectral qualities of some lights may affect such tasks as product inspection. Whether or not fluorescent lamps with their flicker really cause production difficulties is not known. And as we have seen in Chapter 2 (page 32), illumination alone may not be a critical factor in production.

Noise. While there are indications that noise reduces work performance, there is as yet no clear-cut evidence in support of such a contention. Although it is known that continuous exposure to high noise levels above 80 db contributes to hearing loss, it is not known just what continuous industrial noises below the injury level may do to some people. Possibly the noise may be of only nuisance value. But how extensively does this irritate people? A drip in the sink may be more annoying under certain conditions than a very loud noise under other conditions. If there is high morale in a group, it may well stand much greater noise levels without complaint than would another group with low morale (see page 213). Most people probably have some capacity to adapt to annoying characteristics of noise, but under precisely what conditions is not known. High intensities, high frequencies, intermittency, and reverberation are characteristics of noises that cause them to be annoying. Very high tones and extremely low tones are judged to be more irritating than those in the middle ranges. Such knowledge as this has made it possible to sound-treat work areas in order to reduce some of the irritating effects of the noise.

Atmospheric Conditions. In spite of the highly subjective nature of measuring comfort, researchers have been able to come up with ranges of temperature, humidity, and ventilation suitable for the average person under specified conditions. These studies make it apparent that it is important to distinguish between comfortable conditions and conditions, not necessarily comfortable, in which work can be carried on without loss in efficiency.

The temperatures under which most people feel comfortable in the summer range from 69 to 73°F and in the winter from about 65 to 70°F. Feelings of comfort are associated with humidity conditions and with skin temperatures (optimum 91 to 93°F).

Although the most comfortable working temperature may be around 65°F, one study showed that performance did not begin to deteriorate until around 90°F. In higher temperatures more errors occur. The relationship between temperature and humidity is known to all of us in terms of a comfort index. A person can tolerate a hotter temperature if the air is dry. He finds it harder to work when the air is sticky as well as hot. Production drops and mistakes increase when the temperature and humidity rise above certain limits. What these limits are depends on the nature of the work, the freshness of the air, and the amount of exertion of the worker. Roughly, the temperature limits range from 65 to 85°F. It has been found that in low temperatures (in the 50s) production decreases and accident rates increase.

Both physical and mental work are affected by atmospheric conditions, but the latter is not affected until the conditions become extreme. Fortunately, industry can do several things to reduce production loss under temperature extremes. Besides changing the physical environment through heating and air conditioning, industry can select men for jobs on the basis of their temperature tolerance; it can rotate workers on difficult jobs. In addition certain physiological conditions can be maintained; for example, men who work around hot furnaces can take salt pills.

Some Other Conditions. All else being equal, we are probably safe in saying that a comfortable physical environment is good for work output up to a point. We may go to sleep, however, in a chair that is too comfortable or become careless in a situation that does not demand enough of our attention to keep us vigilant. Noise, cold, and dampness may affect work adversely by hampering the worker's activities, or they may be sources of complaint for those who are simply looking for excuses in the environment to warrant their unhappiness. Air conditioning, for example, is an excellent whipping boy for the modern office. In one office a record was kept of complaints over a period of five days. Six people complained that the air was too cold, five reported that it was too humid, two people said they liked the office better before air conditioning was installed. Three office workers complained of the draft created by the air conditioning fan. (You guessed it! The air conditioning had not been on during the entire five days.)

The work system itself is an important condition for work. Some typists may prefer to work in a centralized stenographic pool for the very same reasons that others do not like the system. One girl may prefer the condition that allows for work simplification which another girl dislikes. One man may prefer to work on the assembly line because he likes to have his pace standardized and mechanically controlled where there is a minimum of skill and mental attention required as he repeats over and over his simple assembly motions. Another man may not produce as well there because he dislikes the monotony.

No matter what physical and systems changes in work conditions will come with technological advances, the psychological conditions of work will continue to be of importance. Managers and engineers will still be faced with human problems such as that described by Davis [5]. On the plains of Texas at the beginning of World War II one of the first blackout aircraft factories was constructed without windows or skylights. The building was conditioned to control temperature, humidity, and air circulation. Since the ceiling was over 50 feet from the floor, most of the air vents were up rather high.

From the beginning employees began to complain about the inadequacy of the air conditioning. It was too humid, too hot, and too close. A thorough check was made of the system, and it was found to be in excellent order, providing exactly the atmospheric conditions needed. Still the complaints persisted, until it was recognized that the workers were rural people who were new to both industry and air conditioning. They felt cooped up in a windowless plant where they could not feel a breeze blowing. Since the vents were too high for the workers to feel the air, they needed to see that it was stirring. When tissue streamers were tied to the ventilators high on the walls, the workers could see that the air was moving, and the frequency of employee complaints soon became negligible.

ANALYSIS AND EVALUATION OF WORK

The analysis of work can be thought of in terms of two things. First, the job itself centers around some end product, such as the letter that is typed and ready for signature or the structural steel that is put in place with the aid of a hoist. Second, what the person does in typing the letter or moving appropriate levers of the electric hoist is important. Hence, both in terms of job analysis and man analysis, the psychologist is interested in helping make evaluations, because they impinge upon so many things—for example, personnel requirements, training content, job efficiency, wage rates, ratings for promotions.

Knowing just what is expected of the worker, the supervisor, or the executive is of importance not only to the organization, but to the individual as well. Through job analysis one can spell out who does what; by means of these descriptions, frictions within the office may be lessened, jurisdictional disputes between unions may be adjusted more easily, and the executive may have a better idea of his responsibilities and authority. Job analyses were discussed in the chapter on training (see page 130). Here we shall amplify only a few points in order to set the stage for discussing problems of work evaluation.

Job and man analyses are important to understand in terms of informal structures as well as formal ones. Formally, supervisor A may have as his boss manager A. However, manager A, for some reason or other, may not have the actual power in the organization to "protect" or "manage" comparable to manager B, who formally has nothing to do with the job of supervisor A. Informally, however, manager B may be in such a power position that he actually controls manager A, and hence is the real boss of supervisor A. If our supervisor in this case has a good perception of the informal workings within the organization, he will make a point of knowing who gives orders to whom.

The forms of job analysis are many, and their uses vary. Generally, job analysis forms include items such as job titles, descriptions of the work performed, supervision given and received, equipment used, physical activities, working conditions, pay scales, levels of difficulty, and measures of work performed. They do not include, however, such situations as the one described in the paragraph above.

There are numerous ways to describe different jobs. For the worker, the description may center around manual skills, effort, and responsibility. For managerial operations, it may include such activities as planning, organizing, controlling, making decisions, and delegating authority.

Job Breakdown. Basic to evaluation is knowing just what is expected of the worker, the supervisor, or the manager in his job. With this knowledge, it is a fairly simple matter to list the skills, abilities, and traits that are important on any given job. Let us illustrate what is involved in breaking down *just one aspect of a job,* for instance, the principles underlying the motions that a person goes through in setting printing type. Blair [3] lists fifteen principles of motion economy applicable to this task:

1. Minimize the number of motions.
2. Minimize the lengths of motions.
3. Provide for the use of continuous-curved motions.
4. Minimize the number of parts of the body involved.
5. Minimize the necessity of motion control by muscular effort.
6. Minimize muscular force required for motion.
7. Provide for constant motion paths which encourage the quick establishment of effective habit patterns.
8. Provide for easy and natural motions with respect to the physiological characteristics of the body.
9. Minimize the number of eye fixations required.
10. Minimize the distance apart of eye fixations required.
11. Minimize the eye-fixation time required for perception when this is a controlling factor.
12. Distribute actions among the used members of the body in accordance with the inherent capacities of members.
13. Provide for intermittent use of different muscles.
14. Provide for simultaneous motions of both arms.
15. Provide for symmetrical motions of both arms.

Analysis of work sequences of jobs helps us to develop more effective methods and procedures for work, to develop better tools and equipment for a job. Through the analysis of movements of jobs requiring motor skill and through the analysis of duties of supervisory and managerial-type jobs, we have ways of getting at job evaluation. Through evaluation we obtain criteria which we can use to pay for work, consider promotions, and improve performance.

Merit Rating. The evaluation of an employee by his supervisor or by some other qualified person familiar with his performance is called "merit rating." Industrial practices have included various schemes of evaluation, and over the years psychologists have worked with industrialists to improve these ratings. In 1959 Tiffin [19] analyzed six merit-rating systems which have been in use long enough to talk about in terms of their practical values. Let us summarize here his findings.

The most widely used method today involves a *graphic rating scale* of several different employee characteristics, with the employee rated by his superior separately on each factor. The factors vary from company to company, depending on what any given management thinks is important. In using the graphic-chart system it is customary to add the ratings given to each man on all the traits used; this results in a single over-all rating for the person in question. One of the weaknesses of this system is the tendency of a rater to place a man high or low in every respect because he knows, or thinks he knows, the man is high or low in one particular respect. The result of this "halo" effect is that ratings on ten or twelve different traits do not actually result in ten or twelve different ratings at all. They are simply ten or twelve repetitions of essentially one rating of the man.

Another weakness of this method is the tendency to put all the men high if the rater is lenient or low if he is hard-boiled. Experience has shown that most men on fairly high level jobs are rated higher than most men on fairly low level jobs.

A second merit-rating system has the rater rank his men from *highest to lowest*. This is customarily done on the basis of over-all job performance. It can be done by each supervisor several different times on characteristics that are considered by the company to be important.

A third method of employee rating is the *employee-comparisons system*. In this plan all employees working under a given supervisor are arranged into pairs, each man being paired to every other one. Periodically the supervisor checks the man in each pair who is better in over-all job performance. Tiffin reports that time and time again this method of rating has shown greater agreement between ratings of the same men by different supervisors than has any other rating system. The system, however, has limitations. It cannot be used for promotional purposes, counseling, employee improvement, transfer, or layoff, because the system does not show, for a man rated low, why he was rated low.

A fourth system is that of *forced distribution*. Here again the raters evaluate the men on over-all job performance. Cards are prepared for each man, and the rater is asked to distribute them in five piles: low (10 per cent), low average (20 per cent), average (40 per cent), high average (20 per cent), and high (10 per cent). This method forces a distribution. It shows quite high agreement when different raters evaluate the same group of men.

A fifth system is the *forced-choice method,* which requires considerable preliminary work in developing the scale. Pairs of statements about job performance must be found where the members of each pair of statements express equally favorable or unfavorable things about a man, but with only one of the statements in each pair actually differentiating between the men known to differ in job performance. The statements are then printed on the rating form in groups of four. Two of the four statements are favorable (and equally favorable) and the remaining two are unfavorable (and equally unfavorable). The rater is asked to check two of the four statements—the one which most accurately describes and the one which least accurately describes the man being rated. This plan has been used very little in industry because it is expensive and it is impossible to keep the keys secret. The name "forced-choice" also has proved to be a red flag to the officers who were asked to use the scale.

The sixth method is the *critical-incidents rating system* described earlier in Chapter 6 (page 113). The plan consists of determining, through extensive interviews with superiors on the job, those things people do or fail to do which are critical to success or failure in a given job. Once such a list is compiled, supervisors are asked to watch for these and similar instances of critical behaviors. If a considerable number of good critical incidents are noted about a worker over a given period of time and few negative critical incidents have been observed, the man's rating will be high. Conversely, if most of the incidents noted are negative, his rating will be low. In this rating we are getting reports of actual behavior, not just opinions about behavior.

Merit rating is at best a most difficult task in which to get reliability and validity. But one cannot withdraw from the problem of making ratings and remain in a supervisory position very long. Unions tend to distrust company rating systems; they prefer to depend on the seniority principle in job bidding for promotions. This, of course, handicaps the better man who has low seniority, but it means security for the worker with years on the job. Seniority is an easy measure to use. Until less contestable rating systems are produced, seniority is likely to remain a big problem in labor-management negotiations.

SETTING PERFORMANCE STANDARDS

Production control in the factory is one practical way to describe "work" since its results can be measured. Poor production control is revealed in terms of parts shortages, failure to get orders out on time, excessive overtime, and waste. Good production control shows up in finished products made at a profit.

Production control involves preparation and planning, work routing, scheduling, and dispatching. It involves receiving orders for products from the sales department, determining materials requirements, machine requirements, and the sequence of operations. Making sure that all facilities for production are available, that jobs are assigned to particular men and machines, that operations programming is put into effect in ways providing for meeting delivery dates—all these activities become a part of the "general system" described in Chapter 17. The human being is the key to the entire operation. It is here that incentives are basic to people at work.

There are many types of incentive plans in operation, but almost all are based on some system of measuring the time a worker takes to do a particular job. In spite of the criticisms of time-and-motion studies and the search for better ways to determine the criteria for wage payments in the factory, the number of units produced per unit of time, the number of insurance policies sold in a given period, the number of pages typed per day are related in some way or other to getting people to produce.

Example of a Job Study. One of the oldest incentive systems providing employees with an opportunity to earn extra money for producing extra work is the Procter and Gamble time-bonus plan which has been in effect since 1928 [14]. We can see how the bonus system works by taking a look at Frank Handy on his job of sealing boxes of soap in the packing room. Frank's job requires him to put glue on the flaps of boxes with a brush and push them into the sealing belt as they pass down the line. The job has been studied to find both the correct method of doing the work and the average time normally taken to do it. The standard time for this job has been set up as thirty-six seconds, or .01 of an hour per box. The rate of 100 boxes an hour means, of course, 800 boxes per eight-hour day. However, since Frank can and does seal 125 boxes an hour, or a total of 1,000 boxes per day, he gets bonus credit for *two extra hours,* for which he receives a bonus of a full two hours' pay.

This system benefits Frank by setting up a standard of a fair day's work. It provides a means by which he can earn extra money when he wishes. The company benefits by employing the most efficient work methods, by knowing how many machines to buy and maintain, and by having a criterion for production. The customer may benefit by getting a quality product at a lower price.

How does this *job study* work? The steps are simple enough. First an examination is made of the various methods of doing the job; this is followed by the selection of the best method as indicated by external criteria. This method is now written out according to the elements of the job, and the employees are trained to use the correct method. Next comes finding the average time it takes Frank (and the other employees) to do the job. For this, the job-study engineer uses a stop watch which measures time in hundredths and thousandths of an hour. As Frank seals the boxes the engineer records the time for each element of the job, over and over again. The worker's performance is considered in terms of how *smooth* his motions are, how *quickly* he seals the boxes and pushes them into the sealing belt. Other criteria include *accuracy* in applying glue and *carefulness* in lining the flaps up squarely. How well Frank *plans ahead* in filling his gluepot is important. Is Frank *physically* fit to do the lifting required, and is he the right height to reach the machine? Does he seem to wish to follow the established method for doing the job? These things are important for the job study.

After studying Frank on his job, the engineer finds that Frank's skill and effort are better than normal. Based on the company's established skill and effort values, it was judged that 16 per cent *more time* should be added to make Frank's actual time equal to a fair normal time. This addition amounted to 7.2 minutes per 100 boxes.

In addition to the time required to do the work, an allowance is made in the "standard" for personal needs and tiring. Studies show that on this job, as the day goes on, the person becomes tired. Therefore, a "fatigue allowance" is added to compensate the worker for the effects of getting tired when he maintains a consistent working pace throughout the day. By comparing Frank's job with typical fatigue allowances based on company experiences, the job-study engineer determined that this allowance should be 15 per cent of the normal time. This addition amounted to 7.8 minutes per 100 boxes.

When we add together the time for each step in the study of Frank's jobs, we get the final standard time that is allowed for doing the work:

	Per 100 boxes, min	Per box, hr
1. Frank's actual average time	45.0	0.0075
2. Allowance for skills and efforts	7.2	0.0012
3. Personal needs and fatigue	7.8	0.0013
Final standard time	60	.0100

Now that we have seen how the time-bonus plan works in this case, let us consider some important features of the plan. The worker always knows where he stands in his production and hence can pace himself. When employees work in groups, and it is sometimes impractical to keep each person's work separate, the average for the group suffices. Generally the worker is not required to work at a pace that will produce more than a standard day's work unless he really wants to. Since standards are set to cover emergencies and contingencies, rarely does allowance have to be made because of difficulties of production control.

The model described above is one of a number of ways that work criteria are established. Such objectivity is possible when one is able to "time" and "count." Ratings or measures of a fair day's work in the office, or other non-production-line endeavors, means that more subjectivity enters into the criteria for such work. For management personnel, profits are often used as incentive criteria. In some companies all employees are on a profit-sharing incentive system.

Most profit-sharing plans do not define the relationship between work and share of profit, and this baffles some employees. Nevertheless, profit sharing is favored in many companies. One survey made in 1955 showed there were about twenty-one thousand such plans in operation in the United States, and they seem to be on the increase.

Incentive systems do not necessarily make a man want to work harder and produce more. Production, after all, depends upon the interaction of the individual and his total work environment. Formal incentive systems are only a part of the total climate favorable for work. Just where the employee fits into the organization as a whole is also an important factor.

ORGANIZATIONAL CHANGES AND THE WORKER

In Chapter 4 we discussed the influence of Frederick W. Taylor's *scientific management* on shaping the design of business operating procedures (see page 74). During the first two decades of this century, the influence of Taylorism brought about a shift in the position of the production worker. Instead of being completely independent, he was now being told "the what," "the how," and "the when" to do. Gradually industrial organizations moved toward *participative management,* still leaving the worker in the position of having someone else plan for him. More recently, a third phase of organizational change is beginning to appear, that of *information technology* [9].

Information technology is epitomized by the high-speed computer, represented by techniques like mathematical programming and by methodologies like operations research. Whereas scientific management concentrated on the hourly worker, taking much initiative from him, participative management aimed higher, giving increased status to the people in middle management. This had the effect of relegating the worker to an even lower position in the hierarchy. With the coming of information technology, it now appears that the man in middle management may himself be pushed down in importance, separating the production worker still farther from the rest of the organization. In effect, information technology promises to allow fewer people to do more work, but in a way which will cause the worker to become "programmed" more than ever.

In the following three chapters we shall spell out the changes which are occurring in industrial work as we consider the human problems of man-machine systems in safety, engineering psychology, and systems development.

SUGGESTIONS FOR FURTHER READING

Barnes, R. M. *Motion and time study.* New York: Wiley, 1958. This book gives a well-illustrated description of the applications of time-and-motion study within modern industry.

Bartley, S. H., & Chute, E. *Fatigue and impairment in man.* New York: McGraw-Hill, 1947. Some of the practical implications of fatigue and work.

Marrow, A. J. *Making management human.* New York: McGraw-Hill, 1957. This book describes practical ways of improving the psychological work climate.

Ryan, T. A. *Work and effort.* New York: Ronald, 1947. This book gives a systematic survey of psychological investigations concerned with the productivity of men and women at work.

15

ACCIDENTS

AND SAFETY

Harry W. Karn

Of the many and varied problems related to men working in industry one of the most costly is industrial accidents. The cost in terms of money is enormous, but in terms of life and limb it is tragic. In this chapter we shall describe the nature of the problems leading to accidents and what can be done to improve safety.

The practical application of psychological principles to the behavior of men at work is a matter of prime concern in the field of accident prevention. There are many indications that industry has not fully recognized the psychological ramifications of the problem of preventing accidents. Safety engineers charged with accident prevention are not ordinarily trained in the field of human behavior. Apparently, accident prevention is looked upon as an engineering problem to be solved through the proper design of mechanical safety devices. It is certainly true that the engineer has a real contribution to make toward achieving the goal of accident-free behavior. But the contribution of the psychologist must not be minimized. Actually, the answer to the question of how to prevent accidents requires a cooperative effort of psychologist and engineer.

Is it possible for an engineer to design a safety device that is foolproof regardless of what the operator does? Generally speaking, the answer is "no"—at least, not one that can be operated efficiently and economically. Foolproof safety devices have an uncanny property of becoming hazardous in the hands of certain operators.

Building a safety device that is foolproof requires sound equipment design plus a consideration of the human element. The safety of a mechanical device is to a large degree a function of its meaningfulness to and acceptance by the worker who is operating it.

THE CONCEPT OF AN ACCIDENT

Having stressed the importance of the human element in accidents, let us now explore the problem of accident behavior more concretely by asking just what constitutes an accident. Suppose a workman falls off a ladder with no more serious consequences than bruised dignity and dirt on the seat of his trousers. Is this an accident? Suppose he sprains his ankle in falling off the ladder. Is this an accident? What about the worker who falls off the ladder and rubs the skin from his elbows—shall we call this occurrence an accident? Indeed, in each of these cases we have an act or instance of behavior which we can call an accident. But of course there are differences. In one case the results are inconsequential, in another there is a skin abrasion, and in another an incapacitating sprained ankle. However, common to each of these instances is the act of falling off the ladder. The differences lie in the results of falling off the ladder.

There are many instances of behavior involving acts with common features and different results and, of course, there are other instances where the acts are different but the results are similar. In general, we can say that an accident is an undesirable or unfortunate event that occurs unexpectedly. But a complete understanding of the nature of accidents and their prevention requires that a careful distinction be made between acts and the results of these acts.

Accident Results. Some of the major classes or categories of accident results can be enumerated without difficulty. First, there are results which do not involve injuries of any consequence. These are the no-injury accidents. Harry bumps against a piece of moving machinery; result—just grease on his overalls and a button ripped off his suspenders. Second, there are minor-injury accidents. Joe bumps against the same piece of moving machinery and suffers a slight laceration of the skin on his forearm. Third, there are accidents involving major injuries. Sam's contact with the moving machinery results in a mangled hand which has to be amputated. And of course there are accidents in which there is damage to equipment. Ed bumps into the moving machinery and his recoil causes a nearby wrench to fall into revolving gears. There is no injury, but there is a damaged machine. Widely different results are apparent in each of these cases, but each result stems from the same or nearly the same happening.

LOST-TIME ACCIDENTS

In studying accidents the importance of distinguishing between acts and their results is brought into sharp focus when we consider the emphasis which industry puts upon lost-time accidents. This emphasis merits special treatment because it confuses the problem of accident prevention, the solution of which is, of course, the aim of all safety programs.

While the elimination of lost-time accidents is a desirable goal, this goal will never be achieved by concentrating only upon those accidents involving loss of working time. Unfortunately, many safety directors think that it can be. The safety director who boasts of a good record because his company has had relatively few lost-time accidents is typical. Some companies do not keep records of accidents which involve no loss of time.

Such emphasis upon lost-time accidents fails to take into account the necessity of concentrating upon the causes of accidents. The results are important but they can only be eliminated if we know what causes them. And this means that there should be a careful analysis of all accidents. Focusing attention on results will no more solve the accident problem than focusing attention on the results of cancer will lead to its cure. A cure for cancer will come only when the cause of this disease is discovered.

Thus, accident prevention must begin with a discovery of causes. These causal factors can be ascertained only through a systematic collection of observations in a wide variety of situations. The act which led to no loss of time today may next week lead to a major injury and the loss of a month's time. In studying accident causes, one must consider all accidents important. There is not a sufficient number of lost-time accidents to provide the information which will tell us what we need to know about causes. One authority in the field of accident prevention [7] states that non-lost-time accidents outnumber lost-time accidents by a ratio of 29 to 1. To neglect information provided by non-lost-time accidents is to make the whole problem of accident prevention practically insoluble.

THE CAUSES OF ACCIDENTS

Every enlightened student of behavior knows that behavior is caused, and accident behavior is no exception. A close examination of accident causes reveals two general classes or categories: unsafe conditions and unsafe acts. Unsafe conditions involve some aspect of the physical environment which sets up or makes probable the occurrence of an accident. Cluttered arrangement of machinery, poor lighting, unguarded moving parts, and oily floors are examples of unsafe conditions. Unsafe acts are those behaviors which lead to an accident, or those failures in performance which result in an accident. In the cases previously cited in which three workers bumped into a piece of machinery, the unsafe act was the act of making contact with the machine. The results were different in each case, but if the act of bumping had not occurred, there wouldn't have been any results to worry about. Failure to engage a safety device is an example of neglectful behavior which frequently leads to an accident.

Interaction of Acts and Conditions. Unsafe acts and unsafe conditions may interact in such a way that an accident may be caused by both. Too, an accident may be caused by a number of unsafe conditions or by a number of unsafe acts. The careful investigator or observer always seeks to determine all the factors which lead to the accident.

Let us now push our analysis of causes a little further and ask the question: What causes the unsafe condition or the unsafe act? Since we are getting further and further removed from the actual accident, we can call these matters indirect causes of accidents. The unsafe-act and unsafe-condition categories we can conveniently call the direct causes of accidents.

What causes a man to perform an unsafe act? A number of possibilities are immediately apparent, such as faulty vision, illness, worry, intoxication, poor coordination, lack of job know-how, and the like. All these states or conditions reside within the individual; they make up the so-called "human element," and we may justifiably call them human factors.

Human Element in Accidents. Analyzing the nature of causes to the point where we are dealing with human factors is helpful in understanding accident causation, because we are now dealing with something which can tell us why the unsafe act was performed. If we can isolate a human element responsible for the unsafe act we are in a position to do something constructive. Thus, if one of the human elements responsible for the unsafe act is lack of job know-how, we can eliminate this causative factor by training. If the cause is faulty vision, corrective glasses may remedy the situation. If the human element is uncorrectible, the offender can be removed from the job and placed in a less hazardous type of work.

Are human factors ever responsible for unsafe conditions? Indeed, yes. John overloads a conveyor belt and leaves the scene; later the belt breaks, and the result is an accident to John or some other worker. The direct cause of the accident—the broken belt—is an unsafe condition caused by John's unsafe act. But why did John commit the unsafe act, why did he overload the belt and walk away? Was he distracted by worry over unpaid bills? If we trace the accident back to its primal source, we find that John's state of mind (the human factor) is the indirect cause, out of which the direct causes originated.

As a matter of fact, it is not hard to present a strong case for the contention that all unsafe conditions have their origin in human factors. Worn-out machinery can create an unsafe condition which might cause an accident. But if the machine had been properly maintained and the wearing parts replaced soon enough, the wearing out would have been avoided and the unsafe condition would never have occurred. Why did a worker fail to maintain the machine in proper working order? What human factor in him caused the neglect? A steampipe may burst and be the cause of an accident. This looks like an unsafe condition where no human factor is involved. But steampipes are supposed to be periodically tested for stress potential, and failure to do this is an unsafe act by a human operator. Once again we may ask: Why was the operator negligent? Cases like these are frequently classified as unsafe conditions caused by nonhuman factors, but it is obvious that the classification is an arbitrary one. It is used when the causative human agent is not readily identifiable.

If all accidents are caused, then careful analysis and observation should lead to the discovery of the causes. The next obvious step is to remove the causes. The inevitable result will be no accidents. Accident prevention has been retarded by the failure to identify in some systematic fashion the conditions which cause accidents.

THE ACCIDENT REPORT

So far, we have clarified the complex nature of the accident problem, distinguished between accidents and their results, and focused attention upon accident causality. Where shall we turn to obtain reliable data or information useful for an accident-prevention program? The basic source of such information is the accident report. A good accident report should include data on the items discussed below.

1. DATE, HOUR OF THE DAY, SHIFT, AND LOCATION. Working conditions often change, sometimes in a systematic manner from day to day, from hour to hour, and from shift to shift. For example, the day-shift worker usually comes to work after a full night's sleep and breakfast. The preceding activity of the night-shift worker is usually more varied. Fatigue effects are more pronounced during the latter part of the working day. These and other factors under this category can influence accident behavior.

2. JOB CLASSIFICATION, JOB OPERATION, AND JOB UNIT. These data give specific information about the type of work in which the accident occurs. The hazard potential of different jobs and operations within jobs can thus be determined. Suppose a painter fell from a ladder while descending with his back to the rungs of the ladder. His job classification would be painter; his job operation, using a ladder; his job operation unit, descending the ladder.

3. ACCIDENT TYPE. Information in this category should include an exact description of the nature of the accident including a description of the contact agent. These descriptive data are not necessarily extensive and detailed. For the painter who fell from the ladder, a statement like "fell to the floor" would be sufficient.

4. IMMEDIATE CAUSE OF THE ACCIDENT. This information covers the cause of the accident in terms of specific unsafe acts or conditions or combinations of both. Among other findings we get from this information an answer to the question: What violation of a commonly accepted safety procedure resulted in a particular accident?

5. RESULTS OF THE ACCIDENT. Data under this heading cover bodily

location of the injury, description of the injury, and extent of property damage. Frequently the person who fills out the accident report cannot immediately describe the injury or property damage precisely. Medical assistance and help from someone responsible for assessing property damage are needed.

6. EXPERIENCE. How important experience on the job is in relation to type of accident can be determined only by a careful analysis of reliable data, the source of which must be the accident report. Data of this kind can be of great help in planning a safety-training program.

7. PSYCHOLOGICAL DATA. Scores on aptitude tests, personality inventories, and achievement tests should be included in the accident report if available. The analysis of such data may provide information for identifying some of the personal factors contributing to accident behavior.

Complete data within each of the categories discussed above constitute the minimum requirements for useful accident reporting. Large bodies of data carefully gathered on the various items of the report provide the basic information for the design of a successful accident-prevention program. All accidents should of course be reported, not only those involving injury and property damage. From our previous discussion it will be recalled that information about accident type and causes is just as valuable for the study and prevention of accidents when no injury or damage occurs as when the opposite is true.

The practical problem of obtaining complete accident data is not entirely solved with a carefully designed accident-report form. A report provides information only to the extent that the person filling out the report conscientiously does what the report asks him to do. The foreman or supervisor charged with the responsibility of reporting an accident must be trained in this task. The trainee should be given a complete story of an accident and then asked to fill out a formal accident-report form. He should then compare his report with an accurate model prepared by an expert. Any discrepancies should be discussed and corrected. Practice of this sort prevents careless and incomplete accident reporting.

There is scarcely an industrial organization today which does not have some kind of accident-prevention program and some kind of accident reporting. It is difficult, however, to assess the degree to which published data on accidents have been derived from well-designed reports and reliable reporting. The best we can do is to take representative published investigations and examine them critically in the light of available information.

INVESTIGATIONS OF PERSONAL FACTORS RELATED TO ACCIDENTS

Here we shall summarize some information about accidents in relation to intelligence, muscular coordination, and other factors, showing in some instances that popular opinion and research evidence do not always agree.

Intelligence. Popular thinking seems to assume that dumb people have accidents and smart people do not. There is no evidence available to support this generalization. One investigator [3] studied the problem and could find no correlation of any significance between scores on intelligence tests and accident frequency among dockyard apprentices. It has been suggested [16] that we should expect intelligence to be related to accidents involving errors of judgment but not to accidents involving manual skills. This suggestion may account for the lack of relationship in the dockyard study. Until further carefully controlled studies have been conducted there is little justification except conjecture for assuming that intelligence is related to accident liability.

Defective Vision. How well a person can see would appear to be a factor contributing to accident susceptibility, and there is some indication that this is so. In one investigation [10] the visual requirements of each worker in twelve groups were determined. The workers were then tested in order to find out whether or not they met the usual requirements of their respective jobs. Findings revealed that in eleven of the job groups, the percentage of safe workers was higher among those who passed the test than among those who failed it. No differences were found in the one exceptional group, which consisted entirely of laborers. Another investigator [17] found that only 37 per cent of a group of machine operators who passed visual tests had accidents during a given year, whereas 67 per cent of those who did not pass the vision tests had accidents.

Coordination. Muscular coordination has been a factor singled out by some investigators as having a possible bearing upon accident susceptibility. It would seem reasonable to suppose that slowness of response and clumsiness would contribute to accident frequency. Yet speed of reaction in and of itself has been found to have no significant relation to accident frequency in industry [3]. But more complex reaction tendencies are apparently important. For example, one investigator used a battery of tests consisting of a dotting test, a device for measuring speed of reaction to a signal, and a test which required the subject to change his muscular performance in accordance with changing signals [3]. When 500 employees were divided into two groups on the basis of high and low test scores, the poorer performers had 48 per cent more accidents than the better half. Also, the poorer quarter had 51 per cent more accidents than the better three-quarters. These findings have in general been supported by other investigations of muscular coordination and accidents [15].

Personality Characteristics. Some writers in the field of safety have argued that the personality characteristics of an individual have a great deal to do with his susceptibility to accidents. This may be true, but as yet we do not have a convincing body of evidence to substantiate the claim.

Some support comes from a study of the accident records of taxicab drivers who took a battery of psychological tests, including tests of emotional stability [14]. The latter tests are alleged to be very valuable in spotting the accident-susceptible drivers. Another investigator [8] determined the emotional condition or mood of industrial workers through observation and conversation and concluded that a significantly high percentage of accidents could be attributed to the fact that the worker was worried, apprehensive, or in some other low emotional state. The relationship between personality characteristics and accidents is a fertile field for investigation. However, real progress awaits the development of adequate instruments for assessing personality.

Experience. Common sense, plus a knowledge of the psychology of learning, plus actual research findings point toward inexperience on the job as a factor contributing to accidents. Table 7 summarizes the data from one study [3] which shows a close relationship between accident rate and amount of job experience.

TABLE 7
JOB EXPERIENCE AS RELATED TO ACCIDENT RATE

Length of service	Accident rate (per cent of total)
Less than 1 month	181
1–3 months	127
3–8 months	87
8–12 months	62
1–5 years	57

Another study carried out in England [6] shows that the accident rate continues to decrease among young workers up to eighteen months after employment. Still another analyst [16] reports the striking fact that accidents among workers on a stamping press dropped from 77 on the first day of work to an average of 13 for the next six days.

The fact that job experience and accidents are related calls attention to the importance of proper safety training for all new employees. Job know-how is of course usually acquired with experience on the job. But sometimes this know-how is acquired in a trial-and-error fashion as the result of bitter experience. Making the process of acquiring know-how a safer matter through training and guidance is clearly a means of reducing accidents. We shall look into the problem of safety training later in this chapter.

Fatigue. The critical point at which fatigue becomes an accident determinant in any individual has not been ascertained, but we are fairly certain that extreme fatigue leads to increased accident frequency. For example, in a shell factory in England during World War II the accident rate among women workers was reduced by more than 60 per cent when the factory changed from a twelve-hour to a ten-hour day [16].

Caution must be exercised in attributing accidents to fatigue if there is an accompanying change in production rate. What may seem to be a fatigue factor may really be a tendency to overlook accident dangers because one is working faster. The way to separate these two factors may be illustrated by an analysis of accidents made by the United States Public Health Service in which the effect of production rate was held constant. The technique was to divide the accident index by the production index for a given work period, in other words, to report in terms of accidents per unit of output. Results showed that in the earlier hours of the day the accident index rises and falls with the output rate. Increases in production bring about a corresponding increase in the number of accidents. However, this relation breaks down in the closing hours of the working day. Here the accident rate remains high relative to the production rate. Such an analysis makes it possible to show the importance of the fatigue factor.

Motor and Perceptual Speed. There is an indication that the ratio between an individual's speed of reaction and his perceptual speed bears a relation to accident behavior. In the single available study of this relationship [2], individuals whose speed of muscular reaction was above their perceptual speed had more accidents than those whose muscular reaction speed was below their perceptual speed. In other words, the person who reacts quicker than he can perceive is more likely to have accidents than is the person who can perceive quicker than he can react. The results are interesting and may signal a new approach to the measurement of human factors in accident behavior.

ENVIRONMENTAL CONDITIONS RELATED TO ACCIDENTS

Besides personal factors or conditions within the individual, there are also external or environmental factors which contribute to accidents.

Lighting and Temperature. Scarcely anyone would argue that lighting or conditions of visibility do not effect accident rate in some situations. Certainly it is true that fewer accidents occur in daylight than in any kind of artificial illumination. One insurance company estimated from survey results that 25 per cent of all industrial accidents were due to poor lighting. In an old survey carried out in Great Britain [16] it was found that artificial lighting caused an over-all increase in accidents of 25 per cent.

Temperature has an effect upon the worker which can increase his accident liability. One set of results [13] from a study of this problem indicates that there are fewer accidents among factory workers when the temperature is in the vicinity of 70°F, but there is an increase when the temperature falls below or rises above this figure.

Another study made in coal mines [16] shows a progressive increase in minor accidents as the temperature in different pits ranged from 62 to 85°F. In pits having the highest temperature, the minor accident frequency was three times greater than that of pits having the lowest temperature. The precise optimal temperature for safe work in different occupations is a problem which has not been solved.

Severity of Work. Physical demands upon the worker probably contribute to accidents, although substantiating evidence of this is scant. In one of the few investigations of this factor it was found that for factory workers engaged in muscular work the ratio of afternoon to morning accidents did not differ from that for persons engaged in machine or hand work [6]. The afternoon productivity of the men engaged in the heavier work, however, was less than that for the men engaged in the lighter work. In terms of accidents per productive unit, therefore, the workers on the jobs which were more demanding physically appeared to be at a disadvantage. This conclusion suggests that as the working day proceeds the number of accidents per unit of production increases for men in jobs requiring more physical effort.

Reactions to Environmental Organization. It is reasonable to assume that certain policies, attitudes, and conditions within a work group may cause individuals to have accidents. Low morale, rare opportunities for promotion, the presence of a large number of young workers, disinterested workers: these are examples of environmental factors which may be related to accident behavior. Such possibilities seem to receive support from a study of fifty-three departments of the Camden works of the Radio Corporation of America [11]. The investigator found that accidents occurred more frequently in those departments with low promotion probability, low intracompany transfer mobility, and high noise level. Greater accident severity was found in departments with a predominance of male workers, low promotion probability, low suggestion record, nonyouthfulness of employees, and high average tenure of workers.

ACCIDENT PRONENESS

So far in this account nothing has been said directly about the accident-prone individual, i.e., the person who, because of a peculiar set of biological and psychological characteristics, is more susceptible to accidents than are his fellows. The discussion of this topic has been postponed because of its highly controversial nature. The question is: Are we justified in postulating the presence of accident-prone characteristics as a cause of accident behavior?

The evidence which is frequently claimed to support the principle of accident proneness stems from the finding that some people have repeated accidents and that a relatively large proportion of accidents are experienced by a relatively small proportion of individuals. But is this evidence admissible? Statistical studies of the way accidents are distributed among the worker population show that a certain proportion of the workers should be expected to have repeated accidents purely by chance and that a concentration of the majority of accidents in a minority of the individuals is a mathematical necessity [12]. Thus, the only support for the principle of accident proneness comes from instances of repeated accidents in excess of chance. Even when there is evidence of repetition in excess of chance we must be certain that all cases had equal exposure to risk. Certain workers may have had an excessive number of accidents because they were in unusually hazardous situations or because they were exposed to hazard more often than their fellows.

Accident proneness may well exist and be a general factor which makes a worker susceptible in a wide variety of potential accident situations. Or it may exist in a restricted sense as a human factor or factors which lead to susceptibility in certain kinds of occupations; that is, a man may be accident-prone as a truck driver but not as a steel mill worker. The investigations reported suggest that the latter conception is probably the most valid. The fact remains, however, that studies have not been sufficiently well controlled in their reporting and interpretation to establish a clear case for or against any single position. Perhaps the safest position to take at present is the conclusion reached by two investigators who carried out an analysis of the literature in accident proneness and accident statistics [1]: "This does not mean that accident proneness does not exist, but so far we have not succeeded in defining it, assessing its dimensions and constituent elements, nor evolved a technique for putting it into practical use."

THE PROBLEM OF ACCIDENT-PREVENTION TRAINING

From the preceding discussion it is obvious that much remains to be done in isolating the specific physical and psychological conditions which lead to accidents. The ideal accident-prevention program awaits the answers to questions so far unanswered because of the lack of adequate research. Let us now tackle the problem of accident-prevention training in the light of what can be done with our present knowledge and consider what further knowledge we need before additional progress can be made.

Training deals with the applied psychology of learning, as we discussed in Chapter 7. The specific function of training is to cause the trainee to learn some new way of behaving (see page 129). In the area of accident prevention, the function of training is to reduce accidents. The trainer must bring about a change of behavior in the trainee, and the criterion of success is a change from accident-producing behavior to safe behavior. Everything else is secondary. Apparent cooperation in a safety training program as evidenced by good attendance at safety meetings is of little or no importance unless accidents are reduced. Employees may be entertained by safety films and say they like a training program, but these things are of little consequence unless accidents are reduced. Lectures by safety engineers are largely a waste of time unless they bring about a reduction in accidents. Training in accident prevention must measure up to one basic criterion: accident reduction does occur as a consequence of the training effort.

Knowing and Doing. Accident reduction is achieved through training only if the worker learns to exhibit safe behavior on the job. If a new worker does not know the company safety regulations and he is given this knowledge and demonstrates that he knows it, has he been trained in accident prevention? Not necessarily. Knowing will not always ensure doing. The problem of training clearly involves two phases: first, the worker must learn how to behave in a safe way; second, he must be stimulated to do it. Thus the safety slogan of United States Steel—"Knowing's Not Enough."

When Is Training Indicated? The obvious first step in determining when training is needed is to examine the accident reports. Suppose such an examination reveals that a significant percentage of accidents are associated with a certain kind of unsafe act. Does such a finding indicate lack of knowledge or a failure to put that knowledge into practice? We should find the answer to this question, for there is no point in trying to teach a worker something that he already knows.

If the records on unsafe acts do not tell what is known and what is not known, the sensible thing to do is to use some kind of job know-how test. Such a test should cover all aspects of the job which relate to safety. The test should be objective; and it should be so designed that it requires a minimum amount of time for administration. Relatively few industries use such tests, but they are clearly helpful since they tell the safety director where to start in setting up an accident-prevention training program. If the tests reveal lack of knowledge about how to perform a job safely, then training should meet this lack. If the workers possess the knowledge but are still having accidents, the problem is one of stimulating the worker to put into practice what he knows.

A legitimate question that should be considered at this point concerns training for the new employee or for the old employee who is put on a new job where accident records are not available. How shall we proceed when we cannot turn to records for information about specific job operations, accident types, and causes of accidents? The only safe procedure is to assume a need for all types of training. That is, the worker should be trained not only in what to do but also in how to apply this knowledge while he is on the job.

Content of Training Program. Suppose a determination of training needs reveals a lack of knowledge of how to do a job in a safe way. What kind of knowledge or information should be given to the workers? A careful examination of the accident reports will answer this question. Good accident reports contain data on the kinds of accidents that are occurring, the type of activity in which the accidents occur, the specific job operations having to do with accidents, the cause or causes of accidents, and on the results. Training content should be built around these specific items. If analysis shows operation X to be highly hazardous, then it is reasonable to spend more training on this operation than on operation Y, which is shown to be a low-hazard operation. Accident-prevention training should be directed toward those job phases in which accidents have been frequent.

If a training program is starting from scratch, that is, with no accident data available, the content should be determined through a job analysis by a safety-minded industrial engineer. This analyst reviews a job in its entirety, considering each step in the job sequence. He considers each operation in terms of its hazard potential and then formulates a safe way to deal with this hazard. Suppose an operation involves several specific acts, one of which is lifting a heavy steel bar. The engineer asks himself which of these acts is likely to lead to an accident? He may decide that the act of lifting is potentially hazardous. Therefore, in working up training content he will emphasize the proper way to lift. A discerning analyst can recognize the important accident hazards in most jobs.

Executing the Training. Once the need for training has been determined and the training content has been formulated, how will the training program be executed? A completely satisfactory answer to this question is difficult to determine because training techniques have seldom been systematically evaluated. There are some general training principles, however, which can be safely followed.

A good way to begin is to have the trainer demonstrate to the trainee the safe way to perform a job act. Seeing an act performed gives the learner an over-all idea of how it should be done. After the demonstration there should be a question-and-answer session to determine whether the trainee can tell in his own words what he should do.

Following the demonstration the trainee should be called upon to perform the act himself. He should repeat this performance until it is clear that he has mastered it with an acceptable degree of skill. Too many trainers stop with the demonstration phase of training. Demonstration only shows the trainee what he should do. People learn only when they do something themselves.

Written material, flip-chart talks, and movies can be used to clarify some of the important points in safety training. They can serve the useful purpose of dramatizing the importance of safety. As training aids they are widely used but probably overrated. Certainly they should never be substituted for firsthand demonstration and active performance under the supervision of an experienced trainer.

Who Should Do the Training? The practices which have been recommended so far will not succeed unless the training job is in the hands of a responsible trainer. Sometimes an outsider who is an expert in the field is assigned the training responsibility. Generally, this is an unwise practice. Outsiders usually do not know the work atmosphere of a particular plant well enough to handle the day-to-day problems peculiar to a plant's operations. Also, outsiders are frequently looked upon by the workers as disinterested individuals who are here today and gone tomorrow.

The safety engineer and his assistants are sometimes given the job of accident-prevention training. This policy also has shortcomings, since safety personnel must necessarily give off-the-job training in capsule form. That is, trainees are taken aside in a classroom and given special instruction in accident prevention. Safety personnel are not sufficiently close to the actual work operations to do the best job of training.

The one man who is closest to the worker, as was pointed out in the chapter on human relations in supervision, is the man's foreman or immediate supervisor (see page 159). The responsibility for the detection and correction of training deficiencies falls squarely into the lap of the immediate supervisor. Safety department personnel should clearly define, step by step, the specific responsibilities of first-line supervision, and then see that the foremen carry out these responsibilities. If the supervisor does not insist upon safe practices by his men, safe practices will not be forthcoming, regardless of what top management or the safety engineer does in the way of promoting accident prevention.

Supervisors are frequently reluctant to accept the responsibility for safety training on the grounds that they already have too much to do. Top management then has the problem of getting foremen to accept responsibility for safety. This may require a reorganization of the supervisor's over-all duties, or it may mean providing him with assistants.

When supervisors do an inadequate job in the field of safety, it is because upper management tolerates an inadequate job. Reprimand and recognition will usually bring about an improvement in the supervisor who has been lax in his safety duties. If he sends in a poor accident report, returning it to him for correction and completion will usually lead to improved reporting in the future. Accident-prevention training is most effective when there is an insistence upon safe practices from the office of the president all the way down to the front-line supervisor.

TECHNIQUES IN MOTIVATING SAFETY

As we pointed out earlier in the discussion of accident-prevention training, part of the problem is how to stimulate the worker to practice what he knows. The problem of motivation has been repeatedly referred to, but it merits additional treatment because of its complex nature and the difficulty that is often experienced in bringing about motivation in a practical situation.

The Long-range Point of View. Suppose an analysis of accident data reveals that on a particular job a number of accidents are caused by metal dust which gets into the workers' eyes. To eliminate this cause of accidents, the safety department issues a regulation stating that safety glasses must be worn at all times on the job. Not wearing the glasses is alleged to be an unsafe act. "But," says the worker who won't wear glasses, "I've been on the job for years, have never worn glasses, and have never had an accident." Suppose there is a safety regulation which says that descending a ladder with the back to the rungs is an unsafe act. Many workers can truthfully state that they have been descending ladders in this way for years and have never had an accident. Automobile drivers are told that driving a car above the speed limit is unsafe, but many people habitually exceed the speed limit and don't have accidents. There would probably be no motivational problem in these examples if an accident occurred every time the glasses were not worn, every time the ladder was descended in the wrong way, every time the speed limit was exceeded.

How shall we convince the worker of the fallacy of his reasoning? The important thing is to emphasize the need to take the long-range view— the point of view that in the long run an accident will catch up with him if he persists in violating safety practices. Pertinent evidence should be presented to the skeptical worker. Every industry's accident files contain cases of individuals who went accident-free for months and years and finally had an accident which could be attributed to a specific unsafe act.

Employee Participation. Within recent years a large amount of evidence has been accumulating which shows that employee participation in matters affecting their own welfare is strongly motivating [9]. This principle can be applied to the problem of motivating safety among a group of workers by having the workers themselves engage in the decision making that brings the change.

As a practical example of the effect of employee participation in decision making, consider the case of introducing the practice of wearing safety shoes in a steel-mill operation. Certain workers were selected who were well liked and held in high regard by their coworkers. They were presented with data from accident reports which showed a large percentage of foot injuries and were asked to come up with suggestions or recommendations for preventing such injuries. The supervisors met with the men on company time for several sessions during which the problem was discussed from many angles. The practice of wearing safety shoes was eventually suggested by the members of the group. Then the question of the best kind of safety shoes was brought up, and it was decided to try out different makes of shoes for several days on an experimental basis. During the meetings the safety engineer sat in on all sessions but never made a decision himself. His sole role was to stimulate discussion among members of the group and to get them to arrive at a unanimous decision. Significantly, the members of the committee reported that they had from time to time discussed the problem with their fellow workers. Finally, the group decided to institute the practice of wearing a certain kind of safety shoe on the job at all times. The policy was wholeheartedly accepted by the working group with scarcely even a minor infraction of the regulation.

There are a number of important reasons why the motivational problem just described was solved so effectively. First, the decision was made by the people who were to be directly affected by the decision. It is becoming axiomatic in psychology that people are more effectively motivated when they are permitted some degree of participation in the determination of their own activity (see page 210). Contrary to popular opinion, many people like to assume some responsibility. Allowing a person to make a decision amounts to paying him a compliment, because respect for his judgment is being shown.

A second reason for the effectiveness of the group decision was that, by the very nature of the group process, the change was introduced gradually. Almost everyone resists abrupt changes. Old, habitual ways are highly motivating by the very fact that they are deep-seated or well learned. It requires less time and effort to do something the old way than it does to learn a new way, even though the new way, when learned, will be easier and quicker. The countermotivation to offset resistance to change involves, among other things, a gradual introduction of the new way, and an avoidance, if possible, of an arbitrary decision by someone who will not be directly affected by the change.

Safety Campaigns and Posters. The use of posters and campaigns aimed at stimulating safe behavior is a common practice in industrial organizations. Their effectiveness is somewhat questionable, although under certain conditions they seem to have merit.

Posters which convey a general message, particularly in negative terms, probably do little good. A gruesome picture showing some mutilated part of the body with the caption, "Don't let this happen to you," is of little value in preventing accidents. It creates resentment, fear, and sometimes anger. No one wants to get killed or injured, and it is an insult to a workman to imply that he or anyone else is so motivated. Posters should carry a simple, reasonable, and constructive message in positive terms. Statements like the following, placed in appropriate places, are examples of positive and informative poster material:

Wear Hard Hats Here
Deposit Cigarette Butts in This Container
Cross at This Point
Lower Safety Guard before Starting Machine

Poster material should be used which attracts the maximum amount of attention. Legibility and the proper use of color are attention-getting determinants. Locating the poster so that it will be readily seen is obviously important. And there should not be so many posters that they clutter the working landscape. The fact that one or two posters are effective does not mean that additional posters will be more effective. A poster which is unique or different catches the workers' attention most quickly. If posters are everywhere, people cease paying attention to them.

Safety campaigns or contests in which workers strive for a safety record over a certain period of time tend to sensitize the worker to be safety conscious. The best kind of safety campaign is that which never really ends. Rewards of some kind should be given to the individual who has a good safety record. Indeed, there is no good reason why a man's accident record should not be a permanent part of his personnel file to be used in determining his fitness for promotion, job transfer, or increase in pay.

THE ENGINEERING PHASE OF THE SAFETY PROBLEM

So far, the discussion in this chapter has been focused on the human element in accident behavior. We have been concerned with understanding the nature of the worker so that we can predict and control his behavior. The mechanical or engineering side of the story should not, of course, be neglected. A well-designed working environment can do much to eliminate accidents in some cases, and in others it can make the handling of the human factor a lot easier. On this latter point, for example, the problem of getting men to wear safety clothing may be largely a psychological problem. Whether it will be a difficult psychological problem or an easy one may depend on the design of the safety apparel. If the clothing is uncomfortable, the problem will be more difficult. Of course, there are so many different safety devices in use in modern industry that specific treatment of each and every kind is impossible. But we do know that all good safety devices have certain common features.

Foolproof Devices. From the mechanical standpoint, a good safety device should be as foolpoof as possible. At the beginning of this chapter it was pointed out that it is probably impossible to create a completely foolproof device. But from a practical standpoint, there are degrees of foolproofness, and the engineer with originality and ingenuity can make fairly accurate estimates on this matter. A rotary saw blade which will not start until a guard is in place is more foolproof than one which can be started with the guard disengaged. An ingenious worker may locate the wiring which leads to the motor and arrange it in such a way as to bypass the safety guard. But this kind of action is much less likely to occur than is starting the saw with a disengaged guard.

Production Interference by a Safety Device. Another major requirement of a good safety device is that it does not interfere with production. Safety devices that interfere with production are resisted by both workers and management. A well-designed device not only does not interfere with production but actually facilitates it. Most unsafe operations are perceived as such to some degree, and the perceived hazard hampers production. When the worker knows he is safe, he is free from worry and strain and has a greater fund of energy available to devote to production.

Proper Maintenance of Equipment. Keeping equipment in good order is an important safety measure. Poorly maintained machinery creates unsafe conditions just as surely as does properly maintained equipment without specifically designed safety devices. The success of the safety department depends upon the cooperation and efficiency of the maintenance department, and the former can do much to ensure prompt repair and maintenance by stressing the safety need.

A common failing in this regard is the lag between the time of the report of need for repair and maintenance and the execution of the work itself. Sometimes hazardous conditions are spotted but not corrected for a long time. During the interval the unsafe conditions are often responsible for a rash of accidents. An otherwise good safety program can easily bog down if maintenance men are so overworked that they cannot keep mechanical equipment safe and in good working order. Slipshod and nonprofessional repair and maintenance by the workers themselves is a poor substitute for the work of the maintenance crew. This practice creates a false sense of security which may lead to more accidents than if no attempts at all are made at correction.

Good Housekeeping. Essential for accident-free behavior is orderly housekeeping. Some plants lack adequate storage space for equipment and tools. There are an insufficient number of depositories for waste materials. Windows and floors are not kept clean, and machinery is not properly loaded. All these housekeeping details must be attended to if a safe work atmosphere is to be maintained. One reporter cites a variety of accidents attributable to poor housekeeping [5]: (1) slipping on greasy, wet, or dirty floors; (2) bumping against poorly stacked or misplaced materials; (3)

tripping over loose objects on floors, stairs, and platforms; (4) injuring parts of the body on projecting nails, hooks, or sticks.

The Need for Research on Design of Industrial Equipment. Although it is true that most modern industrial equipment incorporates safety devices of one kind or another, there is need for further research on the design of safe equipment. There are certain subtle features about a piece of equipment which seemingly have little to do with its safe operation but which may actually contribute considerably to unsafe behavior. Thus, the faulty design of control levers may contribute to accidents. Or a gauge may be so poorly designed that errors in reading it are frequently made.

The design of safe equipment calls for a careful consideration of the worker's perceptual abilities and his intellectual and manual response equipment. Even the automaticity of a piece of equipment should be examined in terms of its safety properties. How automatic should a device be in order to get maximum efficiency from the operator? The obvious answer, "Make it as automatic as possible," is not always psychologically sound; for, if a human operator is needed at all, he must have enough to do so that he will not become bored. Lack of attention may well be the cause of accidents in certain machine operations. The principles underlying good equipment design are covered in the following chapter on engineering psychology.

SUGGESTIONS FOR FURTHER READING

Heinrich, H. W. *Industrial accident prevention.* New York: McGraw-Hill, 1941. An old stand-by in the accident-prevention field for practical and sound suggestions.

Karn, H. W., & Gilmer, B. *v.* H. *Readings in industrial and business psychology.* Section VI "Accidents and Safety." New York: McGraw-Hill, 1952. Four research articles on the causes and prevention of industrial accidents.

Metropolitan Life Insurance Co. *Industrial safety.* A practical look at accident prevention.

Thorndike, R. L. *Human factors in accidents.* United States Air Force School of Aviation Medicine, Feb., 1951. A review of the problems and researches of industrial and military accidents.

16

ENGINEERING

PSYCHOLOGY

Lee W. Gregg

Many of the problems of work involve the interrelationships between man and the machines that man must use in performing the work. We have indicated a few of these problems in preceding chapters. Engineering psychology—which attempts to handle the problems of machine design for optimum human use—has grown out of the professions of engineering and experimental psychology. Since we are familiar by now with what the psychologist does, let us begin by describing where the engineer fits into our picture. Later on in the chapter we will describe man-machine systems in modern-day industrial psychology.

THE JOB OF THE ENGINEER

Contriving, designing, and producing structures and machines useful to man is the job of the engineer. He applies his knowledge of the mechanical, electrical, chemical, or other properties of matter to the task of creating all kinds of functional devices—safety pins and automobiles, mousetraps and missiles. Since the ultimate user of these devices is man himself, human characteristics must be considered in their construction. Human muscular frailty provided the necessity for and dictated the design of such devices as the lever, the pulley, the screw, and hand tools of all sorts. Similarly, our more complex machines represent a direct outgrowth of human needs.

As more tools have been invented, they have become increasingly difficult to manage. Some of the simpler control mechanisms of the earlier machines—levers or wheels—no longer provide the sensitivity required for optimum human use. More important perhaps is the fact that the machines themselves have created new needs that can often be met only by contriving new machines. Man is no longer satisfied with the speeds which earlier automobiles provided; he must go faster. He also wants to be able to do this more easily and more comfortably. Hence, we find windows operated by remote control, power steering, fuel injectors, and many, many more of these speeding objects to bump into on the highways.

With the introduction of an independent source of power, the simple and direct link between man and the machine was broken. Very often we know the nature of our environment only in an indirect way. For example, most people traveling in a modern automobile on the modern highway have an inadequate sense of speed. Even though they see the changing roadway, they do not perceive accurately their rate of travel. The engineer must provide the means for transmitting to these people the necessary information for safe and efficient control of the vehicle.

THE PROBLEM OF COMPLETE AUTOMATION

One solution to the problems that arise in dealing indirectly with the environment is to make the machines so fully automatic that no human control of them is ever required. To a limited extent modern industry has been able to eliminate the human element. In certain specialized tools and even in more elaborate systems, automation may be almost complete. A reasonably stable process, such as that exemplified by modern petroleum production, can be carried on in plants which are almost wholly automatic. But even here we find a few operators watching over the complex instrument panels, monitoring them, and being ready to respond to the automatic warning signals that indicate that conditions have arisen which the machines cannot handle. These men are performing different tasks from the workers before them, but they are nonetheless exercising the ultimate control functions.

Machines and the User. It might be possible to anticipate some of these conditions which the machines themselves cannot handle, and build into the systems the means for dealing with them. For example, one could provide auxiliary power units to be used when the primary ones are damaged in a storm. In this way, the *range of environmental conditions* which the machine can cope with is extended—not without cost, however. Adding parts which may be used but infrequently is expensive. We pay for the parts themselves, for the space they fill, and for the increased complexity of the system, because the parts must be integrated into the over-all structure.

Moreover, we must remember that the machines are created to satisfy the needs of the user. As the needs change, different functions are required of the machines. The stable processes and products of the refineries will, in fact, be modified as new petroleum products are found. Needs also change in the short run. The automobile which can get you back and forth to work most economically is not necessarily the one which can take you to a distant destination with speed and comfort, or provide the needed space for camping and fishing gear on a vacation trip. Flexible and adaptable multipurpose machines are, necessarily, complex machines.

Complexity limits the development of complete automation. Each of the separate quantities that influences the behavior of the complex system must be measurable and subject to physical control. All of the facts about the performance of the separate parts must be linked with one another and related to the goals that the machine must achieve. This can only be accomplished through a very complex central processing unit, a multipurpose control device flexible enough to handle the variety of facts given to it— a giant brain. Some of the high-speed digital computers presently available are beginning to approach the degree of complexity necessary to tie in these many and varied facts. In effect, these machines partially simulate the generalized abilities that man already has.

THE FIELD OF ENGINEERING PSYCHOLOGY

The task which confronts engineering psychology is to describe these special abilities of man in such a way that design engineers can effectively incorporate the human operator as a component in the man-machine system. We must specify the "engineering properties of the man" [15]. This task requires a degree of precision difficult to attain, because psychology is a relatively young science, and human behavior is clearly complex.

A Problem in Communication. Communicating with the engineer is also a part of the task. The descriptive material must be presented not necessarily in terms that other psychologists can understand, but rather in such a way that the design engineer can use it. Only by treating both the animate and inanimate components in terms of common conceptualizations can the psychologist and the engineer attain an understanding of their joint actions. For this reason, the bias that has arisen is to treat people as if they were machines rather than to treat machines as people. As a result, the psychologist working in this field has had to learn the language of physical science.

The field of engineering psychology has evolved only within the past fifteen to twenty years. During World War II psychologists were called upon to assist engineers in the development of weapons systems. At first this help involved suggestions for the design of knobs, levers, and dials. A number of investigations were concerned simply with the evaluation of these devices in terms of the speed or accuracy of human response. Later the team approach to systems design enabled psychologists to use their knowledge of the various sensory and motor aspects of man's behavior. In the team, the psychologist served as an advisor to the engineer and in some instances participated in designing various components of the systems. At present the field of engineering psychology, while it draws upon findings within the general field of experimental psychology, is basically concerned with specifying, in physical terms, those properties of human behavior which are important for the control of machines. Once these properties have been appropriately specified, and mechanical or electronic means for simulating them have been developed, unmanned systems of increasing complexity will be possible.

THE NATURE OF MAN-MACHINE SYSTEMS

What is a system? How does the man fit into it? The systems concept is the basic idea that enables us to put the man and the machine on even

Fig. 16.1. The elements of control systems. In a control system there is an *open loop* when the action follows the path from input through control to output, as represented by the solid arrows. The broken arrow shows the output being fed back into the system so that the output itself is modified; this is called a *closed-loop* system.

terms. The word "system" suggests more than one component part. It is bigger than the elements that compose it. The way the parts act toward one another determines the nature of the system. In Figure 16.1 the elements of a system are represented by the blocks. Let us first look at two systems which involve machines only.

The Open Loop. Suppose that we wish to turn on some outside lights at dusk. In setting up a system to accomplish this, we might use a photocell which would react to the change in the outside level of illumination. The quantity of light entering the photocell is the input variable. Whenever this input falls below some previously established level, a switch is activated. The lights come on and the output of the system, also a quantity of light, is modified. When the general out-of-doors illumination—the input—increases again at dawn, the quantity of light entering the photocell exceeds the level set for turning off the lights, and the control switch is deactivated. The control system, consisting of the photocell and some additional electronic equipment, produces a change in the output which depends on a change in the input. Notice in Figure 16.1 that the action follows the solid arrows from left to right. Once the switch is deactivated, further changes in the input do not influence it. This is the simple open loop.

The Closed Loop. Suppose, however, that we now wish to control the temperature of a room. In this case the input variable is the temperature variation that acts upon a thermostat. Whenever the temperature of the room falls too low, a switch turns on the furnace. The result is a greater output of heat for the room. Is this, too, the open loop? It is not, because here the output quantity acts back on the input element. The broken arrow indicates this fact in Figure 16.1. Feeding back the output or some part of the output quantity so that the output is itself modified is characteristic of the closed-loop system.

Specifications in Control. Both of these examples represent types of control. We can see that the word "control" means "holding some specified quantity constant." In the first instance we wish to maintain the conditions of illumination and, in the second, to maintain the level of temperature. Open-loop systems—which lack feedback—are necessarily limited in their scope of operation. They must be calibrated to work properly under some particular set of conditions. Of more interest is the self-regulating system which results when we close the loop. Devices of this type provide rather precise control over a wide range of input values. It is not easy to design an instrument which attains this precision, however.

Suppose for the moment that we try to make a closed-loop system out of the photocell and floodlights. We might do this by letting one of the lamps shine on the photocell. If we incorporate a time lag into the control element, a condition of unstable operation is set up. All night long, the lights go on, then off, then on again. The system oscillates or hunts and cannot settle down. This illustration points up problems—some of them not particularly obvious—which confront the design engineer in building complex interacting mechanisms of the self-regulating type. Their design requires the precise specification of many values having to do with time lags, inertia of moving parts, sensitivity of the detector elements, and so on.

These same complications are present in the systems where men perform the controlling acts. It is, therefore, just as necessary to specify human values with precision as it is to do so for the parts of the machine itself. Let us now turn our attention to man as a control system playing his part in the larger man-machine structure.

An Example of a Man-Machine System. In Figure 16.2 we have represented a very small part of an aircraft system. It suggests a single control function, namely, that of regulating the speed of the aircraft. We may think of the first-level control system as the pilot—the human operator himself. Presumably, he too possesses input, control, and output elements, but for the moment, let's keep him intact. The input to the pilot is derived from the air-speed indicator—a pointer reading on a dial. We must specify a quantity to be controlled, a constant value of perhaps 350 miles per hour. It is the same as setting the thermostat at 70° or adjusting the photocell to turn on the lights at a given level of darkness. By convention, any input element that provides the direct sensory stimulus for the human operator is called a "display." The operator receives information from the display

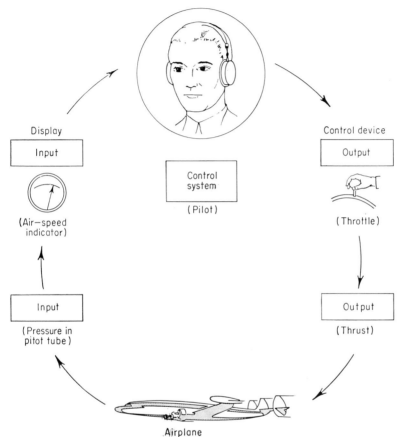

Fig. 16.2. Controlling air speed of an aircraft. The pilot is a control system, receiving inputs from the display (air-speed indicator) and providing outputs to the control device (throttle).

that may lead to a decision to advance the throttle; this is accomplished by a movement on the part of the pilot. The object through which the operator's control decision is carried out is a control mechanism or, simply, a control. The output at this level is a change in position of the control. In a sense the throttle lever is made to follow inversely the movements of the pointer so that any discrepancy or error is kept to a minimum. It is a closed-loop system since the output modifies the input.

It is important that we realize that this description is possible only when the particular level is defined. For example, a new set of input and output quantities is indicated in Figure 16.3. At the next higher level, the display, human operator, and the control device become the control system which receives information, processes it, and provides an output in a somewhat different form. In some instances the remoteness of the human operator from the environmental variable to be controlled is quite great. At each successive level, time lags are introduced which in general reduce the system's effectiveness.

As the number of levels increases, another interesting result can occur. More than one pathway for feeding back information about the output

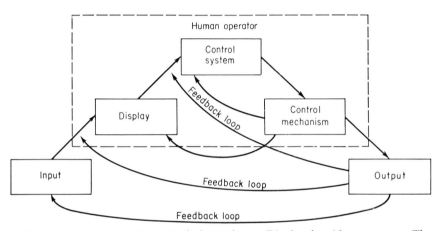

Fig. 16.3. A variety of feedback loops is possible in closed-loop systems. The human operator may "feel" the position or resistance of the control device; he may sense the changes in output directly as increased or decreased pressures; the state of a control device may be directly displayed on an instrument panel; or the state of the unit on which the control device acts may be displayed. The basic feedback loop is that created by the effect of output on input.

quantities may exist. In the diagram of Figure 16.3 some of the possibilities are shown. Most direct is the feedback which an operator receives as he manipulates the control mechanism itself. He sees and feels the extent to which a lever is pushed or a wheel is turned. Sometimes the position of the control is reflected as an integral part of the display. The nature of the feedback, where it comes from and where it goes, is a very important determiner of the behavior of self-regulating systems.

THE BEHAVIOR OF THE HUMAN OPERATOR

In observing what the man actually does in his role as controller of the man-machine system, three aspects of his behavior can be identified. These correspond to the parts of any generalized control system as outlined in Figure 16.1. The man, by analogy, is considered to be such a system.

From Information to Action. Man's first act in the control system is to receive information. What information he receives depends on the nature of his immediate environment or more specifically, the kinds of machine displays the system provides. Next, he decides what to do—he thinks. Actually it is difficult for us to know exactly what occurs, but we infer that processing of the information received from the display goes on within the central nervous structures of the man. In psychology this control activity has been studied extensively, and is identified as higher mental processes, thinking, problem solving, cognition, reasoning, and the like. We will identify this aspect of the human operator's performance as "complex information processing." Finally, the man initiates some physical action. His output is in the form of a response or movement by means of which he manipulates the control. Precisely what course of action he follows depends on the decision he makes and the instruments of the machine.

Each of these aspects of the human operator's behavior will be dealt with in the sections that follow. But before turning to these accounts of the elements of human control, let us consider the behavior as it appears in a specific task in order to see just what the job of the human operator is.

Tracking. A much-studied task which arises in many different settings is that of tracking a moving target. In driving an automobile, aiming a shotgun at a flying bird, or sewing a seam by machine, some of the elements of tracking are involved. The task calls for a change in the output of the system so that a change in the input is matched or followed in space. This amounts to holding constant at some value (usually zero) the discrepancy between the target and an indicator of some sort which reflects the spatial location of the tracking object. Thus, the quantity to be controlled may be thought of as "error."

In the psychological laboratory, tracking tasks related to certain military systems have been so constructed that they permit us to observe the operator in action and to measure his accuracy. One such arrangement uses the cathode ray tube for the display. This is an electronic tube used in radar which operates in a fashion similar to the television picture tube. A spot of light moves over the face of the tube in two dimensions. Its movement represents the movement of the target through space. The indicator or cursor may be a small lighted circle. The job of the operator is to manipulate a joystick control so that the target is kept within the circle.

Pursuit and Compensatory Tracking. If, as suggested in Figure 16.4, the system's input causes the target to move over the face of the screen and the control mechanism permits changes in the cursor so that the operator can follow the target about, the task is referred to as "pursuit tracking." Contrasted with this procedure is one in which the cursor remains at a fixed place in the center of the screen, and movement of the joystick control counteracts the movement of the target as represented on the face of the tube. This is called "compensatory tracking." Notice that the difference between these two modes of tracking lies in the way in which the information is presented. In pursuit tracking, the target course can be observed by the operator. He attempts to match the motion of the cursor to that of the target. In the compensatory task, the target course is not so clearly defined. Instead, what the operator sees is the result of the target and the corrective or adjustive effects produced by the control.

Making Corrections. In the analysis of human operator performance in a tracking task, certain statements can be made about his gross behavior.

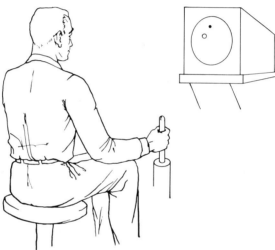

Fig. 16.4. Pursuit tracking. The target (solid dot) moves in two dimensions over the face of the oscilloscope. A cursor (open circle) is controlled by the stick.

Anyone who has carefully studied his own behavior in such tasks will probably be able to recall these same features. First, there is an initial misalignment and an attempt to correct it. Generally, accuracy in making corrections is poor in the early stages. It takes more time for the operator to detect the discrepancy, to decide in what direction and by how much the stick should be moved, and even to move it, than is required after considerable practice. There is a tendency, in making the corrective movement, to overshoot or undershoot so that, instead of smooth-flowing movements, jerky, discrete adjustments are made. Each attempt represents a separate "chunk" of behavior rather than a continuous flow. In this way the tracking behavior proceeds. Later on there is a considerable smoothing out of the adjustments because the individual learns to anticipate changes and to organize movements in sequences. This erratic feature of the human operator's behavior led the late K. J. W. Craik, a British psychologist, to apply the term "intermittent" to the definite corrective behavior of the man in this kind of situation [2].

Transduction. A second characteristic of the human operator's gross behavior is that the man changes the form of the input and output. In physical terms, the energy form which the operator receives is a pattern of light which, during the course of interpretation and processing, comes out as a pattern of movement, i.e., mechanical energy. The engineer's word for this behavior in a machine is "transduction." The radio loudspeaker, for example, is a device which changes electrical energy to sound energy. We find that the human operator has special abilities with respect to transducing energy, and systems design requires matching the needs of the system's variables to the abilities exhibited by the man. In other words, certain kinds of inputs from displays lead more readily to certain specific output movements. This problem has been treated in psychology as the "stimulus-response correspondence."

Amplification. A third important characteristic of the human operator's over-all behavior may be called "amplification." This means that small amounts of energy give rise to larger amounts when passed through the system. Amplification is basic to almost all control systems, whether they include the human operator or not. It is through the expenditure of small amounts of energy that larger energy sources are manipulated in performing the system's work. Relatively little work, in the physical sense, is required in throwing a switch on or off, but the work performed by a motor energized by the switch can be very great. At the level of the human controller, small changes in the discrepancy between target and cursor may give rise to greater changes in his responsive movements.

With these features of the human operator's behavior in mind, we return to the analogy of man as a control system in his own right. Our first concern is with the inputs to the man.

INPUTS AND THE HUMAN SENSORY PROCESSES

The human operator receives information from his environment through the special senses—sight, sound, and touch, smell, and taste. The information which he receives is presented by machine displays and thus only indirectly tells him of the changes in the input variables. We do, of course, receive much of the useful information directly. We may observe that the light on our desk is insufficient for reading and may on the basis of this observation, turn on a lamp. The input variable, level of illumination, is received directly through the visual sense. Sometimes, greater precision is required than is afforded by the unaided visual mechanisms. Perhaps we wish to photograph a scene and this requires a fairly precise setting of the aperture of our camera. The same input variable is involved when we measure the reflected light from the surface of objects with a light meter. In this case, the information is displayed as a needle deflection. We get information represented by the scale symbols which may be converted readily to the proper setting for the camera. The display is a visual one, but the information presented tells us only indirectly of the input.

Design of Displays. The engineering problem is to determine how to construct displays so that the information required is received quickly and accurately by the machine operator. Thus, the engineering psychologist treats the sensory mechanisms of the human being as detector devices.

In designing displays for the more complex systems where many inputs must be represented, it is important to provide as much of the relevant information as possible in a single display. For example, in a task which requires locating objects in space, it is easy to build a display which yields information about a single dimension, say the distance of an approaching aircraft from the end of a runway. However, to give this information *and* information about its altitude, heading, or speed of approach in a single simple display is very difficult. Hence, much of the time and effort expended in display design is directed toward finding ways to simplify the presentation of many separate pieces of information and incorporate them into a single meaningful display.

The problems of presenting information to the operator can be illustrated most easily by a look at the simpler systems where we have single inputs. We have previously suggested that the behavior of the human operator is intermittent. The information provided by a single dial or gauge, the numbers or other symbols, is attended to by the observer discretely. This means that, although the input variable itself may be constantly changing, as in the tracking task, the human observer can grasp the meaning or detect the state of the signal only as a fixed unit in time. For purposes of control action, the information is apprehended as a stationary discrepancy or value. Thus, if two or more displays are presented to the controller, only one of them can be attended to and hence provide a usable signal at one time. In reading, for example, successive fixation of the eyes on separate parts of the written material occurs. Although the better reader exhibits fewer such fixations per line of type, he nevertheless shows the same general pattern. He is able to assimilate a larger number of individual symbols within a single fixation than can the slower reader, but in performance he behaves in essentially the same way.

In the task of presenting information to an operator, the time needed to acquire units of the message contained in the signal must be specified for the many different kinds of sensory inputs that may be used.

Information Theory. In engineering psychology, a convenient analogy has been drawn between the sensory mechanisms of the human being and their counterparts in communication engineering. The concept of a "channel" has come to refer to means by which sensory data are conveyed to the person, just as the television channel stands for the means whereby the audio and video signals are transmitted and received. Information is put into one end of the channel and comes out the other end. This is an almost exact counterpart of the human being receiving information from a display. The display "sends" patterns of light or sound that symbolically denote the changes in the input variable. These patterns are the message. Reception of the message and the perception of its meaning come about through the specialized organs of the man.

Each of the sensory modalities is considered a sensory channel. The sense of sight constitutes the means by which information from visual displays is transmitted to the consciousness of the human controller. The usefulness of this analogy becomes apparent when we recognize that with a suitable

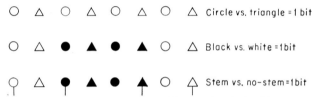

Fig. 16.5. Eight alternatives and three bits. Each of the binary cues—circle vs. triangle, black vs. white, stem vs. no-stem—halves the number of alternatives, so that one of eight alternatives can be selected.

measure for the amount of information contained in a display and a procedure for determining how much of the information presented is received by the observer of the display, a precise technique is available to us for improving displays.

The Bit. A measure has been developed by communications engineers [8, 11, 14] called the "bit" (a contraction of binary digit). A bit is the information in a single choice between two alternatives. Thus, if we know that one of two events is to occur, but are uncertain which it will be, one bit of information which resolves this uncertainty is transmitted by a signal. Paul Revere's "one, if by land; two, if by sea" signal system transmitted "one bit." Any signal, then, that has just two states, or any language with only two symbols, can provide one bit of information. Now let us suppose that there are eight buttons on a panel before you, and you are to push one of them. How much information must be given to enable you to push the correct one?

If as in the first row of Figure 16.5 half of the buttons are circular and half of them triangular, the message "press the circular button" reduces your uncertainty and provides some of the information you need. In fact, it halves the number of alternatives. If the message reads, "press the circular button that is colored black," the number of alternatives is again halved. You finally know what to do when the message reads, "press the circular button that is painted black and has a projecting stem." Three bits of information are contained in the message; they reduce the eight alternatives to just the one specific object, button number three. This information could have been transmitted in many other ways, of course. Relays that are open or closed, lights that are on or off, or currents that either flow or do not flow are all possibilities. But in a strict sense, precise specification is possible only when information is given in quantitative terms.

Of course the message could have read, "Press button number three." On the surface, this appears considerably easier and more efficient and seems to contain fewer units of information than indicated above. Our language is a highly developed code and provides us with a great deal of flexibility, so that there frequently are many ways of saying the same thing. Notice, however, that in setting up the simple number code, eight possible messages "one, two, three, . . . eight" would have to be established in advance, i.e., eight *different* signals would be necessary. From a communication point of view, it is usually easier to think of and provide the means for sending just the three binary symbols. Thus, in teletype, five "on" or "off" punches in a tape can be used to designate 32 possible symbols— enough for the 26 letters of the alphabet and a few punctuation marks.

Redundancy in Communication. The fact is that messages in our language often contain the same information several times. Constraints of the language (the letter u always follows q) create redundancy in normal verbal communication. The context of speech gives us information about what the next symbol is going to be. Hence, when that symbol occurs, some of the information it would have contained has already been received. Shannon [14] has estimated the redundancy of English based on the statistical structure of the language over distances of about eight letters to be 50 per cent. Students have long known that textbooks need be only half as long as they usually are.

These concepts are valuable for the field of engineering psychology because they help us to devise a means of quantitatively describing inputs to the human operator. Quite apart from language communication, as such, we may apply these concepts to any kind of display in which stimulus objects with varying characteristics provide knowledge of changes external to the system. We can compute the capacity of the observer to receive information per unit of time. Or we can find how much information can be transmitted by certain displays, if the observer is given sufficiently great amounts of time to observe them.

Amount of Information in a Display. Hake and Garner [6] determined the amount of information transmitted to observers who made judgments about the value represented by a pointer position between scale marks as on an instrument dial. In this experiment, the pointer was allowed to take on 5, 10, 20, or 50 different positions within the interpolation interval. The greater the number of pointer positions, the greater is the amount of information contained in the display. However, we might reasonably expect that there would be more errors with the larger numbers of values to detect, so that what the observer gets out of the display represents what is there minus the error factors. Hake and Garner found that above a certain minimal number of allowed positions, the amount of information was approximately constant. Very little additional information is transmitted by allowing more than 10 pointer positions. For the particular size of scale that they used, slightly more than 3 bits of information per pointer presentation were obtained from the 10, 20, and 50 positions whereas only 2.31 bits were transmitted in the 5-position case.

Informational analysis of displays is a useful device in treating some of the problems of equipment design for human use. However, a great deal of study devoted to the understanding of the sensory mechanisms—the channels through which the observer picks up the inputs—has yielded basic data about the receptor processes. These results have not often been obtained in information theory terms. They nevertheless identify important factors that are related to the design of displays and the operator's role in the machine system.

CONTROL AND HUMAN INFORMATION PROCESSING

The human operator serves as a living link between the inanimate parts of the man-machine system. The information obtained from the system displays passes through him, but not in the same way that a message passes through a telephone wire. Such a procedure would be wasteful of man's unique talents as a decision-making machine. Rather, the information presented to the operator is assimilated, processed in the light of previously acquired information stored in memory, and evaluated for future action. In many systems, the amount and complexity of this processing is fantastically great. In other practical situations, man's controlling acts are quite simple, and if it were not convenient to keep the man around for other reasons, his control functions might well be eliminated.

The design engineer needs to know which tasks are best performed by machines and which are best carried out by a human operator. If we are to assist the engineer in this, we must look more closely at the information processing which the operator carries out in his role as the data-transmission link in the system. The operator comes to the system with certain previously learned habits and knowledge. He knows what it is that the system is to do.

In the earlier example of the aircraft pilot, the pilot had to know that he was to maintain an air-speed of 350 miles per hour. He retained this figure in his memory—stored away, but available for purposes of comparison with the figure designating his actual air-speed at any time. He received the latter value whenever he directed his attention to the air-speed indicator on his instrument panel. Next, he compared the two values, and determined whether his present air speed was greater or less than the desired value. As a result of this test or comparison, he made his decision: "My air speed is greater than the desired value; therefore I will reduce it." The decision he made is neither more nor less than pulling forth certain pieces of information—also stored in memory—associated with the possible outcomes of the test.

Complex Information Processing. The chain of mental acts that leads to the final decision of the operator begins with the *perceptual responses* which enable him to interpret the data of the display. The patches of light and patterns and shapes are meaningful objects or quantities; the operator recognizes them and distinguishes among them pieces of information for subsequent comparisons. For more complex situations, there may be many steps or stages along the way to reaching the decision. For this reason, we will call the final comparison that the operator makes—the one which leads to one of several alternative courses of action—the *decision.* The comparisons that he must make after the recognition or identification of the objects, but prior to this final step are *judgments.* The distinction between judgments and decisions is simply that we can make a judgment and not do anything about it; when we make a decision, however, the implication is that some course of overt action will follow.

Perceptions, judgments, and decisions, then, are the kinds of mental activities that are included within the broader framework of complex information processing. All three of these activities require basically the same sort of processing. In general, at least two pieces of information must be appropriately specified and at least one test comparing the pieces of information must be carried out. The distinctions among perceptions, judgments, and decisions are made in terms of the kinds of information compared, the bases for the comparison, and what happens as a result of the comparison. In the following sections we will present brief descriptions of these activities.

Perceptual Processes. We are constantly being stimulated by sights and sounds of which only a small fraction have significance for our present behavior. What we attend to and how we interpret the stimuli are determined by our perceptual processes. We recognize or identify an object for what it is because, in the past, experiences of a particular kind were associated with the object. A perception, then, comes about when certain aspects of the stimulus are observed and compared with a stored impression. Let's see how this process works.

Scanning. In perceiving, we draw meaning from the sensory impression by first distinguishing the properties or characteristics of the objects. We must observe the relevant attributes that will permit us to determine whether or not the object matches the stored representation. Since there are many ways in which any given object may be characterized, we speak of a "scanning" or search process as a part of the general perceptual act. Normally we think of applying this term to a rather broad and vague field of view, for example, in scanning an expanse of water or land. But even relatively small displays such as the screen of a radar set can be scanned too. Carried further, the scanning idea permits us to describe the way in which an observer attends successively to input elements whether large or small. In perceiving, we seek distinguishing characteristics of the object by scanning first one property, then another, then still another. Paying attention to the right things enables us to put similar things in the same class and to distinguish other things which do not belong in that class.

The operator, in learning to use the machine, comes to recognize the location of particular instruments. He identifies the uses of the dials and controls. He finds out what they do and how they do it. The sensory inputs that he receives take on meaning as his experience with the machine components broadens. Since our perceptions are based on learning of this sort, we might expect that enough practice would enable us to perform effectively under any circumstances. But this is only partially true. In the more complex systems there are many inputs to the operator—many displays and many input variables denoted by them. There is always the possibility of confusion and interference within the system itself. Moreover, some of our perceptual responses are so well habituated, and so continually practiced, that to create meanings which oppose them in the design of the system would not only increase training time but would pose an ever-present opportunity for errors in interpretation.

Coding. In engineering psychology, the problem posed by the need to present stimuli in meaningful ways is often called a problem in "coding." We want to represent the input variables in such a way that they can make sense to the human operator. One way of doing this is to provide a simple, single cue for the recognition of the stimuli. This method was used in an experiment on a complex job involving the control of air traffic. The study was conducted by investigators at the Ohio State University [12]. The problem made use of a system that was designed to simulate aircraft flying under instrument conditions while being guided into a landing field. The human controller observes the location of incoming aircraft on a radar screen and gives instructions to the pilots so that their aircraft maintain a safe operation in the air and yet are brought into their destination as quickly and efficiently as possible. Usually the targets appear on the radar as small blobs of light, and it is possible to determine which blob stands for which airplane only by remembering the relative positions, headings, and speeds, as obtained from the display. This task is a complex one. The controller must keep in mind a plan of the arrival sequence and guide the flight of the planes to match the sequence that he sets up. He tells the pilots what direction they should go, where they should turn, how fast they should be traveling, and at what altitude they should fly. The perceptual task of the controller was made easier by the use of a clock code which served to identify each of the aircraft which entered the traffic patterns. This coding allowed the controller to differentiate among the blips on the radar, and in this way gave meaning to each of the individual elements of the display. In terms of such measures as control time and fuel consumption for the simulated aircraft in the problem, the improvement in the over-all effectiveness of the operator attributable to the identifying code was quite great.

The Ohio State University experiment demonstrates the principle which applies to the perceptual problem in complex information processing. The perception of an object depends on there being some unambiguous cue which enables the person to distinguish that object from others. Speed of recognition can be increased by reducing the time required for scanning the properties of the object, since only one unequivocal aspect is important.

Processes of Judgment and Estimation. Of great importance in the sequence of the operator's behavior are the judgments and estimates that are derived from consideration of the sensory inputs. As a result of perceptions, things are categorized into classes; objects are recognized or identified as belonging or not belonging to a particular class. Judgments, on the other hand, typically involve comparisons of quantities along a dimension. A few examples will help make this distinction clear. We recognize an object which is before us as a book. This is a perception. We can ask the question, "Is it a long book or a short book? Our answer is, in effect, a judgment or an estimate. We could also estimate how much the book weighs, or, along another dimension, we could judge the literary merit of the book. Similarly, when we see an object flying through the sky, the categorical answer to the question of whether it is a bird, or a plane, or Superman is again found in our perception of the object. But estimating the distance or altitude or size of the object, once it has been identified as an airplane, requires additional processing.

The fundamental comparison operation between information presented to the senses and information stored in memory is once more called into play in carrying out such estimates and judgments. The outcomes, as before, depend on what has been learned in the past about the properties of objects.

Making Judgments. We can distinguish two methods of making judgments. An *absolute judgment* is one in which a value is assigned to the object; the value represents a point on the dimensional continuum. To say that the book weighs 2 pounds or that the airplane is 3 miles away is an absolute judgment. Stored information is called forth for comparison purposes. *Comparative judgments* make use of information provided by two or more objects. Thus, to judge that one book is heavier than another is a comparative judgment.

Judgments of time, size, brightness, extent, and the like may be required in a variety of systems where such dimensions of the displayed stimuli are utilized by the operator for later decisions. An example of an absolute judgment in the context of a man-machine system performance is the judgment reached in determining from the pointer position of a gasoline gauge in an automobile that there are 7 gallons of fuel remaining in the tank. Another dial may provide information which leads to the absolute judgment that the engine is hot. These judgments are *not* decisions. They do, however, yield the information necessary for the last step in the complex processing exhibited by the human operator.

Decision Rules. The final step in the sequence of mental events which leads to overt action by the operator is the decision. The pieces of information available in immediate memory which are compared in reaching the decision are the perceptions and estimates which the operator has derived from the inputs presented him by the machine displays. Associated with the alternative outcomes of the comparison are the courses of action that the operator must then follow if he is to complete his role as a transmission link in the system. Depending on what it is that the system is to do, we get relationships, such as "If this . . . , then I must do that." Essentially, a rule of some sort is established which defines the manner in which the system must behave to accomplish the control function. Such terminal relationships are "decision rules."

Consider the tracking problem described earlier in the chapter. The task of the operator is to keep the spot of light centered on the cross hairs of a screen. He is to do this by moving a joystick control that will change the position of the spot of light on the screen. A target generator causes the spot of light to move about haphazardly over the face of the screen. This is the compensatory tracking task. The goal of the operator is to minimize the discrepancy or error introduced by the target generator. More specifically, we can formulate a decision rule which states the relationship between the momentary position of the target and the position which is desired and also the required action associated with such relationships. If the target is too far to the right of center, then the operator moves the joystick to the right. As a result of the perceptual acts that define "target and center," and as a result of the judgments or estimates of "too far," he is enabled through the associated spatial relationships to go into action and make the necessary corrective movements.

Making Decisions. The precise statement of the rule depends on how the system actually works. The operator must learn which way the spot will move when he moves the stick in a given direction. He must also become familiar with the rate and extent of movement of the spot on the screen for given amounts of stick displacement. Furthermore, he must gain a general idea of the way in which the target moves—how fast the changes in position take place and the like. The decision rule then expresses the prescribed course of action, so that one of several possible outcomes prevails. Decision rules are not always openly stated in words in the way we have described them here. Very often, in complex and variable situations, people make decisions which lead to effective action and then find it impossible to say just what it was that prompted them to decide to do what they did. Sometimes we find that skilled individuals reach decisions quickly, and yet are unable to instruct the novice in their techniques.

Behavior of this sort frequently seems so automatic that it is difficult to conceive of anyone engaging in the elaborate process outlined here. A partial explanation of this observation lies in the fact that the behavior of the operator is intermittent or sequential—as we described earlier. There is a limit to the amount of information that can be held in immediate memory at any one time. To try to think about a problem and *at the same time* to try to make the process that you are going through the object of thought is difficult, if not impossible. The skilled performer is not required normally to produce in language form the mental steps that he goes through. In fact, to do so would probably affect the efficiency of his performance. Hence, the cues and subtle interpretations of them are lost to immediate recall.

Our description of the decision-making processes, though not complete, nevertheless contains the essential ingredients. If human decisions seem more mysterious, more "human" than this, it is *only* because statements of the rules have not been made formally. Certainly some of these decision rules build up slowly in the course of time. Indeed, they may be modified from time to time as the decision maker acquires greater knowledge of the alternatives and the outcomes to which they load. It is also true that many decisions must be based on partial and imperfect knowledge. This simply means that the perceptual interpretations and judgments made along the way are themselves fallible.

The implications for equipment and systems design are clear. Don't let situations arise where more than one perceptual interpretation is possible. Keep the cues for recognition unambiguous. Provide an adequate basis for the kinds of judgments or estimates that must be made. Define the decision rules explicitly.

OUTPUTS AND THE HUMAN MOTOR RESPONSES

After the information has been received and processed by the operator, action of some sort is initiated. The operator responds. Responses that involve throwing switches, turning wheels, moving levers, and the like are called "motor responses." They require the activation of body members through muscular work.

Sometimes the responses of interest to the system's designer are verbal responses made by the operator in communicating with others in the system. Since these systems are very much more complex, we still continue to focus our attention on the system in which a single control receives inputs from and provides outputs to machine components. Although some bowlers try to "talk" to the ball after it has been released, we will assume that what is done with hands and arms while the ball is still in contact with the bowler has a greater bearing on the number of pins knocked down than do verbal responses.

The Study of Motor Skills. A great deal of early work in psychology was devoted to the study of psychomotor skills. The word *"psychomotor"* suggests that some higher activity precedes the motor response, even if it involves only the recognition of a simple signal that initiates action. In early studies, devices of one sort or another were constructed, and the performance of individuals carrying out the tasks was assessed. At first, these tests were very simple; the psychological investigators focused their attention on movements and muscular adjustments alone. Measures of the movements and of their form and accuracy were obtained. Later the devices used to study motor skills became quite complex and, in fact, approximated miniature systems. Such devices called for perceptual and cognitive behavior as well as motor responses, and during World War II many of these complex instruments were developed as selection devices or training aids. Identification of the basic features of motor action becomes difficult when the complexity of the task is increased.

In the field of industrial engineering a somewhat different approach has been used. Time-and-motion studies have led to the isolation of certain basic patterns of movement. These elements are then combined to describe various tasks. The very practical reason for this approach is that it enables us to predict, in some quantitative way, how difficult the job is, what its time requirements are, and what rest allowances are desirable for it. Such studies give little more than a crude approximation of the nature of the motor responses. The job elements of time-and-motion study are assumed to be independent; it is assumed that recombining the elements in different ways will not change the values assigned to them. That this is not a safe assumption was demonstrated in an experiment using a device called the "Universal Motion Analyzer" developed by K. U. Smith at the University of Wisconsin [7].

The Motion Analyzer. The motion analyzer provides time measures for various components of motor behavior. For example, one measure is travel time—the time required in moving the hand from one location to another over the surface of a large panel. On the panel are switches or buttons or other objects that can be manipulated by the operator. Manipulation time, then, is another measure which can be obtained from the device. A number of experiments show that travel time, even though the length of the movement is constant, depends on the terminal manipulation—its kind or extent. This means that allowances for the various elements cannot be set up independently of the context in which the movements are carried out. They cannot be added up as columns of numbers.

Apart from the purely psychological and engineering approaches to the investigation of the motor skills, there is the physiological study in which the structures of the body as separate organs are investigated. Although little is known of the underlying physiology of the higher mental processes discussed in the preceding section, considerably more information is available about muscles and the way they are activated. Hence, the knowledge gained from measures of electrical activity in muscles, anatomical studies of muscular structure, and biochemical studies of the properties of living tissue provide a foundation for the systematic treatment of motor skills.

The Classification of Movements. Descriptively, the forms of muscular activity that are important to the human operator of the man-machine system include the following: First, we frequently find that the basic movement is that of *simple positioning.* In this movement, the body part moves from one particular spatial location to another. Muscle groups initiate action and the movement is stopped by opposing muscle groups when the new position in space is attained. A corrective movement in tracking, the act of reaching for an object, or the twisting of a knob from one setting to another are examples of such movements. Of course, the direction, force, or amplitude required by the task may vary. Then measures of the speed and accuracy with which the movement is carried will change. If, for example, the person is called upon to move his hand in the horizontal plane a fixed distance of say 14 inches, the accuracy will change with the direction of movement [1]. The relationship between accuracy and angle of movement is shown in Figure 16.6.

Other movements of a similar nature are *tense* and *ballistic* movements. In the tense movement the body member is caused to shift in position, but opposing muscular structures are activated while the movement is carried out. Such movements occur whenever variable forces act upon the body member during the course of the action. In driving an automobile over smoothly paved roads, the corrective steering movements are essentially simple positioning movements; but driving over a bumpy, country road, where rocks or ruts may cause forces to be applied that either add to or subtract from the force produced by the driver, leads to the tense kind of movement pattern. The ballistic movement, in contrast, is one in which little or no subsequent forces are applied, either externally or internally, once the initial force is applied. Activation for this type of movement is produced by the sudden, full effect of a well-defined muscle pattern. There is no opposition then from muscle groups that normally in the simple positioning movement would stop the response. Throwing a baseball or swinging a golf club are ballistic movements. The final position of the body member is not quite so important as the initial direction and force, although without the proper follow-through and provision for stopping the body part, the unskilled or unpracticed amateur can "throw his arm out." Although the true ballistic movement is not commonly found in most human-operator

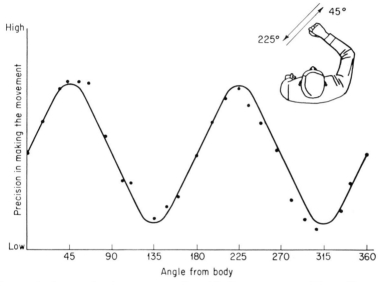

Fig. 16.6. Changes in the accuracy of positioning movements. Depending on the direction of movement, accuracy in tracking a slowly moving target varies. (After Corrigan, R. E., & Brogden, W. J. *Amer. J. Psychol.,* 1950, 62, 90–98.)

performances, it may occur when a person flips on a switch or in the very special case of eye movements.

Static Responses. Positioning movements are dynamic in the sense that the body member and the control device manipulated by the body member move through space. Static responses are similar to these movements in the patterns of activation, but the extent of movement in the static response is relatively small. These responses produce pressure variations; they are used to exert force on objects—brake pedals and the like—but the movement required is minimal or not present at all. They are extremely important in manipulating objects, in grasping, holding, or picking things up. As much physical energy may be expended in this type of motor response as in the dynamic movement patterns. However, such responses have not been thoroughly observed and studied, because there are no obvious ways of detecting them. One approach to a more adequate description of these special muscular patterns is through the use of biological amplifiers that detect the electrical activity generated in muscle tissue whenever it is activated. Since the amount of electrical activity is proportional to the amount or strength of contraction, description of the patterns of activity and of the extent of energy expended is possible even though work in the physical sense cannot be observed.

The more complex movement patterns are built up from the simple positioning responses. Series of movements can be performed because they are learned as a unit. This chaining of responses becomes very critical in many systems, because the relatively independent sequences can be triggered by the operator's decision—once they have been well learned—and can then proceed with little cognitive effort on the part of the operator. The apparent automaticity of certain motor behaviors carries with it both advantages and disadvantages for the design of the man-machine system. The chief advantage, of course, stems from the improved performance which usually results from the reduction of central processing time. The chief disadvantage is the loss of flexibility.

Sequential Movement. The simplest form of sequential movement is the "repetitive movement" in which a unique pattern is itself repeated many times. Tapping tasks and wheel-turning movements are of this sort. When a fairly long sequence of relatively independent movements is carried out as a unit, the term "serial movements" is applied. It should be emphasized that these movement patterns are descriptive of the human motor output alone and do not refer to the information-processing activities and decision-making acts of the operator. While we are learning to make such responses, we must think a good deal about what we are doing, but once these patterns have been established, they can be carried out as a unit. Central control, thinking about them, is, therefore, unnecessary. Hence, the term "continuous movements" is fallacious. The output of the human system is intermittent. The apparent smoothness results from the integration of varying components into larger and larger units.

HUMAN MOTOR-ABILITY FACTORS

In the psychological study of motor responses, a wide variety of instruments have been constructed; each purports to measure certain aspects of the operator's behavior that might be important in the control of man-machine systems. As we mentioned earlier, some of these psychomotor tests are quite simple; others are extremely complex. Since these tests conform roughly to the kinds of controller activities which may be expected in different kinds of systems, the identification of common abilities which are reasonably independent of one another can provide a useful basis for describing motor behavior.

The technique of factor analysis has been applied to this problem [4]. By obtaining the intercorrelations of performance measures on a large number of these tests administered to the same individuals, psychologists can determine clusters of tests that have similar ability requirements. Inspection of tests which are closely related gives some idea of the common characteristic which underlies good performance on them. Certain abilities have thus been identified and named.

Motor-ability Tests. Among the factors represented in a sample of forty tests was one called "wrist-finger speed." Tapping tests, which involve moving a stylus back and forth from one plate to another, and aiming tests, which require the person to place pencil marks in small circles, contain this factor. The basic muscular-movement patterns are essentially simple repetitive or serial movements of the fingers or wrist. It was found that this factor reflected primarily the rapidity of movement rather than the careful positioning of the stylus or pencil. In fact, as the circles were made progressively smaller, less and less of this particular ability seemed to be required for high scoring on the tests.

Other factors were found in the study which provide a framework for describing kinds of motor skills. In addition to wrist-finger speed, rate of arm movement was important. The two factors appear to be similar, but the latter involves the larger muscle groups of the arm. Accuracy of the movements did not appear to be critical. Instead, an entirely distinct factor emerged that accounted for the ability to perform quickly and precisely a series of accurately directed movements. This factor was called "aiming." For other movements in which a number of different muscle groups were employed simultaneously to produce a coordinated pattern of response, the factors of finger dexterity, manual dexterity, and psychomotor coordination were found. These factors seem to be related to the size of the muscle groups which work together in performing the coordinated act. Finger dexterity involves fine manipulation, such as those of the skilled watchmaker who uses the finger tips primarily in executing his task. The gross involvement of the larger muscles of the back, arm, legs, and wrists of the baseball player typifies the factor of psychomotor coordination.

These factors and others, including reaction time and steadiness, help us to understand the outputs of the human operator. In contrast to the job elements of time-and-motion studies, these factors, it seems, may be treated as components of skill. This means that we should not necessarily expect an individual to be able to execute an equally skilled performance in a task involving finger dexterity and in a task requiring psychomotor coordination. What the watchmaker learns to do and what the ballplayer learns are quite different things.

Measures of Motor Performance. Movements made by the operator are observable. We can measure the effectiveness of the various motor responses by obtaining quantities that reflect speed and accuracy of the movements. These determinations are important in their own right, because these human outputs limit the output of the entire system. We can think ahead, for example, faster than we can write down our ideas on paper.

In general, measures of speed and accuracy exhibit a reciprocal relation. What we gain in one typically results in a loss in the other. The generality of this relationship is seen in a unique approach to the problem of determining the limits of motor behavior. In an attempt to provide a more precise, quantitative statement of such a limit, Fitts used ideas taken from the information theory that we discussed earlier in the chapter [3].

He compared several different tasks that involved the factors we have identified as wrist-finger speed, finger dexterity, and aiming. The difficulty of the tasks was changed by introducing greater or lesser distances over which movements were to be made and by changing the tolerances that were allowable for the accurate performance of the tasks. The subjects were permitted to adjust their rate of working so that a constant level of accuracy was maintained. For the different tasks, approximately the same over-all effectiveness was observed when the balance between speed and accuracy was expressed in terms of the information capacity of the motor performance. Thus, when the difficulty of the task was increased, the subjects worked more slowly. But in quantitative terms the measure of motor output was essentially constant.

Just as the engineer evaluates the performance of the machine components by subjecting them to certain standard tests, so too the engineering psychologist evaluates the performance of the man. One such standard procedure by the engineer for testing a variety of mechanical and electrical systems is to apply a sudden load on the system and obtain measures of the response. By analogy, such a "step input function" is frequently utilized in evaluating human performance.

Reaction-time Study. One study investigated the reaction time of operators who were to make a simple corrective movement when the step input function consisted of a sudden displacement of a spot of light on a screen similar to those used in radar presentations [13]. Reaction time was essentially constant no matter what the size of the displacement (see Figure 16.7). More surprising, perhaps, was the finding that the time required to make the response itself was much the same for different extents of movement. Changes in the acceleration and deceleration of the movement compensated for the greater length of travel. Whether this knowledge of a fixed time lag is or is not important to the design engineer depends on the other properties of the particular system. However, in some instances, knowledge of the maximum rates of change in the corrective movement becomes critical; in order to keep overeager operators from imposing changes which are too great or which will produce overcorrection and jerkiness, the design engineer takes special steps to offset these possibilities. For example, the display can be "quickened" so that the effects of the operator's adjustment are fed back faster than the system can respond. Thus, the operator actually receives information from the display about the future state of the system.

The System Components. The measures of motor performance are important for reasons other than simply quantifying the controller's output. Since these measures provide our only means of observing the behavior of the man, it is through their relationships to the inputs that we can infer that

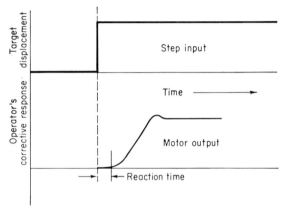

Fig. 16.7. Response to a step input function. Displacement of the target is almost instantaneous, but the operator's response lags in a predictable way in following the target.

such processes as perception, judgment, decision making, and many other things psychological exist as we have described them. Learning, for example, cannot be measured directly. We infer that such a process takes place from observed changes in behavior. The nature of these processes is defined in terms of the overt behavior and its relation to changes in stimuli that we provide.

This same methodology permits us to evaluate the effectiveness of the system components—the displays and controls—which the human operator must use. By holding the response constant and varying the input from several displays, we can determine which display is best for a particular system. By holding the inputs and other requirements constant and varying the responses—devising different kinds of control devices or changing the movements in some way—we get the kind of information that permits us to determine the effectiveness of the movements and to evaluate the different controls themselves.

THE ANALYSIS OF MAN-MACHINE SYSTEMS

Although the field of engineering psychology is young, and the precise specification of the engineering properties of the human operator is far from realized, enough data are available from studies of the sensory, cognitive, and motor abilities of man to suggest tentative ways of approaching the design of equipment for human use. We at least know what we must look for in any attempt to evaluate the performance of the man-machine system.

What to Look For. At the outset, we identify the control functions of the system. This is roughly equivalent to saying that we must first understand the purpose or goal of the system's performance before we can recommend a way of reaching that goal. Complications may arise because a given system may entail control functions simultaneously directed toward two or more goals. For example, a highway traffic control system may be required that has as its ultimate purpose moving vehicles through a congested area quickly and safely. But speed of movement and safe operation of the vehicles in the traffic patterns are incompatible.

We next must determine the nature of the input to the operator, the output from the operator, and the knowledge required by the operator if he is to effect the appropriate control decisions. What the operator already knows or can learn in a reasonably short period of time will determine how to best display the operator inputs and provide for his outputs. Any modification that simplifies the conceptual scheme of the operator and thereby allows faster recognition, fewer steps in the central processing, more clear-cut alternatives for decision, or a change that takes advantage of the better-learned motor-response sequences may improve the effectiveness of the system.

Since we are almost always dealing with systems of the closed-loop type, a further consideration is that of identifying the feedback links. These, too, supply input changes to the operator, and may actually be reflected in the primary display of the machine. However, we also recognize that the feedback may be intrinsic to the human operator's behavior itself. For example, both visual and proprioceptive cues, the latter arising within the musculature during performance, provide information to the operator that may be useful in directing his behavior. In many systems we may wish to provide special displays that monitor the internal changes in the system. These displays may be as simple, for example, as a red warning light to indicate when engine temperatures are too high.

How to Look. A system is a complicated mass of interconnected parts. In order to be able to identify the critical elements in meaningful ways, it is necessary to represent the relationships among the parts in some fashion. A device used by the engineer is the flow diagram. Figure 16.1

(see page 327) is essentially a very simple example of such a diagram. The blocks represent physical or sometimes conceptual elements and the connecting lines indicate the way in which these parts are connected, including the direction of energy flow. In general, such diagrams present only a static picture of the state of affairs existing within the system at a particular point in time. Only by analyzing changes in the flow diagram over a period of time do we obtain some idea of the dynamic picture of the system.

Mathematical representations of a system's operation may give precise statements of the relationships that exist within the system. In order to obtain these equations, ways of measuring the variable quantities must, of course, be known. One kind of mathematical representation which is often employed, for example, is that of determining the *transfer function* of the system. In this particular case, the output quantities, frequently obtained as a time-varying measure, are determined as a function of the input. Since dimensional size of the quantities within the equation must be maintained, one of the basic problems in engineering psychology is that of finding appropriate ways of measuring dimensionally equivalent inputs and outputs. The meaning attached to such mathematical representations of systems then depends on the nature of the dimensions involved.

In a physical system, say the amplifier in your radio, the meaning of the transfer function is fairly clear, since we put in a small voltage and get out a larger one. The gain of the system can be described by the equation that expresses the output as a function of the input. For example, $E_o = KE_I$ tells us that the magnitude of the output is greater than the magnitude of the input by a factor of K. The constant K is the gain of the system and has meaning because we have maintained dimensionality within the equation. There are voltages on both sides of the equals sign.

Such transfer functions have been derived for systems with the human operator imbedded in the system. It is as if both machine and human components were stuck in a "black box." But the task of obtaining transfer functions for the human operator himself—where he alone is in the black box—can only be accomplished when dimensionally equivalent human inputs and human outputs can be found.

GENERALIZED PRINCIPLES OF SYSTEMS DESIGN

There are essentially three things that we must consider in systems design. The first is the loading imposed on the information channels. In the man-machine system we must make sure that the sensory input channels and the motor outputs do not become overloaded. This may be accomplished by appropriately coding the inputs or modifying the task requirements.

A second area of concern is the matching of inputs and outputs throughout the system. In the case of the machine components this may take the form of providing the proper mechanical links, adjusting lengths of lever arms, and the like, or matching the impedance of an amplifier output to the loudspeaker of the radio to obtain maximum power transfer. For the human operator, the matching concept is seen in the problem of choosing appropriate directions of motion for display elements, such as pointers and control devices. The idea of display-response compatibility recognizes the importance of proper choice of these relationships.

Finally, effective systems design requires the adjustment of the time constants of the parts within the system. In the physical realm, inertial and frictional forces govern the motions of objects. A heavy flywheel keeps spining, but it takes longer to start than does a light wheel. The time constants are here derived from the properties of the objects. The human operator has time constants, too. We shall discuss systems in somewhat more detail in the following chapter.

SUGGESTIONS FOR FURTHER READING

Chapanis, A. *Research techniques in human engineering.* Baltimore: Johns Hopkins Press, 1959. Recommended for the technically qualified person, both the engineer and the psychologist.

———, Garner, W. R. & Morgan, C. T. *Applied experimental psychology.* New York: Wiley, 1949. A systematically developed text that provides a background for the detailed study of engineering psychology.

Geldard, F. A. *The human senses.* New York: Wiley, 1953. A readable description of all the human senses.

Handbook of human engineering data. (2d ed.) Medford, Mass.: Tufts College, 1952. A handbook of useful facts.

McCormick, E. J. *Human engineering.* New York: McGraw-Hill, 1957. A readable text covering in breadth the field of engineering psychology.

Stevens, S. S. *Handbook of experimental psychology.* New York: Wiley, 1951. A basic source related to engineering psychology. See chapters "Engineering Psychology and Equipment Design" and "Work and Motor Performance."

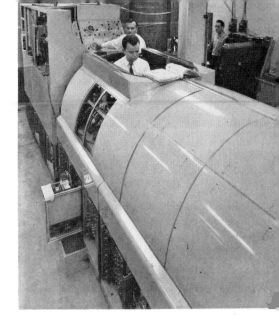

17

THE NEWER ROLES

OF THE INDUSTRIAL

PSYCHOLOGIST

Robert B. Miller

As the preceding chapters in this book suggest, psychologists in industry, although often dealing with a wide range of personnel problems, have tended to cluster into specialties. They may be specialists in safety, in selection testing, in training, or in human engineering. There are perhaps a dozen or more such specializations. In many cases, the specialist has been making worthwhile contributions within his sphere of operations. As a consultant to management, he may offer advice from data he has collected on a specific problem, from general principles, or from a collection of personal observations and wisdom. Occasionally he may have the time, energy, facility, and support to do experiments in which he tests a hypothesis or validates a procedure. The industrial psychologist usually works within fairly restricted limits as to what changes he can make; these limits may be prescribed by budget, management policy, or union practices. He recognizes that his principal responsibility is to keep a going concern moving forward.

EXPANSION OF PSYCHOLOGICAL PROBLEMS

We have already discussed many of the problems with which industrial psychologists work and have seen how they go about solving them. We have also mentioned that problem areas are expanding, and we have seen evidence of how the applications of psychology in industry are branching out. What does this mean for the psychologist? How does he attack problems that seem to be coming from all sides? More specifically, what are the newer roles now appearing for industrial psychologists? Generally, the industrial psychologist has a problem context defined for him when his management thinks that there is something wrong somewhere in company operations and suspects that, somehow, human beings are to blame. The problems are numerous, as we know. Too much labor turnover. Too many accidents. Too many misfits hired. Too few people with managerial talent. Too many troublemakers in Plant Four. Too many grievances in Plant Six. Too many complaints about the incentive system. Too many complaints about the lighting system, the rest rooms, the dining facilities, the vernier markings on the inspection gauges. The rapid growth of technology in the space age has created new problems for human beings. What can be done about the changing context of our human problems?

There are signs pointing to different kinds of questions that will be asked the psychologist in the future. These will be broader questions demanding of him different working relationships with his associates. We shall begin by looking at two examples.

Effects of Automation. Let us assume that an industry is planning to become fully automated in the next five years. This may mean the elimination of many jobs and major changes in others. The industry wants to avoid imposing major hardships on its employees—on its executive officers, its line workers, and others. How does it go about planning for and carrying out this transition? Clearly, the problem will take several specific forms. The psychological problems will include building up different attitudes in supervisory and working personnel. New skill requirements will have to be predicted for managerial and line workers. New job structures may have to be designed not only for a man's present capabilities, but also for the pattern of abilities he must superimpose on what he knows now and is able to learn. Training techniques will have to be developed. In some ways, the new plant facilities may be restricted by policies that permit only the easiest and least costly transition. But most important of all, the entire task must be accomplished within strict budgets of time and money.

Obviously, the psychologist cannot hope to solve such a problem by himself. He will work with associates who have engineering knowledge, with cost accountants and economists, market analysts, production specialists, and many others [6, 8, 13]. He will not make decisions by himself, but he will make recommendations as a member of a team. He will arrive at recommendations partly by interacting with other specialists. But on what evidence will he be able to base his suggestions? That is the subject of later parts of this chapter.

Operations Analysis. Let us look at another example. A large company believes that the installation of a huge automatic computer will be of benefit. But before committing itself to a costly investment in equipment, it wants to know what such an installation will entail; it wants to be given an estimate not only of the cost of the equipment, but of its total demands. The company also wants to know what services the computer can provide, what kinds of data can be profitably analyzed, and how useful the analyses will be. The psychologist may be asked to *participate* in making estimates both of cost and of return. Again, he is a team member, not a lone wolf. Functioning as a member of an operations-analysis group, the psychologist contributes to information technology (see page 303).

The psychologist will look into the present personnel cost of getting and processing company data; he will make estimates of costs for new or re-trained personnel; he will examine supervisory and maintenance personnel requirements, potential dissatisfactions, rerouting in the communication system, shifts in supervisory and executive functions, etc. In assessing the potential usefulness of the new equipment, he may have in mind the processing of personnel information which heretofore would have been too costly an operation, but which in the future may give him the equivalent of experimental data. However, his thinking cannot be that of the psychologist alone. His ideas will have to be adapted to those of the accounting depart-ment, the production department, the inventory and sales departments— all of which are likely to be represented in the operations-analysis group. And the psychologist will have to be able to converse with these people in some common set of terms [9].

RESEARCH AND DEVELOPMENT

Psychologists have always engaged in research, a fact underlined many times in the preceding chapters. Now something new is being added: cer-tain psychologists are finding themselves on a "development team." More and more, the newer roles of the industrial psychologist place him at one time in research and at another time in development. What are the differ-ences between research and development?

Research is the quest for knowledge. *Development* is making something that does something. The remainder of this section will enlarge on this main distinction and on the different roles and operations this distinction implies for the psychologist. Let us begin our discussion with a brief review of what we mean by research so that we may better understand the newer role of the psychologist in development.

Research in Science. Research has many meanings in popular and tech-nical usage. A writer of historical novels says he is "doing research" when he is reading historical documents of the era about which he plans to write. When a scientist looks into existing references about a scientific topic, he generally feels that it would be pretentious to call this research. Instead, he calls it "literature search." Generally, the term "research" implies that facts are being discovered rather than merely reviewed, although important contributions can be made merely by bringing known facts together.

Research itself can be done in many ways. A researcher may begin by asking the question, "I wonder what will happen if I put object X in situation Y?" He then proceeds to do so, and notes the outcome. This approach is *exploratory research* and results in some kind of *demonstration*. A more advanced kind of study may begin with the question, "Is condition A really essential in producing condition B?" The answer requires an experimental group subjected to condition A and a control group in which condition A is presumably absent. The addition of a control group makes it *experimental research*. Experimental research usually aims at testing the validity of a hypothesis, and a hypothesis is a statement of relationships. A group of hypotheses that are logically related to each other is called a *theory*. These are very superficial definitions, but it can be seen that research results in facts producing knowledge. The facts may lead to support or rejection of a hypothesis or theory. Knowledge and trained observation are important requirements for forming hypotheses, but they are not the same things as hypotheses.

Laboratory Research Example. A psychologist in a laboratory observes that the closer hungry rats are to the food box, the faster they seem to run, and the harder it is to get them to make detours. The psychologist wonders if people behave in the same way. His wondering brings him nearly to the formation of a hypothesis. He states a hypothesis when he says, "Human beings will crowd each other more when they are closer to a goal (such as food) than when they are more distant from the goal." So he measures the distance between people in line at a cafeteria. He compares distances between people at the entrance to the serving counter with distances between people 20 feet away from it. The reader may try the experimental measurements himself to test the hypothesis that, in this respect at least, people are more like primitive animals. By making observations of the average number of people per foot from the food tray to the edge of the steam table, one can get a continuous or functional relationship between distance from goal and human density. This quantification is often more useful than merely knowing that some relationship exists.

Notice carefully that the facts (in this case the measurements) *test* the validity of the hypothesis. Depending on how the facts are gathered and analyzed, a more or less general statement can be made about the nearness of a goal and crowding behavior. Does the same phenomenon hold true at a box office? For the persons waiting turns in a doctor's office? Qualifications may have to be made in the generalization, or in the way in which a term like "goal" is defined.

Applied Research Example. Now let us shift to an experiment which is aimed less at achieving a general statement than at discovering whether object or process A is superior in some way to object or process B. This kind of study is generally thought of as "applied research," although the distinction between it and laboratory research is often a small one. We may want to know if test A predicts superior salesmen better than does test B. Or whether a formal training course in the fundamentals of electricity produces more adaptable maintenance men than does a policy of merely shifting them around in a number of jobs. So we set up an experiment and get a body of facts. On the basis of these facts we may or may not recommend to management that alternative A is better than alternative B.

In such exercises, the ingenuity of the psychologist is directed toward efficient ways of reaching a conclusion that will stand up outside the special conditions imposed by his experiment. But his ingenuity may have to be supplemented by sound working knowledge of the probable influence of the many factors and conditions which he has *not* varied in making his experiment. A professional psychologist who has practical and industrial experience in setting up and running an experiment and in drawing conclusions from it is, therefore, more likely to arrive at the correct recommendation than is a layman who is less experienced in these matters.

These conditions should not dismay the prospective researcher; rather they should emphasize the challenge and creative effort that a good research job, like any other nonstandardized situation, calls for. We should bear in mind that creative effort is invariably aided by extensive knowledge, especially if the knowledge can be readily drawn upon while one is setting up the experimental conditions and preparing the conclusions. But we must remember that the knowledge itself does not guarantee that the effort will be creative. A question must be asked and the answer sought.

Research, then, is the process of asking questions and getting sample answers about relationships between events A and B. In general, the better the research, the more certainly can we predict B by efficient control or description of A. Research leads to knowledge.

The Nature of Development. Development, in contrast to research, leads to objects and procedures. For example, we may know, from a body of research, the principles of operating an automobile by gas turbine or by nuclear energy. This does not mean that we would be able to build a workable automobile driven by gas turbine or nuclear energy. Development is hedged by two important considerations: cost and efficiency to produce, and cost and efficiency to operate. Development consists of taking knowledge and using it to invent objects or procedures that serve practical purposes and have dollar denominators to them.

Examples of Development. An industrial psychologist is asked by his management, "What can the company do to reduce technological obsolescence of our design engineers?" The company wishes to keep inventors up to date on technical knowledge, but with minimum cost and dislocation both to the men and the company. A completely practical and successful solution still has to be found.

A more modest problem may arise. Because of various accidents, a company has installed safety guards on a number of its machines. But the men on piecework complain that their work rate is reduced and that the safety guards interfere with their ability to see what they are doing. Some men even remove the guards. Disciplinary actions are taken, and grievances arise. The industrial psychologist may be called in to develop the best all-around compromise between safety, work rate, job satisfaction, and cost to the company. This problem is a "development" problem. There is no formula, no textbook, no standard set of rules for solving this specific problem in its particular context.

In another situation, the psychologist is asked to assist in designing the display control panel for an airplane that the company is developing for commercial use. After studying the problem he prepares a sketch which is submitted to the engineering department. "Look," says the engineer with a good deal of vexation, "this airplane has to fly. Also, it has to carry a cargo. We can give you only 12 inches in height and 29 inches across for the whole panel. The instruments can be only 7 inches deep, and the whole business can't weigh more than 44 pounds." The psychologist says, "I can't give you a device that will meet the requirements for the pilot to operate the aircraft and still fall within your limits." To which the engineer will reply, "Look, bub, people have been flying airplanes without your help for fifty years. This airplane is going to be designed and ready to fly in nine months—with or without your assistance. You get back and work out a panel 12 by 29 by 7 inches, weighing no more than 44 pounds, and there will be a bonus for every pound less. Oh, yes, I forgot to mention that the cost of the panel, including instruments, controls, and accessories, must be less than $950 for production items. This includes development costs, and *that* includes your salary. Incidentally, I hear our competitor has a control panel that meets these specifications and costs less; the Navy is getting ready to buy it. Better get busy, son."

The Variables in Development. The engineer's hard-boiled speech sums up practically all the variables that go into development. It should be clear the development, like any form of practical inventing, proceeds by a series of compromises with competing factors. An object that is ideal with respect to any single set of principles—psychological, engineering, or other—is a fantasy. The professional man responsible for human factors must, of course, maintain the goal of perfection in his job, but he must recognize that his demands must be coordinated and compromised with those of others who may have equally lofty aspirations similarly compromised.

The point at which the psychologist feels that management demands more compromises than his ingenuity can overcome or his integrity can tolerate rests in the area of professional ethics. The question of whether to keep on and be satisfied with small gains and contributions, or to throw in the towel and seek another job, may be going on continuously until the psychologist becomes identified with team effort and objectives.

At present, the majority of professional psychologists, especially those with new Ph.D.s, tend to be oriented toward research and experimentation rather than development and application. It is, of course, essential that we have good research or the wellsprings of our science will dry up. On the other hand, it is equally necessary that we have highly competent professionals dedicated to development. More and more psychologists are entering industry each year in this new role.

Consultancy in a Development Project. Sometimes the professional researcher may undertake the temporary role of consultant in a development project; under these circumstances he generally offers advice, but does not identify himself with a project and its outcome. He risks only a second fee, rather than his job in a company. Furthermore, he may find the role of critic more congenial than that of responsible collaborator. Thus, he will make surveys and field studies, or experimental evaluations, of objects and procedures already designed. This is important work, too, and it is not so risky as trying to design and install an incentive plan which is acceptable both to management and the union as well as effective for the worker, or designing an airplane control panel which suits the engineer as well as the pilot, or creating a training device which is guaranteed to develop skills that will transfer to the job situation. The researcher is more interested in getting information than in having to make decisions based on given information. His professional training, by and large, teaches him how to hedge against making decisions.

Intermesh of Research and Development. It is not impossible, however, for the person who directs or conducts research to put the knowledge thus gained to practical use through inventiveness in development. These functions may merge, for example, when, through the study of job requirements of maintenance mechanics, sets of trouble-shooting principles or strategies are devised, and these become incorporated in special training devices. Research into the factors that influence the fastest and most error-free translation of information by the human being, for instance, when one uses a keyboard as in typing, may lead to a new concept in keyboard design. Obviously, the extent to which research and development can be made to intermesh is limited by the way, and by the breadth with which, the research problem and development problems are stated. In the behavioral sciences some effort is beginning that may lead to a "language" and a theory which will more readily permit translation of specific development objectives into broad-scale research activities, *and* the translation of research into development. Some writers believe that a step in this direction will be made when we have a good means of classifying and showing relationships among human tasks in objective as well as in psychological terms.

As the reader may guess from the foregoing discussion, there is at present a considerable gulf between theoretical research in psychology and so-called "applied experimentation and development." Some of the reasons for this gulf have been proposed above. Let us turn now, however, to some growing problem areas for the industrial psychologist.

THE INDUSTRIAL PSYCHOLOGIST AS PROBLEM SOLVER

The industrial psychologist has for a long time addressed himself to a specific applied problem and/or to general applied problems. More recently some psychologists have become concerned with what we will call "systems" problems. A few examples will illuminate the differences between specific, general, and systems problems, as they involve research and development.

Specific Applied Problems. These problems can be exemplified by a hypothetical case. The personnel director of the Ace Box Factory asks the industrial psychologist to "find out what accounted for the high turnover rate of women in the factory during 1957 as opposed to the low turnover rate in 1956." Without stirring from his seat, the psychologist could reply, "More women wanted to do something other than work in the Ace Box Factory in 1957 than in 1956." This answer is quite incontrovertible, so why is the personnel director unlikely to accept it? The reason is that he can't do anything constructive with such an answer. The first requirement in finding the answer to an applied problem is (or should be!) to uncover information which permits a *decision* to be made and some constructive *action* to be taken by the person who asks the question.

In general, the first step is to test the validity of the question. *Did* more women leave Ace during 1957 than in 1956? Did Ace perhaps employ twice as many women in 1957 as in 1956, and was this accompanied by double the turnover? If this was the case, then the turnover *rate* was the same for both years, even though the absolute number that left was doubled.

If an inspection of the records indicates that the actual turnover rate *is* increasing, then the personnel manager should be shown the actual figures. A judgment should then be made as to whether the problem is of practical importance; that is, will management spend money not only to find out what the causes of the increase are but also to underwrite some remedial action. Let us assume that the answer is "yes" to both questions.

The next logical step would be to determine how many women left voluntarily and how many were fired, and compare 1957 with 1956 rates. After this step, the inquiry would radiate out to matters over which the company has immediate control: the procedures by which the women were selected, indoctrinated, trained, assigned, supervised, grouped, motivated to work, communicated with by management, etc. A sample of those who quit, and of those who did not quit, would be questioned. Perhaps the questions would include background and precipitating incidents that led to quitting or to near quitting.

Let's suppose that the actual quit rate increased 20 per cent in 1957 over 1956—this is something about which to worry. But it is discovered that in 1957 about 30 per cent of the quits left in order to go to work for Zantex Electronics, a new firm that was hiring young engineers, many of whom were probably bachelors. Most of these girls who went to Zantex quite frankly said that they went there not because that firm paid more money (it paid less) but in order to be near eligible men. These and other findings are reported to the personnel manager. It is at this point that *research* ends. Development *begins* with the question, "What can we do about it?"

The study could easily be broadened. Why didn't the married women also quit? Were there some conditions at Ace that were particularly discouraging for the unmarried girls? Yes, there were: there was a tightly knit married women's club in the plant, but none had been organized by or for unmarried women; furthermore, it was Ace policy to send all young unmarried men out on the road for training in sales immediately after hiring. This often resulted in their courting and marrying girls they met in their sales territory. Examination of the causes behind the causes may reveal a good many more alternatives than appear on the surface. This study so far has been specific to conditions at Ace; hence we would classify it as a *specific applied problem*.

As you might expect, the approach to a solution, or a development, for a situation revealed by specific research would also be specific. Ace might organize and support a young unmarried men's and women's club, with the help of an energetic entertainment chairman, and bring their men in from the road for regular club affairs. Or if the company can hire enough married women, it might reduce the hiring of unmarried women in 1959. Of course, by doing this, it might invite a new family of troubles, but one always takes some risk when trying a new development.

General Applied Problems. Dealing with general problems gives us another view of the psychologist's role. An industrial psychologist working for Acme Industrials proposes a plan for studying the relationship that fatigue, stress, and incentives have to various kinds of work decrement in industrial situations. The plan is to get data from a *variety* of existing and experimentally controlled work situations, tasks, and task settings, such as wire winding, punch-press operations, routine operations, semiroutine operations, and even problem-solving situations such as tool and die design. The major task variables may include difficult or complex discriminations and perceptions, human information processing and decision making, and manipulations; or the scope may be restricted to any one of these psychological factors. But whatever activities are studied, the problem is a general one.

Psychological Variables. It should be noticed at once that the above proposal is couched primarily in terms of psychological variables rather than in terms that the company might use, such as the question, "Why can't we get more sustained productivity out of the wire winders?" To the extent that the psychologist will examine a sufficiently broad sample of situations, he may arrive at general conclusions relating fatigue, stress, and incentives to falling off of productivity during the daily and weekly cycle. Such conclusions, if stated in operational terms, may lead to constructive development not only by Acme but other companies as well.

It is not likely that a company will gamble the amount of time and money that such a study will take unless it has considerable confidence in the researcher and his ability to translate at least some of his findings into worthwhile developments. The fact that the researcher may be reluctant to accept responsibility for converting findings into developments useful to the company is often a realistic reason for the company's reluctance to foot the research bill. Moreover, even though the salary of the researcher is paid by a university, the company must provide one or more persons to show him around, and it may also have to accept interference with the normal flow of production. These things are costly.

Systems Problems. Systems methods are ways of stating, thinking about, and solving problems that take into account *complex interrelationships* [6]. Among these interrelationships are those of objects, processes, and human components. Since a description of systems approaches is contained in the following section, we will merely point out here that the industrial psychologist's role in industry is not necessarily that of a solver of either specific or general problems. To the extent that he is designing something useful as a team member working with architects, engineers, accountants, production specialists, mathematicians, operating and maintenance personnel, he will be engaged in a systems enterprise.

The "systems man" will generally not be in a staff position that provides direct recommendations or information to management. He will, instead, tend to be closely associated with a company project such as the development of a new aircraft for military or commercial use. If he is responsible primarily for human factors, he will have to think about the interplay of all human factors with the equipment and the requirements imposed on the man-machine team. These considerations will cover a wide range. He may be concerned with the selection and training, say, of the pilot, copilot, and flight engineer, as well as with the design of facilities for the elimination of body wastes of passengers. Coping with unusual, but possible, contingencies during operation, prediction of kinds and amount of human error and undependability, calls for team action [15].

The psychologist may, through interest or opportunity, elect to follow the "systems approach." By so doing he becomes a more active collaborator with other research and development specialists, such as physicists, design engineers. Furthermore, his responsibility will entail across-the-board consideration of the many human factors that affect the eventual operation and maintenance of the man-machine organism.

THE GENERAL SYSTEM

The student can get a unique global view of an industrial organization from studying the blueprint of a general system.

In order for the industrial psychologist to participate effectively in the planning or redesign of a system, he must have a thorough knowledge of it and all its parts. In some respects, he may have to know more about it than do the planners of equipment and facilities. Such knowledge permits him to suggest what activities are best assigned to machines and what functions should be taken over by human beings. He may help to show how human beings can be used to best advantage in the enterprise, but he can do so only through thorough familiarity with system requirements as well as with human capabilities and limitations. At later stages of participation and development he can use information about the system in determining precisely and concretely what the human work requirements will be. He can then frame selection procedures for the various tasks and jobs assigned to human beings, and proceed to the design of training, training devices and job aids, and evaluation procedures. He can also play a vital role in conducting tests of the adequacy of *the system as a whole* to perform its intended purposes.

Human Factors Specialists. Because of his varied roles and his integration with the design team, the psychologist may even change his title to that of "human factors specialist." His decisions cannot be based solely on what is optimum for the human beings in the system; they must be tempered by what is good (that is, economical and efficient) for the system as a whole. The following sections describe how this newer type of industrial psychologist becomes informed so that he can play his complex role effectively.

System Requirements and Definition. A system may be described in any one of a number of ways, depending upon the purpose that the description is to serve. In its broadest sense, it should aid in obtaining and recording information about the existing or proposed system in terms that will aid in planning, designing, or modifying it. The description should permit maximum freedom in suggesting alternatives; at the same time it should express the various restraints and fixed conditions imposed upon, and accepted by, designers.

The description should permit:

1. Maximum freedom in suggesting alternatives in design and the implications of these alternatives

2. Reminders of all the kinds of information which it is important to have for planning and design purposes

3. Ease in expanding the description to permit coupling of subsystems descriptions into broader systems

4. Ease in coupling the description of the system with descriptions of functionally or physically interconnected systems

5. Differentiation of functions that can be performed by human beings versus functions that can be performed by machines

6. Ease in determining similarities to and differences from other systems

7. Quantification of operations

The main purpose of the description is to keep all pertinent information in view at the same time so that ideas can be readily shifted around like building blocks.

The definition of a *general system* is really very simple. We can define a system roughly as *any planned group of man and machine entities and procedures that convert "input" signals or materials to "output" signals or materials according to some human purpose.*

GENERAL SYSTEM FACTORS

The factors in a system contain some two dozen kinds of information. Rarely can all of this information be obtained at one time; rather the information tends to grow and be filled in as the system becomes designed or invented. Let us describe the various factors below. We shall use an automobile service station as our illustration, since most readers are familiar with the nature of this business.

Purposes, Functions, Processes, Process-links. All four of these terms are related to each other in common usage. *Purpose* is what the system should accomplish, stated in simple, general terms. Thus the function of a service-station system is to provide gasoline, water, and oil to automobiles with a minimum of average waiting time. *Function* may refer to the purpose of the over-all system or the action of some part of the system. It is the most flexible of all terms used in the description, because functions can always be divided into subfunctions. Function names are arbitrary. Thus, a pump may perform a sucking-up function and a pushing-out function, and a measuring function. The measuring function may be divided into a flow-sensing function and a flow-indicating function, and each of these may be divided into rate of flow and absolute amount. A function is an abstraction, but since a function may be thought of independently of the object which performs it, the concept of function is perhaps the most powerful of all concepts for human inventing purposes.

Process is identified by the description of change in a signal or substance, usually in the context of the instrument effecting or responsible for the change. Inflating a tire with air is a process, as is also the condensation of moisture in a gasoline storage tank. *Process-links* are sequences of changes and activities.

Outputs, Criterion Variables, Criterion Tolerances, Waste. These terms describe what comes out of a system. An *output* is information, material, or an object that comes out of a system or one of its components. The gross outputs of a filling station include gasoline in gas tanks, oil in crankcases, water in batteries and radiators, compressed air in tires, and—not altogether incidentally—satisfied customers. Output is a convenient term because it can be used in so many different contexts.

A *criterion variable* is some factor of an output that identifies a quantity or quality variable to be controlled. Thus, the amount of time that a customer must, on the average, have to wait for service is likely to be one criterion variable of some importance to a service station. Another may be the cost of the gasoline. Another may be the customer's notion of how well the gasoline performs.

A *criterion tolerance* is the range through which values of a criterion variable may fluctuate and still result in an acceptable output. A customer may accept an average three-minute wait for service, but perhaps he is unlikely to return if he has to wait more than seven minutes. A criterion tolerance may also be thought of as a working limit of some variable.

Waste is a form of output for which there is no customer, or which is an annoyance or disturbance. Waste may be in the form of energy, objects, or interference with gainful outputs. Gasoline slopped over from a filled tank is a loss either to the customer or to the station owner, or both. A leaking air hose creates waste. So do the errors of the tire changer who occasionally punctures an inner tube through carelessness or lack of skill. Waste can be measured as the ratio of costs of useless output to costs of useful output.

Environments, Inputs, Contingencies, Emergencies, Noise. An *environment* is a context of conditions that has some more or less general effects on system operation. Thus a filling station may be on a side road or a main road, near a city, or out in a desert. All of these and many more environmental conditions will affect the number and kind of customers, demands, distribution of busy and slack periods, length of waiting periods that will be acceptable, and so on.

Environmental conditions change. Some changes are slow, some are rapid. Some are progressive, some are cyclic, some are temporary and intermittent. A slow, progressive change occurs when a residential community becomes a business community. A more rapid change is that from one season to another when buying habits and demands for services change. A rapid, temporary change in an environment occurs when the first heavy snowfall brings a demand for chains, their installation, and for being towed out of snowdrifts, in addition to the regular demand for gasoline and oil. Although immediate returns may not compensate for the heavy investment required to keep everything running smoothly under extraordinary demands, the services provided at such a time may result in additional permanent customers for the gasoline station.

Some environments, such as that of a punch press, are relatively unchanging, or undergo only subtle changes such as those accompanying progressive deterioration of air-conditioning equipment and increase of dust. But a systems planner will attempt to predict and identify as many of these changes as he can in order to provide for them, or be aware of their possible cost if he does nothing about them.

An *input* is anything that comes into the objective parts of the system. It may be the customers and their cars coming into the gasoline station, the materials to be sold, replacement parts for the pumps, and the people who come in to operate and maintain equipment and provide services. An environment is a very general form of input. Somewhat more specifically, an input is information which the system senses, or material which the system can accept for processing. Inputs have variables and tolerances just as outputs do, and some inspection arrangement is usually provided. The food and drink tasters used by the Medicis to determine if poison was present is a medieval example of testing the input to the system.

A *contingency* is a generally unscheduled event which demands some unusual mode of operation for the system. A contingency may arise from an *environmental* condition such as a heavy snowstorm, or it may be a large load of cheap tires that the dealer can buy if he has ample credit and storage space. It may come about through equipment *malfunction,* such as a pump failure. Contingencies also arise through *human error,* such as the failure to note the amount of gasoline pumped into a customer's car registered on a pump before returning the register to zero.

People who plan systems generally pay less attention to the ways in which contingencies can arise and how to cope with them than they do to normal situations. This deficiency is one reason why the development of systems is so costly; it also accounts for the great number of trial-and-error corrections which, from hindsight, seem unwarranted. This deficiency may also be one reason why, once a system is fixed and manages to survive, it is difficult to introduce major changes in concept—such changes, for example, as the drive-in, the self-service store, the assembly line, or the recent trend toward automation.

It is especially important for persons who deal with human factors to anticipate as thoroughly as possible the contingencies and *emergencies* that may beset a system, because ordinarily the human operator, considering "operator" in the broad sense, will have to fill in the gaps left by planning. Whatever the machine will **not** do automatically must obviously be done by the human beings. Improvising to meet unexpected conditions almost certainly will be less efficient in the long run than preparing to meet conditions through planning. A trade-off against planning time is time budgeted for learning how to adapt a new system to the stresses imposed on it or arising from within itself. When the human beings in the system must cope with a large variety of contingencies, the situation may be taken care of by selecting personnel for intelligence and aptitude and by training.

The description of a contingency should include answers to three questions:

1. How is the contingency detected and identified?
2. What is the likely consequence if the contingency or emergency is not detected?
3. What corrective action can be taken? What stand-by is needed?

Many of these data will be difficult to collect. The information they provide will be of substantial assistance in preparing training content, or for making special provisions in the design of the equipment or facilities whereby the operator is better able to cope with situations that otherwise might be catastrophic.

Noise is any disturbing or irrelevant signal, object, or process. It is the input counterpart of waste. The concept of noise includes not only an auditory disturbance, but any kind of disturbance, actual or potential, to operations. With this broader definition, it is a convenient term to have. An example of noise in the filling station may be the presence and activities of young loafers who congregate, and perhaps the passing motorist who stops in merely to get route directions. Glare on display panels is a form of visual noise. Noise may not only be a system input, but may arise within or between components in a system. Noise, like waste, can sometimes be converted to gainful use. Usually, however, it is a nuisance and provisions may have to be taken against it.

Areas and Physical Locations of the Installation. These are relatively permanent parts of the system's environment, and constitute the space and physical support for the installation of the system. The area available for off-street parking may be an important factor in designing a filling station. Whether the storage tanks must be dug into rock or soft earth is another.

Objects, Equipment, and Materials. These are the factors most self-evident in a system, and attention is characteristically concentrated almost exclusively on them. Important as they are in planning and operations, let us defer their implications for human factors to a later section of the chapter, Task Analysis.

People. We are now ready to add to our general system the all-important factor of people. We can approach the problem of dealing with people as if they were individuals or as if they were teams. Both viewpoints are important to system design. The features about people which are of most interest to us in this chapter are:

APTITUDES. What the individual can learn in given periods of time and under given training conditions

KNOWLEDGES. The range of actual and symbolic situations to which the individual can make symbolic (thinking or verbal) responses, and the range of these symbolic responses

SKILLS. The abilities of the individual to perceive and to make appropriate muscle and "work" responses

MOTIVATIONS. The incentives that induce the worker to give some quantity and quality level of work and also enable him to resist distractions

ATTITUDES. Relatively persistent and habitual patterns of like and dislike (as of approach and avoidance) that the individual has for various objects, symbols, and states of affairs

ROLE. Whether supervisor, peer, or subordinate. There are many other kinds of roles that people assume, but these are of main interest to us here.

Procedures, Rules, and Strategies. A *procedure* is some routine way of responding to a more or less standard or normal situation. A *rule* is a procedure that must not be changed under any circumstances, or practically any circumstances. A *strategy* is a procedure which has alternatives at various steps, and the choice of the alternatives depends on what shows up at each step. Familiar examples appear in games. A less familiar example, but extremely important for systems work, is the trouble-shooting technique in which a strategic selection of check points will speed up the location of a defective part.

The human factors specialist may often make substantial contributions to the design of a system by helping specify work procedures and strategies. This is an extension of the kind of work done by methods engineers, or time-and-motion people.

Values. As we continue with our service-station illustration, we soon come face to face with *values.* These are the priorities and relative weights given (under various conditions) to such system factors as different inputs, system components, or different outputs. For example, during rush periods, checking the radiator or battery may be given, at least to some customers, less priority than cleaning the windshield. Value priorities usually show up when the system is under stress and something has to give. However, values also appear under normal operating conditions in the decision as to what kinds of error can occasionally be tolerated without redesigning some part of the system. Values are often contained in the operating policies of a company, department, or supervisor.

Monitoring Arrangements. Monitoring is the comparison of some actual input or output with a criterion input or output, plus a mechanism for action if the actual value disagrees with the standard value. Monitoring is the attempt to maintain the operating integrity of the system as it was designed to operate. It may detect emergency conditions and switch to alternative modes of action; the monitoring function may also extend to coordinating the action of the system as a whole with input availability and output demands. Subfunctions of monitoring include: (1) data sensing (inspection), (2) data storing (records), (3) data interpretation, and (4) channels for executive response and control. There are optimal points in a system where inspection should be performed.

Monitoring may be as informal as a foreman looking over the shoulders of his employees, or as formal as the elaborate mechanisms in an automated chemical industry. A term in common usage that, in a restricted way, is related to the function of monitoring is "process control."

Research and Development (R&D). These are, in part, an extension of the monitoring function. But in this function, data are ordinarily stored for longer periods of time and analyzed with the intent not of maintaining the *status quo* of the system, but of introducing improvements in equipment design, operating procedures, training or selection of personnel, or monitoring procedures. The more precisely errors and waste can be analyzed, the more likely it is that a useful by-product can be found, or that means can be invented for reducing waste. The identification of the variables constituting errors and waste is therefore highly important to the efficiency of the research and development function of the system. Without suitable data channeling, however, the function becomes impotent.

It is axiomatic that systems left to run by themselves become progressively degraded. The better their design and monitoring, of course, the more gradual the degradation. R&D activity can resist and reverse this trend of systems towards death.

R&D may, like monitoring, be formal or informal. Observant individuals within the system may think of ideas for improvements, and carry them out; or a huge agency may be established for this function.

Parenthetically, the reader should notice that monitoring and R&D are not "factors" in a strict sense; they are really a combination of factors already mentioned in the text. Their importance, and the fact that they are so often neglected in thinking and working with systems, justifies mentioning them somewhat out of context.

Suppliers of Inputs and Buyers of Outputs. In some cases, such as that of the filling station, the buyer of the output also supplies some of the input. But the dealer also has to get his pumps, gasoline, tires, tools, and personnel from the outside. The buyer of the output is only partially controlled by what the system does for him. He looks for competing prices and services, or may dispense with all filling-station outputs if he rides by public transportation.

Probabilities of Occurrence and Recurrence. These are the probabilities that, under any particular set of conditions, or within some time period such as an hour, day, week, or year, some event will occur which demands system action. The decision to install one, two, or three sets of gasoline pumps will depend in part on the peak demands for gasoline, how often these peaks occur during a day, the chance of one or more pumps going bad and requiring a stand-by, or the frequency with which a profitable repair job is missed when the one mechanic is off duty. These frequencies and probabilities have to be weighed in two ways. One is the cost of providing against losing a sale, customer, or other benefit. The other is the profit to be obtained from the provision that is made.

As can be seen from the examples, probabilities influence what should be done under normal and exceptional circumstances, and in fact are the main determiners of what will be normal and what will be exceptional. These factors are reflected directly in the kind of personnel who are hired, and the training that is given to them.

OVERLAP WITHIN A GENERAL SYSTEM

It should be noted that the factors of a general system as described above overlap in many ways. This overlap is inescapable in any plan based on things, ideas, and processes that interact with each other.

Whether designing a new system or redesigning an existing one, it is almost a practical necessity to itemize on paper the kinds of information described above. A convenient way of doing so is to begin with the general and fill in the particulars to trace a typical cycle of the system from beginning to end. In planning a filling station, this cycle would start with a potential customer driving along the highway and looking for a gasoline station. It would end with the customer back on the highway. At each stage between these extremes, one would list the variety of input variables and environments, and the contingencies which might occur in the particular locality in mind. Then one would itemize what provisions might be taken against them. The end product will be a systems flow chart that can be used as a master planning document. It will help in remembering what goes with what, and for checking the consequences of any particular development that is proposed. The preparation of this chart is no simple exercise

SYSTEM

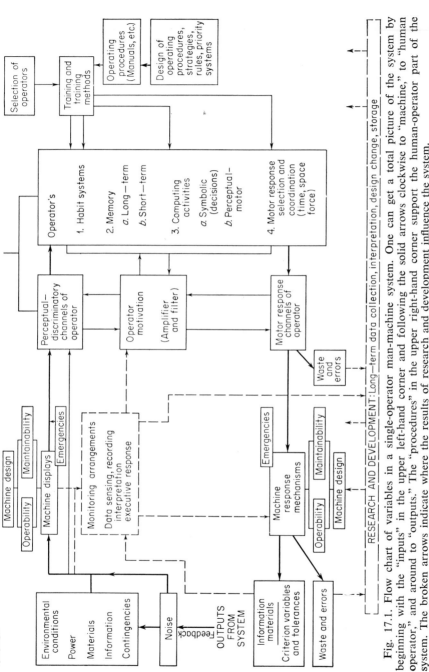

Fig. 17.1. Flow chart of variables in a single-operator man-machine system. One can get a total picture of the system by beginning with the "inputs" in the upper left-hand corner and following the solid arrows clockwise to "machine," to "human operator," and around to "outputs." The "procedures" in the upper right-hand corner support the human-operator part of the system. The broken arrows indicate where the results of research and development influence the system.

RESEARCH AND DEVELOPMENT: Long-term data collection, interpretation, design change, storage

371

even for a relatively simple system, such as may exist between a man and his secretary, or a telephone intercommunication network linked to outside telephone service in a five-office company.

The system flow chart may or may not be prepared by a psychologist. It certainly cannot be prepared by one man alone. As we will see in the next section, much of the information it contains will be vital to the psychologist in determining the human factors requirements imposed by any system that has gone beyond planning stages.

If all else in this section is forgotten, the reader should remember that *every* industrial and business system includes men and procedures; some systems also include machines. Let us take a look at one way a general system can be charted by giving some study to Figure 17.1. We suggest to the reader that he not try to absorb this diagram all at once. This figure appears quite complicated when first viewed. However, it is really no more complicated than an organizational flow chart such as the one we described in Chapter 3 (see page 45). As a matter of fact, one may think of this as a man-machine flow chart.

TASK ANALYSIS

Task analysis is a procedure for describing in specific terms what the human operator or maintenance mechanic is required to do. In many respects, it is like a very complete manual of instructions, although it includes information not found in such manuals. Task analysis is most important for the industrial psychologist. A statement of job requirements is the backbone of any work in human factors. The extent of completeness and concreteness of the statement of job requirements is the limiting factor in the directness and efficiency with which *any* personnel work can be done. Without such information, human factors work is shooting in the dark.

Pitfalls in Analyses. There are several major pitfalls in making job and task descriptions and analyses. One is that general statements about the job may lead to assumptions that are not valid. Thus, some toolmakers must use numbers in their work. The assumption that the toolmaker requires a thorough grounding in mathematics is invalid if it means that he must know math up to and through differential equations and calculus. Actually, he may do no more than compute angles and surfaces, for which rather simple procedures in geometry may suffice. It would then be improper to say that he needs to "know" geometry. In fact, he may be able to do quite well with simple skill in arithmetic and the proper tables to consult. This is the pitfall of *irrelevant job requirements*. It comes from superficial and general statements.

A second pitfall is the converse of the first. A job may seem to be made up of a number of simple steps or elements. But in practice the trick is to figure out how to do these steps in the right order on a particular occasion, and use judgment as to which steps should be omitted. This is like assuming that playing chess is no more than knowing the rules of the game. The result is an *underestimation of the job* requirements.

A third pitfall arises from paying too much attention to normal operating conditions and failing to identify *contingencies, emergencies, and other situations,* that are out of the routine. This will inevitably result in training people who have to have additional years of on-the-job experience before they can be trusted to work without close supervision.

The fourth pitfall is the opposite of the third. This consists in *overemphasizing the occasional situation* which might occur on the job. No doubt occasions arise when it would be helpful if a carpenter also knew how to wire a house, but the cost of carpenters would be much higher than it is if a knowledge of house wiring were made a standard requirement for them. Similarly, there are circumstances when the ability to make any kind of repair on a machine would be an asset, but paying for an additional skill that is used very infrequently may not be worth the asset it provides. Furthermore, an infrequently practiced skill gets rusty and unreliable, and a half-learned skill may be worse than none at all. These considerations should temper the tendency to emphasize the "might be helpful" skill or knowledge (which can be multiplied infinitely for any job). This emphasis should be especially deplored if training on the more frequent and essential job requirements are thereby penalized. This pitfall accommodates many professional educators who go into the field of industrial training.

Kinds of Tasks. No classification scheme exists whereby one task can be absolutely distinguished from another task on psychological grounds. However, it is convenient to make various differentiations on grounds of utility.

A *tracking task* is one in which continuous adjustments are made to a continuously changing signal. Aiming a gun at a moving target or from a moving platform is an example of a tracking task. Many lathe operations have tracking components. So does steering a vehicle, or controlling its rate according to some perceived relationship. The chapter on engineering psychology discussed at greater length the characteristics of tracking tasks (see page 331).

Procedural tasks are those which are performed more or less one step at a time. They can be broken into separate units of action such as punchpress operations, or assembling a relay. Most of the tasks in our daily work are procedural tasks. Procedures may range from highly standardized routines, where the same series of responses is invariably made to the same series of signals or cues, to nonstandardized procedures such as trouble shooting and other forms of problem solving on the job. Fighting a fire will have both standard and nonstandard ingredients.

The importance of making at least a rough classification of tasks in this way is that different aptitudes may be tapped in selection of personnel, and different training conditions will have to be set up. Problem solving and other nonroutine tasks may call for special knowledge that will not be required of standard routines. And whereas one can learn to perform quite a complex number of things at about the same time if they occur in the same order every time (such as in piano playing), one must be more careful of piling up simultaneous activities which are nonroutinized. Laying one task on top of another, such as watching a radarscope at the same time that the functioning of the equipment is being monitored, is called "time sharing."

The modern trend in equipment design is to reduce the extent to which the human being does tracking and standard routine tasks and to increase the extent to which he makes complex decisions. In other words, the human being is a problem solver in contingencies and emergencies, and can take over from the machine.

Task Description. In its simplest terms, a task description is a statement of the cues or signals that are the stimulus to a required action, and a statement of the required action that results in work being done. For example: "When the lamp turns red, turn switch X to the right as far as it will go." This is a fairly simple statement of a signal-response relationship. When all these individual signal-response relationships are described in the order in which they are properly done, the result is a task description.

Let us look, however, more carefully at the elements within the example cited. We find on the stimulus or signal side two components. One of these is the lamp itself. Call this the *indicator*. The state of the lamp (whether on or off) is the *indication*. On the response side of the statement we also find several elements. Switch X is the *control object*. Turning it to the right is the *control response*. In addition there is another signal element in the example. This is the phrase "as far as it will go." Let us think of this as an *indication of response adequacy,* or response feedback. Its function is to inform the operator that he has or has not made the correct response. Many tasks, of course, have action steps that have no direct indications of response adequacy. These tasks or task elements are usually more difficult to learn than those which have immediate continuous and unambiguous response feedback. The immediacy of response feedback in bicycle riding may be one reason why it can be learned rather rapidly as compared with riding a horse. (There may be some who dispute the example.)

Notice that the ingredients of a task description are those of any good instruction: what will give the signal, what the signal will be, what to do, and what to do it with. Also, how to know when the correct response has been made. Many of our everyday instructions take some of these ingredients for granted. Such ambiguity has its hazards in everyday life and in task description.

Special Circumstances and Contingent Conditions. It is now time to recall the section in system description that stressed the importance of identifying contingencies, emergencies, special environmental conditions, and other out-of-the-normal situations. Failure to include such information in a task description is like giving a person a pictorial description of the inside of a strange house without telling him he will have to find his way around in it in total darkness. Thus, pouring liquid from a can into a receptacle may be a simple task indoors, but a difficult one outdoors in a strong wind. Putting a nut on a bolt is a fairly simple operation, unless it has to be done in a space barely large enough to accommodate two fingers. It is easy enough to learn to drive down a road without traffic; it is another matter on city streets during rush hours.

Task descriptions should therefore be accompanied by statements of the environmental conditions and the range of circumstances that may complicate performance. A clear statement of the cues that indicate when a task is, or is not, to be performed is also necessary. Failure to do so is a pitfall with obviously serious consequences for personnel planning.

Work-cycle Analysis. The following procedure is proposed for completeness in job-task description. It consists of tracing through a typical work cycle from the beginning of a sequence to its end. It is important to go back to the real beginning of the cycle, rather than somewhere along in it. For example, the work cycle of flying an airplane mission begins not on the starting ramp, or even in the hangar, but back in the briefing room. It ends when the pilot turns in his flight papers or is debriefed. The start of a maintenance work cycle begins with a work order of some kind. Thence to selection of tools, perhaps of diagrams and proper work manuals. Then transport to the site of the job. And so on to the turning in of a completed work order and the replacement of tools and disposal of parts.

It is good policy first to list the gross tasks in sequence in a work cycle before making a step-by-step description of activities within each gross task. Contingencies and special circumstances may be listed under each title of a gross task. It should be remembered that the title of gross tasks and the number of behavior activities that get lumped into a gross task are quite arbitrary. Different persons making the same analysis will have different gross-task titles. But the heart of the description is finally in the detailed, step-by-step activity description of indicator, indication, control response, and feedback. Skilled individuals should prepare quite similar descriptions of the same tasks.

Task descriptions can be made from direct observation. But they can also be made from blueprint descriptions of equipment or equipment prototypes and information as to how it should be operated, plus systems data.

Let us presume that a work cycle has been sketched out in the form of a series of gross-task titles, and these in turn have been filled in with detailed descriptions of the activities that compromise the task. We also have identified the varieties of contingencies and malfunctions, environmental conditions, and other factors that may complicate the task requirements. All of the work thus far could be done quite well by a nonspecialist in human factors, such as an engineer or operations analyst. The next phase undertakes a behavioral analysis of this description.

Although the human being acts as a unified entity, it is nevertheless useful to distinguish, at times, various kinds of psychological function [16]. These have been divided into perceptual processes, recall processes, problem-solving (decision-making) processes, and muscular (motor) processes. It should be underscored that these divisions are for convenience in analysis. Perceptual processes, for example, are strongly influenced by recall from previous experience, and even from motor processes. Each task as a whole, as well as each group of specific activities, is studied with each of these functions in mind. The patterns of events likely to produce errors in perception, recall, decision making or responses on the machine controls are noted, and the nature of the expected error is described. Time-shared activities are scrutinized with particular care, especially where the signal-response patterns are not precisely the same from one work cycle to another.

THE HUMAN FACTORS SUBSYSTEM

Now that we have a system description and a comprehensive set of job-task requirements through task description and analysis, what can be done with the information? A number of scattered examples were cited, but they were specific to the context in which they were given. We are now in a position to put the elements of the human factors "subsystem" into a general map (see Figure 17.2). This map can be used for planning a strategy for dealing with human factors. It should also make explicit what will have to happen with respect to human beings, whether the outcome is the result of an explicit plan or of implicit improvisations.

The big map is an extension of the systems approach to laying out the most efficient route to a distant, but identified, goal. It is also the most efficient way of bearing in mind and selecting alternative routes for either small or large detours. The principal advantage of maps is that they present not only the main route but also other options that are available for getting from a starting point to a destination.

The ultimate objective in personnel actions is getting jobs done, tasks performed. The system descriptions, and especially the task descriptions, identify the over-all task requirements for a given stage of system development. From these descriptions comprehensive plans can be formulated for job design, human engineering of the work environment, proficiency testing, training and training aids, selection procedures, and other areas within the province of industrial psychology. These factors are interrelated like the roads on a road map, and the segments of a route to a destination. Changes

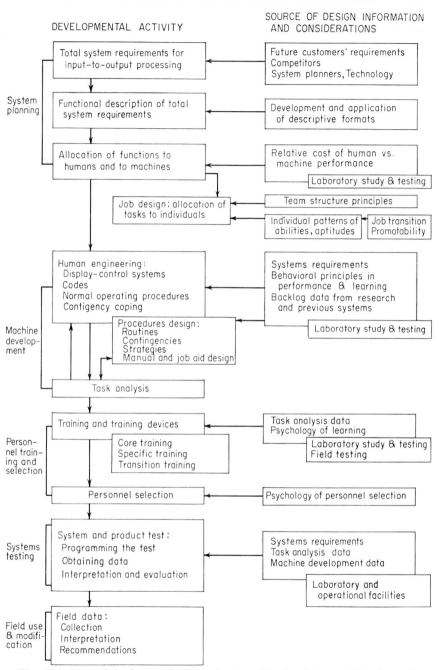

Fig. 17.2. Map of the human factors subsystem. The breakdown within the system can be seen by following the arrows, beginning with "system planning" in the upper left-hand corner.

in any of these factors inevitably cause changes in the other factors. Some of the changes may be inconsequential; others may have practical importance.

DESIGN VARIABLES OF A SUBSYSTEM

The following outline contains the design variables that make up the "personnel subsystem" (as it is called in the military).

Job Design. Let us here define a *job* as all the tasks that will be assigned to a man holding a given job title. Job design has practical meaning when there are two or more persons interacting in a system. Relevant considerations in job design are:

1. TASK RATE AND FREQUENCY. Can one man handle all that needs to be done? Will a stand-by be required for peak loads, and what else should be done with the stand-by?

2. PHYSICAL LOCATION. One man can be in only one place at one time, and time is required to transport him from one location to another.

3. KEEPING BUSY. A job should keep a man reasonably busy throughout the typical work period of system operation.

4. COMMON KNOWLEDGES AND SKILLS. In general, the tasks given to one position should be "psychologically homogeneous"; that is, they should require about the same level and pattern of ability. This will help both in selecting and in training personnel.

5. COMPATIBILITY WITH EXISTING JOB STRUCTURES. This will help persons who are making a transition from a previous system to the new system.

6. SUPERVISORY POSITIONS. These require special attention and skills quite different from technical abilities.

7. OPPORTUNITY FOR ADVANCEMENT. Planning for career structures within a system will provide incentives.

8. SPECIAL OVERRIDING FACTORS. There will be cases where all the foregoing considerations may have to be violated in fulfilling a given set of system requirements. Notice also that many of the considerations above are in conflict with each other. This conflict is resolved by the principle of trade-offs: factors have to be juggled until you get the best with what you have to work with.

Proficiency Criteria. Ideally, these are performance tests of the actual tasks where a wide sampling of environmental conditions, contingencies, and malfunctions (and even human errors) are introduced into the tests. A criterion includes both performance rate and accuracy requirements.

Training. This should consist of experiences that provide the least costly route between being a novice to a job and meeting the proficiency criteria for that job. Training ordinarily includes much education in irrelevant knowledges, and it often neglects teaching the person how to meet the practical contingencies of his job. The reason is that in many cases training is directed to some job titles ("maintenance of data processing systems") rather than to precisely identified task requirements.

Personnel Selection. Job- and task-requirements data should be used in devising procedures for selecting personnel for jobs; such data will cut down the usually large error in prediction of most selection tests.

Human Engineering. This general area has been expanded from "knob-and-dial" design safety and a concern with environmental factors to handbooks of instruction, job aids, procedure design, and the extremely important task of determining what functions in a system will be performed by machines and what will be performed by human operators. Human factors engineering is also extended to motivations and incentive conditions in the design of tasks and task environments.

Systems and Product Test. More and more psychologists (such as those in RAND and the System Development Corporation) are developing complex techniques for the testing of man-machine systems in order to predict their efficacy in real-world conditions. Both human engineering check lists and complex system models have been found useful.

Field-data Collection. Another task in which the psychologist may assist is in the collection and interpretation of field data after the system actually gets into operation. Not only is such data of potential use in modifying existing systems, but it can be tremendously useful in the next "generation" of systems.

FIVE ROLES OF THE INDUSTRIAL PSYCHOLOGIST

The reader has seen that the industrial psychologist may do research in which he plays the role of *critic* by testing proposed design solution, and that as a *problem solver* he may develop solutions for concrete applications. He may tackle problems that are highly *specific* to a work situation, or frame his problem in *general,* psychological variables. If he is engaged in systems work, he will tend to solve personnel problems *as a pattern.* The broader his base of knowledge of psychological and industrial factors, the more likely it is that his creativity and inventiveness will deal effectively with interrelationships among people, work environments, and the processes whereby they interact.

SUGGESTIONS FOR FURTHER READING

Cherry, C. *On human communication.* New York: Wiley, 1957. A review of the diverse studies of communication of an interdisciplinary nature.

Churchman, C. W., Ackoff, R. L., & Arnoff, E. L. *Introduction to operations research.* New York: Wiley, 1957. A detailed account of the applications of operations research in industry.

Ferguson, R. O., & Sargent, L. F. *Linear programming: fundamentals and applications.* New York: McGraw-Hill, 1958. A readable book for those with some mathematical sophistication on the uses of linear programming in industrial management.

Goode, H. H., & Machal, R. E. *Systems engineering.* New York: McGraw-Hill, 1957. A nonpsychological description of systems engineering.

McCloskey, J. F. *Operations research for management.* Baltimore: Johns Hopkins Press, 1956. Another book describing the relatively new field of operations research applied to management problems.

Mann, F. C., & Hoffman, L. R. *Automation and the worker.* New York: Holt, 1960. A study of social change in a plant brought about through automation.

PART VI: INFLUENCE AND SOCIAL INTERACTION

18

THE

MARKETING

MIX

W. J. E. Crissy and
Kathleen A. Thompson

The American economy is unique in the business history of the world. Our gross national product is near half a trillion dollars! Three factors have contributed to our amazing economic growth—*mass production, research and development,* and *marketing and distribution.* In the preceding chapters we have discussed the human factors related to production, research, and development. In this chapter we are concerned with the human aspects of marketing and distribution, and how the methods and content of psychology contribute to two major aspects of it—advertising and selling.

THE INGREDIENTS OF THE MIX

There is an increasing awareness on the part of industrialists that the marketing and distribution of goods and services involves the careful planning and administration of many diverse but *interdependent* activities—advertising, selling, sales promotion, customer service, public relations, credit, transportation and delivery, and market and marketing research. None of these can stand alone. Neglect of one weakens the others. In combination these activities comprise the company's "marketing mix."

Obviously, the mix will vary depending on the goods or services being produced, the market being served, current economic conditions, and the men and money allocable to the marketing and distribution function. Even companies producing competitive lines differ in their marketing mix. One may stress intensive advertising coverage and direct-mail promotion with minimal personal selling. Another may do relatively little advertising but reach the market with a large sales force. The more competitive the industry, the more challenge to each company to utilize fully all its interrelated marketing media. In general, though, *all* companies have a common objective for the marketing mix, that is, *profitable distribution of goods or services.*

What is involved in each ingredient of the mix?

Advertising. The dictionary defines advertising as "any form of public announcement intended to aid directly or indirectly in the sale of goods." In America, advertising media include newspapers, glossy and pulp magazines, trade papers and magazines, billboards, throwaways, car cards, sky writing, and local and national radio and television. Each company must decide which combination of media will be most effective for marketing its goods or services and the extent to which each is to be used.

Selling. Selling involves influencing customers to buy through the efforts of individual members of the sales organization. For some companies the customer is the ultimate user of the goods or services. For others, the customer is a wholesaler, distributor, or agent who, in turn, has his own marketing mix for the distribution of the goods for sale.

Sales Promotion. Usually included here are direct-mail promotion, point-of-sale display pieces, and selling aids. The specific promotional activities and their relative importance vary markedly from one company to another. However, this part of the marketing mix is generally larger in companies producing consumer goods than in those manufacturing industrial products.

Customer Service. Depending on the nature of the product, customer service may be a nonexistent or a major mix ingredient. Such activities include maintenance and repair of products, technical and professional assistance in problem solving, help in training the customer's personnel in operating the equipment, market and marketing research on the customer's products.

Public Relations. Since the reputation the company has in its industry, in the business world, and in the community markedly influences the sale of its products, public relations is an important ingredient of the marketing mix. All employees informally contribute to the public relations of the company. Some companies employ a specialized staff or an outside agency to coordinate this aspect of the marketing mix.

Credit. This ingredient varies in importance from company to company, depending on the goods or services sold, policy with regard to payment, and precedent within the industry. This function may be administered either by the sales department or by a separate credit department.

Transportation and Delivery. Promptness, cost, and customer convenience must all be considered in this mix ingredient. Often, in a highly competitive industry this becomes the crucial factor in the customer's decision to buy or not to buy from a particular supplier. Its importance varies considerably from industry to industry, and even among companies selling similar lines.

Market and Marketing Research. The basic objective here is to substitute facts and data for guesswork in the marketing and distribution of goods or services.

With the above discussion as background we can now turn our attention to how psychology applies to advertising and selling. In the ensuing discussion one can apply some of the principles set forth to the other mix ingredients. It must be remembered, however, that the contributions of psychology to the vast areas of advertising and selling are limited. It must also be recognized that some important findings do not get published in professional journals because the data are held confidential for competitive reasons. Some research findings in this chapter appear in print for the first time.

ADVERTISING

Today, we can correctly refer to an advertising *industry*. Approximately $10 billion is spent annually in America on this ingredient of the marketing mix. Over 350 companies spend $1 million or more on their advertising each year. What a far cry from the announcements painted on the bathhouse walls in ancient Rome!

What kinds of advertising are there? There are many bases of classification—by media, coverage of the market, source of the money, size, and frequency—but perhaps the soundest method of classification for the psychologist is by the objectives to be met.

Direct Sell. The great bulk of advertising is in the direct-sell category and is designed to influence directly the purchase of goods or services. A department store's full-page spread in your Sunday newspaper and the spot commercial on your local television station urging you to buy an album of hit-tune records are commonplace examples.

Brand Reinforcement. During the twentieth century there has been a phenomenal increase in emphasis on buying by brand. Advertising has brought this about and, today, a large segment of consumer-goods advertising is designed to reinforce the brand name. Examples abound in the advertising of clothing, foods, and appliances. A variant of this type of advertising is aimed at reinforcing the company name as a guide to the purchaser.

Institutional. Many companies, particularly those which do not have consumer products for sale, use a large portion of their advertising dollars to establish themselves as good corporate citizens. Examples of such institutional advertising include an oil company's campaign stressing safety on the road, a major life insurance company's award-winning series of advertisements furnishing career information, and the dramatic program on network television sponsored by a nationally renowned steel company. Often, in this kind of advertising one or more companies furnish publicity for national or community endeavors, including car cards, and newspaper, radio, and television announcements for fund raising.

All advertising, regardless of kind, is aimed at triggering perceptual, cognitive, and affective responses in each individual reached. Although we respond as total beings and these processes are interactive, we can, for discussion and analysis, consider each of them separately.

Perceptual Factors. Printed advertisements, regardless of media, involve visual perceptual processes exclusively. Radio advertising, in contrast, depends exclusively on auditory perception. The advent of television complicated matters. In this increasingly important advertising medium an optimal combination of visual and auditory stimulation must be used if the message is to be maximally effective.

Such perceptual variables as the following have undergone research scrutiny; size, color, kind of illustration, amount of copy, and frequency and duration in the case of radio and television commercial "spots." Some of the research is done under the precise conditions of the laboratory; *much of it must be conducted in the field with some sacrifice of accuracy.* Set forth below are synopses of several studies which will serve as illustrations of how perceptual factors in advertising are studied.

Investigators [22] studied the influence of color on legibility of copy; they used a procedure similar to that of visual acuity tests except that the subject moved forward until he could just read the characters correctly. Forty-two color combinations were employed, and it was found that legibility depends on the brightness difference between the color of the lettering and that of the background. Further, dark-colored lettering on a light background, rather than the reverse, is more legible in daylight. Gray was found to form the best background for the legibility of colored lettering. A fairly high positive rank difference correlation (rho .54) exists between legibility and affective preference of color combinations. For example, blue lettering on a gray background was given an average legibility rank of 1.0 and an average affective preference rank of 1.0; red lettering on a gray background was given an average legibility rank of 4.0, and an average affective preference rank of 3.0. In this connection, it was also found that color-combination preference depends more on brightness difference than on legibility.

In another study, the same author measured the relevancy of illustrations to copy in thirty-nine advertisements from *House Beautiful, House and Garden,* and *The Saturday Evening Post.* The pictures were cut from the copy and mounted on a white cardboard background. The subjects, ninety-four college students, were instructed to indicate whether they had or had not seen each of the pictures before, what commodity was featured in the picture, and what desirable feature or features of the commodity were in evidence. It was found that in those pictures in which commodity had a high relevancy to copy (those judged correctly by 80 to 100 per cent of the subjects), the commodity was the conspicuous, and in most cases the centermost, object. Additional features of highly relevant-to-copy illustrations included the label or trademark on the commodity, and lack of an excessive number of extraneous objects surrounding the commodity. In those illustrations in which desirable feature of the commodity had a very high relevancy to copy (those judged correctly by 80 to 100 per cent of the subjects), the plain and unambiguous representation of the product features was characteristic. Further, these pictures contained within their borders printed words which tersely informed the reader of the desirable features, and the human subjects of the illustrations reflected happiness and contentment in their faces. The investigator concluded that the relevancy of pictures to copy was lower than it should be since the average reader rarely reads the copy and pays only fleeting attention to the illustrations.

Cognitive Factors. Each advertisement not only must be perceived, its message must be understood. Word choice and sentence structure are key variables to study to ensure understanding on the part of the audience or readers. The investigations summarized below are typical of the research being done on this aspect of advertising.

Trenchard and Crissy [44] studied the readability of prewar (1936 to 1940) and postwar (1945 to 1949) advertising and editorial copy in the two national news weeklies, *Time* and *Newsweek*. Using Flesch's operational definition of readability and employing his formulas for determining reading ease, a trend toward harder-to-read advertising copy in both magazines was found, although only in *Time* was the trend statistically significant. In contrast, the trend was toward easier-to-read editorial copy, a trend which was significant in the case of *Newsweek*. Prewar advertising was significantly easier to read than the editorial copy in juxtaposition to it. The authors note that there appears to be nothing desirable in the trend toward more difficult-to-read advertising copy, although, from the standpoint of the advertiser, there would seem to be evident advantage in the fact that advertising copy is easier to understand than the editorial copy with which it competes. When the educational level of readers was considered in relation to reading-ease scores, it was found that all copy was within the comprehension of the majority of the readers of both magazines.

Determination of Readership and Comprehension. The Psychological Corporation, a consulting firm, undertook the determination of readership and comprehension of Union Carbide and Carbon newspaper advertising in Charleston, West Virginia. Interviewers questioned 363 men and women on the Sunday the advertisements appeared in the two local papers as well as on the following Monday. Of those who reported having read either of the two newspapers 74 per cent reported having seen the advertising, and 40 per cent of that group reported having read it. Of these latter 145 cases, 84 per cent gave at least one idea which showed a good or fair understanding of the advertisements; 12 per cent had only a poor understanding; and 4 per cent had no idea whatsoever. These figures are based on answers to the question, "What ideas did you get from that advertisement?" which was put to the respondents after the newspaper had been taken out of sight. It is interesting to note that 86 per cent of those who reported having read the advertisement thought it was worthwhile; that is, they had gained something from reading it.

In an effort to determine the optimum length of advertisement headlines, researchers investigated the ability of the reader to remember headlines under varying conditions [25]. Headlines ranging from four to fifteen words, each set in a uniform size and style of type face, were presented to 100 university students for recall and recognition. The results indicated that brevity had a decided advantage if readers spent a uniform, brief period of time on each headline. When a variable exposure time was allowed, almost all the advantages of brevity disappeared. It is a matter of conjecture whether the shorter headlines were better remembered because they could be read so much more quickly and easily, or whether the apparent advantage was due to other factors influencing ease of recall, as illustrated by the fact that the immediate recall scores for some of the shorter headlines were low, and others were high. It is reasonable to assume that the length of time spent on a headline is influenced greatly by context and length of the headline itself. The study did not indicate clearly exactly how long a good headline may be. However, it was found that almost nine-tenths of the subjects remembered one headline containing nine words. Since the subjects were all college students these results cannot be applied to average magazine readers without allowance for the more limited buying interests of students and the lower average memory span of the population as a whole.

Spot Advertising Study. A packaged-drugs firm was interested in determining the effectiveness of its spot advertising in printed media. To study the impact of the copy, key words were extracted from sample advertisements and respondents asked to free-associate to each, to give a definition, and to indicate the degree of affectivity (strongly dislike, dislike, strongly like, and like). The phrase setting in which the word occurred was then mentioned and the interviewee again asked to free-associate. The final question posed was, "What product or service does this remind you of?" For example, when seventeen male and fourteen female subjects were asked to free-associate to the word "membrane," 42 per cent responded with "form of skin or tissue." This phrase was also the modal definition given. A mixed emotional attitude was found; 57 per cent of the subjects expressed like and 42 per cent dislike. The modal response to the captive phrase "shrinks swollen nasal membranes" was "colds." Further, the word had a high brand-associative value for the company. The research indicated that very favorable affective attitudes existed toward such words and phrases as "penetrating ingredient," "stimulates," and "gives you a lift." Such words as "antiseptic," "aromatic," and "medicates" aroused predominantly favorable reactions, whereas unfavorable affective reactions were elicited by "bacteria," "congestion," and "inflamed." The investigators note that when negative emotional reactions are involved the advertisement should "provide a way out."

The importance of affective factors in advertising is exemplified by other unpublished research available to the authors. An artist was commissioned to prepare some illustrations suitable for insurance advertisements. Safety, protection, and security were to be the central themes. One picture showed a mother fastening a safety gate in front of a small boy as the father descended the stairs. Pretesting of the illustration through depth interviewing revealed that the man was regarded as the focal point and that the family was breaking up; hence respondents failed to relate the picture to insurance. When the father was removed and the illustration depicted a child playing while the mother fastened the safety gate, the desired safety theme became apparent to the viewers.

Affective Factors. Regardless of type of advertising, or of product or service for sale, affective responses must be considered. Feelings can be aroused by the illustration, the wording, even by the location of the advertisement in the medium. A leading manufacturer of perfumes pays a premium rate to ensure that his advertisements appear on a page with a love story! Two unpublished research projects, done for client companies by the writers and an associate, serve to indicate how affective factors can be studied. Let us consider these next in showing the importance of pretesting advertisements.

Pretesting. Advertisements are usually tested before they are used. This testing may involve people's reactions to each advertisement as a whole or to its component parts. It may be done under laboratory conditions within the agency or in the field. Often alternative forms of the advertisement are tested in order to choose the most effective one.

If advertisements are checked within the agency an intensive study is made, using a relatively small number of subjects. Three pieces of laboratory equipment are valuable aids—the tachistoscope, the chronoscope, and the eye camera. The first is used to present split-second exposures of either the whole ad, the illustration, or the headline. The purpose is to determine whether the material presented can be perceived speedily. For example, there is a consistent finding that more than six words in a headline prevents its perception in a single act of attention. The chronoscope is useful in measuring precisely the time needed for forming associations with stimulus words or illustrations, for reading the body copy, etc. The eye camera, often used in a combination with a device for turning pages at a constant, known speed, provides a means for determining the attention-getting parts of the advertisement. It is also used for studying this factor in an entire issue of a magazine or newspaper.

To systematize the collection of data on people's reactions to advertisements as wholes, several advertisement tests or check lists have been developed. The most elaborate one is the Thompson-Luce test, which consists of thirty-five factors found to contribute to reader interest in an advertisement. These variables include page, color, visual emphasis, baby, animal, food, shock, pathos, danger, news, slogan, etc. When analysis of several thousand advertisements on the basis of these controlled factors was compared with later consumer-readership reports, the Thompson-Luce preevaluation was found to be accurate within 2 per cent in predicting the ratings later reported by advertisement-checking services. Further, the Thompson-Luce factors were weighted on the basis of statistical studies of good and poor advertisements. Results indicated, for example, that babies appeared in the illustrations of high-ranking advertisements four times more frequently than in the low; and visual emphasis, lack of confusion in the advertisement's appearance, was found eight times more often.

A number of people have suggested rating advertisements on the basis of "attention," "meaning," "feeling," "memory," and "action."

Consumer Panels. When advertisements are taken into the field for pretesting, less intensive data are obtained from larger numbers of subjects. Inherent in field testing is the problem of ensuring an appropriate sampling of the desired segment of the population. This latter factor has caused many large advertising agencies to maintain a consumer panel, that is, people who have been selected on the basis of prescribed criteria and who may be used, as need arises, for testing purposes.

There are four common types of panels.

1. THE CONSUMER JURY. A group who may be asked to give judgments on pieces of copy, to listen to radio programs, or to act as advisors on other matters of interest to an advertiser.

2. THE CONSUMER TESTING GROUP. Individuals who are available to make blind tests of products.

3. THE OPINION PANEL. A group of persons or families who can be relied upon to answer questionnaires on various subjects, ranging from product-use habits to opinions on public affairs.

4. THE CONTINUOUS PURCHASE-RECORD TYPE OF PANEL. Individuals or families who keep adequate records of their purchases of specified products over a period of time. Thus a continuous case history of certain kinds of purchases is provided.

Information may be obtained from the panel members by mail, personal interviews, or group meetings. Individuals are carefully chosen to include representative samplings of the population with regard to age, income, education, and any other identifying characteristics of importance to the sponsoring advertiser. Panel members are often compensated for their cooperation by "points" which may be used in selecting premiums or merchandise from a special catalogue. An alternative is to draw a prescribed sample from each study. If this method is used, the field interviewers are given criteria to be met in selecting respondents.

Obviously the advertisements which can be taken for testing to the interviewee's home or place of business are limited to printed media. Pretesting of radio and television advertising involves bringing the subjects to a central location. However, there is one important exception to this. In the last few years such advertising has been pretested over a single local station prior to widespread use.

Posttesting. Testing advertising after use is easier to accomplish than pretesting. However, once the advertising money is spent it is too late to make changes! Yet this "after the fact" evaluation is useful in several ways.

1. It provides a guide for the formulation of future advertising.

2. If several advertisements have been used, it yields data concerning their relative effectiveness.

3. If several media have been used, the relative merits of the media can be appraised.

4. It furnishes information on the yield of advertising in the company's marketing mix.

The most precise posttesting method is "direct return." If a printed medium is used, a coupon is provided for answering the advertisement. Often a prize or premium is offered the respondent. With an estimate of readership, or audience, it is possible to determine percentage of response. If radio or television is used, a phone number or a mailing address is presented. A variant of this method is "split run." If the company has alternative forms of the advertisement, these can be run alternately in a particular issue of the magazine or newspaper and the relative effectiveness of each determined.

Another method is similar to field pretesting. Either a consumer panel or a sample is interviewed. If unprompted recall is sought, the respondent is asked which advertisements he remembers in a particular issue of a magazine or newspaper. If radio or television commercials are being studied he is asked which ones he remembers on a particular channel or station or on a designated program. Those who recall the advertisements being tested are then interrogated in detail. If prompted recall is desired, the interviewee may be shown the advertisement and then asked detailed questions concerning his reactions to it.

Since the advertiser usually wants to know how his messages are faring with competition, posttesting is done by outside research organizations. Interest in this type of research has grown. The advertiser can obtain readership and listenership information on his own advertising as well as on that of his competitors by subscribing to such services as Starch and

Gallup in printed media and Nielsen, Trendex, Pulse, and American Research Bureau in broadcast media. As a specific example, a Starch report reveals for half-page and larger ads those which have been noted, seen-associated, and read most.

The ultimate test of direct-sell advertising is the profitable sale of goods or services. For this reason an important posttesting method is the advertisement's impact on sales volume. A nationally known manufacturer of cold remedies places newspapers, radio, and television spots depending on local weather conditions. Whenever colds are likely, the advertising is intensified. An immediate follow-up on retail outlets is then made to determine the effect on sales of the company's products.

The following is illustrative of the methods used in posttesting advertisements. In its study to determine the effectiveness of the advertising of the detergent Silver Dust, the Psychological Corporation employed a pretested questionnaire which encompassed three basic approaches. The sample consisted of 400 cases. The interviewees lived in one- two- or three-family houses rather than apartment houses, and the bulk of them were in the $2,000 to $5,000 income bracket. In the *recognition* test five advertisements were shown simultaneously and the interviewees asked whether they had seen them. This is a variation of the usual recognition test in which only one advertisement is shown at a time and the interviewee required to answer "yes," "no," or "don't know." The latter method tends to produce a higher percentage of "yes" answers, while the method used in this study is more conservative. The *aided-recall* segment of the study utilized an introductory question designed to eliminate confusion with the advertising of other soaps, followed by the question, "Have you noticed any other wash soap advertising recently?" This was the most rigorous test since the individual is asked to produce, from all the competitive advertising influences, the one brand that stood out. The succeeding questions dealt with the outstanding features of the Silver Dust advertisements. Finally, the *controlled opinion,* or *consumer jury test,* was employed to get some idea about the different advertisements themselves. The respondents were asked to look at and read the advertisements again, to choose the one which was most interesting, and to describe what they liked about it.

SELLING

In most companies, selling comprises the largest part of the marketing mix, whether viewed in terms of dollars spent or people employed. Selling is classifiable in many ways—by what is sold, by channel of distribution, and by ultimate purchaser.

When we approach the subject of what is sold, the simplest classification of selling consists of industrial goods, consumer goods, and intangibles. Examples of each of these would be selling steel to the automobile manufacturer, selling vacuum cleaners door to door, and selling air travel to newlyweds. Obviously each of these general groupings can be made more specific, depending on the needs of the person who is describing selling. A common practice in business with regard to industrial goods is to categorize such selling by industries—rubber, chemicals, steel, etc. Another practice is to subdivide consumer goods into hard and soft, the latter being expendable items. Similarly intangibles may be broken down into such subcategories as investments, insurance, etc.

Kinds of Selling. Should the approach to classification be through channel of distribution, three kinds of selling can be distinguished: direct to purchaser, wholesale, and retail. Each of these in turn admits of further refinement. Thus the direct sale of consumer goods may be accomplished by personal selling or by direct mail. In the case of industrial goods, direct selling may be subdivided into selling an established line of products or selling goods made to customer specifications. Similarly, wholesale selling can be subdivided into selling through jobbers or selling through exclusive agents or franchisees that are independent businesses, though they sell only one company's products. In the industrial field there is still another grouping which cuts across both wholesale and direct selling: manufacturers' representatives. Such persons do direct selling, but for several companies, and are in many ways independent businessmen. Retail selling can be broken down, depending on the goods or services sold, to department store, specialty shop, and miscellaneous kinds of retail outlets. The characteristic factor of retail selling is that the customer is induced to come to the outlet for the goods or services.

When an attempt is made to classify selling by kind of customer, obviously the simplest classification is whether an individual or a company is the purchaser. Some firms sell goods and services to a wide range of both individuals and companies. For example, an automobile manufacturer may distribute his cars through dealers to a wide range of people of both sexes. The same company may make a large number of fleet sales, that is, quantities of automobiles to companies for use by their sales and executive personnel. Other businesses may find the market for their goods exclusively in a small and homogeneous group of individuals. An example of the latter would be a firm selling hearing aids. Still other companies may have no individuals as customers and their market may be limited to homogenous groups of companies. An example of this would be a tool steel manufacturer; the product is sold only to a restricted number of companies for making tools, dies, and the like.

Still another way of classifying selling might be the mode of payment. Our economy is characterized by a tremendous amount of credit buying. Many retail outlets sell for both cash and credit. Others operate exclusively on a cash basis or exclusively on a credit basis.

Since the above classifications are not mutually exclusive, the best way to describe a particular field of selling is to make a composite description, using all the above categories. For example, the selling engaged in by the Polychemicals Department of E. I. Du Pont de Nemours and Company can be classified, in terms of the above, as industrial, direct, and company. Yet, even when a composite description such as this is made, little insight is gained concerning the nature of the selling process involved. For this reason it is better to state the nature of the selling process itself and to relate the principles and techniques of psychology to it.

ANALYSIS OF THE SELLING PROCESS

Books on salesmanship and treatments of selling typically discuss the selling process in one or more of these three ways:

1. *Stimulus-response,* exemplified in its extreme by the canned sales talk

2. *Formula,* the most common being AIDA (Attract attention, arouse interest, create a desire, get action)

3. *Customer need satisfaction,* in which selling is thought of as a buying process induced by the salesman

Each of these analyses has some merit and application. Each one also has its limitations, depending on the goods and services being sold, the channels of distribution being used, and the customers being reached.

Stimulus-Response. The premise underlying this approach is that a sales message can be prepared which will stimulate action in a large enough number of prospects to make a profit. It also minimizes the company's dependence on the salesman's thought processes and ability to formulate sales strategy and tactics on his own. This approach probably has greatest applicability when these conditions are met:

1. Sales are made door to door to individuals.

2. The dollar value of the purchase is small.

3. Little preselection can be made of prospects.

4. Income for the salesman is low.

Because of 2 and 4 above, the company cannot invest in extensive recruitment, selection, and training of salesmen.

Formula. This method of analysis allows for more flexibility on the part of the salesman, though it too is focused more on selling behavior than on buying behavior. There are several basic assumptions underlying the AIDA method. With regard to attention, it is assumed that a repertoire of visual and auditory stimuli provided by the salesman will get and hold the attention of any prospect. If attention is attracted, it is assumed that the presentation by the salesman will arouse interest. If interests are sufficiently aroused, it is supposed that a desire will be created for the goods or services. Once the desire is intense enough, the action of buying will occur. There are many difficulties with this method in actual practice. First, people's attention waxes and wanes. Further, even when there is interest, there may be competing desires present. For example, the adept salesman may arouse considerable interest in a new car, yet the prospect's desire at the moment may be to use his money for many other things. Even when a desire is created, the act of buying may not necessarily follow. The fundamental problem is posed by the salesman; namely, he has so much talking and demonstrating to do that he has no opportunity to determine what the customer's needs actually are. This method is likely to be most effective when the following conditions are met:

1. The prospect has been presold by other ingredients of the marketing mix.

2. There is the possibility of preselection of prospects.

3. The goods or services sold are complex enough to require visual and auditory presentation.

4. The unit sale is not great enough to warrant intensive training of salesmen.

5. The likelihood of repeat sales is small, so that it is unprofitable to develop customer information on the basis of several personal calls.

Customer Need Satisfaction. This approach differs from the other two in that selling is viewed as a buying process. The salesman's first objective is to arouse needs, if none are verbalized, and to determine what the particular customer's needs are. Having determined the customer's needs and made the customer aware of them, his next objective is to demonstrate how his goods or services are the best need satisfiers available. What is being sold includes not only the goods or services, but the salesman as a person, the company, and its reputation, price, credit, availability, delivery, technical advice and assistance, etc. The salesman deals with these in terms of the particular prospect's or customer's needs; thus no two presentations are exactly alike. His next objective is not to sell but to induce purchase. Then the next objective is to make sure that the customer is satisfied with the action he has taken. For example, an industrial chemicals salesman may call on an account after a purchase to make sure that the goods have been delivered and meet the specifications set. This analysis of the selling process can be diagramed as follows, after E. K. Strong [42, 43]:

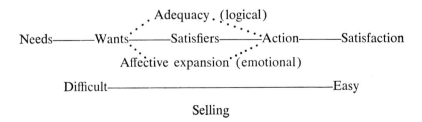

Selling

In treating this method of analysis with business groups, the writers substitute the term "gut reaction" for "affective expansion" and spell out the way emotions spill over from a prompting stimulus to other unrelated aspects of a total stimulus situation. The following incident illustrates the significance of feelings in buying. The president of a small firm was a hot prospect for some key-man insurance. The insurance company's representative called for an appointment, arrived promptly, and gave an adequate presentation, but the president did not buy because of an unfavorable gut reaction to the salesman. The two men sat in the president's office, smoking as they discussed the proposition; however, the salesman failed to use the ashtray provided. His ashes grew longer and longer; they finally fell down the front of his shirt and onto the freshly waxed floor. As the refuse collected on the floor, the president became more and more certain he would not buy from that company, even if it were the only one in the business.

It will be noted that with regard to satisfiers the salesman has a twofold task; he must provide logical reasons why his satisfiers are the best, and at the same time he must take account of emotional appeals. Further, it will be observed that a difficult sale is one that begins with the customer having no awareness of needs. A sale is increasingly easy as the customer is predisposed to buy in advance of the salesman's call. This approach to selling is likely to be best when the following conditions are met:

1. Repeat sales are likely.
2. The dollar value of the purchase is large.
3. It is economical to train the sales force intensively.
4. The line of goods or services is relatively complex.
5. There is a considerable diversity of likely purchasers.
6. Several people must be influenced before a purchase is made, as is the case with most industrial selling.

PERCEPTUAL FACTORS IN SELLING

The importance of perception in selling stems from the fact that the sales interview involves a unique interaction between the salesman and the customer. Each provides a continuing stimulus for the other. What the salesman says and does must be perceived by the customer and responded to favorably if a sale is to take place. For this reason the focus of the salesman's attention is the customer. He must catch the small cues in the customer's behavior which tell him which points to stress, which ones to gloss over.

Many aspects of perception have a direct application in selling—selectivity of attention, span of attention, subjectivity of perception, and sensory reinforcement. Examples will illustrate these.

Selectivity of Attention. The casualty insurance salesman cited earlier allowed the prospect's attention to shift from his presentation to the ashes growing longer and longer on the cigarette he was smoking! The salesman failed to catch the cues which would have told him of the mounting displeasure of the prospect at having the freshly waxed floor dirtied by the salesman's ashes.

Span of Attention. An office supplies salesman was getting along fine with a prospect until he spread out several selling aids, leaflets describing in detail the quality and benefits of the line. The prospect leafed through them and said, "I don't have time to read these now. Leave them with me and I'll give you a ring."

Subjectivity of Perception. It has often been said that we see what we want to see, hear what we want to hear. The purchaser of an electric typewriter complained bitterly when he was billed for his service contract. He thought that a year's service was included in the price of the typewriter. The salesman was certain he had made the point clear in his presentation. Further, the purchase agreement signed by the customer clearly mentioned the service and cited the price for it.

Sensory Reinforcement. A good many years ago when the dairy companies first introduced bottled fruit juice on their milk routes, one firm set up an excellent sales presentation. The route man was instructed to ring the bell, and, as the housewife opened the door, to hand her a bottle of the juice. Then he was to say, "Pardon me, please hold this for me." Imagine the impact of feeling the cold bottle, seeing the contents, and hearing the sales story!

Affective Factors. Feelings and emotions can significantly influence the outcome of a sales call. Three characteristics of affective responses have particular application in selling:

1. Such responses tend to radiate to other aspects of the physical and social environment than to those which provoked them.

2. Once aroused, they are likely to last for a substantial period of time.

3. They can be positive (euphoric) or negative.

In everyday conversation these three points are alluded to when a person is described as being in a good or bad mood.

When the casualty insurance salesman failed to use the ash tray, for example, he aroused a negative affective response in the prospect. Once triggered off, it generalized to the salesman as a person, to the company, even to the sales proposition itself!

The salesman as a person and his conduct provide the primary stimulation of the prospect's and customer's feeling during the sales call. It is incumbent upon him to arouse positive affective reactions. These do much to ensure his success with the prospective customer.

The proper handling of a complaint offers a dramatic application of what has been discussed. The following incident is illustrative. An electric typewriter had been purchased. The secretary had just begun to use it when she noticed that it skipped as she typed. She became irritated (negative affective response) and complained to her supervisor. The salesman was called and, very shortly, a serviceman arrived. As the serviceman entered the office he asked: "Is this the typewriter?" (It was the only one in the room.) "Yes, and it's a lemon," the secretary replied. The serviceman quickly made an adjustment on it and said, "You could have done that yourself if you had read the manual." The secretary, angrier than ever, said, "If it were a good machine, it wouldn't need fixing. I'm a secretary, not a mechanic." It is doubtful whether this customer will ever buy another typewriter from that firm. The serviceman adjusted the typewriter but ignored completely the feelings of the customer.

Cognitive Factors. The customer's mental processes induced by the salesman must also be considered in selling. Obviously, the sales presentation must be made so that it is understandable to each prospect or customer. Particularly in industrial sales work, technical features and properties of the line must often be explained to purchasing agents without technical or professional educational background. Concreteness of language and aptness of illustrations or examples often spell the difference between success or failure in a sales call.

Too frequently, salesmen interject trade jargon during a presentation. The prospect or customer, though not understanding it, is reluctant to betray his ignorance. As the call continues the person becomes more confused and the end result may be a lost sale.

Because the customer's needs and wants are the focus of the sale, the presentation should center upon customer benefits to be derived from the purchase rather than upon features and qualities of the product. An automobile salesman is likely to be more successful saying, "The horespower of this car gives you a fast pickup at a light," than stating, "This car has 315 horsepower." In general, benefits are more easily understood than product features. There is a personal stake in the former!

Table 8 summarizes the perceptual, affective, and cognitive differences between advertising and selling. The reader might find it a valuable exercise to make a table setting forth ways in which they are similar.

There is one other fundamental psychological difference between the two which warrants discussion. Advertising, necessarily, is designed to influence a mass audience; selling is most often directed to an individual prospect or customer. The former must, therefore, employ a *type* approach to human behavior. The latter can and should utilize a *trait* approach. A particular advertisement for a household detergent may contain a repertoire of appeals (stimuli) designed to influence all housewives who see it to purchase the product. The appeals may include economy, ease of storage, use with all kinds of fabrics. On the other hand, a housewife who had not seen the advertisement might be induced to buy the product by her local storekeeper, primarily because she wished something to wash her new dacron dress. Mention of the economy appeal might have blocked the sale. She might not have wanted to use an inexpensive detergent on her expensive dress.

TABLE 8

PERCEPTUAL, AFFECTIVE, AND COGNITIVE DIFFERENCES BETWEEN ADVERTISING AND SELLING

Advertising	Selling
Perceptual	
1. Most media, except television, stimulate only one sensory modality.	1. Vision and audition and sometimes other senses are stimulated.
2. Attention is voluntary once arrested.	2. Once salesman gets to see prospect, he has a "captive audience."
3. Message must be perceived in short time period, may be reinforced by repetition.	3. Message developed over a long time period, often on basis of several calls.
4. Often the full message is not perceived, e.g., dial is turned to another channel.	4. Salesman can leave with customer reminders of his visit, e.g., samples, descriptive literature.
Affective	
1. Once feelings are aroused, either positively or negatively, no immediate way to exploit or change them.	1. Feelings can be aroused *and changed* by the salesman during the call.
2. Negative feelings may permanently block purchase.	2. Negative feelings, if changed by salesman, may result in purchase.
3. Primary affective stimulus is the ad and its components.	3. Primary affective stimulus is the salesman and his behavior.
Cognitive	
1. Vocabulary, sentence structure, etc., must be understandable to *all* prospective purchasers.	1. Except in "canned sales talks," language and expression can be related to each prospect's background.
2. No direct method of knowing whether message is understood.	2. Prospect's responses indicate to the salesman whether his message is being received.
3. Brevity is at a premium.	3. Message can be expanded and stated in different ways.

The advertiser has to determine the characteristics held in common by those persons comprising the market for his products or services. This by inference reduces the market to a type. In contrast, the salesman has to learn the characteristics or traits of each individual prospect or customer. Each must be treated uniquely.

PSYCHOLOGICAL PRINCIPLES AND CONCEPTS APPLIED
TO ADVERTISING AND SELLING

Since this book is devoted to the application of psychology to business, it will be helpful to see, concretely, how various psychological principles and concepts are applied to advertising and selling.

Learning, an Active Process. Learning, as well as forgetting, involves active response to stimulation, as we discussed in the chapter on training. It is not surprising then that advertising, whatever the medium, repetitively suggests action, real or stimulated: "Try some today." "Road-test it and see." "Imagine yourself basking on the sands of Waikiki." "Let your taste be the judge." "Ask the man who owns one."

The effective salesman uses this principle every day in his work. When he uses a questioning approach in his calls, he induces action in the form of responses to his inquiries. During his presentation he urges the prospect to handle the sample, to operate the machine. He knows that the prospect must get into the act if a sale is to take place.

In both advertising and selling it is safe to say that the more action is induced, the greater the conviction or belief on the part of the prospect or customer. Ultimately, this means more sales!

Overlearning. The jingle used to advertise Pepsi-Cola had such an impact that the company found it could play the tune and omit the words and still get its message across. This is a dramatic example of overlearning. Brand-reinforcement advertising is designed to cause overlearning. Once a particular need is felt it is hoped that the company's brand line will be sought as *the* satisfier.

Storekeepers have reported housewives asking for "the tea Arthur Godfrey advertises." In this instance they may have learned the brand, but they did not have it at a point of automatic recall. They had overlearned the fact that the famous redhead advertised tea.

In successful selling it is necessary for the salesman to overlearn his products, especially the benefits to be derived from their use. If he has learned his product information only to the point of bare recall, he is likely to encounter difficulty. An unexpected question or reaction on the part of the customer may cause a mental block just when he needs a ready answer. If the salesman has to interrupt his presentation to check his price list or to find technical information, he is likely to lose the prospect's attention. Worse still, the customer's confidence in him as the knower may be undermined.

Similarly it is important for the salesman who expects repeat sales to overlearn the relevant facts about each of his accounts. Basically, this is a twofold body of knowledge. He has to know "who's who" and the traits of each person with whom he has contact. He also must know the uses the company makes of his products and the related production and marketing problems that require solution.

Temporal Summation. A commonplace example of this phenomenon is to be absorbed in a book, when the telephone rings. We may not be consciously aware of the sound until the phone has rung several times. We rush to answer it before it stops. All our sensory modalities are subject to temporal summation.

In advertising, repetition is used to penetrate the awareness of readers or listeners. It is no happenstance that repetitive jingles are effective in inducing the purchase of goods. Most companies keep their logo (special name plate of an advertiser, usually cast in unique lettering) the same over a period of years in advertising and packaging. The familiar *Coca-Cola* scroll is an effective example.[1] Similarly, companies maintain the same package shape and color to utilize temporal summation.

The salesman makes two general applications of this principle—during each call and on repeat calls. In the course of his sales presentation he may make the same point in several different ways. For example, a paper salesman calling on an industrial prospect wished to stress the shelf-life of his product in inventory. He said, "The last ream you draw from the storeroom will be as good as the first." "Our paper is treated so it won't fade." "The wrappers are sealed to keep out dust and moisture." "This paper won't curl and ripple after it's around for awhile."

In another instance, a salesman said, "I don't know what happened to that fellow today. I finally got an order. This was my fifth call on him." Perhaps the salesman honestly felt that the successful call was the last one. A more likely explanation, however, is that the successive calls had a *summating* effect on the prospect. The message finally got through to him. Where the nature of the business requires repeated calls to close the sale, or where repeat orders are sought, temporal summation is an important principle to employ. On each call the salesman should review with the prospect or customer the ground previously covered, and then build his presentation on that foundation.

Spatial Summation. The world around us is perceived through our several senses. Our nervous system is so structured that when the same stimulus is received through two or more of the senses, reinforcement of the message occurs.

Only television among the major advertising media illustrates this perceptual phenomenon. The TV commercial reaches the listener through both the eyes and the ears. Radio, magazines, newspapers, billboards, all depend on one sense to convey the advertising message. An important

[1] *Coca-Cola* is the registered trademark which distinguishes the product of The Coca-Cola Company. It is reproduced here by special permission.

research problem exists in television: how to maximize perception with visual and auditory stimuli available for simultaneous presentation.

In selling, the application of this principle is more widespread. Remember the dairy route man and his orange juice? This is an illustrative example of spatial summation. Most salesmen are provided with visual aids in the form of pictures, diagrams, descriptive literature, etc. When these are used to reinforce the oral presentation, the chance of getting the message across is increased and the likelihood of a sale is enhanced. However, if visuals are in sight at inappropriate times they may only serve to distract the prospect's or customer's attention from the salesman's message.

Affective Expansion. This peculiarity of human emotions and feelings has direct application in all forms of advertising. The testimonial of an attractive movie star may influence thousands of young girls to buy a particular cosmetic. If they love her, by affective expansion they like the product she uses. The chairman of the board of a well-known advertising agency once declared, "With a baby and a kitten for illustrations I can sell anything." This statement may be an exaggeration, but the fact remains that emotional appeals do induce people to buy.

It is important for the salesman to be aware of this characteristic of the feelings and emotions. His primary application of this principle is to customer behavior. However, he can also better understand his own adjustments, if he is aware of affective expansion. Every salesman is likely to have discouraging days when, despite his efforts, he fails to close a single sale. He must guard against letting his ill feelings become cumulative; otherwise he is apt to express them toward customers and prospects. It is sound planning for a salesman to make his first call on a satisfied customer, even if no order is in prospect. It will serve to build up his positive feelings and to bolster him for the more difficult calls that must be made later in the day.

Projection. People tend to perceive their own strengths and weaknesses, likes and dislikes, virtues and vices in others. Think about the gifts you have purchased for your family and friends. Didn't you buy things you would like to receive? If you have been in an automobile accident, or have witnessed one, you may have observed each driver blaming the other fellow, perhaps even accusing him of committing the very fault he himself was guilty of. Moyer and Gilmer [28] found that adults buying toys for children often buy those with parent appeal rather than those which have child appeal.

The advertising agency that bypasses research and structures a campaign on appeals that agency personnel like, rather than determining the likes and wants of the market, is using projection. The manufacturer of a well-known home permanent sought to enter the Latin American market. Erroneously the advertising campaign emphasized economy because this appeal had proven effective in the United States. Had research been done in advance, the advertiser would have known that the product did not compete in price with a wave done at the beauty parlor in any Latin American country. When sales proved disappointing, subsequent research revealed that safety was an effective appeal because of the ineptness of beauticians in that market. The same research, incidentally, revealed that there was an untapped market for home permanents, namely, young girls preparing for communion and confirmation. A modification of the product was manufactured for this juvenile market and subsequently also marketed in the United States.

The salesman, too often, is likely to stress in his presentation what he would like to hear were he the customer. The following anecdote from *The American Salesman* is illustrative:

A Manhattan real estate salesman and his wife were planning to have a family in the next few years and felt they should acquire a home in the suburbs and pay for it before the wife left her job. Their chief concern about a home in the suburbs was that it be located so as to ensure easy transportation to the heart of the city. They finally found one that met their needs. After a few months in their new residence, the salesman decided to sell suburban real estate rather than continue working in the city. As he showed various pieces of property to prospects, he continually pointed out the convenience of travel to and from the city. One of his prospects was completely unimpressed by his presentation and, as a result, sought the services of another real estate broker. Information later obtained indicated that the prospect was moving to the suburbs to get away from his troublesome mother-in-law; consequently, the last thing he wanted in a new home was to make it easy for her to reach him.

Rationalization. It is part of human adjustment to justify our behavior in our own eyes. Few persons can claim never to have used after-the-fact reasons for doing something. The extreme example of rationalization is the alibi artist. He always has a ready excuse for anything he says or does. This mechanism is illustrated daily in consumer advertising. "Limited quantity." "Order some now before the supply is exhausted." "Buy now; prices are going up." "These coats would cost twice as much in the regular season." As an experiment, scan the ads in your daily newspaper. See how many examples of rationalization you find. The advertiser who uses this principle attempts to provide reasons *in advance* for purchasing his product. It is especially effective with luxury items.

The salesman bases part of his strategy on rationalization. It is his job to furnish the prospect or customer with reasons for justifying the purchase of the goods or services he has for sale. An automobile salesman closed a sale with a customer just before the model change-over by using these points: "At this price your first year of depreciation is already deducted from the list price." "The new models have only minor changes."

"Financing rates are going up." "Think of the trips you can take before winter sets in." "The amount you save will pay your youngster's tuition for a whole year."

Functional Autonomy of Habits. Nowhere is this principle better illustrated in advertising and selling than in the cigarette industry. Well over two-thirds of the adolescent and adult population smoke cigarettes. Yet few people can tell you why they smoke. Heavy smokers often light up without being conscious of it. Companies in the industry strive to "brand lock" their customers. The marketing objective is to have the customer think not of a cigarette, but of Fumos!

A considerable amount of our behavior is a matter of habit. Habits, once established, are difficult to break. Brand-reinforcing advertising is designed to make a brand name a matter of habit in buying a particular item or line of goods. Often advertising copy contains such phrases as "Make it a habit to buy at. . . . "; "Fiftieth anniversary sale"; "A way of life for knowing people."

The salesman with a long-established account has a concrete example of the force of habit. His competitors have a difficult task to take away such a customer. The longer the seller-buyer relationship lasts, the less likely the customer is to change to another source of supply.

It is sound sales strategy to study carefully the habits of each customer. To the extent that the salesman knows them he is able to make buying from him a habit which fits into the habitual behavior of the customer. A salesman learned that a particular purchasing agent obtained purchase requisitions from the various departments of the plant each Friday afternoon. Habitually the purchasing agent took them home with him to study over the week end. The salesman also found out that he and the purchasing agent attended the same church. The salesman, without being obvious about it, arranged to meet the purchasing agent almost every Sunday and to chat with him on these occasions. The salesman also rearranged his call schedule so that he saw the purchasing agent on Monday mornings. The salesman reasoned that through the Sunday contacts he would become a part of the purchasing agent's thought processes regarding prospective purchases. The Monday morning calls provided the salesman an opportunity to interview him before his competitors got there.

CHANGES IN RESEARCH DIRECTIONS

Earlier in the chapter, research was mentioned as an integral part of the marketing mix. Properly designed and executed, research helps to provide answers to such questions as:

1. What is the market potential for a particular product?
2. What is the likely share of the market for brand X?

3. If a consumer product sold through retailers is involved, what are the best outlets for the product?

In psychological terms we might say that market research deals with "actual" and "likely" responses in the market place to marketing stimuli, especially to advertising, sales promotion, and selling. Recently attention has been given to a relatively new approach, *motivation research,* which is concerned with the "why" underlying buying behavior. The objective is to find out what happens inside the individual which prompts his response. Why is tea drinking perceived as feminine? Why are some words liked, others disliked? What feelings are aroused by car ownership? Why do people smoke? These are questions which might be investigated through motivation research.

Motivation research *is not* a substitute for market research. It adds meaning to cold statistics, such as the percentage of teen-agers who use home permanents, by indicating the satisfactions the users derive, the unique features they perceive in the brands they use, or what improvements they feel might be made in such a product. Motivation research has helped to indicate why particular products have not gained acceptance. Some advertising agencies use it to stimulate copy-writing ideas. It has shed considerable light on "product personality," i.e., the characteristics users attribute to a particular product. For example, motivation research revealed that a particular cigarette was feminine. An advertising campaign featuring he-men smokers complete with tatoos changed its gender in the minds and feelings of the smoking public.

One of the early psychologists in motivation research was Ernest Dichter [11] who wrote, in 1947, that in making marketing decisions, we should give attention to how people think and feel, in addition to paying attention to what they say.

The methods of motivation research have been derived from the behavioral sciences. For example, depth interviewing, projective tests and techniques, and free association have their origins in clinical psychology and psychoanalysis. Content analysis has been borrowed from sociology and anthropology. The following descriptions of these illustrative methods with examples and applications of findings suggest an understanding of what motivation research is, how it is conducted, and how results are used.

Depth Interviewing. In the use of this method, respondents are asked open-ended questions, which elicit conversation rather than one-word answers. Usually the first questions are as broad and general as possible. Subsequent ones are focused more directly on what is being sought. Extraneous matters may be interjected during the interview to mask the topic under investigation. To ensure fullness of response, interviewers use such methods as expectant pauses, interjections, such as "I see," "Uh-huh," and follow-up questions, such as, "Could you tell me more?"

Obviously, the skill of the interviewer, the degree of cooperation of the interviewee, the content covered, and the analysis of the data will influence the utility of the findings. Smith [36] points out three levels of awareness encountered in respondents:

1. *Material discussed,* e.g., women's preference for a cleanser with sudsing action.

2. *Material rarely discussed,* e.g., desire to impress one's neighbors with a bigger TV set.

3. *Material unanalyzed, not discussed,* e.g., the origins of some "common colds" in the need for attention and the loss of security.

The goal of the depth interview is to encompass all levels, especially level 3. Smith cites a study using this method in which it was found that candy eating tended to be "associated with the accomplishment of a job that the person who ate candy considered disagreeable. The candy was a sort of reward or compensation for doing a tough job." A switch in advertising theme from "smooth, rich, creamy-coated chocolate—everybody likes 'em" to "make that tough job easier—you deserve M and M candy" yielded a promising increase in sales.

Projective Tests and Techniques. The Rorschach, Murray's Thematic Apperception Test, and the Rosenzweig Picture-frustration Study have been used in motivational research. Adaptations of the latter two have been made to investigate special problems.

One investigation cites a study in which the Rorschach was used to determine personality characteristics of obese women compared with ideal-weight women, noting that "it helps to destroy the myth of the happy fat girl and to replace it with a picture of anxiety and introspection, of passivity and low energization toward a goal" [36]. A variant on the TAT was used in another study designed to determine attitudes toward magazine reading. "A picture was included which showed a family sitting in a living room reading. In making up stories for this picture, respondents revealed many of their views about magazines, the family and home, what the husband reads, what the wife reads, and so on."

Content Analysis. This has been defined as "a process of identifying and classifying certain elements of a verbal communication for the purpose of making quantitative statements about the content of the communication." It has use in the analysis of depth interviews and projective test protocols. Responses can be tallied according to an a priori classification, or the classification can be derived empirically. As an example of the former, it might be desired to find out how often like or dislike was expressed for the color of the wrapper of a package. The latter is illustrated by the study cited earlier of why people eat candy. Reward for the accomplishment of a distasteful job was derived from its recurrent mention by respondents.

Content analysis may also be applied to the analysis of a company's advertising copy as it has appeared in various media. This may be useful in itself, for example, to determine recurrent uses of words and phrases. It may provide a frame of reference for determining reader and listener reactions to elements of the advertisements.

A Professional Attitude. Industrial psychology today is giving increasing attention to the human aspects of marketing. It is critical of research techniques and it is critical of its own role in the marketing mix. Such an attitude, however, may add to the importance of psychology in its future relationships with advertising and selling.

SUGGESTIONS FOR FURTHER READING

Coleman, L. R. *The practice of successful advertising. Pydge Bus. J.*, Sydney, Australia, 1959. The applications of psychology to advertising at the practical level where research data are lacking.

Hepner, H. W. *Modern advertising: practices and principles.* New York: McGraw-Hill, 1956. Written by a psychologist, this book goes into the fundamentals of advertising and selling.

Husband, R. W. *The psychology of successful selling.* New York: Harper, 1953. A description of the psychological principles underlying salesmanship.

Katona, G. *The powerful consumer.* New York: McGraw-Hill, 1960. A research-oriented book of economic psychology related to consumer attitudes, social groupings, levels of aspiration, and economic fluctuations.

McNair, M. P., & Hansen, H. L. *Readings in marketing.* New York: McGraw-Hill, 1956. An over-all view of the marketing mix.

Martineau, P. *Motivation in advertising.* New York: McGraw-Hill, 1957. A discussion of motivation research and buying.

19

THE INDUSTRIAL
COMMUNITY

B. von Haller Gilmer

With the increasing effort of states and local communities to obtain new industries, and with the desire of industry to improve its public relations within the local community, a new emphasis is being given to industry-community cooperation. The problem, however, is not simple, for we must remember that the union also enters the picture in the struggle for power and status. What kind of people does industry like to see in a community? Why do communities seek certain types of new industries? How have technological changes affected community living? Does absentee ownership lead to bad labor relations? Is a man's work affected by the community in which he lives? Should the local plant manager strive for leadership within the community? These are the types of questions we will deal with in this chapter. Modern industry can no longer ignore the fact that how a man lives is related to how he works.

IMPORTANCE OF KNOWING THE COMMUNITY

Social scientists have long been interested in the human problems of industry-community relations. Psychologists are interested not only in the man at work, but also in how the place where he lives affects his work, his attitudes, and his productivity. With the increasing diversifications within industry, with the dispersion of plants into the rural areas, and with the growth of the new suburbia, understanding the industrial community itself is becoming more and more important to the psychologist.

American industry is becoming increasingly aware of the importance of the *human relations* factors in seeking plant locations. To indicate this growing awareness, let us quote a portion of a letter from the president of a medium-sized corporation to an industrial consultant.

Our industrial engineering department is favorably disposed to having us locate our new processing plant just outside of the town of Middlebrook. The town is well located in terms of raw materials, transportation facilities, and markets. We are told that we can be given favorable tax rates. Before we take option on various properties in the region, we would like to have you survey the community and get us answers to such questions as: What is the potential labor supply of men in the age bracket of 20 to 50? What is the potential supply of women for seasonal and part-time employment? What kind of people live there? What are the attitudes of these people toward organized labor? Who runs the town? What are the prevailing wage rates for skilled and unskilled labor? How prosperous are the nearby farmers? Are there enough people we could select locally who could fill our needs for foremen within a reasonable period of time?

The letter continued with the request that, if the labor supply looked good and if a program of selection, training, and orientation of workers could be worked out, the consultant also try to determine what the company would need to do in the way of public relations in order to gain acceptance in the community?

Why is industry paying more attention to the human environment? Although answers to this question depend on many circumstances and change with different locales, one historical example can give us a conceptual base for better understanding the problems of industrial behavior, namely, the Yankee City studies [16].

THE YANKEE CITY STUDIES

Yankee City is the fictitious name given to a real town founded early in the 1600s on a harbor at the mouth of a large river in New England. When these studies began, during the early thirties, there were some seventeen thousand people living there. Slightly over half of the population were born in or near the town; a little less than a quarter of the population were foreign-born; and the remainder were born elsewhere in the United States. About one-fourth of the employable population worked in the shoe industry.

The purpose of the studies was to find out through the gathering of economic data, through the observations of individual and group behaviors, and through intensive interviewing, how the worker in the plant, his activities, and his attitudes are related to the total community in which he lives. The worker brings his outside life with him into the factory; when he returns home at night to his family and friends, he takes part of his factory life with him. How do these two lives influence each other?

An Old Community. Yankee City's social make-up had become firmly organized over a long period of time and the relations of the various members of the society were exactly placed and known by the individuals who made up the group. The town had a life of its own; it was not a satellite of a large metropolitan area. An intensive study of the total community was made by putting field men in various strategic places. Some went into factories to observe the behavior and relationships there; others were placed among the workers at home. Still others conducted interviews and collected budgets. Some men were put to work studying associations; others investigated the churches. The community gave wholehearted cooperation to the researchers. Personal data were gathered on practically all of the seventeen thousand men, women, and children of Yankee City.

In Yankee City's social system, economic wealth did not guarantee the highest social position. People were ranked by the members of the community into socially superior and socially inferior positions. Members of a class tended to marry within their own group, although marriages up and down did occur. One could better himself by a "fine marriage" or lower his status by "marrying beneath himself." Some wealthy families were found outside the top-status class because "they do not belong to the right families," "they do not go around with the right people," "they don't know how to act." The researchers found that if a man's education, occupation, wealth, income, family, intimate friends, clubs and fraternities, as well as his manners, speech, and general outward behavior were known, it was not difficult for his fellow citizens to give a fairly exact estimate of his status. It was easy to classify the whole community in terms of a status hierarchy.

The profile of Yankee City then could be said to be like that of many other towns of its size, age, and location, with its "old families" and "new families," "the people on the 'hill' and those who live in the 'flats,' " those who were "going up in the world" and those "on the way down."

The largest and most important industry in Yankee City was shoe manufacturing. Other industries included building trades, transportation, clamming, and silverware manufacturing. At the time of the studies, a number of workers classed as auto-body and cotton textile employees were unemployed, since these industries had left the city and surrounding areas. Farming was a negligible pursuit in the economic life of the town. Four different faiths cared for the religious needs of the Yankee City community; the majority of the population were of the Protestant faith. The schools were typical of those in a New England community of this size.

Although the voters among the lower classes far outnumbered those in the higher classes, they had a disproportionately small percentage of officers in the political hierarchy.

The Community's First Strike. This was Yankee City in March, 1933, the year of *the strike*. As strikes go, it was a small one, involving only seven shoe factories and 1,500 workers. It involved little money; and it was not a rough strike, in terms of people getting physically hurt or property being damaged. The strike did not even last long, only a month. But at Yankee City it was important, because it occurred at a time when the city was being studied by a team of social anthropologists. The record of the dramatic conflict in this small town represents the most complete and definitive study we have of the factory in the community and what the problems of *people* are during a community crisis. It tells us about the nature of human needs and how people in groups react to frustration. It gives us at least some insight into the nature of industrial behavior.

Here in the worst year of the Great Depression all the workers in all the factories of the principal industry in the Yankee City community walked out. They struck with little or no warning. Management had said the workers would never strike, for they were sensible and dependable, and through a long peaceful history had proved they would always stay on the job. Even union men outside the city agreed that the workers could not be organized. Most of the townspeople said the workers would never strike—but they did.

The strike went through three phrases. First, the workers organized themselves, joined an industrial union, and became strong union members. Management was unsuccessful in regaining control over the workers. The second period began with frontal attacks on management. The union won the support of the public, and most of Yankee City sided with the strikers. Finally, mediation and peace negotiations began when the government stepped in and, after a series of negotiations, helped end the strike.

The researchers talked with people all over the city and questioned them about the strike. The answers tended to reveal more about the life and status of the men who talked than about the causes of the strike. The secrets of the strike seemed to lie in the whole life of the community in which the workers and owners were but a part. Five "why" questions basic to the whole problem soon came out.

Why the Workers Struck. In a community where there had been very few strikes and *no* successful ones in a 300-year history, why did the workers in *all* the shoe factories strike, win all their demands, and after a severe struggle, soundly defeat management?

Why in a "nonunion community" could a union be successful in separating the workers from management?

Why was the union successful in organizing *all* the workers in *all* the shoe factories in the community?

Why was the union successful despite efforts to break it up?

Why did Yankee City change from a nonunion to a union town almost overnight?

All groups in the Yankee City community became involved in the strike. Each person interviewed had his own version of the cause of the crisis: the people blamed economic factors associated with the Depression; they blamed minority groups; and they blamed a dozen other things. One old lady put the problem in a nutshell: "Our todays are made out of yesterday. In fact, sometimes I think we are yesterday."

Technology and Social Change. For some 300 years, Yankee City had grown slowly, and rigid class structures had become ingrained in the community. Status differences were apparent at every level. In the nineteenth century, the worker accepted the role of dependent child, and the owner or the manager played the role of humanitarian or kind father, who knew what was best. By the early part of the twentieth century, the managers of industry acted like gods: "They had become the heroes to labor as well as to management." In short, Yankee City had come to accept paternalism as the normal pattern of human relationships, not only in the shoe industry, not only in worker-employer relationships, but also in the totality of community life.

Following the long history of Yankee City paternalism came the influence of technological development and economic change. Shoemaking had progressed from the early times when the family was the productive unit through the periods of early and late small-city capitalism. By the beginning of the 1930s, mass production was in effect, the machine dominated the industry, *and* control had shifted to the new owners in New York City. The Depression was on, and before national relief appeared on the scene, fears and antagonisms raised among the workers by their economic *and* psychological position helped to precipitate the strike, a community strike as it were.

Local townspeople contributed to strike funds. Sympathy with the strikers came from small merchants and other business people of comparable status with the workers. Technological changes had hampered the chances of a man's working his way up. Instead of a simple, universally agreed upon hierarchy of statuses in technological jobs, the researchers found the situation to be confused and tense; there was suspicion and conflict between workers and managers. Confusion spread into the community itself. More than just a skill hierarchy was lost when the manufacture of shoes shifted from a craft industry into the mass-production pattern. A feeling of worker pride was lost. The skill hierarchy which had dominated the very lives of the workers and helped establish their place in the community was gone.

The workers had many frustrations in common. They dismissed small differences among themselves and united in one industrial union, national in scope. They were now part of a growing labor movement.

In the early days of the shoe industry, the owners and managers were residents of Yankee City. Their loyalties were in the community. There were feelings of neighborliness and friendship between worker and manager and feelings of mutual community responsibilities. The local owners were accepted leaders of the community.

When absentee ownership took over Yankee City, and manufacturers' associations and labor unions grew strong, the "local boy" managers who remained on their jobs lost both power and status. In the eyes of the workers, the "father figure" had changed. In the days before big-city financiers took control, the local enterpriser was financed by Yankee City banks. The people made their investments locally. These local leaders of finance who were subject to local control, influenced by sentiments within the community, lost status also. There was a resentment on the part of these nonworker groups against the outside operators.

The extension of the industrial hierarchy to the big city reduced the local leaders to inferior positions in the hierarchy where they were incapable of making decisions and could not initiate actions which would give them the power to lead the workers and the rest of the town.

Thus Yankee City offers us one picture of a way in which business and industry were closely integrated with the community. Time changed a way of life. What happened in Yankee City gives us an idea of the importance of community human relations as well as individual human relations.

DIFFERENT TYPES OF COMMUNITIES

Paternalism has very few advocates today. Its decline has been due to the breakdown in the isolation of industrial villages. Industrial plants have grown in size and organization to such an extent that paternalism would be most impractical. With the growth of unions, the worker is no longer suited to the role of the dependent child.

The Boom Town. Much of the global picture of human relations problems in industry can be seen through descriptions of various types of industrial communities. The company-dominated community has its advantages and disadvantages for worker-manager relationships. Boom towns and mushroom communities have their peculiar problems. A different pattern of community living was established at Oak Ridge, Tennessee, in 1942: in three years, 75,000 people gathered to live in this town in a "semi-hush-hush" manner where special interest clubs became a basis for social relationships.

A Steel Town. Another community, described by Walker in the book *Steeltown,* gives us a somewhat different picture of the social variables in the industrial community [14]. Here is a steel town of 14,000 people, Ellwood City, Pennsylvania, where there are few status differences of importance. In contrast to the 300-year-old Yankee City, this steel town was established around the turn of the century. People had moved there voluntarily to work in steel plants. The managers always lived near workers, and still do. Worker-manager relations are a part of "big steel"; few real decisions are made at the local level. It is most unlikely that Ellwood City will ever show community behavior similar to that of the Yankee City crisis. The communities are just different and always have been.

The Industrial South. With the recent industrialization of the South, still another kind of community can be found in which labor has not been readily accepted, where strikes are hard to foment when the industry is locally owned and operated. Labor has had more organizational success in the South where industry control is not local, but labor organizers have found that organizational techniques used up North had to be modified to conform to the community patterns of the South.

The New Suburbia. What may be a threat to one community, such as the moving in of a minority group, may prove to be an asset to another. Racial or ethnic discrimination and social or economic stratification, with their related fears and resentments, help determine community patterns. The community not only contributes to the security or insecurity of the individual, but is a place where behaviors can be manifested through informal organizations. One interesting description of how this can occur is found in some examples of the new suburbia described in Whyte's *Organization Man* [18].

In contrast with the rigidities of the traditional community, where interlocking family relationships fix the individual's position and where he can move upward only by sanction of the next upper group, we find that the new suburbia offers more in the way of classlessness.

Levittown, Pennsylvania, is representative of a type of the new suburbia where the goal is not to keep up with the Joneses; rather, it is, as Whyte puts it, to "keep down with them." Conspicious display is frowned upon. Even in a single neighborhood, an item which would be quite acceptable in one block might be regarded as flagrant showing off in another. True, the new suburbia is fraught with problems and conflicts as is any other community, but here a man is more on his own in his chances for upward mobility. This melting pot of people from many industries, of men with many interests and varied backgrounds, is a growing pattern of a community life which contrasts with the Yankee Cities and Steeltowns. The more education the person has, the more mobility he shows. The higher the educational level, the more extensive is the migration.

One study shows, for example, that of those who worked their way through college outside their home state, 69 per cent did not return [3].

And it is of interest that long-distance movers report that almost half of their business is composed of company people being transferred from one place to another.

As the seats of economic power continue to shift from local institutions to national organizations, the middle-management group of people will move more often, some "up" and some "out." The new suburbia provides something of a temporary home for the interim, not unlike army-post life for the family.

The new suburbia helps provide a place of "declassification" of people from the older standards of family background. It is a new chance for a new social order where personal tastes and even religious affiliations change. But for many there is always the fear of "slipping back."

The Large City. Within a city proper there are many and varied communities. Miller and Form [8] have shown that the uneven distribution of rent and occupations in the large city supports the notion that the city is made up of a lot of local and self-contained industrial neighborhoods which are relatively isolated from one another. The lack of interaction among these neighborhoods reinforces the prejudices that each group has toward the others. Some of the tensions of work may well be related to the fact that, the larger the city, the less its different segments appreciate the lives, habits, institutions, and culture of those in other areas.

How a man lives may well be related to the way he works, thinks, and acts. In one large city, there are two railroads belonging to a steel empire. One railroad, which serves a number of steel mills, is located within city boundaries, and most of its workers live in crowded, run-down, "tough" neighborhoods. This railroad has a history of frequent labor complaints, strikes, and threats of strikes. The other railroad, owned and managed by the same people, serves as a connection between the steel mills and ore supply. It employs about the same number of people. This railroad has a history of good labor relations and few strikes. Its workers live in small settlements along the railroad, and, for the most part, own their modest homes and a couple of acres of land. Although the workers of both railroads receive the same pay rates and belong to the same national union, their behavior on the job is different. One reason for this difference seems apparent to the common management of the two railroads: the community way of living affects job satisfactions.

POWER STRUCTURES IN THE COMMUNITY

We have seen in the Yankee City studies how power in the community shifted away from industry as paternalism died out and absentee management took over; in its place, the union found acceptance and power. Variations of this power shift and struggle in the last two decades have been duplicated all over the country. As communities have grown in size, common participation by the entire population has decreased. Businessmen who long held an advantage over the workers through organization, legal knowledge, and resources have found that national unions can now compete with them on even terms. Both power groups have become public relations conscious. They vie for community approval and compete with each other in providing community service programs, athletic teams, and youth organizations. But out of this power struggle has come much good. As one looks at the successful growth of community charities, one sees that they have been made possible by labor and management organizations joining in harmony with each other and with the rest of the community. Both the union and industry have learned the importance of good community relations. Social welfare has developed as one area in which the two can cooperate *and* compete. National union leaders have extended their welfare activities beyond union membership. In the struggle for power, the "lack of welfare" can become a threat to union loyalty and allegiance.

Competition for Power. Both management and labor are conscious of trying to win the loyalty of the workers. They struggle for the confidence of both the workers and the community. One's loss may be the other's gain. We have seen industry lose the power struggle in Yankee City. We have an example of the union losing status and membership in the recent Teamsters' Union difficulties.

Labor and management both have a stake in education, and in local, state, and national politics. Labor-union attempts to influence formal education have been limited primarily to participating in educational conferences at the college level and trying to influence local school systems to abstain from antilabor teaching at the high school level. Industries, on the other hand, have become a primary source of support to independent colleges and for years have supplied funds for huge college scholarship and fellowship programs. At the secondary school level, particularly in the vocational skills, industry has had a marked influence on education. The Du Pont Company, for example, has an elaborate program for supplying educational information on our free-enterprise system; this information has been successfully integrated with the regular courses in a number of schools. At the higher education level, the Standard Oil Company of New Jersey has been most progressive in setting up top-level conferences between college teachers and industrial leaders. Such programs, of course, are not antilabor in any sense, but are designed to acquaint educators with the philosophies of industry. Fortunately for education, the public schools have not become an area where labor and management have fought for power.

In the area of leisure and recreation, labor is going all out to win community support in its power struggle for the workers' loyalty. During working hours, industry has control over the worker. A good work situation itself can provide an excellent medium for building up loyalty to the company, and this threatens loyalty to the union. To combat this, union locals have turned their attention to getting the workers together for cards, beer, athletic events, and family picnics, since they have long since found out that, save for emergency situations, union meetings themselves draw small audiences of members. So successful have the unions been in using the leisure time of workers, that management is beginning to support more of what once was regarded as recreational "frills." Businessmen are learning that cliques formed at work often feed back into community activities in ways that reinforce group ties between industry and the community.

THE BUSINESS CLIMATE

The business climate has been defined as the net result of all "outside conditions" affecting the cost and ease of operating a business in a community. These conditions may be social, economic, or political, and they may have their origin at the local, state, or national level. These conditions represent such tangible things as tax rates and such intangible things as the general attitude of the community toward the business.

The success of any industry depends upon employees, customers, stockholders, and related businesses; and management has long been conscious of this. More recently, however, the business climate has come to be a new dimension of management responsibility.

Business-climate Elements. The General Electric Company has been in the forefront in applying survey methods to appraise the business climate in the community. Some of the questions used in their appraisal guide require answers based on observation and judgment. Others require extensive investigation to come up with accurate facts and figures [2].

General Electric has determined that a favorable business climate is a composite of some eight elements:[1]

1. COMMUNITY PROGRESSIVENESS: A realistically progressive attitude on the part of political, religious, and professional leaders toward sound community growth and city planning, along with citizen understanding of community and business problems.

2. GOVERNMENT: Honest and efficient government, supported by a safe majority of alert, intelligent voters who have the balanced best interests of the community at heart, with an absence of unreasonably restrictive regulations or financial handicaps imposed by the local, state, and federal governments.

3. LABOR RELATIONS: A sound working relationship between employers and employees as evidenced by an absence of unwarranted strikes and slowdowns over a number of years and, where collective bargaining contracts are in effect,

[1] Reproduced here by permission of the General Electric Company.

a constructive and fair union leadership which acts as the servant rather than the master of its membership.

4. PEOPLE: An adequate supply of people to fill employment needs who have a good work attitude, who are properly educated, who are in good physical condition, and who have a good understanding of how our business system operates and their stake in its success.

5. LABOR COSTS: Wage and salary rates and payment methods which are fair to employees, and at the same time provide an opportunity for employers to operate profitably in competition with other manufacturers of their product lines.

6. COMMUNITY SERVICES & FACILITIES: Adequate community services and facilities such as banks, hotels, utilities, shopping facilities, health facilities, and the required commercial services needed in operating businesses.

7. SOCIAL, CULTURAL & EDUCATIONAL INSTITUTIONS: A social and cultural atmosphere that will attract and hold good professional employees, including good and adequate schools, an enlightened press, radio and TV, and an abundance of healthful recreational opportunities.

8. BUSINESS CITIZENSHIP: A serious-minded assumption of business citizenship responsibilities on the part of all employers in the community as evidenced by consistently good employee relations and courageous leadership in civic and political affairs.

General Electric reports that the payoff in business-climate research is somewhat analogous to the payoff in product research: both are long-term propositions. Years of time, effort, and money may be required before an investment in product research begins to net a return in sales and profits, and so it is with business-climate research. The same sustained effort is required in evolving marketable products from research.

To a large extent the measure of any business climate is a measure of people's behavior. And the attitudes and behaviors of people are related to community classes. Let us now take a look at this aspect of the industrial community.

COMMUNITY CLASSES

Much has been written about classes of people by anthropologists, sociologists, psychologists, and other behavioral scientists. In the following sections of this chapter, we wish simply to present those descriptions which we feel are relevant to understanding some of the human problems of the industrial community. These descriptions have been selected from many scholarly writings.

White-collar Workers and Wageworkers. Any small industrial community may be divided, in general terms, into three social classes: the manager group, the wageworkers, and somewhere in between and sharing characteristics of both, the white-collar workers.

White-collar people share with wageworkers the characteristic that they both rely on occupation rather than property for their source of income. Mills [9], in his book *White Collar,* points out that in the early nineteenth century probably four-fifths of the occupied population were self-employed enterprisers. At the present time, only about one-fifth of the people come within this category. The four-fifths of the people who now earn a living do so by working for the 2 or 3 per cent of the population who own 40 or 50 per cent of the private property in this country. This four-fifths includes both wageworkers and white-collar workers. The importance of the white-collar worker may be indicated partly by the fact that the selling of services, which determines the livelihood of most white-collar workers, has grown until the money now paid out for "services" exceeds that paid out for "things."

Though white-collar employees and wageworkers are alike in that they are both without income from property, their characteristics differ in other respects. In terms of prestige, white-collar employees claim higher status than wageworkers. Partly, this is assured, because their income in general is higher. But they also gain status because they live on prestige borrowed from the firm itself; they are the assistants of authority, and hence exercise a derived power. Psychologically, white-collar groups have successfully claimed and maintained more prestige than wageworkers. How permanent this position will remain is in question. Its defense is a part of the power struggle now going on between management and labor organizations.

White-collar workers are themselves divided into two groups, particularly in a smaller community. The higher group includes high-income salesmen and professional and managerial employees. The lower group includes clerks and sales persons. Despite this clear distinction, members of the wageworking class blend all white-collar workers, both higher and lower, into a group called "business" and make little distinction between them. To them, these "business" people are all "pencil pushers who sit around and don't work."

Views about the Management World. The white-collar workers and the wageworkers have diverse pictures of management. To the worker, management is "something one reports to in the office," "the printed instruction," "a sign on the bulletin board." To the white-collar group, management is "one-part people who give you the nod, one-part system, one-part yourself." Mills makes the point that, as one of the managed sees it, "you are on view from above. The money you handle is somebody else's money, the papers you sort and shuffle already bear somebody else's marks. You are the servant of decision, the assistant of authority."

Of course, to the people at the top, management is the place where power is concentrated. Management sees its job as one of making both wageworkers and white-collar workers feel a part of the organization and willing to carry out company policy and procedures. Communication between top and bottom must be so structured, management believes, that commands can go down and be understood and accepted, and that information can come up and be understood and acted upon. Thus, the image of itself which management presents to each of the other groups is very important.

Influences within the City. In the city, industrial influence is different. Human relations are more impersonal. White-collar workers live apart from wageworkers as well as from top-management people. A look at Figure 19.1, taken from the work-plant ecology study of Miller and Form [8] shows the residential distribution of male semiskilled workers in Flint, Michigan. From this map one can see that these workers are not distributed evenly over the city. They tend to live around those plants which employ them. Kantner [4] has shown that within a one-mile radius of each of these General Motors factories rents are lower than average for the city. There was apparently selective recruitment in these communities. Here they are to a large extent "company communities," but each is a self-contained neighborhood isolated from the other.

This isolation, and the communication patterns which grow up, may account for the tension between industry and various parts of the community, conclude Miller and Form. They go on to generalize that, the larger the city, the less its different segments appreciate the lives, institutions, and culture of those in other areas.

Resistances to Change. When work and residence are in the same neighborhood, the community is more family oriented than in those instances where the breadwinner has to travel distances to work. There is evidence to show that a man may be unhappy about a promotion, if it means breaking into established habit structures. The author is familiar with one such case which led one man to ask for his old job back.

Jack was a general supervisor for a railroad. He had worked his way up from trainman over a period of twenty years. He had lived in the house where he was born nearly forty years earlier. Jack was a respected "white-collar" leader in the community of 25,000 inhabitants and enjoyed his "businessman's" status. Promotion into headquarters of the railroad in a city of some 1,500,000 people was offered Jack, and he accepted the new job. He was quite successful as far as the technical aspects of the job were concerned, but he was very unhappy about being in a "new suburbia" of the city. In less than two years he asked for a transfer back to his old supervisory job in his home town. When I asked him why he was willing to give up status and more pay to return home, his answer was simple—"I liked my old way of life better."

No doubt there are those who would dislike moving from the city to the country. People resist change, perhaps they resist change in community living habits as much as or more than changes in habits of work. This

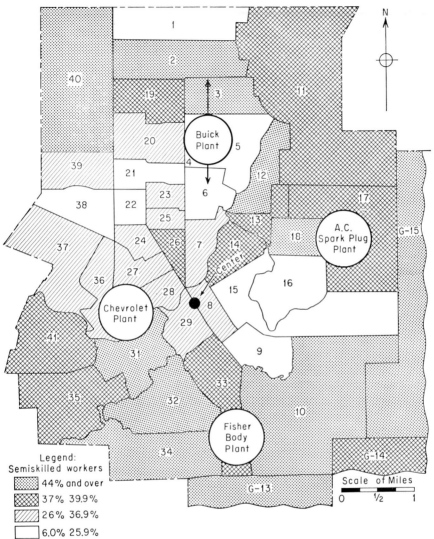

Fig. 19.1. Four major factories of Flint, Michigan. An ecological study of Flint shows that around each of its four main plants low socioeconomic areas appear. Most male workers in these mill circles are semiskilled and are employed in neighboring plants. This map indicates selective recruitment of industrial labor in the urban community. To a large extent these are "company communities," each of which is a self-contained neighborhood. (From Miller, D. C., & Form, W. H. *Industrial sociology*. New York: Harper, 1951.)

is a problem that has to be reckoned with in moving industries. Industrial decentralization may mean changing the routines of the city dweller as he moves to the smaller town. Here he finds things "too small." It may mean just as big a change for the farmer who turns to the factory to supplement his income. He finds things "too large." Thus we can see how, apart from uprooting both groups from their past social patterns, the rural-urban conflict can become a morale problem within the plant itself.

Work Shifts. With the decline in agriculture many rural workers are virtually forced into industry. Although a few divide their time between working on the farm and in the factory, more and more are migrating to industrial communities. Here they find almost everything different from their previous mode of living. One of the biggest problems in adjustment is having the "workday" come in the middle of the night. The U.S. Department of Labor points out that more and more industries are employing second and third shifts during "good times." One-third of the production workers in the automobile industry normally work other than in the daytime.

With the growth of continuous-process manufacturing, many machines have to be manned around the clock. In the plastics industry, for example, it is not economically feasible to shut down certain machines. It costs too much to get them heated up properly, and stopping the operation gums up the liquid materials. Again, many plants are so costly to build that they have to be kept going two or three shifts to justify the capital expenditures.

For men on the second or third shift, family life is all but disrupted. Particularly is this true where more than one member of a family works. Coordinating shifts or "turns" within a family is almost impossible, since turns for any one man change so often.

COMMUNITY TIES

Arensberg [1] emphasizes the importance of knowing how people live in order to understand the relationship between community and industry. Although the tie between work and community may often be indirect, it is most important. He illustrates the point through a firsthand observation of the behaviors underlying a paper mill strike. Fortunately for his study, he was accepted by both union and management. Each gave him access to records and allowed him to hold interviews both on and off the job.

The strike, it turned out, had been called by the paper-machine crew. To management it seemed strange, since this particular department was not involved in an incentive scheme which had been introduced in the cutting room. The incentive scheme was said to be the reason for calling the strike. But why would another department, seemingly unaffected, call the men out? To management, unaccustomed to thinking about the close relationship between the work situation and the community, it seemed incomprehensible that men, in no way connected during working hours with the crucial department, should feel themselves aggrieved.

On investigation it was found that the company's incentive scheme had its effects at a level, as Arensberg put it, "far beyond the formal industrial relationships prescribed by the company's organization chart." The two sets of workers were bound by ties of kinship and by traditional patterns of age and occupational prestige, entirely outside the factory. The company's engineers had done far more than merely provide a better output in a single working department. They had, in fact, reversed the customary patterns of authority. The new incentive scheme had set juniors and inferiors to hurrying up their seniors and superiors. The machine-room men had struck against the disturbance of their community.

This incident brings out another important point when we consider problems of classes. Here we find illustrated the lack of perception on the part of management of the way the workers look at problems. Differences in "class perception" often underly industrial conflict, even though something more specific may be named as the cause.

SOCIAL FORCES WITHIN THE COMMUNITY

Whether one comes from the city, the town, or the rural community, he is aware, somewhat at least, of the system of caste and class which governs American life. He is interested in getting a picture of the social influences shaping his own career. The college student has no doubt seen firsthand instances where some families have stayed at one level for generations, while others rise to the top and stay, or fall to the bottom. What are the factors that determine social position; what is the subtle interplay of education, money, profession, club and business associations that builds the social pyramid? What are the secrets which have made some men victims of downward mobility and carried others to high places of power and prestige? Such were the questions that led to Warner's study of a representative community in the Midwestern part of the United States. In his book, *Democracy in Jonesville,* Warner [15] describes the social forces that make the American community run. He and his associates began their studies during World War II; they continued for most of a decade. In the pages to follow we shall summarize some of the findings of this unusual study.

The Jonesville Study. Jonesville, a code name, has a population of a little more than six thousand people. It is a town where, in terms of social hierarchy, "everybody knows everybody's place." The upper class divides into old families and new families. The first group includes those who have enjoyed wealth and position for several generations, or those who have managed to retain their social position despite loss of much of their wealth. The new families include those who have climbed into top position and have succeeded in being accepted by those already there. Not every wealthy family reaches the top position. This upper class constitutes less than 3 per cent of the population in Jonesville.

The upper-middle class, active in all community activities, have less wealth than those at the top. They are the prominent, substantial people to whom common men often pay deference. But they are anxious people, fearful of doing something wrong and ruining their chances for advancement. They are constantly on the alert to enter into worthy civic enterprises, particularly those of which the elite are active sponsors.

Among the people who "belong to nice families but are nobody socially" are the small shopkeepers, the skilled workers, and the clerks. Below these are the little people, the poor but honest workers who live around the mill in the less well kept part of town. Finally comes a fifth lower-lower class who live across the tracks.

The young people of each class tend to marry at their own level. Their children acquire the status of the parents, learn their way of life, and help ensure the permanence of the class system. The citizens of Jonesville know and think about class behavior, and this knowledge is one of the basic guides to proper and adaptive behavior for them all.

In Jonesville, as in all American communities, the class structure is fluid. Families or individuals may not remain in one class. Mobility may be up or down. People do not quite openly admit that there are different classes, yet through their actions they place themselves and each other in a social class. While the boy from across the tracks does not often reach the mansion, he frequently ends up with a small business on Main Street. On the other hand, there is also downward mobility. Whether movement is up or down, in or out of social groups, the social class of a person's family is the zero point for indicating a change in status.

Mobility Indicators. Eight categories of indicators of mobility emerged from the studies. First comes *educational difference.* This is a prerequisite for mobility into, or through, the middle classes. Second comes *occupational variance,* where a person is in an occupation which is evaluated as different from that of his father's status. This is basic to socioeconomic status. *Membership transference,* such as becoming a member of the Rotary Club, indicates a movement into upper-middle-class status. A fourth area of change seen in upward mobility Warner has called *activity deviation,* exemplified by the man who changes his church affiliation to improve prestige.

A fifth pattern of mobility up and down is the *clique change,* where the mobile person meets socially with individuals who have a different status from the one he or his family held originally. Related to this is a sixth factor, *role revision,* where to move upward a person must be accepted and evaluated positively by others; he must adapt the roles he plays to his new social position.

Interclass marriage is a seventh aspect of mobility, which more often results in a change of social status for the woman than for the man. Acceptance of a woman who marries a man of high status doesn't always come easily. Her behavior is carefully observed and related to her background.

The eighth factor related to mobility is the *residential movement.* Where one lives is a very strong symbol of status.

THE STRUGGLE FOR UPWARD MOBILITY

What makes people want to move up? Certainly upward mobility is related to progress, at both the individual and the group level, but at what price? Some psychiatrists have voiced the opinion that the struggle for upward mobility is one of the big contributing causes of mental illness in the United States.

There are two aspects of mobility. The *situation* the person finds himself in is of importance. The person is given opportunity to move ahead employment-wise by the offer of a job, or he finds himself trapped in a situation where he has to work his way out and up. The situational conditions favoring or hindering upward mobility are many. As a rule, they are easy to spot. It is more difficult, however, to get at the second aspect involved in mobility: *personal motivation.*

Levels of Aspiration. Before we go on with the subject of mobility, however, let us consider some experimental studies on *levels of aspiration.* Here, in a simpler setting, we can find some useful facts for our consideration. Lewin, Dembo, Festinger, and Sears [6] have discussed the many facets of the subject. They pose the following simple problem: A person has scored 6 in shooting at a target with ring 10 at the center. He decides the next time to try for 8. He attains 5, is much disappointed, and decides to try the next time to reach 6 once more.

Within such a sequence there are four main points as illustrated in Figure 19.2.

Here in our level-of-aspiration situation, the subject begins a typical sequence of events. His last performance ("has scored 6") has set his level of aspiration for the next performance ("try for 8"). The new performance was below what he tried for ("attains 5"); hence, there is a "goal discrepancy." The difference between the goal level and that of the new performance is the "attainment discrepancy." This difference is one of the bases of the reaction at point 4 in the figure.

In our example the subject is really trying to hit center. This is his ideal goal. Knowing that this is too difficult for him, at least at the present, he sets his goal at 8, his "action level." It is the level of the action goal which is usually taken as the criterion for the level of aspiration for an individual at a given time. It has been found that nearly all individuals of Western culture, when first exposed to a level-of-aspiration situation, give initially a level of aspiration which is above the previous performance, and under most conditions tend to keep the goal discrepancy positive.

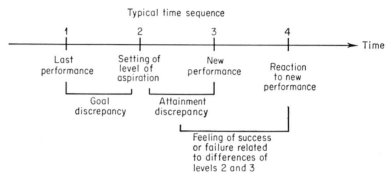

Fig. 19.2. Level of aspiration. Four main points are distinguished in a typical sequence of events in a level-of-aspiration situation: (1) last performance, (2) setting of level of aspiration for the next performance, (3) new performance, and (4) psychological reaction to the new performance. The difference between the level of the last performance and that of the new goal is called "goal discrepancy." The difference between the goal level and that of the new performance is called "attainment discrepancy." This difference is one of the bases of the reaction at (4). (From Lewin, K., Dembo, T., Festinger, L., & Sears, P. S. Levels of Aspiration. In Hunt, J. McV. (Ed.), *Personality and behavior disorders.* Vol. I, New York: Ronald, 1944. Pp. 333–378.)

Generalizations about Aspirations. Being a realist about it, the individual will place his expectation somewhere within the boundary zone of this ability. Three facts we know from experiments:

1. People tend to seek a relatively high level of aspiration.

2. There is a tendency for the level of aspiration to go up only to certain limits.

3. There is a tendency for the person in his level of aspiration to stay out of an area too difficult or too easy.

The judgment of the probability of success or failure on a given level is determined by past experiences, certain realistic situations, and, in addition, by wishes and fears. A recent failure will tend to lower the level of aspiration, and the level will decrease more after resounding failure than after a near success. Success and failure also have their cumulative effects. Experiments show that the feeling of success and failure does not depend on the absolute level of achievement. What may mean success for one person may mean failure for another; and even for the same person, the same achievement will lead sometimes to feelings of failure and sometimes to feelings of success.

Factors in Mobility. Let us now return to the question of individual motivation and upward mobility. In his studies of community life, Warner points out that the primary factor for upward mobility is a high achievement level. What is expected of a person in relation to his age level sets a standard. Traditionally, there are two basic areas for achievement. The first involves obtaining an education, and the second finding a place in the occupational hierarchy. Says Warner [17], "Success in one or both of these areas is almost a basis for achievement in other aspects of living. It is an expression of the ambition drive of an individual."

Achievement level is, of course, dependent upon individual ability, a sort of "special talent" for science, athletics, art, and so forth.

A third factor in mobility concerns an individual's social techniques. This means behaving in ways that fit the situation. And the ability to perceive the situation and react appropriately to it is important in upward mobility.

A fourth factor that emerged from the Jonesville studies concerns the person's ambitions for getting ahead. This has been called "status anxiety." Here the person places too high a value on status symbols, or seeks recognition from those in superior positions, or strives for roles which may bring prestige. The person who overreacts in trying for status lowers his chances for upward mobility.

A fifth factor in evaluating potential mobility involves what Warner has called "situational responses"—a sort of "how do other people evaluate us?" kind of thing. We are all familiar with the words to describe the man with this asset—"knows what to do," "has a pleasant personality," "always says the right things."

Club Status Symbols. In any community one can find the club status symbols that go with upward mobility—country club, hospital charities, Daughters of the American Revolution, Rotary. Of the upper-class families in Jonesville, three-fourths of the families belonged to at least two, and half belonged to three or all four of these clubs. In the Lions, Masons, and Eastern Star, the majority of the members came from the upper- and lower-middle classes. For the lower-lower class of the Jonesville community "there isn't much."

Associations are very important for upward mobility. For some "the old school tie" has its importance. Membership in women's clubs, the PTA, and the Red Cross provide associations at another level. Individuals at the top of the social ladder are ready to identify with their own social status; those at the bottom derive little ego satisfaction from such identification. At the bottom of the socioeconomic hierarchy there is less feeling of "belongingness." Maybe belongingness is *the* basic need underlying the struggles for upward mobility.

Study of a High-status Community. Lest one conclude that the struggle is over when high socioeconomic status has been attained, he should take a look at what is involved in staying up there. The sociological study of a high-status suburban community of 17,000 people has been described in the book *Crestwood Heights* [12]. Here is pictured the community of material abundance, the "dream community where many aspire to live, but only a few can," populated to a large extent by those who have achieved rapid personal mobility. Here is described a community where the child, who in more static social situations might be permitted to take certain aspects of the common life for granted, is made to "appreciate" the close connection between effort and achievement; it is a community where one cannot take anything for granted.

The person who aspires to the Heights in his upward mobility must be prepared to follow the highly developed pattern of movement from one job to another, from one place of residence to another, from one city to another, from one class position to another. The man and woman of Crestwood Heights have few bonds that cannot be broken at the promise of a promotion. They have been prepared for this from the cradle, if they were born into this society.

Mobility must be matched by opportunity for training, for employment, and for advancement. To the man bent upon an executive career, training includes both the necessary technical skills and the social graces, plus the strong desire to manage. The executive or professional man of the Heights must be ready to abandon cherished usages and techniques as new ones arise. He must be willing to acquire new conceptions of life and organization, and to revise constantly in later life his procedures within his chosen field.

The authors make the point that the differences between the careers of the person who has risen by his own effort and the person who has been born and brought up in Crestwood Heights have a relation to the flexibility which is so essential to the executive in a rapidly changing society. The person who is "born into a good start" is more likely to accept current techniques and practices than is the individual who is struggling upward. Psychologically, in work or in play, the key to survival in the Heights is *competition.* Success in making the Heights or staying there may well depend upon how well the person is prepared for competition at this high level, particularly in the more subtle phases of the status struggle.

SOCIAL CLASS AND PERSONALITY

Many of the problems found in industry and in the industrial community are related to social classes, and to the individual behavior of each person in the lower class, the middle class, and the upper class. Shaffer and Shoben

[13] in their book on the psychology of adjustment have presented a summary picture of how social-class membership determines in large measure personality traits. The neighborhood in which an individual lives, the groups to which he belongs, the rewards and punishments to which he is exposed determine in large part the child's learning environment and what he becomes as an adult.

The Lower Class. These authors describe the mother in the lower class as being closer to her baby in many ways than the mother in the middle and upper classes. Nursing continues longer, and weaning is far less abrupt than is usual in the middle-class home. Toilet training is delayed, infantile genital play is not inhibited. The child is permitted greater freedom in his explorations and given more prompt and affectionate attention when he gets into difficulty. On the other hand, the lower-class parents are quick to anger. As the child grows up these parents resort to ridicule, shaming, whipping, and other forms of physical punishment. It is easy to see that growing up under both economic and psychological privation conditions one to belonging to protective groups, to exhibiting "irrational" behavior (from the viewpoint of higher classes), such as overeating when food is abundant or overheating the home when fuel is plentiful. When viewed from above, these people are often considered shiftless and lacking in thrift and foresight. Their behavior in spending is as irrational as that of the person who has been under the strain of prolonged unemployment. Because they are generally deprived of "things," lower-class people have a strong urge to overbuy when they get money. These "have-not" frustrations tend to strengthen the drives for immediate gratification. Not only is there an attitude of seizing upon the pleasures of the moment, but these people tend to react with a greater freedom of emotional expression than is found among the middle class.

Children and adolescents from the lower class are less inhibited in their expression of sex and anger. Fights of a physical nature between husband and wife are frequent. Parents even teach their children to fight with fists and knives and to hit first. Dirty fighting appears to be one way of attaining considerable status both within the family and from one's peers. Interestingly enough, seeking protection from parents and fellow gang members is quite acceptable in contrast to the middle-class emphasis on self-reliance.

Through connections with industrial supervisors in several different kinds of industries, the author has accumulated a number of instances of "low-class behaviors" of workers which by middle-class standards would be regarded as crude. One of the most difficult tasks with which the industrial supervisor has to contend is trying to break through the barriers of low-level behavior. One foreman expressed it thus: "These people don't know any better and don't want to know better."

The Middle Class. Unlike the lower class, middle-class parents make a great effort to get the child to "live right," do well in school, and to think in terms of long-range goals and delayed rewards. A conscious effort is often made to subdue immediate gratifications and learn to discipline oneself. Education is designed to facilitate future achievement. In contrast to their lower-class counterparts, the children from the middle classes are taught responsibilities, independence, and self-reliance. Physical aggression is frowned upon, overt sex expression is regarded as indecent, courtship and marriage are regulated by rules of right and wrong conduct.

The middle-class person develops within a pattern of denying impulse gratifications in favor of developing initiative. He strives to learn appropriate social as well as technical skills. He struggles for improvement, but at some risk. With attainment being a dominant goal, failure becomes an ever-present threat.

The Upper Class. What of the upper class? Here, with a strong emphasis on taste, manners, good form, and family reputation, a child is taught that he is superior. This may be an asset to the person, if he does not have to face too much of the reality of rough and tough competition. It can be a liability where exaggerated values are overly stressed. The secure status of an upper-class member is somewhat automatically conferred by his family, and it can be retained so long as the person does not step out of line. Sometimes the individual brought up in the protection of his upper-class standing finds the going rough when finances become depleted and "family security" is gone.

Achievement Needs. Modern-day industrial communities offer a ready-made laboratory situation for studying achievement needs. The industrial worker who has grown up in a lower-class society is not interested in long periods of preparation and work which will lead to later rewards. He wants his rewards now. Pension plans and programs of future security have little or no motivational value for this person.

To the middle-class person in industry, achievement needs are most important. Sacrifices for education are willingly made; marriage may be delayed to provide for the period of professional training. But these achievement needs come at a price, as we shall see in a later chapter dealing with personal adjustments. The struggle for achievement often brings on anxiety which leaves in its wake compulsions to hard work or rationalization to cover up failures.

The attitudes, the feelings, the strivings, and the complacencies of many people at the same or at different levels in industry are more easily understood when we analyze their class background. One complaint frequently heard from the successful man with a high achievement drive is that "so many people in industry do not want responsibility." And there are those, perhaps, with a low achievement drive, who wonder "why so many people in industry want to be president."

INDUSTRIALIZATION AND THE FAMILY

The man at work, be he an executive or a laborer, does not function alone in his industrial environment. It is almost inevitable that his problems of work are shared with his family, and the feedback from family life affects his work. Essential to the study of the whole man in his total community is the study of the family. It has been estimated that of the over forty million families in the United States about thirty-six million are connected with the labor force [7, 8, 11]. About two-thirds of these families have one or more members earning a wage or salary in a nonagricultural industry.

Socioeconomic Environment. Industry directly and indirectly helps establish the socioeconomic environment within the community, even to the extent of influencing marriages. In their jobs, large numbers of men and women become acquainted. Several studies have shown that one of the primary factors related to who marries whom is proximity. Men and women who live within relatively short distances of each other tend to marry. People who live in the same neighborhood usually come from the same class and often from the same status groups. Marriages occur between people who are thrown together at work or who meet through their positions in the social structure.

The modern industrial-urban family has a high degree of equality among its members. The father is less of an authoritarian figure than in the patriarchal family, particularly where the wife and/or children work for pay. Although those who work may leave their problems at the office or not talk about their work at home, much about these problems is revealed by attitudes, particularly where feelings are involved. Men at all levels of society concentrate daily at their place of work, leaving their homes for a world of often different values and traditions. In all levels of society, says our industrial sociologist, the husband is but a part-time member of the family who must somehow adjust his work life to the demands of the family life. Some men here succeed, but many fail. One man may see his "work self" dominate; another may see the "family self" win out. Here one may find a key to personal adjustment. How a man behaves with his family often reveals something about how well his needs are being satisfied at work.

Work and the Family. To the man in the upper levels of society with prestige and authority gained at work, there may be little carry-over into his family life. The pressure of life at the high occupational levels may mean the man has little time to devote to his family. In either case one's work self differs from the family self. This is particularly true where the wife may have adequate funds of her own to allow her some independence.

To the middle-class white-collar man, the situation is often different.

The income of the white-collar worker is usually superior to his wife's; hence, the family is wholly or in part dependent on the husband's wages. But still his family has not a complete idea of what the man has to put up with in his work. He has difficulty transferring his feelings of accomplishment or lack of accomplishment to his family. The family may observe the strains of his failure or try to share in his victories, but with little real success.

The status position of the worker may be as low within his family as it is at work. If the wife or the children work as wage earners, they may make out as well as or better than the husband. This very weakness of the father's position may cause him to play an authoritarian role in the family as a defensive behavior.

THE TOTAL ENVIRONMENT

In Part I of this text we presented the place of psychology in industry. Part II described the industrial environment in terms of the formal and informal structures of organizations. The ways and means of operating a business gave us a view of how procedures and rules influence what a man in industry does. Part III of the text described how man's needs can become satisfied through selection, training, and individual development. Special kinds of problems dealing with labor, and the special segments of the labor market, were covered in Part IV of the text. The problems related to work were considered in Part V where we described the advances we are making in coordinating man-machine systems. Influence and the social aspects of industry constituted Part VI.

To put it simply, the total environment for the individual consists of "problems in the office and the factory" and "problems where we live." Automation, technological changes, world conditions, all impinge upon the individual. Invention has a way of opening up opportunities for some and denying them to others; perhaps we should remember along with Thoreau: "The mass of men lead lives of quiet desperation." Although we have covered many and varied influences of our total environment, there is one other important aspect of the study of the man and woman in industry: What influence does all this interaction have on the individual in terms of the over-all climate for mental health, for personal adjustments? We shall deal with this question in the final chapters of the text.

SUGGESTIONS FOR FURTHER READING

Form, W. H., & Miller, D. C. *Industry, labor and community*. New York: Harper, 1960. This sociological book deals with the network of business, labor, and community relations in terms of perspective, power structures, and applied problems.

Hodges, W. *Company and community.* New York: Harper, 1958. A study showing why some community projects succeed and others fail.

Mills, C. W. *White collar: the American middle-class.* New York: Oxford, 1951. This book describes some of the positive and negative aspects of men in business and in the professions, and their place in the community.

Purcell, T. V. *Blue collar man.* Cambridge, Mass.: Harvard Univer. Press, 1960. This book examines three packing-house unions in the context of union leadership and urban relations and presents some new ways of thinking about dual allegiance in industrial operations.

Seeley, J. R., Sim, R. A., & Loosley, E. W. *Crestwood Heights.* New York: Basic Books, 1956. A description of what life is like for those people living in a high socioeconomic residential community.

Warner, W. L. *Democracy in Jonesville: a study in quality and inequality.* New York: Harper, 1949. A description of what life is like for those people living in a small, midwestern community.

Zelomek, A. W. *A changing America: at work and play.* New York: Wiley, 1959. A view of changing community life.

PART VII: THE INDIVIDUAL
IN INDUSTRY

20

INDUSTRIAL

MENTAL HEALTH

Emanuel Kay

A prominent business magazine recently started an article on industrial mental hygiene with the following leads:

¶ 2 million problem drinkers lose from 22 to 25 workdays a year, cost industry about $500 million.

¶ 100,000 workers become so mentally ill each year that they enter state hospitals, lose about six months from work apiece.

¶ 85% of industrial medical service goes to 30% of the workers in one plant, and the same 30% cause most of the "headaches" in labor relations.

¶ Seriously troubled employees have three times as many safety shop rule violations in one large company.

¶ Personality study of 300 executives indicates that failures can be traced directly to character traits.

¶ Character traits account for 90% of causes for firings, 76% of the reasons why promotions were not granted in a major oil company.

Aside from the obvious importance of these assertions to industry, one might seriously wonder about the factors which give rise to these situations. Are these statements accurate? Are they solely the reflection of individual peculiarities? Are they caused primarily by conditions of work? Are they just a reflection of our times? Or what? The best answers to these questions are that these statements probably have some bases in fact, although they have been overgeneralized. They are not unusual, however. They are not due solely to individual peculiarities. They are not due primarily to conditions of work, nor are they just a reflection of our times. The statements cited above represent the end products of a complex interaction between personal work and general social factors. They are indicative of the problems which individuals have in adjusting to certain demands made on them. We shall describe these problems of adjustment in this and in the following chapter.

THE MEANING OF MENTAL HEALTH

Mental health is concerned with the adjustments individuals make to situations and the factors which influence these adjustments. As individuals develop, as they approach and reach adulthood, they are faced with a continuing series of adjustments. Consider, for example, the transition from high school to college. The student must adjust to the increased demands that college makes on him in terms of study hours and the responsibility for his own actions. Failure to behave in accordance with these demands can lead to a maladjustment and possible expulsion from college. In the case of college, the new demands are merely transitions from adjustments previously made in high school. If the student has made a good adjustment to the demands made on him in high school, he should be on a firm basis for adjusting to the additional demands made upon him in college.

Stresses in the Work Situation. A similar situation exists in respect to the work situation. Certain modes of behavior are expected of an individual when he is employed. These expectations have to do with such things as hours of work, dress, social relationships, acceptance of authority, and type of work to be performed. On the other hand, the individual has a certain set of needs which he hopes to satisfy through the work situation. He expects to achieve a certain degree of financial security, to achieve a position which will give him status, and to derive satisfaction from his work, as we described in Chapter 10. If the work situation enables the individual to achieve his goals to a sufficient degree, then it is quite reasonable to assume that the individual will accept the demands made upon him by the work situation. If, on the other hand, the demands made by the work situation conflict excessively with the individual's personal goals, then it is reasonable to expect a certain amount of difficulty in adjusting to the demands of the work situation. These difficulties in adjusting will be manifested in such things as labor turnover, absences, and poor morale. The particular behavior involved will depend upon the individual's position in the company, the financial pressures which keep him tied to the job, and the way he perceives his particular job. In this chapter we shall analyze problems of adjustment to work in terms of psychological processes, demands imposed by the work situation, and the interaction between basic psychological processes and the demands imposed by the work situation. These factors, of course, are not sufficient to account for all adjustment and maladjustment. There are factors outside the work situation which also lead to adjustment difficulties, such as personal and domestic problems. This chapter will be limited, however, to those stresses which occur in the *work situation*. The following chapter will deal with the more personal aspects of adjustment.

THE NATURE AND EXTENT OF MALADJUSTMENTS IN INDUSTRY

One of the major social, medical, and economic problems of our century has been the increase in the proportion of the population who are identified as having some form of emotional disorder. The persons so identified have emotional disturbances which range from mild neuroses with little apparent effect on their everyday adjustment to severe psychoses which require hospitalization and special care. Regardless of whether the increase in numbers of persons identified with emotional disorders stems from improved diagnostic procedures, or from an actual increase in the percentage of these persons in our population, it should be recognized that this represents an important problem for industry. Industry draws its manpower resources from the general population, and the prevalence of persons in industry with emotional disorders, particularly mild disorders, should closely parallel the number found in the general population.

Emotional Disorders in Industry. Several estimates have been made of the instances of persons in industry with emotional disorders. We shall illustrate with an example. In one study an investigator reported the incidence of neuroses among factory workers [4]. A sample drawn from approximately three thousand male and female factory employees was given a battery of psychological tests, an interview with a social worker, and a medical and psychiatric examination. On the basis of these examinations 10 per cent of the male and female employees were judged as having a severe neurosis and 20 per cent were affected with a minor neurosis. In addition, neurotic illness was judged as causing between one-quarter and one-third of all absences from work due to illness.

Emotional disorders manifest themselves in different ways. In school, for example, an emotional disturbance in a child may manifest itself in an inability to learn. In industry, emotional disturbances are usually discussed in terms of such on-the-job behaviors as absenteeism, accidents, alcoholism, and grievances. There are a number of studies which have led to attempts to relate emotional disturbances to these job behaviors. Not all the studies have been definitive, but we shall mention several important ones.

Absenteeism. The direct costs of absenteeism to industry have been estimated at 5 billion dollars a year, with the indirect costs estimated at four to five times this amount. This is a sizable sum, the reduction of which could lead to important gains to industry, to individual employees, and to the national economy [2].

Absenteeism is a complex problem. It would be unreasonable to expect that one factor, such as emotional disorders, could account for all absences. Such other factors as age, organizational climate, and community conditions should also be evaluated for their effects on absenteeism. Here, the discussion of absenteeism will be limited to those absences caused by emotional disorders.

It has been judged that emotional illness causes between a quarter and a third of all absences from work due to illness, as we said above. This is equivalent to three working days of absence per year for male employees and six days of absence per year for female employees just as a result of what were judged to be emotional disorders.

One investigator [21] compared the personality characteristics of male machine-shop employees who had six to twelve days of uncertified absence during a two-year period with those who had three or fewer days of uncertified absence during the same period. The employees were alike, otherwise, in respect to type of work, age, length of service, and the distance from home to place of work. On the Guilford-Zimmerman Temperament Survey, the high-absence employees were found to have a lower drive level and to be less emotionally stable than the low-absence employees.

Two other researchers conducted a unique and interesting study of emotional factors in female employees of a telephone company [23]. From 1,297 female employees they selected 20 individuals with at least twenty years of service who had the highest absence records. From among the low-absence individuals with twenty years of service, they selected another 20 cases at random. The medical case histories of the two groups, which had accumulated during the twenty-year period, were compared. The high-absence group had a greater number of recorded instances of emotional disorders and other disorders with an underlying emotional basis. There was nothing in the preemployment physical examination which would have suggested these different patterns over the twenty-year period.

The author [13] has studied 132 female clerical employees whose absences were a reaction to frustration in the work situation. This study differs from those just cited in that emotional factors were not considered. The results of this study show that the employees who tended to react to frustration in the work by withdrawal mechanisms had the greatest number of absences. This suggests the possibility that some absences are a reaction to frustrating work conditions and are used as a means of temporarily avoiding the work situation.

Although no one of the above studies is conclusive in its own right, when taken together they strongly suggest that a significant portion of absenteeism has an underlying emotional basis.

Grievances. The grievance procedure is a standard part of almost all union-management contracts, as we described in Chapter 11. Grievance procedures are designed to provide a method for resolving problems which stem from the interpretation of the formal contract and from problems stemming from the employee's interpretation of what is due him on the basis of past practice and tradition. While many grievances stem from real problems, and others can be accounted for in terms of "local politics," it is interesting to consider the possibility that some grievances arise as a result of emotional disorders, or as an act of aggression. A number of attempts have been made to identify the special personality characteristics of persons who submit a disproportionately large number of grievances. Stagner reports a study of two groups of workers on this [24]. The two groups differed only in the respect that the men in one group had filed *at least* one grievance during the previous year, while the men in the second group had filed none. On the Guilford-Martin Personnel Inventory, the two groups differed on trait O which is a measure of objectivity-sensitivity. The high-grievance group was found to be sensitive with a tendency to be more easily offended. This group also showed a tendency to be more aggressive and critical than the nongrievance group. The results from the test are shown in Figure 20.1.

Although this is just one study with a small group, it does have some important implications worthy of further thought. Personality traits were found to be associated with a tendency to submit grievances. This raises the possibility that persons in industry who are hypersensitive to the conditions of their work environment use an established and recognized channel, the grievance procedure, for expressing their dissatisfaction.

Accidents. A great deal has been written and said about the relationship between personal adjustment and accidents, as we described in Chapter 15. Although these efforts at times give the impression that there is a distinct relationship between personal adjustment factors and accidents, the reader must be cautioned that the entire problem of accident causation has generally been oversimplified, as we indicated in the chapter on accidents and safety. Accidents can stem from a number of sources, both within and outside the individual, and these must be analyzed in detail in order to understand the role of human factors in accidents. Perhaps through the study of accidents we will learn more about the problems of mental health.

Alcoholism. In itself alcoholism is a manifestation of a general lack of adjustment. Industry's direct concern with alcoholism is that many alcoholics are employed actively, and that the effects of alcoholism are quite manifest on the job.

The exact number of alcoholics in the United States is not known with any precision. In 1949, one writer [12] estimated that there were 963,000 persons who had reached an advanced phase of alcoholism. It was concluded that approximately 3,850,000 persons in the United States were in some stage of alcoholism. As of 1953, this figure was revised upwards to an estimated 4,590,000 alcoholics [14]. This is a rate of approximately

4,400 per 100,000 adults. The number of alcoholics employed in industry has been estimated at 3 per cent of the total work force [3, 22]. This means that there are approximately two million alcoholics employed in industry, including people all along the line from workers to executives.

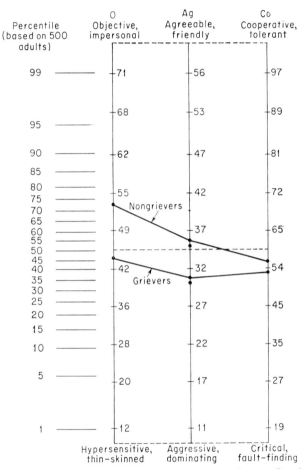

Fig. 20.1. Personality differences in grievers and nongrievers. On the Guilford-Martin Personnel Inventory, grievers and nongrievers differed significantly on trait O ("objectivity"). The grievers tended more toward thin-skinned sensitivity in such things as having their feelings hurt more easily. There was a slight tendency for the grievers to be more aggressive and critical than the nongrievers. (From Stagner, R. *The psychology of industrial conflict.* New York: Wiley, 1956.)

The extent and nature of this probem is difficult to ignore. An increasing number of companies are doing away with the cover-up and discharge methods of dealing with alcoholics and are taking direct steps to restore the alcoholic to a normal and productive state. These rehabilitation programs are of direct benefit to the company, the employee and his family, and to society at large.

Alcoholic Rehabilitation Program. The alcoholic rehabilitation program of the Consolidated Edison Company of New York is an excellent example of a program conducted and later sponsored by an industry [3]. The program was initially conducted by the company's Alcoholic Unit, but since 1952 Consolidated Edison, among others, has been active in supporting an outside rehabilitation organization for use by its employees. This organization's within-company program and its results may be summarized as follows:

CRITERIA FOR IDENTIFYING ALCOHOLICS. The organization relies heavily on supervisors in identifying alcoholic employees. Supervisory personnel are given concrete guideposts for this purpose. Among the guideposts are such things as:

1. Consistent tardiness or absence on Monday morning and frequent occurrences of leaving early on Friday afternoon.

2. Unexpected disappearance from an assigned post during a tour of duty.

3. Recurring excuses for absence due to minor illnesses, such as colds, bronchitis, stomach upsets, or too frequent off-duty accidents, particularly with assault as a factor.

4. Personality changes in a previously good worker; such as arguments or criticism of others, recurring mistakes for which he defends himself, minor accidents which he blames on others or on equipment, marked variation in mood, and disinterest in his work.

Identifying alcoholics places a special burden on supervisors which they are not always willing to accept, as it may appear to be a form of ratting, or as a reflection on the supervisor's ability. Full cooperation of supervisors in this program is dependent upon the climate which the company creates for dealing with alcoholics after they are identified. If the climate is punitive, little cooperation can be expected from supervisors. The supervisors must be made to feel that their participation in the program ultimately will be of benefit to the alcoholic employee as well as the company.

CRITERIA FOR ACCEPTANCE OF THE EMPLOYEE FOR REHABILITATION. If the alcoholic employee has been with the company for less than two years, he may be discharged for his first violation. Employees with two to fifteen years of service are put on probation, pending the development of a rehabilitation program. Employees with more than fifteen years of service may be placed on the disability payroll if it is judged that their condition is chronic.

DEVELOPMENT OF A REHABILITATION PROGRAM FOR EMPLOYEES. The company medical director has the responsibility for the physical and psychological examination of the employee. Specialists from outside the organization are used in the examinaiton as needed. The medical director reports his findings and recommendations to the company personnel director. Steps are then taken to carry out a rehabilitation program for the employee with the facilities available to the company. Recurrence of an offense due to alcoholism results in immediate suspension and action against the employee in accordance with established company procedures and policies.

RESULTS OF REHABILITATION PROGRAM. Between 1948 and 1951, Consolidated Edison dealt with 155 cases of alcoholism. Of these, 51 per cent were rehabilitated. Since 1952 the Company has supported the Consultation Clinic for Alcoholism of the New York University-Bellevue Medical Center. Other large organizations also have joined in the support of the clinic. Employees now are referred directly to the clinic where an expert staff carries out the rehabilitation programs. During its first two years of operation, the clinic staff rehabilitated 63 per cent of the Consolidated Edison employees referred to them. These rehabilitated employees were found not to have relapsed into drinking more than a year after their treatment. In addition, the days-absent rate of the rehabilitated employees had dropped by more than one-third, to just below the company average.

The initial Consolidated Edison program and the Consultation Clinic for Alcoholism Program, now subscribed to by Consolidated Edison and other large companies, are excellent examples of how organized efforts can lead to significant gains by the company, its employees, and society at large. Many companies desirous of such a program, however, may find the costs prohibitive. The Yale Plan Clinic at Yale University offers a consultant service designed to help companies to determine the prevalence of alcoholism in their companies, to develop educational programs and policies relevant to alcoholism, and to help companies develop in-company or community rehabilitation programs.

Job Behaviors and Maladjustment. Maladjustment is reflected in more than one way by an employee. Thus, the maladjusted employee may not limit himself to either absences, grievances, accidents, or some other undesirable job behavior. He may engage in several or all. Investigators [10] analyzed the relationship between accidents and certain classes of absences and found that persons with the greatest number of accidents had a greater number of unsanctioned absences, a greater number of sickness absences, and a smaller number of absences in which permission was granted beforehand. Another writer [18] compared 105 "safety-prones" with 85 "accident-prones" in terms of their numbers of sick excuses, other absence excuses, reprimands, rule violations, suspensions, and incidents of drunkenness. With the exception of the number of incidents of drunkenness, the accident-prone group showed a significantly greater incidence of the above job behaviors than the safety-prone group.

It is evident from studies that there is a relationship between some of the job behaviors which are considered to be indications of maladjustment. While these relationships are in need of further research, they do, even now, have a very practical implication. Studies of these relationships would seem to suggest that a single individual is capable of generating a large variety of problems. Not only is the maladjusted individual absent more frequently, but he would also seem to have a greater number of accidents, be a greater disciplinary problem, and in general, create problems which interfere with the orderly business process. By effecting a better adjustment for one individual, quite a number of problems will disappear. Multiply this single individual by the estimated 20 per cent of the work force who are estimated to have varying degrees of maladjustment which interfere with their work, and it is evident that a concentrated effort at identifying these individuals and helping them resolve their problems will result in a dramatic reduction in on-the-job behavior problems.

ADJUSTMENTS OF THE PRODUCTION WORKER

Organization practices of job simplification, chain of command, unity of direction, and span of supervision make different demands upon persons in different levels of the organization. Let us examine the special adjustment problems which these practices create for production workers, first-line supervisors, and for managers. These groups have been selected for special attention because of the availability of information. This does not imply that other groups, such as engineers, scientists, and sales persons, also do not have special adjustment problems stemming from organization demands [15].

At the level of the production employee, job specialization, chain of command, unity of direction, and span of supervision practices are most pronounced. The production worker's job usually shows the greatest specialization and simplification. He is *at the bottom* of the chain of command; he looks upward for directions and information, and he may be one of a large number of employees under one supervisor. In brief, he has been "programmed" to an extensive degree. What effects do practices of this type have on the work adjustment of production employees?

Worries about Work. Neel conducted a survey of the adjustment problems of a large group of production employees [20]. The workers were asked to indicate how often they were bothered by certain factors in their work and by other domestic and personal factors. Let us summarize what they said.

1. Failure to advance is of great concern to approximately 50 to 60 per cent of the employees.

2. Almost half of the employees sometimes or often worried about working conditions which would lead to sickness or absence.

3. Almost half of the employees sometimes or often worried about how they would get along when they were too old to work.

4. Approximately 40 per cent of the employees sometimes or often worried about temporary layoffs.

5. Approximately 30 per cent of the employees sometimes or often worried about losing their jobs.

6. Approximately 25 per cent of the employees worried about lack of skills required for their jobs.

The above findings are given in the order in which the employees showed concern. It is interesting to note that this group of employees worried most about their inability to advance. The next four sources of concern were related to security factors. Disabling accidents seemed to be the greatest security concern, followed in turn by old age, layoffs, and loss of jobs. Least concern was shown over a lack of skills needed for jobs. Thus, it would seem that the production employee, who is at the bottom of the administrative hierarchy, is worried most by his inability to move upward in the company. His present position also causes a great deal of concern over job and retirement security. There is little concern over acquiring needed skills. This would suggest that most employees have the necessary skills, that acquiring skills poses no special problems, or that the worker may not perceive his position adequately. If job simplification is a common practice in the plant, then acquiring skills probably would not represent a major source of worry.

In-plant Conditions. Neel, in his study, also related three in-plant conditions to the employee's feeling of jumpiness or worry about his work [20].

1. SUPERVISORY PRACTICES AND WORRY. Employees worried because supervisors often placed unwarranted responsibility on them, because they often failed to tell the workers where they stood.

2. WORKING CONDITIONS AND WORRY. A number of working conditions caused an amount of worry among employees. Dust, fumes, poor maintenance, dirt, oil, grease, and old machinery were related to worries about health and the possibility of accidents.

3. TIME-STUDY PRACTICES AND WORRY. It was shown that time standards cause some worry and concern among employees. Employees who felt that they could not achieve the 100 per cent productivity level set for their job, and employees who had trouble in getting their work done, tended to worry more and to feel nervous.

TYPES OF WORK AND MALADJUSTMENTS

An industrial psychologist and psychiatrist has defined some of the psychological hazards and special adjustment problems associated with certain kinds of work. Three specific types of work are considered to be particularly hazardous from a psychological point of view, says Cameron [1].

First, work requiring intense utilization of a limited range of abilities or parts of the body can cause problems. Certain jobs require the employee to make intensive use of a limited range of abilities or parts of the body. Cameron cites the work of telegraphers as an example of such a job requirement. We wish to use this somewhat outdated, but classic example because, in his medical practice, this psychologist has encountered a number of cases of telegrapher's cramp which he feels stem from the requirements made by the work. Telegrapher's cramp is characterized by muscle spasms in the hand used for operating the sending key. It occurs *only* when the telegrapher attempts to perform his work. Otherwise, the telegrapher is quite capable of performing other tasks with his hand, such as putting on gloves and lighting a cigarette. The cramp is a psychological disorder and not a physical one. It would seem to stem directly from the nature of the work performed by the individual. He also cites cases of the loss of voice among switchboard operators and school teachers as examples of similar reactions to a job requiring intensive use of a limited part of the body.

Second, relatively simple, highly repetitive, and highly paced work brings about difficulties. Many production processes have been "fragmented" so that individuals are required only to perform a small segment of the work needed to complete the product. In most cases, if the work is relatively simple and highly repetitive, the pace will vary according to the production demands of the particular plant. Cameron considers this type of work to be psychologically hazardous, particularly when the pace is rapid and sustained.

Third, jobs failing to require the full participation of the worker induce problems. There are jobs in which the work, while never permitting the man complete freedom or relaxation, does not demand his full attention. Many people in jobs of this type will attempt to maintain interest and fill time by conversations with other workers. Where this is not possible, the employees' interests may turn inward and result in the development of obsessive thinking or tensions.

Job Tensions and Hazards. The author had a recent experience related to jobs which create tension in the employee. A number of machinists, discussing their jobs, mentioned as a common experience that tension builds up to a high state near the end of a job. This seemed to stem from the fact that the unit being produced was worth more near the end of the process than at the beginning. Any error made at the end would result in a greater loss, and hence, possible greater repercussions, than an error made near the beginning of the process.

Job hazards are a special characteristic of the work situation which would seem to cause special adjustment problems. Halliday [8] has reported on the psychoneurotic disorders found in coal miners. He reported that 33 per cent of 1,000 miners certified as incapable of work were found to be psychoneurotic. He identified certain hazardous aspects of the work environment which he felt were predisposing to psychoneurosis. For example, wet working conditions caused problems. Some underground mine environments are relatively dry, and others are relatively wet. Wet workings are considered to be hazardous. According to the writer, miners who were switching from dry to wet mines would become tense and anxious over the increased possibility of illnesses or accidents. Also, change from above-ground to below-ground work was found to affect mental health. In mining, above-ground jobs are considered to be very safe in comparison with below-ground jobs. Miners who had become accustomed to the relative safety of above-ground work would become quite upset and anxious when reassigned to underground operations. The stress produced by this change in work was an important factor in predisposing to psychoneurotic and psychosomatic ailments.

Accidents in the mine reinforce anxiety. For most miners, it is difficult not to observe and know the effects of accidents on individual miners and their families. This knowledge serves as a constant source of stress and tension.

It would appear that where the job hazards are high and well known, they become a constant source of tension and stress to individual employees. This stress may be lessened, however, when there is a strong feeling of accomplishment from the work (see page 213).

WHAT MANAGEMENT CAN DO

The production employee's position at the bottom of the organization hierarchy, in all probability, results in other job factors which influence job adjustment. Consider, for example, some of the combined effects of practices stemming from unity of direction, chain of command, and span of supervision on the adjustment of the production worker. *The production employee has little control over what he does and over his security.* All information comes to him from above, or at least this is the direction in which he looks for information pertinent to his job and security. He is placed in a position of complete dependency. Worry over personal and job security is quite prevalent. It is therefore not unreasonable to expect the employee to interpret or consider events which happen in the plant primarily in terms of his need for security. Regardless of the reasons for certain actions stemming from higher levels in the organization, the production employee, who has no real knowledge of mangement's reasoning, will worry about the implications these actions have for him.

In dealing with the adjustment problems of employees, there are a number of approaches available to mangement. First, management can establish programs which deal directly with the problems of individual employees. Programs of this type, which are referred to as "counseling," include provisions for specially trained persons to deal with the problems of the individual employee.

Another approach available to management, and the one which fits in with the emphasis on organization practices and adjustment, is that of introducing practices which will relieve certain stresses on production employees. There are several practices which management can consider for this purpose.

Job Enlargement. Let us begin with job enlargement. This is the opposite of job simplification or shred-out, which we discussed in Chapter 7 (see page 135). Job enlargement would consist of increasing the number and scope of job operations performed by an employee. The recommendation for job enlargement is based on the assumption that it will reverse some of the undesirable effects on employees of job simplification by reducing monotony and giving greater meaning to the job. One may, of course, raise the question as to whether job enlargement will reduce productivity. On the basis of a limited number of studies, the answer to this question would seem to be in the negative. In fact, there are some opinions which suggest that job simplification has gone so far as to reduce productive efficiency in some instances. There are two studies which bear on the relationship between job enlargement and productivity.

JOB ENLARGEMENT STUDY AT IBM. The IBM job enlargement program has been reported by Walker [26]. This program came about as a deliberate policy on the part of top management to increase employees' feelings of responsibility for their work and to give employees additional opportunities for increasing their skills. The program, initially, was applied to machine operators who performed a single operation. Normally they were assisted at the start of a job by setup men and at the end of a job by inspectors. The job enlargement program was designed to give the machine operators the skills needed for the setup and inspector functions. These skills included the ability to do the following things: to sharpen tools, to set up a job from blueprints, and make a complete check and inspection of the completed part with the use of specialized test instruments.

A follow-up of the program showed several things. There was a better quality product with less scrap and defects and less idle time, both for machines and operators; and the cost of setting up and inspecting was reduced by 95 per cent.

SEARS, ROEBUCK and COMPANY STUDY. A study at Sears, Roebuck and Company has also given some observations on the effects of job enlargement in which Worthy points out that jobs can be broken down too finely, lowering both output and morale. Conversely, the most sustained efforts are exerted by those groups of employees who perform the most complete sets of tasks. These people also exhibit the highest levels of morale [29].

Jobs can be enlarged by the addition of work operations which require the same level of skill as an existing job. Doing this would seem to be just a matter of technique. One of the very promising outcomes of systems analysis, presented in Chapter 17, is a technique for analyzing job operations in terms of the skills which they require. This technique, which is referred to as "skills analysis," could lead to the design of jobs with a variety of work operations all requiring the same skill level (see page 372). In this way jobs could be enlarged without imposing unrealistic skill requirements. It would also seem desirable, within practical limits, to vary the levels of skill required within a job. Although there is only indirect evidence to support this view, this practice would offer another source of variety and importance to the job.

Job Rotation. Job rotation is another way to deal with the problem of helping the worker. It consists of periodic changes in work assignments, and in many respects, it resembles job enlargement. Job rotation offers the employee opportunities to perform a variety of work, although for any given period of time the employee may be working on one small aspect of the total job.

Supervisory Practices. Changes in supervisory practices will also help to make employees satisfied. The first-line supervisor is invariably at a focal point as far as the production worker is concerned. The production employee looks to the supervisor for direction, support, and approval, as we pointed out in Chapter 8. If the supervisor's practices create tension, there is very little the employees in the work group can do to avoid it. Although the supervisor may be forced into tension-producing practices by the nature of the supervision he receives, and by the demands which are made upon him from above, he must do his best to become aware of and avoid practices which create tension in the work group.

The supervisor's position makes production employees very dependent upon him for information pertaining to their security and status. If the workers feel insecure to begin with, "no news" will quite often be interpreted as "bad news." While it is recognized that the failure of supervisors to pass important information on to employees stems quite often from the fact that they themselves do not receive this information, supervisors must become more aware of the importance of doing this whenever they can.

Job Status. Increased social significance of the work is another possibility in our practical considerations. In addition to increasing the significance of the work through job enlargement, management can take steps to give jobs greater status both in the plant and in the community. In one report of a survey on company practices for giving greater social significance to the work, it was found that even glamorizing the jobs and stressing the significance of jobs in company publications had a beneficial effect. Community status is given to jobs by displays of company products, by open-hours programs, and by pointing out the special significance of the products to the community. Programs such as these are important steps in giving the employee a feeling that his work efforts are meaningful.

ADJUSTMENTS OF THE FIRST-LINE SUPERVISOR

Although the supervisor's job has received considerable attention, very little study has been given to the adjustment problem of supervisors themselves. There is reason to expect that they have their share of difficulties in making adjustments, as was pointed out in Chapter 8 on human relations in supervision.

The Nature of the Production Foreman's Job. The foreman is the final link in the chain of command. He may have between him and the topmost position in the organization anywhere from six to ten levels of management. The levels of management above him represent a large variety of work activities, many of which are directed at making plans which will ultimately determine what the foremen will do. The sales department, for example, in an effort to win out over a competitor, may have promised an exceptionally early delivery date for the product. The production planning department then schedules the product to meet the promised delivery date. The foremen whose work groups are involved in making the product then have special demands placed on them. They may have to interrupt their current production runs, retool, and reassign personnel.

Several types of people directly or indirectly create problems for the foreman. These people are employees in the foreman's work group, inspectors, dispatchers, design engineers, production clerks, employees from other work groups, stock-room clerks, other foremen, superintendents, examining personnel, planners, field engineers, cost-reduction personnel, time-study and methods personnel, labor relations personnel, human-factors specialists, and quality-control personnel. In addition, the foreman receives a large number of written materials, such as defect slips, parts records, engineering drawings, and grievance notices, which also require his action. Each person and written document has the potential for initiating some activity on the part of the foreman.

Another basic characteristic of the production foreman's job is the unpredictable nature of his work load. The many persons who can bring problems to the foreman are not necessarily coordinating their activities with each other. Thus, at any given moment of time, the foreman may have "nothing" to do, or his office may be crowded with persons from the production planning department who want to discuss a schedule change, with an inspector who has complaints about the quality of the current product run, with an employee who wants the foreman to help him clarify a drawing for the product he is currently making, and with a dispatcher who cannot locate a missing part. It is probably more usual for the foreman's work load to be between these extremes, but conditions of underload or overload are not unusual.

Example of Supervisory Activity Sequence. Minute-by-minute observations of a foreman's day have been made. Let us give below one simplified and brief segment from an afternoon of one such description recorded in *The Foreman on the Assembly Line* (27).[1]

Time	Description
2:15 P.M.	Pat checks with scheduler S. Looks at hourly report of number of cars coming through body shop.
2:16	Walks over to R (repair man) on pickup line and checks to see if earlier repair trouble was corrected.
2:17	Calls over inspection foreman to show him a hole missing in a piece. Inspection foreman acknowledges he will notify the trim department.
2:19	Pat tells repair man to locate the hole by eye until it comes through all right.
2:19½	Pat has a drink.
2:20	Pat walks over to station 5 and asks his utility man how many men he still has to relieve.
2:20½	Moves along the line—stations 5, 6, 7—checking visually on the quality of work.
2:21	Checks a loose nut on a fixture at station 7. Speaks with operator.
2:22	Man at station 3 calls for materials.
2:22½	Pat tells man at subassembly bench E to make up more material.
2:23	Walks over to MH (stock man). Tells stock man the line is getting low on hinges. They discuss the number short and agree there is enough for tomorrow.
2:25	Pat walks from MH to station 1 and makes visual inspection of the car body to check on the hole discussed earlier at the pickup line.
2:26	Pat sees foreman from preceding section and tells him about the missing hole.
2:27	Gets a hand signal from welder W.

Foremen who were shown a log of their activities were somewhat amazed at the number of things which they had done during the day. The number of activities for the foremen observed ranged from 237 to 1,073 for an eight-hour day. The average number of activities was 583 per day, or *one every forty-eight seconds.*

[1] This material is reproduced with permission from Walker, C. R., Guest, R. H., & Turner, A. N. *The foreman on the assembly line.* Cambridge, Mass.: Harvard Univer. Press, 1956.

As was mentioned previously, very little is known about the adjustment problems which are created by the demands the work situation makes on foremen. It would seem quite reasonable to expect that the pressures, the interruptions, and the many persons with whom the foreman must deal every day result in tensions which can lead to adjustment problems. These adjustment problems may be manifested by such things as emotional outbursts, chronic irritability, high fatigue, psychosomatic symptoms, and a sense of inadequacy. These we shall discuss in the following chapter.

Change in Foreman's Position. In addition to the job demands, there are a number of other conditions surrounding the foreman's jobs which may lead to a certain degree of tension in some supervisors.

The foreman's job has and is undergoing considerable change. It has evolved from a clear-cut job as the "boss" to one in which the amount of authority is decreasing. The job is ill-defined and susceptible to challenge by sources internal and external to the plant. A second change has taken place along the lines of the type of work which foremen are expected to do. In Chapter 8 we discussed the multiple roles of the foreman ranging from hiring to firing (see page 156). This is an impressive array of requirements and it leads one to wonder seriously whether one individual has the capabilities for performing each function adequately all the time. These heavy demands, coupled with diminishing and uncertain authority and status, also should be thought of as a possible source of tension and concern to foremen.

Reducing Tensions of Supervisory Jobs. What can management do? There are several steps which management can take to reduce the tensions in the foreman's jobs. These are to reorganize the job and select persons who are psychologically as well as technically qualified to be foremen.

Recognition must be given to the fact that the work which the first-line supervisor does has changed considerably during the past decades. Changes in work must lead to changes in the job and changes in the relationship of the job to the organization hierarchy. Perhaps the job of foreman, as we know it today, is outmoded. Perhaps it should be scrapped and reorganized on a basis which is in keeping with the results expected from production workers.

The first step in reorganizing the foreman's job is a clear statement of the work required just prior to initiation of production activities and the work required to keep production going. Some person, probably with the title of foreman, but at a level somewhat higher than the current first-line foreman, should be responsible for seeing that this work is done. However, he should not be responsible for actually doing the work. The total work load is too demanding for one person in terms of amounts and skills required.

Organizational changes could reduce the pressures on a single individual in terms of time and skill demands. It would be possible to create a climate of "general" versus "close" supervision for the production employees, as the foreman would be concerned most with the supervision of his staff. The foreman's contacts with production employees would not always be concerned with production problems, since these would be dealt with by the staff specialists. This would give the foreman opportunities to develop more friendly and informal relationships with the production employees.

Restructuring Job. A restructuring of the foreman's job along the lines suggested above has been carried out and evaluated in a number of organizations. One writer [19] has reported on the restructuring of the foreman's job in two organizations. In one, a steel plant, the restructuring resulted in the foreman's job being expanded to add a staff of specialists such as metallurgists and power and fuel technicians. The specialists worked directly with the foreman on the work group's special problems. Within a year the plant emerged as the top-ranking producer in the company. A similar restructuring was carried out in another plant requiring highly skilled machinery and assembly operations. In this case, the staff persons, planners, wage raters, and methods specialists were assigned to the general foreman (one level of supervision above the first-line foreman). This change resulted in a marked improvement in the work climate as well as greater job satisfaction.

Another way to improve the situation is to select persons who are psychologically, as well as technically, qualified to do the work of foreman. This can be done by determining the psychological requirements for the foreman's job *as it now exists* and by selecting foremen who can meet these requirements. There is evidence to suggest that the foreman's work consists of a continuous series of short and varied tasks which are performed under time pressures and which are subject to constant interruptions. Clearly then, persons who are being considered for the job of foreman should have the psychological attributes to work under these conditions.

ADJUSTMENTS OF THE EXECUTIVE

Executives have heavy responsibilities of leadership, as was described in Chapter 9. As persons high in the chain of command, they must develop and implement through groups at lower levels the plans which will enable the company to achieve its goals. The stakes are high for persons in executive positions. Success can bring high financial and status rewards, *whereas one failure can do away with years of hard work.*

It is important to examine the special demands which executive positions make on individuals, to identify the indications of maladjustment stemming from these demands, and to examine the means for alleviating tensions without compromising company goals. The characteristics of successful executives give some indication of the demands which executive positions make on individuals. They have been described in Chapter 9 (see page 184), and can be summarized in one word: *pressure*.

The Effects of Pressure. The day-to-day effects of the pressures in the executive's job can include outbreaks of temper, much anxiety, poor relations with subordinates, psychosomatic upsets, defensiveness, avoidance of making major decisions, movement from job to job. These symptoms are comparable to those which appear in persons who have been subjected to great pressures. For the executive, a high level of pressure is a constant feature of the job. It is not unreasonable to expect these symptoms to be chronic.

The executive has been characterized as an individual who, as a result of his strong need for success, makes many sacrifices in other aspects of his life. There are apt to be periods in the executive's life when it becomes apparent that he will not achieve his desired goal. After all, only one person out of a relatively large and potentially qualified group in a company will become president of the organization. There are other periods in life, such as middle age, when one begins to reexamine one's goals and the sacrifices still required to achieve them. These periods are likely to produce special adjustment problems for the executive.

The Lost Goal in Middle Age. Company mergers, changes in company organization, and limitations in capabilities of executives, may lead to the sudden realization that certain goals will not be achieved. To an individual who has invested a considerable portion of his life in working toward achieving these goals, at the expense of other interests, this realization can leave a considerable void. Take away the goal and what remains?

Relieving Job Pressures. Since the executives themselves are management, it becomes, to a very large degree, the responsibility of individual executives to adopt a program which will relieve pressures.

There are practices which can serve as goal-achievement and pressure-reduction devices. Increased emphasis should be placed on *lateral* growth and development as opposed to growth and development upward through the chain of command. This is particularly important for persons who are not regarded as highly promotable. Lateral growth can be achieved through such things as acquiring new skills for the present job and by special temporary assignments and missions within the company. Broadening one's skills and participating in special assignments, in themselves, can serve as important goals and achievements. Increased significance can be given to management jobs by such special organization practices as decentralization. Decentralization practices invest greater authority and responsibility at the point in the organization where they are needed most. For many persons, this increase in authority and responsibility is a desired goal. Making it available at lower levels in the organization should reduce strivings for upward mobility and the pressures associated with these strivings.

PROVISIONS FOR GOOD MENTAL HEALTH

In the preceding sections we described how mental health is related to productivity, accidents, absenteeism, and alcoholism. We pictured the adjustment problems of the unpromotable executive and showed how the fear of failure comes readily in our highly competitive society. These are often "statistics" that never get tabulated when we are adding up the costs of mental illness, because most of these people never become hospitalized. But the *adjustment* problems facing executives and managers, industrial scientists, supervisors, and workers are real problems, too.

Fortunately, a number of industrial organizations have been making progress toward reducing personal maladjustments among their personnel. We have discussed several aspects of this in other connections, but let us review ten points here for our mental-health reference.

1. The selection and training of personnel helps to reduce personal conflicts by better matching abilities, personality factors, and desires with the job and the job climate.

2. The provisions for formal counseling services gives the worker a chance to release his tensions in an approved way, both those related to the job and those outside of work.

3. The informal counseling that is now assumed to be one of the roles of the good supervisor can help relieve worker stress.

4. The increased attention given by industry to helping the worker satisfy his psychological needs for recognition and belonging is favorable to establishing a good mental-health climate at work.

5. The physical examinations now given many executive personnel include mental as well as physical health, and are becoming more of a routine part of industrial preventive medicine.

6. Researches into problems related to productivity, attitudes, and morale are uncovering a lot of cause-effect behaviors related to mental health that previously we were unaware of.

7. Analysis of accidents, absenteeism, and labor turnover is giving us some newer insights into the causes of maladjustments.

8. The increased interest being paid to the problems of the handicapped and aged is opening up ways of compensating for personal losses.

9. Research on how the person lives in his community has made us better aware of the health of the individual. Such research has also made it possible for industry to join with the community in attacking the over-all problems of mental health.

10. Paradoxical as it may seem, some understanding of the problems

of industrial mental health have come through the analyses of labor-management conflicts.

THE NEED FOR UNDERSTANDING PERSONAL ADJUSTMENT

The college graduate who plans to work in industry can himself be helped to live a mentally healthy life, if he comes to know what kinds of problems to expect in industry. The following chapter discusses what many of these problems are and what difficulties some persons have in meeting them.

SUGGESTIONS FOR FURTHER READING

Argyris, C. *Personality and organization.* New York: Harper, 1957. A discussion of organizational behavior, the conflict between system and the individual.

McLean, A. A., & Taylor, G. C. *Mental health in industry.* New York: McGraw-Hill, 1958. Two industrial psychiatrists discuss the nature of emotional disorders found in the industrial climate.

Metropolitan Life Insurance Co. *The alcoholic.* New York: 1951. A practical description of alcoholism.

North American Association of Alcoholism Programs. Research conference on problems of alcohol and alcoholism. *Quart. J. Stud. Alc.* 1959, 20, 415–672. An excellent review of the many aspects of alcoholism.

Portal House Publication. *The problem drinker: a challenge to industry.* Chicago: Portal House, 1953. A practical description of alcoholism.

21

PERSONAL

ADJUSTMENTS

IN INDUSTRY

Robert M. Morgan

"Who is the new shop foreman going to be?"

"They decided to give it to Bill Smith."

"Why didn't they give it to Joe Freeman? Isn't he a better man for it?"

"Well, he might have been better in some ways. But he would have blown the organization apart if he had been put in charge. He has so much nervous energy that he can't even sit still during a conversation with you."

"He usually gets a lot done though."

"You would think so if you watched him. He charges ahead from one thing to another all day, but he doesn't necessarily keep his objective in mind. He just charges."

"What job did they give him?"

"He is in a line job where there is a lot of detail and where he can push people around without upsetting the entire organization. He'll get the job done, too."

In this hypothetical case, we have an example of the adjustment pattern of a man in an industrial position. Joe Freeman "has a lot of nervous energy" and "pushes people around." He may be competent, though he doesn't always keep his objectives in mind. And, most important of all, he did not get the position of shop foreman because of some of his personal characteristics.

The personal characteristics of a mother affect the atmosphere of the home and the way in which the children develop. So, too, the personal characteristics of an instructor affect the atmosphere of the classroom. In the same way, the personal characteristics of the man in industry, both the manager and the worker, affect the atmosphere of the plant or the office.

TOWARD UNDERSTANDING ADJUSTMENT PROBLEMS

Workers are constantly adjusting both to each other and to the general conditions in the office or shop, but they react in a variety of ways. One man angrily loses his temper when he feels that someone is taking unfair advantage of him. A second man reacts to the same situation by retiring into silence or slowing down. And a third man quits his job. Still another man decides to work harder to make sure that no one can take advantage of him again. And still another seeks out a good listener.

Reference has been made to these and other adjustments in previous chapters. You have read about some of the problems connected with the dissatisfied worker, the authoritarian supervisor, the alcoholic, the man with too many accidents. The medical department of any large industry can provide evidence of many other adjustments, for they are constantly dealing with workers suffering from headaches, backaches, menstrual discomfort, and other physical ailments. For many industries, the amount of absenteeism related to these physical ailments constitutes a very real administrative problem.

The adjustments which these workers make cannot be thought of as related solely to working conditions, for men do not drop one set of adjustments at the gate when they report for work in the morning and pick up another set for use during the day. Workers react during the day to conditions which affect them at home, and they react at home to conditions which affect them at work. It is impossible to separate their on-the-job adjustments from their off-the-job adjustments.

It is important for anyone who works alongside other men, and that includes nearly everyone in the population, to have some explanation of the meaning of the adjustments men use. If we understand other men, it helps us in our work with them. It helps us to work if we have some understanding of ourselves, and realize that adjustment itself is a continuing process.

In this chapter we shall piece together in an organized way the different kinds of adjustment patterns found in industry and brought out from time to time in several of the preceding chapters. Here we shall talk about adjustments in terms of on- and off-the-job frustrations, conflicts, stress, defensive behaviors, and neurotic reactions, and we shall mention the few things that industry can do to help people deal with these problems.

FRUSTRATION AND CONFLICT

The adjustments which people use are like the revolving doors of a department store. They never really start at any one point or stop at any one point. But a central feature of any adjustment pattern is the concept of frustration and conflict and the stress which accompanies them. Almost all desires are blocked in some way by barriers or obstacles, and it is at the point where wants and desires are blocked that frustration and conflict occur. (See the basic model of behavior on page 92.) Frustration occurs when a personal or an environmental obstacle stands in the individual's way. Conflict occurs when the individual has opposing desires and wishes.

Personal or Environmental Obstacles. There may be physical limitations that prevent us from attaining some of our goals. An executive may have the skills it takes to be a leader, but his efforts may be limited because he lacks physical energy or suffers from an ulcer. A truck driver is seriously handicapped if he does not have adequate vision for night driving.

Intellectual limitations may hinder some individuals from reaching desired goals. A worker may be highly skilled in mechanical operations and yet lack the intellectual ability to train or supervise others.

The various personal adjustments which an individual habitually makes may also become obstacles to some of his goals. Our worker, Joe Freeman, introduced at the beginning of this chapter, serves as an illustration. His very nervous energy itself probably kept him from getting a promotion. At another extreme, one man with good potential may lack ambition, and, in effect, "go into virtual retirement" before his career gets off the ground. Too much drive can create adjustment problems, but so can too little ambition and effort.

There are also numerous environmental obstacles which lead to frustration. Mechanical failures, inadequate materials, incompetent supervisors, monotonous routine, competition for a better job, or long, hard bargaining sessions—all of these can pile one frustration upon another.

Conflict. When an individual wants to engage in two activities which are in opposition to each other, he is in a state of conflict. Sometimes these conflicts occur when there are two attractive alternatives, which cannot both be done at the same time. A young manager may have to decide between two jobs where one has a better salary, but the other has more prospects for advancement. The middle-aged manager may have to decide between "mediocre success" or living on "ulcer avenue."

Almost exactly the same kind of conflict exists when the alternative actions seem to be equally unattractive. A worker may be in the position where he has to choose between taking orders from a supervisor whom he dislikes or quitting his job. He doesn't really want to do either one. The advertising executive may have to decide between "his conscience" and some "dishonest hard sell." The industrial psychologist may get into state of conflict in attempting to work out a compromise between what is a good experimental design for some study and the limitations imposed by practical circumstances.

MOTIVES AND EMOTIONS

Frustration and conflict occur because individuals have motives which they want to satisfy, but these motives get blocked in some way or other. The behavior of an individual can be explained only when we determine what he was trying to accomplish when he acted as he did. We look for the motive behind the behavior. The needs of individuals differ, as we described in Chapter 5, and no listing of them could possibly be adequate.

Motives begin to develop during infancy and continue to develop during childhood and adolescence; they often become quite visible on the job. They are affected by all experiences, and just as experiences differ from one individual to another, so the motives differ both in their nature and in their strength.

An individual is apt to be completely aware of many of his motives, but he will probably be unaware of others. Few young men can admit to themselves that much of their behavior stems from their desire to equal or better the record set by their father, by an older brother, or by the man who works at the next desk, and yet their overabundant energy may be a direct result of this competition. Some foremen who find it hard to decide what to do, without referring matters upstairs, are completely unaware of their need to depend upon more powerful individuals. It is not unusual for a man to refuse a promotion. He may give what appears to be a good reason to explain his behavior, but in actuality he may be trying to avoid any chance of failure.

When a supervisor asks a machinist to do a job a certain way, and the machinist argues that there is a better way, we say that a simple disagreement has arisen. But if they begin to yell at each other, if their faces become flushed, and if they end up swinging their fists at each other, then we say that they are angry and that the behavior has become emotional.

Emotions are sometimes aroused when behavior is strongly motivated. Let us assume that our supervisor is trying to prove his own value to the company. He is trying to improve both the quality and quantity of the materials his machinist produces. It is only when he runs into a machinist who resists his suggestions that he is aroused. Correspondingly, the machinist may be trying especially hard to avoid any sign that his behavior is incompetent, that he must depend upon the wisdom of others. For both men, the motivation had to be strong in order for them to become emotional.

Emotional behavior involves many organs of the body. When an individual reacts with anger, fear, love, joy, or hate, the nervous system, the glands, the muscles, and the visceral organs are all involved. The angry man feels his muscles tighten and his heart beat more vigorously and rapidly.

Principles of Adjustment. The following case illustrates several of the principles of adjustment.

James S reported to the clinic asking for help because he was not making the progress which he thought he should in his job. He was a bachelor of thirty, a graduate engineer, one of a team of researchers for a large industry. He knew that much of his difficulty stemmed from the stuttering which had bothered him since childhood. He described himself as competent but cautious and precise. His supervisor appreciated his long hours of overtime and his carefully prepared reports, but complained that he was too slow. Many of James's complaints stemmed more from his lack of friends and general lonesomeness than from his job situation.

James was the second son of a moderately prosperous family. Bill, the older brother, was always considered quite superior. From the very beginning, James was compared with this brother. His father never seemed quite satisfied with anything James did. James was aware, even as a child, that he was being watched and compared. He felt that nothing he said or did appeared to be right in his father's eyes, and his own uncertainty began to show up in his speech. His stuttering further infuriated the father who used to pound the table and order him to stop talking that way. During the year before James started kindergarten, Bill received a double promotion. This apparently upset James still more, for when the family tried to start him in school he used to run away every morning. His performance in elementary school was adequate, but his stuttering increased. In high school his performance was superior, but his social adjustment was poor. He refused to date any of the girls because of his stuttering.

James is in a state of disequilibrium which probably includes muscular tension. He feels that his stuttering keeps him from making the desired progress in his job and in his personal life. He is frustrated and is in a state of considerable stress.

James is an ambitious young man. Somewhere along the line he developed a motive to learn and to perform well in his job. The origin of this motive is not clear in the facts as presented, but much of the current tension results from the frustration of this motive. His desire to avoid disapproval is also apparent; the origin and development of this motive is more obvious. The unwarranted comparisons and the disapproval which his father showed seem to have affected him even in his early years. He became more unsure of himself and showed it in his speech. It is quite possible that his fear of his father's disapproval at this time was so intense as to be emotional in nature, and it may be that the stuttering itself was a result of the muscular tension which came as an after-effect of the involvement of the nervous system, the visceral organs, and the glands. During high school and college he continued to be motivated to avoid situations which would bring disapproval. Even now as an adult in industry, he is motivated to do cautious and precise work, on the one hand, and to live a lonely social existence on the other. Both his vocational adjustment and his social adjustment were frustrating. When the stress became too great, he came to the clinic for help.

STRESS AND DEFENSIVE REACTIONS

Stress, as has been described earlier, is the condition which accompanies frustration and conflict [13]. When an individual is motivated toward a certain end, but meets an obstacle which stops or delays him, he is frustrated and there is a certain amount of stress. We come to a description of the varieties of behavior which individuals use to handle the frustration and reduce the stress.

Stress is an unpleasant state of affairs. At the very least it is irritating or annoying to have some conflict or barrier stand in the way of an objective. Many times the conflict or frustration is a major one, and then the individual reacts emotionally. The stress which he feels may involve a change in the functioning of the lungs, stomach, or other visceral organs. There may be tight or strained feelings in the musculature of the body.

Stress in Motivation. The condition of stress is highly motivating in itself. Because it is unpleasant, the individual is stimulated to look for some behavior which will lead to a reduction of stress. He develops adjustment techniques which help him to overcome, avoid, circumvent, escape from, or ignore the frustration or conflict which is stressful. Usually these adjustment techniques become habitual and he resorts to them whenever there is stress. But occasions do arise when old adjustment patterns no longer remove the frustration or conflict and he must develop new adjustment patterns.

There are, of course, tremendous differences in the adjustment patterns which different individuals use. We will look at some of the defensive reactions to which a limited number of individuals resort when the stress is too great to be handled in any other way.

The adjustment patterns which individuals commonly use to defend themselves against the stress which accompanies frustration and conflict are usually called defense mechanisms. They can be classified in various ways, but will be referred to here in a nontechnical way as aggressive reactions, withdrawal reactions, and the like.

Aggressive Reactions. The simplest kind of reaction to frustration is the direct attack. It is a very effective adjustment technique used by most individuals throughout their lives. The housewife uses it when she is tired. The bully on the playground uses it very effectively in reducing certain of his frustrations, although society may view the behavior as socially undesirable. In industry, aggressive reactions may even include physical attack, which has been known to happen even in some of our most esteemed companies. In one corporation, the president actually floored the chairman of the board during an argument. (He soon lost his position.) Usually, however, aggressions are more subtle at this level of the organization, and take such forms as "cutting one out socially."

Most antisocial acts which occur can be labeled as psychological aggression. It may seem strange to label embezzlement, or sexual attacks, for that matter, as "aggression," but that is exactly what they are. They represent an individual's method of reacting to a very definite frustration.

The direct attack is frequently a form of displaced aggression. The individual attacks objects which he regards as less dangerous than the one which is frustrating him. Some people displace their anger against an entire group. Displaced aggression probably accounts for much of the racial prejudice which exists. Industrial settings in the plant and in the office offer vast opportunities for one to displace his aggressions, as we have seen in several of the instances throughout this book. The woman who stopped up the commode (see page 96) was an obvious example of a person showing displaced aggression. Less obvious are some of the displaced aggressions that get categorized as "labor grievances" or "policy disagreements."

Withdrawal Reactions. When a motivated individual is frustrated by an obstacle that prevents him from reaching his goal, there are various ways of withdrawing from the situation. One of the most common is the use of *fantasy.* The individual reduces the frustration and the feelings of stress by imagining the satisfactions which he cannot otherwise attain. Temporary escape from reality by daydreaming is apparently a universal characteristic. It serves many useful functions because it tends to strengthen aspirations during a period when goals might otherwise disappear. The worker with a routine, unstimulating job probably relies heavily upon fantasy to help him pass the time. There is danger only when the individual relies too heavily upon fantasy and makes no attempt to carry out realistic, more aggressive, adjustment patterns. Fantasy can become too pleasant and lull the individual into inactivity. Not many employers would put up for long with a secretary whose thoughts were more on Hollywood than on her typing. Safety directors are well aware of the accident potential present on certain jobs which require vigilance, but often lead to mind wandering.

Identification. An individual may react to the characteristics and achievements of another person as if they were his own. When the identification becomes too real and engrossing, it serves as a substitute for realistic endeavor. Identification is often, however, a constructive method for learning adjustment patterns. The young boy picks up the characteristics of manhood by identifying with his father or another older male adult.

The importance of identification as a defense mechanism in industry is frequently overlooked. In the first place, it is a very powerful tool in the training of new employees. The beginning worker is in a stressful situation because he does not know exactly what is expected of him—just when he wants to make a good impression. He will very likely handle this frustration by identifying with one of the other workers, or at least with the standards which he feels several of the workers set for themselves. He will learn more from identifying with the worker at the next bench than from listening to the formal instructions of one of his supervisors. This may be good, or bad, for him.

Individuals also tend to identify themselves with groups and to pick up the characteristics and achievements of the group as if they were their own characteristics and achievements. The workers identify themselves with the rest of the labor force, and usually, of course, with the union. The supervisors and executives tend to identify themselves with management. Individuals in both groups accept the traditional likes and dislikes as well as the misconceptions of their fellows.

Insulation. An adjustive technique which some people use to reduce the stress they feel from repeated frustrations is to "insulate" themselves. A person who uses insulation tries to protect himself by keeping his distance from others. He may appear self-sufficient, detached, even cold, but the careful observer will soon notice that he maintains this behavior as a protection rather than because he enjoys it. Let us illustrate with a case.

Miss G is the manager of the credit department in a large department store. Now forty-five years of age, she is a competent executive who supervises closely all those who work under her. She is respected by all, but not one person in the store calls her by her first name. She was the only child of elderly parents and had almost no playmates during her early years. Because she lacked skill in getting along with other children her own age, she approached the primary grades with timidity. She always stayed on the sidelines watching others, but never daring to participate.

The child who learns to fear situations where he will fail or be ridiculed is particularly apt to adjust by using the mechanism of insulation. The author knows this is true in the above case. Even in her early years, Miss G was afraid to join the group, and since she does not participate, she doesn't develop new skills as others are developing them. It becomes a self-perpetuating process, for she can never feel skillful enough to get over the fear of failure. Such a person frequently ends up choosing a vocation where he or she can be somewhat isolated. If this is impossible, the person often isolates himself by his haughty, detached manner.

Regression and Fixation. Two related mechanisms for handling stress, commonly found in industry, are regression and fixation. When an individual uses the mechanism of fixation, he continues to rely upon an adjustment pattern which was appropriate at an earlier age, but is no longer appropriate. When he uses regression, he returns to an adjustment pattern which was appropriate at an earlier age. Both are frequently seen in young children when a new baby arrives in the family. The slightly older sibling tends to fixate on his current adjustment pattern, or regress to a pattern more appropriate for a child younger than he. In industry the pattern is seen most frequently in the individual who is completely dependent upon the suggestions and advice of others. Extreme dependency is quite appropriate in the young child but hardly expected of a mature employee. No doubt some of the wet nursing which first-line supervisors have to employ in dealing with workers falls within this category. Let us mention a case in point at a higher organizational level.

Mr. C, a college graduate of some five years, has been promoted from a position of test engineer to assistant chief engineer. As test engineer he was thought of as a conservative, follow-the-rules sort of person, quite appropriate for the job he held. The new job, however, called for quick decision on new problems with which Mr. C just couldn't cope. In defending himself he overplayed being conservative so much that it soon became apparent that his conservatism was a protection from facing problems. This conservative behavior was in actuality a regression to earlier habits where it was used as a cover-up for inadequacy.

Repression. Probably one of the most important mechanisms by which individuals handle stress is repression. It is the process whereby the individual excludes from his conscious awareness an undesirable thought, feeling, or memory that causes him shame, pain, or guilt. Because of its very nature, however, repression is not often observed. It is only the aftereffects of repression that can be observed either by the individual himself or his associates. The aftereffects of repression may be annoying, but not too important. An individual may forget an appointment, or not remember the name of a man he is about to introduce. On the other hand, the aftereffects of repression may also be seen in several of the adjustment patterns usually referred to as neurotic behavior.

Compromise Reactions. One of the most obvious compromises which an individual can make when he is blocked in attaining his goal is compensation. He simply substitutes a second goal and satisfies it. The second goal may be his second choice, but it still satisfies him. It is not always possible to tell when compensation is being used, for the observer seldom knows that the individual is substituting a second goal for a more important one. The individual himself may not be sure either.

Overcompensation is an adjustive technique whereby an individual overemphasizes a certain type of behavior as a compromise. The worker who has always felt physically inferior may be the first to become physically aggressive in an argument. He is, in effect, trying to cover up his own shortcomings and avoid criticisms for an area of weakness. Many a man who boasts about his amorous adventures really doubts his own masculinity. In a sense he is substituting his tall stories for the behavior he would like, but has never achieved. At the same time he is trying to keep others from sensing what he believes to be a shortcoming. One illustration from the author's experience tells of a first-line supervisor who overcompensated for his lack of education by using big words with his men. Unfortunately for him, the men caught on all too quickly to this bit of compensation.

Rationalization. Rationalization is an adjustment technique whereby an individual reduces tension by accounting for his behavior by a socially approved reason rather than by the real reason. One rationalizes when he gives a good reason rather than the true reason for his behavior. We do not have to look very far to see the motive that would lead to the use of rationalization. Just watch any employee try to explain why he made a mistake! Or why he was late to work! The motive to avoid criticism and disapproval is quite strong in most people.

Projection. Still another adjustive technique by which individuals attempt to cover up weaknesses is projection. One really does not have to be troubled about a weakness that everyone else has; if you can project that weakness onto other people, you do not have to worry about it in yourself. The man on the drill press who slows down because "no one else is beating his heart out for the company" is projecting his feelings onto others. The dishonest employee eases his guilt by saying that "everyone has his price" and would take what he could get away with under certain conditions. The department head who does not feel that he is getting due recognition for his efforts may project his feelings against "the system."

NEUROTIC REACTIONS

It is all too frequent in our modern industrial society that an individual will adjust to stress by more abnormal reactions than by the defense mechanisms which we have just described. Our industrial climates are not always favorable to good mental health, and medical directors of our large corporations are finding that they must be as active in keeping workers and executives mentally healthy as they are in trying to keep them in good physical shape [8].

It is not uncommon for people to refer to an abnormal reaction as a "nervous breakdown" or to say that so-and-so is "all on edge." Psychologists and psychiatrists prefer to call these behaviors "neurotic reactions" [3]. They take several forms.

When the stress from a frustration or conflict is intense, the individual feels that the very essence of his personality is threatened. His intense reaction is an emotional one, and it thus involves the whole body. Intense and emotional reactions to frustrations and conflict produce a state of anxiety.

Neurotic anxiety is usually brought on by a conflict of long standing, and the individual is not aware of its exact nature. The industrial environment may not be responsible for the origin of these anxiety states, but it often provides the setting within which many of them develop. Industry cannot ignore the disruption which anxiety states create. Workers and managers who cannot stand competition, who are fearful that they cannot produce what is expected of them, who are angry whenever they receive orders from a superior, may develop such a severe state of anxiety that they have to defend themselves in some way. It is this attempt to defend oneself against anxiety which may lead a person to any one or combination of several of the following neurotic patterns.

Hypochondria. This is one of the most obvious adjustments an individual can make in response to anxiety. Anxiety involves the emotions and the emotions are accompanied by physiological reactions. The hypochondriac focuses his complaint on one or several of the organs that are influenced by emotional reactions. He may think something is wrong with the heart, lungs, stomach, intestines, kidneys, genital organs, nervous system, or muscles. He worries about his digestion and constantly watches his diet. The hypochondriac worries about his heart and tries to avoid the kind of exertion which might cause it to start beating vigorously again. He might better worry about the conflict or frustration which caused the anxiety and emotional reaction in the first place.

It should be fairly obvious that the hypochondriac with his overconcern about some part of his body is going to haunt the medical office of the plant. He is all set to catch the least sign that there is anything wrong, and just as he sees it, he will either begin to doctor himself or run to the infirmary. All of this means time away from the job, and often special problems for the supervisor.

Fatigue Syndrome. This maladjustment, sometimes referred to as "neurasthenia," is another frequent adjustment by which the anxious person shrinks his problem to a level where he can cope with it. Prolonged tension and the aches and pains that accompany it can be very fatiguing. It can, as a matter of fact, interfere with sleep and leave the individual prone to rest a good bit in the daytime. This in turn increases the chance that he will not sleep well at night. He becomes discouraged, perhaps apathetic, and restricts his activities to those involving the least possible exertion. This way of living may further block the satisfaction of the motive that produced the conflict and anxiety in the first place and thus may tend to perpetuate the pattern. Decrease in productivity adds to the complications.

Individuals with hypochondriacal or fatigue complaints usually talk freely about their troubles and frequently demand attention and sympathy. They arouse the anger of their fellow workers by their complaining and their frequent absences.

A public relations man for a well-known corporation began appearing at the office in a more or less haggard or distraught condition. He claimed to his associates that he was not sleeping well at night. It was obvious that he was less alert during the daytime than he had been previously. Several times during the day he would sit back in his chair to rest or he would even go to the lounge for a short nap. When he also complained about slight nausea and lack of appetite, others in the company encouraged him to get medical and then psychiatric assistance. While undergoing psychotherapy, he reviewed his enthusiastic approach to the public relations field some twenty years earlier. He had felt that he had all the qualifications to move quickly toward one of the top public relations posts in the nation. To reach this goal, he had traveled extensively and worked long hours both in the office and at home. He had known all along that he was sacrificing family welfare for his own vocational aspirations. It was only when he passed his fiftieth birthday that he became dimly aware that he was never going to be the great man in his field that he had dreamed of becoming. This dimly sensed realization was apparently responsible for the insomnia. Both the insomnia and the anxiety over not reaching a top position were responsible for the generalized fatigue reaction.

The Phobias. Here we have still another method for handling anxiety. The individual focuses all his anxiety on one specific object even though he cannot account for the tremendous effect that object has on him. Theoretically, any object or situation can become the focal point for the phobia, but the most common ones are animals, germs, small rooms, elevators, trains, closed-in places, wide-open places, high places, and the dark. The individual does not react to his anxiety in general and is not aware of the conflict that is troubling him. Instead he blames something in particular, such as cats. He is thrown into a panic by the presence of a cat, and perhaps by the picture of a cat or even the spoken word "cat." He realizes that his behavior is silly and illogical but he cannot avoid reacting. The choice of the object usually goes back to a time when the object or situation was present, quite incidentally, when anxiety was rather extreme.

A recent graduate of an engineering college was hired by one of the industries in his home town. In spite of his mild protests, he was asked to assist two other employees with some rather complicated mathematical calculations. His desk was crowded into an already small office where the other two men were working. After a few months, he began to complain that the office seemed stuffy and that he felt as if the walls were closing in on him. He would frequently go off on errands or just go outside to get a breath of fresh air. After a period of about six months, his feelings became so intense that it was necessary to change his assignment. In the conversations that took place at this time, it became obvious that he felt very unsure of himself whenever he was dealing with mathematics. His reaction toward the work he was doing generalized to the room itself, and claustrophobia was the result.

Compulsions. These behaviors help an individual reduce the effects of his anxiety. The individual who uses compulsive patterns is in effect distracting himself from the real conflict by focusing his attention on the irresistible urge to do, say, or think something in a particular way. Repetitive acts, such as hand washing, are probably among the most dramatic of the compulsions. Every few minutes the individual feels that he must wash his hands. He knows the act is silly, tries to resist it, feels increasingly uncomfortable, and finally gets relief by giving in once again. One individual who worked in an accounting department would check the safe, time and time again, before leaving the office. This type of behavior often goes unnoticed as being abnormal.

Excessive orderliness or rigidity is a less dramatic compulsive pattern, but probably a far more common one. Orderliness is usually considered to be a desirable trait, but excessive orderliness can dominate an individual's entire life. It may mean that all his possessions must be in exactly the right place. It may lead to a kind of cleanliness to which one becomes a slave. Or it may lead to a rigid pattern of thinking. The individual surrounds himself with rules to govern all his actions and goes to any length to avoid doubt and uncertainty. Office procedures must be exact and unvaried. The individual cannot accept new plans until he is certain that they will succeed.

The Hysterias. Here we find a group of disorders in which a part of the body or a function of the body is either inactivated or involuntarily activated. When inactivation is involved, the individual loses the ability to feel or use a part of the body. He may be unable to walk or see or hear or speak. Amnesia is a hysterical disorder in which the individual has a partial or complete loss of memory.

Occasionally a part of the body is activated and seemingly inexplicable behavior occurs. There may be muscular tremors of the head or hands, muscular cramps which may affect the hand just when the individual wants to write, tics which involve repetitive movements of some part of the body such as the shoulders. Some individuals, usually children, are activated to walk in their sleep.

Most, if not all, of the hysterical disorders can also occur as a result of organ or tissue pathology. They are diagnosed as hysterical only where there is no evidence that anything is wrong with the organs or tissues involved.

In hysterical disorders, the individual transfers an emotional problem into a physical disorder. It is the bragging soldier who is not consciously aware of his fear of battle who loses the use of his right arm and trigger finger. It is the girl who cannot face the possibility that her lover is unfaithful who develops hysterical blindness. And it is the man who feels terribly guilty over some incident in the office who develops amnesia, and who thus excludes from memory the guilt-provoking incident and all other memories including the memory of his own identity as well.

Let us take a look at an illustration that exemplifies a form of hysteria. The author is familiar with a middle-management official who had difficulty writing his name when it involved signing contract agreements. He blamed the difficulty on writer's cramp. After being given a change of jobs which took him out of his responsible position in labor relations, the writing difficulty did not occur again until some two years later. At this particular time the man had to place his signature on an important document. The interesting point of this case is that the writer's cramp went away with the change of job responsibility, *but* a new physical complaint came into being. The man got a stomach-ache each time he went to lunch with a customer. You guessed it, his new job was in sales!

Alcoholic Addiction. Nearly any individual who uses a little alcohol becomes more relaxed. He talks more fluently and is less inhibited in his actions. Excessive use of alcohol leads to a more severe disturbance and withdrawal becomes increasingly difficult. One physician of our acquaintance says that one of his biggest concerns about some of his high-pressure industrial patients is the fear of their turning to excessive use of alcohol.

It is easy to see why the anxious person might seek the relaxation that comes with alcohol. As we have seen, the anxiety itself is frequently a result of the individual's fears, and the alcohol provides him with a period during which he is not afraid.

The Anxiety State. When no other neurotic pattern develops for handling anxiety, the individual is left in an anxiety state. Anxiety is first of all a feeling of vague apprehension accompanied by visceral and muscular changes in the body. This condition stimulates the individual to develop one of the neurotic adjustment patterns—hypochondria, fatigue, compulsions, hysteria, or drug and alcohol addiction—to reduce the anxiety to a level where he can face and handle it. But if he does not develop one of these patterns, or if no one of them works adequately for him, he remains in an anxiety state.

The chronically anxious person makes the usual complaints regarding headaches, backaches, or upsets involving any of the visceral organs. He usually states that he can't think clearly or concentrate. Unexpected noises bother him. He is tired all the time. There is a feeling of general apprehension and dread and yet he does not know what it is that he is afraid of.

PSYCHOTIC DISORDERS

Sometimes an individual's reaction to stress and anxiety is so extreme that he breaks with reality and develops hallucinations, delusions, and distorted emotional tone. Although it is possible that chemical imbalance and even heredity may influence the development of psychotic behavior, it is still generally considered to be an extreme reaction to stress [10]. Let us briefly discuss three psychotic disorders found occasionally in industry.

Paranoid Disorders. These abnormalities are characterized by systematic delusions but do not include any change in emotional tone. The delusions are false beliefs. The individual believes perhaps that someone is persecuting him or talking about him, or that some person or machine has gained an influence over him. He may develop ideas of grandeur and feel that he is an extremely important person or has some extremely important power. Anxiety underlies the development of the paranoid disorders, for the paranoid individual always has some area about which he is insecure or guilty. He broods about it, usually in solitude, and works out a delusion which either accounts for something that bothers him or sets up the possibility that it will free him from the situation.

An expert tool and die maker had made a real name for himself in a large steel plant. When he reached about fifty years of age, he began to be very critical of the work of others around him and suspicious of his supervisors and the company as a whole. He told fantastic tales about the way he was being treated and, in spite of his good record, the company was forced to let him go. The medical department recommended that he get psychiatric treatment, but after one appointment with a specialist, he refused to go back. He went to work for a smaller company, but in only two or three months the same pattern began to repeat itself. Even though he had no supervisory responsibility, he insisted on instructing and criticizing other workers. This company also had to discharge him. His family too was aware that something was wrong, for at home he spent most of his time brooding about the "injustice" of the way he had been treated.

Schizophrenic Disorders. These classifications probably account for over half of the psychotic population. The entire personality of the schizophrenic is disorganized and distorted, for he reacts mostly to the world he creates in his private fantasy. Because of this, his emotional reactions seem completely incongruous to the observer. He can talk of the disintegration of all his internal organs without seeming to be disturbed by it in the least. In effect, the schizophrenic puts a barrier around himself which no person, no event, not even any guilt reaction of his own, can penetrate.

When the disorder develops slowly and has its origin in anxieties which begin during childhood and adolescence, the individual is always considered to be a little queer and detached. Some people, however, maintain a precarious balance for years and develop the psychosis suddenly when some event precipitates a crisis. Before his friends realize what is happening, such an individual may begin to talk wildly or commit a number of foolish acts.

Manic and Depressive Disorders. Here are psychotic behaviors that tend to develop later in life than the schizophrenic disorders. There is usually a feeling of guilt and the individual broods about it until he begins to feel worthless and depressed. The manic excitement, if it occurs at all, is probably an overcompensation, a reaction chosen solely to avoid impending depression. The depressed individual may be either apathetic and hopeless or tense and hopeless. But he is always hopeless. The manic individual is excited. He comes up with fantastically wonderful schemes and turns out a voluminous amount of work. Individuals who are either manic or depressed are obviously dangerous both to themselves and to others.

DEALING WITH PEOPLE WHO HAVE PSYCHOLOGICAL PROBLEMS

There is no one set of rules which one can follow in dealing with all people who have personal adjustment difficulties. Their patterns are far too varied. One would scarcely treat an alcoholic in the same way that one would treat a person who is distracted by his worry about his son's delinquency.

Some companies give a fair amount of attention to people with psychological problems. They have made studies and carried out plans for improvement in the areas of absenteeism, safety, morale, promotion policies, and supervisory practices, as we described in previous chapters. Some industries have recognized that the adjustment of their workers improves only when there is an attempt made to make their work meaningful and dignified.

Some of the techniques which industry uses for handling psychological problems are formal ones which have been crystallized into company policy. There are departments which have the welfare of the employees as their major concern. There are other techniques, less formal ones, which cannot be put into individual departments, which men in industry can use to advantage in dealing with individual workers who have personal psychological problems. As all men in industry learn the nature of behavior and its relation to motivation and conflict, they also see new ways of dealing with individuals. One reason that psychology is becoming increasingly more accepted in industry is because industry is becoming more aware of the human element [6, 7, 14].

Selection, Guidance, and Training. The function of personnel and training departments in industry has been discussed in earlier chapters. The work of these departments in the proper hiring, placement, and training of

employees goes a long way toward reducing the personal adjustment problems which arise out of the nature of the day's work and the working conditions which exist. Good personnel departments attempt to find the proper
job for each employee by making a study of both the job applicant and the
functions of the job to be performed. Orientation, vocational counseling,
and job training may all be involved.

The personnel office frequently extends its activities beyond the original
placement of the applicants, and assists in periodic evaluation of employees. Such evaluations may serve as the basis for raises, promotions,
transfers, and, in addition, indirectly aid in personal adjustments.

In some industries, the personnel office conducts or arranges human
relations courses designed to indoctrinate managers and supervisors with
a point of view to guide them in their handling of the men who work under
them. Such courses usually help the men to see more clearly the personal
adjustment patterns which they encounter daily among the men in their
departments.

Medical Department. The industrial physician and industrial nurse are
in the forefront of those within industry who deal with people having
psychological difficulties. Since adjustment patterns frequently involve
aches and pains as well as other physical symptoms, the medical staff
spends a high proportion of its time with workers whose complaints may
be related to emotional conflicts. They provide medication for the woman
with menstrual irregularities or for the man with a tension headache. They
use massage or a heat lamp for the worker with a backache. And while they
bandage fingers or dispense aspirin they also listen. They often give a re-
assuring kind of attention, and they may be able to say the right thing to
take the mystery out of a physical condition that has the worker worried.
The efforts of the doctors and nurses may not often get at the roots of the
anxiety and conflict, but they do sometimes alleviate many of the
symptoms.

The staff in the medical office may also be among the first to recognize
the possibility of a disturbing neurosis or an actual psychosis. They know
the symptoms, and they know that there will be occasional severe mental
illness coming out here and there [4].

In some industries there is a psychiatric consultant available part time,
or a full-time psychiatrist may even be on the staff. In some industries
there are psychological counselors who, although they are not psychiatrists
and do not have a medical degree, are trained to provide therapy within
the industrial setting.

Not the least of the contributions of the medical office has been the
attention paid to company executives. It takes years to train a competent
executive, and the investment is lost when the pressure of the job brings
on hypertension, an ulcer, or a heart attack. Now that this problem has

been brought to their attention, some companies not only insist upon regular physical examinations, but also have designed plans for reducing the pressure on their executives.

A Problem in Education. Industry is already doing some helpful things for those employees who exhibit disturbing patterns of adjustment by providing professional help for mental as well as physical problems. Individual workers can also do some things to aid their fellow workers who have disturbing problems; they can provide an atmosphere of friendliness and understanding. One of the main aims of both formal and informal educational programs in human relations in industry is to provide some understanding of why people behave as they do.

One thing is certain. We have a long way to go in the area of mental health. McLean and Taylor [8] point out in their book *Mental Health in Industry* that the psychiatrist has no nostrums, no panaceas, and no gimmicks to offer an industrial society.

SUGGESTIONS FOR FURTHER READINGS

Brown, J. A. C. *The social psychology of industry.* Pelican Series. Baltimore: Penguin, 1954. A description of the formal and informal organizations in industry and how they are related to personal adjustments.

Cameron, N. *The psychology of behavior disorders.* Boston: Houghton Mifflin, 1947. A biosocial interpretation of adjustment problems with excellent descriptions of abnormal behaviors.

McKinney, F. *Psychology of personal adjustment.* New York: Wiley, 1960. A student-centered book well organized and highlighted by numerous cases.

Shaffer, L. F., & Shoben, E. J., Jr. *The psychology of adjustment.* Boston: Houghton Mifflin, 1956. A thorough and readable text on problems of personal adjustment.

BIBLIOGRAPHY

CHAPTERS 1 AND 2

1. Blum, M. L. *Readings in experimental industrial psychology.* Englewood Cliffs, N. J.: Prentice-Hall, 1952.
2. Boynton, P. W. *So you want a better job?* New York: Socony-Vacuum Oil Co., 1947.
3. Brown, C. W., & Ghiselli, E. E. *Scientific method in psychology.* New York: McGraw-Hill, 1955.
4. Clark, K. E. *America's psychologists.* Washington: American Psychological Association, 1957.
5. Ferguson, L. W. Industrial psychology. *Annu. Rev. Psychol.* 1958, 9, 243–266.
6. Gilmer, B. v. H. Industrial psychology. *Annu. Rev. Psychol.,* 1960, 11, 323–350.
7. Greenly, R. J. Job training. National Association of Manufacturers, *Labor Relations Bull.,* 1945, No. 35.
8. Haire, M. Business is too important to be studied only by economists. *Amer. Psychologist,* 1960, 15, 271–272.
9. Havemann, E. The age of psychology in the U.S. *Life,* Jan. 7, 1957, 68–82.
10. Karn, H. W., & Gilmer, B. v. H. *Readings in industrial and business psychology.* New York: McGraw-Hill, 1952.
11. Katzell, R. A. Industrial psychology. *Annu. Rev. Psychol.,* 1957, 8, 237–268.
12. Kendall, W. E. Industrial psychology. *Annu. Rev. Psychol.,* 1956, 7, 197–232.
13. Leavitt, H. J., & Whisler, T. L. Management in the 1980's. *Harvard Bus. Rev.,* 1958, 36, 41–48.

14. Levinson, H. The psychologist in industry. *Harvard Bus. Rev.*, 1959, 37, 93–99.
15. McCollom, I. N. Psychologists in industry in the United States. *Amer. Psychologist,* 1959, 14, 704–708.
16. Ogg, E. Psychologists in action. American Psychological Association. Public Affairs Pamphlet No. 229. Washington: Public Affairs Press, 1955.
17. Osgood, C. E. *Method and theory in experimental psychology.* New York: Oxford Univer. Press, 1953.
18. Roethlisberger, F. J., & Dickson, W. J. *Management and the worker.* Cambridge: Harvard Univer. Press, 1939.
19. Symposium. Blueprinting the next ten years of industrial psychology. *Personnel Psychol.,* 1959, 12, 29–48.
20. Townsend, J. C. *Introduction to experimental method.* New York: Mc-Graw-Hill, 1953.
21. Viteles, M. S. *Industrial psychology.* New York: Norton, 1932.
22. Wallace, S. R., Jr., & Weitz, J. Industrial Psychology, *Annu. Rev. Psychol.,* 1955, 6, 217–250.

CHAPTER 3

1. Buchele, R. B. Company character and the effectiveness of personnel management. *Personnel,* 1955, 31, 289–302.
2. Cornell, W. B. *Organization and management in industry and business.* New York: Ronald, 1958.
3. Editors. Executive staff and distaff. *Duns Rev. and Modern Industry,* 1957, 69, 70–75.
4. Fleishman, E. A. Leadership climate, human relations training, and supervisory behavior. *Personnel Psychol.,* 1953, 6, 205–222.
5. Gellerman, S. W. The company personality. *Mgmt. Rev.,* 1959, 48, 69–76.
6. Gorsuch, J. H. Good management men delegate authority. *Advanc. Mgmt.,* Sept., 1954, 5–8.
7. Jones, E. D. *The administration of industrial enterprises.* New York: Longmans, 1925.
8. Leavitt, H. J. *Managerial psychology.* Chicago: Univer. of Chicago Press, 1958.
9. Mandell, M. M. The effect of organizational environment on personnel selection. *Personnel,* 1953, 30, 13–16.
10. Mayo, E. *The social problems of an industrial civilization.* Cambridge: Harvard Univer. Press, 1945.
11. Problem for the front office. *Fortune,* May, 1951.
12. Schoen, D. R. Human relations: boon or bogle? *Harvard Bus. Rev.,* 1957, 35, 41–47.
13. Sayles, L. R. *Behavior of industrial work groups: prediction and control.* New York: Wiley, 1958.
14. Simon, H. A. *Administrative behavior.* New York: Macmillan, 1957.
15. Stryker, P. Can management be managed? *Fortune,* July, 1953, 100–101.

16. Warner, W. L., & Abegglen, J. C. *Occupational mobility in American business and industry.* Minneapolis: Univer. Minn. Press, 1955.

17. Warner, W. L., & Abegglen, J. C. Successful wives of successful executives. *Harvard Bus. Rev.,* 1956, 34, 64–70.

18. Worthy, J. C. Organizational structure and employee morale. *Amer. Sociological Rev.,* 1950, 15, 169–179.

19. Zerfoss, L. F., & O'Connor, R. F. The atmosphere in which people grow. *Atlanta Econ. Rev.* 1960, 10, 11–14.

CHAPTER 4

1. Ashby, W. R. *An introduction to cybernetics.* New York: Wiley, 1956.

2. Bruner, J. S., Goodnow, J. J., & Austin, G. A. *A study of thinking.* New York: Wiley, 1956.

3. Gilbreth, F. B., & Gilbreth, L. M. *Applied motion study.* New York: Sturgis & Walton, 1917.

4. Gouldner, A. W. *Patterns of industrial bureaucracy.* Glencoe, Ill.: Free Press, 1954.

5. Henderson, J. M., & Quandt, R. E. *Microeconomic theory.* New York: McGraw-Hill, 1958.

6. Lamperti, F. A., & Thurston, J. B. *Interval auditing for management.* Englewood Cliffs, N. J.: Prentice-Hall, 1953.

7. Macy, J., Jr., Christie, L. S., & Luce, R. D. Coding noise in a task-oriented group. *J. Abnorm. Soc. Psychol.,* 1953, 48, 401–409.

8. March, J. G., & Simon, H. A. *Organizations.* New York: Wiley, 1958.

9. Roethlisberger, F. J., & Dickson, W. J. *Management and the worker.* Cambridge: Harvard Univer. Press, 1939.

10. Selznick, P. *TVA and the grass roots.* Berkeley: Univer. of Calif. Press, 1949.

11. Simon, H. A. *Models of man: social and rational.* New York: Wiley, 1957.

12. Taylor, F. W. *The principles of scientific management.* New York: Harper, 1911.

13. Trueblood, R. M., & Cyert, R. M. *Sampling techniques in accounting.* Englewood Cliffs, N. J.: Prentice-Hall, 1957.

CHAPTER 5

1. Atkinson, J. W. *Motives in fantasy, action, and society: a method of assessment and study.* Princeton, N. J.: Van Nostrand, 1958.

2. Baldamus, W. Type of work and motivation. *British J. Sociol.,* 1951, 2, 44–58.

3. Bergler, E. *The revolt of the middle-age man.* New York: Wyn, 1954.

4. Brayfield, A. H., & Crockett, W. H. Employee attitudes and employee performance. *Psychol. Bull.,* 1955, 52, 396–424.

5. Cleeton, G. U. *Making work human.* Yellow Springs, Ohio: Antioch Press, 1949.
6. Dill, W. R., Hilton, T. L., & Reitman, W. R. How aspiring managers promote their own careers. *Calif. Mgmt. Rev.,* 1960, 2, No. 4, 9–15.
7. Eaton, W. H. Hypotheses related to worker frustration. *J. Soc. Psychol.,* 1952, 35, 59–68.
8. Gordon, G. How to "live" with your job. *National Office Management Association Conference,* Montreal, May, 1960.
9. Homans, G. C. The Western Electric researches. In G. C. Homans (Ed.), *Fatigue of workers: its relation to production.* New York: Reinhold, 1941.
10. Homans, G. C. *The human group.* New York: Harcourt, Brace, 1950.
11. Leavitt, H. J. *Managerial psychology.* Chicago: Univer. of Chicago Press, 1958.
12. Lewin, K. Forces behind food habits and methods of change. *Bull. National Res. Council,* 1943, 108, 35–65.
13. McGregor, D., & Knickerbocker, I. Industrial relations and national defense: a challenge to management. *Personnel,* 1941, 18, 49–63.
14. Maier, N. R. F. *Principles of human relations.* New York: Wiley, 1952.
15. Moore, H. Basic needs of industrial workers. *Personnel J.,* 1949, 27, 344–348.
16. Selye, H. *The stress of life.* New York: McGraw-Hill, 1956.
17. Smith, F., & Kerr, W. A. Turnover factors as assessed by the exit interview. *J. App. Psychol.,* 1953, 37, 352–355.
18. Stagner, R. Psychological aspects of industrial conflict. II. Motivation. *Personnel Psychol.,* 1950, 3, 1–5.
19. Wyatt, S., Frost, L., & Stock, F. G. L. *Incentives in repetitive work.* London: Industrial Health Research Board, 1934, No. 69.

CHAPTER 6

1. Brogden, H. C., & Taylor, E. K. The dollar criterion—applying the cost accounting concept to criterion construction. *Personnel Psychol.,* 1950, 3, 133–154.
2. Buros, O. K. *The fourth mental measurements yearbook.* New Brunswick, N. J.: Rutgers Univer. Press, 1953.
3. Cronbach, L. J. *Essentials of psychological testing.* New York: Harper, 1949.
4. Cronbach, L. J., & Gleser, G. *Psychological tests and personnel decisions.* Urbana: Univer. of Ill. Press, 1957.
5. DuBois, P. *Multivariate correlational analysis.* New York: Harper, 1957.
6. Flanagan, J. C. The critical incident technique. *Psychol. Bull.,* 1954, 51, 327–358.
7. Freeman, F. S. *Theory and practice of psychological testing.* New York: Henry Holt, 1955.
8. Greene, E. B. *Measurements of human behavior.* New York: Odyssey Press, 1952.
9. Guilford, J. P. The structure of intellect. *Psychol. Bull.,* 1956, 53, 267–293.

10. Horst, A. P. A technique for the development of a differential prediction battery. *Psychol. Monogr.*, 1954, 68, No. 9.

11. Horst, A. P. A technique for the development of a multiple absolute prediction battery. *Psychol. Monogr.*, 1955, 69, No. 5.

12. Primoff, E. J. *Test selection by job analysis.* U. S. Civil Service Commission Assembled Test Technical Series No. 20, May, 1955.

13. Sisson, D. E. Forced-choice: the new army rating. *Personnel Psychol.*, 1948, 1, 365–381.

14. Taylor, H. C., & Russell, J. T. The relationship of validity coefficients to the practical effectiveness of tests in selection: discussion and tables. *J. Appl. Psychol.*, 1939, 23, 565–578.

15. Thorndike, R. L. *Personnel selection.* New York: Wiley, 1949.

16. Thorndike, R. L., & Hagen, E. *Measurement and evaluation in psychology and education.* New York: Wiley, 1955.

17. U. S. Employment Service. *Estimates of worker trait requirements for 4,000 jobs.* Washington: U. S. Department of Labor, 1957.

18. Wherry, R. J. Criteria and validity. In D. H. Fryer, and E. R. Henry, *Handbook of applied psychology.* Vol. 1. New York: Rinehart, 1950, Chap. 27.

19. Wherry, R. J. *A comparison of various rating methods, PRB Report No. 921.* Washington: The Adjutant General's Office, Feb., 1952.

20. Wherry, R. J. The past and future of criterion evaluation. *Personnel Psychol.*, 1957, 10, 1–5.

CHAPTER 7

1. Birmingham, H. D., Kahn, A., & Taylor, F. M. Demonstration of the effects of quickening in multiple-coordinate control tasks. Washington: Naval Research Laboratory, 1954.

2. Braun, H. W., Wedekind, C. E., & Smudski, J. F. The effect of an irrelevant drive on maze learning in the rat. *J. Exp. Psychol.*, 1957, 54, (2), 148–152.

3. Bryan, G. L. Empirical evaluation of various job-analysis methods. In *Symposium on Electronics Maintenance.* Washington: U. S. Government Printing Office, August, 1955.

4. Ebel, R. L. Obtaining and reporting evidence on content validity. *Educ. Psychol. Measmt.*, 1956, 16, 269–282.

5. Frederiksen, N., Saunders, D. R., & Wand, B. The in-basket test. *Psychol. Monogr.*, 1957, 71, No. 9 (Whole No. 438).

6. Fryer, D. H., Feinberg, M. R., & Zalkind, S. S. *Developing people in industry.* New York: Harper, 1956.

7. Gagne, R. M. Training devices and simulators: some research issues. *Amer. Psychologist*, 1954, 9, 95–107.

8. Gagne, R. M. Methods of forecasting maintenance job requirements. In *Symposium on Electronics Maintenance.* Washington: U. S. Government Printing Office, August, 1955.

9. Glaser, R., Damrin, Dora E., & Gardner, F. M. The tab item: a technique

for the measurement of proficiency in diagnostic problem solving tasks. *Educ. Psychol. Measmt.*, 1954, 14, 283–293.

10. Guthrie, E. R. (Ed.) Conditioning: a theory of learning in terms of stimulus, response, and association. *Yearb. Nat. Soc. Stud. Educ.*, 1942, 41, 17–60.

11. Harlow, H. The formation of learning sets. *Psychol. Rev.*, 1949, 56, 51–65.

12. Keller, F. S., & Schoenfeld, W. N. *Principles of psychology*. New York: Appleton-Century-Crofts, 1950.

13. Kendler, H. H. Drive interaction: I. Learning as a function of the simultaneous presence of the hunger and thirst drives. *J. Exp. Psychol.*, 1945, 35, 96–107.

14. Lindahl, L. G. Movement analysis as an industrial training method. *J. App. Psychol.*, 1945, 29, 420–436.

15. Miller, R. B. Psychological considerations for the design of training equipment. *Wright Air Development Center Technical Report 54-563*. Pittsburgh: American Institute for Research, 1954.

16. Saul, E. V., et al. A review of the literature pertinent to the design and use of effective graphic training aids. *SpecDevCen Technical Report 494-08-1*. New York: Special Devices Center, 1954.

17. Skinner, B. F. *Science and human behavior*. New York: Macmillan, 1953.

18. Spence, K. W. *Behavior theory and conditioning*. New Haven: Yale Univer. Press, 1956.

19. Taylor, H. C., & Russell, J. T. The relationship of validity coefficients to the practical effectiveness of tests in selection. *J. App. Psychol.*, 1939, 23, 565–578.

20. Taylor, Janet A. Drive theory and manifest anxiety. *Psychol. Bull.*, 1956, 53, 4, 303–320.

21. Thorndike, R. L. *Personnel selection*. New York: Wiley, 1949.

22. VanCott, H. P., & Altman, J. W. Procedures for including human engineering factors in the development of weapon systems. *Wright Air Development Center Technical Report 56-488*, October, 1956.

23. Wolfle, D. L. Training. In S. S. Stevens (Ed.), *Handbook of experimental psychology*. New York: Wiley, 1951.

Chapter 8

1. Arensberg, C. M., & McGregor, D. Determination of morale in an industrial company. *App. Anthrop.*, 1942, 1, 12–34.

2. Armstrong, T. O. Developing effective supervisor-employee communication. *Personnel*, 1950, 27, 70–75.

3. Bingham, W. V. Making work worthwhile. In E. M. East, (Ed.), *Biology in human affairs*. New York: McGraw-Hill, 1931.

4. File, Q. W., & Remmers, H. H. How supervise? New York: Psychological Corporation, 1948.

5. Habbe, S. Job attitudes of life insurance agents. *J. App. Psychol.*, 1947, 31, 111–128.

6. Hersey, R. *Better foremanship.* Philadelphia: Chilton, 1955.

7. Herzberg, F., Mausner, B., Peterson, R. O., & Capwell, D. F. Job attitudes: review of research and opinion. Pittsburgh: Psychological Service of Pittsburgh, 1957.

8. Jarrard, L. E. Empathy: the concept and industrial application. *Personnel Psychol.*, 1956, 9, 157–167.

9. Kerr, W. A., & Speroff, B. J. *The empathy test.* Chicago: Psychometric Affiliates, 1951.

10. Life Insurance Agency Management Association. *Buddy ratings—a technique for supervisory selection.* Research Report No. 10. Hartford: Author, 1957.

11. Maccoby, N. A quantitative comparison of certain psychological conditions related to group productivity in two widely different industrial situations. Unpublished doctoral dissertation, Univer. of Mich., 1950.

12. McMurry, R. N. Psychological problems of industrial supervision. *J. Consult. Psychol.*, 1944, 8, 175–181.

13. Maier, N. R. F. *Principles of human relations.* New York: Wiley, 1952.

14. Mann, F. C., & Dent, J. *Appraisals of supervisors and attitudes of their employees in an electric power company.* Ann Arbor: Univer. of Mich. Survey Research Center, 1954.

15. Nagle, B. F. Productivity, employee attitude, and supervisor sensitivity. *Personnel Psychol.*, 1954, 7, 219–233.

16. Parker, W. E. J., & Kleemeier, R. W. *Human relations in supervision.* New York: McGraw-Hill, 1951.

17. Patton, W. M., Jr. Studies in industrial empathy. III. A study of supervisory empathy in the textile industry. *J. App. Psychol.*, 1954, 38, 285–288.

18. Pelz, D. C. Influence: a key to effective leadership in the first-line supervisor. *Personnel*, 1952, 29, 209–217.

19. Pfiffner, J. M. The effective supervisor: an organization research study. *Personnel*, 1955, 31, 530–540.

20. Remmers, L. J., & Remmers, H. H. Studies in industrial empathy: labor leaders' attitudes toward industrial supervision and their estimates of management's attitudes. *Personnel Psychol.*, 1949, 2, 427–436.

21. Roethlisberger, F. J., & Dickson, W. J. *Management and the worker.* Cambridge: Harvard Univer. Press, 1939.

22. Rogers, C. R. *Client-centered therapy.* Boston: Houghton Mifflin, 1951.

23. Siegel, A. I. An experimental evaluation of the sensitivity of The Empathy Test. *J. App. Psychol.*, 1954, 38, 222–223.

24. Stagner, R. Psychological aspects of industrial conflict. *Personnel Psychol.*, 1950, 3, 1–15.

25. Thorne, F. C. Directive counseling in psychotherapy. *Amer. Psychologist*, 1948, 3, 160–165.

26. Viteles, M. S. *Motivation and morale in industry.* New York: Norton, 1953.

27. Wallen, R. Improving supervision by reducing anxiety. *Personnel J.*, 1951, 30, 9–13.

28. Weschler, I. R., Tannenbaum, R., & Zenger, J. H. *Yardsticks for human relations training.* Institute of Industrial Relations, No. 66. Berkeley: Univer. of California, 1957.

29. Wilson, R. C., High, W. S., & Comrey, A. L. An iterative analysis of supervisory and group dimensions. *J. App. Psychol.,* 1955, 39, 85–91.

30. Wray, D. E. Marginal men of industry: the foremen. *Amer. J. Sociol.,* 1949, 55, 298.

CHAPTER 9

1. Ahren, E. Executive appraisal—a new approach. *Mgmt. News,* American Management Association, March 31, 1950.

2. Anshen, M. Management development. Western Electric Company, Skytop Conference, May 23, 1957.

3. Argyris, C. *Executive leadership—an appraisal of a manager in action.* New York: Harper, 1953.

4. Barnard, C. I. *The functions of the executive.* Cambridge: Harvard Univer. Press, 1950.

5. Carlson, S. Executive behavior. Stockholm: Strömbergs, 1951.

6. Cattell, R. B., & Stice, G. F. *The psychodynamics of small groups.* Urbana: Univer. of Illinois, 1953.

7. Cleeton, G. U., & Mason, C. W. *Executive ability: its discovery and development.* Yellow Springs, Ohio: Antioch Press, 1946.

8. Coates, C. H., & Pelligrim, R. J. Executives and supervisors: a situational theory of differential occupational mobility. *Social Forces,* 1956, 35, 121–126.

9. Fleishman, E. A., Harris, E. F., & Burtt, H. E. *Leadership and supervision in industry—an evaluation of a supervisory training program.* Columbus: Ohio State Univer. Bur. Educ. Res., No. 33, 1955.

10. Fortune Editors. The nine hundred. In W. M. Fox, *Readings in personnel management.* New York: Holt, 1957, 18–25.

11. Gardner, B. B. Executives: their personality and its appraisal. *Advanc. Mgmt.,* Jan., 1953, 13–15.

12. Gibb, C. A. Leadership. In G. Lindzey, *Handbook of social psychology.* Cambridge: Addison-Wesley, 1954.

13. Ginzberg, E. *What makes an executive.* New York: Columbia Univer. Press, 1955.

14. Guetzkow, H., & Kriesberg, M. Executive use of the administrative conference. *Personnel,* 1950, Mar., 2–7.

15. Henry, W. E. The business executive: the psychodynamics of a social role. *Amer. J. Sociol.,* 1949, 54, 286–291.

16. Homans, G. C. *The human group.* New York: Harcourt, Brace, 1950.

17. Johnson, E. P. A new kind of performance review emphasizes executives' development. *Personnel J.,* 1954, 33, 131–133.

18. Kellogg, M. S. Appraising the performance of management personnel; a case study. *Personnel,* 1955, 31, 442–455.

19. Knickerbocker, I. Leadership, a conception and some implications. *J. Soc. Issues,* 1948, 4, 24–41.

20. Leavitt, H. J., & Whisler, T. L. Management in the 1980's. *Harvard Bus. Rev.,* 1958, 36, 41–48.

21. Lewin, K. *A dynamic theory of personality.* New York: McGraw-Hill, 1935.

22. Lewin, K. *Field theory in social science.* New York: Harper, 1951.

23. Mace, M. L. *The growth and development of executives.* Cambridge: Harvard Univer. Press, 1950.

24. Machaver, W. C., & Erickson, W. E. A new approach to executive appraisal. *Personnel,* 1958, 35, 8–14.

25. Mahler, W. R., & Guyot, F. Appraisal of executive performance, the "Achilles Heel" of management development. *Personnel,* 1955, 31, 429–441.

26. Moyer, K. E. Conference communication and executive development. Pittsburgh: Carnegie Institute of Technology, 1959, 1–41. (Mimeographed.)

27. OSS Assessment Staff. *The assessment of men.* New York: Rinehart, 1948.

28. Peck, R. F., & Thompson, J. M. Use of individual assessments in a management development program: a case study. *J. Personnel Administr. & Industr. Relat.,* Apr., 1954, 79–98.

29. Pellegrin, R. J., & Coates, C. H. Executives and supervisors: contrasting definitions of career success. *Administrative Sci. Quart.,* 1957, 1, 506–517.

30. Planty, E. G., & Efferson, C. E. Counseling executives after merit rating or evaluation. *Personnel,* 1951, 27, 384–402.

31. Ramfalk, C. W. Top management selection. Stockholm: Swedish Council for Personnel Administration, 1957.

32. Randle, C. W. How to identify promotable executives. *Harvard Bus. Rev.,* 1956, 34, 122–134.

33. *What makes an executive?* Round Table on Executive Potential and Performance. New York: Columbia Univer. Press, 1955.

34. Schleh, E. C. Make your executive merit rating realistic. *Personnel,* 1953, 29, 480–484.

35. Schneirla, T. C. Social organization in insects as related to individual function. *Psychol. Rev.,* 1941, 48, 465–486.

36. Shartle, C. L. *Executive performance and leadership.* Englewood Cliffs, N. J.: Prentice-Hall, 1956.

37. Standard Oil Company of California. A practical approach to executive development. San Francisco: Author, 1948.

38. Stogdill, R. M. Personal factors associated with leadership: a survey of the literature. *J. Psychol.,* 1948, 25, 35–71.

39. Stryker, P. On the meaning of executive qualities. *Fortune,* 1958, 57, 116–119.

40. U. S. Naval Institute. Personnel administration at the executive level. Annapolis: Author, 1948.

41. Ward, B. Worker's management in Yugoslavia. *J. Political Econom.,* 1957, 45, 373–387.

42. Whyte, W. F. *The organization man.* New York: Simon & Schuster, 1956.

CHAPTER 10

1. Bavelas, A. Communication patterns in task-oriented groups. *J. Acoust. Soc. Amer.,* 1950, 22, 725–750.
2. Bellows, R. M. *Psychology of personnel in business and industry.* Englewood Cliffs, N. J.: Prentice-Hall, 1954.
3. Blum, M. L. *Industrial psychology and its social foundations.* New York: Harper, 1956.
4. Brown, J. A. C. *The social psychology of industry.* Pelican Series. Baltimore: Penguin, 1954.
5. Browne, C. G. Executive leadership in business. IV. Sociometric pattern. *J. App. Psychol.,* 1951, 35, 34–37.
6. Coch, L., & French, J. R. P., Jr. Overcoming resistance to change. *Human Relat.,* 1949, 1, 512–532.
7. Dalton, M. Worker response and social background. *J. Political Econom.,* 1947, 55, 323–332.
8. Davis, A. The motivation of the underprivileged worker. In W. F. Whyte, *Industry and society.* New York: McGraw-Hill, 1946.
9. Felton, J. S., & Spencer, C. *Morale of workers exposed to high levels of occupational noise.* Norman, Okla.: Univer. of Oklahoma School of Medicine, 1957, 1–59.
10. Guest, R. H. Men and machines: an assembly-line worker looks at his job. *Personnel,* 1955, 31, 496–503.
11. Guetzkow, H., & Simon, H. A. The impact of certain communication nets in task-oriented groups. *Mgmt. Sci.,* 1955, 1, 233–250.
12. Hatchel, E. Why workers go sour. *Forbes,* 1929, 24, 38–42.
13. Herzberg, F., Mausner, B., Peterson, R. O., & Capwell, D. F. *Job attitudes: review of research and opinion.* Pittsburgh: Psychological Service of Pittsburgh, 1957.
14. Jacobsen, E. H. Foreman-steward participation practices and worker attitudes in a unionized factory. Unpublished doctoral dissertation, Univer. of Michigan, 1951.
15. Katz, D. Employee groups: what motivates them and how they perform. *Advanc. Mgmt.,* 1949, 14, 119–124.
16. Lawrence, P. R. How to deal with resistance to change. *Harvard Bus. Rev.,* 1954, 32, 49–57.
17. Marrow, A., & French, J. R. P., Jr. Changing a stereotype in industry. *J. Soc. Issues,* 1945, 3, 33–37.
18. Miles, W. R. *Immediate psychological effects in an exploratory study of the biological effects of noise.* Benox Report. Chicago: Univer. of Chicago Press, 1953.
19. Moreno, J. *Who shall survive.* Washington: Nervous and Mental Diseases Publishing Co., 1934.
20. Morse, N. C. *Satisfactions in the white collar job.* Ann Arbor: Univer. of Michigan Institute for Social Research, 1953.
21. Paterson, D. G., & Stone, C. H. Dissatisfaction with life work among adult workers. *Occupations,* 1942, 21, 219–221.

22. Rice, A. K. Productivity and social organization in an Indian weaving shed. *Human Relat.,* 1953, 6, 297–329.
23. Roethlisberger, F. J., & Dickson, W. J. *Management and the worker.* Cambridge: Harvard Univer. Press, 1939.
24. Seashore, S. E. *Group cohesiveness in the industrial work group.* Ann Arbor: Univer. Mich. Press, 1954.
25. Shaw, M. E. Some effects of unequal distribution of information upon group performance in various communication nets. *J. Abnorm. Soc. Psychol.,* 1954, 49, 547–553.
26. Trist, E. L., & Bamforth, K. W. Some social psychological consequences of the long-wall method of coal-getting. *Human Relat.,* 1951, 4, 3–38.
27. Trow, D. B. Autonomy and job satisfaction in task-oriented groups. *J. Abnorm. Soc. Psychol.,* 1957, 54, 204–209.
28. van Zelst, R. H. Worker popularity and job satisfaction. *Personnel Psychol.,* 1951, 4, 405–412.
29. Viteles, M. S. *Motivation and morale in industry.* New York: Norton, 1953.
30. Wickert, F. R. Turnover and employees' feelings of ego-involvement in the day-to-day operations of a company. *Personnel Psychol.,* 1951, 4, 185–197.

CHAPTER 11

1. Bakke, E. W. Why workers join unions. *Personnel,* 1945, 22, 2–11.
2. Bakke, E. W. *Mutual survival, the goal of unions and management.* New York: Harper, 1946.
3. Brooks, G. W., & Koons, G. R. Bargaining table techniques. *Amer. Mgmt. Ass. Personnel Ser.,* 1957, No. 172.
4. Chamberlain, N. W. *Collective bargaining.* New York: McGraw-Hill, 1951.
5. Coleman, J. The compulsive pressures of democracy in unionism. *Amer. J. Sociol.* May, 1956, 519–526.
6. Dalton, M. Unofficial union-management relations. *Amer. Social. Rev.,* 1950, 15, 611–619.
7. Dean, L. Union activity and dual loyalty. *Int. Labor Relat. Rev.,* 1954, 7, 526.
8. Herberg, W. Bureaucracy and democracy in labor unions. *Antioch Rev.,* 1943, 3, 405–417.
9. Kennedy, V. D. Grievance negotiation. In A. W. Kornhauser et al., *Industrial conflict.* New York: McGraw-Hill, 1954.
10. Kerr, C., & Fisher, L. Multiple-employee bargaining: the San Francisco experience. In R. A. Lester and J. Shister, *Insight into labor issues.* New York: Macmillan, 1948, 25–61.
11. Killingsworth, C. Arbitration as an industrial relations technique; the Bethlehem experience. *Proc. of IRRA,* 1954.
12. Levinson, H. M. *Unionism, wage trends, and income distribution, 1914–1947.* Ann Arbor: Univer. Mich. Press, 1951.
13. Perlman, S. *A theory of the labor movement.* New York: Macmillan, 1928.

14. Purcell, T. V. *The worker speaks his mind on company and union.* Cambridge: Harvard Univer. Press, 1953.
15. Rose, A. M. *Union solidarity, the internal cohesion of a labor union.* Minneapolis: Univer. Minn. Press, 1952.
16. Ross, A. M. *Trade union wage policy.* Berkeley: Univer. Calif. Press, 1948.
17. Sayles, L. R., & Strauss, G. *The local union: its place in the industrial plant.* New York: Harper, 1953.
18. Schelling, T. C. An essay on bargaining. *Amer. Econom. Rev.,* 1956, 46, 281–306.
19. Seidman, J. The labor union as an organization. In A. W. Kornhauser et al., *Industrial conflict.* New York: McGraw-Hill, 1954.
20. Seidman, J. Some requirements for union democracy. *Proc. Amer. Econ. Ass.,* May, 1958, 35–43.
21. Seidman, J., London, J., Karsh, B., & Tagliacozzo, D. L. *The worker views his union.* Chicago: Univer. Chicago Press, 1958.
22. Selekman, B. Varieties of labor relations. *Harvard Bus. Rev.,* 1949, 27, 175–199.
23. Stagner, R. *The psychology of industrial conflict.* New York: Wiley, 1956.
24. Stagner, R., Purcell, T. V., Kerr, W. A., Rosen, J., & Gruen, W. Dual allegiance to union and management; a symposium. *Personnel Psychol.,* 1954, 7, 41–80.
25. Taft, P. *The structure and government of labor unions.* Cambridge: Harvard Univer. Press, 1954.

CHAPTER 12

1. Abrams, A. J. Job engineering and job re-assignment for the older worker in American industry. New York State Legislative Committee, 1954, 99–107.
2. Anderson, N. *Men on the move.* Chicago: Univer. of Chicago Press, 1940.
3. Bakke, E. W. *Citizens without work; a study of the effects of unemployment upon the workers' social relations and practices.* London: Oxford Univer. Press, 1940.
4. Barrow, M. L. Attacking prejudices against the aged. New York State Legislative Committee, 1954, 56–58.
5. Blum, M. L. *Industrial psychology and its social foundations.* New York: Harper, 1956.
6. Bowers, W. H. An appraisal of worker characteristic as related to age. *J. App. Psychol.,* 1952, 36, 296–300.
7. Cavan, R. S., Burgess, E. W., Havighurst, R. J., & Goldhamer, H. *Personal adjustments in old age.* Chicago: Science Research Assoc., 1949.
8. Ginsberg, E. *The unemployed.* New York: Harper, 1943.
9. Ginsburg, S. W. What unemployment does to people. *Amer. J. Psychiat.,* 1942, 99, 439–446.
10. Hall, Harold R. Company stimulation of individual retirement programming. In *Some observations of executive retirement.* Cambridge: Harvard Univer. Press, 1953.

11. Jacobs, A. T. *How to use handicapped workers.* New York: National Foreman's Institute, Inc., 1946.
12. Kahne, H. R., Ryder, C. F., Snegireff, L. S., & Wyshak, G. Don't Take older workers for granted. *Harvard Bus. Rev.,* 1957, 35, 90–94.
13. Komarovsky, M. *The unemployed man and his family.* New York: Dryden, 1940.
14. Lehman, H. C. *Age and achievement.* Princeton: Princeton Univer. Press, 1953.
15. McFarland, R. A. The older worker in industry. *Harvard Bus. Rev.,* 1943, 22, 505–520.
16. McFarland, R. A. Physically handicapped workers. *Harvard Bus. Rev.,* 1944, 23, 1–31.
17. McFarland, R. A. The psychological aspects of aging. *Bulletin N.Y. Academy of Medicine,* 1956, 32, 14–32.
18. Miller, D. C., & Form, W. H. *Industrial sociology.* New York: Harper, 1951.
19. Pennsylvania State Bureau of Rehabilitation. Harrisburg: Author, 1955.
20. Pressey, S. L. The new division of maturity and old age: its history and service. *Amer. Psychologist,* 1948, 3, 107–109.
21. Pressey, S. L. Certain findings and proposals regarding professional retirement. *AAUP. Bull.,* 1955, 41, 503–509.
22. Pressey, S. L., & Kuhlen, R. G. *Psychological development through the life span.* New York: Harper, 1957.
23. *Psychological aspects of physical disability.* Rehabilitation Service Series, No. 10. Washington: U. S. Government Printing Office, 1957.
24. Selye, H. *The stress of life.* New York: McGraw-Hill, 1956.
25. Stanton, J. E. Some factors affecting employment in relation to age. Ohio State Univer. Press, *Abst. dissertation,* 1955, No. 66, 337–343.
26. Switzer, M. E., & Rusk, H. A. *Doing something for the disabled.* Public Affairs Pamphlet No. 197. Washington: Public Affairs Press, 1953.
27. Tiffin, J. *Industrial psychology.* Englewood Cliffs, N. J.: Prentice-Hall, 1942.
28. Travis, H. The structure of unemployment in recent years. *Monthly Labor Rev.,* 1956, 79, 1147–1151.
29. Turner, A. N. The older worker: new light on employment and retirement problems. *Personnel,* 1955, 32, 264–257.
30. U. S. Department of Education. *Education in the aging: a selected annotated bibliography.* Washington: Author, 1958, No. 11, 1–145.

Chapter 13

1. Baetjer, A. M. *Women in industry: their health and efficiency.* Philadelphia: Saunders, 1946.
2. Bell, D. Women and business: II. The great back to work movement. *Fortune,* July, 1956.
3. Davis, N. Some psychological effects on women workers of payment by industrial bonus method. *Occup. Psychol.,* 1944, 18, 53–62.

4. Deutsch, H. *The psychology of women.* New York: Grune & Stratton, 1944.

5. Fisher, D. A. *Steel in the war.* New York: United States Steel Corp., 1946.

6. Fuller, F. M., & Batchelder, M. B. Opportunities for women at the administrative level. *Harvard Bus. Rev.,* 1953, 31, 111–128.

7. Gadel, M. S. Productivity and satisfaction of full- and part-time female employees. *Personnel Psychol.,* 1953, 6, 327–342.

8. Gilmer, B. v. H. Psychological aspects of women in industry. *Personnel Psychol.,* 1957, 10, 439–452.

9. Kehoe, K. Woman's place in tomorrow's workforce. American Management Association, Personnel Series, 1955, 24–26, No. 165.

10. Livingston, E. Attitudes of women operatives to promotion. *Occup. Psychol.,* Oct., 1953, 191–199.

11. National Manpower Council. *Womanpower.* New York: Columbia Univer. Press, 1957.

12. Russia: Medical aspects of women in industry. *J. Akush. i. Zhensk. Boliez.,* Vol. 43, 1932.

13. Strong, E. K. *Vocational interest of men and women.* Stanford, Calif.: Stanford Univer. Press, 1943.

14. U. S. Department of Labor. *Night work for women.* Washington: Author, Women's Bureau, 1949, No. 233.

15. U. S. Department of Labor. *Older women as office workers.* Washington: Author, Women's Bureau, 1953, 1–64, No. 248.

16. U. S. Department of Labor. *Fact book on manpower.* Washington: Author, Bureau of Labor Statistics, Sept., 1954, 1–88.

17. U. S. Department of Labor. *Handbook on women workers.* Washington: Author, 1954, 1–75, No. 255.

18. U. S. Department of Labor. *Training mature women for employment.* Washington: Author, Women's Bureau, 1955, 1–46, No. 256.

19. Wolfle, D. L. *Commission on human resources and advanced training.* New York: Harper, 1954.

20. Zapoleon, M. W. Working girl: bibliography. *Personnel & Guidance J.,* 1953, 32, 68–71.

CHAPTER 14

1. Barnes, R. M. *Motion and time study.* New York: Wiley, 1958.

2. Bartley, S. H., & Chute, E. *Fatigue and impairment in man.* New York: McGraw-Hill, 1947.

3. Blair, R. N. A fresh look at the principles of motion economy. *J. of Industr. Engng.,* 1958, 9, 3–5.

4. Cleeton, G. U. Making work human. Yellow Springs, Ohio: Antioch Press, 1949.

5. Davis, K. *Human relations in business.* New York: McGraw-Hill, 1957.

6. Floyd, W. F., & Welford, A. T. *Symposium on fatigue.* London: Lewis, Ltd., 1953.

7. Ghiselli, E. E., & Brown, C. W. *Personnel and industrial psychology.* New York: McGraw-Hill, 1955.
8. Gregg, L. W., & Jarrard, L. E. Changes in muscle action potentials during prolonged work. *J. Comp. Physiol. Psychol.,* 1958, 51, 532–535.
9. Leavitt, H. J. *Managerial psychology.* Chicago: Univer. of Chicago Press, 1958.
10. McGehee, W., & Owen, E. B. Authorized and unauthorized rest pauses in clerical work. *J. App. Psychol.,* 1940, 24, 605–614.
11. Moore, F. G. Production control. New York: McGraw-Hill, 1951.
12. Nadler, G. *Work simplification.* New York: McGraw-Hill, 1957.
13. Patton, J. A., & Littlefield, C. L. *Job evaluation.* Homewood, Ill.: Irwin, 1957.
14. Procter & Gamble Company. *Time bonus.* Cincinnati: Author, 1946.
15. Ryan, T. A. *Work and effort.* New York: Ronald, 1947.
16. Schwab, R. S., & Prichard, J. S. Neurologic aspects of fatigue. *Neurology,* 1951, 1, 133–135.
17. Seyle, H., & Heuser, G. *Fifth annual report on stress.* Montreal: Acta, 1956.
18. Solomon, R. L. The influence of work on behavior. *Psychol. Bull.,* 1948, 45, 1–40.
19. Tiffin, J. 6 merit rating systems. *Personnel J.,* 1959, 37, 288–291, 300.
20. Wyatt, S., Langdon, J. N., & Stock, F. G. L. *Fatigue and boredom in repetitive work.* London: Industrial Health Research Board, Report No. 77, 1938.

CHAPTER 15

1. Arbous, A. G., & Kerrick, J. E. Accident statistics and the concept of accident proneness. *Biometrics,* 1951, 7, 370–432.
2. Drake, C. A. Accident-proneness: an hypothesis. *Character & Personality,* 1940, 8, 335–341.
3. Farmers, E., & Chambers, E. G. *A psychological study of individual differences in accident rates.* London: Industrial Fatigue Research Board, 1926, No. 38.
4. Fisher, B. *Mental causes of accidents.* Boston: Houghton Mifflin, 1922.
5. Gimbel, M. A. Industrial safety. In R. P. Blake (Ed.), *Industrial engineering.* Englewood Cliffs, N. J.: Prentice-Hall, 1943.
6. Goldmark, J., Hopkins, M. D., Florence, P. S., & Lee, F. S. Studies in industrial physiology: fatigue in relation to working capacity. *Pub. Hlth. Bull.,* 1920, No. 106.
7. Heinrich, H. W. *Industrial accident prevention.* New York: McGraw-Hill, 1941.
8. Hersey, R. B. Emotional factors in accidents. *Personnel J.,* 1936, 15, 59–65.
9. Katz, D. Employee groups: what motivates them and how they perform. *Advanc. Mgmt.,* 1949, 14, 119–124.

10. Kephart, N. C., & Tiffin, J. Vision and accident experience. *National Safety News,* 1950, 62, 90–91.

11. Kerr, W. A. Accident proneness in factory departments. *J. App. Psychol.,* 1950, 34, 167–170.

12. Mintz, A., & Blum, M. L. A re-examination of the accident proneness concept. *J. App. Psychol.,* 1949, 33, 195–211.

13. Osborne, E. G., & Vernon, H. M. *Contributions to the study of accident causation.* London: Industrial Fatigue Research Board, 1922, No. 19.

14. Snow, A. J. Tests for chauffers. *Indust. Psychol.,* 1926, 1, 30–45.

15. Vernon, H. M. *Accidents and their prevention.* London: Cambridge Univer. Press, 1936.

16. Vernon, H. M. Prevention of accidents. *British J. Industr. Med.,* 1945, 2, 3.

17. Wirt, S. E., & Leedke, H. N. Skillful eyes prevent accidents. National Safety Council Industrial Nursing Section, *Newsletter,* 1945.

CHAPTER 16

1. Corrigan, R. E., & Brogden, W. J. The trigometric relationship of precision and angle of linear pursuit movements. *Amer. J. Psychol.,* 1949, 62, 90–98.

2. Craik, K. J. W. Theory of the human operator in control systems. II. Man as an element in a control system. *British J. Psychol.,* 1948, 38, 142–157.

3. Fitts, P. M. The information capacity of the human motor system in controlling the amplitude of movement. *J. Exp. Psychol.,* 1954, 47, 381–391.

4. Fleishman, E. A. Dimensional analysis of psychomotor abilities. *J. Exp. Psychol.,* 1954, 48, 437–454.

5. Geldard, F. A. *The human senses.* New York: Wiley, 1953.

6. Hake, H. W., & Garner, W. R. The effect of presenting various numbers of discrete steps on scale reading accuracy. *J. Exp. Psychol.,* 1951, 42, 358–366.

7. Harris, S. J., & Smith, K. U. Dimensional analysis of motion: VII. Extent and direction of manipulative movements as factors in defining motions. *J. App. Psychol.,* 1954, 38, 126–130.

8. Hartley, R. V. The transmission of information. *Bell System Tech. J.,* 1928, 17, 535–550.

9. Henneman, R. H. Vision and audition as sensory channels for commuication. *Quart. J. Speech,* 1952, 38, 161–166.

10. McCormick, E. J. *Human engineering.* New York: McGraw-Hill, 1957.

11. Miller, G. A. What is information measurement? *Amer. Psychologist,* 1953, 8, 3–11.

12. Schipper, L. M., Kraft, C. L., Smode, A. F., & Fitts, P. M. The use of displays showing identity versus no-identity. *WADC Tech. Rep.,* 57–12, Wright Air Development Center, Feb., 1957.

13. Searle, L. V., & Taylor, F. V. Studies of tracking behavior. I. Rate and time characteristics of simple corrective movements. *J. Exp. Psychol.,* 1948, 38, 615–631.

14. Shannon, C. E. A mathematical theory of communication. *Bell System Tech. J.,* 1948, 27, 379–423, 623–656.
15. Taylor, F. V. Psychology and the design of machines. *Amer. Psychologist,* 1957, 12, 249–258.

CHAPTER 17

1. American Management Association. *Operations research applied: new uses and extensions.* New York: Author, 1957.
2. Barish, N. N. *Systems analysis for effective administration.* New York: Funk & Wagnalls, 1951.
3. Case Institute of Technology. *Proceedings of the conference on operations research.* Cleveland: Author, 1951.
4. Churchman, C. W., Ackoff, R. L., & Arnoff, E. L. *Introduction to operations research.* New York: Wiley, 1957.
5. Ferguson, R. O., & Sargent, L. F. *Linear programming: fundamentals and applications.* New York: McGraw-Hill, 1958.
6. Goode, H. H., & Machal, R. E. *Systems engineering.* New York: McGraw-Hill, 1957.
7. Grabbe, E. M. (Ed.) *Handbook of automation, computation, and control.* New York: Wiley, 1958.
8. Jacobs, H. H., Schreiber, R. J., & Littaner, S. B. Mathematical, psychological, and engineering aspects of accident phenomena. *Trans. N.Y. Acad. Sci.,* 1956, 18, 261–277.
9. McCloskey, J. F. *Operations research for management.* Baltimore: Johns Hopkins Press, 1956.
10. McKean, R. N. *Efficiency in government through systems analysis.* New York: Wiley, 1958.
11. Mackworth, J. F., & Mackworth, N. H. The overlapping of signals for decisions. *Amer. J. Psychol.,* 1956, 69, 26–47.
12. Miller, R. B. Some working concepts of systems analysis. *Amer. Inst. Res.,* Feb., 1954, 1–6.
13. Miller, R. B. *A study of the developmental history of selected complex electronic systems.* AFPTRC TR56-1, PBI25975, San Antonio, 1956.
14. Taylor, F. V. Psychology in the design of machines. *Amer. Psychologist,* 1957, 12, 249–258.
15. Warren, N. D. Automation, human engineering, and psychology. *Amer. Psychologist,* 1956, 11, 531–536.
16. Wissel, J. W., & Hall, S. A. Human engineering research—who should do it and why. *Amer. Psychologist,* 1957, 12, 92–94.

CHAPTER 18

1. Blankenship, A. B. *How to conduct consumer and opinion research.* New York: Harper, 1946.
2. Britt, S. H. Four hazards of motivation research—how to avoid them. *Printers' Ink,* 1955, 250, 40–48.

3. Brown, L. O. What motivation research is and how it works: its advantages and shortcomings. *Advertising Age,* 1955, 26, 65–69.
4. Burtt, H. E. *Psychology of advertising.* Boston: Houghton Mifflin, 1938.
5. Cash, H. C. Old research technique turns out to be "motivation" study. *Printers' Ink,* 1955, 252, 40–41.
6. Cash, H. C., & Crissy, W. J. E. *A point of view for salesmen.* New York: Personnel Development, Inc., 1957.
7. Cash, H. C., & Crissy, W. J. E. *The use of appeals in selling.* New York: Personnel Development, Inc., 1957.
8. Committee Appointed by Advertising Research Foundation. *Copy testing.* New York: Ronald, 1939.
9. Crissy, W. J. E., & Cash, H. C. *Motivation in selling.* New York: Personnel Development, Inc., 1958.
10. Cunningham, R. M. Brand loyalty—what, where, how much? *Harvard Bus. Rev.* Jan., Feb., 1956, 116–128.
11. Dichter, E. Public relations and mass motivations. *J. Communication,* 1953, 3, 90–96.
12. Dix, A. H. Here's what happens when Starch scores are checked by mail. *Printers' Ink,* 1955, 257, 24–27.
13. Frederick, J. G. *Introduction to motivation research.* New York: Business Bourse, 1957.
14. Frey, A. W. *Advertising.* (2d ed.) New York: Ronald, 1953.
15. Gray, J. S. (Ed.) *Psychology in use.* New York: American Book, 1941.
16. Hattwick, M. S. *How to use psychology for better advertising.* Englewood Cliffs, N. J.: Prentice-Hall, 1950.
17. Hepner, H. W. *Modern advertising: practices and principles.* New York: McGraw-Hill, 1956.
18. Hepner, H. W. *Psychology applied to life and work.* Englewood Cliffs, N. J.: Prentice-Hall, 1957.
19. Husband, R. W. *Applied psychology.* New York: Harper, 1949.
20. Husband, R. W. *The psychology of successful selling.* New York: Harper, 1953.
21. Ivey, P. W. *Successful salesmanship.* Englewood Cliffs, N. J.: Prentice-Hall, 1947.
22. Jones, E. H., & Sumner, F. C. Relation of the brightness differences of colors to their apparent distances. *J. Psychol.,* 1948, 26, 25–29.
23. Kenyon, O. A. *Readership and audience studies.* New York: Advertising Research Foundation, 1948.
24. Kleppner, O. *Advertising procedures.* Englewood Cliffs, N. J.: Prentice-Hall, 1950.
25. Lucas, E. B., & Murphy, M. J. False identification of advertisements in recognition tests. *J. App. Psychol.,* 1939, 23, 264–269.
26. McKinney, F. An empirical method of analyzing a sales interview. *J. App. Psychol.,* 1937, 21, 280.
27. Martineau, P. *Motivation in advertising.* New York: McGraw-Hill, 1957.

28. Moyer, K. E., & Gilmer, B. v. H. Attention spans of children for experimentally designed toys. *J. Genet. Psychol.*, 1955, 87, 187–201.

29. Nafziger, R. O. Problems in reader-interest surveys. *J. of Marketing*, April, 1945, 359–363.

30. Newman, J. W. *Motivation research and marketing management.* Boston: Harvard Univer., Graduate School of Business Administration, Division of Research, 1957.

31. Nielsen, A. C. *Advances in scientific marketing research.* Chicago: A. C. Nielsen, 1944.

32. Nixon, H. K. *Principles of advertising.* New York: McGraw-Hill, 1937.

33. Packard, V. *The hidden persuaders.* New York: McKay, 1957.

34. Poffenberger, A. T. *Psychology in advertising.* New York: McGraw-Hill, 1932.

35. Rudolph, H. J. *Attention and interest factors in advertising.* New York: Funk & Wagnalls, 1947.

36. Smith, G. H. *An introductory bibliography of motivation research.* New York: Advertising Research Foundation, 1953.

37. Spires, A. M., & LeBlanc, A. G. The relative effectiveness of absolute size in advertisements: a pilot study. *Bull. Marit. Psychol. Ass.*, 1956, 5, 16–20.

38. Starch, D. Testing the effectiveness of advertisements. *Harvard Bus. Rev.*, 1923, 1, 464–474.

39. Starch, D. What is new about motivation research? *Printers' Ink*, 1955, 252, 58–61.

40. Starch, D. How well do people read long advertisements? *Advertising Agency*, 1956, 49, 66–67.

41. Starch, D. How well-read are comic strip ads? *Advertising Agency*, 1956, 49, 72–74.

42. Strong, E. K., Jr. *Psychology of selling and advertising.* New York: McGraw-Hill, 1925.

43. Strong, E. K., Jr. *Psychological aspects of business.* New York: McGraw-Hill, 1938.

44. Trenchard, K. E., & Crissy, W. J. E. Trends in the use of certain attention-getting devices in newsweekly advertising. *J. App. Psychol.*, 1951, 35, 287–288.

45. Twedt, D. W. How good are multi-page ads? *Printers' Ink*, 1956, 255, 30–31.

46. Van Bortel, F. J. Motivation research and the confusing consumer. *J. Home Econom.*, 1956, 48, 22–24.

47. Wiseman, M. *The anatomy of advertising.* New York: Harper, 1942.

48. Wolf, H. A. (Ed.) *Motivation research, a new aid to understanding your market.* Boston: Motivation Research Associates, 1955.

49. Wulfeck, J. W., & Bennett, E. M. *The language of dynamic psychology as related to motivation research.* New York: McGraw-Hill, 1954.

50. Zubin, J., & Peatman, J. G. Testing the pulling power of advertisements by the split-run copy method. *J. App. Psychol.*, 1945, 29, 40–57.

CHAPTER 19

1. Arensberg, C. M. Industry and the community. *Amer. J. Sociol.*, 1942, 48, 1–12.
2. General Electric Company, Schenectady, N.Y., *Guide to making a business climate appraisal:* Author, 1955.
3. Havemann, E. *They went to college.* New York: Harcourt, Brace, 1952.
4. Kantner, J. *The relationship between accessibility and socio-economic status of residential lands.* Ann Arbor, Michigan: Univer. Mich. Press, 1948.
5. Knox, J. B. *The sociology of industrial relations: as introduction to industrial sociology.* New York: Random House, 1955.
6. Lewin, K., Dembo, T., Festinger, L., & Sears, P. S. Levers of aspiration. In J. McV. Hunt, *Personality and behavior disorders,* Vol. I. New York: Ronald, 1944, 333–378.
7. Lipset, S. M., & Bendix, R. *Social mobility in industrial society.* Berkeley: Univer. of Calif. Press, 1959.
8. Miller, D. C., & Form, W. H. *Industrial sociology.* New York: Harper, 1951.
9. Mills, C. W. *White collar: the American middle class.* New York: Oxford Univer. Press, 1951.
10. National Industrial Conference Board. *Public relations in industry.* New York: Author, 1956, 13–14, No. 80.
11. Schneider, E. V. *Industrial sociology.* New York: McGraw-Hill, 1957.
12. Seeley, J. R., Sim, R. A., & Loosley, E. W. *Crestwood heights.* New York: Basic Books, 1956.
13. Shaffer, L. F., & Shoben, E. J., Jr. *The psychology of adjustment.* Boston: Houghton Mifflin, 1956.
14. Walker, C. R. *Steeltown.* New York: Harper, 1950.
15. Warner, W. L. *Democracy in Jonesville: a study in quality and inequality.* New York: Harper, 1949.
16. Warner, W. L., & Low, J. O. *The social system of the modern factory. The strike: a social analysis.* Yankee City Series IV. New Haven: Yale Univer. Press, 1947.
17. Warner, W. L., & Lunt, P. S. *The social life of a modern community.* New Haven: Yale Univer. Press, 1941.
18. Whyte, W. H., Jr., *The organization man.* New York: Simon & Schuster, 1956.

CHAPTER 20

1. Cameron, N. *The psychology of behavior disorders.* Boston: Houghton Mifflin, 1947.
2. Ewing, O. *The nation's health: a report to the President.* Washington: U. S. Government Printing Office, 1948.
3. Franco, S. C. Problem drinking and industry: policies and procedures. *Quart. J. Stud. Alc.,* 1954, 15, 453–468.

4. Fraser, R. *The incidence of neurosis among factory workers.* London: H. M. Stationery Office, Ind. Health Res. Board, 1947, No. 90.

5. Gardner, J. W. The relation of certain personality variables to level of aspiration. *J. Psychol.,* 1940, 9, 191–206.

6. Gordon, G. Industry's problem children. *National Safety News,* Feb., 1953, 32–33, 81–84.

7. Guilford, J. P. *Personality.* New York: McGraw-Hill, 1959.

8. Halliday, J. L. *Psychosocial medicine.* New York: Norton, 1948.

9. Henderson, R. M., & Bacon, S. D. Problem drinking: the Yale Plan for business and industry. *Quart. J. Stud. Alc.,* 1953, 14, 247–262.

10. Hill, J., & Trist, E. A consideration of industrial accidents as a means of withdrawal from the work situation. *Human Relat.,* 1953, 6, 357–380.

11. Hills, J. R. The measurement of levels of aspiration. *J. Soc. Psychol.,* 1955, 41, 221–239.

12. Jellinek, E. M. The estimate of the number of alcoholics in the U. S. A. for 1949 in the light of the sixth revision of the international lists of causes of death. *Quart. J. Stud. Alc.,* 1952, 13, 215–218.

13. Kay, E. *An experimental study of some methodological and psychological aspects of industrial absenteeism.* Unpublished doctoral dissertation, Carnegie Institute of Technology, 1956.

14. Keller, M., & Efron, V. The prevalence of alcoholism. *Quart. J. Stud. Alc.,* 1955, 16, 619–644.

15. Kubie, L. S. "Socio-economic problems of the young scientist." *Amer. Scientist,* 1954, 42, 104–112.

16. McClelland, D. C., Atkinson, J. W., Clark, R. A., & Lowell, E. L. *The achievement motive.* New York: Appleton-Century-Crofts, 1953.

17. Markowe, M., & Barber, L. Psychological handicap in relation to productivity and occupational adjustment. *British J. Industr. Med.,* 1953, 10, 125–131.

18. Metzger, F. *A verification of the Drake hypothesis of accident proneness.* Unpublished thesis, Carnegie Institute of Technology, 1953.

19. Muller-Thym, B. J. Reconstructing the supervisory job. *Personnel,* 1954, 30, 396–405.

20. Neel, R. G. Nervous stress in the industrial situation. *Personnel Psychol.,* 1955, 8, 405–415.

21. Newton, R. An investigation of certain personality factors in relation to industrial absenteeism. Unpublished thesis, Pennsylvania State Univer., 1950.

22. Page, R. C., Thorpe, J. J., & Caldwell, D. W. The problem drinker in industry. *Quart. J. Stud. Alc.,* 1952, 13, 370–396.

23. Plummer, N., & Hinkle, L. Life stress and industrial absenteeism; concentration of illness and absenteeism in one segment of a working population: New York Telephone Company. *Industr. Med.,* 1952, 22, 363–375.

24. Stagner, R. *The psychology of industrial conflict.* New York: Wiley, 1956.

25. Taylor, J. A. Drive theory and manifest anxiety. *Psychol. Bull.,* 1956, 53, 303–320.

26. Walker, C. R. The problem of the repetitive job. *Harvard Bus. Rev.,* 1950, 28, 54–58.
27. Walker, C. R., Guest, R. H., & Turner, A. N. *The foreman on the assembly line.* Cambridge: Harvard Univer. Press, 1956.
28. Wittmer, J. J. Alcoholism in industry: new policy of the Consolidated Edison Company of New York. *Quart. J. Stud. Alc.,* 1949, 10, 376–379.
29. Worthy, J. C. Factors influencing employee morale. *Harvard Bus. Rev.,* 1950, 28, 61–73.

CHAPTER 21

1. Brodman, K. Absenteeism, working efficiency, and emotional maladjustments. *Industr. Med.,* 1945, 15, 1–5.
2. Brown, J. A. C. *The social psychology of industry.* Pelican Series. Baltimore: Penguin, 1954.
3. Cameron, N. *The psychology of behavior disorders.* Boston: Houghton Mifflin, 1947.
4. Cantoni, L. J. 21 signs that suggest serious emotional disturbance. *Personnel J.,* 1955, 33, 300–301.
5. Dollard, J., & Miller, N. E. *Personality and psychotherapy.* New York: McGraw-Hill, 1950.
6. Kubie, L. S. Psychiatry in industry. *Personnel J.,* 1945, 24, 50–55.
7. Ling, T. M. *Mental health and human relations in industry.* London: H. K. Lewis, 1954.
8. McLean, A. A., & Taylor, G. C. *Mental health in industry.* New York: McGraw-Hill, 1958.
9. McMurry, R. N. The executive neurosis. *Harvard Bus. Rev.* 1952, 30, 33–47.
10. Menninger, W. C. Men, machines, and mental health. *Ment. Hyg., N.Y.,* 1952, 36, 184–196.
11. Menninger, W. C., & Levinson, H. Psychiatry in industry: some trends and perspectives. *Personnel,* 1955, 32, 90–99.
12. Mindus, E. Industrial psychiatry in Great Britain, the United States, and Canada: a report to the World Health Organization. Stockholm: Univer. of Stockholm, Institute of Applied Psychology, 1954.
13. Neel, R. G. Nervous stress in the industrial situation. *Personnel Psychol.,* 1955, 8, 405–415.
14. Shaffer, L. F. & Shoben, E. J., Jr. *The psychology of adjustment.* Boston: Houghton Mifflin, 1956.

INDEX

Abegglen, J. C., 52
Ability and job analysis, 133
Abrams, A. J., 260, 261
Absenteeism, 439–440
  and accidents, 444–445
  and age, 253
  and attitudes, 191
  and the handicapped, 245
  and personality, 440
Accident concept, 306
Accident index, 313
Accident prevention, 315–318
Accident proneness, 314–315
Accident report, 309–310
Accident results, 306
Accidents, and absenteeism, 444–445
  and age, 253
  causes, 307–309
    indirect, 308
  and coordination, 311
  and emotions, 312
  environmental conditions, 313–314
  and fatigue, 312–313
  and the handicapped, 245
  human elements in, 308–309
  intelligence and, 311
  lost-time, 306–307
  personal factors in, 310–313
  and speed, 313
Accomplishment, feelings of, 101–102
Accuracy in training, 138–139
Achievement needs and class, 430

Ackoff, R. L., 379
Acquisition in work, 287–288
Activity change, 293–294
Adjustment problems, understanding, 459
Adjutant General's Office, 23
Administrative structure and status, 57
Advertising, 385–392
  affective factors, 389
  attention in, 389–390
  brand reinforcement, 385, 400, 404
  cognitive factors, 387
  consumer panels, 390–391
  definition, 384
  depth interviewing, 389, 405–406
  direct sell, 385
  emotional attitudes, 388–389
  headlines, 388
  kinds, 385–386
  motivation research, 17, 404–407
  overlearning, 400–401
  perception factors, 386–387
  posttesting, 391–392
  pretesting, 389–390
  product personality, 405
  and selling, differences between, 399
    habits in, 404
    principles and concepts, 400–404
    projection in, 402–403
    rationalization in, 403–404
    summation in, spatial, 401–402
    temporal, 401

Advertising, spot, 388
  Thompson-Luce test, 390
Affective expansion, 396, 402
AFL-CIO structure, 46–48
Agate Club, 19
Age, and absenteeism, 253
  and accidents, 253
  and hobbies, 256–257
  and isolation, 263
  and job demands, 264
  and job reassignment, 261–262
  and job redesign, 260–261
  myth of, 253–255
  and needs, 93–94
  and productivity, 251–253
  and speed, 259
  and status differentials, 253
  and status loss, 256
Aged, attitudes toward, 259–260
  prejudices against, 263
Aggression, 96–97, 463–464
Aging, criteria, 251
  individual differences, 256
  trend of thinking on, 264–265
  and work, 250–255
AIDA formula in selling, 394–395
Air conditioning and attitudes, 296–297
Alcoholism, 441–444
  criteria for, 443
  extent, 441–442
  rehabilitation, 443–444
Altman, J. W., 131
Ambition, differences in, 95
Amplification in control, 333
Anatomy of company, 43–44
Anderson, N., 249
Anshen, M., 184
Antitrust laws, 224
Antiunion campaigns, 227
Anxiety, neurotic, 468
  reinforcements, 448
  state, 471–472
  status, 94–95
Application blanks, first, 21
  in selection, 116–117
Aptitude tests, future of, 125–127
Arbitration, 234, 239
Arbous, A. G., 315
Areas in systems, 367
Arensberg, C. M., 155, 422
Argyris, C., 66, 457
Armstrong, T. O., 157
Army Alpha Test, 23
Army Beta Test, 23
Arnoff, E. L., 379
Ashby, W. R., 77

Aspiration, generalizations about, 426–427
  levels, 103–104, 425–427
  and productivity, 204–205
  and reinforcement, 139
  with success and failure, 94
  and unemployment, 249–250
Associated Senior Executives, 265
Association of Life Insurance Officers, 28
Atmospheric conditions and work, 295–296
Attainment discrepancy, 425–426
Attention, in advertising, 389–390
  in selling, 396–397
Attitude differences, men and women, 270–271
Attitudes, toward aged, 259–260
  and air conditioning, 296–297
  information about, 198–199
  and needs, 100–101
  and productivity, 203–205
  and reinforcement, 141–142
  and turnover, 204
  about women, 276
  and work, 204
  and work systems, 296
Austin, G. A., 85
Authority, delegation, 50
  rejection, 97–98
Autocratic climate, 49
Automatic control in management, 77
Automation, complete, 325–326
  effects, 354
  and women's jobs, 270
Autonomy and job satisfaction, 209

Baker, Newton D., 23
Bakke, E. W., 230, 248
Ballistic movements, 344–345
Balmer, Thomas K., 18
Bamforth, K. W., 210
Barbash, J., 241
Barnard, C. I., 196
Barnes, R. M., 304
Barron, M. L., 263
Bartley, S. H., 304
Batchelder, M. B., 275, 276
Bavelas, A., 208
Behavioral sciences, list, 10
Bell, D., 269, 275, 276
Bellows, R. M., 199
Bendix, R., 431
Benefits and attitudes, 220
Bergler, E., 93
Bingham, Walter V., 19

Birmingham, H. D., 135
Bit, definition, 335
Blair, R. N., 298
Blanks, application, first, 21
  in selection, 116–117
Blum, M. L., 151, 198, 206, 248, 315
Bonus systems, 301
Boomtown, 413
Boredom, 293–294
Borrowed prestige, 419
Bowers, W. H., 263
Boynton, P. W., 5
Brand lock of customers, 404
Brand reinforcement in advertising, 385, 400, 404
Braun, H. W., 147
Brogden, H. C., 114
Brogden, W. J., 344, 345
Brooks, G. W., 231
Brown, J. A. C., 205, 220
Bruner, J. S., 85
Bryan, G. L., 134
Buchele, R. B., 49, 50
Bureau of Personnel Research, 30
Bureau of Salesmanship Research, 20, 23–24, 26
Burgess, E. W., 257
Burtt, H. E., 180
Business climate, 417–418
Business decision constraints, 226
Buyers in systems, 370

Caldwell, D. W., 440
Cameron, N., 447, 467, 475
Cannell, C. F., 128
Cantoni, L. J., 474
Capwell, D. F., 155, 197, 200, 204, 216
Career planning, 5, 205
  and unemployment, 247
  for women, 276–277
Career training and community, 428
Cattell, R. B., 182
Cause-effect complexities, 9–10
Cause-effect relations, 8–10
Cavan, R. S., 257
Chamberlain, N. W., 236
Chambers, E. G., 311, 312
Change, in climates, 50–51
  resistance to, 78–79, 210–212, 420–422
Channel concept, 335
Channels in routing, 82
Chapanis, A., 352
Chart, informal organization, 54
Charters, W. W., 26
Cherry, C., 379

Christensen, C. R., 105
Christie, L. E., 84
Churchman, C. W., 379
Chute, E., 304
City as community, 415, 420
Class, and achievement needs, 430
  lower, 429
  middle, 429–430
  and personality, 428–430
  upper, 430
Class differences and needs, 94
Classes in community, 418–422, 424
Cleeton, G. U., 185
Climate, autocratic, 49
  business, 417–418
  democratic, 49
  in leadership training, 191
  permissive, 49
  for work, 205–207
Climates (see Psychological climates)
Clinical information, 13
Closed-circuit model of behavior, 92
Closed-loop system, 328
Clothier, Robert C., 24
Coates, C. H., 180
Coch, L., 211, 212
Code in communication, 84, 336
Coding, 339–340
Coefficient, validity, interpretation, 121–124
Cognitive factors in advertising, 387
Coleman, J., 233
Coleman, L. R., 407
Collective bargaining, behavior in, 230–231
  contract, 239–241
College Board tests, 120–121
Committee on Classification of Personnel, 23, 28
Communication, and attitudes, 219
  and departmentalization, 82
  lack of, 450
Communication code, 84, 336
Communication networks, 208–209
Communities, company, 420
  types, 413–415
Community, charities, 416
  classes, 418–422, 424
  crises, 411–413
  declassification, 415
  high-status, 428
  industry relations, 408–409
  labor relations, 415
  power structures, 415–417
  social forces, 423–425
  ties, 422–423

Company, anatomy, 43–44
  and attitudes, 217
  communities, 420
  definition, 41
  size, 44, 46
Compensatory tracking, 331–332
Complaint handling, 397–398
Complex information processing, 338
Comprehension and readership, 387–388
Compromise reactions, 466–467
Compulsions, 470
Comrey, A. L., 155
Conference groups in training, 192–194
Conference leadership, 168–169
Conflict and frustration, 460–461
Consulting, first organization for, 23–26
Consumer panels, types, 390–391
Consumer readership reports, 390
Content analysis in motivation research, 406–407
Content validity in training, 149
Contingencies in job study, 302
Contingency in systems, 366
Contingent conditions, 374–375
Continuous-process manufacturing, 422
Contract, labor-management, 239–241
Control, managerial, 77–78
  through records, 76–77
Control specifications in systems, 328
Coordination and accidents, 311
Cornell, W. B., 66
Correlation coefficient, 117–118
Corrigan, R. E., 344, 345
Counseling, directive, 167
  evaluation, 165
  formal, 164–165
  industrial beginning, 33
  informal, 165–166
  nondirective, 166–167
  union reaction to, 165
  Western Electric, 164–165
Cowdery, Karl, 32
Craft rules, 75
Craik, K. J. W., 333
Credit in marketing mix, 384
Credit buying, 393
Crestwood Heights, 428
Crissy, W. J. E., 387
Criteria, of aging, 251
  for alcoholism, 443
  company records as, 111–112
  critical incidents as, 113
  error in, 109
  of leadership, 178–181
  problem, 107–111
  for retirement, 255–256
  salary as, 179

Criteria, use of ratings, 112–113
  weighting, 114
Criterion, definition, 107
  for production, 301
  scores, first comparison, 21
Criterion behaviors, 107
Criterion development, steps in, 110–111
Criterion measures, availability, 111–113
  combination, 113–114
  dollar, 114
  establishing, 108–109
Criterion tolerance in systems, 365
Criterion variable in systems, 365
Critical incidents as criteria, 113
Critical-incidents rating, 300
Cronbach, L. J., 116, 127
Crook, G. H., 265
Cultural attitudes and women, 269
Customer feelings, 397–398
Customer needs, 395–396, 398–399
Customer service, 384
Cyert, R. M., 78

Dalton, M., 196, 210, 238
Damrin, D. E., 145
Davis, A., 200
Davis, K., 174, 296
Decision making, participation in, 211–212
  records for, 79–80
  in systems, 341–342
Decision rules in systems, 341
Decrement in work, 287–288
Defensive reactions, 463–467
Delegation of authority, 50
De Martino, M. F., 105
Dembo, T., 425, 426
Democratic climate, 49
Dent, J., 154, 156
Depth interviewing in advertising, 389, 405–406
Development, examples, 357–358
  nature, 357
  team, 355
  variables in, 358–359
Dickson, W. J., 32, 208
Dill, W. R., 104
Direct sell in advertising, 385
Displays, definition, 329
  design, 334
  and information, 336–337
  quickening, 349
Dollar criterion, 114
Drake, C. A., 313
Dubin, R., 241
Dubois, P., 128

Ebel, R. L., 149
Education and training, 134–135
Effort, and learning, 143
  physiological measures, 288–289
  psychological measures, 289–290
Ego identification and morale, 63–64
Ego involvement, and morale, 215
  in supervision, 158
Electrical potentials, from muscles,
  346
  in work, 289
Elliott, O., 196
Emergencies, in job study, 302
  in systems, 367
Emotions, and accidents, 312
  and motives, 461–463
Empathy in supervision, 157–158
Employee comparison rating, 299
Employee participation, 210–213, 319–
  320
Employee recruitment, 124–125
Employment of women, barriers to,
  271–272
Employment interview, first study, 20
End product in training, 131
End spurt in work, 287–288
Engineering psychology, beginning, 35
  field, 326–327
Engineer's job, 324–325
Entrepreneurship, meaning, 42
Environment, and accidents, 313–314
  in systems, 365
Environmental conditions, control,
  325–326
  and morale, 213–216
Equipment design and safety, 323
Equipment redesign for women, 273
Escape through work, 98
Ewing, O., 439
Executive, adjustments, 454–456
  development, 194–195
  functions, 175–177
  selection, 186–187
  successful, portrait, 195–196
  training, 187–194
Executives, clinical description, 179–
  180
  educational programs, 188–189
  empirical view, 176
  source, 187
  theoretical view, 176–177
  wives, 51–52
Experimental method, limitations, 11–12
Experimental variables, description, 12–
  13
Extinction in training, 141–142

Failure, and aspiration, 94
  criteria for, 103–104
  excuses for, 98–99
Families, industrial, 431–432
  number, 431
Farmers, E., 311, 312
Fatigue, 290–292
  and accidents, 312–313
  in job study, 302
Fatigue syndrome, 468–469
Feedback, response, 374
Feinberg, M. R., 150, 151
Felton, J. S., 213
Ferguson, R. O., 380
Festinger, L., 425, 426
Fictions about organizations, 53
File, Q. W., 158
File and Remmers test, 158
Filtering, selective, 83–84
Filtering rules, 82
Firm, definition, 41
Firms, planning, 84–86
First graduate school, applied psychol-
  ogy, 19
Fisher, D. A., 269, 281
Fitts, P. M., 339, 348
Fixation and regression, 465–466
Flanagan, J. C., 113
Fleishman, E. A., 49, 190, 347
Flexibility and management success, 79
Florence, P. S., 312
Forced-choice rating, 299
Forced-distribution rating, 299
Foreman's status, 58–59
Form, W. H., 246, 415, 420, 421, 432
Franco, S. C., 440
Fraser, R., 439
Frederiksen, N., 145
Freeman, F. S., 116
French, J. R. P., Jr., 211, 212
Freyd, Max, 31
Frost, L., 102
Frustration, accumulation, 99
  and conflict, 460–461
  reaction to, 96–99
Fryer, D. H., 128, 150, 151
Fuller, F. M., 275, 276
Function in systems, 364
Functional organization, 43

Gagne, R. M., 133, 145, 148
Gale, H., 19
Gardner, B. B., 220
Gardner, F. M., 145
Gardner, W. R., 352
Garner, W. R., 336

Geldard, F. A., 352
Gellerman, S. W., 50
General system, definition, 364
  factors, 364–370
  overlap within, 370–372
Georgia Association of Life Insurers, 21
Gibb, C. A., 182, 183, 196
Gilbreth, F. B., 74
Gilbreth, L. M., 74
Gilmer, B. v. H., 151, 268, 271, 323, 402
Gimbel, M. A., 322
Ginsberg, E., 247, 265
Ginsburg, S. W., 250
Glaser, R., 145
Gleser, G., 127
Goal discrepancy, 425–426
Goldhamer, H., 257
Goldmark, J., 312
Goode, H. H., 362, 380
Goodnow, J. J., 85
Gordon, G., 104
Gorsuch, J. H., 50
Gouldner, A. W., 68
Grabbe, E. M., 354
Graphic rating scale, 299
Greene, E. B., 116
Greenly, R. J., 6
Gregg, L. W., 289
Grievances, 440–442
  and personality, 441
  settlement, 237–239
Grimshaw, A., 87
Group decisions, procedures, 167–171
  in safety, 319–320
Group problem solving, case study, 169–171
Groups, need variations in, 95–96
Guest, R. H., 220, 452
Guetzkow, H., 177, 208
Guilford, J. P., 126
Gulliksen, H., 128
Guthrie, E. R., 145

Habbe, S., 155
Haberstroh, C. J., 66
Habits in advertising and selling, 404
Haire, M., 87
Hake, H. W., 336
Hall, S. A., 376
Halliday, J. L., 448
Hamerschlag, Arthur A., 19
Handicapped worker, 242–245
  as economic asset, 243
  employment, 245
  number, 245
  productivity, 242–243

Hansen, H. L., 407
Harlow, H., 145
Harris, E. F., 180
Hartley, R. V., 335
Hatchel, E., 210
Havemann, E., 6, 414
Havighurst, R. J., 257
Hawthorne studies, 32–34, 75
Hayes, Mary H. S., 25
Henderson, J. M., 68
Heinrich, H. W., 307, 323
Heinstein, M., 265
Hennessey, J. W., 87
Henry, E. R., 128
Hepner, H. W., 407
Hersey, R., 161, 174
Hersey, R. B., 312, 319
Herzberg, F., 155, 157, 197, 200, 204, 216, 220
High, W. S., 155
Higher positions, women in, 275–276
Hill, J., 444
Hilton, T. L., 104
Hinkle, L., 440
Hiring, decisions in, 125
  some attitudes, 279
Hobby, 293
Hodges, W., 433
Hoffman, L. R., 380
Homans, G. C., 32, 97, 104
Hopkins, Louis B., 24
Hopkins, M. D., 312
Human factors specialist, 363
Human factors subsystem, 376–379
  design variables, 378–379
  map, 377
Human relations, elements, 65
  emphasis on, 153
  and plant location, 409
  problem solving in, 171–173
Hurlock, E. B., 252
Husband, R. W., 407
Hypochondria, 468
Hysterias, 470–471

Identification, 464–465
Illumination, and production study, 33–34
  and work, 294
Incentive pay and reinforcement, 140
Incentive plans, 301
Incentive scheme strike, 422–423
Incentive systems, 303
Incentives in work, 102
Income and job dissatisfaction, 200
Individual and situation, 8–9

Industrial morale, definition, 198
Industrial South, 414
Industrialization and family, 431–432
Industry, definition, 42
Industry-community relations, 408–409
Informal organization, 52–55
Information, confusion in, 81
  flow, 81
  in general system, 364–370
  handling rules, 80–84
  processing, 337–342
  sources, 80–81
  technology, 46, 303
  theory, 334–335
  useful and unuseful, 82–83
Injunction, 224
Input in systems, 333–337, 366
Institutional advertising, 385–386
Insulation, 465
Intelligence and accidents, 311
Interests, early research, 30–32
Interviewing, depth, in advertising, 389, 405–406
  indirect, beginning, 33
  in selection, 117
Irrational spending, and class, 429
  and unemployment, 248–249

Jacobs, H. H., 354
Jacobsen, E. H., 211
Jarrard, L. E., 157, 289
Jennings, E. E., 66
Job analysis, and ability, 133
  early types, 27
  methods, 134
  pitfalls, 372–373
  and safety, 317
  in systems, 372–376
  and training specifications, 130–131
  and work evaluation, 297–300
Job application blank, 116–117
Job aspects, and attitudes, 218, 219
Job attitudes, definition, 198
  factors, 216–220
Job breakdown, 298
Job climate, 48–52
Job demands and age, 264
Job description, 131–132
  categories, 133–134
Job dissatisfaction, extent, 199–200
  and income, 200
Job engineering, older workers, 260–261
Job enlargement, 449–450
  IBM study, 449
  Sears, Roebuck study, 449–450

Job expectancy and class, 94
Job factor comparisons, 201–203
Job hazards, and morale, 213–216
  and tensions, 447–448
Job know-how test and safety, 316–317
Job need satisfactions, 102–103
Job pressures, relief from, 455
Job proficiency, requirements for, 130
Job reassignment and age, 261–263
Job redesign, for aged, 260–261
  and training, 131
Job rotation, 450
Job satisfaction, and autonomy, 209
  and community living, 415
  definition, 198
  men and women, 270–271
  and occupation level, 200
  and position, 209
Job security and attitudes, 216
Job shred-out, 135
Job simplification, 135
Job study, example, 301–303
Job tensions, and hazards, 447–448
Jobs of women, 274–278
Jones, E. D., 63
Jones, E. H., 386
Jonesville study, 423–425
Judgments, absolute, 340–341
  comparative, 341

Kahn, A., 135
Kahn, R. L., 128
Kahne, H. R., 253
Kantner, J., 420
Karn, H. W., 151, 323
Karsh, B., 226
Katona, G., 407
Katz, D., 212
Kaufmann, Edgar J., 26
Kaufmann Department Stores, Inc., 26
Kay, E., 440
Keller, F. S., 140
Kendler, H. H., 147
Kennedy, V. D., 238
Kephart, N. C., 311
Kerr, W. A., 158, 314
Kerr and Speroff test, 158
Kerrick, J. E., 315
Killingsworth, C., 239
Kinship and group behavior, 422–423
Kleemeier, R. W., 163, 174
Knickerbocher, I., 95, 183
Koons, G. R., 231
Kornhauser, Arthur W., 24, 241
Kraft, C. L., 339
Kriesberg, M., 177

Kubie, L. S., 445, 473
Kuhlen, R. G., 265

Labor force, women in, 266
Labor-management bargaining, 236–237
Labor-management contract, 239–241
Labor-management cooperation, 241
Labor organizational structures, 46–48
Labor reserve, 268
Labor union (see Union)
Lamperti, F. A., 77
Langdon, J. N., 293
Lateral growth, 455
Lawrence, P. R., 66, 211
Leadership, climate, 49
  composite picture, 184–185
  conference, 168–169
  criteria, 178–181
  and environment, 181–184
  generalizations about, 183
  individual differences in, 181
  methods, 183
  personality variables, 182
  and self-evaluation, 185–186
  and situations, 182
  and social interaction, 182
  and social setting, 191–192
  stereotypes, 181
Learning, active, 145–146
  aversive consequences, 144
  and effort, 143
  meaningfulness of material, 134–144
  and task guidance, 138–139
  and training procedures, 137–148
  variables, 137–138
Leavitt, H. J., 46, 65, 66, 91, 208
Lee, F. S., 312
Leedke, H. N., 311
Lehman, H. C., 251
Level of occupation and dissatisfaction, 200
Levels of aspiration, 425–427
Levinson, H. M., 240
Lewin, K., 35, 100, 425, 426
Life insurance selling, early courses in, 29
Lighting and accidents, 313–314
Limitations in psychology, 7
Lindzey, G., 104
Line organization, 43
  and committee, 44
  and functional staff, 44
  and staff, 43
Ling, T. M., 473
Lipset, S. M., 431
Littaner, S. B., 354

Locations in systems, 367
Logo in advertising, 401
London, J., 226, 241
Loosley, E. W., 428, 433
Lost-time accidents, 306–307
Lott, Merrill, 25
Lovelace, Griffin M., 29
Low, J. O., 409
Lower class, 429
Lucas, E. B., 388
Luce, R. D., 84
Lunt, P. S., 427

McCloskey, J. F., 355, 380
Maccoby, N., 154
McCollom, I. N., 4
McCormick, E. J., 352
McFarland, R. A., 245, 264
McGehee, W., 292
McGregor, D., 66, 95, 155, 185
Machal, R. E., 362, 380
McKinney, F., 475
McLean, A. A., 457, 475
McMurry, R. N., 157
McNair, M. P., 407
Macy, J., Jr., 84
Maier, A. A., 151
Maier, N. R. F., 103, 151, 167
Makin, John Lee, 19
Maladjustments, extent, 439–445
  reduction in, 456–457
  and work, 446–448
Man-machine systems, analysis, 350–351
  example, 328–330
  flow chart, 371
  human operator in, 330–333
  nature, 327–330
  (See also Systems)
Management and worker adjustment, 448–451
Management-union contact levels, 48
Management wives, 51–52
Mandell, M. M., 50
Manic-depressive disorders, 473
Mann, F. C., 154, 156, 380
March, J. G., 79, 87
Market research, 405
Marketing mix, ingredients, 383–385
Marrow, A. J., 211, 304
Martineau, P., 407
Mason, C. W., 185
Mausner, B., 155, 197, 200, 204, 216, 220
Mayo, Elton, 32, 50

Measurement, of proficiency, 148–150
  of work output, 286–288
Medical departments, 474–475
Memory in information processing, 337
Mental health, meaning, 438–439
  provisions for, 456–457
Merit rating, 298–300
Methods, psychological, **11–13**
Metzger, F., 444
Middle age, lost goals, **455**
  needs in, 93–94
  revolt, 93–94, 200
Middle class, 429–430
Migrant workers, 246
Miles, W. R., 213
Miller, D. C., 246, 415, 420, 421, 432
Miller, G. A., 335
Miller, R. B., 148, 354
Mills, C. W., 419, 433
Miner, James B., 26
Mintz, A., 315
Mobility, aspects, 425
  belongingness need, 427
  factors in, 427
  indicators, 424–428
  upward, 425–428
Model of behavior, 91–92
Monitoring in systems, 369
Moore, Bruce V., 30
Moore, D. G., 220
Morale, and accidents, 314
  and communication nets, 208–209
  definition, 198
  dimensions, 212
  early interest in, 27–28
  and ego identification, 63–64
  and ego involvement, 215
  and organizations, 207–210
  and participation, 211
  and permissiveness, 155–156
  in small companies, 200
  of supervisor, 212–213
  and training, 148
  training, 143–144
  and work environment, 213–216
Moreno, J., 206
Morgan, C. T., 352
Morse, N. C., 204
Motion analyzer, 343–344
Motion economy, 298
Motivation, personal development, 194–196
  in training, 146–147
  (*See also* Needs)
Motivation research in advertising, 7, 404–407
Motives and emotions, 461–463

Motor-ability factors, 346–349
Motor-performance measures, 348
Motor skills, 343
Movements, classification, 344–346
Moyer, K. E., 192, 193, 402
Multiple regression, 117–118
Münsterberg, Hugo, 19
Murphy, M. J., 388
Muscular coordination and accidents, 311

Nagle, B. F., 155, 158
National Association of Life Under-
  writers, 20
National Manpower Council, 268, 279, 281
Need satisfaction, 100–103
  on job, 102–103
  and status, 56
Need variations, 92–96
Needs, and age, 93–94
  and attitudes, 100–101
  and class differences, 94
  in middle age, 93–94
  substitutes for, 101
  variations across groups, 95–96
  in youth, 93
Neel, R. G., 445
Neurasthenia, 468
Neurotic reactions, 467–471
New suburbia, 414–415
Newton, R., 440
Nightwork of women, 273
Noise, in systems, 367
  and work, 295

Old age (*see* Aged; Aging)
Old community, 410
Open-loop system, 327–328
Operating procedures, types, 72–73
Operations analysis, 354–355
Opportunity and attitudes, 217
Organization, character, 49
  control by training, 75–76
  elements, 177
  first consulting, 23–26
  informal, 52–55
  and system, 363–364
  of training, 150–151
Organization charts, 45, 47
Organizational changes, 70–71
  and supervisor, 453–454
  and worker, 303
Organizational clichés, 53–54

Organizational climates (*see* Psychological climates)

Organizational complexity and human relations, 63–64

Organizational demands and behavior, 78

Organizational fictions, 53

Organizational needs of union, 228

Organizational planning, 84–86

Organizational theory, 65–66

Organizations, administrative types, 43–44

  economist's view, 68

  informal, 205–206

  and morale, 207–210

  psychologist's view, 68

  sociologist's view, 68

O'Rourke, L. J., 24

Osborne, E. G., 313

OSS (Office of Strategic Services), 186

Output in systems, 342–346, 365

Overbuying and class, 429

Overlearning in advertising, 400–401

Owen, E. B., 292

Pacing and tension, 447

Page, R. C., 440

Paradoxes in status, 57

Paranoia, 472

Parker, W. E. J., 163, 174

Part-time work, 271

Participation, in decisions, 100–101, 211–212

  employee, 210–213

  lack, 101

  and morale, 211

Participative management, 303

Paternalism, 412

Patton, W. M., Jr., 158

Pauses, rest, 291

PEDOS training formula, 27

Pellegrin, R. J., 180

Pelz, D. C., 154

People in systems, 368

Perception in information processing, 338

Perception factors in advertising, 386–387

Performance standards, 300–303

Permissive climate, 49

Personal-history blanks, first, 21

Personality, and accidents, 311–312

  and social class, 428–430

Personnel consulting, first organization, 23–26

Personnel selection, future, 125–127

Peters, Thomas L., 21

Peterson, R. O., 155, 197, 200, 204, 216

Pfiffner, J. M., 155

Phases in planning, 85–86

Phobias, 469–470

Physical demands and accidents, 314

Piece rates and boredom, 294

Piecework and reinforcement, 140

Pilot selection, 119–120

Planning phases, 85–86

Planning rules, 84–86

Plant, definition, 42

Plateaus, in training, 144–145

  in work, 287–288

Plummer, N., 440

Point systems, first evaluation, 24–25

Position and status, 55–56

Positioning in movements, 344

Positions, high, women in, 275–276

Posttesting in advertising, 391–392

Power structures, community, 415–417

Predictor-criterion relationships, 117–119

Predictor field, definition, 115

Predictor variables, 114–115

President's status, 61

Pressey, S. L., 264, 265

Pressure effects, 455

Pretesting in advertising, 389–390

Probabilities in systems, 370

Problem-solving conferences, stages in, 167–168

Problem-solving outline, 171–173

Problems, general, 361–362

  specific, 360–361

  systems, 362–363

Procedural changes, resistance to, 78–79

Procedural tasks, 373–374

Procedures in systems, 368

Process in systems, 365

Process-links in systems, 365

Product personality in advertising, 405

Production and illumination, study, 33–34

Production control, 300

Productivity, and age, 251–253

  and aspiration, 204–205

  and attitudes, 203–205

  and job enlargement, 449

Proficiency measurement, 148–150

Proficiency tests, 149–150

Profit-sharing plans, 303

Programming worker, 303

Projection, 467

  in advertising and selling, 402–403

Projective tests, 406

Property ownership, 419

Psychological climates, 48–52
  change, 50–51
  for work, 205–207
Psychomotor skills, 343
Psychoses, 472–473
Public relations in marketing mix, 384
Purcell, T. V., 433
Purposes in systems, 364
Pursuit tracking, 331–332

Quality control, 78
Quandt, R. E., 68

Rank-order rating, 299
Rate buster, 97, 210
Rating scale, first graphic, 25
Ratings, as criteria, 112–113
  of executives, 179
  forced-choice, 113
  halo-effect, 299
  merit, 298–300
Rationalization, 98–99, 467
  in advertising and selling, 403–404
Reaction-time study, 348–349
Readership and comprehension, 387–388
Ream, Merrill J., 31
Records, for control, 76–77
  and decision-making, 79–80
  for prediction, 79
  and reports, 76–80
Recruitment, of employees, 124–125
  urban, 421
Redundancy in communication, 336
Regression, and fixation, 465–466
  multiple, 117–118
Regression equation, 118
Rehabilitation effects, 244
Reinforcement, and aspiration, 139
  in training, 139–140
Reinforcement schedules, 139–140
Reitman, W. R., 104
Rejection of authority, 97–98
Relationships, classes, 10
Relevancy of illustrations, 386–387
Remmers, H. H., 158
Remmers, L. J., 158
Repetition in training, 138
Repetitive movement, 346
Repression, 466
Research, aspects, 355–357
  and development, 355–360
    intermesh, 359–360
  first sponsors, 20
  in marketing mix, 385
  motivation, 404–407

Research Bureau of Retail Training, 26–28
Research Center for Group Dynamics, 35
Resistance, to change, 78–79, 210–212, 420–422
  and prediction, 85
Response in systems, 342–346
Response extinction, 141
Response feedback, 374
Response tolerance in training, 143
Responsibility lines, 44
Rest pauses, 291–292
Retail training, early principles, 26–28
Retirement, 255–257
  criteria for, 255
  individual differences in, 257–259
Revolt in middle age, 93–94
Roethlisberger, F. J., 32, 105, 209
Rogers, C. R., 166
Rose, A. M., 227
Ross, A. M., 229, 240, 241
Routing rules, 82
Rubenstein, A. H., 66
Rules, craft, 75
  filtering, 82
  information handling, 80–84
  need for, 73
  planning, 84–86
  routing, 82
  in systems, 368
  task performance, 73–76
Ruml, Beardsley, 24
Rusk, H. A., 243, 245, 265
Russell, J. T., 136
Russell, Winslow, 28
Ryan, T. A., 290, 293, 304
Ryder, C. F., 253

Safety, engineering phase, 321–322
  and equipment design, 323
  group decisions, 319–320
  housekeeping, 322–323
  and job know-how, 316–317
  knowing and doing, 316
  motivating techniques, 319–321
  through training, 312
  training content, 317
Safety campaigns and posters, 320–321
Safety devices, 321–322
Safety director, 307
Safety engineer, 318
Sales promotion in marketing mix, 384
Salesmanship, early courses in, 29
  first insurance school, 28–29
Salesmanship congress, first, 20

Salesmen, first aids in selection, 21–22
Sargent, L. F., 380
Saul, E. V., 148
Saunders, D. R., 145
Sayles, L. R., 66, 339
Scanning, 339
Schelling, T. C., 236
Schipper, L. M., 339
Schizophrenia, 472–473
Schoen, D. R., 64
Schoenfeld, W. N., 140
School of Life Insurance Salesmanship, 29, 31
Schreiber, R. J., 354
Schutte, W. M., 220
Scientific management, 74–75
Scott, W. G., 174
Scott, Walter D., 18
Scott Company, 23–26
Searle, L. V., 348
Sears, P. S., 425–426
Seashore, S. E., 210
Seeley, J. R., 428, 433
Seidman, J., 226–241
Selection, academic example, 120–121
    current status, 119–124
    future of, 125–127
    of handicapped, 243
    industrial example, 120–122
    military example, 119–120
    potential executives, 186–187
    problem, 106–107
    of trainees, 135–136
Selekman, B., 235
Seller-buyer relationship, 404
Selling, 392–394
    and advertising (see Advertising)
    affective factors in, 397–398
    analysis, 394–396
    cognitive factors in, 398–399
    concept, 384
    kinds, 393
    perceptual factors in, 396–398
Selye, H., 104, 251, 256
Selznick, P., 68, 87
Senility, 257
Seniority in rating, 300
Sensory processes in systems, 333–337
Sensory reinforcement, 397
Sequential movement, 346
Serial movements, 346
Servomechanism theory in management control, 77
Shaffer, L. F., 429, 473, 475
Shannon, C. E., 335, 336
Shartle, C. L., 176, 196
Shaw, M. E., 208

Shifts, work, 422
Shoben, E. J., Jr., 429, 473, 475
Shop steward, 48
Shred-out, job, 135
Signal-response relation, 374
Sill, J. W., 252
Sim, R. A., 428, 433
Simon, H. A., 50, 70, 79, 87, 208
Sisson, D. E., 113
Situations, and individual, 8–9
    and leadership, 182
Skill-level variance, 450
Skinner, B. F., 140, 143, 151
Smith, G. H., 406
Smode, A. F., 339
Smudski, J. F., 147
Snegireff, L. S., 253
Snow, A. J., 312
Snyderman, B., 220
Social change and technology, 412–413
Sociograms, 206–207, 214
Solem, A. R., 151
Spatial summation in advertising and selling, 401–402
Speed, and accidents, 313
    and accuracy, in training, 138–139
    and age, 259
Spence, K. W., 147
Spencer, C., 213
Speroff, B. J., 158
Spot advertising, 388
Stacey, C. L., 105
Stagner, R., 101, 158, 241, 442
Standard operating procedures, advantages, 71
    persistence, 69–70
    psychological consequences, 86
    why used, 86
Standards of work, 73–74
Stanine in selection, 119–120
Starch, Daniel, 19
Static response, 345–346
Status, and administrative structure, 57
    and community, 410, 413, 414
    differences, 55–56
    at different ranks, 58–61
    hierarchies, 55–57
    illogical aspects, 57
    loss with age, 256
    in middle age, 93
    subtle indications, 57
    and unemployment, 247
    within union, 61–63
    and wages, 57
Status anxiety, 94–95, 427
Status position, constancy, 55–56
Status symbols, 56, 427

Steeltown, 413–414
Steinberg, E. R., 220
Stevens, S. S., 352
Steward, shop, 48
Stimulus-response in selling, 394
Stimulus-response correspondence, 333
Stock, F. G. L., 102, 293
Stogdill, R. M., 182
Strategy in systems, 368
Strauss, G., 233
Stress, and defensive reactions, 463–467
    and goals, 104
    in work situation, 438–439
Strike, incentive scheme example, 422–423
    Yankee City example, 411
Strikes and bargaining, 236–237
Strong, Edward K., Jr., 29, 395
Strong Vocational Interest Blanks, 30–32, 126
Stryker, P., 52, 53, 54
Success, and aspiration, 94
    criteria for, 103–104, 178–181
    and failure, and aspiration, 426–427
        relation to unemployment, 248
    flexibility and, 79
    multidimentionality, 109–110
Sumner, F. C., 386
Superstitious responses, 141
Supervision, and attitudes, 218
    ego involvement in, 158
    empathy in, 157–158
    good, 153–156
    history, 152–153
    merit rating, 298–300
    overgeneralization in, 162–163
Supervisor, activity sequence, 452
    adjustments, 451–454
    and individual, 163–164
    jobs, 158–163
    loyalty, 156–157
    morale, 212–213
    responsibilities, 158–160
    restructuring job, 454
    roles, 156–157
    in safety training, 318
    work load variance, 451–452
    worker relations, 161–162
Supervisory complexities, 155–156
Supervisory practices check list, 160–161
Supervisory results, measurement, 154–155
Supervisory training, evaluation, 189–192
Suppliers in systems, 370
Survey Research Center, 36

Surveys, data from, 13
Switzer, M. E., 243, 245, 265
Symbols of status, 56, 427
System, components, 349
    concept, 327
    closed-loop, 328
    description, 364
    general, 363–364
    open-loop, 327–328
    requirements, 363–364
Systems, decision making, 341–342
    decision rules, 341
    inputs, 333–337
    man-machine (see Man-machine systems)
    outputs, 342–346
    transfer function, 351
Systems design principles, 351–352

Taft, P., 230
Tagliacozzo, D. L., 226, 241
Task, analysis, 372–376
    pitfalls in, 372–373
    description, 132–133, 374–376
    performance rules, 73–76
    specifications, 73–74
Task guidance and learning, 138–139
Task redesign in job simplification, 135
Task response and extinction, 142
Tasks, kinds, 373
Taylor, E. K., 114
Taylor, F. M., 135
Taylor, F. V., 326, 348
Taylor, F. W., 74, 303
Taylor, G. C., 457, 475
Taylor, H. C., 136
Taylor, J. A., 147
Taylor-Russell tables, 123
Technology, and social change, 412–413
    and women, 270
Temperature and accidents, 313–314
Temperature tolerance, 296
Temporal summation in advertising and selling, 401
Tense movements, 344–345
Tensions, accumulation, 99
    and job hazards, 447–448
    and job status, 450–451
    in supervision, 450
    of supervision, 453–454
Test scores and criterion, first comparison, 21
Testing, situational, 186–187
    and training, 136
Testing advertising, 389–392

Tests, evaluation, 115–116
  motor ability, 347
  proficiency, 149–150
  (*See also* Selection)
Textbook use, 16–17
Thompson-Luce test in advertising, 390
Thorndike, R. L., 113, 116, 128, 136, 323
Thorpe, J. J., 440
Thurston, J. B., 77
Tiffin, J., 253, 298, 311
Time, estimation, 294
Time-and-motion methods, 285
  and skills, 343
Time-and-motion study, 74–75, 301–303
Time sharing, 374
Tiredness, 290
Tracking, 331–373
Trainee, individual differences, 147
Training, accident prevention, 315–318
  accident reports, 310
  accuracy and speed, 138–139
  advantages in, 6
  aids, devices, and simulators, 148
  attitudinal conditioning, 147–148
  aversive consequences, 144
  and company climate, 191
  through conferences, 192–194
  costs, 136
  definition, 129
  and education, 134–135
  effects, 189–192
  equipment changes, 146
  of executives, 187–192
  and experimentation, 151
  extinction, 141–142
  generalization in, 140–141
  and identification, 465
  kinds, 150–151
  motivation in, 146–147
  needs, 136
  objectives, 129–130
  of older women, 271–273
  and organization control, 75–76
  plateaus, 144–145
  procedures, 137–148
  reinforcement in, 139–140
  repetition in, 138
  response tolerance in, 143
  retail, 26–28
  safety, 312
  sequences, 142–143
  and testing, 136
  transfer, 146
Transduction in control, 333
Transportation in marketing mix, 384–385

Trenchard, K. E., 387
Trist, E. L., 210, 444
Trow, D. B., 208
Trueblood, R. M., 78
Turner, A. N., 259, 452
Turnover, and attitudes, 204
  and job reassignment, 262
  of new men, 163
  and participation, 211
Turns, work, 422

Unemployed, behavior, 248–249
  number, 246
  psychological aspects, 245–250
  seasonal, 246–247
  sex differences, 246, 250
  status, 247
Unemployment, and aspirations, 249–250
  effects on individuals, 247–249
  lasting influences, 250
Union, bargaining policy, 231
  committeeman, 48
  constraints on management, 225–226
  contract violations, 237
  democracy, 231
  executive committee of local, 48
  goals, 227–229
  growth, 223–225
  locals, 48
  membership ratification, 230, 231
  officer power, 229–230, 233
  officer status, 62–63
  organization, 229–231
  organizer, 234–235
  power delegation in, 229
  rivalry, 228
  rule of two, 233
  shop, 226
  shop steward, 48
  status loss, 416
  status structure, 61–63
Unions, early hardships, 223–225
  internal problems, 227
  and mass production, 225
  organizational paradox, 232
  percentage, 225
  and rating systems, 300
  threats to survival, 227
  women in, 275
Upper class, 430

Validity coefficient, interpretation, 121–124
Values in systems, 368

Van Cott, H. P., 131
Van Zelst, R. H., 204
Variations in work, 287–288
Vernon, H. M., 311–313
Vision and accidents, 311
Vitality, 256
Viteles, M. S., 105, 157
Vocational guidance, beginnings, 29–32

Wages and attitudes, 217
Walker, C. R., 220, 414, 449, 452
Wand, B., 145
Warm-up in work, 287–288
Warner, W. L., 52, 409, 423, 427, 433
Warren, N. D., 363
Waste in systems, 365
Watson, John B., 24
Weapons systems and psychology, 326–327
Wedekind, C. E., 147
Western Electric, early researches, 32–34
    in counseling, 164–165
Wherry, R. J., 111, 126
Whipple, Guy Montrose, 20
White-collar worker, 419
Whyte, W. F., 105, 174
Whyte, W. H., Jr., 66, 414
Wickert, F. R., 204
Williams, Whiting, 28
Wilson, R. C., 155
Wirt, S. E., 311
Wissel, J. W., 376
Withdrawal, 99, 464
Wives in industry, 51–52
Womanpower in future, 280–281
Women, discrimination against, 274–275
    in expanding economy, 278–281
    jobs for, 274–278
    limitations to advancement, 277–278
    and nightwork, 273
    opportunities for, 276–277
    supervisors, 278
    in World War II, 268–269
Women workers, married, 271, 278
Woods, Edward A., 19
Work, and aging, 250–255
    analysis, 297–300
    and attitudes, 204
    capacity for, 290–291

Work, characteristics, 287–288
    conditions, 294–297
    context, 292
    decrement, 287–288
    as escape, 98
    evaluation, 297–300
    and family, 431–432
    hazardous types, 213–216, 447
    incentives for, 102
    and maladjustments, 446–448
    pacing, 302
    part-time, 271
    pauses, 287
    plant ecology, 420
    reasons for, 216–220
    shifts, 422
    standards, 73–74
    turns, 422
Work-cycle analysis, 375
Work environment and morale, 213–216
Work output, measurement, 286–288
    reduction, 290–291
Worker, adjustments, 445–446
    dependency, 448
    early philosophy about, 25
    handicapped, 242–245
    and organizational changes, 303
    programming, 303
    worries, 445–446
Worker-supervisor relations, 161–162
Working conditions, and attitudes, 219
    perception, 215–216
World War I, psychology in, 22–23
World War II, psychology in, 34–35
    women in, 268–269
Worries about work, 445–446
Worthy, J. C., 63, 450
Wright, B. A., 265
Wyatt, S., 102, 293
Wyshak, C., 253

Yankee City studies, 409–413
Yerkes, Robert M., 22
Yoakum, Clarence S., 30
Youth, needs in, 93

Zalenzik, A., 105
Zalkind, S. S., 150–151
Zelomek, A. W., 433